Foreword by
KATHERINE BRUNT

Editor
BENJ MOOREHEAD

Design
ROB WHITEHOUSE

This edition first published in the UK by TriNorth Ltd

ISBN: 978-1-909811-48-5

 A CIP Catalogue record for this book is available from the British Library.

Published by Jellyfish Publishing
www.jellyfishsolutions.co.uk

Editor: *Benj Moorehead;* Research and editorial: *Jo Harman, Phil Walker, James Wallace*
Design: *Rob Whitehouse;* Images: *Getty Images unless stated;*
Print: *Jellyfish Print Solutions*

Acknowledgements
The publishers would like to thank the county clubs and the players for their assistance in helping to put together this book. Additional information has been gathered from espncricinfo.com and cricketarchive.com. Thanks also to Nick Wood of Unshaken Photography for providing an image.

CONTENTS

Openers

FOREWORD

By Katherine Brunt

It's a pleasure to write the foreword for *The Cricketers' Who's Who*, but sad to be doing so in such troubling times. I hope above all that this finds you and your family safe, and that you manage to get through the difficult months ahead. The cricket season will certainly be affected, and the thought of not playing is very strange indeed. But I'm sure some day soon we'll all be back on the field having fun.

It was only a few weeks ago that I was playing for England in the T20 World Cup in Australia. Unfortunately we weren't able to win that tournament – we had a bad stroke of luck with the weather – but it's still brilliant to be able to say that the England women's and men's team are the current 50-over World Cup holders. It's awesome to share that title with the men and put England at the top of the leaderboard in terms of ODI cricket.

Much has changed in the last decade of women's cricket. A lot of countries are catching up with the likes of us and Australia really quickly, and they're also getting more support now, which I think is fantastic for women's cricket.

But Australia have been dominant recently. They seem to have a lot of players in their prime. It's more difficult for us because we've had a lot of retirements of late. In fact since we won the 2017 World Cup in England there's been a lot of change and that's what we're trying to deal with at the moment.

Lisa Keightley taking over as our head coach earlier this year was good timing because the side was changing. She's taken to it like a duck to water. Lisa has coached in England before and saw a lot of the girls grow up when she was head coach of England Women's Academy. She's all about creating confidence and letting people lead in their own way. We're all really happy to have her.

I don't think my role in the team will change that much. For several years now I've felt like one of the leaders – or grandmas! As a player my role might change, because you can't just stand still. You've got to keep evolving or else someone else will overtake you. I'm still really enjoying it and as long as that's the case I'll keep going.

The Hundred will be a big change for us. Women's domestic cricket was not in a great way a few years back. No one knew about it, you didn't get paid to play it – you paid your own way and bought your own kit. It had to change. The T20 Kia Super League was great, but I think it was always only an introduction to something bigger. I'd say The Hundred will benefit the women most because it's giving us the opportunity to play alongside the men

– the same kit, same venues, same team names. It makes us feel part of something bigger. And it's been really important that it has attracted all the best players in the world – the Kia Super League didn't always do that. It's certainly the start of another shift forward for women's cricket.

So I welcome the new format, even though I am a traditionalist who loves Test cricket. As well as keeping people in love with the game we also need people to fall in love with the game.

This is also an exciting time for me outside of cricket. Last October me and my England teammate Nat Sciver announced our engagement on National Coming Out Day. The public reaction was brilliant. I actually expected a lot of negativity because that's the impression I've had over the years of how people see these things. But for the reaction to have been 99.99% positive has made me feel really great about it.

The teams that I have played in have always been very supportive and have never given me any reason to believe that if I wanted to say something, or be something, that that wouldn't be ok. It was easy to be myself around the team but a lot harder to be myself in the wider world. But you shouldn't have to live your life behind closed doors because you are ashamed of who you are. Putting ourselves out there has actually shown us how good people can be. There's a lot of bad stuff in the world right now – why not send a bit of positivity out there?

We've not really had time to celebrate or plan so far. The wedding is due to be two days after the last England game of the summer so it's going to get pretty stressful. But no wedding planner needed – I'm a Yorkshire lass and my dad was a miner so I'm as tight as they come! Anything I can do myself I'll do!

Whatever the summer brings, I wish you all the best.

Katherine Brunt
March 2020

EDITOR'S NOTES

By Benj Moorehead

This was supposed to be the season after the season before. ("By the *barest* of all margins! Absolute ecstasy for England. Agony – AGONY – for New Zealand.") Or the season which launches a bold/foolhardy new era in our domestic game. (You guessed it, The Hundred.) But right now it would be wonderful, just wonderful, to have any season at all. As I write the sporting world is in lockdown, along with well over 100 million people worldwide, and the thought of some white-cladded figures strolling out to the sound of pitter-patter clapping at Fenner's, Hove, Worcester – wherever – anytime soon seems like a distant dream.

But let us dream…

The Hundred is due to launch this year. At last. Not because we all welcome it, but because its arrival might curb the rankling that has proliferated since the competition was announced nearly two years ago, particularly on social media. At times it has felt like cricket's Brexit, with trenches being dug so deep that all perspective is lost.

In the Comment section we have attempted, with some success I believe, to have a balanced debate about The Hundred, featuring seven different stakeholders, from its brainchild Tom Harrison via Bumble through to the founder of the pressure group Oppose The Hundred. A personal view – from someone who is largely underwhelmed by abbreviated cricket – is that The Hundred will be a success: it has attracted the superstars, it will likely draw the crowds, and it will be distinct from other global franchise tournaments.

It seems to have the support of the players, to judge from their response to our question in the survey they all received about what excites them about The Hundred. True, some left the field blank, perhaps diplomatically, while a few said they most look forward to the free crisps (KP Snacks are the main sponsors). But the majority are looking forward to having new teammates, to be playing with and against the best, and to be working with world-class coaches. And we are not talking exclusively about the younger generation. Consider Wayne Madsen for instance, a superb batsman for Derbyshire for more than a decade now but someone who has never played international cricket and only rarely experienced a 'big-game' atmosphere. What excites him about The Hundred? "Playing at Old Trafford in front of a full house for the Manchester Originals!" You bet. For the women it is even more significant, for they will be playing in double-headers with men's fixtures at the big grounds in front of large crowds.

Nevertheless, the arrival of the new format does raise a number of questions. Should we still view the T20 Blast as a tournament in its own right, or will it inevitably become the tame little brother? How about the One-Day Cup, due to take place in the shadow of The

Hundred – sub-standard fare for second-raters or, as Middlesex coach Stuart Law puts it on page 11, "an opportunity for us to grow a great young team, and a competition where they can really stamp their authority"? Will the fact that the best short-format players won't be playing 50-over cricket harm England's chances of winning another World Cup? The women won't be playing any T20 cricket whatsoever.

And what of the County Championship which, year after year, provides gripping narrative? Well, it's still there, a remarkable achievement in itself given how out of step it is with modern 'entertainment'. In fact one of the best things about the four-day game is that it runs counter to the neon noise of modern sport, a blessed sedative whose survival we should cherish. Just one thing though, which Bumble puts best on page 15 "I'd move heaven and earth to come up with a solution that ensures it is played in the summer months."

Enough politics. With a nod to The Hundred, our Comment section also includes Tim Wigmore and Freddie Wilde's fascinating insight into the tactical impact of Twenty20 when it first arrived on these shores 17 years ago. Then we slow things right down with William Fiennes's beautiful elegy to old-school wicketkeepers, worth reading for the first sentence alone. But you'd be mad not to read the rest.

And, of course, we have asked the players – some 450 of them – to answer our annual questionnaire. Or, to put more accurately, we have poked and prodded each county's media manager all through the winter to shake the tree one more time and hope that some more apples will fall. We are hugely grateful for their support, and to all those players who responded to the call. Sometimes they throw up a few surprises. Would you have guessed, for instance, that players still talk about crosswords in the dressing room (admittedly there's a lot of football chat too, along with an obsession with something called *Love Island*)?

We also asked the players which animal they would be. There was a honey badger, a poison dart frog, an ibis, a mayfly, a Toy Poodle, Bagpuss, and a "Psychrolutes marcidus" (a blobfish to you and me).

But in the present circumstances it feels fitting to pick out the choice of Hampshire's Mason Crane: "A tortoise – because it's always at home." Just like we all are as I write this. But don't forget the fable about the tortoise and the hare. Patience. Cricket will be back.

Benj Moorehead
March 2020

THE HUNDRED AND ITS WIDER IMPACT

Seven stakeholders with different roles in the game share their thoughts on the opinion-dividing new competition and how it will affect the overall landscape of English cricket

THE PANEL

Will Brown, Gloucestershire chief executive

James Buttler, journalist and founder of Oppose The Hundred

Becky Fairlie-Clarke, Cricket Supporters' Association chief executive

Tom Harrison, ECB chief executive

Stuart Law, Middlesex coach and former Australia batsman

David Lloyd, Sky Sports broadcaster, former player and coach

Daryl Mitchell, Worcestershire batsman and Professional Cricketers' Association chairman

Are you in favour of The Hundred?

Brown: I don't have an issue at all with the tournament in many respects, having seen a lot of the figures around recreational cricket and participation. I can absolutely see the need for it and Gloucestershire have been supportive from a very early point in the process. What I worry about is that we're dropping a stone into the middle of the pond. I don't have an issue with the stone; what I worry about are the ripples it'll create.

Mitchell: A quiet optimism is probably the best way of putting it. It's happening and, as players, I think we've got to do all we can now to get behind it. Obviously there's been a lot of opposition but for the good of English cricket we need it to be a success now.

Buttler: Absolutely not. What the ECB have done with The Hundred is a massive gamble with the future of our game. For existing cricket fans who now feel disenfranchised, it is a gimmick and not cricket. For the targeted new audience, it is still cricket and therefore why are they likely to be any easier to seduce? By centring the tournament around seven cities, a huge raft of the country is being geographically excluded from attending matches. And what about the allegiance that supporters have with their current county? Cricket needs to move with the times and open itself up to all communities. The problem is The Hundred is not the right way to do it.

Lloyd: It will be a success because it has got the best players. It is going to be great fun – the broadcasters will ensure that it absolutely zings. There's a lot of resistance on social media but in my experience social media is wrong the majority of the time. I'm a massive champion of county cricket – I owe it everything – but it can't stand still.

Law: Everyone fears change, and it is a massive change. We can't really make an educated assumption on its success or otherwise until we've seen a couple of editions. No one thought the IPL would take off, and here we are a decade later and it's stronger than ever. Personally I'm focusing on the 50-over competition with Middlesex. I see it as an opportunity for us to grow a great young team, and a competition where they can really stamp their authority.

Fairlie-Clarke: In our recent Cricket Supporters' Association (CSA) survey, only 12 per cent of fans showed any intention to watch The Hundred at a ground, although this rose to 28 per cent for 16-24-year-olds. Slightly more intend to watch online or on TV, with the average figure at 29 per cent, rising to 53 per cent for 16-24-year-olds.

What do you foresee as the biggest obstacles to the success of The Hundred?

Brown: There's certainly a prevalence of opinions around The Hundred but actually most of the target market are probably still waking up to it. There will be those who aren't yet sure if they'll give it go, and there are those who aren't even aware of it yet. And they are the ones I suspect the game is trying to go after.

Mitchell: It'll be judged on how many people we get in the ground and what the spectacle looks like on TV. It's great having some of the games on free-to-air. To get cricket into primetime BBC slots can only benefit the game as a whole.

Buttler: My communication with fans suggests that the vast majority will not attend games. Some are open and a few are excited, but the construct of the competition and the way it was promoted has disenfranchised many, geographically excluded others and selling tickets will be a tough task. Tickets may be cheap but people still have to get to games.

Harrison (right): We know we are competing for attention in an ever-changing world. We all have so much choice for how we spend our time, and we know that this challenge is most pronounced across younger generations, who spend on average 30-plus hours a week online. However, I am convinced that both new and existing fans of cricket will want to watch some of the best players in the world compete in a new and exciting format of the game. Aside from inclement weather, our biggest obstacle to success is the unknown. Whilst we are confident in the insights we've explored and the enormous amount of work we have done, we also acknowledge that anything new and innovative is often accompanied by concerns.

Brown: A big challenge for Gloucestershire is the name of the franchise that we're affiliated to (Welsh Fire). I understand there was a big bidding process behind it, with a huge amount of support from the Welsh Assembly and Cardiff City Council, and the expectation was that it would have a strong Welsh feel to it. Do I think there will be lots of people crossing the bridge from Bristol to Cardiff? I think that's a challenge, and it's even more of a challenge from Taunton to Cardiff. The challenge we've got is hosting women's Welsh Fire. Where we're lucky is that women's cricket has a strong footing in our part of the world, and it's not as tribalistic as men's cricket. I think people will come because we've got Meg Lanning in our team. But it is a challenge.

Does cricket need a fourth format?

Mitchell: No is the honest answer, but I can understand why they've got to it. A new eight-team competition was going to be directly competing with the Blast. I think the change of format is a lot to do with that and not having two T20 competitions in the same summer.

Law: When I first played county cricket we had four competitions. We haven't actually moved the bar that far forward. Whether or not 100-ball is going to be the answer remains to be seen.

Harrison: The 100-ball format itself emerged from a significant amount of research with current and potential fans. Through this research we uncovered that more people would engage with cricket if the game was simpler to understand and took less time. We also want to ensure cricket is positioned as a game for everyone. At an elite level, it is also very important for us to ensure the competition is differentiated from our existing short-format competitions, which a new format enables. Our plan for The Hundred is for it to grow the interest in cricket and complement existing formats by acting as a gateway for people to engage with our sport for the first time, and then go on to become loyal fans of the game in all its forms.

Buttler: Three formats is tough enough to fit into the English summer. Divide the T20 Blast into two divisions. Make the top tier the Premier League and spend a fraction of The Hundred budget on marketing the living daylights out of it. The beauty of that idea is that all 18 counties are involved, they all have existing support that doesn't need creating from scratch. How a T20 is any more complex for a new audience to get their collective heads around than The Hundred is beyond me.

Will 100 rather than 120 balls make much difference to the cricket itself?

Mitchell: No, not really. I played a number of the trial games and I was captain as well. It probably took half an innings to get my head around the five and 10-ball blocks but after that it felt pretty natural. The skillset is identical. I don't think there's any problem with the format.

Law: A five- or 10-ball over, that's a massive thing to get used to. It takes a lot out of a bowler in T20 cricket to bowl six balls in a row. If they're going to bowl 10, it makes it very interesting.

Lloyd (above right): From a broadcasting point of view, we will demystify the game for new people. We cannot, as commentators, be saying things like, 'He's just moved from a short-leg position to a backward of square-leg position' or anything like that. It's new people that we want. If you look at Lord's, who get 25,000 spectators every match for a T20 – they ain't MCC members, most aren't Middlesex fans. Of course you can pick holes in it but it's a night out and it's a lot of fun.

Buttler: If you can get around some of the gimmicks, it probably won't be much different. I'm sure there will be some very entertaining games. It isn't the games themselves that put me off; it is the potential repercussions to the wider game that massively worries me.

Does the new competition threaten the 18-county model? And, if so, why did 17 of the 18 counties support the proposals (with only Surrey vetoing)?

Lloyd: The 18 counties will benefit massively from the city set-up. It is absolutely necessary. Take a county that draws in £200k through membership per annum – two players alone could take that.

Law (right): This hasn't just come about recently. I remember talking to [former chairman of selectors] David Graveney 15 or 20 years ago, about cutting down the teams from 18 to six or eight, as they do in other countries. But look, county cricket is special. It's special for reasons that other countries probably don't understand. Unfortunately everyone's looking at the bottom line, which is how much money it's making. First-class cricket around the world doesn't make any money. It needs a strong national set-up to help produce and nurture the talent coming through. I think if we keep looking at the stuff going on below to find the dollars, then we're kidding ourselves.

Harrison: The Hundred protects the 18-county model. It is all about growing the game, which is fundamental in protecting cricket's long-term future, and with it our 18-county structure, Test cricket and all the other non-negotiables. I can assure you that the ECB is committed to the 18 first-class county model.

Buttler: It has to threaten some of the smaller counties. If the eight-team model works, the ECB can potentially point to the success of The Hundred and say that the other competitions should trim down to similar numbers of teams. In my view Surrey got it right, and they would be OK whatever happens. Glamorgan, Hampshire, Lancashire, Nottinghamshire, Warwickshire and Yorkshire will survive as they are operating from the same grounds as sides in The Hundred. Middlesex don't own Lord's but you'd expect them to be fine too. Of the other sides, the only reason they can possibly have voted in favour of the new format is the £1.3m bribe they have been promised each year. That is big money for some smaller counties. If we scroll on a few years and that money is potentially withdrawn, will they still view that vote as wise?

Brown: I believe that the people at the top of the ECB, and Tom [Harrison] in particular, do care about the 18 counties and they want them all to be there. At every single meeting that I've been to every CEO has been supportive of the other 17. I believe we've got a group of CEOs who are supportive, though if things were to get tough, it'd be interesting to see who broke ranks first.

Will the four-day game be pushed further to the margins by The Hundred?

Mitchell (right): If you look back at the last few years there's been a lot of Championship cricket played in April and September anyway. I think it's another easy thing to kick The Hundred about without actually looking at the bigger picture.

Law: We're getting caught up in the glamorisation of cricket, which has taken place since the inception of T20. Phenomenal sums of money, TV rights deals going through the roof – but you'll find that the best cricketers come from the four-day system. Four-day cricket produces a higher-skilled and mentally tougher cricketer – someone who can work out a problem, and fix it. You can't do that from the crash-bang-wallop of the T20 format. What T20 cricket has created is a player who plays one way. You stand, you step, and you swing through the line.

Harrison: The current domestic structure was agreed by the first-class counties, after a review process led by the first-class county CEOs and directors of cricket, so it predominantly reflects where counties themselves want the balance of the red- and white-ball season to be. The domestic season is not something the ECB has control over. Test cricket remains a priority for the ECB at domestic and international level, which is why England men's red-ball cricketers will be available for every Test match throughout the summer.

Brown: Red-ball cricket in 2020 is actually no different. We're playing Championship cricket through to the middle of July, then breaking while we host another tournament. Now it just so happens that over the last three years that's been T20 cricket rather than 100-ball cricket, but the ECB's first feeling has been: let's protect the sanctity of the four-day game and not do anything to marginalise it, or anything that could be perceived as marginalising it.

Lloyd: This issue isn't about The Hundred. As it stands, I don't think Championship cricket is developing cricketers in the proper way, because of the surfaces. Putting my coach's hat on – with 14 Championship matches, the 50-over competition, the T20 Blast and The Hundred, there is no way you can prepare players properly. By reducing the Championship to 10 matches, the players would be primed to give the best possible performance. My solution would be three divisions, six teams in each, playing each other twice. And I'd move heaven and earth to come up with a solution that ensures it is played in the summer months.

THE GIMMICK

With a new format due to take off this summer, Tim Wigmore and Freddie Wilde recall the birth of England's Twenty20 Cup

On a sultry evening at The Oval cricket ground in London in June 2003, Surrey's captain Adam Hollioake won the toss against Middlesex. "We're going to bowl first," he announced, "because I haven't got a clue what's going to happen."

This was how professional T20 cricket began, in a spirit of ignorance, innocence and sheer bedlam. Professional sport fleetingly became a world of children playing a game for the first time. No room for tactical smarts here. Just figuring out the new rules – the threat of an incoming batsman being 'timed out' if they took more than 90 seconds to take guard at the crease, and the need to bowl all 20 overs within 75 minutes or be penalised six runs for every over unbowled – was challenging enough.

"Like many, we took it as a bit of a joke to begin with," Hollioake later admitted. Alex Tudor, who played for Surrey at the time, recalled before the tournament: "I remember Keith Medlycott, our coach at the time, was saying, 'Who wants to play?' I was very much a longer-formats player, and obviously had ambitions of getting back into the Test team, so I couldn't care less about it."

Surrey were the Twenty20 Cup's first champions. This was largely a triumph for simply having the best players, though Hollioake immediately grasped that T20 was not merely a shorter version of one-day cricket so much as a drastically different game. Before the tournament, he addressed the side, saying: "Lads, we're not going to worry too much about ones and twos, we're just going to try and hit more sixes than the other team."

In this way, Hollioake stumbled on an essential truth about the nature of T20, and how it diverged from the longer formats. "We went in with the theory that basically a one run here and there in a T20 game isn't a big deal but if you had a six it's a big chunk. You hit a couple of sixes and that could be 10 per cent of your total – that's a big swing. We went in to bat with the mentality of hitting sixes."

In many ways the point of T20 was to make people forget they were watching cricket at all. In that first, heady summer of 2003, evenings at the cricket were about pitchside Jacuzzis, bouncy castles, cheerleaders, speed-dating and copious alcohol, with the cricket itself incidental. This was very deliberate; the very point of T20 was to create a product that appealed to those who would never normally go to cricket.

At the start of the new century, the English game seemed moribund: domestic attendances fell 17 per cent in the five years to 2001. John Carr, director of cricket operations for the England and Wales Cricket Board (ECB), gave Stuart Robertson, the marketing manager, £250,000 to undertake the biggest consumer survey in cricket history.

"We specifically wanted to ask people who were non-cricket fans but we felt might be convertible why they weren't attending – we spoke to young people, children, ethnic minorities, inner-city communities, women," Robertson recalled. "The key reason why people weren't attending cricket was summed up in a word: inaccessible. The game was perceived as being socially inaccessible. Some people thought it was a posh sport and they had to go to county games in a suit and tie." Over the course of their research, the ECB found that one-third of the population were "cricket-tolerators". They neither disliked the game nor attended matches.

The research made clear what this demographic wanted: a condensed format of the game on midweek evenings or weekends, lasting no more than three hours. "The killer finding was we found 19 million people who were there for convincing," Robertson said. "The format that they were keen about and would come along to was the 20-over format."

The concept was not new – T20 was a staple of club cricket around the country – but it had never been played at professional level before. The ECB executives, in need of a cure for the ailing summer game, were ardently in favour. The trouble was, those with the votes – the county chairmen – were not.

On the morning of 21 April 2002, English cricket was on the brink of rejecting T20. As the vote at Lord's loomed, the ECB's chairman Lord MacLaurin – whose cricketing instincts were always far more radical than might have been expected of a Conservative member of the House of Lords – decided to "flatter the f***" out of the county chairmen, as one observer recalled.

Some were wooed, but it did not look like enough, as became apparent in the meeting of the county chairmen immediately prior to the vote. Minutes before the vote, Bill Midgley, the 60-year-old Durham chairman who had previously opposed T20, gave a speech likening the debate to the staunch opposition to the creation of one-day cricket 40 years earlier. It proved decisive: the vote of the counties and the Marylebone Cricket Club (MCC) was won 11-7, with the MCC abstaining. T20 cricket was born.

For all the gimmicks, T20 looked just enough like cricket that it was still recognisable. Cricket remained an 11-a-side game, played with six-ball overs; a mooted "golden over", in which the batting side would choose an over for runs to count double, was rejected as too manufactured. Earlier innovations – Cricket Max, an abbreviated form of the game, designed by the former New Zealand batsman Martin Crowe; and the Hong Kong Sixes, a five-overs-a-side game played by teams of six – had been a qualified success without taking off, and were considered to have deviated too much from the sport's underlying norms.

The first-ever delivery in a professional T20 match – between Hampshire and Sussex on June 13, 2003 – was a wide, from Sussex's James Kirtley. Thereafter the first year of English domestic T20 was a resounding success. The notorious English rain stayed away: all 48 games in 2003 were played to a conclusion and the 20-over format produced an accelerated form of the game, with all the action of a 50-over match crammed into less than half the time. Over 18 exhilarating days, Robertson's target of an average attendance of 5,000 was cleared; it would have been considerably higher than 5,300 had county grounds had greater capacity. No county chief executive would ever again question whether they should play T20. The *Wisden Cricketers' Almanack*, regarded as the sport's bible, noted that the competition "struck the motherlode of public affection for cricket that runs just below the surface crust of apparent indifference". The ECB had got very lucky, but they had also got a lot right.

Even as the game's popularity snowballed – South Africa immediately launched a domestic T20 competition of their own, to great acclaim, and a swathe of other countries including Pakistan, Australia and New Zealand soon followed – its fundamental image as nothing more than frivolous fun remained.

When New Zealand hosted Australia in the inaugural T20 international in 2005, the match drew more resemblance to a charity fundraiser than elite-level sport. The New Zealand players dressed up in retro kits and outfits – batsman Hamish Marshall wore frizzy hair more at home in a 1970s disco and Glenn McGrath did an impersonation of Trevor Chappell's notorious underarm delivery. The sport itself was a sideshow. Australian captain Ricky Ponting scored 98 not out in his side's victory yet, after the game, regarded the whole spectacle as a gimmick: "I think it's difficult to play seriously. If it does become an international game then I'm sure the novelty won't be there all the time."

Because of its brevity, T20 completely transformed how risk was conceived in cricket. In longer formats, the number of balls available to a batting team compelled batsmen to manage risk, to ensure that the team were not bowled out prematurely. In T20 the number of balls available to a batting team (120) was under half that in 50-over cricket (300) – but they still possessed 11 batsmen. A team could lose a wicket every 12 balls and still bat out their full allocation of 20 overs. Even Chris Martin, the New Zealand bowler regarded as the worst Test batsman of the 21st century, was dismissed only every 11.82 balls in Test cricket. In T20, then, defence virtually ceased to matter.

Defence had historically formed the bedrock of batting because the tactical and technical foundation of cricket was the first-class game – the oldest format to be played at professional level. That first-class cricket was played across multiple days placed an emphasis on wicket preservation to enable batsmen to bat for as long as possible and steadily accumulate as many runs as possible. Traditional cricket coaching has therefore always prescribed the foundation of a strong batting technique to be a solid defence.

In Test cricket, the bowlers were charged with attacking – in order to take wickets – while batsmen traditionally emphasised defence in order to stay in for as long as possible while they steadily accumulated runs. The framework of T20 cricket inverted this relationship – suddenly batsmen were on the offence as they looked to score as many runs as fast as possible and bowlers on the defence as they looked to prevent batsmen from doing so.

This was a paradigm shift. T20 was not merely a shorter version of one-day cricket; the difference was altogether more profound, necessitating a wholly different approach to playing.

The format's incipient years were defined by an underlying tactical anarchy. "Nobody knows anything," the screenwriter William Goldman once said of the entertainment industry. So it was in the first skirmishes of T20.

Worcestershire began the first summer by virtually inverting their batting order, aiming to use their bowlers' big-hitting skills to exploit the fielding restrictions in the first six overs. They even signed a big-hitting club player, David Taylor, on a specialist T20 contract, a harbinger of how the new format would encourage specialisation. Yet such attempts to innovate looked more like over-complication; Taylor harrumphed 46 on his debut but averaged 11.71 in seven county T20 matches. The promoted bowlers, meanwhile, set about proving that uncultured hoicking was no way to score runs in T20. On the second day of professional T20, Matt Mason, a hulking Australian fast bowler, was sent in to bat at No.4, imbued with intent to clear the ropes. Every ball he swung, with ever more ferocity. Every ball he missed, until he was caught for nought off 10 balls; Worcestershire's specialist batsmen were left with insufficient time and the team stumbled to 122 all out. It was a salutary lesson in the pitfalls of wrong-headed strategy in T20.

Yet even in the bedlam of T20's first years, there were glimpses of sides succeeding through recognising what could be achieved by taking the game a little more seriously. John Inverarity, the coach of Warwickshire, used to bellow "two' to his players, reflecting a belief that the side who scored the most twos would win. His side reached the final in 2003. Derbyshire, convinced that the six Powerplay overs – with only two fielders permitted outside the 30-yard circle – were pivotal and that batsmen were more dangerous if they could line up a particular bowler, used six different bowlers across the six overs.

Leicestershire were the first to succeed through embracing how, for all that T20 is seen as the most instinctive and spontaneous format of the game, it also lends itself best to planning. They overcame the limitations of a small playing squad and budget to triumph in the Twenty20 Cup in 2004 and 2006, giving a glimpse of what was possible.

"No one had really decided how to play it. They basically just thought it was 'slog it as far as you can and that's it', and that spinners wouldn't even be a factor in the game," recalled fast

bowler Charles Dagnall. Leicestershire took a different approach. "We weren't great in other competitions, and we thought we've got a chance here."

"We were ahead of our time as far as planning and game management," remembered the wicketkeeper Paul Nixon. "Having the right opportunities at the right times, reading pitches, knowing the right times for hitters, the right times to be able to box clever, and save hitters for the end, to get a new batsman in, not losing two wickets together, change of orders, having certain batsmen that can target spin – certain things that you can really latch on to that you can take on most pitches."

Leicestershire managed the pace of the game intelligently, slowing things down when they were batting to help them think and speeding things up when they were bowling to rush the opposition batsmen.

At a time when many teams experimented opening with pinch-hitters – weaker batsmen with a penchant for scoring quickly – their batting followed a simple mantra. Leicestershire put their best batsman, Brad Hodge, at the top of the order so he could face the most balls. They planned where they wanted to be after the end of the six-over Powerplay and mapped out the progression of their innings. They emphasised having partnerships between a hitter and a player who would rotate the strike. They believed this combination meant they avoided a build-up of dot balls if two hitters struggled to get going or avoided falling behind the required rate if they had two strike rotators at the crease. The top eight batsmen were always padded up and ready to go, enabling Leicester to have a flexible batting order. They would send in players to target certain bowling types; the earliest intimation of a team playing to 'match-ups', well before the advent of data analysis elevated it to become a major part of the game.

With the ball, Leicestershire attacked early on, even if it meant leaking boundaries, believing that ultimately the best way to contain a T20 innings was to take regular wickets. They played with two frontline spinners – Claude Henderson and Jeremy Snape – with Hodge offering an extra spin option, and extended the boundaries at Grace Road to make the slow bowlers harder to hit; sometimes Hodge would even open the bowling with his off-spin. They put mandatory men in the 30-yard circle to save one, rather than leaving them on the edge of the circle, reasoning that they could not afford to let the opposition score off every ball of the innings. They used Dagnall's in-swing in the middle overs, believing that it was harder for batsmen to free their arms than against out-swingers.

And they innovated. At T20 practice sessions, bowlers experimented audaciously – running in, stopping again, and then restarting; bowling with no front arm; looking away as they ran in – to try to put batsmen off. Bowlers were encouraged to master not just one slower ball, but several. Tweaks were made to the field before a bowler delivered a slower ball.

Now, none of these steps look revolutionary or, perhaps, anything more than an implementation of the obvious. But low-budget Leicestershire's triumphs were a hint of what it was possible to achieve by embracing T20 not simply as an abridged version of limited-overs cricket, but an entirely different sport.

This is an extract from Cricket 2.0: Inside the T20 Revolution *by Tim Wigmore and Freddie Wilde (Arena Sport, £17.99)*

KEEPING

William Fiennes recalls some dreamy bye-less afternoons

My father had been a wicketkeeper, widely admired, playing at Lord's aged 18 in the summer of 1939, maybe good enough for a county trial if war hadn't barged in, and it was still in his bone and muscle memory in his eighties and nineties, throwing an apple up and catching it and nudging the bails off, or just miming a take to one side of the body, his fingers and palms opening into a bowl or cradle, a little give with the elbows as the ball invisibly landed, not "caught" so much as greeted and received, the evidence there when he held his hands up and you could see the fingers all crooked where balls had crocked the joints, corroborated too when old friends of his encountered with Rover tickets in the Warner or Allen stands would look down at me and remember not just my father's batting but his keeping too: "A *very good* wicketkeeper, your father..."

So when at school they asked for a volunteer, I raised my hand. The gloves in the communal kitbags were huge, cumbersome gauntlets, sweat-soaked leather hardened in the off-season, the plastic finger guards like burly thimbles, the pimpled catching surface worn smooth and shiny. The chamois inner gloves were hard and creased when you first put them on but would melt and soften with sweat from your hands so that after a short sequence of catches the paraphernalia of inner and outer gloves seemed to meld with your own body and be forgotten. I don't remember any coaching, it was more a matter of imitation, mimicking the squats and nimble sidestep dances of Bob Taylor and Jeff Dujon, relishing not just their diving one-handed catches but the lovely soundless grace of the task done right, understanding from Dad that the point was to go beneath notice, taking each catch so cleanly the ball made no sound in the gloves, the good wicketkeeper dissolving into each passage of play with Zen-like self-effacement. That was my father's ideal, increasingly remote in an era when keepers were expected to lead the psychological attack, being right under the batsman's nose and eyes, mouth in his ears, lips almost brushing the stump mic, expected to chirp and heckle like Healy, Boucher, Prior, Nixon, Wade, even the ineffably dignified Kumar Sangakkara haranguing Shaun Pollock with some entry-level psy-ops in the 2003 World Cup: "Lots of pressure for the skipper now, yeah? Gonna let his whole country down if he fails! Oh man, the weight of all these expectations, fellas! The weight of the country, chaps! Forty-two million supporters right here!"

And not just the relentless dreary chiselling at the batsman's sporting and sexual self-esteem – now the keeper had to be chief of geeing-up and morale-boosting too, as if he were the afternoon's host and compère, calling everyone "buddy" and filling the pauses – "Good areas, Frankie!" – like a radio DJ scared of dead air. Of course no one's better placed to jab the needle, but even Paul Nixon must have felt something more complicated than enmity for the batsman standing just across the line. You're so close to the batsman's talents and shortcomings it's hard not to feel solidarity as well as opposition, so that the celebrations of a stumping might simply be a way of disguising the feeling you'd betrayed a friend. You can hear them breathing, hear the mantras of concentration and self-reproach they murmur to themselves, read forearm tattoos and bat labels, see where they take guard and how they mark it, how their feet settle and shuffle. When the ball approaches, keeper and batsman are alone together inside a world of movement and sound – the flurry of backlift and batswing, the faint creaking of leather boots and pads, the fabric swish and rustle, the expulsions of breath, the bat-and-ball percussion all bursting out of the still, silent moment when you and the batsman waited together in squat and stance.

Baseball has a catcher, cricket has a keeper: you *keep* wicket, like a diary or a secret, the verb rich with suggestions of ownership and intimacy. The keeper standing up to slow or medium-paced bowling is eye-level with the bails' rolled beads and spigots, breathes woody stump varnish, knows each agricultural miniscape of grooving and abrasion made by bat toes and dragged studs across the batting crease – the guards, guidelines and small August dust bowls. The idea was to stay low and rise with the ball, weight in the balls of your feet, thigh muscles driving out of the squat to spring to left or right. I liked the athletic possibilities of standing back to quick bowlers – at university I took one off the inside edge, a fast Neil Coulson out-swinger that first had me moving slipwards before a drive scrambled the trajectories and I dived full-length down the leg side, the ball landing snug in my left glove, just off the ground. And how about that flier off the outside edge at Burleigh Park, right-handed, slips dispersed to boundaries for a batsman on 99, or that guy trying to cut a wide one at Stonor so I was already moving in front of first slip and could plunge in front of second to land it one-handed inches off the grass… Now approaching 50, I'm aware of those reflexes waning, balls diverted off the edge already yards past me before my nerves convey the message of a chance, and sometimes I watch the YouTube clips – Tim Ludeman's full-stretch zero-gravity left-hander, a Brad Haddin screamer in front of first slip, where in slo-mo you can see Shane Watson raising his hands in awe or prayer at the flying man under his eyes – and dream of just one more before it's over.

Aged 12 I got *Gordon's Gin's Wicketkeepers of the World* by Godfrey Evans for Christmas, and the author's Dickensian white muttonchops and ritual siesta in the lunch interval seemed part of a strain of eccentricity running through English keepers, via Alan Knott who warmed his hands in hot water before taking the field and reinforced his chamois inners with strips of plasticine, and Jack Russell who drove between games wearing a specially-adapted sleeping bag to keep his back and legs warm, and reportedly used the same tea bag through all five days of an Oval Test against Australia, which Derek Randall estimated amounted to a hundred cups. Dad liked Russell especially for his "tidiness", and I'd absorbed the idea that this was the highest accolade available for keepers, whose mistakes – a drop, a bye, a fumbled stumping chance – could loom so unfairly over hours of quiet, unnoticed competence. This was the goalkeeper's burden too, and both keepers shared that Wim Wenders existential loneliness, the only one of their kind: a handful of batters, a handful of bowlers, only one keeper. And added to this was the way the game continually circulated the ball (and so also the focus of players and spectators) through the keeper like blood through the heart, not just when batters played and missed or let it go, but almost every time fielders gathered and sent it back in, as if the keeper were really the ball's home, the place to which it always returned.

My Godfrey Evans book featured Jeff Dujon – who could go a whole innings without standing up to the stumps, at home midway between wicket and boundary while Marshall, Holding, Garner and Croft took turns stretching him like a goalie to posts, top corners and crossbar – and Farokh Engineer, who could go a whole day anchored to the stumps by the spin quartet of Bedi, Prasanna, Chandrasekhar and Venkataraghavan.

Hard to imagine a book like that now, in the post-Gilchrist era, when keepers earn their place as much for their batting as their glovework, and when keeping is more an interchangeable athletic discipline than an art for which you might have natural gift and style. Admirable sportsmen, of course, but who's talking about "art" or "style" in the keeping of Ramdin, Karthik, Pant, Watling, Bairstow, Wade, Paine? The speed of Dhoni's hands in a stumping off Harbhajan is objectively astonishing, but there's a stiff, machine efficiency to the transaction that leaves me cold. Give me Sarah Taylor standing up to Nat Sciver or Anya Shrubsole, moving to leg as Ellyse Perry or Trisha Chetty or Suné Luus shape for a glance or flick but get nothing on it. Taylor has spoken of "flowing with the line" and it's true there's something silky or liquid in the way her hands and body track the angle to make the catch then spirit the ball back as if through her own slipstream to the bails, batter teetering off-balance, Taylor already rushing towards teammates with arms fully outstretched, beaming.

Standing back, each ball had the glory-potential of a one-handed grab; up close, I could only dream of leg-side stumpings like Taylor's. Maybe you have to have kept wicket yourself to grasp the challenge: you're in a squat outside off, and when the bowler sends it down leg it's not just that you have a fraction of a second to adjust position, body following the advance party of your hands, but for a large fraction of that fraction the ball will be completely invisible behind the batsman, on the dark side of the moon, your hands moving blind, by dead reckoning. So it's not just an exhibition of physical speed and balance, but a computational miracle that Taylor can "know" where and when the ball will arrive and be there to meet it. Sciver couldn't have been bowling more than 70mph, so think about Jack Russell in early January 1991, the third Test against Australia at Sydney, when Dean Jones on 60 has been batting out of his crease, so Russell is standing up (no helmet!) to *Gladstone Small* to keep the batsman honest. Small fires it at 80-odd clicks down leg, Jones tries to glance but misses, and in blink-speed Russell has followed his hands blind a couple of yards to his left and the bails are gone, Jones already walking. No way Jack Russell ran out that morning wondering how he was going to "get in the batsman's head". And Russell was dropped for the next Test, replaced by Alec Stewart, the superior batsman…

"Well taken": I must have learned the phrase from my father, and that verb had resonance too – not "caught" but "taken", as if each ball were a criticism or compliment the keeper had to absorb and process. It was more than catching. You made your broad, webbed hands into a berth or nest, and gave with the elbows to cushion the landing. The technique evolved to protect the palms from repeated heavy impacts – the ball a meat hammer tenderising the fillets – but origin stories didn't matter when you saw or made those cradle shapes in the arms and the ball sank home so naturally you barely felt it. I don't remember when I last really talked about wicket-keeping with my father. Maybe it was around the time Russell faded from view, and Adam Gilchrist's phenomenal impact as a batsman forced everyone to think differently about the keeper's role – who cares about "flowing with the line" when you can score an Ashes century off 57 balls? But the conversation was still there when he lobbed an apple in the kitchen and made the stumping (Mum said he did the same when she threw him a pair of balled-up socks to put in his sock drawer) or held up his hands in silhouette with the window behind them, his fingers crooked like an old oak's staghead branches, and in those dreamy bye-less afternoons when each catch landed true, all the half-volley throws, wides and leg-side surprises, Dad's voice among my teammates' saying: "Well taken, Will. Well taken."

This article appeared in the 2019 autumn edition of The Nightwatchman, *the Wisden Cricket Quarterly which specialises in long-form articles by an array of international authors*

CAPTAIN: Joe Root (Test), Eoin Morgan (ODI/T20I)
COACH: Chris Silverwood

2020 SUMMER FIXTURES

June 4
England vs West Indies
1st Test
The Oval

June 12
England vs West Indies
2nd Test
Edgbaston

June 25
England vs West Indies
3rd Test
Lord's

July 3
England vs Australia
1st T20I
Chester-le-Street

July 5
England vs Australia
2nd T20I
Old Trafford

July 7
England vs Australia
3rd T20I
Headingley

July 11
England vs Australia
1st ODI
Lord's

July 14
England vs Australia
2nd ODI
Southampton

July 16
England vs Australia
3rd ODI
Bristol

July 30
England vs Pakistan
1st Test
Lord's

August 7
England vs Pakistan
2nd Test
Old Trafford

August 20
England vs Pakistan
3rd Test
Trent Bridge

August 29
England vs Pakistan
1st T20I
Headingley

August 31
England vs Pakistan
2nd T20I
Cardiff

September 2
England vs Pakistan
3rd T20I
Southampton

September 10
England vs Ireland
1st ODI
Trent Bridge

September 12
England vs Ireland
2nd ODI
Edgbaston

September 15
England vs Ireland
3rd ODI
The Oval

2020 KEY DATES

April 12-May 25
First phase of County Championship

May 28-July 12
T20 Blast group stage

June 17-July 8
Second phase of County Championship

July 17-August 13
The Hundred group stage (men and women)

July 19-August 16
One-Day Cup group and knockout stages

August 14
The Hundred – women's Finals Day, Hove

August 15
The Hundred – men's Finals Day, Lord's

August 26-September 25
Final phase of County Championship

September 5
T20 Blast Finals Day, Edgbaston

September 19
One-Day Cup final, Trent Bridge

As this book went to press the ECB announced that the county season would not begin before May 28 due to the coronavirus crisis

KEY

THE PLAYERS

LHB – Left-hand batsman
LB – Leg-break bowler
LF – Left-arm fast bowler
LFM – Left-arm fast-medium bowler
LM – Left-arm medium bowler
LMF – Left-arm medium-fast bowler
MCCU – Marylebone Cricket Club University
MVP – Denotes a player's presence in the top 100 places of the 2019 PCA County MVP Rankings (the number next to 'MVP' denotes the player's specific placing)
OB – Off-break bowler
R – 1,000 or more first-class runs in an English season (the number next to 'R' denotes how many times the player has achieved this feat)
RF – Right-arm fast bowler
RFM – Right-arm fast-medium bowler
RHB – Right-hand batsman
RM – Right-arm medium bowler
RMF – Right-arm medium-fast bowler
SLA – Slow left-arm orthodox bowler
SLW – Slow left-arm wrist-spin bowler
UCCE – University Centre of Cricketing Excellence
W – 50 or more first-class wickets in an English season (the number next to 'W' denotes how many times the player has achieved this feat)
WK – Wicketkeeper
* – Not-out innings (e.g. 137*)

THE TEAMS

(s) – A competition has been shared between two or more winners
C&G – Cheltenham & Gloucester Trophy (English domestic 50-over competition, 2001-2006)
CB40 – Clydesdale Bank 40 (English domestic 40-over competition, 2010-2012)
CC1/CC2 – County Championship Division One/Division Two
FP Trophy – Friends Provident Trophy (English domestic 50-over competition, 2007-2009)
Gillette – Gillette Cup (English domestic limited-overs competition, 1963-1980)
NatWest – NatWest Trophy (English domestic limited-overs competition, 1981-2000)
Pro40 – NatWest Pro40 (English domestic 40-over competition, 2005-2009)
REL – A player has been released by the relevant county
RET – A player has retired
RL50 – Royal London One-Day Cup (English domestic 50-over competition, 2014-2020)
T20 Cup – English domestic T20 competition (2003-2020)
YB40 – Yorkshire Bank 40 (English domestic 40-over competition, 2013)

NOTES: The statistics given for a player's best batting and best bowling performance are limited to first-class cricket, except where indicated. A field within a player's career statistics which is marked with an '-' indicates that a particular statistic is inapplicable, e.g. a player has never bowled a ball in first-class cricket. All stats correct as of March 16, 2020.

The
Teams

DERBYSHIRE

FORMED: 1870
HOME GROUND: The Pattonair County Ground, Derby
ONE-DAY NAME: Derbyshire Falcons
CAPTAIN: Billy Godleman
2019 RESULTS: CC2: 7/10; RL50: 5/9 North Group; T20: Semi-finalists
HONOURS: Championship: 1936; Gillette/NatWest/C&G/FP Trophy: 1981; Benson & Hedges Cup: 1993; Sunday League: 1990

THE LOWDOWN

Derbyshire appear at last to have found some backroom stability under head of cricket Dave Houghton, and there are signs it is paying off. The club reached their first Finals Day last year, inspired by T20 coach Dominic Cork. Club captain Billy Godleman, spared the off-field distractions of recent seasons, passed 1,000 Championship runs for the second time in his career and amassed another 974 in white-ball cricket. The evergreen Ravi Rampaul seems to have rediscovered his mojo, while Luis Reece – who opens with bat and ball in four-day cricket – has matured into one of the best allrounders on the circuit. And there is Fynn Hudson-Prentice, the 24-year-old allrounder who was plucked from MCC Young Cricketers last May and became an instant hit. They will miss the runs of Tom Lace, who has returned to Middlesex after a loan spell, and England U19 spinner Hamidullah Qadri has moved on to Kent. Australian paceman Sean Abbott will bolster the attack in the first half of the season, and Derbyshire have taken a punt on 21-year-old Michael Cohen, a South African left-armer who qualifies on an EU passport. Daryn Smit retired in January to take on a development role aimed at nurturing the county's local talent.

IN: Michael Cohen (SA, EU passport), Sean Abbott (Aus, CC/T20), Ben McDermott (Aus, RL50/T20
OUT: Hamidullah Qadri (Ken), James Taylor (Sur), Alfie Gleadall (REL), Daryn Smit (RET)

HEAD OF CRICKET: DAVE HOUGHTON

A former Zimbabwe captain, Houghton averaged 43 from 22 Tests after his country acquired Test status in 1992. He has vast experience on the county circuit, with previous stints as batting coach for Derbyshire, Somerset and Middlesex. He was head coach at Derbyshire between 2004 and 2007, returning to the club in October 2018 as head of cricket. Club icon Dominic Cork stays on for a second successive season as T20 head coach.

COUNTY CHAMPIONSHIP AVERAGES 2019

Batting

	Mat	Inns	NO	Runs	HS	Ave	SR	100	50	4s	6s
TC Lace	10	19	1	780	143	43.33	49.87	3	3	102	1
JL du Plooy	10	17	3	554	118	39.57	47.18	2	2	66	4
BA Godleman	14	26	0	1008	227	38.76	58.46	4	2	131	3
WL Madsen	13	24	1	794	204*	34.52	60.70	1	3	119	1
FJ Hudson-Prentice	7	12	2	342	99	34.20	69.09	0	2	48	4
LM Reece	14	26	0	785	184	30.19	52.71	2	1	119	1
HR Hosein	14	25	3	618	91*	28.09	49.00	0	5	68	0
AL Hughes	11	20	1	510	109*	26.84	41.09	1	1	60	1
MJJ Critchley	14	23	2	461	79*	21.95	60.18	0	3	62	3
AK Dal	9	16	3	278	92	21.38	43.57	0	2	23	0
S Conners	2	2	1	20	14	20.00	28.98	0	0	2	0
LV van Beek	9	12	3	127	34*	14.11	41.10	0	0	17	1
R Rampaul	12	19	5	186	30	13.28	72.37	0	0	19	8
Hamidullah Qadri	2	4	2	23	17*	11.50	67.64	0	0	3	0
AP Palladino	10	15	3	134	58	11.16	40.97	0	1	16	0
MH McKiernan	1	2	0	7	7	3.50	25.92	0	0	1	0
DR Melton	2	2	1	1	1*	1.00	6.66	0	0	0	0

Bowling

	Overs	Mdns	Runs	Wkts	BBI	BBM	Ave	Econ	SR	5w	10w
LM Reece	371.0	105	1022	52	6/58	6/62	19.65	2.75	42.8	3	0
AK Dal	45.4	8	142	7	3/11	3/11	20.28	3.10	39.1	0	0
FJ Hudson-Prentice	148.0	38	465	20	3/27	6/69	23.25	3.14	44.4	0	0
AP Palladino	282.5	99	652	27	5/29	7/59	24.14	2.30	62.8	1	0
R Rampaul	374.0	79	1139	44	5/77	8/130	25.88	3.04	51.0	2	0
Hamidullah Qadri	31.3	3	140	5	2/24	4/70	28.00	4.44	37.8	0	0
LV van Beek	219.2	34	726	19	3/20	4/53	38.21	3.31	69.2	0	0
S Conners	23.0	3	77	2	1/36	1/36	38.50	3.34	69.0	0	0
MJJ Critchley	229.1	26	841	19	4/107	5/121	44.26	3.66	72.3	0	0
JL du Plooy	46.3	2	182	4	2/24	2/42	45.50	3.91	69.7	0	0
WL Madsen	59.0	12	188	4	1/12	1/12	47.00	3.18	88.5	0	0
DR Melton	17.5	1	94	2	1/24	2/54	47.00	5.27	53.5	0	0
AL Hughes	81.0	14	219	3	1/11	1/11	73.00	2.70	162.0	0	0

Catches/Stumpings:

32 Hosein (inc 2st), 21 Madsen, 14 Critchley, 11 Hughes, 10 Lace, 9 du Plooy, 5 Dal, Reece, van Beek, 3 McKiernan, 2 Godleman, Rampaul, 1 Hudson-Prentice, Melton

ROYAL LONDON ONE-DAY CUP AVERAGES 2019

Batting

	Mat	Inns	NO	Runs	HS	Ave	SR	100	50	4s	6s
BA Godleman	8	8	1	521	116	74.42	88.30	3	1	40	10
MJJ Critchley	8	8	5	208	64*	69.33	113.04	0	1	14	5
WL Madsen	8	8	1	406	119*	58.00	106.84	2	1	42	11
JL du Plooy	5	5	1	222	75	55.50	108.29	0	2	19	7
LM Reece	8	8	0	310	128	38.75	95.67	1	1	35	4
AL Hughes	8	6	1	139	69	27.80	108.59	0	1	11	4
AK Dal	4	2	0	54	52	27.00	128.57	0	1	3	1
HR Hosein	8	6	2	87	41*	21.75	104.81	0	0	5	1
TC Lace	8	6	0	108	48	18.00	85.03	0	0	6	3
LV van Beek	5	3	2	9	6*	9.00	75.00	0	0	0	0
S Conners	3	1	0	4	4	4.00	200.00	0	0	1	0
MRJ Watt	6	1	0	1	1	1.00	100.00	0	0	0	0
AP Palladino	1	1	1	1	1*	-	100.00	0	0	0	0
AF Gleadall	2	-	-	-	-	-	-	-	-	-	-
R Rampaul	6	-	-	-	-	-	-	-	-	-	-

Bowling

	Overs	Mdns	Runs	Wkts	BBI	Ave	Econ	SR	4w	5w
WL Madsen	35.0	1	183	2	1/18	91.50	5.22	105.0	0	0
R Rampaul	51.0	3	267	8	2/25	33.37	5.23	38.2	0	0
AP Palladino	7.0	0	38	0	-	-	5.42	-	0	0
MRJ Watt	46.2	0	275	6	2/32	45.83	5.93	46.3	0	0
MJJ Critchley	50.0	0	313	5	3/73	62.60	6.26	60.0	0	0
AL Hughes	42.0	2	264	7	4/44	37.71	6.28	36.0	1	0
LM Reece	53.0	0	334	5	2/59	66.80	6.30	63.6	0	0
S Conners	23.0	1	150	2	1/45	75.00	6.52	69.0	0	0
LV van Beek	37.0	0	264	7	3/50	37.71	7.13	31.7	0	0
AF Gleadall	14.0	0	101	3	3/43	33.66	7.21	28.0	0	0
JL du Plooy	1.4	0	13	0	-	-	7.80	-	0	0
TC Lace	2.0	0	20	2	2/20	10.00	10.00	6.0	0	0

Catches/Stumpings:
9 Hosein (inc 2st), 6 Madsen, 4 Hughes, 3 Reece, 2 Critchley, Conners, Godleman, Lace, van Beek, 1 Dal, du Plooy, Rampaul

VITALITY BLAST AVERAGES 2019

Batting

	Mat	Inns	NO	Runs	HS	Ave	SR	100	50	4s	6s
WL Madsen	14	14	4	464	69	46.40	146.83	0	4	52	13
BA Godleman	14	14	3	453	92	41.18	115.85	0	4	36	14
D Smit	14	5	3	80	29*	40.00	111.11	0	0	6	1
JL du Plooy	14	12	4	312	70	39.00	133.33	0	3	24	9
LM Reece	14	13	0	325	61	25.00	126.95	0	3	30	13
AL Hughes	12	8	4	87	23	21.75	119.17	0	0	8	2
FJ Hudson-Prentice	14	7	2	94	31*	18.80	111.90	0	0	9	1
LV van Beek	12	4	2	34	16*	17.00	100.00	0	0	1	2
MJJ Critchley	14	10	1	94	21	10.44	100.00	0	0	6	2
DI Stevens	4	4	1	31	26*	10.33	110.71	0	0	2	1
R Rampaul	14	4	2	15	7	7.50	78.94	0	0	0	1
MRJ Watt	5	2	0	14	11	7.00	87.50	0	0	2	0
AK Dal	4	1	0	0	0	0.00	0.00	0	0	0	0
WB Rankin	5	-	-	-	-	-	-	-	-	-	-

Bowling

	Overs	Mdns	Runs	Wkts	BBI	Ave	Econ	SR	4w	5w
R Rampaul	54.0	1	362	23	3/17	15.73	6.70	14.0	0	0
AL Hughes	36.0	0	249	10	3/13	24.90	6.91	21.6	0	0
MJJ Critchley	44.1	0	315	17	4/36	18.52	7.13	15.5	1	0
LM Reece	34.0	0	270	10	2/9	27.00	7.94	20.4	0	0
LV van Beek	31.0	0	264	9	4/17	29.33	8.51	20.6	1	0
FJ Hudson-Prentice	37.0	1	320	11	2/2	29.09	8.64	20.1	0	0
MRJ Watt	20.0	0	181	7	4/19	25.85	9.05	17.1	1	0
WB Rankin	13.0	0	124	2	1/32	62.00	9.53	39.0	0	0
DI Stevens	4.0	0	43	0	-	-	10.75	-	0	0
WL Madsen	1.0	0	15	0	-	-	15.00	-	0	0

Catches/Stumpings:
12 Madsen, 10 Godleman, 9 du Plooy, Smit, 7 Hughes, 6 Reece, 5 Critchley, 4 van Beek, 3 Hudson-Prentice, 1 Dal, Rampaul, Rankin, Stevens

DURHAM

FORMED: 1882
HOME GROUND: Emirates Riverside
CAPTAIN: Cameron Bancroft
2019 RESULTS: CC2: 5/10; RL50: 4/9 North Group; T20: 6/9 North Group
HONOURS: Championship: (3) 2008, 2009, 2013; Gillette/NatWest/C&G/FP Trophy: 2007; Pro40/National League/CB40/YB40/RL50: 2014

THE LOWDOWN

Durham made steady improvements in Marcus North's first season as director of cricket last summer. They were unlucky to miss out on the knockout stages of the One-Day Cup – one victory was needed from their last two group games but both were washouts. The club were also competitive in T20 cricket and weren't far off Championship promotion despite losing their first four games. The pace attack, led by Ben Raine and the veteran Chris Rushworth, is a match for most, even without the injury-prone Mark Wood, but the batting looked bitty last summer. Ned Eckersley and Alex Lees rediscovered their touch but the local youngsters found life tough – with the exception of 20-year-old Scott Steel, who looks a fine prospect at the top of the order in white-ball cricket. South African batsman Farhaan Behardien brings a wealth of experience to the middle order, and compatriot David Bedingham adds more beef to the batting. Allrounder Paul Coughlin returns to the club after an injury-ridden two years at Nottinghamshire, while Australian opener Cameron Bancroft continues to lead the side. Wicketkeeper Stuart Poynter has called time on his Ireland career to qualify as a local player.

IN: Paul Coughlin (Not), David Bedingham (SA, UK visa), Cameron Bancroft (Aus), Farhaan Behardien (SA, Kolpak)
OUT: George Harding, Ryan Pringle (both REL)

DIRECTOR OF CRICKET: MARCUS NORTH

North played 21 Tests for Australia as well as scoring over 4,000 first-class runs for six different counties, including a successful season for Durham in 2004. He was appointed as Durham's director of cricket in September 2018 after three seasons as CEO at South Northumberland CC. As part of a structural overhaul, North appointed former New Zealand and Middlesex allrounder James Franklin as lead high performance coach in January 2019.

D

COUNTY CHAMPIONSHIP AVERAGES 2019

Batting

	Mat	Inns	NO	Runs	HS	Ave	SR	100	50	4s	6s
BJ Watling	2	3	1	139	104*	69.50	48.43	1	0	17	0
CT Bancroft	9	17	1	726	158	45.37	45.17	2	3	76	2
EJH Eckersley	13	22	4	720	118	40.00	45.02	1	4	71	1
AZ Lees	14	25	1	899	181	37.45	46.31	3	3	97	6
NJ Rimmington	6	9	2	210	92	30.00	58.33	0	2	27	2
PSP Handscomb	2	3	0	86	54	28.66	62.31	0	1	12	0
JTA Burnham	13	23	1	598	86	27.18	48.34	0	4	78	5
L Trevaskis	10	17	1	392	64	24.50	37.36	0	2	39	1
GJ Harte	11	21	1	459	77	22.95	37.96	0	3	41	3
BA Raine	14	23	2	464	82	22.09	44.91	0	2	49	1
BA Carse	10	15	3	246	77*	20.50	46.06	0	1	33	0
AJ Robson	4	6	0	97	64	16.16	35.14	0	1	11	0
CT Steel	6	10	0	133	39	13.30	44.48	0	0	18	0
S Steel	2	4	0	48	39	12.00	71.64	0	0	6	0
MJ Potts	3	5	1	46	20	11.50	42.99	0	0	7	0
G Clark	4	8	1	79	26	11.28	41.79	0	0	10	0
RD Pringle	2	4	0	41	30	10.25	87.23	0	0	8	0
MET Salisbury	5	10	1	76	23	8.44	33.77	0	0	10	0
SW Poynter	1	2	0	15	8	7.50	45.45	0	0	2	0
WJ Weighell	3	5	0	37	24	7.40	53.62	0	0	5	0
MJ Richardson	1	2	0	12	7	6.00	24.00	0	0	2	0
C Rushworth	14	19	8	56	12*	5.09	31.81	0	0	7	0
MA Jones	2	3	0	9	9	3.00	20.93	0	0	0	0
WR Smith	1	2	0	4	4	2.00	44.44	0	0	0	0
SJD Bell	1	1	0	1	1	1.00	10.00	0	0	0	0

Bowling

	Overs	Mdns	Runs	Wkts	BBI	BBM	Ave	Econ	SR	5w	10w
CT Steel	10.0	1	35	2	2/35	2/35	17.50	3.50	30.0	0	0
C Rushworth	486.4	127	1271	69	6/39	10/67	18.42	2.61	42.3	4	1
BA Raine	463.4	122	1179	54	6/27	9/96	21.83	2.54	51.5	3	0
MET Salisbury	137.1	27	448	19	4/67	6/71	23.57	3.26	43.3	0	0
NJ Rimmington	140.2	29	392	16	4/42	8/116	24.50	2.79	52.6	0	0
WJ Weighell	75.1	17	222	9	3/41	5/104	24.66	2.95	50.1	0	0
GJ Harte	91.0	23	256	10	4/15	4/36	25.60	2.81	54.6	0	0
BA Carse	250.4	42	940	35	6/26	7/63	26.85	3.75	42.9	3	0
L Trevaskis	149.3	36	410	6	2/96	3/116	68.33	2.74	149.5	0	0
JOI Campbell	28.0	3	87	1	1/43	1/87	87.00	3.10	168.0	0	0
MJ Potts	68.0	13	213	2	1/47	1/75	106.50	3.13	204.0	0	0
S Steel	7.0	3	16	0	-	-	-	2.28	-	0	0
JTA Burnham	10.1	2	17	0	-	-	-	1.67	-	0	0

Catches/Stumpings:

42 Eckersley, 16 Bancroft, 10 Lees, 6 Robson, 5 Richardson, 4 Burnham, Clark, Handscomb, 3 Poynter, Rimmington, Rushworth, 2 Harte, C Steel, Trevaskis, 1 Carse, Pringle, Potts, Smith, S Steel, Watling, Weighell

D

ROYAL LONDON ONE-DAY CUP AVERAGES 2019

Batting

	Mat	Inns	NO	Runs	HS	Ave	SR	100	50	4s	6s
CT Bancroft	8	7	3	377	151*	94.25	95.44	2	0	26	9
AZ Lees	8	7	3	361	115	90.25	83.37	1	4	25	5
MJ Richardson	6	4	1	215	102	71.66	91.88	1	1	13	6
GJ Harte	4	2	1	65	51*	65.00	91.54	0	1	6	0
JTA Burnham	8	4	2	70	45	35.00	100.00	0	0	4	2
S Steel	8	7	0	227	68	32.42	80.78	0	2	31	0
BA Raine	8	4	2	62	32	31.00	86.11	0	0	8	1
MJ Potts	7	1	0	22	22	22.00	95.65	0	0	3	0
G Clark	6	6	0	89	66	14.83	80.90	0	1	10	1
L Trevaskis	8	3	0	16	16	5.33	84.21	0	0	3	0
BA Carse	7	1	0	2	2	2.00	28.57	0	0	0	0
WJ Weighell	2	1	0	1	1	1.00	33.33	0	0	0	0
MET Salisbury	6	1	1	2	2*	-	66.66	0	0	0	0
MA Wood	2	-	-	-	-	-	-	-	-	-	-

Bowling

	Overs	Mdns	Runs	Wkts	BBI	Ave	Econ	SR	4w	5w
L Trevaskis	42.0	2	187	7	2/37	26.71	4.45	36.0	0	0
BA Raine	47.4	3	220	7	2/25	31.42	4.61	40.8	0	0
WJ Weighell	17.0	1	83	2	2/43	41.50	4.88	51.0	0	0
MJ Potts	44.0	2	236	10	4/62	23.60	5.36	26.4	1	0
MET Salisbury	52.0	3	279	9	3/51	31.00	5.36	34.6	0	0
BA Carse	40.5	5	223	10	3/52	22.30	5.46	24.5	0	0
S Steel	9.0	0	53	1	1/38	53.00	5.88	54.0	0	0
GJ Harte	13.0	0	81	1	1/53	81.00	6.23	78.0	0	0

Catches/Stumpings:
9 Bancroft, 4 Burnham, Raine, 3 Clark, S Steel, 2 Carse, Harte, Lees, 1 Potts

VITALITY BLAST AVERAGES 2019

Batting

	Mat	Inns	NO	Runs	HS	Ave	SR	100	50	4s	6s
DJM Short	12	12	1	483	77*	43.90	139.59	0	4	59	14
PSP Handscomb	9	8	2	206	65*	34.33	120.46	0	1	11	2
S Steel	11	11	0	369	70	33.54	136.66	0	2	28	15
AZ Lees	8	7	2	128	44	25.60	107.56	0	0	5	4
G Clark	11	11	2	196	59*	21.77	134.24	0	1	16	6
HRD Adair	3	3	0	45	32	15.00	93.75	0	0	2	1
SW Poynter	9	7	3	51	19*	12.75	124.39	0	0	3	0
BA Carse	10	5	0	42	14	8.40	127.27	0	0	3	1
JTA Burnham	8	5	0	39	23	7.80	97.50	0	0	2	1
BA Raine	9	8	1	44	13	6.28	86.27	0	0	5	0
L Trevaskis	12	8	2	30	7*	5.00	83.33	0	0	0	1
MJ Potts	12	5	3	8	3*	4.00	88.88	0	0	0	0
GJ Harte	3	2	0	7	6	3.50	63.63	0	0	1	0
NJ Rimmington	12	3	2	3	2	3.00	60.00	0	0	0	0
WJ Weighell	2	2	2	2	2*	-	100.00	0	0	0	0
C Rushworth	1	-	-	-	-	-	-	-	-	-	-

Bowling

	Overs	Mdns	Runs	Wkts	BBI	Ave	Econ	SR	4w	5w
S Steel	16.0	0	99	5	1/6	19.80	6.18	19.2	0	0
GJ Harte	3.0	0	20	1	1/11	20.00	6.66	18.0	0	0
NJ Rimmington	43.5	0	305	16	3/15	19.06	6.95	16.4	0	0
L Trevaskis	40.1	0	281	12	3/16	23.41	6.99	20.0	0	0
DJM Short	40.2	0	318	13	2/19	24.46	7.88	18.6	0	0
MJ Potts	39.5	0	332	17	3/22	19.52	8.33	14.0	0	0
BA Carse	33.0	1	294	7	1/21	42.00	8.90	28.2	0	0
C Rushworth	2.0	0	19	0	-	-	9.50	-	0	0
BA Raine	7.0	0	74	1	1/23	74.00	10.57	42.0	0	0
WJ Weighell	2.0	0	29	0	-	-	14.50	-	0	0

Catches/Stumpings:
7 Clark, 6 Burnham, 5 Carse, Short, 4 Handscomb, Potts, Trevaskis, 3 Poynter (inc 2st), Lees, 2 Adair, Harte, Raine, Rimmington, 1 Rushworth, S Steel

ESSEX

FORMED: 1876
HOME GROUND: The Cloudfm County Ground, Chelmsford
ONE-DAY NAME: Essex Eagles
CAPTAIN: Tom Westley, Simon Harmer (T20)
2019 RESULTS: CC1: Winners; RL50: 8/9 South Group; T20: Winners
HONOURS: Championship: (8) 1979, 1983, 1984, 1986, 1991, 1992, 2017, 2019; Gillette/NatWest/C&G/FP Trophy: (3) 1985, 1997, 2008; B&H Cup: (2) 1979, 1998; Pro40/National League/CB40/YB40/RL50: (2) 2005, 2006; Sunday League: (3) 1981, 1984, 1985; T20 Cup: 2019

THE LOWDOWN

This Essex team are on the cusp of greatness. Last summer's Championship title was their second in three seasons, and they doubled up with a long-awaited first T20 trophy. Much more of this and we'll soon be talking about an Essex era. The portents are good, even if the club have lost their talismanic allrounder Ravi Bopara – who scored nearly 20,000 runs in 18 years at Chelmsford – and begin their title defence under a new captain, with Ryan ten Doeschate handing over the captaincy to Tom Westley. Alastair Cook has pledged to play "for another year at least", while ten Doeschate – who turns 40 in June – signed a new one-year deal in October. Jamie Porter and Simon Harmer have taken the bowling plaudits but the young pace duo of Sam Cook and Aaron Beard have also been outstanding. Meanwhile the tireless Peter Siddle returns for his fourth summer at Chelmsford. In the T20 Blast Essex can count on South African batsman Cameron Delport – one of the most destructive hitters in the land – and Aussie leg-spinner Adam Zampa, who will resume his potent spin partnership with Harmer. Perhaps the only concern is in the wicketkeeping department, with Adam Wheater yet to fully convince.

IN: Moises Henriques (Aus, T20), Adam Zampa (Aus, T20)
OUT: Ravi Bopara (Sus), Matt Coles (REL)

HEAD COACH: ANTHONY MCGRATH

The club have gone from strength to strength since McGrath joined the backroom staff in 2016. He helped deliver back-to-back titles in Division Two and Division One as assistant coach before securing the Championship-T20 double last season after replacing Chris Silverwood as head coach in 2017. McGrath scored more than 23,000 runs and took 240 wickets in an 18-year career for Yorkshire, retiring in 2013. He played four Tests and 14 ODIs.

COUNTY CHAMPIONSHIP AVERAGES 2019

Batting

	Mat	Inns	NO	Runs	HS	Ave	SR	100	50	4s	6s
AN Cook	14	24	4	913	125	45.65	45.31	1	7	117	0
RS Bopara	10	14	1	514	135	39.53	51.86	2	2	60	2
DW Lawrence	14	22	3	725	147	38.15	52.12	1	5	97	2
T Westley	14	23	1	794	141	36.09	47.65	1	3	113	2
PM Siddle	8	11	4	227	60	32.42	53.41	0	1	20	5
Mohammad Amir	1	2	1	32	28	32.00	74.41	0	0	4	0
NLJ Browne	14	23	1	604	163	27.45	39.45	1	2	93	2
RN ten Doeschate	14	19	1	483	130	26.83	58.47	2	1	54	4
AP Beard	7	9	4	112	41	22.40	42.42	0	0	13	0
RG White	2	2	0	41	39	20.50	45.55	0	0	4	0
SR Harmer	14	19	2	340	62	20.00	51.75	0	2	47	3
RK Patel	4	5	0	87	35	17.40	39.90	0	0	11	0
AJA Wheater	10	12	1	177	30*	16.09	53.79	0	0	25	0
MR Quinn	3	5	2	23	10	7.66	16.66	0	0	2	0
SJ Cook	9	10	2	54	37*	6.75	33.75	0	0	4	1
MS Pepper	1	2	0	8	7	4.00	27.58	0	0	1	0
JA Porter	13	15	5	31	17	3.10	15.50	0	0	3	0
ASS Nijjar	1	1	0	2	2	2.00	66.66	0	0	0	0
WEL Buttleman	1	1	0	0	0	0.00	0.00	0	0	0	0

Bowling

	Overs	Mdns	Runs	Wkts	BBI	BBM	Ave	Econ	SR	5w	10w
Mohammad Amir	30.0	8	64	6	4/48	6/64	10.66	2.13	30.0	0	0
ASS Nijjar	4.4	0	18	1	1/18	1/18	18.00	3.85	28.0	0	0
SR Harmer	595.5	175	1518	83	8/98	12/61	18.28	2.54	43.0	10	2
PM Siddle	263.4	72	683	34	6/104	7/80	20.08	2.59	46.5	2	0
SJ Cook	235.5	61	673	32	7/23	12/65	21.03	2.85	44.2	3	1
AP Beard	114.0	18	406	17	4/23	7/45	23.88	3.56	40.2	0	0
JA Porter	391.2	83	1234	48	5/51	9/73	25.70	3.15	48.9	2	0
RS Bopara	69.0	12	222	6	2/54	2/54	37.00	3.21	69.0	0	0
MR Quinn	89.0	12	327	5	3/104	3/104	65.40	3.67	106.8	0	0
RN ten Doeschate	7.0	0	21	0	-	-	-	3.00	-	0	0
DW Lawrence	23.0	4	52	0	-	-	-	2.26	-	0	0
T Westley	15.0	2	58	0	-	-	-	3.86	-	0	0

Catches/Stumpings:
29 Wheater (inc 3st), 15 A Cook, Harmer, 11 Browne, Westley, 9 Bopara, 8 Lawrence, ten Doeschate, 6 Pepper, White (inc 2st), 3 Beard, Buttleman, Porter, 2 S Cook, Siddle, 1 Lawrence, Patel

ROYAL LONDON ONE-DAY CUP AVERAGES 2019

Batting

	Mat	Inns	NO	Runs	HS	Ave	SR	100	50	4s	6s
V Chopra	5	5	0	421	156	84.20	88.25	3	0	37	5
T Westley	8	8	0	373	77	46.62	99.20	0	4	36	4
RN ten Doeschate	6	6	0	227	89	37.83	128.97	0	1	21	5
DW Lawrence	8	8	0	270	56	33.75	95.74	0	4	20	5
MT Coles	4	3	1	57	34	28.50	126.66	0	0	4	2
AN Cook	8	8	0	204	53	25.50	85.35	0	1	30	1
AP Beard	2	2	1	24	22*	24.00	120.00	0	0	3	0
RS Bopara	8	8	0	179	89	22.37	95.72	0	1	15	2
RG White	8	8	4	87	21*	21.75	114.47	0	0	7	1
RK Patel	3	3	0	65	35	21.66	91.54	0	0	8	0
PI Walter	4	4	1	59	25	19.66	83.09	0	0	5	2
SR Harmer	6	6	1	93	28	18.60	97.89	0	0	5	3
SJ Cook	4	2	1	7	6	7.00	63.63	0	0	0	0
PM Siddle	6	3	1	8	4	4.00	72.72	0	0	1	0
MR Quinn	2	1	0	4	4	4.00	80.00	0	0	1	0
JA Porter	6	3	3	14	7*	-	73.68	0	0	0	0

Bowling

	Overs	Mdns	Runs	Wkts	BBI	Ave	Econ	SR	4w	5w
JA Porter	50.0	2	252	4	2/44	63.00	5.04	75.0	0	0
AP Beard	19.0	0	97	3	3/51	32.33	5.10	38.0	0	0
PM Siddle	49.0	1	265	12	4/60	22.08	5.40	24.5	1	0
SJ Cook	31.0	1	179	6	3/37	29.83	5.77	31.0	0	0
SR Harmer	41.0	0	237	4	2/44	59.25	5.78	61.5	0	0
RS Bopara	54.0	2	326	8	3/26	40.75	6.03	40.5	0	0
T Westley	5.0	0	31	1	1/31	31.00	6.20	30.0	0	0
DW Lawrence	41.3	0	270	5	2/52	54.00	6.50	49.8	0	0
MT Coles	33.4	0	252	9	4/48	28.00	7.48	22.4	1	0
MR Quinn	18.0	0	144	2	2/64	72.00	8.00	54.0	0	0
RN ten Doeschate	2.0	0	16	1	1/16	16.00	8.00	12.0	0	0
PI Walter	12.0	0	108	1	1/56	108.00	9.00	72.0	0	0

Catches/Stumpings:
16 White (inc 2st), 5 Harmer, 4 Porter, 3 Chopra, 2 Coles, A Cook, Lawrence, Walter, Westley, Quinn, ten Doeschate

VITALITY BLAST AVERAGES 2019

Batting

	Mat	Inns	NO	Runs	HS	Ave	SR	100	50	4s	6s
RS Bopara	12	11	5	291	70*	48.50	162.56	0	1	18	14
DW Lawrence	14	13	2	386	69	35.09	152.56	0	4	24	21
RN ten Doeschate	14	13	5	269	74*	33.62	120.62	0	3	18	6
T Westley	14	14	2	363	86*	30.25	130.57	0	1	42	8
CS Delport	14	14	0	409	129	29.21	167.62	1	3	40	24
PI Walter	11	7	4	79	26*	26.33	127.41	0	0	8	1
AP Beard	8	2	1	17	13	17.00	141.66	0	0	1	1
AJA Wheater	14	13	2	178	39	16.18	112.65	0	0	16	2
SR Harmer	14	7	3	43	18*	10.75	138.70	0	0	5	0
V Chopra	3	3	0	31	19	10.33	93.93	0	0	2	1
A Zampa	12	2	1	8	6*	8.00	80.00	0	0	1	0
S Snater	5	2	1	3	2	3.00	60.00	0	0	0	0
Mohammad Amir	8	2	0	2	1	1.00	33.33	0	0	0	0
MR Quinn	4	1	0	1	1	1.00	33.33	0	0	0	0
SJ Cook	1	-	-	-	-	-	-	-	-	-	-
ASS Nijjar	2	-	-	-	-	-	-	-	-	-	-
JA Porter	4	-	-	-	-	-	-	-	-	-	-

Bowling

	Overs	Mdns	Runs	Wkts	BBI	Ave	Econ	SR	4w	5w
ASS Nijjar	8.0	0	57	3	3/26	19.00	7.12	16.0	0	0
Mohammad Amir	27.0	0	201	10	4/29	20.10	7.44	16.2	1	0
RS Bopara	35.0	0	261	12	3/18	21.75	7.45	17.5	0	0
DW Lawrence	9.0	0	70	3	2/26	23.33	7.77	18.0	0	0
A Zampa	43.0	1	347	12	2/31	28.91	8.06	21.5	0	0
SR Harmer	42.4	0	348	17	4/19	20.47	8.15	15.0	1	0
CS Delport	13.4	0	123	3	1/10	41.00	9.00	27.3	0	0
MR Quinn	13.0	0	123	6	3/34	20.50	9.46	13.0	0	0
SJ Cook	2.0	0	19	0	-	-	9.50	-	0	0
JA Porter	12.5	0	122	8	4/38	15.25	9.50	9.6	1	0
AP Beard	20.0	0	193	6	2/31	32.16	9.65	20.0	0	0
PI Walter	7.0	0	73	2	1/12	36.50	10.42	21.0	0	0
S Snater	13.0	0	157	4	2/44	39.25	12.07	19.5	0	0

Catches/Stumpings:
12 Harmer, 9 Bopara, Wheater (inc 4st), 7 Westley, 5 Walter, 4 Lawrence, 3 ten Doeschate, 2 Delport, Snater, 1 Beard, Chopra, Nijjar, Porter, Zampa

GLAMORGAN

FORMED: 1888
HOME GROUND: Sophia Gardens, Cardiff
CAPTAIN: Chris Cooke, David Lloyd (RL50)
2019 RESULTS: CC2: 4/10; RL50: 6/9 South Group; T20: 9/9 South Group
HONOURS: Championship: (3) 1948, 1969, 1997; Pro40/National League/ CB40/YB40/ RL50: (2) 2002, 2004; Sunday League: 1993

THE LOWDOWN

Glamorgan made significant improvements last summer under interim head coach Matthew Maynard, who signed a permanent three-year deal at the end of the season. Bottom of the pile in 2018, the club pushed for Championship promotion right up until September. Marnus Labuschagne was signed last April as the Aussie with the unusual surname and ended the year as one of the best batsmen on the planet. In November he agreed a new two-year deal. Labuschagne passed 1,000 Championship runs in just nine matches, and his firm presence at No.3 brought much-needed stability to the batting. Nick Selman and Billy Root both shone, while David Lloyd – who captains the 50-over side this summer – at last found some consistency. The bowling, however, relies heavily on 38-year-old Michael Hogan. Marchant de Lange will want to make more of an impact with the red ball in 2020. Watch out for 23-year-old Dan Douthwaite, a highly regarded allrounder who broke into the team last year. As for T20, it's a case of starting from scratch after one win in 14 matches last season. Four-day skipper Chris Cooke has replaced Colin Ingram as captain for the Blast.

IN: Marnus Labuschagne (Aus)
OUT: Jeremy Lawlor (REL)

HEAD COACH: MATTHEW MAYNARD

Maynard was appointed interim coach after Robert Croft stepped down in October 2018, before agreeing a three-year deal last November. Previously he had a three-year spell as Glamorgan coach between 2008 and 2010, returning as a batting consultant in 2018 following a stint as Somerset's director of cricket. A dashing batsman for Glamorgan during a 20-year career, Maynard made a club-record 54 centuries and was a key figure in the side that won the County Championship in 1997. He played four Tests and 14 ODIs.

G

COUNTY CHAMPIONSHIP AVERAGES 2019

Batting

	Mat	Inns	NO	Runs	HS	Ave	SR	100	50	4s	6s
M Labuschagne	10	18	1	1114	182	65.52	76.19	5	5	154	8
KC Brathwaite	3	4	1	166	103*	55.33	37.55	1	0	17	1
CB Cooke	7	10	2	368	96	46.00	70.36	0	2	56	3
T van der Gugten	8	10	7	135	30*	45.00	63.38	0	0	14	4
WT Root	14	22	1	768	229	36.57	64.05	2	1	99	1
TN Cullen	9	12	3	319	63	35.44	43.51	0	4	35	0
NJ Selman	14	24	2	752	150	34.18	46.50	1	6	95	0
KS Carlson	3	4	0	130	111	32.50	81.76	1	0	20	0
GG Wagg	10	16	3	418	100	32.15	61.02	1	1	49	9
CR Hemphrey	10	18	1	546	75	32.11	41.71	0	5	77	3
SR Patel	4	6	0	187	66	31.16	66.31	0	2	25	2
DL Lloyd	14	23	1	668	97	30.36	53.26	0	4	97	3
MG Hogan	11	12	6	166	54	27.66	109.93	0	1	22	6
LJ Carey	9	12	3	230	62*	25.55	86.14	0	2	35	3
DA Douthwaite	7	12	0	298	63	24.83	61.95	0	1	44	1
JL Lawlor	2	4	0	74	25	18.50	43.78	0	0	9	1
AO Morgan	4	6	1	82	43	16.40	42.05	0	0	11	1
AG Salter	2	3	0	47	26	15.66	30.92	0	0	3	0
M de Lange	8	10	1	127	45*	14.11	101.60	0	0	16	7
SE Marsh	1	2	0	17	9	8.50	34.69	0	0	1	0
RAJ Smith	3	5	0	35	18	7.00	76.08	0	0	6	1
KA Bull	1	2	0	7	5	3.50	14.89	0	0	0	0

Bowling

	Overs	Mdns	Runs	Wkts	BBI	BBM	Ave	Econ	SR	5w	10w
MG Hogan	349.0	85	974	46	5/62	7/71	21.17	2.79	45.5	1	0
NJ Selman	3.3	0	22	1	1/22	1/22	22.00	6.28	21.0	0	0
SR Patel	122.1	40	292	12	4/58	6/103	24.33	2.39	61.0	0	0
AG Salter	45.0	12	103	4	3/6	4/23	25.75	2.28	67.5	0	0
RAJ Smith	67.0	11	224	7	3/43	3/53	32.00	3.34	57.4	0	0
WT Root	19.0	4	69	2	2/63	2/63	34.50	3.63	57.0	0	0
DA Douthwaite	132.1	10	612	17	4/48	6/137	36.00	4.63	46.6	0	0
M de Lange	244.4	33	950	26	4/64	7/125	36.53	3.88	56.4	0	0
M Labuschagne	192.2	16	724	19	3/52	5/77	38.10	3.76	60.7	0	0
LJ Carey	242.3	50	766	19	4/54	5/89	40.31	3.15	76.5	0	0
DL Lloyd	128.1	22	437	10	2/35	2/31	43.70	3.40	76.9	0	0
GG Wagg	236.0	35	789	17	3/59	5/94	46.41	3.34	83.2	0	0
T van der Gugten	198.0	26	705	15	3/44	5/112	47.00	3.56	79.2	0	0
KA Bull	36.0	6	100	2	2/42	2/100	50.00	2.77	108.0	0	0
CR Hemphrey	43.0	4	163	2	1/17	1/35	81.50	3.79	129.0	0	0
JL Lawlor	6.0	1	15	0	-	-	-	2.50	-	0	0
KS Carlson	15.0	2	52	0	-	-	-	3.46	-	0	0
AO Morgan	31.0	2	108	0	-	-	-	3.48	-	0	0

Catches/Stumpings:

29 Cullen, 20 Cooke (inc 2st), 16 Lloyd, 12 Labuschagne, 10 Selman, 7 Hemphrey, 4 Root, 3 Hogan, Lawlor, 2 Brathwaite, Carlson, de Lange, van der Gugten, Wagg, 1 Bull, Douthwaite, Marsh, Morgan, Patel

ROYAL LONDON ONE-DAY CUP AVERAGES 2019

Batting

	Mat	Inns	NO	Runs	HS	Ave	SR	100	50	4s	6s
WT Root	8	7	1	386	113*	64.33	95.30	1	2	35	4
CB Cooke	8	8	0	337	161	42.12	96.01	1	0	34	9
DL Lloyd	8	8	1	240	84	34.28	93.02	0	2	29	4
M de Lange	8	7	2	159	58*	31.80	152.88	0	1	11	12
LJ Carey	7	4	1	92	39	30.66	101.09	0	0	12	1
DA Douthwaite	3	3	1	61	52*	30.50	141.86	0	1	6	2
GG Wagg	8	7	0	207	68	29.57	102.47	0	2	20	7
JL Lawlor	5	5	0	129	48	25.80	74.13	0	0	12	3
CR Hemphrey	8	6	0	134	87	22.33	93.70	0	1	15	2
M Labuschagne	8	8	1	123	54	17.57	67.95	0	1	9	3
KS Carlson	5	4	0	25	15	6.25	54.34	0	0	1	0
CAJ Meschede	3	3	0	10	10	3.33	41.66	0	0	1	0
T van der Gugten	5	2	2	23	18*	-	79.31	0	0	2	0
MG Hogan	3	2	2	12	10*	-	133.33	0	0	0	1
RI Walker	1	1	1	7	7*	-	233.33	0	0	0	1

Bowling

	Overs	Mdns	Runs	Wkts	BBI	Ave	Econ	SR	4w	5w
LJ Carey	48.0	3	251	4	2/64	62.75	5.22	72.0	0	0
RI Walker	4.0	0	21	0	-	-	5.25	-	0	0
WT Root	20.0	0	115	3	2/36	38.33	5.75	40.0	0	0
M Labuschagne	58.0	0	340	7	3/46	48.57	5.86	49.7	0	0
T van der Gugten	32.1	1	190	4	2/63	47.50	5.90	48.2	0	0
CAJ Meschede	15.0	0	89	1	1/27	89.00	5.93	90.0	0	0
DL Lloyd	4.0	0	24	0	-	-	6.00	-	0	0
MG Hogan	23.0	2	140	3	2/52	46.66	6.08	46.0	0	0
GG Wagg	52.3	1	327	9	3/46	36.33	6.22	35.0	0	0
DA Douthwaite	13.0	1	83	2	2/46	41.50	6.38	39.0	0	0
M de Lange	62.5	2	421	16	4/63	26.31	6.70	23.5	1	0
CR Hemphrey	2.0	0	20	0	-	-	10.00	-	0	0

Catches/Stumpings:
9 Cooke (inc 2st), 4 de Lange, Hemphrey, Lloyd, Root, 3 Labuschagne, 2 Carey, Carlson, Hogan, Lawlor, van der Gugten, Wagg, 1 Meschede

VITALITY BLAST AVERAGES 2019

GLAMORGAN

Batting

	Mat	Inns	NO	Runs	HS	Ave	SR	100	50	4s	6s
DL Lloyd	12	11	0	358	63	32.54	139.84	0	3	46	7
NJ Selman	3	3	0	93	40	31.00	143.07	0	0	11	3
CA Ingram	12	11	1	261	50*	26.10	145.00	0	2	19	15
CZ Taylor	4	3	2	23	16*	23.00	121.05	0	0	2	1
CB Cooke	12	11	2	196	45	21.77	145.18	0	0	8	12
SE Marsh	4	4	0	86	52	21.50	104.87	0	1	9	2
KS Carlson	1	1	0	18	18	18.00	128.57	0	0	1	1
AG Salter	12	6	3	51	39*	17.00	118.60	0	0	2	2
Fakhar Zaman	7	6	0	99	58	16.50	93.39	0	1	12	2
JL Lawlor	6	5	0	60	43	12.00	113.20	0	0	6	1
GG Wagg	9	6	1	55	36*	11.00	110.00	0	0	3	3
DA Douthwaite	8	8	2	64	24	10.66	83.11	0	0	3	2
WT Root	6	6	0	60	24	10.00	95.23	0	0	5	0
M de Lange	12	6	1	35	12	7.00	125.00	0	0	4	1
LJ Carey	5	3	2	7	5	7.00	70.00	0	0	1	0
RAJ Smith	4	2	1	7	7*	7.00	70.00	0	0	1	0
AO Morgan	5	4	1	15	11	5.00	62.50	0	0	0	1
MG Hogan	5	2	1	3	2*	3.00	60.00	0	0	0	0
RI Walker	3	1	0	1	1	1.00	33.33	0	0	0	0
P Sisodiya	2	-	-	-	-	-	-	-	-	-	-

Bowling

	Overs	Mdns	Runs	Wkts	BBI	Ave	Econ	SR	4w	5w
Fakhar Zaman	6.0	0	26	1	1/15	26.00	4.33	36.0	0	0
CZ Taylor	2.0	0	14	0	-	-	7.00	-	0	0
GG Wagg	23.0	0	170	5	2/28	34.00	7.39	27.6	0	0
AO Morgan	5.0	0	38	0	-	-	7.60	-	0	0
DL Lloyd	4.0	0	31	1	1/6	31.00	7.75	24.0	0	0
AG Salter	34.0	0	269	14	4/12	19.21	7.91	14.5	2	0
RAJ Smith	14.0	0	121	5	3/21	24.20	8.64	16.8	0	0
CA Ingram	3.0	0	26	0	-	-	8.66	-	0	0
P Sisodiya	8.0	0	70	1	1/45	70.00	8.75	48.0	0	0
DA Douthwaite	17.0	0	154	3	1/25	51.33	9.05	34.0	0	0
M de Lange	33.1	0	304	13	4/26	23.38	9.16	15.3	1	0
LJ Carey	16.0	0	148	2	1/15	74.00	9.25	48.0	0	0
MG Hogan	12.0	0	117	1	1/48	117.00	9.75	72.0	0	0
RI Walker	11.5	0	119	5	3/39	23.80	10.05	14.2	0	0

Catches/Stumpings:
6 Root, 4 de Lange, 3 Lawlor, Zaman, 2 Hogan, Ingram, Lloyd, Salter, 1 Carey, Douthwaite, Marsh, Selman, Smith, Taylor

GLOUCESTERSHIRE

FORMED: 1871
HOME GROUND: The Brightside Ground, Bristol
CAPTAIN: Chris Dent, TBC (T20)
2019 RESULTS: CC2: 3/10; RL50: 4/9 South Group; T20: Quarter-finalists
HONOURS: Gillette/NatWest/C&G/FP Trophy: (5) 1973, 1999, 2000, 2003, 2004; Benson & Hedges Cup: (3) 1977, 1999, 2000; Pro40/National League/CB40/YB40/RL50: (2) 2000, 2015

THE LOWDOWN

Gloucestershire are back in the top flight for the first time in 15 years, the culmination of an upward trend under coach Richard Dawson and captain Chris Dent, who passed 1,000 Championship runs last season and led the team astutely. Their talisman is 25-year-old Ryan Higgins, who has become one of the most explosive allrounders in county cricket since signing from Middlesex in 2017. Higgins led the club's Championship batting and bowling averages last summer, earning England Lions selection along with 22-year-old teammate James Bracey, who had another consistent season with the bat. Higgins was ably supported by the rest of the seamers but it will be tougher going in Division One. The club will hope for better luck with their overseas recruit after firing three duds last year. India's Cheteshwar Pujara has signed up for the first six Championship matches, while 19-year-old Afghan leggie Qais Ahmad will play in the T20 Blast as well as the last six four-day matches. Ex-West Indies paceman Jerome Taylor has signed a three-year Kolpak deal. Gloucestershire are generally competitive in the shorter formats, although white-ball specialists Michael Klinger and Chris Liddle have both retired.

IN: George Scott (Mid), Josh Shaw (Yor), Jerome Taylor (WI, Kolpak), Cheteshwar Pujara (Ind), Qais Ahmad (Afg, CC/T20)
OUT: Michael Klinger, Chris Liddle (both RET)

HEAD COACH: RICHARD DAWSON

Dawson was appointed in early 2015 after gaining some coaching experience with Yorkshire's Second XI and inspired Gloucestershire to win the One-Day Cup in his first season before guiding the team to Championship promotion last summer. A former Yorkshire and Gloucestershire off-spinner who played seven Tests, Dawson worked as a coach at Bristol following his retirement in 2011. He was head coach of the England Lions for the 2019/20 tour of Australia. Assistant coach Ian Harvey won six one-day trophies at the club between 1999 and 2003.

COUNTY CHAMPIONSHIP AVERAGES 2019

Batting

	Mat	Inns	NO	Runs	HS	Ave	SR	100	50	4s	6s
RF Higgins	14	21	5	958	199	59.87	76.64	4	3	124	9
CDJ Dent	14	24	1	1087	176	47.26	49.31	4	4	142	3
GL van Buuren	10	13	3	363	93	36.30	60.39	0	2	52	0
JR Bracey	13	22	2	677	152	33.85	53.05	2	2	88	0
TMJ Smith	5	8	0	261	84	32.62	35.12	0	2	28	0
GH Roderick	14	24	3	654	158	31.14	49.47	1	2	73	3
BAC Howell	10	15	0	369	76	24.60	50.34	0	2	49	0
BG Charlesworth	5	7	1	145	77*	24.16	36.06	0	1	15	0
MD Taylor	9	10	7	67	28*	22.33	42.40	0	0	5	0
JMR Taylor	9	13	0	279	99	21.46	48.10	0	1	40	0
MAH Hammond	14	23	1	418	82	19.00	40.34	0	2	49	0
DA Payne	12	15	4	205	43	18.63	43.80	0	0	27	3
CJ Sayers	4	4	1	55	33*	18.33	47.41	0	0	5	0
ER Bamber	2	3	1	30	15	15.00	37.03	0	0	3	0
J Shaw	9	12	2	107	38*	10.70	43.14	0	0	15	0
HJ Hankins	1	1	0	9	9	9.00	52.94	0	0	1	0
GT Hankins	4	6	0	23	14	3.83	31.50	0	0	2	0
ST Gabriel	3	3	1	5	2*	2.50	13.15	0	0	0	0
GS Drissell	1	1	0	1	1	1.00	10.00	0	0	0	0
BMJ Allison	1	1	0	0	0	0.00	0.00	0	0	0	0

Bowling

	Overs	Mdns	Runs	Wkts	BBI	BBM	Ave	Econ	SR	5w	10w
CDJ Dent	2.2	0	18	1	1/1	1/18	18.00	7.71	14.0	0	0
RF Higgins	453.4	110	1182	50	5/54	8/89	23.64	2.60	54.4	2	0
J Shaw	225.2	43	737	30	4/33	6/102	24.56	3.27	45.0	0	0
ER Bamber	85.3	15	206	8	3/53	4/103	25.75	2.40	64.1	0	0
DA Payne	403.5	94	1113	43	4/40	6/88	25.88	2.75	56.3	0	0
MD Taylor	245.0	43	760	29	5/57	5/57	26.20	3.10	50.6	1	0
BG Charlesworth	18.0	1	84	3	2/27	2/46	28.00	4.66	36.0	0	0
BMJ Allison	41.0	9	139	4	3/109	4/139	34.75	3.39	61.5	0	0
CJ Sayers	149.4	39	400	11	3/60	5/94	36.36	2.67	81.6	0	0
BAC Howell	97.2	23	262	7	2/19	3/67	37.42	2.69	83.4	0	0
GS Drissell	41.1	5	174	4	4/83	4/174	43.50	4.22	61.7	0	0
TMJ Smith	76.0	14	217	4	2/73	2/74	54.25	2.85	114.0	0	0
ST Gabriel	32.5	0	180	2	2/20	2/59	90.00	5.48	98.5	0	0
GL van Buuren	119.0	16	343	3	3/46	3/46	114.33	2.88	238.0	0	0
JR Bracey	10.0	0	35	0	-	-	-	3.50	-	0	0
JMR Taylor	9.0	0	51	0	-	-	-	5.66	-	0	0
HJ Hankins	33.0	4	101	0	-	-	-	3.06	-	0	0
MAH Hammond	22.0	0	121	0	-	-	-	5.50	-	0	0

Catches/Stumpings:

42 Roderick (inc 1st), 23 Bracey, 14 Hammond, 12 Howell, 8 Dent, 4 Higgins, Payne, van Buuren, 3 Charlesworth, Shaw, Smith, J Taylor

ROYAL LONDON ONE-DAY CUP AVERAGES 2019

Batting

	Mat	Inns	NO	Runs	HS	Ave	SR	100	50	4s	6s
JR Bracey	7	7	1	333	113*	55.50	106.38	1	2	25	9
JMR Taylor	8	8	3	253	75	50.60	108.58	0	2	15	13
GH Roderick	8	8	1	302	100*	43.14	89.34	1	2	25	4
CDJ Dent	8	8	0	345	89	43.12	81.94	0	2	38	3
MAH Hammond	4	4	0	165	95	41.25	73.66	0	1	16	2
RF Higgins	8	7	1	180	45	30.00	111.80	0	0	10	8
GL van Buuren	6	5	1	120	61	30.00	80.00	0	1	11	2
BAC Howell	8	8	1	190	55	27.14	86.75	0	1	12	3
TMJ Smith	8	4	2	38	17*	19.00	61.29	0	0	2	0
CJ Liddle	5	3	0	40	26	13.33	114.28	0	0	3	2
DJ Worrall	2	2	1	13	12*	13.00	108.33	0	0	0	1
GT Hankins	4	4	0	43	33	10.75	60.56	0	0	4	0
IA Cockbain	1	1	0	3	3	3.00	27.27	0	0	0	0
MD Taylor	5	1	0	3	3	3.00	60.00	0	0	0	0
DA Payne	6	2	2	62	36*	-	95.38	0	0	8	0

Bowling

	Overs	Mdns	Runs	Wkts	BBI	Ave	Econ	SR	4w	5w
MD Taylor	37.0	1	179	5	3/39	35.80	4.83	44.4	0	0
GL van Buuren	44.0	0	221	4	1/19	55.25	5.02	66.0	0	0
TMJ Smith	56.0	1	283	8	3/7	35.37	5.05	42.0	0	0
RF Higgins	59.5	2	304	8	2/55	38.00	5.08	44.8	0	0
DJ Worrall	10.0	0	52	4	2/22	13.00	5.20	15.0	0	0
BAC Howell	52.4	1	319	12	3/45	26.58	6.05	26.3	0	0
DA Payne	55.0	0	353	9	2/30	39.22	6.41	36.6	0	0
CJ Liddle	42.0	1	311	9	4/66	34.55	7.40	28.0	1	0
JR Bracey	3.0	0	23	1	1/23	23.00	7.66	18.0	0	0

Catches/Stumpings:
8 Roderick, 6 J Taylor, 4 Dent, 3 Bracey, Hankins, Howell, Liddle, 2 Higgins, Payne, Smith, 1 Hammond, M Taylor, van Buuren, Worrall

VITALITY BLAST AVERAGES 2019

Batting

	Mat	Inns	NO	Runs	HS	Ave	SR	100	50	4s	6s
IA Cockbain	13	12	4	277	61*	34.62	120.96	0	1	24	7
M Klinger	13	12	1	371	102*	33.72	122.44	1	1	33	9
MAH Hammond	13	12	0	322	63	26.83	140.61	0	2	39	10
BAC Howell	7	6	2	106	33	26.50	145.20	0	0	11	3
RF Higgins	13	11	3	206	77*	25.75	137.33	0	1	14	9
JMR Taylor	13	11	3	193	42	24.12	134.96	0	0	16	6
GL van Buuren	8	5	2	71	37*	23.66	165.11	0	0	5	4
JR Bracey	13	12	0	245	64	20.41	118.35	0	1	26	3
TMJ Smith	13	5	4	13	6*	13.00	130.00	0	0	1	0
AJ Tye	13	7	3	51	38*	12.75	150.00	0	0	4	1
DA Payne	13	2	2	3	2*	-	100.00	0	0	0	0
ZJ Chappell	1	-	-	-	-	-	-	-	-	-	-
CJ Liddle	8	-	-	-	-	-	-	-	-	-	-
J Shaw	1	-	-	-	-	-	-	-	-	-	-
MD Taylor	1	-	-	-	-	-	-	-	-	-	-

Bowling

	Overs	Mdns	Runs	Wkts	BBI	Ave	Econ	SR	4w	5w
MD Taylor	3.0	0	19	0	-	-	6.33	-	0	0
BAC Howell	26.0	0	173	10	5/18	17.30	6.65	15.6	0	1
DA Payne	47.0	1	347	16	3/32	21.68	7.38	17.6	0	0
AJ Tye	49.3	0	376	15	2/23	25.06	7.59	19.8	0	0
TMJ Smith	40.0	0	312	8	3/19	39.00	7.80	30.0	0	0
CJ Liddle	23.1	0	184	11	3/25	16.72	7.94	12.6	0	0
RF Higgins	28.2	0	241	8	3/36	30.12	8.50	21.2	0	0
GL van Buuren	17.0	0	154	4	2/27	38.50	9.05	25.5	0	0
ZJ Chappell	4.0	0	39	1	1/39	39.00	9.75	24.0	0	0
J Shaw	4.0	0	42	1	1/42	42.00	10.50	24.0	0	0

Catches/Stumpings:
12 Tye, 10 Bracey (inc 3st), Klinger, 7 Cockbain, 5 Hammond, 4 J Taylor, van Buuren, 3 Smith, 2 Higgins, Howell, 1 Chappell, Payne

HAMPSHIRE

FORMED: 1863
HOME GROUND: The Ageas Bowl, Southampton
CAPTAIN: James Vince
2019 RESULTS: CC1: 3/8; RL50: Runners-up; T20: 7/9 South Group
HONOURS: Championship: (2) 1961, 1973; Gillette/NatWest/C&G/FP Trophy: (3) 1991, 2005, 2009; Benson & Hedges Cup: (2) 1988, 1992; Pro40/National League/CB40/YB40/RL50: (2) 2012, 2018; Sunday League: (3) 1975, 1978, 1986; T20 Cup: (2) 2010, 2012

THE LOWDOWN

Hampshire last won the Championship nearly half a century ago but that elusive third title appears to be in reach. They finished third last summer, their highest position since 2008, led by probably the strongest seam attack on the circuit. Kyle Abbott was the county's leading wicket-taker in every competition and took his tally to 219 first-class wickets in three seasons since joining the club, while Fidel Edwards and Keith Barker were never far behind. And now Hampshire have added a genuine world-class spinner in Nathan Lyon, who has signed a red-ball contract and is due to be with the club all summer. The batting also looks stronger, with Sam Northeast back in the runs and World Cup winner James Vince likely to be more available this summer. Felix Organ, a 20-year-old opening batsman, made a strong impression last summer, but Aneurin Donald may miss the entire 2020 season with a torn cruciate ligament. The club will also be without Gareth Berg, who has joined Northants, while Rilee Rossouw has quit four-day cricket. Hampshire continue to be a strong white-ball side, their T20 struggles notwithstanding, although their 50-over campaign will suffer for the loss of six players to The Hundred.

IN: Nathan Lyon (Aus), Shaheen Afridi (Pak, T20)
OUT: Gareth Berg (Nor)

FIRST-TEAM MANAGER: ADRIAN BIRRELL

The vastly experienced Birrell, who turns 60 at the end of the year, took over from Craig White in December 2018 and led Hampshire to the 50-over final last summer. A former first-class cricketer who played for Eastern Province, Birrell made his name as coach of Ireland, whom he guided to a famous victory over Pakistan in the 2007 World Cup. More recently he was in charge of England U19 before a four-year stint as South Africa's assistant coach.

www.ageasbowl.com / tel: 023 8047 2002

COUNTY CHAMPIONSHIP AVERAGES 2019

Batting

	Mat	Inns	NO	Runs	HS	Ave	SR	100	50	4s	6s
SA Northeast	13	22	3	969	169	51.00	60.07	3	5	122	3
LA Dawson	8	12	1	561	103	51.00	55.00	1	5	63	1
RA Stevenson	1	1	0	51	51	51.00	51.51	0	1	7	0
JM Vince	6	10	1	365	142	40.55	77.82	1	1	60	1
AHT Donald	9	15	1	554	173	39.57	83.30	1	2	74	9
AK Markram	2	3	0	115	63	38.33	64.97	0	1	16	0
RR Rossouw	10	17	1	595	92	37.18	79.22	0	5	84	10
JK Fuller	4	5	1	138	54*	34.50	58.97	0	1	17	3
IG Holland	9	16	1	478	143	31.86	48.08	1	3	56	2
LD McManus	7	10	1	267	61	29.66	53.72	0	1	34	3
JJ Weatherley	8	13	2	322	66	29.27	43.27	0	2	37	0
FS Organ	6	11	0	300	100	27.27	45.73	1	2	32	5
TP Alsop	10	16	3	347	150	26.69	52.73	1	1	43	3
KHD Barker	13	18	4	357	64	25.50	50.92	0	1	40	0
AM Rahane	7	13	0	307	119	23.61	53.76	1	1	40	0
KJ Abbott	13	16	2	207	72	14.78	54.61	0	1	35	1
OC Soames	5	9	0	124	62	13.77	34.54	0	1	15	1
GK Berg	5	8	0	79	33	9.87	45.40	0	0	11	0
MS Crane	6	8	1	65	20	9.28	37.79	0	0	8	1
FH Edwards	14	17	9	32	8*	4.00	34.78	0	0	6	0
HRC Came	1	1	1	23	23*	-	25.84	0	0	1	0

Bowling

	Overs	Mdns	Runs	Wkts	BBI	BBM	Ave	Econ	SR	5w	10w
FS Organ	45.5	9	125	8	5/25	5/25	15.62	2.72	34.3	1	0
KJ Abbott	362.5	78	1117	71	9/40	17/86	15.73	3.07	30.6	6	1
FH Edwards	353.1	55	1240	48	5/49	8/100	25.83	3.51	44.1	4	0
KHD Barker	348.0	78	984	37	5/48	6/88	26.59	2.82	56.4	1	0
JK Fuller	80.4	15	302	9	3/51	3/114	33.55	3.74	53.7	0	0
GK Berg	116.0	24	361	9	2/41	3/57	40.11	3.11	77.3	0	0
LA Dawson	210.1	39	538	10	3/184	3/64	53.80	2.55	126.1	0	0
JJ Weatherley	16.0	0	67	1	1/12	1/12	67.00	4.18	96.0	0	0
IG Holland	146.1	33	378	5	1/14	2/41	75.60	2.58	175.4	0	0
RA Stevenson	25.0	1	87	1	1/87	1/87	87.00	3.48	150.0	0	0
MS Crane	106.5	8	539	5	3/122	3/210	107.80	5.04	128.2	0	0
TP Alsop	1.0	0	3	0	-	-	-	3.00	-	0	0
JM Vince	6.0	0	17	0	-	-	-	2.83	-	0	0

Catches/Stumpings:
21 McManus (inc 1st), 11 Alsop, 8 Weatherley, 6 Dawson, Rahane, 5 Holland, Northeast, 4 Donald, Organ, 3 Edwards, Vince, 2 Barker, Rossouw, Soames, 1 Abbott, Berg, Fuller, Stevenson

ROYAL LONDON ONE-DAY CUP AVERAGES 2019

Batting

	Mat	Inns	NO	Runs	HS	Ave	SR	100	50	4s	6s
JM Vince	7	7	0	509	190	72.71	110.89	1	3	52	8
AK Markram	8	8	0	466	130	58.25	101.96	1	3	57	5
RR Rossouw	10	9	1	388	93	48.50	111.17	0	4	42	2
LA Dawson	9	7	1	274	108	45.66	102.62	1	1	18	5
SA Northeast	10	10	3	280	105*	40.00	81.15	1	2	21	4
TP Alsop	10	10	1	351	130*	39.00	90.00	2	0	42	4
JK Fuller	10	8	2	162	55*	27.00	120.89	0	1	13	7
AHT Donald	7	7	1	131	57	21.83	87.33	0	1	14	3
GK Berg	8	6	1	102	41	20.40	93.57	0	0	7	3
JJ Weatherley	1	1	0	12	12	12.00	48.00	0	0	0	0
CP Wood	4	3	1	17	16*	8.50	130.76	0	0	1	1
KJ Abbott	10	6	1	15	7	3.00	40.54	0	0	1	0
BTJ Wheal	3	2	1	3	3	3.00	37.50	0	0	0	0
MS Crane	9	5	5	44	28*	-	100.00	0	0	5	0
FH Edwards	3	-	-	-	-	-	-	-	-	-	-
BJ Taylor	1	-	-	-	-	-	-	-	-	-	-

Bowling

	Overs	Mdns	Runs	Wkts	BBI	Ave	Econ	SR	4w	5w
LA Dawson	89.0	2	366	18	3/37	20.33	4.11	29.6	0	0
AK Markram	26.0	0	117	5	3/39	23.40	4.50	31.2	0	0
GK Berg	53.4	0	279	9	5/26	31.00	5.19	35.7	0	1
KJ Abbott	81.5	1	471	20	3/36	23.55	5.75	24.5	0	0
CP Wood	28.0	1	167	2	2/47	83.50	5.96	84.0	0	0
MS Crane	74.1	1	446	14	3/42	31.85	6.01	31.7	0	0
FH Edwards	24.3	0	165	5	3/69	33.00	6.73	29.4	0	0
JK Fuller	48.0	0	340	5	2/55	68.00	7.08	57.6	0	0
BTJ Wheal	18.5	0	162	3	2/49	54.00	8.60	37.6	0	0
BJ Taylor	3.0	0	26	0	-	-	8.66	-	0	0

Catches/Stumpings:
19 Alsop (inc 5st), 6 Fuller, Vince, 5 Dawson, Northeast, 4 Crane, 3 Donald, Markram, 2 Abbott, Berg, Rossouw, 1 Wheal, Wood

VITALITY BLAST AVERAGES 2019

Batting

	Mat	Inns	NO	Runs	HS	Ave	SR	100	50	4s	6s
JM Vince	13	12	2	407	87*	40.70	132.14	0	4	48	5
LA Dawson	13	11	4	232	47*	33.14	107.40	0	0	18	1
LD McManus	13	8	4	107	32	26.75	157.35	0	0	6	6
SA Northeast	13	12	0	273	73	22.75	107.90	0	2	25	2
KJ Abbott	13	3	2	21	15	21.00	175.00	0	0	1	1
AHT Donald	11	10	0	203	51	20.30	138.09	0	1	20	7
RR Rossouw	12	11	1	174	60	17.40	124.28	0	1	17	4
CH Morris	11	8	2	86	18*	14.33	114.66	0	0	4	4
JK Fuller	13	9	1	92	28	11.50	133.33	0	0	4	4
CP Wood	13	4	1	18	9	6.00	120.00	0	0	3	0
BJ Taylor	2	1	0	2	2	2.00	66.66	0	0	0	0
IG Holland	3	2	2	12	11*	-	133.33	0	0	1	0
MS Crane	8	2	2	8	5*	-	100.00	0	0	0	0
T Shamsi	4	-	-	-	-	-	-	-	-	-	-
RA Stevenson	1	-	-	-	-	-	-	-	-	-	-

Bowling

	Overs	Mdns	Runs	Wkts	BBI	Ave	Econ	SR	4w	5w
LA Dawson	46.3	0	308	10	3/11	30.80	6.62	27.9	0	0
MS Crane	26.0	0	183	11	3/22	16.63	7.03	14.1	0	0
BJ Taylor	6.0	0	44	1	1/22	44.00	7.33	36.0	0	0
CH Morris	38.0	0	297	12	3/22	24.75	7.81	19.0	0	0
CP Wood	45.4	1	363	14	2/18	25.92	7.94	19.5	0	0
KJ Abbott	43.3	0	356	20	3/15	17.80	8.18	13.0	0	0
IG Holland	2.0	0	17	0	-	-	8.50	-	0	0
T Shamsi	15.0	0	141	3	1/32	47.00	9.40	30.0	0	0
JK Fuller	6.0	0	80	2	1/20	40.00	13.33	18.0	0	0
RA Stevenson	1.0	0	25	0	-	-	25.00	-	0	0

Catches/Stumpings:
13 McManus (inc 3st), 8 Morris, 7 Donald, 6 Dawson, 5 Northeast, Vince, 4 Fuller, Rossouw, 2 Holland, 1 Taylor, Wood

KENT

FORMED: 1870
HOME GROUND: The Spitfire Ground, Canterbury
ONE-DAY NAME: Kent Spitfires
CAPTAIN: Sam Billings
2019 RESULTS: CC1: 4/8; RL50: 7/9 South Group; T20: 5/9 South Group
HONOURS: Championship: (7) 1906, 1909, 1910, 1913, 1970, 1977(s), 1978; Gillette/NatWest/C&G/FP Trophy: (2) 1967, 1974; Pro40/National League/CB40/RL50: 2001; Benson & Hedges Cup: (3) 1973, 1976, 1978; Sunday League: (4) 1972, 1973, 1976, 1995; T20 Cup: 2007

THE LOWDOWN

Promoted in 2018, Kent held firm among the Championship elite last summer and staving off relegation will be the club's prime objective again this year. A fit Sam Billings, the club captain who missed most of last season with a shoulder injury, will be a massive boost. With Joe Denly and Zak Crawley in the England set-up, the onus for runs is on Billings, Daniel Bell-Drummond, new signing Jack Leaning and upcoming keeper-batsman Ollie Robinson, while more will be expected of Heino Kuhn and Sean Dickson. It seems absurd now that the club were ready to release 43-year-old Darren Stevens last September, only for the unstoppable allrounder to produce a late-season blitz of runs and wickets and earn a one-year extension. Why not five? Fellow seamers Matt Milnes and Harry Podmore each passed 50 Championship wickets last summer, while the experienced Tim Groenewald is a handy replacement for Mitchell Claydon. Kent also prised England U19 spinner Hamidullah Qadri from Derbyshire, but the major coup was luring back Kiwi seamer Matt Henry – who took 75 wickets in 11 matches in 2018 – for the opening seven Championship games. Batsman Alex Blake signed a white-ball deal in January, ruling him out of four-day cricket.

IN: Tim Groenewald (Som), Jack Leaning (Yor), Hamidullah Qadri (Der), Matt Henry (NZ), Mohammad Nabi (Afg, T20)
OUT: Mitchell Claydon (Sus)

HEAD COACH: MATT WALKER

Walker was assistant to Jimmy Adams before his promotion to the top job ahead of the 2017 season, having previously worked with Essex. A left-handed batsman, he scored nearly 20,000 runs for Kent and Essex between 1992 and 2011. Allan Donald has left after a two-year spell as assistant coach, while ex-Kent seamer Simon Cook returns as bowling coach and Michael Yardy arrives to oversee the batsmen.

COUNTY CHAMPIONSHIP AVERAGES 2019

Batting

	Mat	Inns	NO	Runs	HS	Ave	SR	100	50	4s	6s
SW Billings	4	7	1	366	138	61.00	73.79	3	0	47	2
JL Denly	6	11	2	504	167*	56.00	60.86	2	1	57	7
DJ Bell-Drummond	14	26	1	892	166	35.68	51.17	1	5	121	1
Z Crawley	13	24	0	820	111	34.16	59.46	2	5	128	2
OG Robinson	14	25	2	765	143	33.26	59.30	2	3	93	2
DI Stevens	12	19	1	597	237	33.16	71.66	1	2	69	17
PWA Mulder	3	6	2	114	68*	28.50	55.07	0	1	15	0
SR Dickson	11	21	0	557	161	26.52	46.07	2	1	68	0
HG Kuhn	14	24	0	605	95	25.20	61.79	0	5	82	0
MT Renshaw	3	6	1	118	48*	23.60	55.66	0	0	22	0
G Stewart	5	7	2	113	59	22.60	61.08	0	1	14	1
F du Plessis	1	2	0	36	36	18.00	60.00	0	0	5	0
JM Cox	3	4	0	71	27	17.75	36.22	0	0	8	0
HW Podmore	14	21	6	265	54*	17.66	51.25	0	1	38	3
OP Rayner	8	10	1	152	40*	16.88	69.40	0	0	23	0
ME Claydon	6	7	4	50	13*	16.66	80.64	0	0	9	0
AJ Blake	5	9	0	136	34	15.11	41.71	0	0	18	0
ME Milnes	14	19	6	174	31	13.38	36.55	0	0	23	0
FJ Klaassen	1	2	0	23	13	11.50	15.54	0	0	1	0
MK O'Riordan	1	2	0	21	12	10.50	26.58	0	0	3	0
AEN Riley	2	3	2	10	7	10.00	15.62	0	0	1	0
Imran Qayyum	1	2	2	15	14*	-	26.31	0	0	0	0

Bowling

	Overs	Mdns	Runs	Wkts	BBI	BBM	Ave	Econ	SR	5w	10w
DI Stevens	403.0	126	914	52	5/20	10/92	17.57	2.26	46.5	5	1
ME Claydon	130.2	20	466	19	5/46	9/112	24.52	3.57	41.1	1	0
ME Milnes	386.4	68	1383	55	5/68	7/111	25.14	3.57	42.1	2	0
HW Podmore	473.3	105	1380	52	5/41	8/123	26.53	2.91	54.6	2	0
DJ Bell-Drummond	60.2	11	163	6	2/7	3/44	27.16	2.70	60.3	0	0
OP Rayner	166.3	76	292	10	2/7	2/7	29.20	1.75	99.9	0	0
PWA Mulder	91.5	22	307	10	4/118	5/159	30.70	3.34	55.1	0	0
G Stewart	135.3	16	514	15	3/37	4/145	34.26	3.79	54.2	0	0
JL Denly	72.0	20	184	4	3/48	3/72	46.00	2.55	108.0	0	0
FJ Klaassen	29.0	0	132	2	1/44	2/132	66.00	4.55	87.0	0	0
AEN Riley	56.0	10	182	2	1/45	2/101	91.00	3.25	168.0	0	0
AJ Blake	1.0	0	9	0	-	-	-	9.00	-	0	0
SR Dickson	4.0	0	9	0	-	-	-	2.25	-	0	0
Z Crawley	11.0	2	33	0	-	-	-	3.00	-	0	0
MK O'Riordan	7.0	0	33	0	-	-	-	4.71	-	0	0
Imran Qayyum	8.0	0	43	0	-	-	-	5.37	-	0	0
MT Renshaw	16.0	2	53	0	-	-	-	3.31	-	0	0

Catches/Stumpings:
54 Robinson, 16 Crawley, 13 Dickson, 11 Kuhn, 5 Milnes, Rayner, 4 Bell-Drummond, Podmore, Riley, 3 du Plessis, Renshaw, 2 Blake, Stevens, 1 Billings, Cox, Denly, Klaassen

Batting

	Mat	Inns	NO	Runs	HS	Ave	SR	100	50	4s	6s
DJ Bell-Drummond	4	4	1	184	120*	61.33	87.20	1	0	23	0
Z Crawley	8	7	0	394	120	56.28	87.55	1	2	45	0
JL Denly	1	1	0	56	56	56.00	81.15	0	1	7	1
MT Renshaw	7	6	1	213	109	42.60	90.25	1	0	21	6
HG Kuhn	6	5	1	116	36*	29.00	109.43	0	0	16	1
AJ Blake	8	6	1	112	43	22.40	83.58	0	0	11	4
AP Rouse	8	6	1	111	45*	22.20	85.38	0	0	7	5
OG Robinson	6	4	0	83	46	20.75	83.00	0	0	8	1
HW Podmore	8	5	0	103	40	20.60	94.49	0	0	11	4
ME Milnes	8	5	0	77	26	15.40	140.00	0	0	6	4
DI Stevens	3	3	0	41	30	13.66	70.68	0	0	2	2
SR Dickson	3	3	0	34	30	11.33	97.14	0	0	3	2
Imran Qayyum	8	5	1	20	7	5.00	51.28	0	0	1	0
ME Claydon	3	1	1	5	5*	-	62.50	0	0	0	0
FJ Klaassen	6	3	3	5	4*	-	83.33	0	0	0	0
SW Billings	1	-	-	-	-	-	-	-	-	-	-

Bowling

	Overs	Mdns	Runs	Wkts	BBI	Ave	Econ	SR	4w	5w
DJ Bell-Drummond	23.0	2	103	5	2/22	20.60	4.47	27.6	0	0
DI Stevens	26.0	0	130	3	2/50	43.33	5.00	52.0	0	0
MT Renshaw	9.0	1	48	2	2/17	24.00	5.33	27.0	0	0
HW Podmore	71.0	4	411	8	2/54	51.37	5.78	53.2	0	0
Imran Qayyum	53.0	0	308	5	2/37	61.60	5.81	63.6	0	0
FJ Klaassen	40.2	1	243	7	2/17	34.71	6.02	34.5	0	0
ME Milnes	71.5	1	494	16	5/79	30.87	6.87	26.9	0	1
ME Claydon	22.0	1	152	2	1/55	76.00	6.90	66.0	0	0
AJ Blake	17.0	0	130	1	1/32	130.00	7.64	102.0	0	0
Z Crawley	2.0	0	17	0	-	-	8.50	-	0	0
SR Dickson	2.0	0	20	0	-	-	10.00	-	0	0

Catches/Stumpings:
8 Rouse (inc 1st), 6 Renshaw, 5 Podmore, 4 Blake, Crawley, Milnes, 2 Klaassen, Kuhn, 1 Bell-Drummond

VITALITY BLAST AVERAGES 2019

Batting

	Mat	Inns	NO	Runs	HS	Ave	SR	100	50	4s	6s
F du Plessis	2	2	0	92	60	46.00	139.39	0	1	8	2
HG Kuhn	10	10	4	255	55*	42.50	132.12	0	2	19	6
Z Crawley	12	11	0	307	89	27.90	144.81	0	2	28	12
DJ Bell-Drummond	12	12	0	317	64	26.41	119.62	0	3	31	4
SW Billings	4	4	1	74	55	24.66	125.42	0	1	2	3
AJ Blake	12	11	2	204	66*	22.66	148.90	0	2	13	12
Mohammad Nabi	9	9	1	147	43*	18.37	153.12	0	0	8	11
Imran Qayyum	9	5	4	16	13*	16.00	133.33	0	0	0	1
JM Cox	7	6	2	58	23*	14.50	100.00	0	0	5	0
OG Robinson	12	10	0	139	53	13.90	104.51	0	1	12	3
AF Milne	9	7	2	60	16	12.00	150.00	0	0	6	2
SR Dickson	2	2	0	19	17	9.50	86.36	0	0	0	0
FJ Klaassen	12	3	2	8	4*	8.00	133.33	0	0	0	0
GC Viljoen	12	7	1	43	15	7.16	153.57	0	0	4	1
ME Claydon	4	3	2	5	4*	5.00	83.33	0	0	0	0
G Stewart	2	1	1	2	2*	-	66.66	0	0	0	0
ME Milnes	1	-	-	-	-	-	-	-	-	-	-
MK O'Riordan	1	-	-	-	-	-	-	-	-	-	-

Bowling

	Overs	Mdns	Runs	Wkts	BBI	Ave	Econ	SR	4w	5w
G Stewart	4.0	0	23	2	2/23	11.50	5.75	12.0	0	0
AJ Blake	5.0	0	29	1	1/17	29.00	5.80	30.0	0	0
MK O'Riordan	2.0	0	13	0	-	-	6.50	-	0	0
Mohammad Nabi	31.0	0	224	8	2/32	28.00	7.22	23.2	0	0
Imran Qayyum	30.1	0	226	12	5/21	18.83	7.49	15.0	0	1
AF Milne	31.3	1	242	10	3/21	24.20	7.68	18.9	0	0
GC Viljoen	45.2	0	355	18	3/15	19.72	7.83	15.1	0	0
ME Claydon	15.0	0	134	1	1/37	134.00	8.93	90.0	0	0
FJ Klaassen	41.1	0	384	10	2/24	38.40	9.32	24.7	0	0
DJ Bell-Drummond	12.3	0	132	5	2/19	26.40	10.56	15.0	0	0
ME Milnes	2.0	0	25	0	-	-	12.50	-	0	0

Catches/Stumpings:

10 Kuhn, 8 Robinson (inc 2st), 7 Klaassen, 5 Crawley, 4 Bell-Drummond, 3 Blake, Nabi, 2 Milne, 1 Cox, du Plessis, Milnes, Stewart

LANCASHIRE

Lancashire County Cricket Club

FORMED: 1864
HOME GROUND: Emirates Old Trafford, Manchester
ONE-DAY NAME: Lancashire Lightning
CAPTAIN: Dane Vilas
2019 RESULTS: CC2: Winners; RL50: Semi-finalists; T20: Quarter-finalists
HONOURS: Championship: (9) 1897, 1904, 1926, 1927, 1928, 1930, 1934, 1950(s), 2011; Gillette/NatWest/C&G/FP Trophy: (7) 1970, 1971, 1972, 1985, 1990, 1996, 1998; Benson & Hedges Cup: (4) 1984, 1990, 1995, 1996; Pro40/National League/CB40/YB40/RL50: 1999; Sunday League: (4) 1969, 1970, 1989, 1998; T20 Cup: 2015

THE LOWDOWN

Lancashire bounced back from a dismal 2018 by returning to the top tier of the Championship as Division Two champions, also coming within a whisker of a Lord's final and T20 Finals Day. Much of the credit must go to South African captain Dane Vilas, who took over after Liam Livingstone's sudden resignation in November 2018. Vilas was the club's leading run-scorer in the Championship last summer but he needs more help. It won't come from Haseeb Hameed, who was released after three excruciating seasons, but Livingstone appears to have recovered some form and signalled his intentions by spurning this year's IPL to focus on red-ball cricket. Keaton Jennings did not make a century last summer, but Rob Jones enjoyed his most consistent season and Josh Bohannon, 22, confirmed his potential with a maiden first-class hundred. Kiwi keeper BJ Watling is a classy addition for the first nine Championship matches. Even without James Anderson, who is likely to have Test duties, a pace attack of Onions, Gleeson, Bailey and Mahmood will test the best. Young leggie Matt Parkinson continues to blossom and forms a potent spin pairing with Livingstone in the T20 Blast, a competition for which Lancashire will again be among the favourites, particularly following the re-signing of Glenn Maxwell.

IN: Luke Wood (Not), BJ Watling (NZ), James Faulkner (Aus, T20), Glenn Maxwell (Aus, T20)
OUT: Haseeb Hameed (Not)

HEAD COACH: GLEN CHAPPLE

Chapple took over in January 2017 following Ashley Giles's decision to return to Warwickshire. After finishing as Championship runners-up in his first season as coach, Lancashire were relegated in 2018 but immediately secured promotion back into Division One last summer. A club legend, Chapple took 1,373 wickets in 664 appearances during a 23-year playing career at Old Trafford and captained the side to the Championship title in 2011.

www.lancashirecricket.co.uk / tel: 0161 282 4000

COUNTY CHAMPIONSHIP AVERAGES 2019

Batting

	Mat	Inns	NO	Runs	HS	Ave	SR	100	50	4s	6s
DJ Vilas	14	17	4	1036	266	79.69	74.63	2	7	146	6
JJ Bohannon	11	12	3	472	174	52.44	53.57	1	2	69	3
DJ Lamb	1	1	0	49	49	49.00	92.45	0	0	7	2
SJ Croft	11	12	2	472	78	47.20	53.21	0	4	60	2
LS Livingstone	11	14	1	599	114	46.07	62.78	1	5	85	6
LJ Hurt	1	1	0	38	38	38.00	48.71	0	0	4	0
RP Jones	14	19	2	624	122	36.70	40.33	1	4	85	0
AL Davies	10	14	1	468	147	36.00	59.24	1	2	79	0
KK Jennings	14	21	2	588	97	30.94	41.52	0	6	78	0
H Hameed	10	15	3	341	117	28.41	43.27	1	1	44	2
TE Bailey	9	10	0	207	68	20.70	55.20	0	2	32	1
GJ Maxwell	4	5	0	96	59	19.20	68.08	0	1	11	0
S Mahmood	9	10	2	136	34	17.00	31.05	0	0	15	0
BD Guest	1	2	0	28	17	14.00	35.89	0	0	3	0
JA Burns	1	1	0	10	10	10.00	43.47	0	0	1	0
JS Lehmann	3	4	0	35	22	8.75	44.87	0	0	5	0
RJ Gleeson	9	8	4	34	11	8.50	34.69	0	0	3	0
G Onions	10	10	1	65	18	7.22	53.71	0	0	7	1
JM Anderson	6	6	2	25	9*	6.25	44.64	0	0	2	1
MW Parkinson	4	4	0	19	14	4.75	46.34	0	0	2	0
SD Parry	1	1	0	0	0	0.00	0.00	0	0	0	0

Bowling

	Overs	Mdns	Runs	Wkts	BBI	BBM	Ave	Econ	SR	5w	10w
JM Anderson	159.4	61	281	30	5/18	9/47	9.36	1.75	31.9	2	0
DJ Lamb	26.0	5	89	6	4/70	6/89	14.83	3.42	26.0	0	0
MW Parkinson	143.5	33	381	20	6/23	10/165	19.05	2.64	43.1	1	1
G Onions	306.1	66	881	45	5/38	8/57	19.57	2.87	40.8	3	0
RJ Gleeson	273.1	61	948	47	6/43	10/113	20.17	3.47	34.8	5	1
GJ Maxwell	109.5	27	287	14	5/40	6/76	20.50	2.61	47.0	1	0
TE Bailey	289.2	81	777	37	5/41	10/119	21.00	2.68	46.9	3	1
LS Livingstone	135.1	42	249	10	2/17	3/85	24.90	1.84	81.1	0	0
SD Parry	55.0	5	156	5	3/59	5/156	31.20	2.83	66.0	0	0
S Mahmood	196.3	31	660	21	4/48	4/69	31.42	3.35	56.1	0	0
SJ Croft	26.0	6	60	1	1/17	1/17	60.00	2.30	156.0	0	0
KK Jennings	26.0	3	68	1	1/8	1/42	68.00	2.61	156.0	0	0
JJ Bohannon	109.4	20	365	5	1/31	2/72	73.00	3.32	131.6	0	0
AL Davies	1.0	0	6	0	-	-	-	6.00	-	0	0
RP Jones	5.0	1	18	0	-	-	-	3.60	-	0	0
LJ Hurt	25.0	6	66	0	-	-	-	2.64	-	0	0

Catches/Stumpings:

48 Vilas, (inc 1st), 17 Jennings, 11 Jones, 7 Livingstone, 5 Bailey, Guest, Hameed, 4 Anderson, Bohannon, Croft, 3 Maxwell, Parkinson, 2 Gleeson, 1 Onions

ROYAL LONDON ONE-DAY CUP AVERAGES 2019

Batting

	Mat	Inns	NO	Runs	HS	Ave	SR	100	50	4s	6s
SJ Croft	10	9	2	516	110	73.71	94.67	1	3	46	13
JS Lehmann	4	4	1	191	77*	63.66	98.45	0	2	15	2
DJ Vilas	10	9	2	439	166	62.71	119.61	1	2	30	16
KK Jennings	10	10	0	416	96	41.60	81.09	0	5	49	0
JJ Bohannon	10	7	2	156	55*	31.20	96.29	0	1	10	5
RP Jones	10	8	2	186	65	31.00	83.40	0	1	11	1
GJ Maxwell	6	5	1	124	35	31.00	110.71	0	0	11	6
H Hameed	8	8	1	168	65	24.00	75.00	0	1	23	0
G Onions	8	4	3	23	16*	23.00	164.28	0	0	0	2
BD Guest	2	2	0	41	36	20.50	78.84	0	0	4	0
S Mahmood	10	4	0	52	45	13.00	89.65	0	0	2	2
LS Livingstone	2	2	0	26	22	13.00	96.29	0	0	3	0
MW Parkinson	9	3	2	13	10	13.00	118.18	0	0	2	0
JM Anderson	6	3	1	5	4	2.50	25.00	0	0	0	0
SD Parry	1	1	0	1	1	1.00	12.50	0	0	0	0
LJ Hurt	4	2	2	19	15*	-	90.47	0	0	2	0

Bowling

	Overs	Mdns	Runs	Wkts	BBI	Ave	Econ	SR	4w	5w
SD Parry	6.0	0	23	1	1/23	23.00	3.83	36.0	0	0
JM Anderson	52.4	4	227	6	3/21	37.83	4.31	52.6	0	0
LJ Hurt	25.0	2	134	5	2/24	26.80	5.36	30.0	0	0
LS Livingstone	13.0	0	70	1	1/49	70.00	5.38	78.0	0	0
S Mahmood	95.3	7	518	28	6/37	18.50	5.42	20.4	1	2
GJ Maxwell	52.5	3	297	8	3/42	37.12	5.62	39.6	0	0
MW Parkinson	77.1	0	436	12	5/51	36.33	5.65	38.5	0	1
G Onions	72.2	2	434	9	2/39	48.22	6.00	48.2	0	0
RP Jones	20.2	0	122	2	1/3	61.00	6.00	61.0	0	0
SJ Croft	34.0	0	211	2	2/20	105.50	6.20	102.0	0	0
JJ Bohannon	15.0	0	142	1	1/33	142.00	9.46	90.0	0	0
KK Jennings	1.0	0	13	0	-	-	13.00	-	0	0

Catches/Stumpings:
14 Vilas (inc 1st), 9 Jennings, 6 Jones, 5 Croft, Maxwell, 3 Anderson, Parkinson, 2 Hameed, Vilas, 1 Bohannon, Guest (inc 1st), Lehmann

VITALITY BLAST AVERAGES 2019

Batting

	Mat	Inns	NO	Runs	HS	Ave	SR	100	50	4s	6s
AL Davies	12	11	3	307	80*	38.37	127.91	0	2	36	5
GJ Maxwell	11	9	1	305	79	38.12	150.99	0	3	27	12
DJ Vilas	12	10	2	259	46	32.37	146.32	0	0	21	8
KK Jennings	12	8	4	119	35	29.75	106.25	0	0	7	2
SJ Croft	12	11	2	247	94	27.44	126.66	0	2	20	9
LS Livingstone	10	10	0	273	70	27.30	135.14	0	2	23	14
JJ Bohannon	12	5	3	40	17*	20.00	108.10	0	0	3	0
JP Faulkner	12	8	4	73	34*	18.25	123.72	0	0	6	2
LJ Hurt	1	1	0	0	0	0.00	0.00	0	0	0	0
DJ Lamb	4	1	1	4	4*	-	44.44	0	0	0	0
S Mahmood	9	1	1	0	0*	-	0.00	0	0	0	0
RJ Gleeson	11	-	-	-	-	-	-	-	-	-	-
TJ Lester	2	-	-	-	-	-	-	-	-	-	-
MW Parkinson	12	-	-	-	-	-	-	-	-	-	-

Bowling

	Overs	Mdns	Runs	Wkts	BBI	Ave	Econ	SR	4w	5w
GJ Maxwell	30.0	0	198	6	3/23	33.00	6.60	30.0	0	0
SJ Croft	8.0	0	53	3	1/8	17.66	6.62	16.0	0	0
MW Parkinson	41.0	0	307	21	4/30	14.61	7.48	11.7	1	0
TJ Lester	2.0	0	15	0	-	-	7.50	-	0	0
LS Livingstone	28.0	0	215	14	3/21	15.35	7.67	12.0	0	0
RJ Gleeson	30.0	0	236	9	2/13	26.22	7.86	20.0	0	0
JP Faulkner	39.5	0	314	11	3/36	28.54	7.88	21.7	0	0
DJ Lamb	10.0	0	80	2	2/25	40.00	8.00	30.0	0	0
S Mahmood	25.0	0	220	8	3/33	27.50	8.80	18.7	0	0
LJ Hurt	2.0	0	25	0	-	-	12.50	-	0	0

Catches/Stumpings:
8 Croft, Maxwell, Vilas (inc 4st), 6 Faulkner, 5 Davies, 4 Bohannon, Gleeson, 2 Jennings, Livingstone, Mahmood, Parkinson, 1 Lamb, Lester

LEICESTERSHIRE

FORMED: 1879
HOME GROUND: Fischer County Ground, Leicester
ONE-DAY NAME: Leicestershire Foxes
CAPTAIN: Colin Ackermann
2019 RESULTS: CC2: 10/10; RL50: 9/9 North Group; T20: 9/9 North Group
HONOURS: Championship: (3) 1975, 1996, 1998; Benson & Hedges Cup: (3) 1972, 1975, 1985; Sunday League: (2) 1974, 1977; T20 Cup: (3) 2004, 2006, 2011

THE LOWDOWN

Leicestershire finished bottom in all three competitions last year which, even for a club of limited means, is just not good enough. In mitigation they were four points away from the T20 knockout stages, while seven draws in the Championship hinted at some resilience. Bowling is the main worry. Chris Wright did a decent job of replacing Ben Raine last summer, but the rest of the attack looked fairly toothless. And this year there will be no Mohammad Abbas, who has moved to Nottinghamshire after taking 79 wickets at 20.67 in two seasons at Grace Road. But Leicestershire do have another Pakistan-born star in the making: opening batsman Hassan Azad, who scored 1,189 runs in his debut Championship season. Azad was ably supported by Paul Horton, Mark Cosgrove and Colin Ackermann, although none of the younger batsmen made much of an impression. The club lean heavily on Ackermann but the signing of South African opener Janneman Malan should ease the run-scoring burden. That no Leicestershire player was signed up to The Hundred means they are well-placed for a tilt at the concurrent 50-over competition.

IN: George Rhodes (Wor), Janneman Malan (SA)
OUT: Aadil Ali, Neil Dexter, Ateeq Javid (all REL)

HEAD COACH: PAUL NIXON

Leicestershire went back to the boot room by appointing Nixon ahead of the 2018 season. The former England wicketkeeper has lived in Leicester for more than 30 years and won two Championship titles in the 1990s. He won the Caribbean Premier League twice as coach of Jamaica Tallawahs and worked in the Bangladesh Premier League over the winter. John Sadler has left his post as assistant coach to take up a similar role at Northants. Matt Mason quit as bowling coach to join Western Australia.

 www.leicestershireccc.co.uk / tel: 0116 283 2128

COUNTY CHAMPIONSHIP AVERAGES 2019

Batting

	Mat	Inns	NO	Runs	HS	Ave	SR	100	50	4s	6s
Hassan Azad	14	26	4	1189	137	54.04	41.57	3	8	124	1
CN Ackermann	14	25	6	675	70*	35.52	42.74	0	7	91	0
MJ Cosgrove	13	23	3	697	107*	34.85	46.65	1	6	98	1
GH Rhodes	3	6	2	128	61*	32.00	38.32	0	1	19	0
NJ Dexter	8	12	0	359	180	29.91	42.78	1	1	42	2
PJ Horton	14	26	1	744	100*	29.76	52.28	1	3	108	0
TAI Taylor	3	4	0	115	57	28.75	48.11	0	1	15	0
CF Parkinson	4	7	0	158	37	22.57	34.27	0	0	14	0
D Klein	6	6	0	122	87	20.33	68.92	0	1	12	0
HE Dearden	13	19	0	375	61	19.73	40.32	0	1	55	1
LJ Hill	7	11	1	196	67	19.60	56.81	0	1	23	2
HJ Swindells	7	10	0	168	37	16.80	35.14	0	0	17	0
CJC Wright	14	21	3	295	60	16.38	42.20	0	1	41	1
WS Davis	10	17	8	142	39*	15.77	41.04	0	0	15	0
A Javid	4	8	0	113	69	14.12	28.17	0	1	16	0
BWM Mike	5	8	1	73	16	10.42	23.93	0	0	10	0
GT Griffiths	4	7	0	41	22	5.85	24.84	0	0	5	0
HA Evans	1	2	1	5	5*	5.00	27.77	0	0	1	0
Mohammad Abbas	9	11	3	22	11	2.75	21.35	0	0	2	0
ST Evans	1	1	0	1	1	1.00	16.66	0	0	0	0

Bowling

	Overs	Mdns	Runs	Wkts	BBI	BBM	Ave	Econ	SR	5w	10w
HA Evans	21.0	3	79	4	3/65	4/79	19.75	3.76	31.5	0	0
TAI Taylor	98.0	16	344	14	6/47	10/122	24.57	3.51	42.0	1	1
Mohammad Abbas	281.5	81	747	29	4/72	6/88	25.75	2.65	58.3	0	0
D Klein	112.0	15	467	16	4/113	4/66	29.18	4.16	42.0	0	0
CJC Wright	424.2	78	1455	47	5/30	7/131	30.95	3.42	54.1	2	0
WS Davis	264.5	59	871	23	4/73	5/104	37.86	3.28	69.0	0	0
GT Griffiths	110.3	19	380	9	3/71	4/107	42.22	3.43	73.6	0	0
BWM Mike	104.3	14	486	11	3/41	4/125	44.18	4.65	57.0	0	0
CF Parkinson	64.4	9	237	5	2/0	2/0	47.40	3.66	77.6	0	0
CN Ackermann	180.0	22	703	12	5/69	5/69	58.58	3.90	90.0	1	0
NJ Dexter	120.3	25	426	3	1/15	2/59	142.00	3.53	241.0	0	0
A Javid	3.0	0	8	0	-	-	-	2.66	-	0	0
HE Dearden	2.0	0	13	0	-	-	-	6.50	-	0	0
GH Rhodes	4.4	0	23	0	-	-	-	4.92	-	0	0
MJ Cosgrove	17.1	5	36	0	-	-	-	2.09	-	0	0

Catches/Stumpings:

24 Hill (inc 1st), 19 Ackermann, 13 Swindells (inc 1st), 11 Horton, 7 Azad, 6 Dearden, 4 Abbas, 3 Wright, 2 Cosgrove, 1 Davis, Dexter, Griffiths, Rhodes, Taylor

ROYAL LONDON ONE-DAY CUP AVERAGES 2019

Batting

	Mat	Inns	NO	Runs	HS	Ave	SR	100	50	4s	6s
CN Ackermann	8	8	1	428	152*	61.14	92.04	2	1	43	7
TAI Taylor	7	7	2	242	98*	48.40	113.61	0	2	26	3
HE Dearden	8	8	0	304	91	38.00	95.29	0	3	44	0
LJ Hill	8	8	0	239	118	29.87	121.93	1	0	28	6
AM Ali	1	1	0	26	26	26.00	113.04	0	0	3	0
CF Parkinson	5	5	1	100	39*	25.00	98.03	0	0	12	0
BWM Mike	3	3	0	70	41	23.33	84.33	0	0	9	0
MJ Cosgrove	8	8	0	184	59	23.00	80.00	0	1	21	1
D Klein	7	6	1	88	46	17.60	84.61	0	0	10	0
CJC Wright	4	4	2	34	16*	17.00	53.96	0	0	4	0
WS Davis	3	2	1	17	15*	17.00	70.83	0	0	0	1
A Javid	2	2	0	33	24	16.50	61.11	0	0	1	0
HJ Swindells	2	1	0	15	15	15.00	51.72	0	0	0	0
PJ Horton	6	6	0	85	36	14.16	93.40	0	0	9	0
Mohammad Abbas	2	2	1	12	8*	12.00	100.00	0	0	2	0
AM Lilley	6	5	0	56	25	11.20	119.14	0	0	6	2
GT Griffiths	6	3	2	5	4	5.00	16.12	0	0	0	0
HG Munsey	2	2	0	7	6	3.50	35.00	0	0	1	0

Bowling

	Overs	Mdns	Runs	Wkts	BBI	Ave	Econ	SR	4w	5w
A Javid	4.0	0	19	1	1/19	19.00	4.75	24.0	0	0
Mohammad Abbas	20.0	1	114	3	2/55	38.00	5.70	40.0	0	0
TAI Taylor	64.0	1	377	8	3/57	47.12	5.89	48.0	0	0
CN Ackermann	35.0	0	210	5	3/55	42.00	6.00	42.0	0	0
PJ Horton	0.1	0	1	0	-	-	6.00	-	0	0
CJC Wright	32.0	1	198	2	1/65	99.00	6.18	96.0	0	0
CF Parkinson	26.0	0	168	2	1/51	84.00	6.46	78.0	0	0
D Klein	60.2	5	404	12	4/72	33.66	6.69	30.1	1	0
GT Griffiths	43.0	1	301	7	3/92	43.00	7.00	36.8	0	0
AM Lilley	25.0	0	177	0	-	-	7.08	-	0	0
WS Davis	22.3	0	178	2	1/60	89.00	7.91	67.5	0	0
BWM Mike	12.0	0	99	1	1/47	99.00	8.25	72.0	0	0
AM Ali	3.0	0	32	1	1/32	32.00	10.66	18.0	0	0

Catches/Stumpings:
6 Hill, Taylor, 4 Horton, 3 Cosgrove, Lilley, 2 Ackermann, Griffiths, Munsey, 1 Abbas, Davis, Javid, Parkinson

VITALITY BLAST AVERAGES 2019

Batting

	Mat	Inns	NO	Runs	HS	Ave	SR	100	50	4s	6s
MJ Cosgrove	12	12	1	319	45	29.00	134.03	0	0	42	5
CN Ackermann	13	12	0	342	58	28.50	127.61	0	2	31	5
LJ Hill	13	11	1	207	58	20.70	131.01	0	1	15	8
AM Lilley	13	12	0	248	66	20.66	167.56	0	1	22	12
HJ Swindells	9	9	0	175	63	19.44	110.06	0	2	17	1
HE Dearden	12	11	2	158	37	17.55	106.04	0	0	9	5
AM Ali	11	8	1	84	18	12.00	110.52	0	0	2	2
NJ Dexter	4	3	0	33	25	11.00	110.00	0	0	2	3
BWM Mike	6	4	1	33	19	11.00	91.66	0	0	2	0
CF Parkinson	13	9	3	57	17	9.50	85.07	0	0	4	0
D Klein	13	10	4	31	9	5.16	75.60	0	0	1	0
WS Davis	9	2	1	2	2	2.00	66.66	0	0	0	0
CJC Wright	4	2	0	2	2	1.00	33.33	0	0	0	0
GT Griffiths	11	6	6	12	4*	-	85.71	0	0	1	0

Bowling

	Overs	Mdns	Runs	Wkts	BBI	Ave	Econ	SR	4w	5w
CN Ackermann	24.4	0	149	12	7/18	12.41	6.04	12.3	0	1
CF Parkinson	41.0	0	309	12	2/17	25.75	7.53	20.5	0	0
GT Griffiths	25.4	0	200	9	3/14	22.22	7.79	17.1	0	0
AM Lilley	17.5	0	140	3	1/11	46.66	7.85	35.6	0	0
WS Davis	22.3	0	183	8	3/24	22.87	8.13	16.8	0	0
NJ Dexter	2.0	0	18	0	-	-	9.00	-	0	0
D Klein	31.0	1	309	5	1/24	61.80	9.96	37.2	0	0
CJC Wright	9.1	0	95	1	1/34	95.00	10.36	55.0	0	0
BWM Mike	11.5	0	145	2	1/12	72.50	12.25	35.5	0	0

Catches/Stumpings:
10 Lilley, 5 Dearden, Hill, 4 Klein, 3 Parkinson, Swindells, 2 Ackermann, Griffiths, 1 Ali, Cosgrove, Davis, Mike

MIDDLESEX

FORMED: 1864
HOME GROUND: Lord's Cricket Ground, London
CAPTAIN: Peter Handscomb, Eoin Morgan (T20)
2019 RESULTS: CC2: 8/10; RL50: Quarter-finalists; T20: Quarter-finalists
HONOURS: Championship: (13) 1903, 1920, 1921, 1947, 1949(s), 1976, 1977(s), 1980, 1982, 1985, 1990, 1993, 2016; Gillette/NatWest/C&G/FP Trophy: (4) 1977, 1980, 1984, 1998; Benson & Hedges Cup: (2) 1983, 1986; Sunday League: 1992; T20 Cup: 2008

THE LOWDOWN

Stuart Law's first season as coach was a baptism of fire. With two notable exceptions, his frontline batsmen failed repeatedly in four-day cricket, much of which explains why the club finished eighth in Division Two. Then in September, Law lost his captain Dawid Malan – the club's leading run-scorer in Championship and T20 cricket last summer – who quit to join Yorkshire. Law will now form part of an Aussie double act with new skipper Peter Handscomb, who signed a two-year deal in November. The pair have work to do. Malan and Sam Robson aside, none of the batsmen averaged above the low-20s in 2019. Middlesex will be delighted to welcome back Tom Lace after a run-laden loan season at Derbyshire. The pace attack, so strong in recent seasons, has been carried by the indefatigable Tim Murtagh, although Toby Roland-Jones made an encouraging return from a long-term injury. Ireland's Paul Stirling left the club because he no longer qualifies as a local player, but Murtagh has quit international cricket to continue his county career. Former West Indies fast bowler Miguel Cummins, 29, has signed a three-year Kolpak deal. Eoin Morgan is the T20 captain.

IN: Miguel Cummins (WI, Kolpak), Peter Handscomb (Aus), Mitchell Marsh (Aus, T20), Mujeeb Ur Rahman (Afg, T20)
OUT: Tom Barber (Not), Dawid Malan (Yor), George Scott (Glo), Ollie Rayner, Paul Stirling (both REL)

HEAD COACH: STUART LAW

Law was appointed after the 2018 season as part of sweeping changes which saw the departure of Richard Scott after nearly a decade as head coach. Law, a Queenslander who scored 65 hundreds for Essex and Lancashire between 1996 and 2008, had a two-year stint as West Indies coach prior to joining Middlesex and performed similar roles with Sri Lanka and Bangladesh. He has also coached Queensland and Brisbane Heat in domestic cricket. Former England allrounder Dimitri Mascarenhas has re-joined the club as a specialist T20 bowling coach.

www.middlesexccc.com / tel: 0207 289 1300

COUNTY CHAMPIONSHIP AVERAGES 2019

Batting

	Mat	Inns	NO	Runs	HS	Ave	SR	100	50	4s	6s
PR Stirling	3	4	1	150	138	50.00	61.98	1	0	15	0
DJ Malan	13	22	1	1005	199	47.85	58.15	4	2	124	4
JA Simpson	14	22	3	773	167*	40.68	50.48	2	4	112	2
SD Robson	14	24	1	858	140*	37.30	51.22	2	4	117	1
JAR Harris	9	16	3	435	80	33.46	41.23	0	3	56	1
MK Andersson	2	3	0	95	83	31.66	45.02	0	1	15	0
TC Lace	1	2	0	55	51	27.50	51.40	0	1	9	0
ST Finn	7	9	3	155	56	25.83	69.19	0	1	23	2
TG Helm	7	9	1	187	46	23.37	50.00	0	0	27	0
TS Roland-Jones	11	17	3	327	54	23.35	54.77	0	2	44	3
EJG Morgan	2	4	1	69	36*	23.00	42.07	0	0	10	0
NRT Gubbins	14	24	0	530	91	22.08	43.83	0	3	77	2
GFB Scott	7	11	1	204	55	20.40	53.40	0	1	19	1
SS Eskinazi	12	21	0	403	75	19.19	53.16	0	1	65	0
NA Sowter	7	11	1	184	57*	18.40	73.60	0	2	23	2
MDE Holden	9	16	0	218	54	13.62	29.70	0	1	27	0
TJ Murtagh	11	15	4	149	33	13.54	88.69	0	0	21	0
OP Rayner	2	4	1	29	28*	9.66	43.28	0	0	5	0
ML Cummins	3	5	1	34	22*	8.50	40.00	0	0	4	1
RG White	2	4	0	22	10	5.50	23.40	0	0	1	0
ER Bamber	5	8	2	30	8	5.00	23.25	0	0	2	0

Bowling

	Overs	Mdns	Runs	Wkts	BBI	BBM	Ave	Econ	SR	5w	10w
PR Stirling	8.0	0	29	2	2/21	2/21	14.50	3.62	24.0	0	0
TJ Murtagh	295.3	93	757	43	6/51	8/76	17.60	2.56	41.2	4	0
SD Robson	9.5	0	44	2	2/4	2/4	22.00	4.47	29.5	0	0
TG Helm	208.0	39	600	24	5/36	6/71	25.00	2.88	52.0	2	0
TS Roland-Jones	302.5	60	963	33	7/52	10/79	29.18	3.17	55.0	3	1
ST Finn	149.5	25	548	17	5/75	7/90	32.23	3.65	52.8	1	0
ML Cummins	81.0	19	266	8	4/77	6/129	33.25	3.28	60.7	0	0
DJ Malan	42.0	3	134	4	3/60	3/74	33.50	3.19	63.0	0	0
ER Bamber	125.0	31	381	11	5/93	5/93	34.63	3.04	68.1	1	0
OP Rayner	72.0	16	183	5	4/58	5/110	36.60	2.54	86.4	0	0
JAR Harris	247.0	41	876	22	4/98	5/76	39.81	3.54	67.3	0	0
GFB Scott	39.0	6	123	3	2/49	2/49	41.00	3.15	78.0	0	0
NA Sowter	180.4	23	650	14	3/42	4/100	46.42	3.59	77.4	0	0
JA Simpson	1.0	0	2	0	-	-	-	2.00	-	0	0
SS Eskinazi	2.0	0	4	0	-	-	-	2.00	-	0	0
EJG Morgan	3.0	1	4	0	-	-	-	1.33	-	0	0
MDE Holden	14.0	1	66	0	-	-	-	4.71	-	0	0

Catches/Stumpings:

35 Simpson, 17 Malan, 12 Eskinazi, 9 Robson, 4 Sowter, 3 Cummins, Gubbins, Roland-Jones, Scott, 2 Finn, Harris, Murtagh, Rayner, Stirling, 1 Helm, Holden

ROYAL LONDON ONE-DAY CUP AVERAGES 2019

Batting

	Mat	Inns	NO	Runs	HS	Ave	SR	100	50	4s	6s
JAR Harris	4	1	0	117	117	117.00	108.33	1	0	11	2
NRT Gubbins	8	8	1	417	98*	59.57	106.64	0	4	57	0
SD Robson	4	4	0	196	106	49.00	87.11	1	1	19	3
SS Eskinazi	9	9	2	327	107*	46.71	106.16	1	1	33	2
MDE Holden	5	5	0	225	166	45.00	98.68	1	0	21	2
TS Roland-Jones	8	5	2	131	45	43.66	122.42	0	0	11	4
GFB Scott	9	8	3	188	63	37.60	138.23	0	1	12	8
DJ Malan	5	5	0	173	95	34.60	92.02	0	1	22	1
EJG Morgan	3	3	0	99	41	33.00	94.28	0	0	10	3
LRPL Taylor	6	6	0	177	94	29.50	87.19	0	2	13	2
JA Simpson	9	9	1	232	74	29.00	111.53	0	1	23	6
PR Stirling	5	5	0	84	23	16.80	103.70	0	0	12	3
NA Sowter	9	5	1	55	31	13.75	82.08	0	0	3	2
TG Helm	9	5	2	27	11	9.00	52.94	0	0	2	0
TJ Murtagh	4	2	0	1	1	0.50	16.66	0	0	0	0
ST Finn	2	2	2	43	30*	-	107.50	0	0	3	2

Bowling

	Overs	Mdns	Runs	Wkts	BBI	Ave	Econ	SR	4w	5w
TJ Murtagh	39.0	4	142	7	3/24	20.28	3.64	33.4	0	0
PR Stirling	29.0	0	163	2	1/34	81.50	5.62	87.0	0	0
NA Sowter	89.2	0	521	25	6/62	20.84	5.83	21.4	3	1
TS Roland-Jones	73.3	1	436	13	3/46	33.53	5.93	33.9	0	0
ST Finn	14.0	0	85	1	1/35	85.00	6.07	84.0	0	0
JAR Harris	38.4	0	237	7	4/65	33.85	6.12	33.1	1	0
GFB Scott	33.0	0	211	1	1/65	211.00	6.39	198.0	0	0
TG Helm	85.0	0	547	19	5/71	28.78	6.43	26.8	1	1
DJ Malan	24.0	0	160	2	1/28	80.00	6.66	72.0	0	0
MDE Holden	6.0	0	43	0	-	-	7.16	-	0	0
SD Robson	6.0	0	43	1	1/27	43.00	7.16	36.0	0	0

Catches/Stumpings:
14 Simpson (inc 3st), 9 Sowter, 5 Helm, Scott, 4 Malan, Stirling, 3 Eskinazi, Robson, 2 Finn, Gubbins, Holden, Murtagh, Taylor, 1 Morgan, Roland-Jones

VITALITY BLAST AVERAGES 2019

MIDDLESEX CRICKET

Batting

	Mat	Inns	NO	Runs	HS	Ave	SR	100	50	4s	6s
AB de Villiers	8	8	3	348	88*	69.60	182.19	0	4	21	20
EJG Morgan	9	9	1	341	83*	42.62	168.81	0	3	18	23
DJ Malan	14	14	2	490	117	40.83	147.59	1	2	54	16
GFB Scott	9	7	5	71	35*	35.50	101.42	0	0	4	2
SS Eskinazi	11	9	1	256	57*	32.00	131.95	0	2	34	2
Mohammad Hafeez	4	4	0	115	48	28.75	112.74	0	0	7	4
JA Simpson	14	11	3	202	42*	25.25	137.41	0	0	7	8
TS Roland-Jones	14	7	2	121	40	24.20	124.74	0	0	7	5
PR Stirling	11	11	0	223	33	20.27	129.65	0	0	30	6
DJ Lincoln	3	3	0	38	30	12.66	108.57	0	0	4	1
NA Sowter	14	5	2	20	13*	6.66	125.00	0	0	3	0
NRT Gubbins	3	2	0	13	12	6.50	81.25	0	0	2	0
TG Helm	14	6	2	16	5	4.00	66.66	0	0	0	0
TE Barber	1	1	0	0	0	0.00	0.00	0	0	0	0
Mujeeb Ur Rahman	10	1	0	0	0	0.00	0.00	0	0	0	0
MDE Holden	1	1	1	30	30*	-	125.00	0	0	4	1
ST Finn	14	3	3	2	1*	-	40.00	0	0	0	0

Bowling

	Overs	Mdns	Runs	Wkts	BBI	Ave	Econ	SR	4w	5w
Mujeeb Ur Rahman	39.0	0	282	7	2/31	40.28	7.23	33.4	0	0
NA Sowter	53.0	0	447	16	4/29	27.93	8.43	19.8	1	0
TS Roland-Jones	44.1	0	378	19	5/21	19.89	8.55	13.9	1	1
Mohammad Hafeez	14.0	0	121	2	1/22	60.50	8.64	42.0	0	0
ST Finn	48.0	0	453	19	5/16	23.84	9.43	15.1	0	1
TG Helm	46.5	0	444	15	3/27	29.60	9.48	18.7	0	0
PR Stirling	6.0	0	61	2	1/6	30.50	10.16	18.0	0	0
TE Barber	1.5	0	20	1	1/20	20.00	10.90	11.0	0	0
DJ Malan	3.0	0	34	0	-	-	11.33	-	0	0
GFB Scott	1.0	0	15	0	-	-	15.00	-	0	0

Catches/Stumpings:

8 Simpson (inc 3st), Sowter, 7 Roland-Jones, Scott, 6 de Villiers, Finn, 4 Eskinazi, 3 Gubbins, Helm, Lincoln, Malan, Mujeeb, 1 Holden, Morgan, Stirling

NORTHAMPTONSHIRE

FORMED: 1878
HOME GROUND: County Ground, Northampton
ONE-DAY NAME: Northamptonshire Steelbacks
CAPTAIN: Adam Rossington, Josh Cobb (RL50 & T20)
2019 RESULTS: CC2: 2/10; RL50: 8/9 North Group; T20: 7/9 North Group
HONOURS: Gillette/NatWest/C&G/FP Trophy: (2) 1976, 1992; Benson & Hedges Cup: 1980; T20 Cup: (2) 2013, 2016

THE LOWDOWN

Even the most optimistic Northants supporter would not have bet on promotion a year ago, but Adam Rossington proved an inspired choice to replace Alex Wakely as captain last June, leading the club to five wins in six matches and second place in Division Two. It would not have been possible without Ben Sanderson, who was the club's leading wicket-taker in all competitions and made up for an unsettled pace attack which felt the losses of Richard Gleeson and Steven Crook. Brett Hutton battled gamely through injury but had ankle surgery in November, while Zimbabwean quick Blessing Muzarabani is still bedding in. Hence the arrivals of Gareth Berg, signed from Hampshire last summer; Jack White, a former Cheshire seamer who was plucked from Australian grade cricket; and 22-year old Netherlands paceman Brandon Glover. Runs were shared around in 2019, with six players making Championship hundreds. Opener Ricardo Vasconcelos, who made 750 runs in 10 matches before an ankle injury, looks a fine prospect. The T20 side have faded of late, although Kieron Pollard and Paul Stirling offer some extra firepower this summer. They will also be targeting the One-Day Cup, with only Rossington signed for The Hundred.

IN: Gareth Berg (Ham), Brandon Glover (Net, EU passport), Jack White (unattached), Faheem Ashraf (Pak), Kieron Pollard (WI, T20), Paul Stirling (Ire, T20)
OUT: None

HEAD COACH: DAVID RIPLEY

Ripley was promoted from Second XI coach in 2012 and led the club to their maiden T20 title the following year, repeating the trick in 2016. As a keeper-batsman, he scored over 10,000 runs for the county and claimed more than 1,000 dismissals. Phil Rowe has retired after 15 years on the club's staff, with John Sadler arriving from Leicestershire as assistant coach. Recently retired left-armer Chris Liddle has joined as bowling coach after a successful stint with Netherlands.

COUNTY CHAMPIONSHIP AVERAGES 2019

Batting

	Mat	Inns	NO	Runs	HS	Ave	SR	100	50	4s	6s
D Pretorius	1	1	0	111	111	111.00	71.15	1	0	15	3
R Vasconcelos	10	18	2	750	184	46.87	53.57	2	3	105	2
AM Rossington	13	19	2	787	82	46.29	61.77	0	8	92	13
T Bavuma	8	15	0	566	134	37.73	63.59	2	1	70	5
AG Wakely	12	16	1	548	102	36.53	47.77	1	2	72	2
LA Procter	14	21	7	510	86*	36.42	49.90	0	2	46	5
RI Keogh	14	22	0	744	150	33.81	50.68	2	2	100	1
SA Zaib	3	5	0	163	54	32.60	58.42	0	1	13	6
NL Buck	10	13	4	287	53	31.88	76.94	0	3	44	5
JJ Cobb	6	10	0	314	68	31.40	63.30	0	3	41	4
RE Levi	4	6	1	144	60	28.80	65.75	0	1	20	0
BJ Curran	7	11	1	273	52	27.30	49.10	0	1	35	0
MT Coles	4	5	1	98	41*	24.50	112.64	0	0	10	6
RI Newton	10	19	2	396	105	23.29	48.58	1	1	47	1
L Wood	4	6	1	116	66	23.20	48.73	0	1	16	0
JO Holder	2	2	0	43	40	21.50	47.25	0	0	5	0
BA Hutton	10	15	4	203	34*	18.45	37.80	0	0	23	0
DAJ Bracewell	3	3	0	54	38	18.00	50.46	0	0	8	1
BW Sanderson	14	17	6	162	28	14.72	52.42	0	0	26	1
J Overton	2	3	0	25	19	8.33	47.16	0	0	3	0
GK Berg	3	3	0	9	5	3.00	22.50	0	0	1	0
B Muzarabani	2	2	1	2	1*	2.00	28.57	0	0	0	0
EN Gay	1	-	-	-	-	-	-	-	-	-	-

Bowling

	Overs	Mdns	Runs	Wkts	BBI	BBM	Ave	Econ	SR	5w	10w
GK Berg	59.3	18	153	8	2/17	4/76	19.12	2.57	44.6	0	0
BW Sanderson	448.2	118	1179	60	6/37	10/55	19.65	2.62	44.8	3	1
BA Hutton	263.3	72	700	35	6/57	7/79	20.00	2.65	45.1	2	0
D Pretorius	20.0	6	54	2	1/21	2/54	27.00	2.70	60.0	0	0
MT Coles	69.0	13	268	9	3/51	3/51	29.77	3.88	46.0	0	0
L Wood	110.0	18	332	9	5/72	5/72	36.88	3.01	73.3	1	0
NL Buck	207.1	38	814	22	5/54	8/107	37.00	3.92	56.5	1	0
J Overton	55.2	3	223	6	3/79	5/137	37.16	4.03	55.3	0	0
B Muzarabani	31.0	2	160	4	2/47	2/47	40.00	5.16	46.5	0	0
LA Procter	204.1	43	697	17	4/26	4/26	41.00	3.41	72.0	0	0
JO Holder	52.0	6	199	4	2/62	2/79	49.75	3.82	78.0	0	0
DAJ Bracewell	54.0	7	212	4	2/44	2/108	53.00	3.92	81.0	0	0
RI Keogh	225.2	37	804	13	3/43	4/93	61.84	3.56	104.0	0	0
JJ Cobb	27.0	4	91	1	1/21	1/52	91.00	3.37	162.0	0	0
T Bavuma	1.0	0	2	0	-	-	-	2.00	-	0	0
R Vasconcelos	1.3	0	9	0	-	-	-	6.00	-	0	0
SA Zaib	4.0	0	16	0	-	-	-	4.00	-	0	0
AM Rossington	5.0	0	20	0	-	-	-	4.00	-	0	0

Catches/Stumpings:
34 Rossington (inc 2st), 16 Vasconcelos, Wakely, 9 Hutton, 7 Bavuma, 4 Holder, Keogh, Procter, 3 Coles, Curran, Wood, 2 Buck, Cobb, Levi, Overton, 1 Gay, Muzurabani, Newton

ROYAL LONDON ONE-DAY CUP AVERAGES 2019

Batting

	Mat	Inns	NO	Runs	HS	Ave	SR	100	50	4s	6s
JO Holder	5	5	1	284	86	71.00	132.09	0	3	30	8
LA Procter	8	8	5	175	50*	58.33	99.43	0	1	13	2
R Vasconcelos	5	5	0	255	112	51.00	98.45	1	2	25	5
RI Keogh	8	8	0	359	102	44.87	87.34	1	3	30	0
BJ Curran	2	2	0	79	69	39.50	97.53	0	1	7	0
AM Rossington	6	6	1	184	68	36.80	129.57	0	1	21	4
AG Wakely	8	8	0	288	66	36.00	92.90	0	3	27	2
JJ Cobb	8	8	0	227	63	28.37	75.91	0	2	21	5
RE Levi	8	8	0	197	58	24.62	90.36	0	1	25	5
CO Thurston	1	1	0	21	21	21.00	105.00	0	0	3	0
SA Zaib	1	1	0	16	16	16.00	133.33	0	0	1	0
B Muzarabani	5	4	2	23	18	11.50	79.31	0	0	1	1
RI Newton	2	2	0	23	14	11.50	52.27	0	0	2	0
BW Sanderson	8	5	0	45	31	9.00	64.28	0	0	4	0
IG Holland	4	4	2	18	9	9.00	163.63	0	0	3	0
NL Buck	7	4	0	19	16	4.75	79.16	0	0	2	0
TB Sole	1	1	0	4	4	4.00	133.33	0	0	1	0
BA Hutton	1	-	-	-	-	-	-	-	-	-	-

Bowling

	Overs	Mdns	Runs	Wkts	BBI	Ave	Econ	SR	4w	5w
LA Procter	59.4	2	296	5	2/51	59.20	4.96	71.6	0	0
B Muzarabani	37.4	1	193	6	3/28	32.16	5.12	37.6	0	0
JJ Cobb	21.0	0	115	3	2/38	38.33	5.47	42.0	0	0
RI Keogh	33.0	0	185	3	2/52	61.66	5.60	66.0	0	0
BA Hutton	10.0	0	57	1	1/57	57.00	5.70	60.0	0	0
BW Sanderson	64.3	5	371	14	3/44	26.50	5.75	27.6	0	0
JO Holder	27.0	1	160	7	3/26	22.85	5.92	23.1	0	0
NL Buck	56.0	1	344	11	3/44	31.27	6.14	30.5	0	0
SA Zaib	5.0	0	36	0	-	-	7.20	-	0	0
IG Holland	21.4	0	158	3	2/38	52.66	7.29	43.3	0	0
TB Sole	2.0	0	17	0	-	-	8.50	-	0	0

Catches/Stumpings:
6 Rossington, 4 Levi, 3 Cobb, Holland, Keogh, Procter, Vasconcelos, 2 Curran, Sanderson, Wakely, 1 Buck, Holder, Hutton, Thurston

VITALITY BLAST AVERAGES 2019

Batting

	Mat	Inns	NO	Runs	HS	Ave	SR	100	50	4s	6s
RI Keogh	10	9	4	177	59*	35.40	105.98	0	1	14	2
RE Levi	7	7	1	156	44	26.00	144.44	0	0	23	2
TB Sole	6	4	2	51	41*	25.50	100.00	0	0	5	1
JJ Cobb	11	10	0	254	84	25.40	137.29	0	2	14	18
D Pretorius	11	10	1	225	50*	25.00	129.31	0	1	18	9
AM Rossington	11	11	1	239	54	23.90	137.35	0	2	26	8
AG Wakely	11	10	2	188	47*	23.50	105.02	0	0	13	3
GG White	11	4	1	44	27*	14.66	118.91	0	0	5	2
B Muzarabani	4	2	1	9	9	9.00	69.23	0	0	1	0
Faheem Ashraf	11	7	2	36	24	7.20	120.00	0	0	4	1
MT Coles	6	5	1	22	14	5.50	110.00	0	0	2	1
CO Thurston	2	2	0	11	8	5.50	57.89	0	0	1	0
NL Buck	8	2	1	5	5*	5.00	71.42	0	0	0	0
BJ Curran	2	2	0	8	5	4.00	50.00	0	0	1	0
BW Sanderson	9	2	1	3	2	3.00	50.00	0	0	0	0
LA Procter	1	1	0	1	1	1.00	50.00	0	0	0	0

Bowling

	Overs	Mdns	Runs	Wkts	BBI	Ave	Econ	SR	4w	5w
JJ Cobb	22.0	0	127	2	1/17	63.50	5.77	66.0	0	0
RI Keogh	20.0	0	130	10	3/30	13.00	6.50	12.0	0	0
GG White	38.0	0	275	10	2/18	27.50	7.23	22.8	0	0
TB Sole	4.0	0	29	0	-	-	7.25	-	0	0
BW Sanderson	27.0	0	211	11	4/28	19.18	7.81	14.7	1	0
Faheem Ashraf	40.1	1	326	11	2/26	29.63	8.11	21.9	0	0
D Pretorius	21.1	0	178	6	3/17	29.66	8.40	21.1	0	0
MT Coles	8.0	0	69	0	-	-	8.62	-	0	0
B Muzarabani	8.0	0	76	1	1/28	76.00	9.50	48.0	0	0
NL Buck	18.3	0	179	5	1/14	35.80	9.67	22.2	0	0
LA Procter	1.0	0	10	0	-	-	10.00	-	0	0

Catches/Stumpings:
7 Rossington (inc 3st), 5 Coles, Sole, Wakely, 4 Ashraf, Buck, 3 Keogh, White, 2 Thurston, 1 Cobb, Muzarabani, Pretorius

NOTTINGHAMSHIRE

FORMED: 1841
HOME GROUND: Trent Bridge, Nottingham
ONE-DAY NAME: Notts Outlaws
CAPTAIN: Steven Mullaney, Dan Christian (T20)
2019 RESULTS: CC1: 8/8; RL50: Semi-finalists; T20: Semi-finalists
HONOURS: County Championship: (6) 1907, 1929, 1981, 1987, 2005, 2010; Gillette/NatWest/C&G/FP Trophy: 1987; Pro40/National League/CB40/YB40/RL50: (2) 2013, 2017; Benson & Hedges Cup: 1989; Sunday League: 1991; T20 Cup: 2017

THE LOWDOWN

Nottinghamshire remain a strong white-ball outfit, reaching the T20 and 50-over semi-finals last summer, but their Championship form has sunk without trace: the club finished bottom of Division One by 64 points. It is a dismal return for a squad of big-name players, and failure to achieve promotion this summer may lead to changes at the top. The batsmen must take a large share of the blame, with only Joe Clarke and Chris Nash scraping an average of 30-plus. Both the Bens – Duckett and Slater – struggled in their debut season at Trent Bridge, while Samit Patel's woes were such that he was loaned out to Glamorgan. The club have now gambled on resurrecting Haseeb Hameed, signed from Lancashire. Beyond the iconic Luke Fletcher, the seam supply looked oddly bare last summer, though the arrival of Mohammad Abbas for the first nine Championship matches should go some way to fixing that. Zak Chappell's first summer at Trent Bridge was blighted by injury, while Paul Coughlin has been sent back to Durham. A brighter note was the emergence of slow left-armer Liam Patterson-White. Peter Trego, 38 but still unquenched, is a handy recruit from Somerset.

IN: Tom Barber (Mid), Haseeb Hameed (Lan), Peter Trego (Som), Mohammad Abbas (Pak), Dan Christian (Aus, T20)
OUT: Paul Coughlin (Dur), Nick Kimber (Sur), Jake Libby (Wor), Luke Wood (Lan)

HEAD COACH: PETER MOORES

Moores replaced Mick Newell (now the director of cricket) in 2016 and immediately led the club to the cup double as well as Championship promotion. Moores had two spells as England head coach and won the Championship with Sussex in 2003 and Lancashire in 2011. As a keeper-batsman he scored 7,000 first-class runs and claimed 517 dismissals for Sussex between 1985 and 1998. Kevin Shine, who worked previously with Moores as England's fast-bowling guru, has replaced Andy Pick as assistant coach.

COUNTY CHAMPIONSHIP AVERAGES 2019

Batting

	Mat	Inns	NO	Runs	HS	Ave	SR	100	50	4s	6s
R Ashwin	5	10	1	339	66*	37.66	55.21	0	2	47	1
JM Clarke	12	21	1	621	125	31.05	57.44	3	1	91	0
CD Nash	12	22	1	641	85	30.52	48.78	0	6	96	0
SJ Mullaney	13	24	0	694	179	28.91	55.52	2	2	88	14
JDM Evison	1	2	0	57	45	28.50	59.37	0	0	11	0
BM Duckett	13	23	0	630	140	27.39	60.81	1	2	85	8
P Coughlin	5	7	0	167	49	23.85	53.52	0	0	25	0
BG Compton	2	3	1	43	16*	21.50	32.08	0	0	7	0
BT Slater	13	24	1	471	76	20.47	43.61	0	1	70	0
JD Libby	5	10	0	189	77	18.90	37.20	0	1	22	0
JL Pattinson	3	5	2	55	22	18.33	26.06	0	0	8	0
SR Patel	9	16	1	258	52	17.20	39.44	0	1	30	0
LA Patterson-White	5	8	2	91	58*	15.16	29.35	0	1	10	1
TJ Moores	13	23	0	323	48	14.04	35.49	0	0	48	4
JT Ball	10	16	11	67	15*	13.40	61.46	0	0	11	1
SCJ Broad	7	13	4	109	30	12.11	42.91	0	0	15	0
ZJ Chappell	3	6	1	59	29	11.80	48.76	0	0	11	0
L Wood	5	9	1	87	52	10.87	48.60	0	1	17	0
LJ Fletcher	12	22	1	209	25*	9.95	32.65	0	0	26	3
M Carter	5	7	0	51	23	7.28	28.65	0	0	6	0
JM Blatherwick	2	2	2	6	4*	-	50.00	0	0	1	0

Bowling

	Overs	Mdns	Runs	Wkts	BBI	BBM	Ave	Econ	SR	5w	10w
LA Patterson-White	134.5	17	420	20	5/73	6/107	21.00	3.11	40.4	1	0
R Ashwin	297.4	73	836	34	6/69	12/144	24.58	2.80	52.5	4	1
LJ Fletcher	326.4	68	926	35	5/50	6/113	26.45	2.83	56.0	2	0
JL Pattinson	74.0	12	235	8	6/73	8/140	29.37	3.17	55.5	1	0
SCJ Broad	195.4	44	509	17	5/73	5/73	29.94	2.60	69.0	1	0
L Wood	93.0	12	349	11	5/67	6/138	31.72	3.75	50.7	1	0
SJ Mullaney	166.0	32	536	13	4/48	4/105	41.23	3.22	76.6	0	0
P Coughlin	135.4	19	530	11	3/37	4/160	48.18	3.90	74.0	0	0
SR Patel	117.5	18	391	7	3/31	3/112	55.85	3.31	101.0	0	0
JT Ball	246.5	42	878	15	2/57	3/106	58.53	3.55	98.7	0	0
M Carter	137.4	14	529	6	3/68	3/102	88.16	3.84	137.6	0	0
JM Blatherwick	34.4	3	192	2	1/82	1/82	96.00	5.53	104.0	0	0
BM Duckett	4.0	0	16	0	-	-	-	4.00	-	0	0
JD Libby	4.0	0	32	0	-	-	-	8.00	-	0	0
JDM Evison	9.0	0	33	0	-	-	-	3.66	-	0	0
ZJ Chappell	40.4	3	178	0	-	-	-	4.37	-	0	0

Catches/Stumpings:

30 Moores (inc 1st), 13 Mullaney, 7 Coughlin, Duckett, 6 Clarke, Slater, 5 Carter, 4 Nash, 3 Ball, Broad, Libby, Patterson-White, 2 Ashwin, Fletcher, Patel, 1 Chappell, Compton, Evison

ROYAL LONDON ONE-DAY CUP AVERAGES 2019

Batting

	Mat	Inns	NO	Runs	HS	Ave	SR	100	50	4s	6s
BT Slater	4	4	0	315	100	78.75	88.23	1	3	40	1
SJ Mullaney	9	8	2	305	81	50.83	114.66	0	3	29	11
AD Hales	3	2	0	90	54	45.00	95.74	0	1	12	1
JM Clarke	9	8	0	340	139	42.50	129.27	1	1	47	8
SR Patel	9	7	2	210	136*	42.00	84.00	1	0	20	2
TJ Moores	9	8	1	281	74	40.14	132.54	0	4	17	21
CD Nash	5	4	0	157	56	39.25	85.79	0	2	19	4
LJ Fletcher	8	6	2	138	46*	34.50	164.28	0	0	8	11
JD Libby	7	5	0	117	66	23.40	101.73	0	1	6	3
JL Pattinson	7	4	1	64	33	21.33	136.17	0	0	5	4
BM Duckett	7	7	0	145	86	20.71	115.07	0	1	18	3
M Carter	8	4	1	33	21*	11.00	84.61	0	0	6	0
JT Ball	8	3	1	14	14	7.00	66.66	0	0	2	0
LW James	1	1	0	0	0	0.00	0.00	0	0	0	0
L Wood	1	1	1	17	17*	-	65.38	0	0	2	0
P Coughlin	1	1	1	11	11*	-	91.66	0	0	0	1
ZJ Chappell	2	1	1	8	8*	-	88.88	0	0	0	0
HF Gurney	1	1	1	1	1*	-	100.00	0	0	0	0

Bowling

	Overs	Mdns	Runs	Wkts	BBI	Ave	Econ	SR	4w	5w
JL Pattinson	49.0	2	264	11	5/61	24.00	5.38	26.7	0	1
SR Patel	63.1	3	364	8	2/42	45.50	5.76	47.3	0	0
LJ Fletcher	63.1	2	368	17	5/56	21.64	5.82	22.2	0	1
M Carter	51.2	4	303	7	3/60	43.28	5.90	44.0	0	0
JT Ball	54.0	0	358	14	4/62	25.57	6.62	23.1	1	0
SJ Mullaney	34.0	0	243	3	1/35	81.00	7.14	68.0	0	0
L Wood	5.0	0	36	2	2/36	18.00	7.20	15.0	0	0
ZJ Chappell	9.0	0	67	0	-	-	7.44	-	0	0
HF Gurney	10.0	0	86	1	1/86	86.00	8.60	60.0	0	0

Catches/Stumpings:
10 Moores (inc 2st), 6 Duckett, 3 Hales, 2 Carter, Fletcher, Mullaney, Patel, 1 Ball, Clarke, James, Libby, Pattinson

VITALITY BLAST AVERAGES 2019

Batting

	Mat	Inns	NO	Runs	HS	Ave	SR	100	50	4s	6s
CD Nash	2	2	1	98	74*	98.00	142.02	0	1	13	2
AD Hales	12	12	1	418	83*	38.00	140.26	0	5	41	18
DT Christian	12	10	5	183	41*	36.60	140.76	0	0	12	8
TJ Moores	12	11	4	218	69	31.14	144.37	0	1	9	14
JD Libby	9	3	0	85	35	28.33	111.84	0	0	8	0
JM Clarke	11	10	1	248	50	27.55	119.23	0	2	24	8
BM Duckett	12	11	1	255	64	25.50	128.78	0	1	26	7
SR Patel	12	7	2	93	34	18.60	127.39	0	0	10	2
Imad Wasim	7	5	2	39	18*	13.00	134.48	0	0	5	0
L Wood	9	3	1	13	7	6.50	86.66	0	0	0	0
M Carter	11	3	0	18	14	6.00	94.73	0	0	2	0
LJ Fletcher	4	2	0	10	6	5.00	111.11	0	0	0	1
ZJ Chappell	1	1	0	0	0	0.00	0.00	0	0	0	0
SJ Mullaney	1	1	0	0	0	0.00	-	0	0	0	0
HF Gurney	12	3	3	5	5*	-	250.00	0	0	1	0
JT Ball	5	1	1	2	2*	-	33.33	0	0	0	0

Bowling

	Overs	Mdns	Runs	Wkts	BBI	Ave	Econ	SR	4w	5w
M Carter	42.0	1	277	14	3/14	19.78	6.59	18.0	0	0
Imad Wasim	25.0	1	166	10	2/21	16.60	6.64	15.0	0	0
SR Patel	39.0	0	263	6	2/26	43.83	6.74	39.0	0	0
L Wood	27.3	0	193	11	3/16	17.54	7.01	15.0	0	0
DT Christian	19.0	0	152	8	3/26	19.00	8.00	14.2	0	0
SJ Mullaney	4.0	0	32	2	2/32	16.00	8.00	12.0	0	0
HF Gurney	44.0	0	396	22	5/30	18.00	9.00	12.0	0	1
LJ Fletcher	9.0	0	82	6	3/17	13.66	9.11	9.0	0	0
JT Ball	15.0	0	143	4	2/21	35.75	9.53	22.5	0	0
ZJ Chappell	3.0	0	29	0	-	-	9.66	-	0	0
JD Libby	1.0	0	11	1	1/11	11.00	11.00	6.0	0	0

Catches/Stumpings:
10 Duckett, 9 Moores (inc 2st), 8 Hales, Libby, 6 Christian, 5 Carter, 4 Wood, 3 Patel, 2 Ball, 1 Clarke, Gurney, Imad, Nash

FORMED: 1875
HOME GROUND: The Cooper Associates County Ground, Taunton
CAPTAIN: Tom Abell, Lewis Gregory (T20)
2019 RESULTS: CC1: 2/8; RL50: Champions; T20: 6/9 South Group
HONOURS: Gillette/NatWest/C&G/FP Trophy: (3) 1979, 1983, 2001; Pro40/National League/CB40/YB40/RL50: 2019; Benson & Hedges Cup: (2) 1981, 1982; Sunday League: 1979; T20 Cup: 2005

THE LOWDOWN

Can you believe it, runners-up again. And so Marcus Trescothick and Peter Trego sign off without a Championship title after 19 summers as teammates and almost as many close shaves. Somerset could have won all three competitions last year but had to settle with winning the last one-day Lord's final. Babar Azam, the Pakistan international who returns this summer, and Tom Banton topped the T20 run-charts, and it was only the wastefulness of the bowlers which stunted their Blast campaign. Banton also starred in the One-Day Cup and has quickly become one of the hottest properties in English cricket; he will miss the start of the season after landing an IPL contract. Will the 21-year-old master the red ball this summer? There was a general batting malaise among Somerset's top order in 2019. Few sides can resist this Somerset bowling attack, whether it's Lewis Gregory – 51 wickets at 15 – the Overtons or the spin twins, Jack Leach and Dom Bess. That the prolific Jack Brooks was occasionally 12th man speaks volumes. And Vernon Philander has arrived on a two-year Kolpak after hanging up his international boots following the 2019/20 Test series against England.

IN: Vernon Philander (SA, Kolpak), Babar Azam (Pak, CC/T20), Corey Anderson (NZ, T20)
OUT: Tim Groenewald (Ken), Peter Trego (Not), Tim Rouse, Paul van Meekeren (both REL), Marcus Trescothick (RET)

HEAD COACH: JASON KERR

A former Somerset allrounder, Kerr was promoted from bowling coach to head coach in 2017 and works alongside director of cricket Andy Hurry. Kerr has been part of the coaching staff since 2005, grooming the club's brightest talent as Academy director. Marcus Trescothick makes an immediate transition from player to assistant coach and the club have also decided to rename Taunton's pavilion in his honour. Gordon Hollins has left his role as ECB managing director of county cricket to become the club's fourth CEO in three years, while former Adidas MD Gordon Baird is the new chairman.

COUNTY CHAMPIONSHIP AVERAGES 2019

	Mat	Inns	NO	Runs	HS	Ave	SR	100	50	4s	6s
TB Abell	14	25	1	756	101	31.50	45.95	1	5	102	1
GA Bartlett	14	24	1	718	137	31.21	57.94	2	3	96	5
T Banton	10	18	0	533	79	29.61	59.02	0	5	73	4
L Gregory	11	18	2	465	129*	29.06	72.54	1	1	51	17
SM Davies	14	24	1	642	109	27.91	48.71	1	3	95	2
RE van der Merwe	4	6	1	132	60	26.40	77.19	0	1	9	6
Azhar Ali	9	16	2	344	79	24.57	47.57	0	3	45	1
DM Bess	7	13	3	233	52*	23.30	43.14	0	2	29	0
JC Hildreth	14	24	0	553	105	23.04	59.91	1	3	77	2
J Overton	8	14	2	252	52*	21.00	83.72	0	1	27	8
Babar Azam	1	2	0	40	40	20.00	38.46	0	0	8	0
C Overton	10	15	1	230	40	16.42	55.15	0	0	30	4
JH Davey	5	9	1	92	36	11.50	56.09	0	0	10	0
JA Brooks	8	12	6	68	35*	11.33	66.66	0	0	10	1
ME Trescothick	5	8	0	86	23	10.75	42.15	0	0	16	0
TD Groenewald	7	13	3	100	17	10.00	34.72	0	0	14	2
EJ Byrom	1	2	0	20	14	10.00	62.50	0	0	4	0
M Vijay	3	5	0	42	29	8.40	32.81	0	0	7	0
MJ Leach	9	13	4	53	11*	5.88	32.91	0	0	6	0

Batting

	Overs	Mdns	Runs	Wkts	BBI	BBM	Ave	Econ	SR	5w	10w
L Gregory	284.1	81	804	51	6/32	11/53	15.76	2.82	33.4	4	1
MJ Leach	250.3	71	596	34	6/36	7/121	17.52	2.37	44.2	2	0
RE van der Merwe	66.5	21	177	10	4/41	4/59	17.70	2.64	40.1	0	0
JH Davey	107.5	29	301	17	5/21	8/51	17.70	2.79	38.0	1	0
J Overton	156.5	29	521	28	5/70	7/94	18.60	3.32	33.6	1	0
C Overton	282.3	64	810	37	5/31	7/69	21.89	2.86	45.8	2	0
DM Bess	174.3	44	447	19	5/59	7/93	23.52	2.56	55.1	1	0
TB Abell	103.2	30	313	13	4/39	6/70	24.07	3.02	47.6	0	0
TD Groenewald	163.3	32	472	18	5/51	7/96	26.22	2.88	54.5	1	0
JA Brooks	214.1	51	728	25	5/33	6/90	29.12	3.39	51.4	1	0
Azhar Ali	2.0	2	0	0	-	-	-	0.00	-	0	0

Bowling

Catches/Stumpings:
50 Davies (inc 3st), 17 Hildreth, 16 J Overton, 13 Abell, 12 C Overton, 10 Gregory, 9 Trescothick, 7 Leach, van der Merwe, 6 Banton, 5 Vijay, 3 Azhar, Bess, Groenewald, 2 Brooks, Byrom, 1 Bartlett, Davey

ROYAL LONDON ONE-DAY CUP AVERAGES 2019

Batting

	Mat	Inns	NO	Runs	HS	Ave	SR	100	50	4s	6s
C Overton	11	9	6	213	66*	71.00	131.48	0	1	12	10
JC Hildreth	11	11	1	457	93	45.70	98.49	0	4	36	8
T Banton	11	11	0	454	112	41.27	94.58	2	3	50	13
Azhar Ali	11	11	0	451	110	41.00	79.96	1	2	36	4
PD Trego	11	11	0	389	141	35.36	96.52	1	1	36	8
GA Bartlett	9	9	3	207	57*	34.50	99.51	0	1	16	2
L Gregory	11	10	1	287	52	31.88	141.37	0	3	17	17
JH Davey	11	6	4	52	23*	26.00	91.22	0	0	5	0
TB Abell	11	10	0	253	44	25.30	86.34	0	0	20	0
RE van der Merwe	11	8	1	145	38	20.71	102.83	0	0	10	4
TD Groenewald	6	4	1	62	28	20.66	108.77	0	0	6	1
J Overton	5	3	1	39	27	19.50	139.28	0	0	2	2
DM Bess	2	2	0	19	14	9.50	95.00	0	0	2	0

Bowling

	Overs	Mdns	Runs	Wkts	BBI	Ave	Econ	SR	4w	5w
TB Abell	6.0	0	26	2	2/19	13.00	4.33	18.0	0	0
C Overton	83.0	3	402	20	5/18	20.10	4.84	24.9	0	1
JH Davey	78.3	6	382	14	4/36	27.28	4.86	33.6	1	0
RE van der Merwe	73.1	2	397	11	3/29	36.09	5.42	39.9	0	0
L Gregory	73.4	1	438	10	2/35	43.80	5.94	44.2	0	0
J Overton	38.0	1	228	8	4/64	28.50	6.00	28.5	1	0
DM Bess	5.0	0	32	0	-	-	6.40	-	0	0
TD Groenewald	38.3	1	253	7	3/34	36.14	6.57	33.0	0	0
Azhar Ali	19.0	1	136	7	5/34	19.42	7.15	16.2	0	1
PD Trego	1.0	0	10	0	-	-	10.00	-	0	0

Catches/Stumpings:
12 Banton (inc 1st), van der Merwe, 8 Azhar, 7 C Overton, 4 Bartlett, Gregory, 3 Abell, Davey, 2 Hildreth, J Overton

VITALITY BLAST AVERAGES 2019

SOMERSET
COUNTY CRICKET CLUB

Batting

	Mat	Inns	NO	Runs	HS	Ave	SR	100	50	4s	6s
Babar Azam	13	13	2	578	102*	52.54	149.35	1	4	60	14
TB Abell	13	10	2	354	101*	44.25	177.88	1	2	38	11
T Banton	13	13	0	549	100	42.23	161.47	1	4	67	23
PD Trego	4	4	1	116	47*	38.66	124.73	0	0	11	4
JE Taylor	13	5	4	38	19*	38.00	146.15	0	0	5	1
EJ Byrom	9	9	1	185	54*	23.12	196.80	0	1	15	12
JC Hildreth	13	13	2	216	40	19.63	122.72	0	0	17	6
TA Lammonby	12	9	3	88	31	14.66	139.68	0	0	9	2
J Overton	4	2	0	28	19	14.00	140.00	0	0	3	1
C Overton	12	7	2	47	19*	9.40	106.81	0	0	0	3
L Gregory	4	3	1	16	10*	8.00	123.07	0	0	3	0
RE van der Merwe	13	8	2	45	17	7.50	104.65	0	0	3	1
MTC Waller	13	4	1	17	7	5.66	106.25	0	0	2	0
TD Groenewald	7	4	1	10	9	3.33	90.90	0	0	2	0

Bowling

	Overs	Mdns	Runs	Wkts	BBI	Ave	Econ	SR	4w	5w
MTC Waller	46.5	0	361	13	3/19	27.76	7.70	21.6	0	0
L Gregory	11.0	0	91	5	3/30	18.20	8.27	13.2	0	0
RE van der Merwe	46.0	0	387	15	5/32	25.80	8.41	18.4	0	1
TD Groenewald	20.0	0	175	8	2/22	21.87	8.75	15.0	0	0
TB Abell	1.0	0	9	0	-	-	9.00	-	0	0
JE Taylor	43.5	0	415	14	2/12	29.64	9.46	18.7	0	0
C Overton	38.0	0	366	11	3/32	33.27	9.63	20.7	0	0
TA Lammonby	20.0	0	218	8	2/32	27.25	10.90	15.0	0	0
J Overton	10.0	0	121	0	-	-	12.10	-	0	0

Catches/Stumpings:
11 Abell, 10 Waller, 7 Banton (inc 1st), van der Merwe, 5 Azam, Lammonby, C Overton, 4 Hildreth, 2 Byrom, Gregory, 1 J Overton, Trego, Taylor

SURREY

FORMED: 1845
GROUND: The Kia Oval, London
CAPTAIN: Rory Burns, Jade Dernbach (T20)
2019 RESULTS: CC1: 6/8; RL50: 9/9 South Group; T20: 8/9 South Group
HONOURS: Championship: (20) 1890, 1891, 1892, 1894, 1895, 1899, 1914, 1950, 1952, 1953, 1954, 1955, 1956, 1957, 1958, 1971, 1999, 2000, 2002, 2018; Gillette/NatWest/C&G/FP Trophy: 1982; Benson & Hedges Cup: (3) 1974, 1997, 2001; Pro40/National League/CB40/YB40/RL50: (2) 2003, 2011; Sunday League: 1996; T20 Cup: 2003

THE LOWDOWN

The champions of 2018 crashed to earth last summer. Putting aside the T20 Blast – in which they were still only modest at best – Surrey won three of 22 matches. The club need only look at their rivals across the Thames to see how the mighty can fall. They go into the new season with a 30-man squad and they'll need to draw on all their resources to cover for England absences. That was a mitigating factor last season, along with a long injury list. Ollie Pope stood head and shoulders above the other batsmen but, like captain Rory Burns, he is now a Test regular. Better returns are needed from the other senior batsmen. After a difficult Ashes summer Jason Roy comes back into the fold – though not before an IPL stint – while Hashim Amla has joined as a Kolpak following his international retirement. Last summer the bowling was too reliant on Rikki Clarke and Morne Morkel, who shared 87 Championship wickets between them, though experienced Aussie seamer Michael Neser should ease the load in the early season. Amar Virdi will battle it out with the ever-resilient Gareth Batty for the spinner's berth. Reece Topley arrives on a white-ball contract.

IN: Nick Kimber (Not), James Taylor (Der), Hashim Amla (SA, Kolpak), Michael Neser (Aus), Reece Topley (Sus, RL50/T20), Shadab Khan (Pak, T20), D'Arcy Short (Aus, T20)
OUT: Stuart Meaker (Sus), Arun Harinath, Freddie van den Bergh (both REL)

HEAD COACH: MICHAEL DI VENUTO

A prolific Tasmanian batsman who played nine ODIs for Australia, Di Venuto scored nearly 15,000 first-class runs for Sussex, Derbyshire and Durham from 1999 to 2012. Di Venuto took over from Graham Ford before the 2016 season, having been Australia's batting coach for three years. He led the club to two Lord's finals in his first two seasons before the Championship triumph of 2018. Vikram Solanki is his deputy, while former Middlesex man Richard Johnson is the bowling coach.

COUNTY CHAMPIONSHIP AVERAGES 2019

Batting

	Mat	Inns	NO	Runs	HS	Ave	SR	100	50	4s	6s
AJ Finch	1	1	0	90	90	90.00	71.42	0	1	12	1
OJ Pope	5	8	1	561	221*	80.14	64.78	2	2	68	1
RJ Burns	8	16	0	603	107	37.68	50.25	1	2	79	2
R Clarke	14	25	5	662	88	33.10	57.16	0	3	96	8
SG Borthwick	13	23	0	705	137	30.65	42.72	2	2	89	0
TK Curran	1	2	1	30	22*	30.00	66.66	0	0	3	2
MD Stoneman	13	23	0	685	100	29.78	56.51	1	4	102	2
SM Curran	5	9	0	265	80	29.44	60.50	0	2	33	6
D Elgar	10	19	0	555	103	29.21	45.86	1	5	76	1
A Virdi	5	6	5	28	14*	28.00	59.57	0	0	4	0
WG Jacks	10	16	0	427	120	26.68	54.18	1	3	70	3
BT Foakes	13	23	1	575	69	26.13	49.39	0	5	79	1
JL Smith	8	14	1	338	57	26.00	45.18	0	2	41	1
J Clark	9	15	4	268	54	24.36	50.47	0	1	36	2
RS Patel	8	14	1	292	100*	22.46	37.00	1	1	45	1
FOE van den Bergh	1	1	0	16	16	16.00	48.48	0	0	3	0
GJ Batty	8	15	4	123	29	11.18	37.73	0	0	20	0
C McKerr	4	5	1	35	17*	8.75	46.66	0	0	6	0
M Morkel	14	22	3	131	27	6.89	37.42	0	0	18	2
MP Dunn	3	5	3	3	2*	1.50	5.55	0	0	0	0
LE Plunkett	3	3	0	2	2	0.66	10.52	0	0	0	0

Bowling

	Overs	Mdns	Runs	Wkts	BBI	BBM	Ave	Econ	SR	5w	10w
A Virdi	140.0	34	452	23	8/61	14/139	19.65	3.22	36.5	2	1
MP Dunn	90.2	18	277	13	5/43	8/128	21.30	3.06	41.6	1	0
R Clarke	332.0	73	1031	43	7/74	8/128	23.97	3.10	46.3	2	0
GJ Batty	234.3	43	678	26	8/64	10/111	26.07	2.89	54.1	1	1
SM Curran	156.5	28	510	19	3/50	5/77	26.84	3.25	49.5	0	0
D Elgar	15.4	2	57	2	1/17	1/17	28.50	3.63	47.0	0	0
M Morkel	413.0	94	1297	44	4/43	7/105	29.47	3.14	56.3	0	0
J Clark	151.4	17	636	21	5/77	5/99	30.28	4.19	43.3	1	0
TK Curran	28.0	6	118	3	3/118	3/118	39.33	4.21	56.0	0	0
C McKerr	89.0	11	366	7	3/94	3/94	52.28	4.11	76.2	0	0
RS Patel	56.3	6	213	4	2/35	2/35	53.25	3.76	84.7	0	0
FOE van den Bergh	21.4	1	88	1	1/88	1/88	88.00	4.06	130.0	0	0
LE Plunkett	33.0	5	160	1	1/85	1/85	160.00	4.84	198.0	0	0
RJ Burns	1.0	1	0	0	-	-	-	0.00	-	0	0
WG Jacks	1.0	1	0	0	-	-	-	0.00	-	0	0
MD Stoneman	2.0	0	15	0	-	-	-	7.50	-	0	0
SG Borthwick	22.0	1	113	0	-	-	-	5.13	-	0	0

Catches/Stumpings:

45 Foakes (inc 6st), 18 Clarke, 16 Borthwick, 13 Jacks, 8 Burns, 6 Elgar, 5 Smith (inc 1st), Stoneman, 4 Pope, 3 Morkel, Patel, 2 Batty, 1 Clark, Finch, McKerr

ROYAL LONDON ONE-DAY CUP AVERAGES 2019

Batting

	Mat	Inns	NO	Runs	HS	Ave	SR	100	50	4s	6s
BT Foakes	7	7	0	328	82	46.85	87.23	0	3	24	2
D Elgar	5	5	1	180	64	45.00	68.96	0	2	11	3
JJ Roy	3	3	1	63	35*	31.50	95.45	0	0	8	1
RS Patel	3	3	1	57	41*	28.50	95.00	0	0	1	3
OJ Pope	3	3	0	85	39	28.33	77.98	0	0	4	2
RJ Burns	8	8	0	198	55	24.75	76.44	0	1	10	2
J Clark	5	5	0	119	79	23.80	88.14	0	1	12	1
JL Smith	5	5	0	110	40	22.00	88.70	0	0	13	2
SC Meaker	4	4	0	83	50	20.75	91.20	0	1	6	2
WG Jacks	8	8	0	164	56	20.50	84.10	0	1	20	3
MD Stoneman	8	8	0	162	70	20.25	79.02	0	1	19	2
C McKerr	6	6	2	56	26*	14.00	88.88	0	0	6	0
FOE van den Bergh	2	2	0	22	22	11.00	91.66	0	0	3	0
LE Plunkett	4	4	1	29	12	9.66	60.41	0	0	2	0
R Clarke	3	3	0	26	19	8.66	92.85	0	0	2	1
TK Curran	2	2	0	16	13	8.00	66.66	0	0	1	0
GJ Batty	6	6	2	20	10*	5.00	68.96	0	0	1	0
M Morkel	6	5	3	4	2*	2.00	40.00	0	0	0	0

Bowling

	Overs	Mdns	Runs	Wkts	BBI	Ave	Econ	SR	4w	5w
TK Curran	19.0	1	63	6	3/26	10.50	3.31	19.0	0	0
M Morkel	52.5	3	239	13	4/23	18.38	4.52	24.3	1	0
GJ Batty	59.0	0	267	9	4/29	29.66	4.52	39.3	1	0
R Clarke	23.1	2	117	4	4/43	29.25	5.05	34.7	1	0
WG Jacks	28.2	0	154	5	2/32	30.80	5.43	34.0	0	0
FOE van den Bergh	10.0	0	55	0	-	-	5.50	-	0	0
SC Meaker	32.5	0	207	5	3/58	41.40	6.30	39.4	0	0
C McKerr	51.5	2	334	8	3/56	41.75	6.44	38.8	0	0
RS Patel	12.0	0	82	2	2/65	41.00	6.83	36.0	0	0
D Elgar	8.0	0	56	0	-	-	7.00	-	0	0
J Clark	32.2	0	227	3	1/33	75.66	7.02	64.6	0	0
LE Plunkett	31.5	0	227	7	4/50	32.42	7.13	27.2	1	0

Catches/Stumpings:
11 Foakes (inc 3st), 6 Jacks, 4 Burns, 3 McKerr, 2 Batty, T Curran, Meaker, Plunkett, Pope, Smith, Stoneman, 1 Clark, Clarke, Elgar, Morkel, Patel, Roy

VITALITY BLAST AVERAGES 2019

Batting

	Mat	Inns	NO	Runs	HS	Ave	SR	100	50	4s	6s
AJ Finch	13	13	2	398	102*	36.18	167.22	1	1	33	23
SM Curran	8	8	1	230	53	32.85	143.75	0	2	24	10
OJ Pope	12	12	2	302	48	30.20	132.45	0	0	25	6
J Clark	13	11	3	203	60	25.37	145.00	0	1	9	12
WG Jacks	13	13	0	272	63	20.92	151.95	0	1	23	17
MD Stoneman	9	8	0	144	53	18.00	97.95	0	1	19	0
TK Curran	10	8	1	110	31	15.71	126.43	0	0	7	3
LE Plunkett	2	2	0	23	18	11.50	121.05	0	0	1	1
BT Foakes	10	6	1	54	29*	10.80	120.00	0	0	3	1
Imran Tahir	13	5	3	17	8*	8.50	100.00	0	0	0	1
GJ Batty	13	6	4	15	6*	7.50	83.33	0	0	0	0
R Clarke	7	6	1	27	16	5.40	71.05	0	0	5	0
JW Dernbach	11	6	2	14	9	3.50	60.86	0	0	0	0
RS Patel	7	3	1	7	5*	3.50	70.00	0	0	0	0
RJ Burns	1	1	1	47	47*	-	180.76	0	0	3	3
JL Smith	1	-	-	-	-	-	-	-	-	-	-

Bowling

	Overs	Mdns	Runs	Wkts	BBI	Ave	Econ	SR	4w	5w
LE Plunkett	4.0	0	29	0	-	-	7.25	-	0	0
GJ Batty	41.5	0	304	13	3/7	23.38	7.26	19.3	0	0
Imran Tahir	47.0	0	385	19	4/25	20.26	8.19	14.8	1	0
JW Dernbach	38.3	0	342	11	2/27	31.09	8.88	21.0	0	0
J Clark	26.0	0	232	6	1/15	38.66	8.92	26.0	0	0
TK Curran	33.1	0	305	17	3/3	17.94	9.19	11.7	0	0
AJ Finch	2.0	0	19	0	-	-	9.50	-	0	0
SM Curran	24.3	0	236	5	2/23	47.20	9.63	29.4	0	0
RS Patel	3.3	0	36	0	-	-	10.28	-	0	0
R Clarke	9.0	0	119	0	-	-	13.22	-	0	0
WG Jacks	1.0	0	14	0	-	-	14.00	-	0	0

Catches/Stumpings:

8 Pope, 7 Finch, Foakes (inc 4st), 6 Tahir, 5 Clarke, S Curran, 4 Jacks, 3 Clark, T Curran, 2 Dernbach, Stoneman, 1 Batty, Patel, Plunkett, Smith

SUSSEX

FORMED: 1839
HOME GROUND: The 1st Central County Ground, Hove
ONE-DAY NAME: Sussex Sharks
CAPTAIN: Ben Brown, Luke Wright (T20)
2019 RESULTS: CC2: 6/10; RL50: 5/9 South Group; T20: Quarter-finalists
HONOURS: Championship: (3) 2003, 2006, 2007; Gillette/NatWest/C&G/FP Trophy: (5) 1963, 1964, 1978, 1986, 2006; Pro40/ National League/CB40/YB40/RL50: (2) 2008, 2009; Sunday League: 1982; T20 Cup: 2009

THE LOWDOWN

At the end of a disappointing 2019 which left the club marooned in Division Two, the overriding sense was that Sussex lacked quality in depth. Ollie Robinson had another outstanding summer – 63 wickets at 16 to follow his 74 at 18 the previous year – but his fellow bowlers often came up short. Similarly, Ben Brown and Stiaan van Zyl were a reliable source of runs but a number of frontline batsmen flopped. Luke Wells made two fifties from 25 Championship innings. The club have wisely brought in three proven county stalwarts who can make an immediate impact: Ravi Bopara, Mitch Claydon and Stuart Meaker. And in Travis Head they have acquired that rare and valuable thing: an overseas player who will stick around all summer for all three formats. There is some exciting talent knocking around at Hove, not least Phil Salt, whose full-throttle batting has already attracted the England selectors, and left-armer George Garton, who was signed up for The Hundred. T20 runners-up in 2018, Sussex impressed again in the 2019 Blast, topping their group and beaten only by a brilliant Moeen Ali hundred in the quarters. Afghan star Rashid Khan is back for a third summer.

IN: Ravi Bopara (Ess), Mitchell Claydon (Ken), Stuart Meaker (Sur), Travis Head (Aus), Rashid Khan (Afg, T20)
OUT: Michael Burgess (War), Reece Topley (Sur), Abi Sakande (REL)

HEAD COACH: JASON GILLESPIE

A serial winner who claimed 402 wickets for Australia, Gillespie took over from Mark Davis ahead of the 2018 season. In five seasons at Yorkshire, Gillespie achieved back-to-back titles in 2014 and 2015. He also coached 2017/18 Big Bash winners Adelaide Strikers and worked with England Lions in Australia over the winter. Last October he extended his contract until the end of 2022. James Kirtley has replaced Jon Lewis as pace-bowling coach.

COUNTY CHAMPIONSHIP AVERAGES 2019

Batting

	Mat	Inns	NO	Runs	HS	Ave	SR	100	50	4s	6s
AT Carey	1	2	1	125	69*	125.00	76.68	0	2	17	4
GHS Garton	3	4	2	112	59*	56.00	75.16	0	2	14	3
S van Zyl	12	20	3	820	173	48.23	50.39	2	4	110	0
BC Brown	14	22	3	812	156	42.73	61.74	3	3	100	3
DMW Rawlins	6	10	1	328	100	36.44	57.95	1	2	42	8
PD Salt	10	19	1	603	122	33.50	77.60	2	3	75	7
WAT Beer	10	15	2	377	97	29.00	38.86	0	3	48	2
CJ Jordan	11	16	1	429	166	28.60	55.85	1	1	61	1
DR Briggs	4	5	2	80	24	26.66	60.15	0	0	13	0
D Wiese	14	20	0	527	77	26.35	63.03	0	5	75	5
LJ Evans	7	11	0	264	113	24.00	52.69	1	1	39	1
LWP Wells	14	25	3	527	98*	23.95	40.25	0	2	70	1
OE Robinson	11	16	4	255	59	21.25	52.25	0	1	40	1
EO Hooper	1	1	0	20	20	20.00	71.42	0	0	3	0
AD Thomason	3	6	0	113	90	18.83	60.75	0	1	14	4
V Chopra	2	4	0	74	32	18.50	45.12	0	0	8	0
TJ Haines	6	11	0	159	39	14.45	41.19	0	0	21	0
TGR Clark	1	1	0	13	13	13.00	38.23	0	0	2	0
HZ Finch	8	14	1	161	48	12.38	45.35	0	0	23	0
A Sakande	5	7	3	38	15	9.50	34.54	0	0	4	0
MGK Burgess	1	1	0	9	9	9.00	50.00	0	0	2	0
RJW Topley	2	2	1	6	5	6.00	23.07	0	0	0	0
Mir Hamza	6	7	2	14	8	2.80	16.86	0	0	1	0
JD Warner	2	2	2	14	13*	-	36.84	0	0	1	0

Bowling

	Overs	Mdns	Runs	Wkts	BBI	BBM	Ave	Econ	SR	5w	10w
RJW Topley	22.3	4	81	6	4/58	6/81	13.50	3.60	22.5	0	0
OE Robinson	380.3	83	1036	63	8/34	14/135	16.44	2.72	36.2	6	3
GHS Garton	30.5	2	107	4	2/29	3/53	26.75	3.47	46.2	0	0
Mir Hamza	195.0	48	577	21	4/51	6/104	27.47	2.95	55.7	0	0
DMW Rawlins	89.0	10	330	10	3/19	3/52	33.00	3.70	53.4	0	0
D Wiese	339.3	68	1048	30	5/26	7/92	34.93	3.08	67.9	2	0
JD Warner	30.2	4	141	4	3/35	3/79	35.25	4.64	45.5	0	0
CJ Jordan	297.0	58	919	26	4/58	5/100	35.34	3.09	68.5	0	0
TJ Haines	70.0	17	198	5	1/9	2/73	39.60	2.82	84.0	0	0
LWP Wells	148.4	21	497	11	5/63	5/63	45.18	3.34	81.0	1	0
A Sakande	111.3	11	458	9	3/74	5/138	50.88	4.10	74.3	0	0
WAT Beer	150.1	24	474	8	2/76	2/76	59.25	3.15	112.6	0	0
DR Briggs	83.3	11	255	4	2/40	2/85	63.75	3.05	125.2	0	0
EO Hooper	20.5	5	65	1	1/65	1/65	65.00	3.12	125.0	0	0
AD Thomason	52.0	2	239	2	1/33	1/65	119.50	4.59	156.0	0	0
BC Brown	2.0	0	15	0	-	-	-	7.50	-	0	0

Catches/Stumpings:

53 Brown (inc 1st), 17 Jordan, 13 Salt, 12 Finch, 6 Evans, 5 Rawlins, Wells, 4 van Zyl, 3 Robinson, 2 Briggs, Chopra, Garton, Haines, Hamza, Sakande, 1 Beer, Carey, Thomason, Wiese

ROYAL LONDON ONE-DAY CUP AVERAGES 2019

Batting

	Mat	Inns	NO	Runs	HS	Ave	SR	100	50	4s	6s
D Wiese	8	7	3	395	171	98.75	120.42	1	3	41	13
LJ Wright	7	7	0	409	166	58.42	97.14	1	2	39	12
LJ Evans	8	8	0	335	110	41.87	96.82	1	1	35	7
PD Salt	7	7	1	241	137*	40.16	114.76	1	0	30	7
BC Brown	8	8	2	172	64	28.66	93.47	0	2	12	2
CJ Jordan	3	1	0	26	26	26.00	83.87	0	0	2	1
HZ Finch	7	7	0	164	89	23.42	88.17	0	1	22	1
WAT Beer	7	5	0	95	75	19.00	77.86	0	1	9	2
DR Briggs	8	6	3	50	37*	16.66	125.00	0	0	8	0
GHS Garton	8	6	0	83	38	13.83	85.56	0	0	10	1
S van Zyl	4	4	0	50	29	12.50	56.17	0	0	4	0
Mir Hamza	8	4	3	10	9*	10.00	52.63	0	0	1	0
A Sakande	5	4	1	3	2	1.00	42.85	0	0	0	0

Bowling

	Overs	Mdns	Runs	Wkts	BBI	Ave	Econ	SR	4w	5w
WAT Beer	62.0	1	327	7	2/49	46.71	5.27	53.1	0	0
DR Briggs	74.0	2	416	11	2/11	37.81	5.62	40.3	0	0
GHS Garton	45.0	0	267	9	3/42	29.66	5.93	30.0	0	0
D Wiese	61.0	2	374	6	3/54	62.33	6.13	61.0	0	0
Mir Hamza	74.5	0	484	18	4/43	26.88	6.46	24.9	1	0
CJ Jordan	22.0	0	148	2	2/42	74.00	6.72	66.0	0	0
A Sakande	40.0	1	274	4	1/32	68.50	6.85	60.0	0	0
LJ Evans	3.0	0	29	1	1/29	29.00	9.66	18.0	0	0

Catches/Stumpings:
8 Brown (inc 2st), 5 Beer, 4 Finch, Garton, 3 Sakande, Salt, Wright, 2 Briggs, van Zyl, Wiese, 1 Evans, Jordan

VITALITY BLAST AVERAGES 2019

Batting

	Mat	Inns	NO	Runs	HS	Ave	SR	100	50	4s	6s
LJ Evans	14	13	5	358	65*	44.75	139.29	0	2	37	9
D Wiese	14	10	3	284	66	40.57	149.47	0	1	22	13
AT Carey	10	8	1	264	78	37.71	152.60	0	2	26	10
PD Salt	14	13	2	406	78*	36.90	161.11	0	4	41	16
LJ Wright	14	12	1	388	76*	35.27	125.97	0	2	48	6
DMW Rawlins	12	9	2	155	69	22.14	159.79	0	1	15	7
DR Briggs	14	5	4	16	7*	16.00	80.00	0	0	2	0
OE Robinson	10	5	3	22	18*	11.00	110.00	0	0	0	1
BC Brown	5	3	0	28	11	9.33	96.55	0	0	2	0
Rashid Khan	9	6	0	41	22	6.83	151.85	0	0	2	4
CJ Jordan	9	6	1	30	19	6.00	76.92	0	0	4	0
WAT Beer	6	3	1	8	4*	4.00	57.14	0	0	0	0
JC Archer	2	1	0	1	1	1.00	33.33	0	0	0	0
JP Behrendorff	2	1	0	1	1	1.00	50.00	0	0	0	0
HZ Finch	1	1	0	0	0	0.00	0.00	0	0	0	0
RJW Topley	11	3	3	7	3*	-	77.77	0	0	0	0
TS Mills	7	-	-	-	-	-	-	-	-	-	-

Bowling

	Overs	Mdns	Runs	Wkts	BBI	Ave	Econ	SR	4w	5w
DMW Rawlins	5.0	0	27	2	2/19	13.50	5.40	15.0	0	0
JC Archer	8.0	0	49	3	2/21	16.33	6.12	16.0	0	0
TS Mills	23.0	0	150	7	3/23	21.42	6.52	19.7	0	0
Rashid Khan	32.0	0	237	7	2/41	33.85	7.40	27.4	0	0
OE Robinson	28.4	0	223	11	4/15	20.27	7.77	15.6	1	0
WAT Beer	21.0	0	164	9	3/22	18.22	7.80	14.0	0	0
JP Behrendorff	8.0	0	66	0	-	-	8.25	-	0	0
DR Briggs	42.0	0	350	8	3/35	43.75	8.33	31.5	0	0
RJW Topley	36.0	0	305	17	4/33	17.94	8.47	12.7	1	0
CJ Jordan	33.0	0	304	10	2/28	30.40	9.21	19.8	0	0
D Wiese	20.0	0	198	4	1/8	49.50	9.90	30.0	0	0

Catches/Stumpings:
13 Salt, 8 Rawlins, 5 Evans, Wiese, 4 Carey, Khan, 3 Brown, Jordan, 2 Behrendorff, Robinson, 1 Beer, Briggs, Mills, Wright

WARWICKSHIRE

FORMED: 1882
HOME GROUND: Edgbaston Stadium, Birmingham
T20 BLAST NAME: Birmingham Bears
CAPTAIN: Will Rhodes, Chris Green (T20)
2019 RESULTS: CC1: 7/8; RL50: 7/9 North Group; T20: 8/9 North Group
HONOURS: Championship: (7) 1911, 1951, 1972, 1994, 1995, 2004, 2012; Gillette/NatWest/C&G/FP Trophy: (5) 1966, 1968, 1989, 1993, 1995; Benson & Hedges Cup: (2) 1994, 2002; Pro40/National League/CB40/YB40/RL50: (2) 2010, 2016; Sunday League: (3) 1980, 1994, 1997; T20 Cup: 2014

THE LOWDOWN

If Warwickshire's results in 2019 were ugly, their injury list was grotesque. Seven seamers were affected – three for the entire season – leaving the admirable Oliver Hannon-Dalby virtually on his own. Throw in the hasty decision to release Keith Barker in 2018 and it's easy to see why Warwickshire were forced to bring in replacements anywhere they could find them. Furthermore, the injured Ian Bell did not face a ball to compound the pain of Jonathan Trott's retirement. Avoiding Championship relegation was therefore some achievement. Everyone should be fit for the new season but a bit of rust is to be expected. Will Rhodes has taken the four-day captaincy from Jeetan Patel, who was the club's leading wicket-taker in red-ball and 50-over cricket, as well as the most economical T20 bowler. Patel retires at the end of this summer – what will they do without him? With Rhodes, the in-form Sam Hain and the 38-year-old Bell, runs should be less of a problem, even with Dom Sibley likely to be taken up by England commitments. Watch out for England U19 left-hander Dan Mousley. Australian off-spinner Chris Green will captain the T20 side if he can correct his action, deemed illegal by Cricket Australia in January.

IN: Michael Burgess (Sus), Chris Green (Aus, T20)
OUT: Alex Mellor, George Panayi (both REL)

FIRST-TEAM COACH: JIM TROUGHTON

Troughton scored more than 13,000 runs for the club and captained Warwickshire to the Championship title in 2012. He was appointed first-team coach in 2016 and works alongside sporting director Paul Farbrace. Second XI coach Ian Westwood will take charge for the 50-over competition when Troughton is on duty at The Hundred. Former Premiership Rugby CEO Mark McCafferty has become the club's first new chairman in nearly a decade, replacing Norman Gascoigne.

COUNTY CHAMPIONSHIP AVERAGES 2019

Batting

	Mat	Inns	NO	Runs	HS	Ave	SR	100	50	4s	6s
DP Sibley	13	21	2	1324	244	69.68	43.78	5	5	151	1
BWM Mike	2	3	1	124	72	62.00	39.87	0	1	19	0
SR Hain	12	19	3	822	129*	51.37	44.07	2	3	112	0
MGK Burgess	5	7	1	248	64	41.33	84.06	0	3	34	4
WMH Rhodes	14	23	0	770	109	33.47	54.14	1	5	106	10
RM Yates	12	19	0	570	141	30.00	40.31	1	2	76	0
LC Norwell	4	6	2	120	64	30.00	75.00	0	1	17	4
MJ Lamb	5	8	1	208	173	29.71	45.02	1	0	30	0
JS Patel	14	22	4	365	70*	20.27	59.54	0	2	50	4
TR Ambrose	12	20	0	399	107	19.95	41.73	1	0	52	0
HJH Brookes	11	17	2	285	84	19.00	49.13	0	1	36	5
AJ Hose	11	20	0	340	111	17.00	39.67	1	0	43	2
L Banks	8	13	0	220	50	16.92	44.71	0	1	33	1
GA Garrett	3	4	2	32	24	16.00	35.16	0	0	4	0
AT Thomson	2	2	0	27	18	13.50	49.09	0	0	3	1
CN Miles	5	8	1	77	27	11.00	41.17	0	0	11	0
OJ Hannon-Dalby	12	15	5	102	17*	10.20	32.58	0	0	15	0
TP Milnes	1	2	0	13	12	6.50	27.65	0	0	2	0
OP Stone	2	4	0	22	21	5.50	30.13	0	0	2	0
DR Mousley	1	2	0	3	3	1.50	14.28	0	0	0	0
EA Brookes	1	1	0	0	0	0.00	0.00	0	0	0	0
RN Sidebottom	1	2	2	31	27*	-	42.46	0	0	4	0
TJ Lester	2	2	2	0	0*	-	0.00	0	0	0	0
JC Wainman	1	-	-	-	-	-	-	-	-	-	-

Bowling

	Overs	Mdns	Runs	Wkts	BBI	BBM	Ave	Econ	SR	5w	10w
OJ Hannon-Dalby	399.0	108	1129	44	5/18	9/137	25.65	2.82	54.4	2	0
LC Norwell	110.5	30	360	14	7/41	9/92	25.71	3.24	47.5	1	0
JS Patel	635.1	182	1712	64	8/36	12/89	26.75	2.69	59.5	4	2
WMH Rhodes	149.1	37	425	15	5/17	9/55	28.33	2.84	59.6	1	0
CN Miles	118.4	14	542	17	5/91	8/149	31.88	4.56	41.8	1	0
JC Wainman	23.0	4	112	3	3/112	3/112	37.33	4.86	46.0	0	0
GA Garrett	84.5	19	302	8	2/53	4/125	37.75	3.55	63.6	0	0
OP Stone	66.3	10	270	7	5/93	5/129	38.57	4.06	57.0	1	0
HJH Brookes	315.3	52	1350	32	3/100	4/59	42.18	4.27	59.1	0	0
TJ Lester	55.0	11	233	5	4/41	4/129	46.60	4.23	66.0	0	0
AT Thomson	10.0	0	54	1	1/21	1/21	54.00	5.40	60.0	0	0
MJ Lamb	34.2	3	166	3	1/15	1/15	55.33	4.83	68.6	0	0
RN Sidebottom	34.0	6	119	2	2/90	2/119	59.50	3.50	102.0	0	0
BWM Mike	36.0	1	163	1	1/75	1/75	163.00	4.52	216.0	0	0
L Banks	3.0	0	9	0	-	-	-	3.00	-	0	0
EA Brookes	12.0	2	41	0	-	-	-	3.41	-	0	0
TP Milnes	13.0	2	50	0	-	-	-	3.84	-	0	0

Catches/Stumpings:

42 Ambrose (inc 3st), 16 Hain, 14 Banks, 13 Rhodes, 10 Yates, 8 Patel, 5 Sibley, 4 H Brookes, Burgess, 3 Hose, 2 Hannon-Dalby, Miles, 1 Lester, Lamb, Norwell, Stone

ROYAL LONDON ONE-DAY CUP AVERAGES 2019

Batting

	Mat	Inns	NO	Runs	HS	Ave	SR	100	50	4s	6s
SR Hain	7	7	2	385	161*	77.00	87.50	1	2	23	7
RM Yates	1	1	0	66	66	66.00	89.18	0	1	6	1
AT Thomson	8	7	2	239	68*	47.80	92.99	0	2	17	4
AJ Mellor	4	3	1	89	58	44.50	105.95	0	1	6	4
TR Ambrose	4	4	0	139	77	34.75	65.87	0	2	7	0
L Banks	8	8	0	250	61	31.25	85.03	0	2	18	5
GD Panayi	7	6	3	90	26	30.00	90.00	0	0	7	2
JS Patel	8	4	2	53	28	26.50	129.26	0	0	6	1
EJ Pollock	8	8	0	188	57	23.50	110.58	0	1	28	5
CR Woakes	4	4	0	83	50	20.75	106.41	0	1	9	1
CN Miles	2	2	0	39	31	19.50	114.70	0	0	5	1
WMH Rhodes	8	8	0	152	43	19.00	76.38	0	0	12	1
DP Sibley	8	8	0	115	29	14.37	65.71	0	0	9	0
HJH Brookes	5	4	1	12	12*	4.00	109.09	0	0	1	1
AD Thomason	1	1	1	23	23*	-	153.33	0	0	1	1
OJ Hannon-Dalby	5	1	1	6	6*	-	75.00	0	0	1	0

Bowling

	Overs	Mdns	Runs	Wkts	BBI	Ave	Econ	SR	4w	5w
AT Thomson	65.0	2	326	10	3/27	32.60	5.01	39.0	0	0
JS Patel	75.0	6	384	16	5/45	24.00	5.12	28.1	0	1
CR Woakes	37.4	3	199	4	3/47	49.75	5.28	56.5	0	0
GD Panayi	58.0	0	372	5	2/44	74.40	6.41	69.6	0	0
AD Thomason	8.0	0	52	1	1/52	52.00	6.50	48.0	0	0
OJ Hannon-Dalby	44.0	1	292	9	3/81	32.44	6.63	29.3	0	0
WMH Rhodes	24.0	0	167	1	1/21	167.00	6.95	144.0	0	0
HJH Brookes	47.2	0	356	8	3/50	44.50	7.52	35.5	0	0
CN Miles	18.0	0	143	1	1/74	143.00	7.94	108.0	0	0

Catches/Stumpings:
5 Patel, 4 Sibley, 3 Mellor, Rhodes, Thomson, Woakes, 2 Ambrose, Hain, Hannon-Dalby, Pollock, 1 Banks

VITALITY BLAST AVERAGES 2019

Batting

	Mat	Inns	NO	Runs	HS	Ave	SR	100	50	4s	6s
SR Hain	12	12	1	459	85	41.72	118.60	0	3	39	8
MJ Lamb	5	5	2	102	35	34.00	130.76	0	0	10	1
AJ Hose	10	10	1	300	69	33.33	149.25	0	2	24	17
DP Sibley	8	8	0	257	64	32.12	125.36	0	2	28	5
AC Agar	4	4	1	95	41*	31.66	148.43	0	0	8	4
EJ Pollock	6	6	0	129	77	21.50	157.31	0	1	15	5
L Banks	6	5	3	34	24*	17.00	161.90	0	0	2	1
WMH Rhodes	12	11	3	129	45	16.12	126.47	0	0	7	5
MGK Burgess	11	10	1	123	28*	13.66	113.88	0	0	11	3
CJ Green	6	5	2	40	23*	13.33	125.00	0	0	5	0
AT Thomson	10	5	3	25	11*	12.50	86.20	0	0	2	0
JS Patel	12	4	1	15	8*	5.00	107.14	0	0	1	0
HJH Brookes	10	4	0	12	6	3.00	75.00	0	0	1	0
OJ Hannon-Dalby	4	1	0	1	1	1.00	50.00	0	0	0	0
FH Edwards	7	3	1	1	1*	0.50	16.66	0	0	0	0
OP Stone	1	1	1	1	1*	-	25.00	0	0	0	0
JC Wainman	5	2	2	1	1*	-	33.33	0	0	0	0
GA Garrett	2	-	-	-	-	-	-	-	-	-	-
AJ Mellor	1	-	-	-	-	-	-	-	-	-	-

Bowling

	Overs	Mdns	Runs	Wkts	BBI	Ave	Econ	SR	4w	5w
CJ Green	21.4	0	145	5	1/19	29.00	6.69	26.0	0	0
OP Stone	4.0	0	29	1	1/29	29.00	7.25	24.0	0	0
JS Patel	45.0	0	327	11	2/21	29.72	7.26	24.5	0	0
AC Agar	16.0	0	119	3	1/22	39.66	7.43	32.0	0	0
AT Thomson	30.0	0	242	6	2/28	40.33	8.06	30.0	0	0
FH Edwards	25.0	0	206	9	4/22	22.88	8.24	16.6	1	0
HJH Brookes	36.4	0	321	13	3/26	24.69	8.75	16.9	0	0
WMH Rhodes	20.0	0	178	8	2/25	22.25	8.90	15.0	0	0
GA Garrett	4.0	0	39	1	1/19	39.00	9.75	24.0	0	0
JC Wainman	15.0	0	150	2	1/28	75.00	10.00	45.0	0	0
OJ Hannon-Dalby	10.0	0	107	1	1/18	107.00	10.70	60.0	0	0
DP Sibley	1.0	0	14	0	-	-	14.00	-	0	0

Catches/Stumpings:
7 Burgess (inc 1st), 5 Hain, Hose, 4 Green, 3 Rhodes, Thomson, 2 Banks, H Brookes, Pollock, Sibley, 1 Edwards, Patel

WORCESTERSHIRE

FORMED: 1865
HOME GROUND: Blackfinch New Road, Worcester
ONE-DAY NAME: Worcestershire Rapids
CAPTAIN: Joe Leach
2019 RESULTS: CC2: 9/10; RL50: Quarter-finalists; T20: Runners-up
HONOURS: Championship: (5) 1964, 1965, 1974, 1988, 1989; Gillette/NatWest/C&G/FP Trophy: 1994; Benson & Hedges Cup: 1991; Pro40/National League/CB40/YB40/RL50: 2007; Sunday League: (3) 1971, 1987, 1988; T20 Cup: 2018

THE LOWDOWN

Worcestershire continue to produce some thrilling white-ball cricket. A stirring defence of the T20 trophy went right down to the last ball of Finals Day, and they also entertained on the way to the 50-over quarter-finals. Starring roles were played by Moeen Ali and Riki Wessels – who in his first season at New Road came within a whisker of being the club's top run-scorer in each format – and the experience and variety of left-armer Wayne Parnell was invaluable. Pat Brown was again effective, earning an England T20I debut over the winter, but he will miss the start of the season after suffering a stress fracture in his lower back. However, Worcestershire are stalling in red-ball cricket, finishing ninth in their first season back in Division Two. No blame is attached to the frontline seamers, three of whom topped 40 wickets. But the batting, shorn of the departed Joe Clarke, fell to pieces; no one tallied 600 runs. Even Daryl Mitchell had a lean time of it – two hundreds but a mid-20s average. Much is hoped of new opener Jake Libby, signed from Notts, and Kiwi left-hander Hamish Rutherford, who returns to play in all formats.

IN: Jake Libby (Not), Hamish Rutherford (NZ), Ashton Turner (Aus, T20)
OUT: George Rhodes (Lei)

FIRST-TEAM COACH: ALEX GIDMAN

Gidman was promoted from Second XI coach after playing a major role in the club's first T20 title in 2018, having joined the backroom staff earlier that year in the wake of Steve Rhodes' departure. A former Gloucestershire captain who scored more than 11,000 first-class runs, Gidman turned to coaching in 2016 after spending one season as a player at New Road. Bowling coach Alan Richardson will take charge of the 50-over team while Gidman is with Birmingham Phoenix for The Hundred. Matt Rawnsley resigned as CEO in October.

www.wccc.co.uk / tel: 01905 748474

COUNTY CHAMPIONSHIP AVERAGES 2019

Batting

	Mat	Inns	NO	Runs	HS	Ave	SR	100	50	4s	6s
HD Rutherford	4	5	0	220	123	44.00	57.74	1	1	37	0
BL D'Oliveira	7	9	1	298	103	37.25	48.69	1	1	34	0
MM Ali	2	4	0	126	42	31.50	63.95	0	0	21	1
CJ Ferguson	9	17	1	503	127	31.43	44.51	1	3	74	0
MH Wessels	14	23	2	593	118	28.23	79.49	1	3	83	7
OB Cox	14	22	2	531	100*	26.55	48.09	1	3	57	2
J Leach	12	20	4	420	54*	26.25	60.78	0	2	68	1
RA Whiteley	10	16	1	391	88	26.06	45.46	0	3	49	6
WD Parnell	7	8	0	205	63	25.62	50.24	0	1	28	0
DKH Mitchell	14	24	2	559	139	25.40	40.83	2	2	72	0
EG Barnard	14	21	2	429	56	22.57	42.81	0	2	53	1
TC Fell	5	7	0	136	40	19.42	41.08	0	0	23	0
JA Haynes	4	6	0	95	31	15.83	40.77	0	0	13	0
JJ Dell	6	11	0	158	61	14.36	31.79	0	1	22	0
CAJ Morris	11	15	8	96	29*	13.71	28.65	0	0	10	0
JC Tongue	4	5	1	51	20*	12.75	49.03	0	0	6	0
GH Rhodes	3	6	0	59	28	9.83	28.78	0	0	9	0
AW Finch	7	9	4	43	17	8.60	21.39	0	0	7	0
DY Pennington	4	8	0	44	18	5.50	36.66	0	0	6	0
AG Milton	3	6	0	17	12	2.83	29.82	0	0	3	0

Bowling

	Overs	Mdns	Runs	Wkts	BBI	BBM	Ave	Econ	SR	5w	10w
JC Tongue	113.3	23	322	17	5/37	6/87	18.94	2.83	40.0	1	0
CAJ Morris	293.0	67	945	44	7/45	8/93	21.47	3.22	39.9	3	0
EG Barnard	371.0	100	993	44	6/42	8/121	22.56	2.67	50.5	1	0
WD Parnell	157.4	42	507	22	5/47	5/47	23.04	3.21	43.0	1	0
J Leach	384.4	83	1081	41	6/79	7/106	26.36	2.81	56.2	1	0
MM Ali	55.3	10	210	7	3/126	4/65	30.00	3.78	47.5	0	0
DY Pennington	115.0	29	301	8	2/92	3/119	37.62	2.61	86.2	0	0
RA Whiteley	79.4	5	303	8	2/35	3/85	37.87	3.80	59.7	0	0
BL D'Oliveira	170.4	22	556	14	7/92	9/182	39.71	3.25	73.1	1	0
AW Finch	152.2	26	583	11	2/23	3/126	53.00	3.82	83.0	0	0
DKH Mitchell	34.0	7	79	1	1/20	1/20	79.00	2.32	204.0	0	0
GH Rhodes	22.2	2	90	0	-	-	-	4.02	-	0	0

Catches/Stumpings:
39 Cox (inc 1st), 21 Wessels, 18 Mitchell, 11 Barnard, 8 Ferguson, 5 Dell, 4 Fell, Milton, Whiteley, 3 Rutherford, D'Oliveira, 2 Ali, Parnell, 1 Haynes, Leach

Batting

	Mat	Inns	NO	Runs	HS	Ave	SR	100	50	4s	6s
HD Rutherford	5	5	0	317	126	63.40	105.66	2	0	33	8
CJ Ferguson	4	4	1	151	103*	50.33	94.37	1	0	13	4
GH Rhodes	3	3	0	126	106	42.00	88.11	1	0	12	2
RA Whiteley	9	9	1	290	131	36.25	118.85	1	0	28	9
MH Wessels	9	9	0	313	130	34.77	137.88	1	1	31	16
OB Cox	8	8	1	238	87	34.00	92.24	0	1	25	1
WD Parnell	9	6	2	134	76	33.50	116.52	0	1	10	4
TC Fell	9	9	1	220	53	27.50	72.60	0	1	24	1
DKH Mitchell	7	7	0	169	101	24.14	96.57	1	0	17	1
EG Barnard	9	7	3	90	61	22.50	91.83	0	1	10	1
JC Tongue	6	4	1	64	34	21.33	103.22	0	0	4	1
BL D'Oliveira	9	9	0	113	57	12.55	70.62	0	1	6	0
CAJ Morris	8	5	3	9	3*	4.50	39.13	0	0	0	0
PR Brown	4	1	0	3	3	3.00	75.00	0	0	0	0

Bowling

	Overs	Mdns	Runs	Wkts	BBI	Ave	Econ	SR	4w	5w
GH Rhodes	2.0	0	9	0	-	-	4.50	-	0	0
DKH Mitchell	51.2	0	268	6	2/40	44.66	5.22	51.3	0	0
EG Barnard	66.0	0	363	7	3/26	51.85	5.50	56.5	0	0
BL D'Oliveira	48.0	3	265	6	2/20	44.16	5.52	48.0	0	0
CAJ Morris	54.0	5	304	11	2/17	27.63	5.62	29.4	0	0
WD Parnell	73.4	2	415	22	5/24	18.86	5.63	20.0	0	2
PR Brown	32.0	0	197	5	3/80	39.40	6.15	38.4	0	0
RA Whiteley	12.0	0	82	2	1/11	41.00	6.83	36.0	0	0
JC Tongue	42.4	0	301	6	2/35	50.16	7.05	42.6	0	0

Catches/Stumpings:
12 Cox (inc 1st), 6 D'Oliveira, Mitchell, 5 Fell, 3 Barnard, Wessels, 2 Brown, Ferguson, Morris, Whiteley, 1 Parnell, Rhodes, Rutherford, Tongue

VITALITY BLAST AVERAGES 2019

Batting

	Mat	Inns	NO	Runs	HS	Ave	SR	100	50	4s	6s
MM Ali	7	7	2	365	121*	73.00	171.36	1	2	25	30
MH Wessels	14	14	1	461	91	35.46	129.85	0	3	46	15
MJ Guptill	9	9	1	259	86*	32.37	145.50	0	1	15	19
OB Cox	14	12	4	203	44*	25.37	114.68	0	0	11	5
WD Parnell	12	9	1	178	81*	22.25	134.84	0	1	7	13
RA Whiteley	14	11	2	198	89*	22.00	150.00	0	1	17	10
EG Barnard	14	11	4	135	42*	19.28	137.75	0	0	12	4
CJ Ferguson	8	8	1	129	37	18.42	112.17	0	0	15	2
TC Fell	4	3	0	38	28	12.66	102.70	0	0	1	1
DKH Mitchell	13	8	2	67	19	11.16	113.55	0	0	6	1
HD Rutherford	5	4	0	42	18	10.50	135.48	0	0	7	1
DY Pennington	12	3	2	9	4	9.00	75.00	0	0	0	0
BL D'Oliveira	6	5	0	33	13	6.60	82.50	0	0	2	0
GH Rhodes	2	1	0	5	5	5.00	71.42	0	0	0	0
J Leach	3	1	0	1	1	1.00	50.00	0	0	0	0
PR Brown	14	4	4	4	3*	-	57.14	0	0	0	0
CAJ Morris	3	1	1	0	0*	-	-	0	0	0	0

Bowling

	Overs	Mdns	Runs	Wkts	BBI	Ave	Econ	SR	4w	5w
DKH Mitchell	36.0	1	231	7	2/17	33.00	6.41	30.8	0	0
MM Ali	26.0	0	174	11	4/18	15.81	6.69	14.1	1	0
GH Rhodes	3.0	0	21	2	2/12	10.50	7.00	9.0	0	0
MJ Guptill	2.0	0	16	0	-	-	8.00	-	0	0
PR Brown	51.5	0	421	17	2/21	24.76	8.12	18.2	0	0
EG Barnard	49.0	0	416	12	2/21	34.66	8.48	24.5	0	0
WD Parnell	45.0	0	388	13	4/25	29.84	8.62	20.7	1	0
BL D'Oliveira	11.0	0	97	2	2/25	48.50	8.81	33.0	0	0
CAJ Morris	8.0	0	73	1	1/37	73.00	9.12	48.0	0	0
DY Pennington	32.0	1	297	9	2/26	33.00	9.28	21.3	0	0
J Leach	4.0	0	59	0	-	-	14.75	-	0	0

Catches/Stumpings:
11 Cox (inc 3st), 9 Wessels, 8 Barnard, 7 Whiteley, 5 Mitchell, 4 Ferguson, 3 Ali, Guptill, Pennington, 2 Brown, Parnell, Rhodes, 1 Rutherford

YORKSHIRE

FORMED: 1863
HOME GROUND: Emerald Headingley Stadium, Leeds
ONE-DAY NAME: Yorkshire Vikings
CAPTAIN: Steven Patterson, David Willey (T20)
2019 RESULTS: CC1: 5/8; RL50: 6/9 North Group; T20: 5/9 North Group
HONOURS: County Championship: (33) 1893, 1896, 1898, 1900, 1901, 1902, 1905, 1908, 1912, 1919, 1922, 1923, 1924, 1925, 1931, 1932, 1933, 1935, 1937, 1938, 1939, 1946, 1949, 1959, 1960, 1962, 1963, 1966, 1967, 1968, 2001, 2014, 2015; Gillette/NatWest/C&G/FP Trophy: (3) 1965, 1969, 2002; Benson & Hedges Cup: 1987; Sunday League: 1983

THE LOWDOWN

Yorkshire are doing enough to stay afloat in Division One without really threatening to pull off the triumph their supporters demand, with too many missing pieces to the jigsaw. To some extent these have now been addressed. Dawid Malan is probably the signing of the winter, a man in prime form and much needed by a batting order that relies on the trio of Adam Lyth, Gary Ballance and Tom Kohler-Cadmore. The club have also plugged the spin-bowling berth, with Ravi Ashwin signed for a minimum of eight Championship matches after the IPL. Keshav Maharaj, who took 38 wickets in just five games last year, returns for a two-match stint in April. Ben Coad continues to lead the pace attack, with Duanne Olivier yet to have the effect some anticipated after signing as a Kolpak in February 2019. Club captain Steven Patterson has retired from T20 cricket, so David Willey leads in the Blast. Willey may provide the driving force the club badly needs; Yorkshire have never won the T20 trophy and have not qualified for the knockout stages in six of the last seven seasons. Adil Rashid has signed a new one-year deal to play white-ball cricket.

IN: Dawid Malan (Mid), Ravi Ashwin (Ind), Keshav Maharaj (SA), Nicholas Pooran (WI, T20)
OUT: Jack Leaning (Ken), Josh Shaw (Glo), Karl Carver (REL)

HEAD COACH: ANDREW GALE

After a 14-year career at Yorkshire – eight as skipper – Gale made the transition from captain to coach following Jason Gillespie's departure in 2016. Gillespie, who led the club to back-to-back titles in 2014 and 2015, has proven a hard act to follow. Gale works alongside director of cricket Martyn Moxon. Former off-spinning allrounder Paul Grayson, who coached Essex between 2007 and 2015, looks after the batsmen while cult hero Richard Pyrah is the bowling coach.

COUNTY CHAMPIONSHIP AVERAGES 2019

Batting

	Mat	Inns	NO	Runs	HS	Ave	SR	100	50	4s	6s
JE Root	2	3	1	297	130*	148.50	57.55	1	2	32	1
TW Loten	1	1	0	58	58	58.00	37.41	0	1	8	0
GS Ballance	14	23	2	975	159	46.42	49.49	5	3	144	1
T Kohler-Cadmore	14	22	1	828	165*	39.42	53.80	2	3	118	3
DM Bess	4	5	1	156	91*	39.00	67.82	0	1	23	0
A Lyth	14	25	2	804	95	34.95	48.63	0	7	107	12
MD Fisher	4	5	1	115	47*	28.75	30.18	0	0	14	1
DJ Willey	5	7	1	171	46	28.50	73.07	0	0	29	0
WAR Fraine	8	15	1	393	106	28.07	52.96	1	0	57	4
JEG Logan	1	2	1	27	20*	27.00	20.14	0	0	4	0
MJ Waite	2	2	1	27	22	27.00	64.28	0	0	2	0
JA Leaning	8	12	1	295	77*	26.81	39.38	0	3	37	0
KA Maharaj	5	9	0	239	85	26.55	92.27	0	2	23	11
JA Tattersall	14	21	1	523	92	26.15	41.97	0	3	60	0
HC Brook	10	16	0	353	101	22.06	66.60	1	0	49	0
D Olivier	13	17	11	130	24	21.66	41.93	0	0	21	0
AY Patel	2	2	1	20	20	20.00	71.42	0	0	3	0
TT Bresnan	4	8	0	143	58	17.87	44.82	0	1	20	1
BO Coad	11	14	2	196	48	16.33	74.24	0	0	29	4
SA Patterson	14	20	2	271	60	15.05	43.49	0	1	36	1
JA Thompson	2	3	0	36	34	12.00	64.28	0	0	5	1
J Shaw	1	1	0	6	6	6.00	17.14	0	0	1	0
ML Revis	1	2	0	9	9	4.50	15.78	0	0	1	0

Bowling

	Overs	Mdns	Runs	Wkts	BBI	BBM	Ave	Econ	SR	5w	10w
JEG Logan	21.0	6	41	4	4/22	4/41	10.25	1.95	31.5	0	0
KA Maharaj	266.0	76	719	38	7/52	10/127	18.92	2.70	42.0	4	2
JA Thompson	40.0	10	105	5	2/28	3/64	21.00	2.62	48.0	0	0
BO Coad	340.0	82	955	37	6/52	9/118	25.81	2.80	55.1	1	0
MD Fisher	82.0	16	288	11	3/59	4/99	26.18	3.51	44.7	0	0
DJ Willey	88.2	21	316	11	3/71	4/127	28.72	3.57	48.1	0	0
SA Patterson	396.4	111	1050	36	5/81	6/83	29.16	2.64	66.1	1	0
JA Leaning	30.0	8	96	3	2/20	2/25	32.00	3.20	60.0	0	0
D Olivier	365.5	66	1390	43	5/96	7/162	32.32	3.79	51.0	2	0
DM Bess	97.0	24	234	7	3/45	3/45	33.42	2.41	83.1	0	0
MJ Waite	59.0	5	235	6	2/38	3/73	39.16	3.98	59.0	0	0
TT Bresnan	82.0	17	262	6	2/47	3/77	43.66	3.19	82.0	0	0
A Lyth	25.0	3	79	1	1/25	1/25	79.00	3.16	150.0	0	0
AY Patel	35.0	0	231	2	1/112	2/231	115.50	6.60	105.0	0	0
J Shaw	8.0	3	24	0	-	-	-	3.00	-	0	0
JE Root	43.0	2	158	0	-	-	-	3.67	-	0	0

Catches/Stumpings:

35 Tattersall (inc 3st), 30 Kohler-Cadmore, 26 Lyth, 8 Fraine, 7 Brook, 6 Patterson, 4 Ballance, 3 Leaning, Olivier, Willey, 2 Root, 1 Bess, Bresnan, Fisher, Maharaj, Revis, Waite

ROYAL LONDON ONE-DAY CUP AVERAGES 2019

Batting

	Mat	Inns	NO	Runs	HS	Ave	SR	100	50	4s	6s
GS Ballance	7	6	0	294	156	49.00	108.08	1	1	26	10
JA Tattersall	7	6	1	232	79	46.40	120.83	0	2	18	5
HC Brook	8	7	1	275	103	45.83	102.23	1	1	33	2
T Kohler-Cadmore	8	7	0	290	97	41.42	81.92	0	3	33	3
DJ Willey	4	4	1	121	72*	40.33	96.03	0	1	17	3
MJ Waite	2	2	1	32	32	32.00	91.42	0	0	2	0
TT Bresnan	6	4	0	117	89	29.25	105.40	0	1	10	3
A Lyth	7	7	0	201	78	28.71	109.23	0	2	25	4
MW Pillans	7	5	1	54	31	13.50	90.00	0	0	6	1
AU Rashid	3	3	1	24	17	12.00	126.31	0	0	3	1
JA Leaning	5	3	0	28	24	9.33	54.90	0	0	3	0
SA Patterson	6	3	1	18	11*	9.00	64.28	0	0	2	0
JE Poysden	8	4	1	2	1	0.66	16.66	0	0	0	0
D Olivier	5	3	3	17	8*	-	58.62	0	0	1	0
BD Birkhead	1	-	-	-	-	-	-	-	-	-	-
WAR Fraine	1	-	-	-	-	-	-	-	-	-	-
TW Loten	1	-	-	-	-	-	-	-	-	-	-
JA Thompson	1	-	-	-	-	-	-	-	-	-	-
JD Warner	1	-	-	-	-	-	-	-	-	-	-

Bowling

	Overs	Mdns	Runs	Wkts	BBI	Ave	Econ	SR	4w	5w
AU Rashid	24.0	0	123	2	1/46	61.50	5.12	72.0	0	0
JE Poysden	55.0	1	303	6	2/31	50.50	5.50	55.0	0	0
TT Bresnan	44.0	0	259	6	2/27	43.16	5.88	44.0	0	0
SA Patterson	43.0	2	263	8	4/45	32.87	6.11	32.2	1	0
DJ Willey	26.0	1	162	5	2/26	32.40	6.23	31.2	0	0
JA Leaning	8.0	0	50	0	-	-	6.25	-	0	0
HC Brook	3.0	0	19	0	-	-	6.33	-	0	0
JD Warner	5.0	0	32	0	-	-	6.40	-	0	0
MW Pillans	52.2	0	344	16	5/29	21.50	6.57	19.6	0	1
D Olivier	39.0	1	262	2	1/44	131.00	6.71	117.0	0	0
MJ Waite	12.3	0	98	3	2/32	32.66	7.84	25.0	0	0
JA Thompson	5.0	0	43	0	-	-	8.60	-	0	0
A Lyth	3.0	0	27	2	2/27	13.50	9.00	9.0	0	0

Catches/Stumpings:

12 Tattersall (inc 2st), 5 Kohler-Cadmore, 4 Leaning, 3 Lyth, Willey, 2 Ballance, Pillans, 1 Birkhead, Bresnan, Brook, Olivier, Rashid

VITALITY BLAST AVERAGES 2019

Batting

	Mat	Inns	NO	Runs	HS	Ave	SR	100	50	4s	6s
T Kohler-Cadmore	10	10	3	435	96*	62.14	141.23	0	5	29	19
N Pooran	3	3	0	122	67	40.66	184.84	0	1	10	10
A Lyth	10	10	0	379	69	37.90	155.96	0	3	45	14
JA Thompson	9	7	4	91	50	30.33	162.50	0	1	6	6
JA Leaning	5	4	0	113	39	28.25	122.82	0	0	8	2
JA Tattersall	8	7	3	110	39*	27.50	122.22	0	0	9	1
HC Brook	7	7	1	123	38	20.50	136.66	0	0	9	6
DJ Willey	10	9	0	136	32	15.11	125.92	0	0	11	8
WAR Fraine	4	3	1	30	16	15.00	107.14	0	0	1	1
TT Bresnan	8	6	2	58	18	14.50	152.63	0	0	4	2
MD Fisher	1	1	0	9	9	9.00	180.00	0	0	0	1
MW Pillans	5	1	0	8	8	8.00	266.66	0	0	2	0
GS Ballance	5	4	0	24	11	6.00	77.41	0	0	1	0
DM Bess	6	3	1	8	5*	4.00	80.00	0	0	1	0
D Olivier	5	2	0	2	1	1.00	50.00	0	0	0	0
JW Shutt	7	2	1	0	0*	0.00	0.00	0	0	0	0
KA Maharaj	5	2	2	10	10*	-	76.92	0	0	0	0
SA Patterson	1	-	-	-	-	-	-	-	-	-	-
JE Poysden	1	-	-	-	-	-	-	-	-	-	-

Bowling

	Overs	Mdns	Runs	Wkts	BBI	Ave	Econ	SR	4w	5w
KA Maharaj	20.0	1	126	2	1/17	63.00	6.30	60.0	0	0
JW Shutt	24.0	0	164	10	5/11	16.40	6.83	14.4	0	1
JA Leaning	2.0	0	15	1	1/15	15.00	7.50	12.0	0	0
DJ Willey	34.4	1	273	9	4/18	30.33	7.87	23.1	1	0
TT Bresnan	15.0	0	121	8	2/15	15.12	8.06	11.2	0	0
A Lyth	18.0	0	147	12	5/31	12.25	8.16	9.0	0	1
JE Poysden	3.0	0	25	0	-	-	8.33	-	0	0
DM Bess	20.0	0	174	4	2/30	43.50	8.70	30.0	0	0
JA Thompson	25.0	0	228	4	1/19	57.00	9.12	37.5	0	0
MW Pillans	12.0	0	118	3	1/25	39.33	9.83	24.0	0	0
D Olivier	17.0	0	191	6	2/29	31.83	11.23	17.0	0	0
MD Fisher	1.0	0	13	0	-	-	13.00	-	0	0
SA Patterson	2.0	0	27	0	-	-	13.50	-	0	0

Catches/Stumpings:
7 Brook, 6 Fraine, Tattersall, 4 Kohler-Cadmore, Lyth, 3 Ballance, Leaning, Willey, 2 Maharaj, Pooran, Shutt, 1 Patterson, Pillans

The
Players

MOHAMMAD ABBAS

RHB / RMF / R0 / W1

FULL NAME: Mohammad Abbas
BORN: March 10, 1990, Sialkot, Punjab, Pakistan
SQUAD NO: 27
TEAMS: Pakistan, Nottinghamshire, Khan Research Laboratories, Islamabad, Leicestershire, Multan Sultans, Pakistan Television, Rawalpindi, Sialkot, Southern Punjab, Sui Northern Gas Pipelines Limited
ROLE: Bowler
DEBUT: Test: 2017; ODI: 2019; First-class: 2009; List A: 2009; T20: 2013

BEST BATTING: 40 Khan Research Laboratories vs Karachi Whites, Karachi, 2016
BEST BOWLING: 8-46 Khan Research Laboratories vs Karachi Whites, Karachi, 2016
COUNTY CAP: 2018 (Leicestershire)

TWITTER: @Mohmmadabbas11
NOTES: Notts have signed the seamer for the first nine Championship matches before he joins up with Pakistan for the Test series against England later this summer. Abbas had a hugely successful spell at Leicestershire in 2018 and 2019, taking 50 Championship wickets at 17.72 in his debut season in county cricket and following it up with 29 at 25.75 last summer. Abbas's career has progressed rapidly in the past few years. He made his first-class debut in 2009 but until the start of 2014 had taken just 74 wickets at an average of 35.45, working in a leather factory, as a welder, and as a helper in a law firm to support his cricket career. Since then he has emerged as one of the most skilful seamers in the world, becoming the joint-second-fastest to take 50 Test wickets for Pakistan (10 matches), behind only Yasir Shah (9)

Batting	Mat	Inns	NO	Runs	HS	Ave	SR	100	50	Ct	St
Tests	18	25	12	94	29	7.23	19.62	0	0	5	0
ODIs	3	-	-	-	-	-	-	-	-	0	0
First-class	106	150	54	669	40	6.96	28.54	0	0	29	0
List A	52	30	13	136	15*	8.00	53.54	0	0	12	0
T20s	24	9	6	32	15*	10.66	152.38	0	0	5	0
Bowling	**Mat**	**Balls**	**Runs**	**Wkts**	**BBI**	**BBM**	**Ave**	**Econ**	**SR**	**5w**	**10**
Tests	18	3814	1557	75	5/33	10/95	20.76	2.44	50.8	4	1
ODIs	3	162	153	1	1/44	1/44	153.00	5.66	162.0	0	0
First-class	106	21011	9550	456	8/46	14/93	20.94	2.72	46.0	34	10
List A	52	2520	2023	67	4/31	4/31	30.19	4.81	37.6	0	0
T20s	24	492	685	20	3/22	3/22	34.25	8.35	24.6	0	0

KYLE ABBOTT RHB / RFM / R0 / W3 / MVP2

FULL NAME: Kyle John Abbott
BORN: June 18, 1987, Empangeni, KwaZulu-Natal, South Africa
SQUAD NO: 11
NICKNAME: Jimmy
EDUCATION: Kearsney College, KwaZulu-Natal
TEAMS: South Africa, Hampshire, London Spirit, Dolphins, Kings XI Punjab, KwaZulu-Natal, Middlesex, Worcestershire
ROLE: Bowler
DEBUT: Test: 2013; ODI: 2013; T20I: 2013; First-class: 2009; List A: 2009; T20: 2011

BEST BATTING: 97* Hampshire vs Lancashire, Old Trafford, 2017
BEST BOWLING: 9-40 Hampshire vs Somerset, Southampton, 2019
COUNTY CAP: 2017 (Hampshire)

TWITTER: Kyle_Abbott87
NOTES: A well-built South African fast bowler and no slouch with the bat, Abbott interrupted his international career to sign a four-year Kolpak deal with Hampshire in January 2017. He had an immediate impact with 60 Championship wickets at 18.20 to help save the county from relegation and followed it up with 51 wickets at 23.18 in 2018. Last summer was even better: an extraordinary 71 wickets at 15.73, which included the best first-class match figures since 1956 – 17-86 against Somerset at the Ageas Bowl in September. He was also Hampshire's leading wicket-taker in both white-ball competitions. Abbott will play in The Hundred for London Spirit, who picked up the 32-year-old in the £50k category

Batting	Mat	Inns	NO	Runs	HS	Ave	SR	100	50	Ct	St
Tests	11	14	0	95	17	6.78	28.10	0	0	4	0
ODIs	28	13	4	76	23	8.44	60.31	0	0	7	0
T20Is	21	6	4	23	9*	11.50	115.00	0	0	7	0
First-class	114	157	30	2427	97*	19.11	47.65	0	9	18	0
List A	104	50	19	485	56	15.64	85.08	0	1	28	0
T20s	153	53	29	320	30	13.33	118.08	0	0	33	0
Bowling	**Mat**	**Balls**	**Runs**	**Wkts**	**BBI**	**BBM**	**Ave**	**Econ**	**SR**	**5w**	**10**
Tests	11	2081	886	39	7/29	9/68	22.71	2.55	53.3	3	0
ODIs	28	1303	1051	34	4/21	4/21	30.91	4.83	38.3	0	0
T20Is	21	436	579	26	3/20	3/20	22.26	7.96	16.7	0	0
First-class	114	19663	9256	442	9/40	17/86	20.94	2.82	44.4	30	4
List A	104	4708	4098	141	4/21	4/21	29.06	5.22	33.3	0	0
T20s	153	3198	4396	155	5/14	5/14	28.36	8.24	20.6	1	0

SEAN ABBOTT RHB / RFM / R0 / W0

FULL NAME: Sean Anthony Abbott
BORN: February 29, 1992, Windsor, New South Wales, Australia
SQUAD NO: 23
HEIGHT: 6ft
TEAMS: Australia, Derbyshire, New South Wales, Royal Challengers Bangalore, Sydney Sixers, Sydney Thunder
ROLE: Bowler
DEBUT: ODI: 2014; T20I: 2014; First-class: 2011; List A: 2010; T20: 2011

BEST BATTING: 86 New South Wales vs Queensland, Sydney, 2019
BEST BOWLING: 7-45 New South Wales vs Tasmania, St Kilda, 2019

TWITTER: @seanabbott77
NOTES: A fast bowler who can swing the bat, Abbott made his first-class debut for New South Wales at the age of 18 in 2011 and rose to prominence two years later, winning the Steve Waugh Medal as his state's Player of the Season. He made his T20I and ODI debuts against Pakistan in 2014 before slipping out of the international reckoning but returned to the set-up in 2019, taking 2-14 on his recall to the T20I side against the same opponents. Abbott has represented Royal Challengers Bangalore in the IPL and was named Sydney Sixers' Player of the Tournament in the 2016/17 Big Bash League after taking 20 wickets in 10 matches. He was part of the Sixers side that won the most recent BBL. Abbott has been signed by Derbyshire for the first half of the 2020 season and is expected to be available for 10 Championship fixtures and the T20 Blast group stage

Batting	Mat	Inns	NO	Runs	HS	Ave	SR	100	50	Ct	St
ODIs	1	1	0	3	3	3.00	42.85	0	0	0	0
T20Is	4	1	0	5	5	5.00	62.50	0	0	2	0
First-class	54	77	6	1283	86	18.07	49.61	0	5	30	0
List A	62	42	6	610	50	16.94	100.82	0	1	25	0
T20s	87	53	11	430	39	10.23	107.76	0	0	49	0
Bowling	**Mat**	**Balls**	**Runs**	**Wkts**	**BBI**	**BBM**	**Ave**	**Econ**	**SR**	**5w**	**10**
ODIs	1	30	25	1	1/25	1/25	25.00	5.00	30.0	0	0
T20Is	4	60	61	3	2/14	2/14	20.33	6.10	20.0	0	0
First-class	54	9260	4885	143	7/45	8/67	34.16	3.16	64.7	3	0
List A	62	2751	2413	97	5/43	5/43	24.87	5.26	28.3	2	0
T20s	87	1630	2288	107	5/16	5/16	21.38	8.42	15.2	1	0

TOM ABELL RHB / RM / R0 / W0 / MVP15

FULL NAME: Thomas Benjamin Abell
BORN: March 5, 1994, Taunton
SQUAD NO: 28
HEIGHT: 5ft 11in
NICKNAME: Siddy
EDUCATION: Taunton School; Exeter University
TEAMS: Somerset, Manchester Originals, England Lions, Rangpur Rangers
ROLE: Allrounder
DEBUT: First-class: 2014; List A: 2015; T20: 2016

BEST BATTING: 135 Somerset vs Lancashire, Old Trafford, 2016
BEST BOWLING: 4-39 Somerset vs Warwickshire, Edgbaston, 2019
COUNTY CAP: 2018

WHAT WAS YOUR FIRST CRICKET CLUB? Taunton CC, Somerset. My first and hopefully my last club team
HOW WOULD YOU DISMISS STEVE SMITH? Lbw
BIGGEST TOPIC OF DISCUSSION IN YOUR DRESSING ROOM? Love Island
MOST INTERESTING TEAMMATE? James Burke
WHICH RULE WOULD YOU CHANGE ABOUT CRICKET? The one that says you need to wait until 5pm before the captains can shake hands on a draw
CRICKET STAR OF THE FUTURE? Will Smeed (England U19, Somerset Second XI)
WHICH BOOK MEANS MOST TO YOU? The Obstacle is the Way – The Timeless Art of Turning Trials into Triumph by Ryan Holiday
IF YOU WERE AN ANIMAL, WHICH WOULD IT BE? A cricket
TWITTER: @tomabell1

Batting	Mat	Inns	NO	Runs	HS	Ave	SR	100	50	Ct	St
First-class	75	135	13	3855	135	31.59	48.19	5	23	50	0
List A	25	21	1	636	106	31.80	79.30	1	1	7	0
T20s	37	32	7	747	101*	29.88	142.28	1	2	25	0
Bowling	**Mat**	**Balls**	**Runs**	**Wkts**	**BBI**	**BBM**	**Ave**	**Econ**	**SR**	**5w**	**10**
First-class	75	1612	958	37	4/39	6/70	25.89	3.56	43.5	0	0
List A	25	36	26	2	2/19	2/19	13.00	4.33	18.0	0	0
T20s	37	58	89	2	1/11	1/11	44.50	9.20	29.0	0	0

COLIN ACKERMANN RHB / OB / R0 / W0 / MVP12

FULL NAME: Colin Niel Ackermann
BORN: April 4, 1991, George, Cape Province, South Africa
SQUAD NO: 48
HEIGHT: 6ft 1in
NICKNAME: Ackers
EDUCATION: Grey High School, Port Elizabeth; University of South Africa
TEAMS: Netherlands, Leicestershire, Eastern Province, South Africa U19, Warriors
ROLE: Allrounder
DEBUT: T20I: 2019; First-class: 2010; List A: 2010; T20: 2011

BEST BATTING: 196* Leicestershire vs Middlesex, Leicester, 2018
BEST BOWLING: 5-69 Leicestershire vs Sussex, Hove, 2019

FAMILY TIES? My dad played a bit and by the age of three I had a bat in my hands. My younger brother Travis Ackermann plays for South Western Districts in South Africa
WHAT WAS YOUR FIRST CRICKET CLUB? Kibworth CC, Leicestershire (my first club in the UK)
BEST ADVICE RECEIVED? Watch the ball
BIGGEST TOPIC OF DISCUSSION IN YOUR DRESSING ROOM? Who is going bald first
CRICKETING HERO? Jacques Kallis
IF YOU WERE AN ANIMAL, WHICH WOULD IT BE? An eagle
TWITTER: @ackers38

Batting	Mat	Inns	NO	Runs	HS	Ave	SR	100	50	Ct	St
T20Is	11	11	3	243	43*	30.37	123.97	0	0	4	0
First-class	125	219	25	7864	196*	40.53	49.17	17	48	112	0
List A	83	76	14	2260	152*	36.45	78.74	2	15	55	0
T20s	107	102	16	2454	79*	28.53	119.88	0	13	52	0
Bowling	**Mat**	**Balls**	**Runs**	**Wkts**	**BBI**	**BBM**	**Ave**	**Econ**	**SR**	**5w**	**10**
T20Is	11	150	147	5	1/6	1/6	29.40	5.88	30.0	0	0
First-class	125	4793	2607	60	5/69	5/69	43.45	3.26	79.8	1	0
List A	83	2065	1663	42	4/48	4/48	39.59	4.83	49.1	0	0
T20s	107	1130	1302	47	7/18	7/18	27.70	6.91	24.0	1	0

SHAHEEN AFRIDI

LHB / LFM

FULL NAME: Shaheen Shah Afridi
BORN: April 6, 2000, Khyber Agency, Pakistan
SQUAD NO: TBC
HEIGHT: 6ft 6in
TEAMS: Pakistan, Hampshire, Birmingham Phoenix, Khan Research Laboratories, Lahore Qalandars, Northern Areas
ROLE: Bowler
DEBUT: Test: 2018; ODI: 2018; T20I: 2018; First-class: 2017; List A: 2018; T20: 2018

BEST BATTING: 4 Lahore Qalandars vs Peshawar Zalmi, Dubai, 2019 (T20)
BEST BOWLING: 5-4 Lahore Qalandars vs Multan Sultans, Dubai, 2018 (T20)

TWITTER: @iShaheenAfridi

NOTES: Afridi will represent Hampshire in this summer's T20 Blast subject to his involvement with the touring Pakistan team, with director of cricket Giles White describing the 20-year-old as "the best death bowler we could possibly find". Tall, fast and with the ability to move the ball, the Pakistani left-armer gave notice of his talent by taking 8-39 on his first-class debut for Khan Research Laboratories in September 2017. Afridi was the leading wicket-taker for his country at the 2018 U19 World Cup and made his T20I, ODI and Test debuts later that year. He took 16 wickets in five matches at last summer's World Cup. Afridi will also play in The Hundred for Birmingham Phoenix

Batting	Mat	Inns	NO	Runs	HS	Ave	SR	100	50	Ct	St
Tests	8	12	2	42	14	4.20	44.68	0	0	0	0
ODIs	19	8	6	42	19*	21.00	65.62	0	0	2	0
T20Is	12	1	1	0	0*	-	0.00	0	0	1	0
First-class	13	17	2	84	25	5.60	44.91	0	0	1	0
List A	24	10	7	45	19*	15.00	62.50	0	0	3	0
T20s	42	11	2	16	4	1.77	34.04	0	0	6	0
Bowling	**Mat**	**Balls**	**Runs**	**Wkts**	**BBI**	**BBM**	**Ave**	**Econ**	**SR**	**5w**	**10**
Tests	8	1607	839	30	5/77	6/128	27.96	3.13	53.5	1	0
ODIs	19	924	847	40	6/35	6/35	21.17	5.50	23.1	1	0
T20Is	12	276	333	16	3/20	3/20	20.81	7.23	17.2	0	0
First-class	13	2559	1342	53	8/39	9/84	25.32	3.14	48.2	2	0
List A	24	1188	1108	45	6/35	6/35	24.62	5.59	26.4	1	0
T20s	42	925	1163	55	5/4	5/4	21.14	7.54	16.8	1	0

QAIS AHMAD RHB / LB / R0 / W0

FULL NAME: Qais Ahmad Kamawal
BORN: August 15, 2000, Nangarhar, Afghanistan
SQUAD NO: 32
TEAMS: Afghanistan, Gloucestershire, Welsh Fire, Guyana Amazon Warriors, Hobart Hurricanes, Speen Ghar Region, Rajshahi Kings, St Lucia Stars
ROLE: Bowler
DEBUT: Test: 2019; First-class: 2018; List A: 2018; T20: 2017

BEST BATTING: 46* Afghanistan A vs Bangladesh A, Khulna, 2019
BEST BOWLING: 7-41 Speen Ghar Region vs Band-e-Amir Region, Jalalabad, 2019

TWITTER: @Qais_AhmadK
NOTES: Gloucestershire have signed the Afghan leg-spinner to play the first six Championship matches and in the T20 Blast. "Qais will help take us to the next level in both the long and short formats with his game-changing skills," said Gloucestershire head coach Richard Dawson. "He is one of the most exciting young spinners in the world." Ahmad burst onto the scene when he took 10 wickets on his first-class debut for Speen Ghar Region in 2018. Leading wicket-taker for Afghanistan at the 2018 U19 World Cup with a haul of 14 at 12.50, he has since been fast-tracked into the senior side, making his Test debut against Bangladesh last September in a famous victory at Chittagong. The 19-year-old has also starred in T20 leagues around the world, taking 19 wickets for Hobart Hurricanes in the 2019/20 Big Bash League, including a match-winning spell of 4-12 on debut against Sydney Sixers. Ahmad will also represent Welsh Fire in The Hundred this summer after being picked up in the £60k wage bracket

Batting	Mat	Inns	NO	Runs	HS	Ave	SR	100	50	Ct	St
Tests	1	2	0	23	14	11.50	56.09	0	0	0	0
T20Is	1	1	1	0	0*	-	-	0	0	0	0
First-class	12	17	2	226	46*	15.06	59.16	0	0	7	0
List A	9	4	1	41	19	13.66	85.41	0	0	5	0
T20s	51	22	5	202	33	11.88	106.31	0	0	17	0
Bowling	**Mat**	**Balls**	**Runs**	**Wkts**	**BBI**	**BBM**	**Ave**	**Econ**	**SR**	**5w**	**10**
Tests	1	54	28	1	1/22	1/28	28.00	3.11	54.0	0	0
T20Is	1	24	25	3	3/25	3/25	8.33	6.25	8.0	0	0
First-class	12	2465	1395	68	7/41	13/127	20.51	3.39	36.2	5	3
List A	9	492	431	12	3/53	3/53	35.91	5.25	41.0	0	0
T20s	51	1032	1252	59	5/18	5/18	21.22	7.27	17.4	1	0

KASEY ALDRIDGE RHB / RFM / R0 / W0

FULL NAME: Kasey Luke Aldridge
BORN: December 24, 2000, Bristol
SQUAD NO: 5
HEIGHT: 6ft 4in
NICKNAME: Fred, Bridge
EDUCATION: Millfield School, Street, Somerset
TEAMS: Somerset, England U19
ROLE: Allrounder

WHAT WAS YOUR FIRST CRICKET CLUB? Glastonbury CC, Somerset
WHAT WERE YOU DOING WHEN ENGLAND WON THE WORLD CUP? Watching it at Loughborough with the England U19 squad
CRICKET STAR OF THE FUTURE? Alex Horton (Glamorgan Academy)
IF YOU WERE AN ANIMAL, WHICH WOULD IT BE? An eagle
TWITTER: @KaseyAldridge1
NOTES: The England U19 fast bowler signed his first contract with Somerset last August having joined the club's Academy the previous year. "Kasey is a real talent," said director of cricket Andy Hurry. "He's tall, he bowls with genuine pace and is capable of generating lateral movement in the air and off the pitch. The way he handled the step-up from the Academy to the Second XI has been very impressive." Aldridge made his England U19 debut last summer and took 5-18 against West Indies at North Sound in December before heading to South Africa with the World Cup squad. A capable batsman down the order, Aldridge has the potential to develop into a genuine allrounder, as he showed when making an unbeaten 58 against Bangladesh U19 last summer. Hurry added: "We all hope that he can continue on his current path and turn the outstanding potential he has shown into performances for the First XI when given the opportunity"

MOEEN ALI

LHB / OB / R2 / W0

FULL NAME: Moeen Munir Ali
BORN: June 18, 1987, Birmingham
SQUAD NO: 8
HEIGHT: 6ft
NICKNAME: Brother Mo
EDUCATION: Moseley School, Birmingham
TEAMS: England, Worcestershire, Birmingham Phoenix, Matabeleland Tuskers, Moors Sports Club, Multan Sultans, Royal Challengers Bangalore, Warwickshire
ROLE: Allrounder
DEBUT: Test: 2014; ODI: 2014; T20I: 2014; First-class: 2005; List A: 2006; T20: 2007

BEST BATTING: 250 Worcestershire vs Glamorgan, Worcester, 2013
BEST BOWLING: 6-29 Worcestershire vs Lancashire, Old Trafford, 2012
COUNTY CAP: 2007 (Worcestershire)

FAMILY TIES? My cousin Kabir played for England and my brother Kadeer played for Worcestershire, Gloucestershire and Leicestershire
WHAT WAS YOUR FIRST CRICKET CLUB? Moseley Ashfield CC, Birmingham
WHAT EXCITES YOU ABOUT THE HUNDRED? Playing for Birmingham Phoenix!
CRICKETING HERO? Saeed Anwar
NOTES: Moeen was retained by Royal Challengers Bangalore for the 2020 edition of the IPL

Batting	Mat	Inns	NO	Runs	HS	Ave	SR	100	50	Ct	St
Tests	60	104	8	2782	155*	28.97	51.12	5	14	32	0
ODIs	102	83	14	1783	128	25.84	104.08	3	5	32	0
T20Is	28	25	7	284	72*	15.77	131.48	0	1	8	0
First-class	194	332	27	11202	250	36.72	55.08	20	69	112	0
List A	219	194	16	5078	158	28.52	102.64	11	20	65	0
T20s	158	149	15	3393	121*	25.32	140.49	2	18	53	0
Bowling	**Mat**	**Balls**	**Runs**	**Wkts**	**BBI**	**BBM**	**Ave**	**Econ**	**SR**	**5w**	**10**
Tests	60	10972	6624	181	6/53	10/112	36.59	3.62	60.6	5	1
ODIs	102	4714	4131	85	4/46	4/46	48.60	5.25	55.4	0	0
T20Is	28	410	588	16	2/21	2/21	36.75	8.60	25.6	0	0
First-class	194	23702	13965	368	6/29	12/96	37.94	3.53	64.4	12	2
List A	219	7825	7014	160	4/33	4/33	43.83	5.37	48.9	0	0
T20s	158	2255	2882	108	5/34	5/34	26.68	7.66	20.8	1	0

FABIAN ALLEN RHB/SLA

FULL NAME: Fabian Anthony Allen
BORN: May 7, 1995, Kingston, Jamaica
SQUAD NO: TBC
HEIGHT: 6ft 2in
TEAMS: West Indies, Oval Invincibles, Jamaica, St Kitts & Nevis Patriots, Sunrisers Hyderabad
ROLE: Allrounder
DEBUT: ODI: 2018; T20I: 2018; First-class: 2016; List A: 2018; T20: 2017

BEST BATTING: 64* St Kitts & Nevis Patriots vs Barbados Tridents, Basseterre, 2018 (T20)
BEST BOWLING: 2-19 West Indies vs Bangladesh, Mirpur, 2018 (T20)

TWITTER: @FabianAllen338
NOTES: An allrounder who bowls left-arm spin, Allen is most noted for his ability to smash runs at the end of the innings and for his spectacular fielding. After being selected in the West Indies squad for the 2014 U19 World Cup, Allen made his first-class debut for Jamaica in 2016. He played his first T20 in the Caribbean Premier League for St Kitts and Nevis Patriots in 2017. The following year he made his ODI and T20I debuts against India and he was part of West Indies' World Cup squad last summer, impressing with a rapid half-century and a spectacular caught-and-bowled against Sri Lanka at Chester-le-Street. He signed his first IPL contract last December and is playing for Sunrisers Hyderabad in the 2020 tournament. Allen was selected by Oval Invincibles for The Hundred in the £50k salary band

Batting	Mat	Inns	NO	Runs	HS	Ave	SR	100	50	Ct	St
ODIs	14	12	3	143	51	15.88	110.00	0	1	6	0
T20Is	13	10	3	67	27	9.57	113.55	0	0	4	0
First-class	13	23	2	696	169*	33.14	61.26	2	4	9	0
List A	24	20	6	300	62*	21.42	91.74	0	2	10	0
T20s	29	24	8	404	64*	25.25	164.89	0	2	9	0
Bowling	**Mat**	**Balls**	**Runs**	**Wkts**	**BBI**	**BBM**	**Ave**	**Econ**	**SR**	**5w**	**10**
ODIs	14	396	397	4	2/40	2/40	99.25	6.01	99.0	0	0
T20Is	13	210	238	11	2/19	2/19	21.63	6.80	19.0	0	0
First-class	13	650	332	10	4/47	5/99	33.20	3.06	65.0	0	0
List A	24	700	617	11	2/18	2/18	56.09	5.28	63.6	0	0
T20s	29	397	492	16	2/19	2/19	30.75	7.43	24.8	0	0

BEN ALLISON

RHB / RFM / R0 / W0

FULL NAME: Benjamin Michael John Allison
BORN: December 18, 1999, Colchester, Essex
SQUAD NO: 65
EDUCATION: New Hall School, Chelmsford; Chelmsford College
TEAMS: Essex, England U19, Gloucestershire
ROLE: Bowler
DEBUT: First-class: 2019

BEST BATTING: 0 Gloucestershire vs Derbyshire, Derby 2019
BEST BOWLING: 3-109 Gloucestershire vs Derbyshire, Derby 2019

NOTES: A right-arm seamer who made his first-class debut last season while on loan at Gloucestershire, Allison has been with Essex since the age of eight. He took four wickets on his County Championship bow last August, dismissing three of the top four in Derbyshire's second innings a week after signing his first professional contract. "All I've ever been focused on is being a professional cricketer, so signing my first professional deal is a very special moment for myself and my family," said the former England U19 paceman. He took 29 wickets at an impressive average of 15.34 in last season's Second XI Championship and nine at 22.44 in the Second XI Trophy. Allison has also played Minor Counties cricket for Bedfordshire and Cambridgeshire. He will be hoping to follow in the footsteps of fellow homegrown seamers Jamie Porter, Sam Cook and Aaron Beard by securing regular first-team cricket at Essex

Batting	Mat	Inns	NO	Runs	HS	Ave	SR	100	50	Ct	St
First-class	1	1	0	0	0	0.00	0.00	0	0	0	0
Bowling	**Mat**	**Balls**	**Runs**	**Wkts**	**BBI**	**BBM**	**Ave**	**Econ**	**SR**	**5w**	**10**
First-class	1	246	139	4	3/109	4/139	34.75	3.39	61.5	0	0

TOM ALSOP

LHB / WK / R0 / W0

FULL NAME: Thomas Philip Alsop
BORN: November 27, 1995, High Wycombe, Buckinghamshire
SQUAD NO: 9
HEIGHT: 5ft 11in
NICKNAME: Deeney, Brodie
EDUCATION: Lavington School; The John Bentley School, Wiltshire
TEAMS: Hampshire, England Lions
ROLE: Wicketkeeper/batsman
DEBUT: First-class: 2014; List A: 2014; T20: 2016

BEST BATTING: 150 Hampshire vs Warwickshire, Edgbaston, 2019
BEST BOWLING: 2-59 Hampshire vs Yorkshire, Headingley, 2016

FAMILY TIES? Dad played for Merchant Taylors' School and my older brother Owen played for Wiltshire CCC and was in the Hampshire Academy. My little (not so little) brother plays for Wiltshire age-groups
WHAT WAS YOUR FIRST CRICKET CLUB? Bishop Canning CC, Wiltshire
WHAT WERE YOU DOING WHEN ENGLAND WON THE WORLD CUP? Parked up listening to it in the car
HOW WOULD YOU DISMISS STEVE SMITH? Take him out for a couple the night before
BIGGEST TOPIC OF DISCUSSION IN YOUR DRESSING ROOM? The best coffee places
MOST INTERESTING TEAMMATE? Joe Weatherley. We're both like old men really, but he just moans about coffee, food, bats... the list is endless. And he doesn't stop talking about Winchester
CRICKETING HERO? Shikhar Dhawan
CRICKET STAR OF THE FUTURE? Fletcha Middleton (Hampshire Academy)
IF YOU WERE AN ANIMAL, WHICH WOULD IT BE? A tiger. We have the same hair colour

Batting	Mat	Inns	NO	Runs	HS	Ave	SR	100	50	Ct	St
First-class	44	74	4	1835	150	26.21	46.93	2	13	60	0
List A	48	48	3	1465	130*	32.55	77.80	4	6	33	5
T20s	31	29	4	575	85	23.00	114.77	0	2	13	2
Bowling	**Mat**	**Balls**	**Runs**	**Wkts**	**BBI**	**BBM**	**Ave**	**Econ**	**SR**	**5w**	**10**
First-class	44	84	81	3	2/59	2/59	27.00	5.78	28.0	0	0
List A	48	-	-	-	-	-	-	-	-	-	-
T20s	31	-	-	-	-	-	-	-	-	-	-

TIM AMBROSE RHB / WK / R0 / W0

FULL NAME: Timothy Raymond Ambrose
BORN: December 1, 1982, Newcastle, New South Wales, Australia
SQUAD NO: 11
HEIGHT: 5ft 7in
NICKNAME: Amby, Shambrose
EDUCATION: Merewether Selective High, NSW; Training and Further Education College, NSW
TEAMS: England, Warwickshire, Sussex
ROLE: Wicketkeeper
DEBUT: Test: 2008; ODI: 2008; T20I: 2008; First-class: 2001; List A: 2001; T20: 2003

BEST BATTING: 251* Warwickshire vs Worcestershire, Worcester, 2007
BEST BOWLING: 1-0 Warwickshire vs Middlesex, Lord's, 2016
COUNTY CAP: 2003 (Sussex); 2007 (Warwickshire); BENEFIT: 2016 (Warwickshire)

FAMILY TIES? My father played for Nelson Bay CC in Australia
BEST MOMENT IN CRICKET? County Championship titles in 2003 and 2012 and becoming T20 champions in 2014. Anytime playing for England
CRICKETING HEROES? Ian Healy for his attention to detail in wicketkeeping. Steve Waugh and Sachin Tendulkar for mental strength and concentration
NON-CRICKETING HERO? Michael Jordan – for his ability to deliver under pressure
SURPRISING FACT ABOUT YOU? I have a three-year-old Puggle named Frank
TWITTER: @timambrose2016

Batting	Mat	Inns	NO	Runs	HS	Ave	SR	100	50	Ct	St
Tests	11	16	1	447	102	29.80	46.41	1	3	31	0
ODIs	5	5	1	10	6	2.50	29.41	0	0	3	0
T20Is	1	-	-	-	-	-	-	-	-	1	1
First-class	251	383	34	11349	251*	32.51	51.43	18	65	678	43
List A	182	148	20	4145	135	32.38	79.01	3	25	172	34
T20s	106	66	19	1138	77	24.21	112.45	0	3	66	24
Bowling	**Mat**	**Balls**	**Runs**	**Wkts**	**BBI**	**BBM**	**Ave**	**Econ**	**SR**	**5w**	**10**
Tests	11	-	-	-	-	-	-	-	-	-	-
ODIs	5	-	-	-	-	-	-	-	-	-	-
T20Is	1	-	-	-	-	-	-	-	-	-	-
First-class	251	17	1	1	1/0	1/0	1.00	0.35	17.0	0	0
List A	182	-	-	-	-	-	-	-	-	-	-
T20s	106	-	-	-	-	-	-	-	-	-	-

MOHAMMAD AMIR LHB / LFM

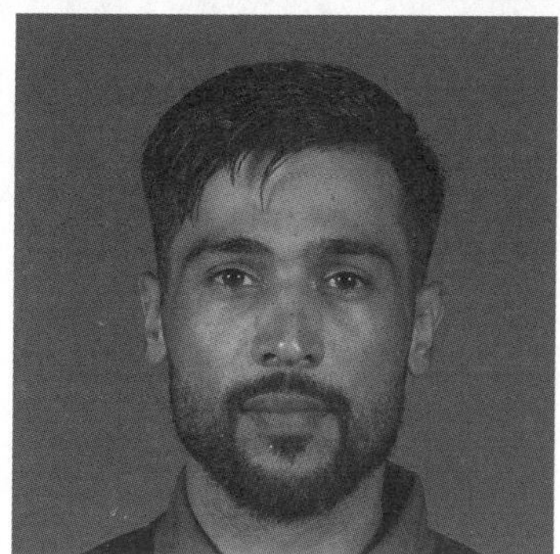

FULL NAME: Mohammad Amir
BORN: April 13, 1992, Gujjar Khan, Pakistan
SQUAD NO: TBC
HEIGHT: 6ft 2in
TEAMS: Pakistan, London Spirit, Chittagong Vikings, Dhaka Dynamites, Essex, Federal Areas, Karachi Kings, Khulna Tigers, National Bank of Pakistan, Sui Southern Gas Corporation
ROLE: Bowler
DEBUT: Test: 2009; ODI: 2009; T20I: 2009; First-class: 2008; List A: 2008; T20: 2008

BEST BATTING: 21* Pakistan vs Australia, Edgbaston, 2010 (T20)
BEST BOWLING: 6-17 Khulna Tigers vs Rajshahi Royals, Dhaka, 2020 (T20)

TWITTER: @iamamirofficial
NOTES: Amir made his T20I debut for Pakistan in 2009 and within a month he had represented his country across all formats. He played every game during the 2009 World T20, helping Pakistan win the tournament. The left-arm paceman served a five-year ban for spot-fixing between 2010 and 2015 but returned to international cricket to play a key role in Pakistan's Champions Trophy victory in 2017. He finished the 2019 World Cup as his country's leading wicket-taker, with 17 victims, including figures of 5-30 against Australia at Taunton. A month later he retired from Test cricket at the age of 27 but he continues to represent Pakistan in the short formats. He has had two stints with Essex, in 2017 and 2019. Amir was signed by London Spirit for The Hundred in the £100k salary band

Batting	Mat	Inns	NO	Runs	HS	Ave	SR	100	50	Ct	St
Tests	36	67	11	751	48	13.41	37.92	0	0	5	0
ODIs	61	30	10	363	73*	18.15	81.75	0	2	8	0
T20Is	48	14	6	59	21*	7.37	81.94	0	0	4	0
First-class	67	102	16	1366	66	15.88	44.78	0	2	15	0
List A	84	38	16	413	73*	18.77	80.35	0	2	13	0
T20s	164	58	26	215	21*	6.71	91.10	0	0	14	0
Bowling	**Mat**	**Balls**	**Runs**	**Wkts**	**BBI**	**BBM**	**Ave**	**Econ**	**SR**	**5w**	**10**
Tests	36	7619	3627	119	6/44	7/64	30.47	2.85	64.0	4	0
ODIs	61	3013	2400	81	5/30	5/30	29.62	4.77	37.1	1	0
T20Is	48	1054	1224	59	4/13	4/13	20.74	6.96	17.8	0	0
First-class	67	12394	5850	260	7/61	10/72	22.50	2.83	47.6	13	2
List A	84	4244	3279	123	5/30	5/30	26.65	4.63	34.5	2	0
T20s	164	3605	4166	199	6/17	6/17	20.93	6.93	18.1	1	0

HASHIM AMLA

RHB / OB / R0 / W0

FULL NAME: Hashim Mahomed Amla
BORN: March 31, 1983, Durban, South Africa
SQUAD NO: 1
HEIGHT: 6ft
TEAMS: South Africa, Surrey, Barbados Tridents, Cape Cobras, Derbyshire, Dolphins, Durban Heat, Essex, Hampshire, Khulna Tigers, Kings XI Punjab, KwaZulu-Natal, Nottinghamshire, Trinbago Knight Riders
ROLE: Batsman
DEBUT: Test: 2004; ODI: 2008; T20I: 2009; First-class: 1999; List A: 2002; T20: 2004

BEST BATTING: 311* South Africa vs England, The Oval, 2012
BEST BOWLING: 1-10 South Africa A vs India A, Kimbereley, 2002
COUNTY CAP: 2010 (Nottinghamshire)

TWITTER: @amlahash
NOTES: After calling time on his illustrious international career last August, Amla signed a two-year Kolpak contract with Surrey and will join forces with his old South African teammate Morne Morkel. He will be available across all formats. The 37-year-old previously represented the county in 2013 and 2014, scoring 663 first-class runs at 47.35. Amla has a wealth of experience in the English domestic game, having also had spells at Derbyshire, Essex, Hampshire and Nottinghamshire. He is still the only South African to have scored a Test triple-century – 311* against England at The Oval in 2012 – and is the fastest batsman to reach 7,000 ODI runs (150 innings). "With several of our players now in or around the international set-up, the opportunity to bring Hashim back to Surrey was too good to ignore," said Surrey director of cricket Alec Stewart

Batting	Mat	Inns	NO	Runs	HS	Ave	SR	100	50	Ct	St
Tests	124	215	16	9282	311*	46.64	49.97	28	41	108	0
ODIs	181	178	14	8113	159	49.46	88.39	27	39	87	0
T20Is	44	44	6	1277	97*	33.60	132.05	0	8	19	0
First-class	237	396	31	17765	311*	48.67		52	88	185	0
List A	243	237	16	9973	159	45.12		30	52	108	0
T20s	155	154	14	4292	104*	30.65	126.16	2	27	38	0
Bowling	**Mat**	**Balls**	**Runs**	**Wkts**	**BBI**	**BBM**	**Ave**	**Econ**	**SR**	**5w**	**10**
Tests	124	54	37	0	-	-	-	4.11	-	0	0
ODIs	181	-	-	-	-	-	-	-	-	-	-
T20Is	44	-	-	-	-	-	-	-	-	-	-
First-class	237	393	277	1	1/10		277.00	4.22	393.0	0	0
List A	243	16	28	0	-	-	-	10.50	-	0	0
T20s	155	2	5	0	-	-	-	15.00	-	0	0

COREY ANDERSON

LHB / LMF / R0 / W0

FULL NAME: Corey James Anderson
BORN: December 13, 1990, Christchurch, Canterbury, New Zealand
SQUAD NO: 78
TEAMS: New Zealand, Somerset, Auckland, Canterbury, Delhi Daredevils, Lahore Qalandars, Mumbai Indians, Northern Districts, Royal Challengers Bangalore
ROLE: Allrounder
DEBUT: Test: 2013; ODI: 2013; T20I: 2012; First-class: 2007; List A: 2007; T20: 2009

BEST BATTING: 95* Mumbai Indians vs Rajasthan Royals, Mumbai, 2014 (T20)
BEST BOWLING: 2-17 New Zealand vs Pakistan, Wellington, 2016 (T20)

TWITTER: @coreyanderson78
NOTES: After two earlier spells as Somerset's hired T20 gun, the big-hitting Kiwi allrounder returns for the third time to Taunton, where he will team up with Pakistan's Babar Azam as the overseas stars spearheading the club's push for a second T20 title. Anderson has form in the competition, hitting 514 runs at a strike rate of 169.07 as Somerset reached Finals Day in 2018. He will be available this season for all 14 group games and a possible quarter-final. Director of cricket Andy Hurry said: "Corey has made a big impression both on and off the field for the club in his two previous stints with us. He was one of the first names mentioned when it came to considering our overseas players for next season because he is one of the best T20 players in the world and he was extremely popular with the playing staff and also with our members and supporters"

Batting	Mat	Inns	NO	Runs	HS	Ave	SR	100	50	Ct	St
Tests	13	22	1	683	116	32.52	56.86	1	4	7	0
ODIs	49	45	5	1109	131*	27.72	108.72	1	4	11	0
T20Is	31	24	4	485	94*	24.25	138.17	0	2	19	0
First-class	53	89	10	2862	167	36.22	58.71	4	13	39	0
List A	85	79	8	1988	131*	28.00	99.79	1	11	28	0
T20s	145	126	24	2717	95*	26.63	139.97	0	10	51	0
Bowling	**Mat**	**Balls**	**Runs**	**Wkts**	**BBI**	**BBM**	**Ave**	**Econ**	**SR**	**5w**	**10**
Tests	13	1302	659	16	3/47	4/69	41.18	3.03	81.3	0	0
ODIs	49	1485	1502	60	5/63	5/63	25.03	6.06	24.7	1	0
T20Is	31	360	495	14	2/17	2/17	35.35	8.25	25.7	0	0
First-class	53	3153	1675	40	5/22	7/60	41.87	3.18	78.8	1	0
List A	85	1740	1708	69	5/26	5/26	24.75	5.88	25.2	2	0
T20s	145	849	1282	36	2/17	2/17	35.61	9.06	23.5	0	0

JAMES ANDERSON

LHB / RFM / R0 / W3

LANCASHIRE

FULL NAME: James Michael Anderson
BORN: July 30, 1982, Burnley, Lancashire
SQUAD NO: 9
HEIGHT: 6ft 2in
NICKNAME: Jimmy, Jimbo, Jimbob
EDUCATION: St Theodore's Roman Catholic High School, Burnley
TEAMS: England, Lancashire, Auckland
ROLE: Bowler
DEBUT: Test: 2003; ODI: 2002; T20I: 2007; First-class: 2002; List A: 2000; T20: 2004

BEST BATTING: 81 England vs India, Trent Bridge, 2014
BEST BOWLING: 7-42 England vs West Indies, Lord's, 2017
COUNTY CAP: 2003; BENEFIT: 2012

FAMILY TIES? My dad played for Burnley CC
CRICKETING HERO? Peter Martin
NON-CRICKETING HERO? Steve Davis (ex-Burnley FC)
SURPRISING FACT? I can peel a potato in 2.4 seconds and I'm allergic to mushrooms
TWITTER: @jimmy9

Batting	Mat	Inns	NO	Runs	HS	Ave	SR	100	50	Ct	St
Tests	151	212	89	1185	81	9.63	39.67	0	1	93	0
ODIs	194	79	43	273	28	7.58	48.66	0	0	53	0
T20Is	19	4	3	1	1*	1.00	50.00	0	0	3	0
First-class	248	319	129	1826	81	9.61		0	1	146	0
List A	261	105	63	376	28	8.95		0	0	68	0
T20s	44	10	6	23	16	5.75	88.46	0	0	8	0
Bowling	**Mat**	**Balls**	**Runs**	**Wkts**	**BBI**	**BBM**	**Ave**	**Econ**	**SR**	**5w**	**10**
Tests	151	32779	15670	584	7/42	11/71	26.83	2.86	56.1	28	3
ODIs	194	9584	7861	269	5/23	5/23	29.22	4.92	35.6	2	0
T20Is	19	422	552	18	3/23	3/23	30.66	7.84	23.4	0	0
First-class	248	49905	23907	959	7/42		24.92	2.87	52.0	48	6
List A	261	12730	10230	358	5/23	5/23	28.57	4.82	35.5	2	0
T20s	44	933	1318	41	3/23	3/23	32.14	8.47	22.7	0	0

MARTIN ANDERSSON RHB / RM / R0 / W0

FULL NAME: Martin Kristoffer Andersson
BORN: September 6, 1996, Reading
SQUAD NO: 24
HEIGHT: 6ft 2in
NICKNAME: Tino, Pasty
EDUCATION: Reading Blue Coat School; University of Leeds
TEAMS: Middlesex, Derbyshire
ROLE: Allrounder
DEBUT: First-class: 2017; T20: 2018

BEST BATTING: 83 Middlesex vs Lancashire, Old Trafford, 2019
BEST BOWLING: 4-25 Derbyshire vs Glamorgan, Derby, 2018

WHAT WAS YOUR FIRST CRICKET CLUB? Reading CC, Berkshire
WHAT WERE YOU DOING WHEN ENGLAND WON THE WORLD CUP? Watching from behind the sofa
BIGGEST TOPIC OF DISCUSSION IN YOUR DRESSING ROOM? Football, football, football
BEST INNINGS YOU'VE SEEN? Kusal Perera's 153 not out for Sri Lanka against South Africa at Durban earlier this year. He single-handedly chased down the target against a great attack
CRICKETING HERO? Hashim Amla
SURPRISING FACT ABOUT YOU? My karaoke song of choice is Basshunter's 'Now You're Gone' in Swedish. I have 90% of my middle finger left – the other 10% was left in a door frame in a building at school
CRICKET STAR OF THE FUTURE? Blake Cullen (Middlesex)
WHICH BOOK MEANS MOST TO YOU? Bounce – The Myth of Talent and the Power of Practice by Matthew Syed
IF YOU WERE AN ANIMAL, WHICH WOULD IT BE? A dolphin
TWITTER: @MartinAnderss11

Batting	Mat	Inns	NO	Runs	HS	Ave	SR	100	50	Ct	St
First-class	8	15	2	194	83	14.92	41.72	0	1	6	0
T20s	1	1	0	1	1	1.00	33.33	0	0	1	0
Bowling	**Mat**	**Balls**	**Runs**	**Wkts**	**BBI**	**BBM**	**Ave**	**Econ**	**SR**	**5w**	**10**
First-class	8	420	239	12	4/25	4/41	19.91	3.41	35.0	0	0
T20s	1	6	7	0	-	-	-	7.00	-	0	0

JOFRA ARCHER

RHB / RF / R0 / W1

FULL NAME: Jofra Chioke Archer
BORN: April 1, 1995, Bridgetown, Barbados
SQUAD NO: 22
HEIGHT: 6ft 2in
NICKNAME: Jof
EDUCATION: Christ Church Foundation School, Bridgetown, Barbados
TEAMS: England, Sussex, Southern Brave, Hobart Hurricanes, Khulna Titans, Quetta Gladiators, Rajasthan Royals, West Indies U19
ROLE: Bowler
DEBUT: Test: 2019; ODI: 2019; T20I: 2019; First-class: 2016; List A: 2016; T20: 2016

BEST BATTING: 81* Sussex vs Northamptonshire, Northampton, 2017
BEST BOWLING: 7-67 Sussex vs Kent, Hove, 2017
COUNTY CAP: 2017

WHAT WAS YOUR FIRST CRICKET CLUB? Pickwick CC, Bridgetown, Barbados
BEST ADVICE RECEIVED? Be the best in your own way
WHAT WERE YOU DOING WHEN ENGLAND WON THE WORLD CUP? I was trying to focus on bowling a super over
HOW WOULD YOU DISMISS STEVE SMITH? Nick him off
MOST INTERESTING TEAMMATE? Adil Rashid – he's just hilarious
CRICKETING HERO? Don't have one
SURPRISING FACT ABOUT YOU? I'm ambidextrous
CRICKET STAR OF THE FUTURE? Tom Clark (Sussex)
IF YOU WERE AN ANIMAL, WHICH WOULD IT BE? An eagle
TWITTER: @craig_arch

Batting	Mat	Inns	NO	Runs	HS	Ave	SR	100	50	Ct	St
Tests	7	12	0	97	30	8.08	49.74	0	0	1	0
ODIs	14	7	3	13	7*	3.25	59.09	0	0	4	0
T20Is	1	-	-	-	-	-	-	-	-	0	0
First-class	36	54	10	1141	81*	25.93	68.11	0	6	20	0
List A	28	18	6	205	45	17.08	113.88	0	0	8	0
T20s	95	49	24	419	36	16.76	139.66	0	0	26	0
Bowling	**Mat**	**Balls**	**Runs**	**Wkts**	**BBI**	**BBM**	**Ave**	**Econ**	**SR**	**5w**	**10**
Tests	7	1644	822	30	6/45	8/85	27.40	3.00	54.8	3	0
ODIs	14	737	569	23	3/27	3/27	24.73	4.63	32.0	0	0
T20Is	1	24	29	2	2/29	2/29	14.50	7.25	12.0	0	0
First-class	36	7783	3985	166	7/67	11/137	24.00	3.07	46.8	8	1
List A	28	1468	1214	44	5/42	5/42	27.59	4.96	33.3	1	0
T20s	95	2090	2719	121	4/18	4/18	22.47	7.80	17.2	0	0

FAHEEM ASHRAF

RHB / RMF / R0 / W0

FULL NAME: Faheem Ashraf
BORN: January 16, 1994, Kasur, Punjab, Pakistan
SQUAD NO: 41
TEAMS: Pakistan, Northamptonshire, Central Punjab, Dhaka Platoon, Faisalabad Wolves, Habib Bank Limited, Islamabad United, Lahore Blues, National Bank of Pakistan
ROLE: Allrounder
DEBUT: Test: 2018; ODI: 2017; T20I: 2017; First-class: 2013; List A: 2013; T20: 2015

BEST BATTING: 116 Faisalabad vs Multan, Faisalabad, 2013
BEST BOWLING: 6-65 Habib Bank Limited vs Khan Research Laboratories, Karachi, 2016

TWITTER: @iFaheemAshraf
NOTES: Northamptonshire have re-signed the Pakistan seam-bowling allrounder to play across all three formats in the first half of the season. Ashraf played for the club in last year's T20 Blast campaign, taking 11 wickets in as many matches, although he rarely had the chance to show off his pinch-hitting qualities with the bat. He has appeared for Pakistan in all forms of the game without yet cementing a place in the side. "The fact he's got the extra pace is key," said Northants head coach David Ripley. "We've got a very fine group of seam bowlers that got us into Division One... but I can see him being a genuine threat when the wickets are flatter. What the seam bowlers in Pakistan tend to have to do is find a way to get people out when those wickets are very flat and pretty slow"

Batting	Mat	Inns	NO	Runs	HS	Ave	SR	100	50	Ct	St
Tests	4	6	0	138	83	23.00	70.05	0	1	0	0
ODIs	23	15	2	162	28	12.46	83.07	0	0	5	0
T20Is	27	18	6	133	21	11.08	120.90	0	0	7	0
First-class	43	62	10	1596	116	30.69	67.54	2	7	22	0
List A	66	50	7	700	71	16.27	83.13	0	2	18	0
T20s	94	65	23	616	54*	14.66	133.33	0	1	25	0
Bowling	**Mat**	**Balls**	**Runs**	**Wkts**	**BBI**	**BBM**	**Ave**	**Econ**	**SR**	**5w**	**10**
Tests	4	540	287	11	3/42	6/99	26.09	3.18	49.0	0	0
ODIs	23	902	744	20	5/22	5/22	37.20	4.94	45.1	1	0
T20Is	27	447	557	24	3/5	3/5	23.20	7.47	18.6	0	0
First-class	43	6695	3409	125	6/65	9/115	27.27	3.05	53.5	6	0
List A	66	2808	2408	89	5/22	5/22	27.05	5.14	31.5	2	0
T20s	94	1818	2506	102	6/19	6/19	24.56	8.27	17.8	1	0

RAVI ASHWIN RHB / OB / R0 / W0

FULL NAME: Ravichandran Ashwin
BORN: September 17, 1986, Chennai, India
SQUAD NO: 99
TEAMS: India, Yorkshire, Chennai Super Kings, Delhi Capitals, Kings XI Punjab, Nottinghamshire, Tamil Nadu, Rising Pune Supergiants, Worcestershire
ROLE: Allrounder
DEBUT: Test: 2011; ODI: 2010; T20I: 2010; First-class: 2006; List A: 2007; T20: 2007

BEST BATTING: 124 India vs West Indies, Kolkata, 2013
BEST BOWLING: 7-59 India vs New Zealand, Indore, 2016

TWITTER: @ashwinravi99
NOTES: The brilliant Indian spinner has been signed by Yorkshire for a minimum of eight Championship matches following the conclusion of the IPL. "I'm thrilled to be joining Yorkshire, a club with a wonderful history and a fantastic fanbase," said Ashwin. "Our team looks extremely talented with some superb pace bowlers and exciting batsmen. Hopefully my role as the spinner will be a key feature in helping the team achieve success." In 2017 Ashwin became the fastest player in history to take 300 Test wickets (54 matches) and last December he was named in Wisden's Test Team of the Decade. The 33-year-old has had productive spells in county cricket with Worcestershire in 2017 (20 Championship wickets at 29.15) and with Nottinghamshire last summer (34 at 24.58)

Batting	Mat	Inns	NO	Runs	HS	Ave	SR	100	50	Ct	St
Tests	71	98	13	2389	124	28.10	54.61	4	11	24	0
ODIs	111	61	19	675	65	16.07	86.98	0	1	30	0
T20Is	46	11	7	123	31*	30.75	106.95	0	0	8	0
First-class	125	171	29	4288	124	30.19	54.86	6	22	48	0
List A	171	101	26	1314	79	17.52	77.15	0	4	49	0
T20s	232	85	32	714	46	13.47	115.16	0	0	56	0
Bowling	**Mat**	**Balls**	**Runs**	**Wkts**	**BBI**	**BBM**	**Ave**	**Econ**	**SR**	**5w**	**10**
Tests	71	19586	9282	365	7/59	13/140	25.43	2.84	53.6	27	7
ODIs	111	6021	4937	150	4/25	4/25	32.91	4.91	40.1	0	0
T20Is	46	1026	1193	52	4/8	4/8	22.94	6.97	19.7	0	0
First-class	125	33642	15649	598	7/59	13/140	26.16	2.79	56.2	45	11
List A	171	9232	7121	230	4/25	4/25	30.96	4.62	40.1	0	0
T20s	232	4988	5721	235	4/8	4/8	24.34	6.88	21.2	0	0

GUS ATKINSON

RHB / RM / R0 / W0

FULL NAME: Angus Alexander Patrick Atkinson
BORN: January 19, 1998, Chelsea, Middlesex
SQUAD NO: 37
HEIGHT: 6ft 2in
NICKNAME: G-bus
EDUCATION: Northcote Lodge, London; Bradfield College, Berkshire
TEAMS: Surrey
ROLE: Bowler

WHAT WAS YOUR FIRST CRICKET CLUB? Spencer CC, London. I still play for them
BEST ADVICE EVER RECEIVED? Don't be afraid to fail
WHAT WERE YOU DOING WHEN ENGLAND WON THE WORLD CUP? Watching it in the pub
BIGGEST TOPIC OF DISCUSSION IN YOUR DRESSING ROOM? Football
MOST INTERESTING TEAMMATE? Rikki Clarke – good stories
BEST INNINGS YOU'VE SEEN? Aaron Finch's 117 not out from 52 balls against Middlesex at The Oval in the 2018 T20 Blast. Never seen anything like it
CRICKETING HERO? Andrew Flintoff
WHICH RULE WOULD YOU CHANGE ABOUT CRICKET? You can be out lbw even if you are hit outside the line of off stump while playing a shot
SURPRISING FACT ABOUT YOU? I had a rugby trial for Harlequins aged 13
CRICKET STAR OF THE FUTURE? Dan Moriarty (Surrey Second XI)
WHICH BOOK MEANS MOST TO YOU? A Clockwork Orange by Anthony Burgess
TWITTER: @gus_atkinson1

HASSAN AZAD

LHB / OB / R1 / W0

FULL NAME: Mohammad Hassan Azad
BORN: January 7, 1994, Quetta, Balochistan, Pakistan
SQUAD NO: 42
EDUCATION: Bilborough Sixth Form College, Nottingham; Loughborough University
TEAMS: Leicestershire
ROLE: Batsman
DEBUT: First-class: 2015

BEST BATTING: 139 Leicestershire vs Loughborough MCCU, Leicester, 2019

TWITTER: @Bat_Pad_Man
NOTES: The Pakistan-born left-hander was a revelation for struggling Leicestershire last summer, scoring 1,189 Championship runs at 54.05 including three hundreds. A gritty batsman, Azad moved to England aged 15 and was briefly on Nottinghamshire's books but he was released by the club in 2014. His game improved while at Loughborough University, where he studied Chemical Engineering, and he was picked up by Leicestershire after a number of impressive performances for the MCCU side. Last August he signed a two-year contract with the club. Leicestershire head coach Paul Nixon said: "We were thrilled to get Hass on board with us. He has been a brilliant addition. He just loves to bat and bat, and places the highest price on his wicket"

Batting	Mat	Inns	NO	Runs	HS	Ave	SR	100	50	Ct	St
First-class	24	38	5	1659	139	50.27	41.32	4	10	11	0
Bowling	**Mat**	**Balls**	**Runs**	**Wkts**	**BBI**	**BBM**	**Ave**	**Econ**	**SR**	**5w**	**10**
First-class	24	6	2	0	-	-	-	2.00	-	0	0

BABAR AZAM

RHB / OB / R0 / W0

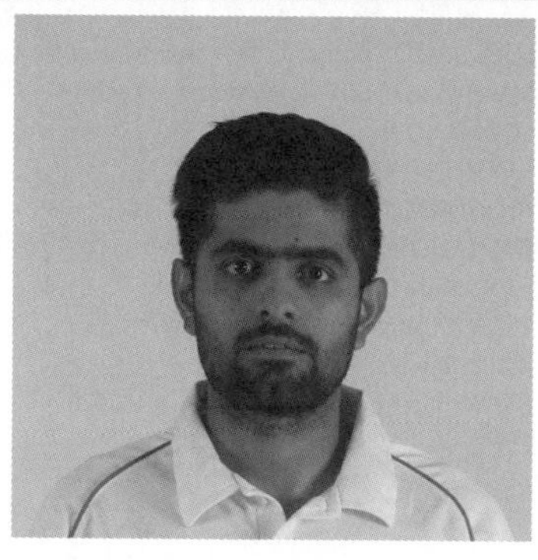

FULL NAME: Mohammad Babar Azam
BORN: October 15, 1994, Lahore, Pakistan
SQUAD NO: 56
TEAMS: Pakistan, Somerset, Central Punjab, Guyana Amazon Warriors, Karachi Kings, Islamabad, Lahore Blues, State Bank of Pakistan, Sui Southern Gas Corporation, Sylhet Sixers, Zarai Taraqiati Bank Limited
ROLE: Batsman
DEBUT: Test: 2016; ODI: 2015; T20I: 2016; First-class: 2010; List A: 2012; T20: 2012

BEST BATTING: 266 State Bank of Pakistan vs Habib Bank Limited, Faisalabad, 2014
BEST BOWLING: 1-13 Zarai Taraqiati Bank Limited vs United Bank Limited, Islamabad, 2012

TWITTER: @babarazam258
NOTES: Somerset have secured the services of one of the world's most prolific and stylish batsmen with the re-signing of the Pakistani run-machine. Babar was the leading run-scorer in last summer's T20 Blast, with 578 runs in 13 innings, and he returns to Taunton for 12 T20 fixtures as well as two mid-summer outings in the Championship ahead of Pakistan's Test series against England later in the season. The 25-year-old scored 1,607 T20 runs in 2019, the most of any batsman worldwide, and captains his country in the shortest format. As of March 2020, Babar sits at No.1 in the ICC's T20I rankings, No.3 in ODIs and No.5 in Tests. "His batting is so easy on the eye and he is so hungry to evolve his game," said Andy Hurry, Somerset's director of cricket. "He will add significant value to the team, both with his batting and leadership"

Batting	Mat	Inns	NO	Runs	HS	Ave	SR	100	50	Ct	St
Tests	26	48	7	1850	143	45.12	56.90	5	13	19	0
ODIs	74	72	10	3359	125*	54.17	87.08	11	15	36	0
T20Is	38	38	9	1471	97*	50.72	128.13	0	13	15	0
First-class	61	100	11	3805	266	42.75	57.73	8	25	41	0
List A	138	135	17	6275	142*	53.17	85.21	21	33	63	0
T20s	142	138	25	4861	102*	43.01	125.31	3	38	62	0
Bowling	**Mat**	**Balls**	**Runs**	**Wkts**	**BBI**	**BBM**	**Ave**	**Econ**	**SR**	**5w**	**10**
Tests	26	-	-	-	-	-	-	-	-	-	-
ODIs	74	-	-	-	-	-	-	-	-	-	-
T20Is	38	-	-	-	-	-	-	-	-	-	-
First-class	61	720	423	5	1/13	1/17	84.60	3.52	144.0	0	0
List A	138	633	555	12	2/20	2/20	46.25	5.26	52.7	0	0
T20s	142	78	85	4	2/20	2/20	21.25	6.53	19.5	0	0

TOM BAILEY

RHB / RFM / R0 / W1

FULL NAME: Thomas Ernest Bailey
BORN: April 21, 1991, Preston, Lancashire
SQUAD NO: 8
HEIGHT: 6ft 4in
NICKNAME: Jeb, Bails
EDUCATION: Myerscough College, Lancashire
TEAMS: Lancashire, England Lions
ROLE: Bowler
DEBUT: First-class: 2012; List A: 2014; T20: 2015

BEST BATTING: 68 Lancashire vs Northamptonshire, Old Trafford, 2019
BEST BOWLING: 5-12 Lancashire vs Leicestershire, Leicester, 2015
COUNTY CAP: 2018

FAMILY TIES? My dad played for a local side and I used to watch him every weekend as a kid
WHAT WAS YOUR FIRST CRICKET CLUB? Vernon Carus CC, Lancashire
WHAT WERE YOU DOING WHEN ENGLAND WON THE WORLD CUP? Enjoying a bit of the bubbly
WHAT EXCITES YOU ABOUT THE HUNDRED? The money
BIGGEST TOPIC OF DISCUSSION IN YOUR DRESSING ROOM? How much our head coach looks like Boris Johnson
CRICKETING HERO? Steve Harmison
SURPRISING FACT ABOUT YOU? I'm actually really smart
CRICKET STAR OF THE FUTURE? Virat Kohli jnr
IF YOU WERE AN ANIMAL, WHICH WOULD IT BE? A peacock
TWITTER: @TomBaildog

Batting	Mat	Inns	NO	Runs	HS	Ave	SR	100	50	Ct	St
First-class	56	76	12	1128	68	17.62	50.35	0	5	14	0
List A	15	11	6	81	33	16.20	89.01	0	0	2	0
T20s	13	4	1	18	10	6.00	112.50	0	0	6	0
Bowling	**Mat**	**Balls**	**Runs**	**Wkts**	**BBI**	**BBM**	**Ave**	**Econ**	**SR**	**5w**	**10**
First-class	56	9957	4873	193	5/12	10/98	25.24	2.93	51.5	9	2
List A	15	679	660	20	3/31	3/31	33.00	5.83	33.9	0	0
T20s	13	216	351	11	2/24	2/24	31.90	9.75	19.6	0	0

JONNY BAIRSTOW

RHB / WK / R3 / W0

FULL NAME: Jonathan Marc Bairstow
BORN: September 26, 1989, Bradford
SQUAD NO: 21
NICKNAME: Bluey
EDUCATION: St Peter's School, York; Leeds Metropolitan University
TEAMS: England, Yorkshire, Welsh Fire, Peshawar Zalmi, Sunrisers Hyderabad
ROLE: Batsman/wicketkeeper
DEBUT: Test: 2012; ODI: 2011; T20I: 2011; First-class: 2009; List A: 2009; T20: 2010

BEST BATTING: 246 Yorkshire vs Hampshire, Headingley, 2016

COUNTY CAP: 2011

FAMILY TIES? My father David played for Yorkshire and England
CRICKETING HERO? Sachin Tendulkar
NON-CRICKETING HERO? Steve Irwin
IF YOU WEREN'T A CRICKETER? I'd be a rugby player
SURPRISING FACT? I played football for the Leeds United Academy for seven years
TWITTER: @jbairstow21
NOTES: Bairstow was retained by Sunrisers Hyderabad for the 2020 IPL

Batting	Mat	Inns	NO	Runs	HS	Ave	SR	100	50	Ct	St
Tests	70	123	7	4030	167*	34.74	55.07	6	21	184	13
ODIs	77	70	8	2923	141*	47.14	104.50	9	11	35	2
T20Is	37	32	6	725	68	27.88	139.42	0	4	32	0
First-class	181	299	33	11576	246	43.51		24	62	470	24
List A	145	132	14	4845	174	41.05	103.50	12	21	86	8
T20s	116	104	19	2423	114	28.50	135.21	2	10	74	12
Bowling	**Mat**	**Balls**	**Runs**	**Wkts**	**BBI**	**BBM**	**Ave**	**Econ**	**SR**	**5w**	**10**
Tests	70	-	-	-	-	-	-	-	-	-	-
ODIs	77	-	-	-	-	-	-	-	-	-	-
T20Is	37	-	-	-	-	-	-	-	-	-	-
First-class	181	6	1	0	-	-	-	1.00	-	0	0
List A	145	-	-	-	-	-	-	-	-	-	-
T20s	116	-	-	-	-	-	-	-	-	-	-

GEORGE BALDERSON LHB / RM / R0 / W0

FULL NAME: George Philip Balderson
BORN: October 11, 2000, Manchester
SQUAD NO: 10
HEIGHT: 5ft 10in
NICKNAME: Baldy
EDUCATION: Cheadle Hulme High School, Greater Manchester
TEAMS: Lancashire, England U19
ROLE: Allrounder

WHAT WAS YOUR FIRST CRICKET CLUB? Cheadle Hulme CC, Greater Manchester. I'd watch my dad play there every Saturday
WHAT WERE YOU DOING WHEN ENGLAND WON THE WORLD CUP? Watching with England U19 at Loughborough University
BIGGEST TOPIC OF DISCUSSION IN YOUR DRESSING ROOM? Lads losing their hair
MOST INTERESTING TEAMMATE? Shiv Chanderpaul – the experience of the game he shared with us was amazing
BIGGEST CRICKETING REGRET? Bowling leg-spin until I was 14
IF YOU WERE AN ANIMAL, WHICH WOULD IT BE? An elephant
TWITTER: @BaldersonGeorge
NOTES: The 19-year-old seam-bowling allrounder signed his first professional contract with Lancashire in November 2018 after featuring regularly for the second team, including both games in the victorious Second XI T20 Finals Day. Last summer he took 10 wickets at 17.80 in four Second XI Championship matches. A left-handed batsman who bowls right-arm pace, Balderson was made England U19 captain for last summer's tri-series against Bangladesh and India. He led the side in the U19 World Cup in South Africa in January, where a narrow defeat against Australia in the group stages cost England a place in the Super League phase. Balderson took seven wickets at 23.71 in five matches at the tournament. He will be hoping to make his first-team debut for Lancashire this summer

JAKE BALL

RHB / RFM / R0 / W1

FULL NAME: Jacob Timothy Ball
BORN: March 14, 1991, Mansfield, Nottinghamshire
SQUAD NO: 28
HEIGHT: 6ft 3in
NICKNAME: Yak
EDUCATION: Meden School, Mansfield
TEAMS: England, Nottinghamshire
ROLE: Bowler
DEBUT: Test: 2016; ODI: 2016; T20I: 2018; First-class: 2011; List A: 2009; T20: 2011

BEST BATTING: 49* Nottinghamshire vs Warwickshire, Trent Bridge, 2015
BEST BOWLING: 6-49 Nottinghamshire vs Sussex, Trent Bridge, 2015
COUNTY CAP: 2016

FAMILY TIES? My uncle Bruce French played for England
WHAT WAS YOUR FIRST CRICKET CLUB? Welbeck Colliery CC, Nottinghamshire
WHAT EXCITES YOU ABOUT THE HUNDRED? Ask me after the wildcards have been picked...
BIGGEST TOPIC OF DISCUSSION IN YOUR DRESSING ROOM? Snap
BEST INNINGS YOU'VE SEEN? Alastair Cook's double century at the MCG in the 2017/18 Ashes. As a member of the squad I got to see how hard he worked for that innings over the whole tour
SURPRISING FACT ABOUT YOU? I was a batter till the age of 15
CRICKET STAR OF THE FUTURE? Joey Evison (Nottinghamshire)
TWITTER: @Jakeball30

Batting	Mat	Inns	NO	Runs	HS	Ave	SR	100	50	Ct	St
Tests	4	8	0	67	31	8.37	53.60	0	0	1	0
ODIs	18	6	2	38	28	9.50	77.55	0	0	5	0
T20Is	2	-	-	-	-	-	-	-	-	1	0
First-class	63	96	23	964	49*	13.20	74.55	0	0	10	0
List A	96	38	15	198	28	8.60	99.00	0	0	19	0
T20s	65	15	10	35	8*	7.00	83.33	0	0	17	0
Bowling	**Mat**	**Balls**	**Runs**	**Wkts**	**BBI**	**BBM**	**Ave**	**Econ**	**SR**	**5w**	**10**
Tests	4	612	343	3	1/47	1/47	114.33	3.36	204.0	0	0
ODIs	18	947	980	21	5/51	5/51	46.66	6.20	45.0	1	0
T20Is	2	42	83	2	1/39	1/39	41.50	11.85	21.0	0	0
First-class	63	9409	5434	191	6/49	9/57	28.45	3.46	49.2	6	0
List A	96	4060	3984	118	5/51	5/51	33.76	5.88	34.4	1	0
T20s	65	1280	1865	70	3/27	3/27	26.64	8.74	18.2	0	0

GARY BALLANCE

LHB / LB / R4 / W0 / MVP70

FULL NAME: Gary Simon Ballance
BORN: November 22, 1989, Harare, Zimbabwe
SQUAD NO: 19
NICKNAME: Gazza, Gaz
EDUCATION: Peterhouse School, Marondera, Zimbabwe; Harrow School, London
TEAMS: England, Yorkshire, Derbyshire, Mid West Rhinos, Zimbabwe U19
ROLE: Batsman
DEBUT: Test: 2014; ODI: 2013; First-class: 2008; List A: 2006; T20: 2010

BEST BATTING: 210 Mid West Rhinos vs Southern Rocks, Masvingo, 2011

COUNTY CAP: 2012 (Yorkshire)

NOTES: A close family friend of former Zimbabwe skipper David Houghton, Ballance signed for Derbyshire aged 16 before joining the Yorkshire Academy in 2008. He played for Zimbabwe at the 2006 U19 World Cup before qualifying to play for England. His ODI debut was in 2013 before his Test debut at Sydney in the 2013/14 Ashes. He had an exceptional summer in Test cricket in 2014, hitting three centuries to cement his place at No.3. Ballance lost his Test spot during the 2015 Ashes and was in and out the side over the next two years. His most recent Test was in 2017. He was made captain of Yorkshire across all formats that year but stood down in 2018 when he took a brief break from cricket for personal reasons. Ballance has been the club's leading run-scorer in the Championship for the past three seasons, scoring 975 runs last summer including five hundreds

Batting	Mat	Inns	NO	Runs	HS	Ave	SR	100	50	Ct	St
Tests	23	42	2	1498	156	37.45	47.16	4	7	22	0
ODIs	16	15	1	297	79	21.21	67.04	0	2	8	0
First-class	160	262	24	11282	210	47.40	51.86	40	51	120	0
List A	110	102	14	4360	156	49.54	90.06	8	26	43	0
T20s	90	80	9	1648	79	23.21	122.16	0	6	46	0
Bowling	**Mat**	**Balls**	**Runs**	**Wkts**	**BBI**	**BBM**	**Ave**	**Econ**	**SR**	**5w**	**10**
Tests	23	12	5	0	-	-	-	2.50	-	0	0
ODIs	16	-	-	-	-	-	-	-	-	-	-
First-class	160	162	154	0	-	-	-	5.70	-	0	0
List A	110	-	-	-	-	-	-	-	-	-	-
T20s	90	-	-	-	-	-	-	-	-	-	-

ETHAN BAMBER

RHB / RFM / R0 / W0

FULL NAME: Ethan Read Bamber
BORN: December 17, 1998, Westminster, London
SQUAD NO: 54
HEIGHT: 5ft 11in
NICKNAME: Sorry, Bambs
EDUCATION: Mill Hill School, London; University of Exeter
TEAMS: Middlesex, England U19, Gloucestershire
ROLE: Bowler
DEBUT: First-class: 2018; T20: 2019

BEST BATTING: 27* Middlesex vs Gloucestershire, Bristol, 2018
BEST BOWLING: 5-93 Middlesex vs Derbyshire, Lord's, 2019

WHAT WAS YOUR FIRST CRICKET CLUB? North Middlesex CC, London. It was about 400 metres from my house
WHAT WERE YOU DOING WHEN ENGLAND WON THE WORLD CUP? Having a barbecue in Bristol
HOW WOULD YOU DISMISS STEVE SMITH? Mankad him
BIGGEST TOPIC OF DISCUSSION IN YOUR DRESSING ROOM? Crosswords
WHICH RULE WOULD YOU CHANGE ABOUT CRICKET? An edge for a four should go down as extras
BIGGEST CRICKETING REGRET? Getting out with a shocking shot when the other batter was on 98
CRICKET STAR OF THE FUTURE? Joe Cracknell (Middlesex Second XI)
IF YOU WERE AN ANIMAL, WHICH WOULD IT BE? An elephant
TWITTER: @etbamber

Batting	Mat	Inns	NO	Runs	HS	Ave	SR	100	50	Ct	St
First-class	13	21	6	136	27*	9.06	29.31	0	0	2	0
T20s	1	1	1	0	0*	-	0.00	0	0	0	0
Bowling	**Mat**	**Balls**	**Runs**	**Wkts**	**BBI**	**BBM**	**Ave**	**Econ**	**SR**	**5w**	**10**
First-class	13	2486	1154	47	5/93	6/70	24.55	2.78	52.8	1	0
T20s	1	24	38	1	1/38	1/38	38.00	9.50	24.0	0	0

CAMERON BANCROFT RHB / WK / R0 / W0 / MVP94

FULL NAME: Cameron Timothy Bancroft
BORN: November 19, 1992, Perth, Australia
SQUAD NO: 4
HEIGHT: 6ft 1in
NICKNAME: Bangers
EDUCATION: Aquinas College, Perth
TEAMS: Australia, Durham, Gloucestershire, Perth Scorchers, Western Australia
ROLE: Batsman
DEBUT: Test: 2017; T20I: 2016; First-class: 2013; List A: 2011; T20: 2014

BEST BATTING: 228* Western Australia vs South Australia, Perth, 2017
BEST BOWLING: 1-10 Western Australia vs Queensland, Brisbane, 2019
COUNTY CAP: 2016 (Gloucestershire)

WHAT WAS YOUR FIRST CRICKET CLUB? Leeming Spartans CC, Perth, Australia
WHAT WERE YOU DOING WHEN ENGLAND WON THE WORLD CUP? Batting out in the middle against Worcestershire
HOW WOULD YOU DISMISS STEVE SMITH? I wouldn't, I'd give up
WHAT EXCITES YOU ABOUT THE HUNDRED? It's a bit of an unknown
BIGGEST TOPIC OF DISCUSSION IN YOUR DRESSING ROOM? Winding up Brydon Carse
MOST INTERESTING TEAMMATE? Gareth Harte – he can be quite funny when he stresses out a bit
IF YOU WERE AN ANIMAL, WHICH WOULD IT BE? A willie wagtail – because I'm always up and at them
TWITTER: @cbancroft4

Batting	Mat	Inns	NO	Runs	HS	Ave	SR	100	50	Ct	St
Tests	10	18	1	446	82*	26.23	42.80	0	3	16	0
T20Is	1	1	1	0	0*	-	-	0	0	1	0
First-class	101	185	15	6355	228*	37.38	42.62	14	26	132	1
List A	56	53	8	1882	176	41.82	83.20	3	12	48	1
T20s	50	44	10	1090	87*	32.05	123.02	0	8	19	5
Bowling	**Mat**	**Balls**	**Runs**	**Wkts**	**BBI**	**BBM**	**Ave**	**Econ**	**SR**	**5w**	**10**
Tests	10	-	-	-	-	-	-	-	-	-	-
T20Is	1	-	-	-	-	-	-	-	-	-	-
First-class	101	66	77	2	1/10	1/10	38.50	7.00	33.0	0	0
List A	56	-	-	-	-	-	-	-	-	-	-
T20s	50	-	-	-	-	-	-	-	-	-	-

LIAM BANKS

RHB / RM / R0 / W0

FULL NAME: Liam Banks
BORN: March 27, 1999, Stoke-on-Trent
SQUAD NO: 8
HEIGHT: 5ft 10in
NICKNAME: Banksy
EDUCATION: Newcastle-under-Lyme School and Sixth Form College
TEAMS: Warwickshire, England U19
ROLE: Batsman
DEBUT: First-class: 2017; List A: 2019; T20: 2019

BEST BATTING: 50 Warwickshire vs Essex, Chelmsford, 2019

WHAT WAS YOUR FIRST CRICKET CLUB? Silverdale CC, Staffordshire
WHICH BOWLER WOULD YOU LEAST LIKE TO FACE? Mitchell Johnson
CRICKETING HERO? Ricky Ponting
BEST INNINGS YOU'VE SEEN? Alastair Cook's first Test hundred on debut against India at Nagpur in 2006. Nerveless
WHO WOULD YOU ASK TO BAT FOR YOUR LIFE? Kane Williamson
WHICH RULE WOULD YOU CHANGE ABOUT CRICKET? Bring DRS into domestic cricket
YOUR BIGGEST CRICKETING REGRET? Getting in and getting out
SURPRISING FACT ABOUT YOU? I love animals and fishing
FAVOURITE QUOTE OR SAYING? You won't have to force anything that's truly meant to be
WHICH BOOK MEANS MOST TO YOU? The Subtle Art of Not Giving a F*** – A Counterintuitive Approach to Living a Good Life by Mark Manson

Batting	Mat	Inns	NO	Runs	HS	Ave	SR	100	50	Ct	St
First-class	10	17	0	277	50	16.29	42.94	0	1	15	0
List A	8	8	0	250	61	31.25	85.03	0	2	1	0
T20s	6	5	3	34	24*	17.00	161.90	0	0	2	0
Bowling	**Mat**	**Balls**	**Runs**	**Wkts**	**BBI**	**BBM**	**Ave**	**Econ**	**SR**	**5w**	**10**
First-class	10	18	9	0	-	-	-	3.00	-	0	0
List A	8	-	-	-	-	-	-	-	-	-	-
T20s	6	-	-	-	-	-	-	-	-	-	-

TOM BANTON

RHB / WK / R0 / W0 / MVP19

SOMERSET / WELSH FIRE

FULL NAME: Thomas Banton
BORN: November 11, 1998, Chiltern, Buckinghamshire
SQUAD NO: 18
HEIGHT: 6ft 2in
NICKNAME: Bants
EDUCATION: Bromsgrove School, Worcestershire; King's College, Taunton
TEAMS: England, Somerset, Welsh Fire, Brisbane Heat, Kolkata Knight Riders, Peshawar Zalmi
ROLE: Batsman/wicketkeeper
DEBUT: ODI: 2020; T20I: 2019; First-class: 2018; List A: 2018; T20: 2017

BEST BATTING: 79 Somerset vs Hampshire, Taunton, 2019

WHAT WAS YOUR FIRST CRICKET CLUB? Sutton CC, London
CRICKETING HERO? Virat Kohli
BEST INNINGS YOU'VE SEEN? Johann Myburgh smashing 103 off 44 balls against Essex in the 2018 T20 Blast. I was batting at the other end as we chased down 136 without losing a wicket
YOUR BIGGEST CRICKETING REGRET? Not playing for Somerset at the age of 10
SURPRISING FACT ABOUT YOU? I love playing hockey
TWITTER: @tombanton18

Batting	Mat	Inns	NO	Runs	HS	Ave	SR	100	50	Ct	St
ODIs	3	2	0	50	32	25.00	90.90	0	0	0	0
T20Is	3	3	0	56	31	18.66	164.70	0	0	4	0
First-class	12	21	0	570	79	27.14	58.22	0	5	7	0
List A	21	19	0	574	112	30.21	86.70	2	3	14	1
T20s	34	33	2	944	100	30.45	157.33	1	7	18	3
Bowling	**Mat**	**Balls**	**Runs**	**Wkts**	**BBI**	**BBM**	**Ave**	**Econ**	**SR**	**5w**	**10**
ODIs	3	-	-	-	-	-	-	-	-	-	-
T20Is	3	-	-	-	-	-	-	-	-	-	-
First-class	12	-	-	-	-	-	-	-	-	-	-
List A	21	-	-	-	-	-	-	-	-	-	-
T20s	34	-	-	-	-	-	-	-	-	-	-

TOM BARBER

RHB / LFM / R0 / W0

FULL NAME: Thomas Edward Barber
BORN: August 8, 1995, Poole, Dorset
SQUAD NO: 18
HEIGHT: 6ft 3in
NICKNAME: Barbs
EDUCATION: Bournemouth Grammar School
TEAMS: Nottinghamshire, England U19, Hampshire, Middlesex
ROLE: Bowler
DEBUT: First-class: 2018; List A: 2014; T20: 2017

BEST BATTING: 3 Middlesex vs Sussex, Hove, 2018

WHAT WAS YOUR FIRST CRICKET CLUB? Parley CC, Dorset. The club also produced David Payne of Gloucestershire
BEST ADVICE RECEIVED? Hit the top of off stump
HOW WOULD YOU DISMISS STEVE SMITH? Swing it back in and take his poles out the ground
WHAT EXCITES YOU ABOUT THE HUNDRED? Less time in the field!
BIGGEST TOPIC OF DISCUSSION IN YOUR DRESSING ROOM? Football warm-ups
MOST INTERESTING TEAMMATE? AB de Villiers at Middlesex last summer – one of the greatest cricketers ever and he has time for everyone
BEST INNINGS YOU'VE SEEN? Paul Stirling's 66 off 36 balls for my old club Middlesex against Surrey in the 2018 T20 Blast. Sixes all over the place
WHICH RULE WOULD YOU CHANGE ABOUT CRICKET? Allow more bouncers per over
SURPRISING FACT ABOUT YOU? I broke the record for the fastest ball bowled in the Vicon testing at Loughborough – 89.6mph
TWITTER: @Tom_Barber20

Batting	Mat	Inns	NO	Runs	HS	Ave	SR	100	50	Ct	St
First-class	2	3	1	3	3	1.50	21.42	0	0	0	0
List A	7	6	0	1	1	0.16	5.88	0	0	0	0
T20s	11	5	0	3	2	0.60	37.50	0	0	1	0
Bowling	**Mat**	**Balls**	**Runs**	**Wkts**	**BBI**	**BBM**	**Ave**	**Econ**	**SR**	**5w**	**10**
First-class	2	204	131	0	-	-	-	3.85	-	0	0
List A	7	300	322	9	3/62	3/62	35.77	6.44	33.3	0	0
T20s	11	209	392	12	4/28	4/28	32.66	11.25	17.4	0	0

KEITH BARKER

LHB / LFM / R0 / W3 / MVP96

FULL NAME: Keith Hubert Douglas Barker
BORN: October 21, 1986, Manchester
SQUAD NO: 10
HEIGHT: 6ft 3in
NICKNAME: Barks
EDUCATION: Moorhead High School, Accrington; Preston College
TEAMS: Hampshire, Warwickshire
ROLE: Allrounder
DEBUT: First-class: 2009; List A: 2009; T20: 2009

BEST BATTING: 125 Warwickshire vs Surrey, Guildford, 2013
BEST BOWLING: 6-40 Warwickshire vs Somerset, Taunton, 2012
COUNTY CAP: 2013 (Warwickshire)

FAMILY TIES? My father, godfather and brothers all played various levels of cricket
WHAT WAS YOUR FIRST CRICKET CLUB? Enfield CC, Lancashire
BEST ADVICE RECEIVED? It's only a game
WHAT WERE YOU DOING WHEN ENGLAND WON THE WORLD CUP? Can't remember
MOST INTERESTING TEAMMATE? Jonathan Trott
CRICKETING HERO? My father
WHICH RULE WOULD YOU CHANGE ABOUT CRICKET? Stop making things easier for batters
SURPRISING FACT ABOUT YOU? I never scored a hundred for the Enfield first team
WHICH BOOK MEANS MOST TO YOU? Rich Dad Poor Dad – What the Rich Teach Their Kids About Money that the Poor and Middle Classes Do Not by Robert Kiyosaki
IF YOU WERE AN ANIMAL, WHICH WOULD IT BE? A silverback gorilla

Batting	Mat	Inns	NO	Runs	HS	Ave	SR	100	50	Ct	St
First-class	127	169	29	3955	125	28.25	57.54	6	17	35	0
List A	62	39	11	560	56	20.00	94.59	0	1	14	0
T20s	65	35	7	383	46	13.67	111.01	0	0	17	0
Bowling	**Mat**	**Balls**	**Runs**	**Wkts**	**BBI**	**BBM**	**Ave**	**Econ**	**SR**	**5w**	**10**
First-class	127	20608	10123	397	6/40	10/70	25.49	2.94	51.9	15	1
List A	62	2342	2263	69	4/33	4/33	32.79	5.79	33.9	0	0
T20s	65	1206	1588	69	4/19	4/19	23.01	7.90	17.4	0	0

ED BARNARD

RHB / RFM / R0 / W0 / MVP14

FULL NAME: Edward George Barnard
BORN: November 20, 1995, Shrewsbury
SQUAD NO: 30
HEIGHT: 6ft
NICKNAME: Barndoor, Earthworm Jim
EDUCATION: Meole Brace School, Shrewsbury; Shrewsbury School
TEAMS: Worcestershire, Northern Superchargers, England Lions
ROLE: Allrounder
DEBUT: First-class: 2015; List A: 2015; T20: 2015

BEST BATTING: 75 Worcestershire vs Durham, Worcester, 2017
BEST BOWLING: 6-37 Worcestershire vs Somerset, Taunton, 2018

FAMILY TIES? Dad (Andy) played for Shropshire; brother (Mike) played for Shropshire and first-class cricket for Oxford MCCU; brother (Steve) played for Shropshire
WHAT WAS YOUR FIRST CRICKET CLUB? Shrewsbury CC, Shropshire. National Knockout champions 1983 and 2011
BEST INNINGS YOU'VE SEEN? Ben Cox's 46 not out to beat Sussex in the 2018 T20 final
BIGGEST TOPIC OF DISCUSSION IN YOUR DRESSING ROOM? Football
MOST INTERESTING TEAMMATE? Richard Oliver
CRICKETING HERO? Andrew Flintoff
CRICKET STAR OF THE FUTURE? Rehan Edavaleth (Worcestershire Academy)
IF YOU WERE AN ANIMAL, WHICH WOULD IT BE? A bird, so that I could fly wherever
TWITTER: @EdBarn95

Batting	Mat	Inns	NO	Runs	HS	Ave	SR	100	50	Ct	St
First-class	60	90	14	2028	75	26.68	53.82	0	12	35	0
List A	44	32	13	554	61	29.15	100.36	0	3	19	0
T20s	66	41	18	410	42*	17.82	133.55	0	0	39	0
Bowling	**Mat**	**Balls**	**Runs**	**Wkts**	**BBI**	**BBM**	**Ave**	**Econ**	**SR**	**5w**	**10**
First-class	60	9261	5086	187	6/37	11/89	27.19	3.29	49.5	5	1
List A	44	1908	1867	53	3/26	3/26	35.22	5.87	36.0	0	0
T20s	66	1028	1536	38	3/29	3/29	40.42	8.96	27.0	0	0

ED BARNES

RHB / RFM / R0 / W0

FULL NAME: Edward Barnes
BORN: November 26, 1997, York
SQUAD NO: 62
EDUCATION: King James School, Knaresborough, North Yorkshire
TEAMS: Yorkshire, England U19
ROLE: Allrounder

NOTES: The 21-year-old seam-bowling allrounder has been a consistent performer for Yorkshire's Academy and Second XI for a number of seasons, one of several players from York to make the grade along with Jonny Bairstow, Matthew Fisher and Jack Leaning. He helped the Yorkshire Academy win the league-and-cup double in 2014 and a year later hit a run-a-ball 177 against Derbyshire U17. Barnes is yet to make his first-team debut but has played two 'Tests' and two 'ODIs' for England U19 against Sri Lanka in 2016, taking nine wickets and playing in the same side as future Test cricketers Ollie Pope and Dom Bess. Up until the start of this season, Barnes has taken 152 wickets for the Yorkshire Academy and Second XI combined. He was loaned out to Sussex for the One-Day Cup last summer but did not make an appeareance for the Sharks

GEORGE BARTLETT

RHB / OB / R0 / W0

FULL NAME: George Anthony Bartlett
BORN: March 14, 1998, Frimley, Surrey
SQUAD NO: 14
HEIGHT: 6ft 1in
NICKNAME: GB
EDUCATION: Millfield School, Street, Somerset
TEAMS: Somerset, England U19
ROLE: Batsman
DEBUT: First-class: 2017; List A: 2019

BEST BATTING: 137 Somerset vs Surrey, Guildford, 2019

WHAT WAS YOUR FIRST CRICKET CLUB? Westlands CC, Yeovil, Somerset
WHAT WERE YOU DOING WHEN ENGLAND WON THE WORLD CUP? Watching it in a hotel reception area in Yorkshire
BIGGEST TOPIC OF DISCUSSION IN YOUR DRESSING ROOM? The weather
MOST INTERESTING TEAMMATE? Azhar Ali
CRICKET STAR OF THE FUTURE? Theodore Hildreth
IF YOU WERE AN ANIMAL, WHICH WOULD IT BE? A bald eagle
TWITTER: @georgebartlett9
NOTES: Bartlett is a product of the Somerset Academy and signed a contract with the club in 2016 before agreeing a two-year extension last October. In 2017 he made 179 for England U19 against India U19 in a four-day match at Nagpur, taking Nasser Hussain's record for the highest score by an England U19 batsman overseas. The 22-year-old made his first-class debut in 2017 and scored his maiden Championship hundred the following year against Lancashire at Old Trafford. Last summer he played in all 14 Championship fixtures, scoring two centuries and three fifties, as well as making his List A debut

Batting	Mat	Inns	NO	Runs	HS	Ave	SR	100	50	Ct	St
First-class	25	45	2	1178	137	27.39	56.99	3	3	6	0
List A	9	9	3	207	57*	34.50	99.51	0	1	4	0
Bowling	**Mat**	**Balls**	**Runs**	**Wkts**	**BBI**	**BBM**	**Ave**	**Econ**	**SR**	**5w**	**10**
First-class	25	20	27	0	-	-	-	8.10	-	0	0
List A	9	-	-	-	-	-	-	-	-	-	-

GARETH BATTY RHB / OB / R0 / W2 / MVP74

FULL NAME: Gareth Jon Batty
BORN: October 13, 1977, Bradford
SQUAD NO: 13
HEIGHT: 5ft 11in
NICKNAME: Bats
EDUCATION: Bingley Grammar School, West Yorkshire
TEAMS: England, Surrey, Worcestershire, Yorkshire
ROLE: Bowler
DEBUT: Test: 2003; ODI: 2002; T20I: 2009; First-class: 1997; List A: 1998; T20: 2003

BEST BATTING: 133 Worcestershire vs Surrey, The Oval, 2004
BEST BOWLING: 8-64 Surrey vs Warwickshire, Edgbaston, 2019
COUNTY CAP: 2011 (Surrey); BENEFIT: 2017 (Surrey)

FAMILY TIES? Dad played for Yorkshire Second XI and my brother Jeremy played for Yorkshire and Somerset
WHAT WAS YOUR FIRST CRICKET CLUB? Bradford and Bingley CC, West Yorkshire
HOW WOULD YOU DISMISS STEVE SMITH? With a 150mph yorker
BIGGEST TOPIC OF DISCUSSION IN YOUR DRESSING ROOM? The Hundred
MOST INTERESTING TEAMMATE? Kumar Sangakkara
CRICKETING HERO? Joel Garner
SURPRISING FACT ABOUT YOU? This is my 24th year as a pro
IF YOU WERE AN ANIMAL, WHICH WOULD IT BE? Bagpuss

Batting	Mat	Inns	NO	Runs	HS	Ave	SR	100	50	Ct	St
Tests	9	12	2	149	38	14.90	25.68	0	0	3	0
ODIs	10	8	2	30	17	5.00	41.09	0	0	4	0
T20Is	1	1	0	4	4	4.00	57.14	0	0	0	0
First-class	261	389	68	7399	133	23.04		3	30	163	0
List A	271	200	44	2374	83*	15.21		0	5	84	0
T20s	171	93	33	623	87	10.38	101.30	0	1	48	0
Bowling	**Mat**	**Balls**	**Runs**	**Wkts**	**BBI**	**BBM**	**Ave**	**Econ**	**SR**	**5w**	**10**
Tests	9	1714	914	15	3/55	5/153	60.93	3.19	114.2	0	0
ODIs	10	440	366	5	2/40	2/40	73.20	4.99	88.0	0	0
T20Is	1	18	17	0	-	-	-	5.66	-	0	0
First-class	261	46183	22356	682	8/64		32.78	2.90	67.7	27	4
List A	271	10713	8283	255	5/35	5/35	32.48	4.63	42.0	3	0
T20s	171	3048	3736	137	4/13	4/13	27.27	7.35	22.2	0	0

AARON BEARD

LHB / RMF / R0 / W0

FULL NAME: Aaron Paul Beard
BORN: October 15, 1997, Chelmsford
SQUAD NO: 14
HEIGHT: 5ft 11in
NICKNAME: Beardo, AB
EDUCATION: The Boswells School, Chelmsford; Great Baddow High School, Chelmsford
TEAMS: Essex, England U19
ROLE: Bowler
DEBUT: First-class: 2016; List A: 2019; T20: 2019

BEST BATTING: 58* Essex vs Durham MCCU, Chelmsford, 2017
BEST BOWLING: 4-23 Essex vs Somerset, Chelmsford, 2019

WHAT WAS YOUR FIRST CRICKET CLUB? Writtle CC, Essex
BEST ADVICE RECEIVED? Play straight, be great
WHAT EXCITES YOU ABOUT THE HUNDRED? The high intensity
BIGGEST TOPIC OF DISCUSSION IN YOUR DRESSING ROOM? Who is the biggest bandit on the golf course
MOST INTERESTING TEAMMATE? Simon Harmer – he has in-depth knowledge of nearly everything
BEST INNINGS YOU'VE SEEN? Dan Lawrence hitting 141 against Lancashire at Chelmsford in 2017. He batted out the final day to get Essex a draw after we had lost some early wickets
CRICKETING HERO? Nick Browne
WHICH RULE WOULD YOU CHANGE ABOUT CRICKET? For DRS and lbws: if it's hitting the stumps it is out, regardless of whether the whole ball or part of the ball is hitting
WHICH BOOK MEANS MOST TO YOU? My passport
IF YOU WERE AN ANIMAL, WHICH WOULD IT BE? A bearded dragon
TWITTER: @aaronbeard_14

Batting	Mat	Inns	NO	Runs	HS	Ave	SR	100	50	Ct	St
First-class	17	18	9	191	58*	21.22	47.98	0	1	4	0
List A	2	2	1	24	22*	24.00	120.00	0	0	0	0
T20s	8	2	1	17	13	17.00	141.66	0	0	1	0
Bowling	**Mat**	**Balls**	**Runs**	**Wkts**	**BBI**	**BBM**	**Ave**	**Econ**	**SR**	**5w**	**10**
First-class	17	2030	1233	38	4/23	7/45	32.44	3.64	53.4	0	0
List A	2	114	97	3	3/51	3/51	32.33	5.10	38.0	0	0
T20s	8	120	193	6	2/31	2/31	32.16	9.65	20.0	0	0

DAVID BEDINGHAM

RHB / OB / R0 / W0

FULL NAME: David Guy Bedingham
BORN: April 22, 1994, George, Western Cape, South Africa
SQUAD NO: 5
TEAMS: Durham, Boland, Cape Cobras, South Africa U19, Western Province
ROLE: Batsman
DEBUT: First-class: 2013; List A: 2013; T20: 2015

BEST BATTING: 147 Boland vs Easterns, Paarl, 2018

NOTES: A promising top-order batsman who has played for South Africa at U19 level, Bedingham signed a one-year contract with Durham in January which means he cannot be selected to play for his country. He qualifies as a domestic player due to having a UK visa through a member of his family. Bedingham has been one of the most consistent batsmen on the South African first-class circuit in recent years, averaging 52.37 for Cape Cobras and Western Province in the 2019/20 campaign, 47.35 in 2018/19 and 52.66 in 2017/18. He played two Youth Tests against England U19 in 2013, scoring 131 at Paarl against a side featuring future internationals Ben Duckett, Olly Stone and Dom Sibley. "It is great to add another young, promising batsman to the Durham squad," said director of cricket Marcus North. "David has made the decision to move and live in the UK to pursue a career in England and we look forward to seeing him develop"

Batting	Mat	Inns	NO	Runs	HS	Ave	SR	100	50	Ct	St
First-class	32	55	6	2242	147	45.75	60.77	7	7	32	0
List A	20	20	3	504	104*	29.64	76.94	2	2	6	0
T20s	22	21	1	500	73	25.00	125.62	0	3	2	0
Bowling	**Mat**	**Balls**	**Runs**	**Wkts**	**BBI**	**BBM**	**Ave**	**Econ**	**SR**	**5w**	**10**
First-class	32	18	18	0	-	-	-	6.00	-	0	0
List A	20	39	25	0	-	-	-	3.84	-	0	0
T20s	22	-	-	-	-	-	-	-	-	-	-

WILL BEER

RHB / LB / R0 / W0

FULL NAME: William Andrew Thomas Beer
BORN: October 8, 1988, Crawley, Sussex
SQUAD NO: 18
HEIGHT: 5ft 10in
NICKNAME: Beery
EDUCATION: Reigate Grammar School; Collyer's Sixth Form College, Horsham
TEAMS: Sussex, England U19
ROLE: Bowler
DEBUT: First-class: 2008; List A: 2009; T20: 2008

BEST BATTING: 97 Sussex vs Gloucestershire, Arundel, 2019
BEST BOWLING: 6-29 Sussex vs South Africa A, Arundel, 2017

WHAT WAS YOUR FIRST CRICKET CLUB? Horsham CC, West Sussex. Best wicket in the UK
HOW WOULD YOU DISMISS STEVE SMITH? Bouncers with the keeper stood up
WHAT EXCITES YOU ABOUT THE HUNDRED? Cricket on terrestrial television again
BIGGEST TOPIC OF DISCUSSION IN YOUR DRESSING ROOM? Fantasy Football
BEST INNINGS YOU'VE SEEN? No.9 Ollie Robinson hitting 41 off 37 balls for a one-wicket win at Colwyn Bay in the Championship in 2017
CRICKETING HERO? Shane Warne
WHICH RULE WOULD YOU CHANGE ABOUT CRICKET? White-ball games should begin early or be shortened if the weather looks really bad – as long as both captains agree
WHICH BOOK MEANS MOST TO YOU? Racing Post Guide to the Jumps 2019–2020 by David Dew
IF YOU WERE AN ANIMAL, WHICH WOULD IT BE? A horse – it's my dream to run in the cross country at the Cheltenham Festival
TWITTER: @willbeer18

Batting	Mat	Inns	NO	Runs	HS	Ave	SR	100	50	Ct	St
First-class	27	34	7	755	97	27.96	36.31	0	4	6	0
List A	60	37	9	444	75	15.85	82.07	0	1	15	0
T20s	111	56	19	337	37	9.10	123.89	0	0	22	0
Bowling	**Mat**	**Balls**	**Runs**	**Wkts**	**BBI**	**BBM**	**Ave**	**Econ**	**SR**	**5w**	**10**
First-class	27	2754	1480	40	6/29	11/91	37.00	3.22	68.8	2	1
List A	60	2598	2246	54	3/27	3/27	41.59	5.18	48.1	0	0
T20s	111	1992	2455	93	3/14	3/14	26.39	7.39	21.4	0	0

FARHAAN BEHARDIEN

RHB / RM / R0 / W0

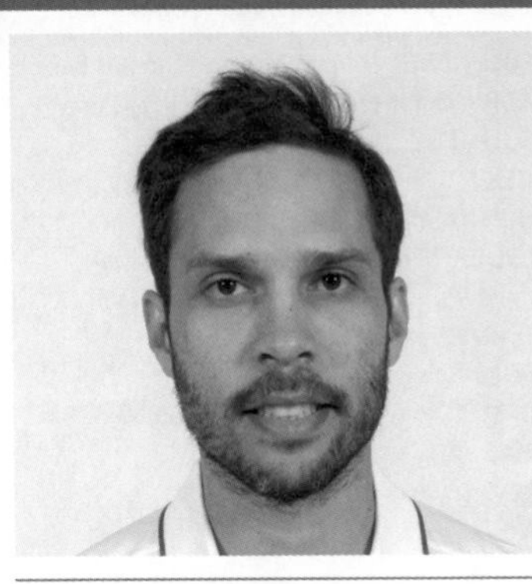

FULL NAME: Farhaan Behardien
BORN: October 9, 1983, Johannesburg, South Africa
SQUAD NO: 36
NICKNAME: Abadi
TEAMS: South Africa, Durham, Kings XI Punjab, Leicestershire, Northerns, Titans, Western Province
ROLE: Batsman
DEBUT: ODI: 2013; T20I: 2012; First-class: 2004; List A: 2004; T20: 2007

BEST BATTING: 150* Titans vs Eagles, Benoni, 2008
BEST BOWLING: 3-48 Western Province vs Eastern Province, Port Elizabeth, 2004

NOTES: The South African middle-order batsman signed on a two-year Kolpak deal with Durham in January and will be available to play in all three formats. He brings a wealth of experience after representing his country in white-ball cricket on 97 occasions between 2012 and 2018, including captaining South Africa's T20 side for a brief spell in 2017. The 36-year-old also played in the 2012 T20 World Cup and the 50-over World Cup in 2015. "Behardien is such an experienced cricketer, and with the young group of players we have in the squad he will help them develop their all-round game," said Durham director of cricket Marcus North

Batting	Mat	Inns	NO	Runs	HS	Ave	SR	100	50	Ct	St
ODIs	59	49	14	1074	70	30.68	97.90	0	6	27	0
T20Is	38	30	14	518	64*	32.37	128.21	0	1	14	0
First-class	114	183	18	6794	150*	41.17	53.82	11	44	74	0
List A	223	191	54	5432	113*	39.64	94.53	5	33	85	0
T20s	175	146	59	3186	72*	36.62	134.60	0	11	76	0
Bowling	**Mat**	**Balls**	**Runs**	**Wkts**	**BBI**	**BBM**	**Ave**	**Econ**	**SR**	**5w**	**10**
ODIs	59	748	719	14	3/19	3/19	51.35	5.76	53.4	0	0
T20Is	38	30	27	3	2/15	2/15	9.00	5.40	10.0	0	0
First-class	114	2248	1199	32	3/48		37.46	3.20	70.2	0	0
List A	223	1901	1774	35	3/16	3/16	50.68	5.59	54.3	0	0
T20s	175	115	176	5	2/15	2/15	35.20	9.18	23.0	0	0

IAN BELL

RHB / RM / R5 / W0

FULL NAME: Ian Ronald Bell
BORN: April 11, 1982, Walsgrave, Coventry
SQUAD NO: 4
HEIGHT: 5ft 10in
NICKNAME: Belly
EDUCATION: Princethorpe College, Rugby
TEAMS: England, Warwickshire, Perth Scorchers
ROLE: Batsman
DEBUT: Test: 2004; ODI: 2004; T20I: 2006; First-class: 1999; List A: 1999; T20: 2003

BEST BATTING: 262* Warwickshire vs Sussex, Horsham, 2004
BEST BOWLING: 4-4 Warwickshire vs Middlesex, Lord's, 2004
COUNTY CAP: 2001; BENEFIT: 2011

BEST MOMENTS IN CRICKET? Winning the County Championship with Warwickshire and Ashes victories
CRICKETING HERO? Dominic Ostler
NON-CRICKETING HERO? Gordon Cowans
IF YOU WEREN'T A CRICKETER? I'd be sitting at the Holte End watching the Villa
SURPRISING FACT ABOUT YOU? I have an honorary doctorate at Coventry University
TWITTER: @Ian_Bell

Batting	Mat	Inns	NO	Runs	HS	Ave	SR	100	50	Ct	St
Tests	118	205	24	7727	235	42.69	49.46	22	46	100	0
ODIs	161	157	14	5416	141	37.87	77.16	4	35	54	0
T20Is	8	8	1	188	60*	26.85	115.33	0	1	4	0
First-class	307	516	55	20256	262*	43.93		57	103	233	0
List A	318	301	31	11130	158	41.22		13	79	109	0
T20s	104	100	12	2749	131	31.23	124.72	1	18	36	0
Bowling	**Mat**	**Balls**	**Runs**	**Wkts**	**BBI**	**BBM**	**Ave**	**Econ**	**SR**	**5w**	**10**
Tests	118	108	76	1	1/33	1/33	76.00	4.22	108.0	0	0
ODIs	161	88	88	6	3/9	3/9	14.66	6.00	14.6	0	0
T20Is	8	-	-	-	-	-	-	-	-	-	-
First-class	307	2875	1615	47	4/4		34.36	3.37	61.1	0	0
List A	318	1290	1138	33	5/41	5/41	34.48	5.29	39.0	1	0
T20s	104	132	186	3	1/12	1/12	62.00	8.45	44.0	0	0

SOL BELL RHB / LB / R0 / W0

FULL NAME: Solomon Jack Bell
BORN: February 27, 2001, Newcastle upon Tyne, Northumberland
SQUAD NO: 27
EDUCATION: Durham School
TEAMS: Durham
ROLE: Batsman
DEBUT: First-class: 2019

BEST BATTING: 1 Durham vs Glamorgan, Chester-le-Street, 2019

TWITTER: @SolBell01

NOTES: A homegrown middle-order batsman, Bell made his first-class debut in Durham's final County Championship match of last season and will hope for further opportunities this summer in what was a misfiring batting line-up last year. Bell played seven Second XI Championship matches in 2019, scoring 263 runs at 29.22 including three half-centuries. The 19-year-old made a brilliant hundred – 109 from 121 balls with 20 fours – to inspire the second team to chase down 282 on the final day of their three-day friendly match against Yorkshire Second XI at Scarborough in September. He was also a key component of the Durham side which reached the final of the Second XI Trophy, averaging 40.60 as they finished runners-up to Kent. Bell signed a youth contract with the county in November last year

Batting	Mat	Inns	NO	Runs	HS	Ave	SR	100	50	Ct	St
First-class	1	1	0	1	1	1.00	10.00	0	0	-	-
Bowling	**Mat**	**Balls**	**Runs**	**Wkts**	**BBI**	**BBM**	**Ave**	**Econ**	**SR**	**5w**	**10**
First-class	1	-	-	-	-	-	-	-	-	-	-

DANIEL BELL-DRUMMOND RHB / RM / R1 / W0 / MVP22

FULL NAME: Daniel James Bell-Drummond
BORN: August 4, 1993, Lewisham, London
SQUAD NO: 23
HEIGHT: 5ft 11in
NICKNAME: DBD, Deebz
EDUCATION: Millfield School, Somerset; Anglia Ruskin University
TEAMS: Kent, Auckland, England Lions, Rajshahi Kings
ROLE: Batsman
DEBUT: First-class: 2011; List A: 2011; T20: 2011

BEST BATTING: 206* Kent vs Loughborough MCCU, Canterbury, 2016
BEST BOWLING: 2-6 Kent vs Loughborough MCCU, Canterbury, 2019
COUNTY CAP: 2015

FAMILY TIES? My father got me into cricket. I've always really enjoyed spending time at my local club Catford Wanderers CC
CRICKETING HERO? Marcus Trescothick
NON-CRICKETING HERO? Thierry Henry
IF YOU WEREN'T A CRICKETER? I'd be a musician
TWITTER: @deebzz23
NOTES: A stylish strokeplayer, Bell-Drummond had been tipped to open the batting for England since he was a teenager but hasn't been able to establish the sort of four-day consistency to attract the national selectors. Last season marked a return to form for the 26-year-old, including a hundred against Warwickshire at Canterbury – his first in the Championship in more than three years. In all he scored 892 runs in 14 matches at a healthy average of 35.68. A key member of the Kent side in the short formats, Bell-Drummond also notched a century in the One-Day Cup last summer. In November 2018 he signed to play for the club until the end of the 2021 season

Batting	Mat	Inns	NO	Runs	HS	Ave	SR	100	50	Ct	St
First-class	112	192	16	5812	206*	33.02	49.86	10	30	44	0
List A	89	88	8	3381	171*	42.26	81.50	6	22	32	0
T20s	90	89	6	2469	112*	29.74	131.75	1	19	26	0
Bowling	**Mat**	**Balls**	**Runs**	**Wkts**	**BBI**	**BBM**	**Ave**	**Econ**	**SR**	**5w**	**10**
First-class	112	493	241	10	2/6	3/44	24.10	2.93	49.3	0	0
List A	89	155	121	5	2/22	2/22	24.20	4.68	31.0	0	0
T20s	90	105	179	5	2/19	2/19	35.80	10.22	21.0	0	0

GARETH BERG

RHB / RMF / R0 / W0

FULL NAME: Gareth Kyle Berg
BORN: January 18, 1981, Cape Town, South Africa
SQUAD NO: 13
HEIGHT: 6ft
NICKNAME: Iceman, Batman, Greb
EDUCATION: South African College School, Cape Town
TEAMS: Italy, Northamptonshire, Hampshire, Middlesex
ROLE: Allrounder
DEBUT: First-class: 2008; List A: 2008; T20: 2009

BEST BATTING: 130* Middlesex vs Leicestershire, Leicester, 2011
BEST BOWLING: 6-56 Hampshire vs Yorkshire, Southampton, 2016
COUNTY CAP: 2010 (Middlesex); 2016 (Hampshire)

WHAT WAS YOUR FIRST CRICKET CLUB? My first English club was Southgate CC, London
WHAT WERE YOU DOING WHEN ENGLAND WON THE WORLD CUP? I was paddle boarding
HOW WOULD YOU DISMISS STEVE SMITH? Tell him the first round is on me
WHAT EXCITES YOU ABOUT THE HUNDRED? I get into the starting XI for the 50-over competition
MOST INTERESTING TEAMMATE? Blessing Muzarabani – because I never see him
BIGGEST TOPIC OF DISCUSSION IN YOUR DRESSING ROOM? Standards of coffee
CRICKETING HERO? I've never had a hero
WHICH RULE WOULD YOU CHANGE ABOUT CRICKET? A longer tea break please
BIGGEST CRICKETING REGRET? Missing out on playing professional sport between the age of 20 to 27
CRICKET STAR OF THE FUTURE? Hudson de Lucchi (Norfolk Cricket Board)
IF YOU WERE AN ANIMAL, WHICH WOULD IT BE? A wolf – family is everything to me
TWITTER: @Bergy646

Batting	Mat	Inns	NO	Runs	HS	Ave	SR	100	50	Ct	St
First-class	131	197	23	4948	130*	28.43	64.41	2	27	65	0
List A	103	77	13	1474	75	23.03	93.05	0	7	39	0
T20s	89	68	22	1063	90	23.10	127.00	0	3	22	0
Bowling	**Mat**	**Balls**	**Runs**	**Wkts**	**BBI**	**BBM**	**Ave**	**Econ**	**SR**	**5w**	**10**
First-class	131	17150	8575	273	6/56	7/45	31.41	3.00	62.8	5	0
List A	103	3634	3184	97	5/26	5/26	32.82	5.25	37.4	1	0
T20s	89	1549	2067	70	4/20	4/20	29.52	8.00	22.1	0	0

DOM BESS

RHB / OB / R0 / W0

FULL NAME: Dominic Mark Bess
BORN: July 22, 1997, Exeter, Devon
SQUAD NO: 22
HEIGHT: 5ft 11in
NICKNAME: Calf, Bessy, Moonhead
EDUCATION: Blundell's School, Tiverton, Devon
TEAMS: England, Somerset, Yorkshire
ROLE: Bowler
DEBUT: Test: 2018; First-class: 2016; List A: 2018; T20: 2016

BEST BATTING: 107 MCC vs Essex, Barbados, 2018
BEST BOWLING: 7-117 Somerset vs Hampshire, Taunton, 2017

WHAT WAS YOUR FIRST CRICKET CLUB? Sidmouth CC, Devon. A beautiful coastal cricket club with a thatched roof
WHAT WERE YOU DOING WHEN ENGLAND WON THE WORLD CUP? Racing back to the hotel in Yorkshire with the lads after a very long day in the field
HOW WOULD YOU DISMISS STEVE SMITH? Bring Jack Leach on to bowl – but tell him to get his foot behind the line
MOST INTERESTING TEAMMATE? Eddie Byrom. That bole is on a different planet. Very funny to sit next to and watch the game
CRICKETING HERO? Graeme Swann
CRICKET STAR OF THE FUTURE? Kasey Aldridge – big fast bowler who can bat and field! Proper athlete
IF YOU WERE AN ANIMAL, WHICH WOULD IT BE? A Panda – just because they like eating
TWITTER: @DomBess99

Batting	Mat	Inns	NO	Runs	HS	Ave	SR	100	50	Ct	St
Tests	4	6	0	112	57	18.66	47.86	0	1	2	0
First-class	42	65	9	1279	107	22.83	52.87	1	6	21	0
List A	15	12	1	100	24*	9.09	66.66	0	0	5	0
T20s	8	4	1	9	5*	3.00	75.00	0	0	0	0
Bowling	**Mat**	**Balls**	**Runs**	**Wkts**	**BBI**	**BBM**	**Ave**	**Econ**	**SR**	**5w**	**10**
Tests	4	868	327	11	5/51	6/87	29.72	2.26	78.9	1	0
First-class	42	7087	3488	121	7/117	10/162	28.82	2.95	58.5	9	1
List A	15	648	616	11	3/35	3/35	56.00	5.70	58.9	0	0
T20s	8	156	216	5	2/30	2/30	43.20	8.30	31.2	0	0

SAM BILLINGS RHB / WK / R0 / W0

FULL NAME: Samuel William Billings
BORN: June 15, 1991, Pembury, Kent
SQUAD NO: 7
HEIGHT: 6ft
NICKNAME: Bilbo, Skittles
EDUCATION: Haileybury & Imperial College, Herts; Loughborough University
TEAMS: England, Kent, Oval Invincibles, Chennai Super Kings, Delhi Daredevils, Islamabad United, Sydney Sixers
ROLE: Batsman/wicketkeeper
DEBUT: ODI: 2015; T20I: 2015; First-class: 2011; List A: 2011; T20: 2011

BEST BATTING: 171 Kent vs Gloucestershire, Bristol, 2016

COUNTY CAP: 2015

WHAT WAS YOUR FIRST CRICKET CLUB? Hartley Country Club, Dartford, Kent
WHAT WERE YOU DOING WHEN ENGLAND WON THE WORLD CUP? At the ground working for Sky because unfortunately I was injured
WHAT EXCITES YOU ABOUT THE HUNDRED? The standard of competition will be as good as anywhere in the world, and it's a great opportunity to grow the game on the back of a great year for English cricket
BIGGEST TOPIC OF DISCUSSION IN YOUR DRESSING ROOM? How does Darren Stevens keep going?
MOST INTERESTING TEAMMATE? Mohammad Nabi – amazing guy who had an incredible journey to become the best T20 allrounder in the world
CRICKETING HERO? Adam Gilchrist
TWITTER: @sambillings

Batting	Mat	Inns	NO	Runs	HS	Ave	SR	100	50	Ct	St
ODIs	15	12	0	271	62	22.58	90.93	0	2	13	0
T20Is	26	23	3	348	87	17.40	136.47	0	2	15	1
First-class	68	102	11	3158	171	34.70	60.25	6	14	165	11
List A	91	80	13	2708	175	40.41	105.41	6	18	82	8
T20s	169	158	24	3138	95*	23.41	130.36	0	18	96	14
Bowling	**Mat**	**Balls**	**Runs**	**Wkts**	**BBI**	**BBM**	**Ave**	**Econ**	**SR**	**5w**	**10**
ODIs	15	-	-	-	-	-	-	-	-	-	-
T20Is	26	-	-	-	-	-	-	-	-	-	-
First-class	68	1	4	0	-	-	-	24.00	-	0	0
List A	91	-	-	-	-	-	-	-	-	-	-
T20s	169	-	-	-	-	-	-	-	-	-	-

ALEX BLAKE

LHB / RM / R0 / W0

FULL NAME: Alexander James Blake
BORN: January 25, 1989, Farnborough, Kent
SQUAD NO: 10
HEIGHT: 6ft 2in
NICKNAME: Blakey, Butler, TS
EDUCATION: Hayes Secondary School, Kent; Leeds Metropolitan University
TEAMS: Kent, Oval Invincibles, England U19
ROLE: Batsman
DEBUT: First-class: 2008; List A: 2007; T20: 2010

BEST BATTING: 71* Kent vs Hampshire, Southampton, 2015 (T20)
BEST BOWLING: 1-17 Kent vs Gloucestershire, Canterbury, 2019 (T20)
COUNTY CAP: 2017

WHAT WAS YOUR FIRST CRICKET CLUB? Bromley Town CC, London
WHICH BOWLER WOULD YOU LEAST LIKE TO FACE? Jonny Darke
BEST INNINGS YOU'VE SEEN? Matt Coles's hundred in the 2015 50-over quarter-final against Surrey. He was switch-hitting sixes
CRICKETING HERO? Graham Thorpe
WHO WOULD YOU ASK TO BAT FOR YOUR LIFE? Steve Waugh
WHICH RULE WOULD YOU CHANGE ABOUT CRICKET? Double plays, like you have in baseball – if you catch a batsman you can also run out the non-striker in the same play
SURPRISING FACT ABOUT YOU? I can name every player's squad number in county cricket (give or take)
SURPRISING FACT ABOUT A TEAMMATE? Adam Riley is an avid trainspotter
FAVOURITE QUOTE OR SAYING? It's definitely Tottenham's year
TWITTER: @aj_blake10
NOTES: Blake signed a white-ball contract with Kent in January 2018 until the end of the 2022 season

Batting	Mat	Inns	NO	Runs	HS	Ave	SR	100	50	Ct	St
First-class	46	72	6	1511	105*	22.89	55.61	1	6	25	0
List A	106	88	18	2125	116	30.35	100.14	1	12	53	0
T20s	117	101	25	1601	71*	21.06	135.33	0	8	59	0
Bowling	**Mat**	**Balls**	**Runs**	**Wkts**	**BBI**	**BBM**	**Ave**	**Econ**	**SR**	**5w**	**10**
First-class	46	210	138	3	2/9	2/9	46.00	3.94	70.0	0	0
List A	106	204	223	4	2/13	2/13	55.75	6.55	51.0	0	0
T20s	117	30	29	1	1/17	1/17	29.00	5.80	30.0	0	0

JACK BLATHERWICK

RHB / RFM / R0 / W0

FULL NAME: Jack Morgan Blatherwick
BORN: June 4, 1998, Nottingham
SQUAD NO: 80
HEIGHT: 6ft 2in
NICKNAME: Blathers, The Milkman
EDUCATION: Holgate Academy, Hucknall; Central College, Nottingham
TEAMS: Nottinghamshire, England U19
ROLE: Bowler
DEBUT: First-class: 2019; List A: 2018

BEST BATTING: 4* Nottinghamshire vs Warwickshire, Trent Bridge, 2019
BEST BOWLING: 1-82 Nottinghamshire vs Surrey, The Oval, 2019

FAMILY TIES? My uncle is the former Nottingham Forest defender Steve Blatherwick
WHAT WAS YOUR FIRST CRICKET CLUB? Kimberley Institute CC, Nottingham. There's a very steep hill on the run-up at one end
WHAT WERE YOU DOING WHEN ENGLAND WON THE WORLD CUP? I was in a beer garden in Southbank, London
WHAT EXCITES YOU ABOUT THE HUNDRED? Seeing the best players in the world at Trent Bridge
BIGGEST TOPIC OF DISCUSSION IN YOUR DRESSING ROOM? Tom Moores's gear
BEST INNINGS YOU'VE SEEN? Jos Buttler's 150 from 77 balls in the ODI at Grenada earlier this year. Twelves sixes and a 360-degree wagon wheel
WHICH RULE WOULD YOU CHANGE ABOUT CRICKET? In T20 it should be a wide rather than a no-ball when it goes over the batsman's head
BIGGEST CRICKETING REGRET? Leaving it until I was 17 years old to really knuckle down with my game
CRICKET STAR OF THE FUTURE? Daniel Blatherwick (Nottinghamshire U17)
IF YOU WERE AN ANIMAL, WHICH WOULD IT BE? A squirrel – they like peanut butter, and I like how they go about life
TWITTER: @BlatherwickJM

Batting	Mat	Inns	NO	Runs	HS	Ave	SR	100	50	Ct	St
First-class	2	2	2	6	4*	-	50.00	0	0	0	0
List A	3	3	2	6	3*	6.00	28.57	0	0	1	0
Bowling	**Mat**	**Balls**	**Runs**	**Wkts**	**BBI**	**BBM**	**Ave**	**Econ**	**SR**	**5w**	**10**
First-class	2	208	192	2	1/82	1/82	96.00	5.53	104.0	0	0
List A	3	48	72	1	1/55	1/55	72.00	9.00	48.0	0	0

JOSH BOHANNON

RHB / RMF / R0 / W0

FULL NAME: Joshua James Bohannon
BORN: April 9, 1997, Bolton, Lancashire
SQUAD NO: 20
HEIGHT: 5ft 9in
NICKNAME: Bo'ey, Bosh
EDUCATION: Harper Green High School, Bolton
TEAMS: Lancashire
ROLE: Allrounder
DEBUT: First-class: 2018; List A: 2018; T20: 2018

BEST BATTING: 174 Lancashire vs Derbyshire, Old Trafford, 2019
BEST BOWLING: 3-46 Lancashire vs Hampshire, Southampton, 2018

WHAT WAS YOUR FIRST CRICKET CLUB? Farnworth CC, Greater Manchester
BEST ADVICE EVER RECEIVED? Train hard, play hard
BEST INNINGS YOU'VE SEEN? Alastair Cook's last Test innings
CRICKETING HERO? Joe Root
SURPRISING FACT ABOUT YOU? I played junior cricket alongside Haseeb Hameed at Farnworth Social Circle CC (Bolton League)
CRICKET STAR OF THE FUTURE? Bradley Barrow (Lancashire U11)
IF YOU WERE AN ANIMAL, WHICH WOULD IT BE? A giraffe – I've always wondered what it would be like to be over 6ft tall
TWITTER: @joshbo97

Batting	Mat	Inns	NO	Runs	HS	Ave	SR	100	50	Ct	St
First-class	16	21	4	727	174	42.76	50.52	1	4	6	0
List A	15	10	2	210	55*	26.25	93.75	0	1	3	0
T20s	14	7	3	67	23	16.75	101.51	0	0	5	0
Bowling	**Mat**	**Balls**	**Runs**	**Wkts**	**BBI**	**BBM**	**Ave**	**Econ**	**SR**	**5w**	**10**
First-class	16	820	468	10	3/46	4/82	46.80	3.42	82.0	0	0
List A	15	150	208	1	1/33	1/33	208.00	8.32	150.0	0	0
T20s	14	-	-	-	-	-	-	-	-	-	-

RAVI BOPARA

RHB / RM / R1 / W0 / MVP40

FULL NAME: Ravinder Singh Bopara
BORN: May 4, 1985, Forest Gate, London
SQUAD NO: 23
HEIGHT: 5ft 10in
NICKNAME: Puppy
EDUCATION: Brampton Manor, London
TEAMS: England, Sussex, Birmingham Phoenix, Auckland, Essex, Gloucestershire, Karachi Kings, Kings XI Punjab, Multan Sultans, Sunrisers Hyderabad, Sydney Sixers
ROLE: Allrounder
DEBUT: Test: 2007; ODI: 2007; T20I: 2008; First-class: 2002; List A: 2002; T20: 2003

BEST BATTING: 229 Essex vs Northamptonshire, Chelmsford, 2007
BEST BOWLING: 5-49 Essex vs Derbyshire, Chelmsford, 2016
COUNTY CAP: 2005 (Essex); BENEFIT: 2015 (Essex)

FAMILY TIES? My brother played Essex age-group cricket
BEST MOMENTS IN CRICKET? Scoring 201* against Leicestershire in a one-day match, playing in the IPL, scoring three centuries in a row for England, and winning trophies with Essex
CRICKETING HERO? Sachin Tendulkar
SURPRISING FACT? I have a fast-food business
TWITTER: @ravibopara

Batting	Mat	Inns	NO	Runs	HS	Ave	SR	100	50	Ct	St
Tests	13	19	1	575	143	31.94	52.89	3	0	6	0
ODIs	120	109	21	2695	101*	30.62	77.84	1	14	35	0
T20Is	38	35	10	711	65*	28.44	118.69	0	3	7	0
First-class	221	357	40	12821	229	40.44	51.54	31	55	118	0
List A	323	301	56	9845	201*	40.18		15	60	103	0
T20s	357	324	72	7113	105*	28.22	121.90	1	35	123	0
Bowling	**Mat**	**Balls**	**Runs**	**Wkts**	**BBI**	**BBM**	**Ave**	**Econ**	**SR**	**5w**	**10**
Tests	13	434	290	1	1/39	1/39	290.00	4.00	434.0	0	0
ODIs	120	1860	1523	40	4/38	4/38	38.07	4.91	46.5	0	0
T20Is	38	322	387	16	4/10	4/10	24.18	7.21	20.1	0	0
First-class	221	15462	9381	257	5/49		36.50	3.64	60.1	3	0
List A	323	8097	7197	248	5/63	5/63	29.02	5.33	32.6	1	0
T20s	357	4701	5875	234	6/16	6/16	25.10	7.49	20.0	1	0

SCOTT BORTHWICK

LHB / LB / R3 / W0

FULL NAME: Scott George Borthwick
BORN: April 19, 1990, Sunderland, County Durham
SQUAD NO: 6
HEIGHT: 5ft 10in
NICKNAME: Badger
EDUCATION: Farringdon Community Sports College, Sunderland
TEAMS: England, Surrey, Chilaw Marians, Durham, Wellington
ROLE: Allrounder
DEBUT: Test: 2014; ODI: 2011; T20I: 2011; First-class 2009; List A: 2009; T20: 2008

BEST BATTING: 216 Durham vs Middlesex, Chester-le-Street, 2014
BEST BOWLING: 6-70 Durham vs Surrey, The Oval, 2013
COUNTY CAP: 2018 (Surrey)

WHAT WAS YOUR FIRST CRICKET CLUB? Eppleton CC, Sunderland. Made my first-team debut aged 13 and I got a 44-ball duck (on a poor pitch)
BEST INNINGS YOU'VE SEEN? Kevin Pietersen's double ton at Adelaide in the 2010/11 Ashes
SURPRISING FACT ABOUT YOU? I know Only Fools and Horses word for word
WHICH BOOK MEANS MOST TO YOU? The Girl on the Train by Paula Hawkins. That was the first time I'd read the book before watching the film (the book is better)
TWITTER: @Borthwick16

Batting	Mat	Inns	NO	Runs	HS	Ave	SR	100	50	Ct	St
Tests	1	2	0	5	4	2.50	26.31	0	0	2	0
ODIs	2	2	0	18	15	9.00	112.50	0	0	0	0
T20Is	1	1	0	14	14	14.00	87.50	0	0	1	0
First-class	164	275	25	9096	216	36.38	53.19	19	48	216	0
List A	99	72	11	1350	87	22.13	78.67	0	7	32	0
T20s	91	49	18	548	62	17.67	95.47	0	1	42	0
Bowling	**Mat**	**Balls**	**Runs**	**Wkts**	**BBI**	**BBM**	**Ave**	**Econ**	**SR**	**5w**	**10**
Tests	1	78	82	4	3/33	4/82	20.50	6.30	19.5	0	0
ODIs	2	54	72	0	-	-	-	8.00	-	0	0
T20Is	1	24	15	1	1/15	1/15	15.00	3.75	24.0	0	0
First-class	164	11983	7940	206	6/70	8/84	38.54	3.97	58.1	3	0
List A	99	2750	2773	69	5/38	5/38	40.18	6.05	39.8	1	0
T20s	91	1106	1506	64	4/18	4/18	23.53	8.16	17.2	0	0

NAT BOWLEY

LHB / OB / R0 / W0

FULL NAME: Nathan John Bowley
BORN: August 3, 2001, Nottingham
SQUAD NO: TBC
HEIGHT: 6ft 3in
EDUCATION: Woodbrook Vale School, Loughborough; Loughborough College
TEAMS: Leicestershire
ROLE: Bowler

WHAT WAS YOUR FIRST CRICKET CLUB? Loughborough Outwoods CC, Leicestershire
WHAT WERE YOU DOING WHEN ENGLAND WON THE WORLD CUP? Jumping around at home
WHAT EXCITES YOU ABOUT THE HUNDRED? The first franchise competition in the UK – more fans for each team
MOST INTERESTING TEAMMATE? Hassan Azad – unbelievably clever
CRICKET STAR OF THE FUTURE? Aryan Patel (Leicestershire Academy)
IF YOU WERE AN ANIMAL, WHICH WOULD IT BE? A bird – to explore
TWITTER: @nat_bowley
NOTES: The 18-year-old off-spinner signed his first professional contract after impressing in the Second XI last season, playing a key role in the team's run to the Championship final against Hampshire. "I am absolutely buzzing," he said. "It is a club that I have been at since I was 13 and is a club really close to me – I'm really excited to be on board." Bowley, who is in his first year of studies at Loughborough University, was also a member of the U17 side that won back-to-back 50-over titles last summer. Leicestershire head coach Paul Nixon said: "Nat has got a great attitude and has been around professional environments for a few years now with his father who works at Leicester City Football Club. He is a wonderful young man with a quality attitude and high skill levels with the ball. It is clear that he has been working hard and making great progress with his batting as well

JAMES BRACEY LHB / WK / R0 / W0 / MVP54

FULL NAME: James Robert Bracey
BORN: May 3, 1997, Bristol
SQUAD NO: 25
HEIGHT: 6ft 1in
NICKNAME: Bob, Brace, Wock
EDUCATION: The Ridings High School, Bristol; SGS Filton College; Loughborough University
TEAMS: Gloucestershire, England Lions
ROLE: Batsman/wicketkeeper
DEBUT: First-class: 2016; List A: 2019; T20: 2019

BEST BATTING: 156 Gloucestershire vs Glamorgan, Cardiff, 2017

COUNTY CAP: 2016

FAMILY TIES? My older brother Sam has played first-class cricket for Cardiff MCCU
WHAT WAS YOUR FIRST CRICKET CLUB? Winterbourne CC, Bristol
WHAT WERE YOU DOING WHEN ENGLAND WON THE WORLD CUP? I was in the England Lions changing room at Canterbury
HOW WOULD YOU DISMISS STEVE SMITH? Medium pace, round and through, sunnies on, three catching midwickets
MOST INTERESTING TEAMMATE? Benny Howell – he's always coming up with new theories
CRICKETING HERO? Alastair Cook
SURPRISING FACT ABOUT YOU? I was probably the only child ever who did not like Ketchup or baked beans
CRICKET STAR OF THE FUTURE? Will Naish (Gloucestershire Academy)
IF YOU WERE AN ANIMAL, WHICH WOULD IT BE? A badger
TWITTER: @bobbybracey114

Batting	Mat	Inns	NO	Runs	HS	Ave	SR	100	50	Ct	St
First-class	38	65	6	2092	156	35.45	47.03	5	8	49	0
List A	9	9	1	487	113*	60.87	108.94	1	4	5	0
T20s	13	12	0	245	64	20.41	118.35	0	1	7	3
Bowling	**Mat**	**Balls**	**Runs**	**Wkts**	**BBI**	**BBM**	**Ave**	**Econ**	**SR**	**5w**	**10**
First-class	38	60	35	0	-	-	-	3.50	-	0	0
List A	9	18	23	1	1/23	1/23	23.00	7.66	18.0	0	0
T20s	13	-	-	-	-	-	-	-	-	-	-

TIM BRESNAN

RHB / RFM / R0 / W0

YORKSHIRE

FULL NAME: Timothy Thomas Bresnan
BORN: February 28, 1985, Pontefract, Yorkshire
SQUAD NO: 16
HEIGHT: 6ft
NICKNAME: Brez, Brezzylad
EDUCATION: Castleford High School, West Yorkshire; New College Pontefract
TEAMS: England, Yorkshire, Hobart Hurricanes, Perth Scorchers, Sylhet Sixers
ROLE: Allrounder
DEBUT: Test: 2009; ODI: 2006; T20I: 2006; First-class: 2003; List A: 2001; T20: 2003

BEST BATTING: 169* Yorkshire vs Durham, Chester-le-Street, 2015
BEST BOWLING: 5-28 Yorkshire vs Hampshire, Headingley, 2018
COUNTY CAP: 2006; BENEFIT: 2014

WHAT WAS YOUR FIRST CRICKET CLUB? Townville CC, Castleford, West Yorkshire
WHAT WERE YOU DOING WHEN ENGLAND WON THE WORLD CUP? Sat on the sofa at home with a beer
MOST INTERESTING TEAMMATE? Andrew Hodd – cliché king, sarcastic optimist. Very very dry, funny man
SURPRISING FACT ABOUT YOU? I'm a qualified scuba-diver
CRICKET STAR OF THE FUTURE? Don't want to jinx anybody. My record of choosing future stars over the last 20 years has been dreadful
IF YOU WERE AN ANIMAL, WHICH WOULD IT BE? A dolphin – play in the surf all day
TWITTER: @timbresnan

Batting	Mat	Inns	NO	Runs	HS	Ave	SR	100	50	Ct	St
Tests	23	26	4	575	91	26.13	39.43	0	3	8	0
ODIs	85	64	20	871	80	19.79	90.25	0	1	20	0
T20Is	34	22	9	216	47*	16.61	127.05	0	0	10	0
First-class	198	272	41	6599	169*	28.56	47.20	6	34	102	0
List A	279	203	54	3221	95*	21.61	91.11	0	10	73	0
T20s	173	127	51	1593	51	20.96	132.41	0	1	58	0
Bowling	**Mat**	**Balls**	**Runs**	**Wkts**	**BBI**	**BBM**	**Ave**	**Econ**	**SR**	**5w**	**10**
Tests	23	4674	2357	72	5/48	8/141	32.73	3.02	64.9	1	0
ODIs	85	4221	3813	109	5/48	5/48	34.98	5.42	38.7	1	0
T20Is	34	663	887	24	3/10	3/10	36.95	8.02	27.6	0	0
First-class	198	32848	17092	552	5/28		30.96	3.12	59.5	9	0
List A	279	12338	10794	315	5/48	5/48	34.26	5.24	39.1	1	0
T20s	173	3272	4422	168	6/19	6/19	26.32	8.10	19.4	1	0

DANNY BRIGGS

RHB / SLA / R0 / W0

FULL NAME: Danny Richard Briggs
BORN: April 30, 1991, Newport, Isle of Wight
SQUAD NO: 21
HEIGHT: 6ft 2in
NICKNAME: Briggsy
EDUCATION: Carisbrooke High School, Isle of Wight
TEAMS: England, Sussex, Welsh Fire, Hampshire
ROLE: Bowler
DEBUT: ODI: 2012; T20I: 2012; First-class: 2009; List A: 2009; T20: 2010

BEST BATTING: 120* Sussex vs South Africa A, Arundel, 2017
BEST BOWLING: 6-45 England Lions vs Windward Islands, Roseau, 2011
COUNTY CAP: 2012 (Hampshire)

WHAT WAS YOUR FIRST CRICKET CLUB? Ventnor CC, Isle of Wight. Gets more sun than anywhere else in the UK
BIGGEST TOPIC OF DISCUSSION IN YOUR DRESSING ROOM? Fantasy Football
MOST INTERESTING TEAMMATE? Neil McKenzie – great stories
BEST INNINGS YOU'VE SEEN? AB de Villiers's record 31-ball hundred in the 2015 ODI against West Indies in Johannesburg
CRICKETING HERO? Daniel Vettori
TWITTER: @DannyBriggs19

Batting	Mat	Inns	NO	Runs	HS	Ave	SR	100	50	Ct	St
ODIs	1	-	-	-	-	-	-	-	-	0	0
T20Is	7	1	1	0	0*	-	-	0	0	1	0
First-class	108	138	38	1769	120*	17.69		1	1	38	0
List A	107	56	24	402	37*	12.56	93.27	0	0	34	0
T20s	158	33	23	97	13	9.70	101.04	0	0	26	0
Bowling	**Mat**	**Balls**	**Runs**	**Wkts**	**BBI**	**BBM**	**Ave**	**Econ**	**SR**	**5w**	**10**
ODIs	1	60	39	2	2/39	2/39	19.50	3.90	30.0	0	0
T20Is	7	108	199	5	2/25	2/25	39.80	11.05	21.6	0	0
First-class	108	18642	9390	270	6/45	9/96	34.77	3.02	69.0	8	0
List A	107	4916	4188	112	4/32	4/32	37.39	5.11	43.8	0	0
T20s	158	3175	3842	174	5/19	5/19	22.08	7.26	18.2	1	0

STUART BROAD LHB / RFM / R0 / W0

NOTTINGHAMSHIRE

FULL NAME: Stuart Christopher John Broad
BORN: June 24, 1986, Nottingham
SQUAD NO: 8
HEIGHT: 6ft 5in
NICKNAME: Broady
EDUCATION: Oakham School, Rutland
TEAMS: England, Nottinghamshire, Hobart Hurricanes, Kings XI Punjab, Leicestershire
ROLE: Bowler
DEBUT: Test: 2007; ODI: 2006; T20I: 2006; First-class: 2005; List A: 2005; T20: 2006

BEST BATTING: 169 England vs Pakistan, Lord's, 2010
BEST BOWLING: 8-15 England vs Australia, Trent Bridge, 2015
COUNTY CAP: 2007 (Leicestershire); 2008 (Notts); BENEFIT: 2019 (Notts)

FAMILY TIES? My father Chris played for England, Nottinghamshire and Gloucestershire and is now an ICC match official
CRICKETING HERO? Shaun Pollock
SURPRISING FACT? I often dream in French
TWITTER: @StuartBroad8
NOTES: The 33-year-old signed a new two-year contract with Notts in February. "Every time I step out at Trent Bridge, it feels just as special as the first time I walked onto the turf at three or four years old," he said. "I love Nottingham being my home, I love playing for the club, and I certainly can't envisage myself playing for any other county"

Batting	Mat	Inns	NO	Runs	HS	Ave	SR	100	50	Ct	St
Tests	138	203	31	3211	169	18.66	64.72	1	12	46	0
ODIs	121	68	25	529	45*	12.30	74.61	0	0	27	0
T20Is	56	26	10	118	18*	7.37	100.00	0	0	21	0
First-class	223	315	51	5181	169	19.62	62.74	1	24	82	0
List A	151	80	28	620	45*	11.92	75.88	0	0	32	0
T20s	85	32	12	152	18*	7.60	102.01	0	0	26	0
Bowling	**Mat**	**Balls**	**Runs**	**Wkts**	**BBI**	**BBM**	**Ave**	**Econ**	**SR**	**5w**	**10**
Tests	138	28079	13827	485	8/15	11/121	28.50	2.95	57.8	17	2
ODIs	121	6109	5364	178	5/23	5/23	30.13	5.26	34.3	1	0
T20Is	56	1173	1491	65	4/24	4/24	22.93	7.62	18.0	0	0
First-class	223	42106	21415	779	8/15		27.49	3.05	54.0	29	3
List A	151	7496	6591	216	5/23	5/23	30.51	5.27	34.7	1	0
T20s	85	1788	2144	100	4/24	4/24	21.44	7.19	17.8	0	0

HARRY BROOK

RHB / RMF / R0 / W0

FULL NAME: Harry Cherrington Brook
BORN: February 22, 1999, Keighley, Yorkshire
SQUAD NO: 88
HEIGHT: 6ft
EDUCATION: Sedbergh School, Cumbria
TEAMS: Yorkshire, England U19
ROLE: Batsman
DEBUT: First-class: 2016; List A: 2017; T20: 2018

BEST BATTING: 124 Yorkshire vs Essex, Chelmsford, 2018
BEST BOWLING: 1-54 Yorkshire vs Somerset, Scarborough, 2017

BEST ADVICE EVER RECEIVED? What will be will be
BEST MOMENT IN CRICKET? My first-class debut for Yorkshire against Pakistan A at Headingley in 2016
SURPRISING FACT ABOUT YOU? I love Tinder
CRICKETING HERO? Jacques Kallis
NON-CRICKETING HERO? Tommy Shelby (Peaky Blinders)
TWITTER: @harry_brook88

Batting	Mat	Inns	NO	Runs	HS	Ave	SR	100	50	Ct	St
First-class	28	47	0	1027	124	21.85	59.32	2	3	15	0
List A	15	12	1	343	103	31.18	99.42	1	1	4	0
T20s	16	16	3	325	44	25.00	141.92	0	0	7	0
Bowling	**Mat**	**Balls**	**Runs**	**Wkts**	**BBI**	**BBM**	**Ave**	**Econ**	**SR**	**5w**	**10**
First-class	28	247	132	1	1/54	1/65	132.00	3.20	247.0	0	0
List A	15	18	19	0	-	-	-	6.33	-	0	0
T20s	16	6	13	0	-	-	-	13.00	-	0	0

ETHAN BROOKES RHB / RMF / R0 / W0

WARWICKSHIRE

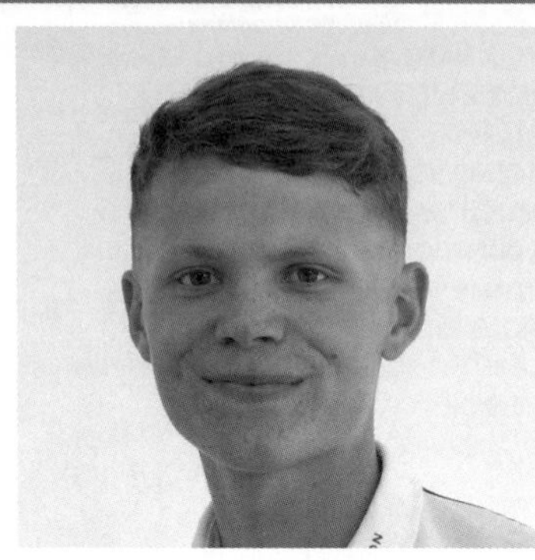

FULL NAME: Ethan Alexander Brookes
BORN: May 23, 2001, Solihull, Warwickshire
SQUAD NO: 77
HEIGHT: 6ft 1in
EDUCATION: Solihull School
TEAMS: Warwickshire
ROLE: Bowler
DEBUT: First-class: 2019

WHAT WAS YOUR FIRST CRICKET CLUB? Olton and West Warwicks CC, Solihull
HOW WOULD YOU DISMISS STEVE SMITH? Round the wicket, leg-stump yorker
WHAT EXCITES YOU ABOUT THE HUNDRED? Fewer teams, bigger names, different structure
BIGGEST TOPIC OF DISCUSSION IN YOUR DRESSING ROOM? Who is the worst at Spikeball (definitely Sam Hain)
MOST INTERESTING TEAMMATE? Rob Yates – known as 'The President' by all
CRICKET STAR OF THE FUTURE? Jacob Bethell (Warwickshire U17)
IF YOU WERE AN ANIMAL, WHICH WOULD IT BE? A golden eagle
TWITTER: @ethanbrookes2

NOTES: The 18-year-old seamer signed a two-year rookie contract with Warwickshire last August after a string of impressive performances for the club's Second XI and for Staffordshire in the Minor Counties Championship. Brookes is the younger brother of fellow seamer and Warwickshire teammate Henry, who has become a regular member of the first team over the last couple of seasons. Another older sibling – Ben Brookes – has also been on Warwickshire's books. Ethan made his first-class debut at the end of last summer in the Championship fixture against champions Essex at Edgbaston

Batting	Mat	Inns	NO	Runs	HS	Ave	SR	100	50	Ct	St
First-class	1	1	0	0	0	0.00	0.00	0	0	0	0
Bowling	**Mat**	**Balls**	**Runs**	**Wkts**	**BBI**	**BBM**	**Ave**	**Econ**	**SR**	**5w**	**10**
First-class	1	72	41	0	-	-	-	3.41	-	0	0

HENRY BROOKES RHB / RFM / R0 / W0 / MVP71

FULL NAME: Henry James Hamilton Brookes
BORN: August 21, 1999, Solihull, Warwickshire
SQUAD NO: 10
HEIGHT: 6ft 4in
NICKNAME: Brookesy
EDUCATION: Tudor Grange Academy, Solihull
TEAMS: Warwickshire, Birmingham Phoenix, England U19
ROLE: Bowler
DEBUT: First-class: 2017; List A: 2018; T20: 2018

BEST BATTING: 84 Warwickshire vs Kent, Edgbaston, 2019
BEST BOWLING: 4-54 Warwickshire vs Northamptonshire, Edgbaston, 2018

FAMILY TIES? My two brothers Ben and Ethan have both played age-group cricket for Warwickshire
WHAT WAS YOUR FIRST CRICKET CLUB? Olton CC, West Midlands
CRICKETING HERO? Ian Botham
BEST MOMENT IN CRICKET? My County Championship debut for Warwickshire in 2017
WHICH BOWLER WOULD YOU LEAST LIKE TO FACE? Brett Lee
WHO WOULD YOU ASK TO BAT FOR YOUR LIFE? Rahul Dravid
WHICH RULE WOULD YOU CHANGE ABOUT CRICKET? Allow free hits in all cricket
IF YOU WEREN'T A CRICKETER? I'd be an engineer
FAVOURITE QUOTE OR SAYING? If you don't back yourself then who is going to back you?
TWITTER: @BrookesHenry

Batting	Mat	Inns	NO	Runs	HS	Ave	SR	100	50	Ct	St
First-class	17	25	3	465	84	21.13	52.01	0	3	7	0
List A	12	5	2	13	12*	4.33	108.33	0	0	1	0
T20s	15	6	0	22	9	3.66	95.65	0	0	3	0
Bowling	**Mat**	**Balls**	**Runs**	**Wkts**	**BBI**	**BBM**	**Ave**	**Econ**	**SR**	**5w**	**10**
First-class	17	2811	1863	53	4/54	8/119	35.15	3.97	53.0	0	0
List A	12	551	601	17	3/50	3/50	35.35	6.54	32.4	0	0
T20s	15	340	491	20	3/26	3/26	24.55	8.66	17.0	0	0

JACK BROOKS RHB / RFM / R0 / W4

FULL NAME: Jack Alexander Brooks
BORN: June 4, 1984, Oxford
SQUAD NO: 70
HEIGHT: 6ft 2in
NICKNAME: Ferret, Headband Warrior
EDUCATION: Wheatley Park School, South Oxfordshire
TEAMS: Somerset, England Lions, Northamptonshire, Yorkshire
ROLE: Bowler
DEBUT: First-class: 2009; List A: 2009; T20: 2010

BEST BATTING: 109* Yorkshire vs Lancashire, Old Trafford, 2017
BEST BOWLING: 6-65 Yorkshire vs Middlesex, Lord's, 2016
COUNTY CAP: 2012 (Northamptonshire); 2013 (Yorkshire)

WHAT WAS YOUR FIRST CRICKET CLUB? Tiddington CC, Oxfordshire. AKA: Oxfordshire's Premier Nightspot
WHAT WERE YOU DOING WHEN ENGLAND WON THE WORLD CUP? Watching it in the Headingley dining room with some Yorkshire and Somerset players
HOW WOULD YOU DISMISS STEVE SMITH? Nick him off. Easy
BIGGEST TOPIC OF DISCUSSION IN YOUR DRESSING ROOM? Who has the bigger head: Dom Bess or Tom Banton
MOST INTERESTING TEAMMATE? Kane Williamson – sees and speaks about the game on a different level
CRICKETING HERO? Dennis Lillee
WHICH RULE WOULD YOU CHANGE ABOUT CRICKET? Make the tea break longer
SURPRISING FACT ABOUT YOU? I breed ferrets
WHICH BOOK MEANS MOST TO YOU? The dictionary
IF YOU WERE AN ANIMAL, WHICH WOULD IT BE? A ferret. I'm already halfway there
TWITTER: @brooksyferret

Batting	Mat	Inns	NO	Runs	HS	Ave	SR	100	50	Ct	St
First-class	128	158	56	1688	109*	16.54	57.06	1	4	31	0
List A	36	15	5	49	10	4.90	52.12	0	0	4	0
T20s	56	10	6	59	33*	14.75	134.09	0	0	16	0
Bowling	**Mat**	**Balls**	**Runs**	**Wkts**	**BBI**	**BBM**	**Ave**	**Econ**	**SR**	**5w**	**10**
First-class	128	21448	12631	462	6/65	9/84	27.33	3.53	46.4	20	0
List A	36	1584	1276	37	3/30	3/30	34.48	4.83	42.8	0	0
T20s	56	1029	1282	47	5/21	5/21	27.27	7.47	21.8	1	0

BEN BROWN

RHB / WK / R1 / W0 / MVP87

FULL NAME: Ben Christopher Brown
BORN: November 23, 1988, Crawley, Sussex
SQUAD NO: 26
HEIGHT: 5ft 8in
NICKNAME: Goblin, The Raisin
EDUCATION: Ardingly College, West Sussex; Manchester Metropolitan University
TEAMS: Sussex, England U19
ROLE: Wicketkeeper/batsman
DEBUT: First-class: 2007; List A: 2007; T20: 2008

BEST BATTING: 163 Sussex vs Durham, Hove, 2014
BEST BOWLING: 1-48 Sussex vs Essex, Colchester, 2016
COUNTY CAP: 2014

WHAT WAS YOUR FIRST CRICKET CLUB? Balcombe CC, West Sussex. My dad won the Sally Miller Trophy when he played for them and hasn't kept quiet about it ever since
WHAT WERE YOU DOING WHEN ENGLAND WON THE WORLD CUP? Watching at Old Trafford after we'd had a shocking day in the field. Really lifted us to see Jofra be a superstar and was amazing to watch with all the boys
HOW WOULD YOU DISMISS STEVE SMITH? Call Neil Wagner
BIGGEST TOPIC OF DISCUSSION IN YOUR DRESSING ROOM? Love Island
CRICKETING HERO? Adam Gilchrist
SURPRISING FACT ABOUT YOU? I don't like cheese
CRICKET STAR OF THE FUTURE? Murray Goodwin's son Jayden (Western Australia)
TWITTER: @Ben_brown26

Batting	Mat	Inns	NO	Runs	HS	Ave	SR	100	50	Ct	St
First-class	140	219	34	7403	163	40.01	62.11	18	40	397	17
List A	74	58	13	1102	73*	24.48	88.65	0	8	67	12
T20s	79	64	8	825	68	14.73	111.03	0	1	39	7
Bowling	**Mat**	**Balls**	**Runs**	**Wkts**	**BBI**	**BBM**	**Ave**	**Econ**	**SR**	**5w**	**10**
First-class	140	120	109	1	1/48	1/48	109.00	5.45	120.0	0	0
List A	74	-	-	-	-	-	-	-	-	-	-
T20s	79	-	-	-	-	-	-	-	-	-	-

CONNOR BROWN

RHB / OB / R0 / W0

FULL NAME: Connor Rhys Brown
BORN: April 28, 1997, Caerphilly, Wales
SQUAD NO: 28
HEIGHT: 6ft
NICKNAME: Browntown, Browny
EDUCATION: Y Pant Comprehensive School, Llantrisant; Cardiff Metropolitan University
TEAMS: Glamorgan
ROLE: Batsman
DEBUT: First-class: 2017; List A: 2018

BEST BATTING: 35 Glamorgan vs Gloucestershire, Cardiff, 2017

WHAT WAS YOUR FIRST CRICKET CLUB? Pentyrch CC, South Wales. My dad also played there for 10 years
HOW WOULD YOU DISMISS STEVE SMITH? I'd play his favourite music
BIGGEST TOPIC OF DISCUSSION IN YOUR DRESSING ROOM? Golf
MOST INTERESTING TEAMMATE? Colin Ingram – you learn a lot from his experience
CRICKETING HERO? Mitchell Starc
WHICH RULE WOULD YOU CHANGE ABOUT CRICKET? Free hits for a wide or a no-ball in every format
BIGGEST CRICKETING REGRET? Falling two runs short of my first List A hundred
CRICKET STAR OF THE FUTURE? Alex Horton (Glamorgan Academy)
IF YOU WERE AN ANIMAL, WHICH WOULD IT BE? A sloth
TWITTER: @connorbrown_97

Batting	Mat	Inns	NO	Runs	HS	Ave	SR	100	50	Ct	St
First-class	10	19	0	249	35	13.10	32.80	0	0	3	0
List A	3	3	0	163	98	54.33	63.67	0	1	1	0
Bowling	**Mat**	**Balls**	**Runs**	**Wkts**	**BBI**	**BBM**	**Ave**	**Econ**	**SR**	**5w**	**10**
First-class	10	24	14	0	-	-	-	3.50	-	0	0
List A	3	-	-	-	-	-	-	-	-	-	-

PAT BROWN

RHB / RFM / R0 / W0

FULL NAME: Patrick Rhys Brown
BORN: August 23, 1998, Peterborough, Cambridgeshire
SQUAD NO: 36
HEIGHT: 6ft 2in
NICKNAME: Brownfish
EDUCATION: Bourne Grammar School, Lincolnshire; University of Worcester
TEAMS: England, Worcestershire, Birmingham Phoenix
ROLE: Bowler
DEBUT: T20I: 2019; First-class: 2017; List A: 2018; T20: 2017

BEST BATTING: 5* Worcestershire vs Sussex, Worcester, 2017
BEST BOWLING: 2-15 Worcestershire vs Gloucestershire, Worcester, 2017

WHAT WAS YOUR FIRST CRICKET CLUB? Market Deeping CC, Lincolnshire
WHAT WERE YOU DOING WHEN ENGLAND WON THE WORLD CUP? Carrying the drinks at Durham
HOW WOULD YOU DISMISS STEVE SMITH? The knuckle ball
CRICKETING HERO? Brett Lee – he offers a fantastic technical framework for bowling fast
WHICH RULE WOULD YOU CHANGE ABOUT CRICKET? The lbw rule should be simpler. If it's hitting the stumps, it's out, right?
SURPRISING FACT ABOUT YOU? I'm not as grumpy as I seem when I am bowling
BIGGEST CRICKETING REGRET? Losing in the final over of the 2018 One-Day Cup semi-final when I was bowling
WHICH BOOK MEANS MOST TO YOU? My Story by Steven Gerrard
TWITTER: @patbrowny6

Batting	Mat	Inns	NO	Runs	HS	Ave	SR	100	50	Ct	St
T20Is	4	1	1	4	4*	-	44.44	0	0	2	0
First-class	5	6	4	14	5*	7.00	25.00	0	0	2	0
List A	10	2	1	3	3	3.00	42.85	0	0	3	0
T20s	40	8	5	8	4*	2.66	36.36	0	0	10	0
Bowling	**Mat**	**Balls**	**Runs**	**Wkts**	**BBI**	**BBM**	**Ave**	**Econ**	**SR**	**5w**	**10**
T20Is	4	78	128	3	1/29	1/29	42.66	9.84	26.0	0	0
First-class	5	376	266	7	2/15	3/70	38.00	4.24	53.7	0	0
List A	10	418	438	12	3/53	3/53	36.50	6.28	34.8	0	0
T20s	40	786	1090	52	4/21	4/21	20.96	8.32	15.1	0	0

NICK BROWNE

LHB / LB / R3 / W0

FULL NAME: Nicholas Laurence Joseph Browne
BORN: March 24, 1991, Leytonstone, Essex
SQUAD NO: 10
HEIGHT: 6ft 3in
NICKNAME: Brownie, Orse
EDUCATION: Trinity Catholic High School, London
TEAMS: Essex
ROLE: Batsman
DEBUT: First-class: 2013; List A: 2015; T20: 2015

BEST BATTING: 255 Essex vs Derbyshire, Chelmsford, 2016

COUNTY CAP: 2015

WHAT WAS YOUR FIRST CRICKET CLUB? South Woodford CC, London. My parents met each other for the first time at the club, and I was practically born into it. I'm lucky that I can play with my two brothers when I get the chance to play for the club
WHICH BOWLER WOULD YOU LEAST LIKE TO FACE? David Masters – I used to face him in the nets most days and he was an unbelievably skilful bowler who could seam the ball both ways and never missed his length
BEST INNINGS YOU'VE SEEN? Alastair Cook's in his final Test. The amount of people who wanted him to score a hundred was a testament to him as a person
YOUR BIGGEST CRICKETING REGRET? The quarter-final against Yorkshire at Chelmsford in the 2015 One-Day Cup. Chasing a low total, Tom Westley and I were flying before we both got out in quick succession. We lost by 20 runs
FAVOURITE QUOTE OR SAYING? Not all superheroes wear capes
TWITTER: @NickBrowne4

Batting	Mat	Inns	NO	Runs	HS	Ave	SR	100	50	Ct	St
First-class	91	149	10	5531	255	39.79	48.94	15	23	69	0
List A	21	18	0	557	99	30.94	89.83	0	3	7	0
T20s	14	12	2	165	38	16.50	114.58	0	0	6	0
Bowling	**Mat**	**Balls**	**Runs**	**Wkts**	**BBI**	**BBM**	**Ave**	**Econ**	**SR**	**5w**	**10**
First-class	91	268	175	0	-	-	-	3.91	-	0	0
List A	21	-	-	-	-	-	-	-	-	-	-
T20s	14	-	-	-	-	-	-	-	-	-	-

NATHAN BUCK RHB / RFM / R0 / W0

FULL NAME: Nathan Liam Buck
BORN: April 26, 1991, Leicester
SQUAD NO: 11
HEIGHT: 6ft 3in
NICKNAME: Bucky
EDUCATION: Ashby Grammar School, Ashby-de-la-Zouch
TEAMS: Northamptonshire, England Lions, Lancashire, Leicestershire
ROLE: Bowler
DEBUT: First-class: 2009; List A: 2009; T20: 2010

BEST BATTING: 53 Northamptonshire vs Glamorgan, Cardiff, 2019
BEST BOWLING: 6-34 Northamptonshire vs Durham, Chester-le-Street, 2017
COUNTY CAP: 2011 (Leicestershire)

WHAT WAS YOUR FIRST CRICKET CLUB? Grace Dieu Park CC, Leicestershire. I got hit into the forest on many occasions
WHAT WERE YOU DOING WHEN ENGLAND WON THE WORLD CUP? Crouched around an iPad with about six other teammates in the changing room during a four-day game against Derbyshire
HOW WOULD YOU DISMISS STEVE SMITH? Caught long-on… again
BIGGEST TOPIC OF DISCUSSION IN YOUR DRESSING ROOM? Horses and football
WHICH RULE WOULD YOU CHANGE ABOUT CRICKET? Bowlers should be allowed more than two bouncers per over
SURPRISING FACT ABOUT YOU? I got seven A stars and three As in my GCSEs
BIGGEST CRICKETING REGRET? Not getting 'off 'em' on debut
CRICKET STAR OF THE FUTURE? Liam Kinch
WHICH BOOK MEANS MOST TO YOU? Of Mice and Men by John Steinbeck (the only book I've read as it was compulsory for my GCSEs)
TWITTER: @nathanbuck17

Batting	Mat	Inns	NO	Runs	HS	Ave	SR	100	50	Ct	St
First-class	94	131	36	1345	53	14.15		0	3	17	0
List A	61	29	11	141	21	7.83	72.30	0	0	13	0
T20s	53	14	8	42	11*	7.00	80.76	0	0	10	0
Bowling	**Mat**	**Balls**	**Runs**	**Wkts**	**BBI**	**BBM**	**Ave**	**Econ**	**SR**	**5w**	**10**
First-class	94	14256	8526	250	6/34	8/107	34.10	3.58	57.0	8	0
List A	61	2527	2632	69	4/39	4/39	38.14	6.24	36.6	0	0
T20s	53	1069	1558	61	4/26	4/26	25.54	8.74	17.5	0	0

SOL BUDINGER

LHB / OB / WK / R0 / W0

FULL NAME: Soloman George Budinger
BORN: August 21, 1999, Colchester, Essex
SQUAD NO: 96
HEIGHT: 6ft
NICKNAME: Lord
EDUCATION: The Southport School, Queensland, Australia
TEAMS: Nottinghamshire
ROLE: Batsman

WHAT WAS YOUR FIRST CRICKET CLUB? Coomera Hope Island CC, Queensland, Australia
BIGGEST TOPIC OF DISCUSSION IN YOUR DRESSING ROOM? Politics
CRICKET STAR OF THE FUTURE? Jordan Cook (Nottinghamshire Academy)
TWITTER: @lordbudinger

NOTES: The 20-year-old left-hander has signed his first contract with Notts to run until the end of the 2021 season. Born in Colchester, Budinger moved to Australia aged six and made his debut for Queensland U19 in 2016. He had a spell with Sussex Second XI before deciding to move back permanently to the UK in 2018. After impressing at Nottinghamshire Premier League side Farnsfield, Budinger was recommended to Notts and joined the club's Academy. He has scored more than 1,000 runs for the Second XI over the past two seasons, earning a reputation for his aggressive batting. "I have watched games at Trent Bridge on TV but before joining the club I had never been here so I was a bit speechless when I first arrived," he said. "I like to put pressure on the bowler when I am batting and now we've got a good competitive rivalry amongst the young players to get the best out of ourselves." Director of cricket Mick Newell added: "He brings a real energy to the game when he's in the side and hopefully he can start pushing for places across all three formats"

KIERAN BULL

RHB / OB / R0 / W0

FULL NAME: Kieran Andrew Bull
BORN: April 5, 1995, Haverfordwest, Pembrokeshire, Wales
SQUAD NO: 11
HEIGHT: 6ft 1in
NICKNAME: Bully, Bulldog
EDUCATION: Queen Elizabeth High School, Haverfordwest; Cardiff Metropolitan University
TEAMS: Glamorgan
ROLE: Bowler
DEBUT: First-class: 2014; List A: 2015

BEST BATTING: 31 Glamorgan vs Gloucestershire, Swansea, 2015
BEST BOWLING: 4-62 Glamorgan vs Kent, Canterbury, 2014

WHAT WAS YOUR FIRST CRICKET CLUB? Carmarthen Wanderers CC, South Wales
BIGGEST TOPIC OF DISCUSSION IN YOUR DRESSING ROOM? FIFA on the PlayStation
MOST INTERESTING TEAMMATE? Ruaidhri Smith – he comes out with some questionable statements
CRICKETING HERO? Darren Gough
SURPRISING FACT ABOUT YOU? I set off an alarm every time I walk into a shop due to the metal screw in my back. I represented Spain at tennis at age-group level and was a ball boy for Rafael Nadal
CRICKET STAR OF THE FUTURE? Joe Cooke (Glamorgan)
IF YOU WERE AN ANIMAL, WHICH WOULD IT BE? A giraffe – so that I wouldn't have to strain my neck to speak to Jack Murphy
TWITTER: @Kieran_Bull89

Batting	Mat	Inns	NO	Runs	HS	Ave	SR	100	50	Ct	St
First-class	12	20	6	152	31	10.85	20.05	0	0	4	0
List A	2	-	-	-	-	-	-	-	-	0	0
Bowling	**Mat**	**Balls**	**Runs**	**Wkts**	**BBI**	**BBM**	**Ave**	**Econ**	**SR**	**5w**	**10**
First-class	12	1474	861	22	4/62	4/62	39.13	3.50	67.0	0	0
List A	2	52	48	1	1/40	1/40	48.00	5.53	52.0	0	0

MICHAEL BURGESS

RHB / WK / R0 / W0

WARWICKSHIRE

FULL NAME: Michael Gregory Kerran Burgess
BORN: July 8, 1994, Epsom
SQUAD NO: 61
HEIGHT: 6ft 1in
NICKNAME: Burge
EDUCATION: Cranleigh School, Surrey; Loughborough University
TEAMS: Warwickshire, Leicestershire, Sussex
ROLE: Wicketkeeper
DEBUT: First-class: 2014; List A: 2015; T20: 2016

BEST BATTING: 146 Sussex vs Nottinghamshire, Hove, 2017

WHAT WAS YOUR FIRST CRICKET CLUB? Reigate Priory CC, Surrey
FAVOURITE CRICKET BAT? My Puma Ballistic – that was my garden cricket bat as a kid
WHICH BOWLER WOULD YOU LEAST LIKE TO FACE? Rashid Khan
BEST INNINGS YOU'VE SEEN? Brendon McCullum's last Test innings when he scored the fastest-ever Test hundred (54 balls), against Australia at Christchurch in 2016
WHICH RULE WOULD YOU CHANGE ABOUT CRICKET? Seven runs should be awarded if you hit it out the ground
YOUR BIGGEST CRICKETING REGRET? Not learning to bowl mystery spin
WHAT WILL YOU BE DOING IN THE YEAR 2040? I'll be suited-up in London
FAVOURITE QUOTE OR SAYING? Hey, there are skittles in there! (The Hangover)
ODDEST SPORT YOU'VE PLAYED? Eton Fives
TWITTER: @mgkburgess

Batting	Mat	Inns	NO	Runs	HS	Ave	SR	100	50	Ct	St
First-class	33	47	4	1688	146	39.25	69.72	2	10	32	0
List A	19	17	0	363	58	21.35	99.45	0	2	10	1
T20s	30	24	5	320	56	16.84	118.95	0	1	12	6
Bowling	**Mat**	**Balls**	**Runs**	**Wkts**	**BBI**	**BBM**	**Ave**	**Econ**	**SR**	**5w**	**10**
First-class	33	36	14	0	-	-	-	2.33	-	0	0
List A	19	-	-	-	-	-	-	-	-	-	-
T20s	30	-	-	-	-	-	-	-	-	-	-

JACK BURNHAM RHB / RM / R0 / W0

FULL NAME: Jack Tony Arthur Burnham
BORN: January 18, 1997, Durham
SQUAD NO: 8
HEIGHT: 6ft 2in
NICKNAME: Burny
EDUCATION: Deerness Valley Comprehensive School, Durham; The Durham Federation
TEAMS: Durham, England U19
ROLE: Batsman
DEBUT: First-class: 2015; List A: 2016; T20: 2016

BEST BATTING: 135 Durham vs Surrey, The Oval, 2016

WHAT WAS YOUR FIRST CRICKET CLUB? Esh Winning CC, County Durham. My mum and dad coached the U13 team for three years
WHAT WERE YOU DOING WHEN ENGLAND WON THE WORLD CUP? Watching it at home with my parents
HOW WOULD YOU DISMISS STEVE SMITH? Caught behind
WHAT EXCITES YOU ABOUT THE HUNDRED? Getting to watch Andre Russell bat
BIGGEST TOPIC OF DISCUSSION IN YOUR DRESSING ROOM? Cricket!
MOST INTERESTING TEAMMATE? Mark Wood – the team joker
CRICKETING HERO? Stephen Harmison
BIGGEST CRICKETING REGRET? Getting a one-year ban
CRICKET STAR OF THE FUTURE? Jonny Bushnell (Durham Academy)
IF YOU WERE AN ANIMAL, WHICH WOULD IT BE? A lion
TWITTER: @BurnhamMorton

Batting	Mat	Inns	NO	Runs	HS	Ave	SR	100	50	Ct	St
First-class	39	67	5	1616	135	26.06	48.09	1	10	13	0
List A	13	8	2	139	45	23.16	79.88	0	0	4	0
T20s	24	18	1	189	53*	11.11	90.43	0	1	10	0
Bowling	**Mat**	**Balls**	**Runs**	**Wkts**	**BBI**	**BBM**	**Ave**	**Econ**	**SR**	**5w**	**10**
First-class	39	61	17	0	-	-	-	1.67	-	0	0
List A	13	-	-	-	-	-	-	-	-	-	-
T20s	24	1	0	0	-	-	-	0.00	-	0	0

RORY BURNS LHB / RM / R6 / W0

FULL NAME: Rory Joseph Burns
BORN: August 26, 1990, Epsom, Surrey
SQUAD NO: 17
HEIGHT: 5ft 10in
NICKNAME: Fong, The Cat (goalkeeper), Niggle
EDUCATION: Whitgift School; City of London Freemen's; Cardiff Metropolitan University
TEAMS: England, Surrey, London Spirit
ROLE: Batsman
DEBUT: Test: 2018; First-class: 2011; List A: 2012; T20: 2012

BEST BATTING: 219* Surrey vs Hampshire, The Oval, 2017
BEST BOWLING: 1-18 Surrey vs Middlesex, Lord's, 2013
COUNTY CAP: 2014

WHAT WAS YOUR FIRST CRICKET CLUB? Banstead CC, Surrey
WHAT WERE YOU DOING WHEN ENGLAND WON THE WORLD CUP? Watching it at the pub at Trent Bridge after finishing a day's play in a Championship match
HOW WOULD YOU DISMISS STEVE SMITH? Caught at leg slip – see day four at The Oval in 2019
WHAT EXCITES YOU ABOUT THE HUNDRED? The possibility that it can capitalise on last summer's cricket and increase the popularity of the game
BIGGEST TOPIC OF DISCUSSION IN YOUR DRESSING ROOM? Current affairs
MOST INTERESTING TEAMMATE? Kumar Sangakkara – he has a wealth of knowledge and is happy to share it with anyone at any time
IF YOU WERE AN ANIMAL, WHICH WOULD IT BE? A leopard – majestic creature
TWITTER: @roryburns17

Batting	Mat	Inns	NO	Runs	HS	Ave	SR	100	50	Ct	St
Tests	15	29	0	979	133	33.75	45.17	2	6	12	0
First-class	132	231	14	9209	219*	42.43	48.95	18	50	114	0
List A	57	55	6	1722	95	35.14	84.78	0	12	29	0
T20s	41	36	5	499	50	16.09	122.60	0	1	13	1
Bowling	**Mat**	**Balls**	**Runs**	**Wkts**	**BBI**	**BBM**	**Ave**	**Econ**	**SR**	**5w**	**10**
Tests	15	-	-	-	-	-	-	-	-	-	-
First-class	132	186	127	2	1/18	1/18	63.50	4.09	93.0	0	0
List A	57	-	-	-	-	-	-	-	-	-	-
T20s	41	-	-	-	-	-	-	-	-	-	-

GEORGE BURROWS RHB / RMF / R0 / W0

FULL NAME: George Davidson Burrows
BORN: June 22, 1998, Wigan, Lancashire
SQUAD NO: 21
HEIGHT: 6ft 4in
EDUCATION: St John Rigby College, Wigan; Liverpool John Moores University
TEAMS: Lancashire
ROLE: Bowler

WHAT WAS YOUR FIRST CRICKET CLUB? Orrell Red Triangle CC, Wigan, Greater Manchester
BIGGEST TOPIC OF DISCUSSION IN YOUR DRESSING ROOM? Danny Lamb's hair
MOST INTERESTING TEAMMATE? James Faulkner
CRICKET STAR OF THE FUTURE? Tom Hartley (Lancashire)
NOTES: A right-arm seamer who studied Sociology at Liverpool John Moores University, Burrows was one of seven Lancashire youngsters handed new contracts towards the end of last season. "I know that this is a club that will give young, local players an opportunity, so hopefully consistent performances for the Second XI will push my case for first-team selection over the coming months," said Burrows. Paul Allott, Lancashire's director of cricket, added: "He has worked really hard on his game over the last few years and I am excited by the progression he continues to show." Burrows was a regular wicket-taker for Lancashire's Second XI last season, claiming 12 victims in the Second XI County Championship including a haul of 5-24 against Derbyshire at Belper. He also lined up alongside a rehabilitating James Anderson in a non-competitive second-team fixture against Leicestershire at Moor Park in Liverpool, comfortably outbowling England's leading Test wicket-taker with figures of 13-4-22-6

WILL BUTTLEMAN RHB / WK / R0 / W0

FULL NAME: William Edward Lewis Buttleman
BORN: April 20, 2000, Chelmsford
SQUAD NO: 9
HEIGHT: 6ft 1in
NICKNAME: Butterz
EDUCATION: Felsted School, Essex
TEAMS: Essex
ROLE: Wicketkeeper
DEBUT: First-class: 2019

BEST BATTING: 0 Essex vs Yorkshire, Headingley, 2019

WHAT WAS YOUR FIRST CRICKET CLUB? Cloghams CC, Essex
WHAT WERE YOU DOING WHEN ENGLAND WON THE WORLD CUP? I was there!
WHAT EXCITES YOU ABOUT THE HUNDRED? The crowds
BIGGEST TOPIC OF DISCUSSION IN YOUR DRESSING ROOM? Trainers
MOST INTERESTING TEAMMATE? Alastair Cook – because he is a Sir
CRICKET STAR OF THE FUTURE? Ishaan Chopra (Varun's son)
IF YOU WERE AN ANIMAL, WHICH WOULD IT BE? A monkey – they have the most fun
TWITTER: @Will_Buttleman
NOTES: The Brentwood CC wicketkeeper was thrust into action in the first Championship game of last summer as a substitute for the injured Adam Wheater. With three Essex keepers injured in June, he was called up for his full senior debut in the four-day match at Headingley – Alastair Cook gave him a lift to the ground. Buttleman signed a one-year contract last August, although first-team opportunities will be limited with Wheater and Michael Pepper ahead in the pecking order

Batting	Mat	Inns	NO	Runs	HS	Ave	SR	100	50	Ct	St
First-class	1	1	0	0	0	0.00	0.00	0	0	3	0
Bowling	**Mat**	**Balls**	**Runs**	**Wkts**	**BBI**	**BBM**	**Ave**	**Econ**	**SR**	**5w**	**10**
First-class	1	-	-	-	-	-	-	-	-	-	-

JOS BUTTLER RHB / WK / R0 / W0

FULL NAME: Joseph Charles Buttler
BORN: September 8, 1990, Taunton
SQUAD NO: 6
NICKNAME: Jose
EDUCATION: King's College, Taunton
TEAMS: England, Lancashire, Manchester Originals, Comilla Victorians, Melbourne Renegades, Mumbai Indians, Rajasthan Royals, Somerset, Sydney Thunder
ROLE: Batsman/wicketkeeper
DEBUT: Test: 2014; ODI: 2012; T20I: 2011; First-class: 2009; List A: 2009; T20: 2009

BEST BATTING: 144 Somerset vs Hampshire, Southampton, 2013

COUNTY CAP: 2013 (Somerset), 2018 (Lancashire)

TWITTER: @josbuttler
NOTES: One of English cricket's most ferocious hitters, Buttler's international duties have restricted him to just 16 Championship appearances since he left Somerset to join Lancashire in 2013. Called up for England's limited-overs squads in 2012, he made his Test debut two years later but has been in and out of the side ever since. Buttler looked to have finally nailed a spot when making his maiden Test hundred in 2018 but his form of late has slipped once more. However, there is no denying his extraordinary skills in the shorter forms, of which the best example was his 46-ball ODI hundred against Pakistan in Dubai in 2015 – the fastest by an England player. And, not forgetting, he is now a World Cup winner. Buttler has been retained by Rajasthan Royals for the 2020 IPL and will turn out for Manchester Originals in The Hundred this summer

Batting	Mat	Inns	NO	Runs	HS	Ave	SR	100	50	Ct	St
Tests	41	73	6	2127	106	31.74	57.84	1	15	88	0
ODIs	142	117	23	3843	150	40.88	119.83	9	20	171	31
T20Is	69	61	11	1334	73*	26.68	139.68	0	8	25	4
First-class	107	173	13	5122	144	32.01	59.32	6	30	209	2
List A	213	177	43	6009	150	44.84	120.22	11	36	223	36
T20s	252	231	41	5782	95*	30.43	144.73	0	40	137	27
Bowling	**Mat**	**Balls**	**Runs**	**Wkts**	**BBI**	**BBM**	**Ave**	**Econ**	**SR**	**5w**	**10**
Tests	41	-	-	-	-	-	-	-	-	-	-
ODIs	142	-	-	-	-	-	-	-	-	-	-
T20Is	69	-	-	-	-	-	-	-	-	-	-
First-class	107	12	11	0	-	-	-	5.50	-	0	0
List A	213	-	-	-	-	-	-	-	-	-	-
T20s	252	-	-	-	-	-	-	-	-	-	-

EDDIE BYROM

LHB / OB / R0 / W0

FULL NAME: Edward James Byrom
BORN: June 17, 1997, Harare, Zimbabwe
SQUAD NO: 97
HEIGHT: 6ft
NICKNAME: Muta
EDUCATION: King's College, Taunton
TEAMS: Somerset, Manchester Originals, Rising Stars
ROLE: Batsman
DEBUT: First-class: 2017; T20: 2019

BEST BATTING: 152 Rising Stars vs Tuskers, Kwekwe, 2017

WHAT WAS YOUR FIRST CRICKET CLUB? Taunton St Andrews CC, Somerset
BIGGEST TOPIC OF DISCUSSION IN YOUR DRESSING ROOM? Carl (this season's good-luck charm)
MOST INTERESTING TEAMMATE? Roelof van der Merwe – because of how loudly he snores
CRICKETING HERO? Brian Lara. Whenever West Indies were playing I would watch him bat and as soon as he got out I would change the channel
WHICH RULE WOULD YOU CHANGE ABOUT CRICKET? We should use the same type of ball all over the world
BIGGEST CRICKETING REGRET? Diving for a ball I was never going to get and dislocating my shoulder
WHICH BOOK MEANS MOST TO YOU? Crushing It! How Great Entrepreneurs Build Their Business and Influence – and How You Can, Too by Gary Vaynerchuk
IF YOU WERE AN ANIMAL, WHICH WOULD IT BE? A sloth
TWITTER: @EddieByrom

Batting	Mat	Inns	NO	Runs	HS	Ave	SR	100	50	Ct	St
First-class	21	40	2	1108	152	29.15	45.13	2	4	12	0
T20s	9	9	1	185	54*	23.12	196.80	0	1	2	0
Bowling	**Mat**	**Balls**	**Runs**	**Wkts**	**BBI**	**BBM**	**Ave**	**Econ**	**SR**	**5w**	**10**
First-class	21	60	39	0	-	-	-	3.90	-	0	0
T20s	9	-	-	-	-	-	-	-	-	-	-

HARRY CAME

RHB / OB / R0 / W0

FULL NAME: Harry Robert Charles Came
BORN: August 27, 1998, Hampshire
SQUAD NO: 4
HEIGHT: 5ft 8in
NICKNAME: Hazza, Camey, Cameo
EDUCATION: Bradfield College, Berkshire
TEAMS: Hampshire
ROLE: Batsman
DEBUT: First-class: 2019

BEST BATTING: 23* Hampshire vs Surrey, The Oval, 2019

WHAT WAS YOUR FIRST CRICKET CLUB? Odiham & Greywell CC, Hampshire
WHAT WERE YOU DOING WHEN ENGLAND WON THE WORLD CUP? Playing in the Cricketer Cup quarter-final
HOW WOULD YOU DISMISS STEVE SMITH? Mankad
BEST INNINGS YOU'VE SEEN? Kusal Perera's match-winning 153 not out for Sri Lanka against South Africa in the Test at Durban in 2019
BIGGEST TOPIC OF DISCUSSION IN YOUR DRESSING ROOM? Football
MOST INTERESTING TEAMMATE? James Fuller – an absolute space cadet
WHICH RULE WOULD YOU CHANGE ABOUT CRICKET? If you are trying to leave the ball and it hits you, 'dead ball' should be called
BIGGEST CRICKETING REGRET? Getting run out for 99 for the Hampshire Academy when I was 16 years old
CRICKET STAR OF THE FUTURE? Scott Currie (Hampshire Academy)
TWITTER: @HarryCame4
NOTES: The 21-year-old batsman turned down a contract at Kent to sign a two-year deal with Hampshire, his home county, in October 2018. Came has come through the age-group ranks at Hampshire and was a key member of the side which won the U17 County Championship in 2015. He made his first-class debut last season as a concussion substitute for Aneurin Donald, making a match-saving 23 not out at The Oval to defy a strong Surrey attack

Batting	Mat	Inns	NO	Runs	HS	Ave	SR	100	50	Ct	St
First-class	1	1	1	23	23*	-	25.84	0	0	0	0
Bowling	**Mat**	**Balls**	**Runs**	**Wkts**	**BBI**	**BBM**	**Ave**	**Econ**	**SR**	**5w**	**10**
First-class	1	-	-	-	-	-	-	-	-	-	-

JACK CAMPBELL

RHB / LMF / R0 / W0

FULL NAME: Jack Oliver Ian Campbell
BORN: November 11, 1999, Portsmouth
SQUAD NO: 21
HEIGHT: 6ft 7in
NICKNAME: JC, Jacko
EDUCATION: Churcher's College, Petersfield, Hampshire
TEAMS: Durham, England U19
ROLE: Bowler
DEBUT: First-class: 2019

BEST BATTING: 2 Durham MCCU vs Durham, Chester-le-Street, 2019
BEST BOWLING: 1-43 Durham vs Leicestershire, Leicester, 2019

WHAT WAS YOUR FIRST CRICKET CLUB? Steep CC, Hampshire
HOW WOULD YOU DISMISS STEVE SMITH? Use two sets of stumps
BIGGEST TOPIC OF DISCUSSION IN YOUR DRESSING ROOM? Golf
MOST INTERESTING TEAMMATE? James Tomlinson – possibly the funniest player I have ever played with
IF YOU WERE AN ANIMAL, WHICH WOULD IT BE? A giraffe – I have long limbs
TWITTER: @jack_campbell11
NOTES: The 6ft 7in left-arm seamer, who has played second-team cricket for Kent and Hampshire, signed his first professional contract in September 2018 after impressing in the Durham Second XI. Campbell made his England U19 debut in 2018, playing in the youth ODI against South Africa at Gosforth. He made his first-class debut at the beginning of last season and played his first Championship match in July at Leicester

Batting	Mat	Inns	NO	Runs	HS	Ave	SR	100	50	Ct	St
First-class	3	4	2	2	2	1.00	9.52	0	0	0	0
Bowling	**Mat**	**Balls**	**Runs**	**Wkts**	**BBI**	**BBM**	**Ave**	**Econ**	**SR**	**5w**	**10**
First-class	3	468	261	1	1/43	1/87	261.00	3.34	468.0	0	0

LUKAS CAREY

RHB / RFM / R0 / W0

FULL NAME: Lukas John Carey
BORN: July 17, 1997, Carmarthen, Wales
SQUAD NO: 17
EDUCATION: Pontarddulais Comprehensive School, Swansea; Gower College Swansea
TEAMS: Glamorgan
ROLE: Bowler
DEBUT: First-class: 2016; List A: 2017; T20: 2017

BEST BATTING: 62* Glamorgan vs Derbyshire, Swansea, 2019
BEST BOWLING: 4-54 Glamorgan vs Middlesex, Cardiff, 2019

TWITTER: @LukasCarey
NOTES: Hailing from Robert Croft's club Pontarddulais, Carey made a promising start to his Glamorgan career in August 2016, picking up seven wickets against Northants with his skiddy fast-medium seamers. He had a breakthrough season in 2017, taking 35 wickets at 30.03 in 10 Championship matches as well as making his maiden first-class half-century. Carey has featured regularly in all three formats over the last two seasons but hasn't been able to have the same impact. A graduate from Glamorgan's Academy, Carey is another in the ranks of talented local products looking to reinvigorate the Welsh club

Batting	Mat	Inns	NO	Runs	HS	Ave	SR	100	50	Ct	St
First-class	29	39	6	519	62*	15.72	76.54	0	3	4	0
List A	18	10	5	124	39	24.80	91.17	0	0	3	0
T20s	9	3	2	7	5	7.00	70.00	0	0	2	0
Bowling	**Mat**	**Balls**	**Runs**	**Wkts**	**BBI**	**BBM**	**Ave**	**Econ**	**SR**	**5w**	**10**
First-class	29	4672	2748	80	4/54	7/151	34.35	3.52	58.4	0	0
List A	18	814	755	12	2/57	2/57	62.91	5.56	67.8	0	0
T20s	9	138	209	4	1/15	1/15	52.25	9.08	34.5	0	0

KIRAN CARLSON

RHB / OB / R0 / W0

FULL NAME: Kiran Shah Carlson
BORN: May 16, 1998, Cardiff, Wales
SQUAD NO: 5
HEIGHT: 5ft 8in
NICKNAME: Dink, Tiki
EDUCATION: Whitchurch High School, Cardiff; Cardiff University
TEAMS: Glamorgan
ROLE: Batsman
DEBUT: First-class: 2016; List A: 2016; T20: 2017

BEST BATTING: 191 Glamorgan vs Gloucestershire, Cardiff, 2017
BEST BOWLING: 5-28 Glamorgan vs Northamptonshire, Northampton, 2016

WHAT WAS YOUR FIRST CRICKET CLUB? Cardiff CC
WHAT WERE YOU DOING WHEN ENGLAND WON THE WORLD CUP? Driving on the M4
HOW WOULD YOU DISMISS STEVE SMITH? Nick Selman from round the wicket with five men on the hook
MOST INTERESTING TEAMMATE? David Lloyd – he used to be part of the Nepalese government
CRICKETING HERO? Sachin Tendulkar
WHICH RULE WOULD YOU CHANGE ABOUT CRICKET? You should get 12 runs for hitting the ball out of the ground
SURPRISING FACT ABOUT YOU? I'm half-Indian
BIGGEST CRICKETING REGRET? Not being 6ft 5in and bowling 90mph
WHICH BOOK MEANS MOST TO YOU? Kama Sutra by Vatsyayana
IF YOU WERE AN ANIMAL, WHICH WOULD IT BE? A squirrel – small and annoying
TWITTER: @kiran_carlson

Batting	Mat	Inns	NO	Runs	HS	Ave	SR	100	50	Ct	St
First-class	30	52	2	1393	191	27.86	57.94	4	3	14	0
List A	17	16	1	341	63	22.73	96.87	0	2	4	0
T20s	17	14	1	316	58	24.30	139.20	0	1	8	0
Bowling	**Mat**	**Balls**	**Runs**	**Wkts**	**BBI**	**BBM**	**Ave**	**Econ**	**SR**	**5w**	**10**
First-class	30	438	293	6	5/28	5/78	48.83	4.01	73.0	1	0
List A	17	42	47	1	1/30	1/30	47.00	6.71	42.0	0	0
T20s	17	1	1	0	-	-	-	6.00	-	0	0

BRYDON CARSE RHB / RFM / R0 / W0 / MVP84

FULL NAME: Brydon Alexander Carse
BORN: July 31, 1995, Port Elizabeth, South Africa
SQUAD NO: 99
HEIGHT: 6ft 2in
NICKNAME: Cheesy, Carsie
EDUCATION: Pearson High School, Port Elizabeth
TEAMS: Durham, Northern Superchargers, Eastern Province, England Lions
ROLE: Bowler
DEBUT: First-class: 2016; List A: 2019; T20: 2014

BEST BATTING: 77* Durham vs Northamptonshire, Chester-le-Street, 2019
BEST BOWLING: 6-26 Durham vs Middlesex, Lord's, 2019

FAMILY TIES? My dad James played for Northants, Rhodesia, Eastern Province, Border and Western Province
WHAT WAS YOUR FIRST CRICKET CLUB? Union CC, South Africa. Best traditional song for newcomers: 'Buffalo Soldier'
BIGGEST TOPIC OF DISCUSSION IN YOUR DRESSING ROOM? You don't want to know...
MOST INTERESTING TEAMMATE? Cameron Bancroft – he's got some outrageous stories
WHICH BOOK MEANS MOST TO YOU? To the Point – The No-Holds-Barred Autobiography by Herschelle Gibbs
IF YOU WERE AN ANIMAL, WHICH WOULD IT BE? A kudu – it jumps high
TWITTER: @CarseBrydon

Batting	Mat	Inns	NO	Runs	HS	Ave	SR	100	50	Ct	St
First-class	22	27	8	543	77*	28.57	48.65	0	2	3	0
List A	7	1	0	2	2	2.00	28.57	0	0	2	0
T20s	13	8	1	47	14	6.71	120.51	0	0	6	0
Bowling	**Mat**	**Balls**	**Runs**	**Wkts**	**BBI**	**BBM**	**Ave**	**Econ**	**SR**	**5w**	**10**
First-class	22	2949	1845	58	6/26	7/63	31.81	3.75	50.8	3	0
List A	7	245	223	10	3/52	3/52	22.30	5.46	24.5	0	0
T20s	13	245	369	9	1/11	1/11	41.00	9.03	27.2	0	0

MATT CARTER RHB / OB / R0 / W0

FULL NAME: Matthew Carter
BORN: May 26, 1996, Lincoln
SQUAD NO: 20
HEIGHT: 6ft 6in
NICKNAME: Carts, Goober, Long Plod
EDUCATION: Branston Community Academy, Lincolnshire
TEAMS: Nottinghamshire, Trent Rockets, England Lions
ROLE: Bowler
DEBUT: First-class: 2015; List A: 2018; T20: 2018

BEST BATTING: 33 Nottinghamshire vs Sussex, Hove, 2017
BEST BOWLING: 7-56 Nottinghamshire vs Somerset, Taunton, 2015

FAMILY TIES? My dad and oldest brother played at village level. My brother Andrew played for Notts, Derby and Hampshire before retiring in 2016
WHAT WAS YOUR FIRST CRICKET CLUB? Market Rasen CC, Lincolnshire
WHAT WERE YOU DOING WHEN ENGLAND WON THE WORLD CUP? Standing on a table in the pavilion at Papplewick CC (Nottingham), trying to see the screen over everyone
WHAT EXCITES YOU ABOUT THE HUNDRED? Working with the analyst
CRICKETING HERO? Andrew Flintoff
SURPRISING FACT ABOUT YOU? Any chance I get, whether for an hour or a full day, it's spent with the dog in the middle of a field shooting. I've had a lot of swimming achievements but now I'm scared of swimming
CRICKET STAR OF THE FUTURE? Qundeel Haider (Nottinghamshire Academy)
IF YOU WERE AN ANIMAL, WHICH WOULD IT BE? A gnat – so that you can bite people who are horrible to you

Batting	Mat	Inns	NO	Runs	HS	Ave	SR	100	50	Ct	St
First-class	14	23	1	191	33	8.68	42.72	0	0	13	0
List A	16	10	1	65	21*	7.22	76.47	0	0	5	0
T20s	13	4	1	34	16*	11.33	136.00	0	0	5	0

Bowling	Mat	Balls	Runs	Wkts	BBI	BBM	Ave	Econ	SR	5w	10
First-class	14	2650	1726	39	7/56	10/195	44.25	3.90	67.9	2	1
List A	16	701	625	23	4/40	4/40	27.17	5.34	30.4	0	0
T20s	13	288	328	16	3/14	3/14	20.50	6.83	18.0	0	0

ZAK CHAPPELL

RHB / RFM / R0 / W0

FULL NAME: Zachariah John Chappell
BORN: August 21, 1996, Grantham, Lincolnshire
SQUAD NO: 32
HEIGHT: 6ft 5in
NICKNAME: Smasher, Chappy
EDUCATION: Stamford School, Lincolnshire
TEAMS: Nottinghamshire, England Lions, Gloucestershire, Leicestershire
ROLE: Bowler
DEBUT: First-class: 2015; List A: 2015; T20: 2015

BEST BATTING: 96 Leicestershire vs Derbyshire, Derby, 2015
BEST BOWLING: 6-44 Leicestershire vs Northamptonshire, Northampton, 2018

WHAT WAS YOUR FIRST CRICKET CLUB? Stamford Town CC, Lincolnshire
BEST ADVICE RECEIVED? Play across, be a boss
WHAT WERE YOU DOING WHEN ENGLAND WON THE WORLD CUP? I was watching in the Trent Bridge dressing room with all the boys
WHAT EXCITES YOU ABOUT THE HUNDRED? Quality players and a new format
BIGGEST TOPIC OF DISCUSSION IN YOUR DRESSING ROOM? Tom Moores's Instagram
CRICKETING HERO? Brett Lee
WHICH RULE WOULD YOU CHANGE ABOUT CRICKET? No cricket when it goes below 10 degrees
SURPRISING FACT ABOUT YOU? I can walk on my hands
TWITTER: @ZakkChappell

Batting	Mat	Inns	NO	Runs	HS	Ave	SR	100	50	Ct	St
First-class	19	30	5	597	96	23.88	57.45	0	2	2	0
List A	17	14	6	141	59*	17.62	64.38	0	1	2	0
T20s	15	10	2	67	16	8.37	131.37	0	0	6	0
Bowling	**Mat**	**Balls**	**Runs**	**Wkts**	**BBI**	**BBM**	**Ave**	**Econ**	**SR**	**5w**	**10**
First-class	19	2057	1369	38	6/44	6/53	36.02	3.99	54.1	1	0
List A	17	731	765	17	3/45	3/45	45.00	6.27	43.0	0	0
T20s	15	268	435	13	3/23	3/23	33.46	9.73	20.6	0	0

BEN CHARLESWORTH LHB / RMF / R0 / W0

FULL NAME: Ben Geoffrey Charlesworth
BORN: November 19, 2000, Oxford
SQUAD NO: 64
HEIGHT: 6ft 3in
NICKNAME: Charlie
EDUCATION: St Edward's School, Oxford
TEAMS: Gloucestershire, England U19
ROLE: Allrounder
DEBUT: First-class: 2018; List A: 2019

BEST BATTING: 77* Gloucestershire vs Middlesex, Bristol, 2018
BEST BOWLING: 3-25 Gloucestershire vs Middlesex, Bristol, 2018
COUNTY CAP: 2018

WHAT WAS YOUR FIRST CRICKET CLUB? Abingdon Vale CC, Oxfordshire. It was 10 minutes down the road from my house. I played and trained there from the age of five to 16
WHAT EXCITES YOU ABOUT THE HUNDRED? The crowds
BIGGEST TOPIC OF DISCUSSION IN YOUR DRESSING ROOM? Football
MOST INTERESTING TEAMMATE? Hamidullah Qadri (with England U19)
CRICKETING HERO? Kumar Sangakkara
WHICH RULE WOULD YOU CHANGE ABOUT CRICKET? Free hits in red-ball cricket to bring more excitement into the longer format – and to punish bowlers for no-balls
BIGGEST CRICKETING REGRET? Not speaking to Eoin Morgan in 2018 when I played against Middlesex. I could have learned a thing or two by having a chat with him
CRICKET STAR OF THE FUTURE? My brother Luke Charlesworth (Gloucestershire Second XI)
WHICH BOOK MEANS MOST TO YOU? Rafa – My Story by Rafael Nadal with John Carlin
IF YOU WERE AN ANIMAL, WHICH WOULD IT BE? A lion – I have South African genes
TWITTER: @Ben_1289

Batting	Mat	Inns	NO	Runs	HS	Ave	SR	100	50	Ct	St
First-class	11	16	2	339	77*	24.21	38.78	0	3	5	0
List A	1	1	0	14	14	14.00	63.63	0	0	0	0
Bowling	**Mat**	**Balls**	**Runs**	**Wkts**	**BBI**	**BBM**	**Ave**	**Econ**	**SR**	**5w**	**10**
First-class	11	235	131	7	3/25	3/25	18.71	3.34	33.5	0	0
List A	1	-	-	-	-	-	-	-	-	-	-

VARUN CHOPRA

RHB / LB / R3 / W0

FULL NAME: Varun Chopra
BORN: June 21, 1987, Barking, Essex
SQUAD NO: 6
HEIGHT: 6ft 1in
NICKNAME: Tiddles, Chops
EDUCATION: Ilford County High School
TEAMS: Essex, England Lions, Sussex, Tamil Union Cricket & Athletic Club, Warwickshire
ROLE: Batsman
DEBUT: First-class: 2006; List A: 2006; T20: 2006

BEST BATTING: 233* Tamil Union vs Sinhalese Sports Club, Colombo, 2012

COUNTY CAP: 2012 (Warwickshire); 2018 (Essex)

WHAT GOT YOU INTO CRICKET? Dad taking me to Joe Hussain's Ilford Cricket School
BEST ADVICE EVER RECEIVED? It's not how, it's how many
BEST MOMENT IN CRICKET? Winning the T20 competition in 2014 off the last ball in front of a packed house at Edgbaston
CRICKETING HERO? Sachin Tendulkar
IF YOU WEREN'T A CRICKETER? I'd be an architect
SURPRISING FACT ABOUT YOU? I love a chin-up
TWITTER: @vchops06

Batting	Mat	Inns	NO	Runs	HS	Ave	SR	100	50	Ct	St
First-class	190	313	20	10154	233*	34.65	50.83	20	50	224	0
List A	114	111	7	4789	160	46.04	77.01	12	28	41	0
T20s	109	106	12	2812	116	29.91	119.30	2	20	23	0
Bowling	**Mat**	**Balls**	**Runs**	**Wkts**	**BBI**	**BBM**	**Ave**	**Econ**	**SR**	**5w**	**10**
First-class	190	204	128	0	-	-	-	3.76	-	0	0
List A	114	18	18	0	-	-	-	6.00	-	0	0
T20s	109	-	-	-	-	-	-	-	-	-	-

DAN CHRISTIAN

RHB / RM / R0 / W0

FULL NAME: Daniel Trevor Christian
BORN: May 4, 1983, Sydney, Australia
SQUAD NO: 54
HEIGHT: 6ft
EDUCATION: St Gregory's College, Sydney
TEAMS: Australia, Notts, Manchester Originals, Brisbane Heat, Delhi Daredevils, Gloucestershire, Hants, Hobart Hurricanes, Melbourne Renegades, Middlesex, Rising Pune Supergiant, South Australia, Victoria
ROLE: Allrounder
DEBUT: ODI: 2012; T20I: 2010; First-class: 2008; List A: 2006; T20: 2006

BEST BATTING: 129 Middlesex vs Kent, Canterbury, 2014 (T20)
BEST BOWLING: 5-14 Hobart Hurricanes vs Adelaide Strikers, Hobart, 2017 (T20)
COUNTY CAP: 2013 (Gloucestershire); 2015 (Nottinghamshire)

WHAT WAS YOUR FIRST CRICKET CLUB? Narrandera CC, New South Wales, Australia
BEST INNINGS YOU'VE SEEN? Chris Gayle's 175 not out in the 2013 IPL (I was carrying the drinks for Bangalore). He took down the Pune Warriors with the cleanest hitting I have ever seen
WHO WOULD YOU ASK TO BAT FOR YOUR LIFE? Steve Waugh
WHICH RULE WOULD YOU CHANGE ABOUT CRICKET? Balls over head height to be no-balls in the T20 Blast
YOUR BIGGEST CRICKETING REGRET? Not nailing down a spot in the Australia team
TWITTER: @danchristian54

Batting	Mat	Inns	NO	Runs	HS	Ave	SR	100	50	Ct	St
ODIs	19	18	5	273	39	21.00	88.92	0	0	10	0
T20Is	16	7	3	27	9	6.75	96.42	0	0	5	0
First-class	83	141	17	3783	131*	30.50	53.77	5	16	90	0
List A	119	108	21	2844	117	32.68	101.64	2	14	43	0
T20s	315	271	70	4671	129	23.23	137.58	2	13	132	0
Bowling	**Mat**	**Balls**	**Runs**	**Wkts**	**BBI**	**BBM**	**Ave**	**Econ**	**SR**	**5w**	**10**
ODIs	19	727	595	20	5/31	5/31	29.75	4.91	36.3	1	0
T20Is	16	213	317	11	3/27	3/27	28.81	8.92	19.3	0	0
First-class	83	10301	5679	163	5/24	9/87	34.84	3.30	63.1	3	0
List A	119	3896	3585	107	6/48	6/48	33.50	5.52	36.4	3	0
T20s	315	4703	6588	231	5/14	5/14	28.51	8.40	20.3	2	0

GRAHAM CLARK

RHB / LB / R0 / W0

FULL NAME: Graham Clark
BORN: March 16, 1993, Whitehaven, Cumbria
SQUAD NO: 7
HEIGHT: 6ft 1in
NICKNAME: Sparky, Schnoz
EDUCATION: St Benedict's Catholic High School, Whitehaven
TEAMS: Durham
ROLE: Batsman
DEBUT: First-class: 2015; List A: 2015; T20: 2015

BEST BATTING: 109 Durham vs Glamorgan, Chester-le-Street, 2017
BEST BOWLING: 1-10 Durham vs Sussex, Arundel, 2018

FAMILY TIES? My older brother Jordan plays for Lancashire
WHAT WAS YOUR FIRST CRICKET CLUB? Cleator CC, Cumbria. They won the National Village Cup at Lord's in 2013 and my dad (Ian) was Man of the Match
HOW WOULD YOU DISMISS STEVE SMITH? Get the other 10 batsmen
BIGGEST TOPIC OF DISCUSSION IN YOUR DRESSING ROOM? You wouldn't want to know
MOST INTERESTING TEAMMATE? Alan Walker (Durham Second XI coach). Hearing about the work he did before he became a professional cricketer and then coach makes you realise how much easier our generation have had it
BIGGEST CRICKETING REGRET? Not believing in myself in my first years as a professional cricketer
IF YOU WERE AN ANIMAL, WHICH WOULD IT BE? The proboscis monkey. We have similar noses
TWITTER: @GrahamClark16

Batting	Mat	Inns	NO	Runs	HS	Ave	SR	100	50	Ct	St
First-class	34	63	1	1543	109	24.88	53.11	1	10	25	0
List A	32	32	1	665	114	21.45	81.19	1	2	11	0
T20s	48	48	4	1061	91*	24.11	137.08	0	7	23	0
Bowling	**Mat**	**Balls**	**Runs**	**Wkts**	**BBI**	**BBM**	**Ave**	**Econ**	**SR**	**5w**	**10**
First-class	34	95	58	2	1/10	1/10	29.00	3.66	47.5	0	0
List A	32	24	18	3	3/18	3/18	6.00	4.50	8.0	0	0
T20s	48	14	29	0	-	-	-	12.42	-	0	0

JORDAN CLARK RHB / RM / R0 / W0 / MVP91

FULL NAME: Jordan Clark
BORN: October 14, 1990, Whitehaven, Cumbria
SQUAD NO: 8
HEIGHT: 6ft 4in
NICKNAME: Clarky
EDUCATION: Sedbergh School, Cumbria
TEAMS: Surrey, Hobart Hurricanes, Lancashire
ROLE: Allounder
DEBUT: First-class: 2015; List A: 2010; T20: 2011

BEST BATTING: 140 Lancashire vs Surrey, The Oval, 2017
BEST BOWLING: 5-58 Lancashire vs Yorkshire, Old Trafford, 2018

FAMILY TIES? My younger brother Graham plays for Durham. My older brother Darren has played Minor Counties with Cumberland and together with my dad won the National Village Cup with Cleator CC in 2013
WHICH BOWLER WOULD YOU LEAST LIKE TO FACE? Darren Stevens – he lands it on a sixpence
BEST INNINGS YOU'VE SEEN? Ashwell Prince's 261 for Lancashire against Glamorgan at Colwyn Bay in 2015. He was playing one-handed reverse-sweeps
WHO WOULD YOU ASK TO BAT FOR YOUR LIFE? Dane Vilas – he always gets his body in the way, especially his shin
SURPRISING FACT ABOUT YOU? I once split a testicle when pole dancing
TWITTER: @Clarksy16

Batting	Mat	Inns	NO	Runs	HS	Ave	SR	100	50	Ct	St
First-class	51	74	8	1884	140	28.54	55.64	1	10	7	0
List A	51	39	8	954	79*	30.77	99.89	0	5	8	0
T20s	85	63	23	914	60	22.85	135.20	0	1	31	0
Bowling	**Mat**	**Balls**	**Runs**	**Wkts**	**BBI**	**BBM**	**Ave**	**Econ**	**SR**	**5w**	**10**
First-class	51	5624	3364	99	5/58	7/97	33.97	3.58	56.8	2	0
List A	51	1452	1536	34	4/34	4/34	45.17	6.34	42.7	0	0
T20s	85	1007	1481	52	4/22	4/22	28.48	8.82	19.3	0	0

TOM CLARK

LHB / RM / R0 / W0

FULL NAME: Thomas Geoffrey Reeves Clark
BORN: July 2, 2001, Haywards Heath, Sussex
SQUAD NO: 27
HEIGHT: 6ft 2in
EDUCATION: Ardingly College, West Sussex
TEAMS: Sussex, England U19
ROLE: Batsman
DEBUT: First-class: 2019

BEST BATTING: 13 Sussex vs Worcestershire, Hove, 2019

WHAT WAS YOUR FIRST CRICKET CLUB? Horsham CC, West Sussex
WHAT WERE YOU DOING WHEN ENGLAND WON THE WORLD CUP? Watching it at Loughborough with the England U19 team
BIGGEST TOPIC OF DISCUSSION IN YOUR DRESSING ROOM? Fantasy Football
CRICKET STAR OF THE FUTURE? Kasey Aldridge (Somerset)
IF YOU WERE AN ANIMAL, WHICH WOULD IT BE? A Labrador
TWITTER: @tomclark2702
NOTES: The left-handed batsman signed his first professional contract with Sussex last November. Clark has been on the club's books since the age of eight and made his first-class debut last summer in the Championship game against Worcestershire at Hove, making a a 46-minute 13 against a strong attack which included the former South Africa international Wayne Parnell. "It was a great moment making my first-class debut at the end of the season and it has given me a good taste of what's to come," said Clark. "I'm looking forward to what the future holds for me." The 18-year-old, who plays his club cricket for Horsham CC, was called up to the England U19 squad last summer and was a playing member on the tour of the Caribbean over the winter and for the U19 World Cup in South Africa which followed

Batting	Mat	Inns	NO	Runs	HS	Ave	SR	100	50	Ct	St
First-class	1	1	0	13	13	13.00	38.23	0	0	-	-
Bowling	**Mat**	**Balls**	**Runs**	**Wkts**	**BBI**	**BBM**	**Ave**	**Econ**	**SR**	**5w**	**10**
First-class	1	-	-	-	-	-	-	-	-	-	-

JOE CLARKE RHB / WK / R1 / W0 / MVP66

FULL NAME: Joseph Michael Clarke
BORN: May 26, 1996, Shrewsbury, Shropshire
SQUAD NO: 33
HEIGHT: 6ft
NICKNAME: Clarkey
EDUCATION: Llanfyllin High School, Powys
TEAMS: Nottinghamshire, Manchester Originals, England Lions, Worcestershire
ROLE: Batsman
DEBUT: First-class: 2015; List A: 2015; T20: 2015

BEST BATTING: 194 Worcestershire vs Derbyshire, Worcester, 2016

WHAT WAS YOUR FIRST CRICKET CLUB? Oswestry CC, Shropshire
WHAT WERE YOU DOING WHEN ENGLAND WON THE WORLD CUP? I was in the Trent Bridge Inn watching on the big screen
MOST INTERESTING TEAMMATE? Ravi Ashwin – I could listen to him talk about life and cricket for hours
BEST INNINGS YOU'VE SEEN? Callum Ferguson's 192 for Worcestershire against Leicestershire in the 2018 One-Day Cup. Pure skill, and so good to watch from the other end
CRICKETING HERO? Adam Gilchrist
SURPRISING FACT ABOUT YOU? I can speak (some) Welsh
BIGGEST CRICKETING REGRET? Being not out overnight before Bank Holiday Monday
CRICKET STAR OF THE FUTURE? Qundeel Haider (Nottinghamshire Academy)
IF YOU WERE AN ANIMAL, WHICH WOULD IT BE? An owl – up all night
TWITTER: @joeclarke10

Batting	Mat	Inns	NO	Runs	HS	Ave	SR	100	50	Ct	St
First-class	75	130	9	4586	194	37.90	61.14	16	15	36	0
List A	62	59	5	1846	139	34.18	92.81	4	9	22	2
T20s	55	53	4	1282	124*	26.16	142.92	1	7	14	0
Bowling	**Mat**	**Balls**	**Runs**	**Wkts**	**BBI**	**BBM**	**Ave**	**Econ**	**SR**	**5w**	**10**
First-class	75	12	22	0	-	-	-	11.00	-	0	0
List A	62	-	-	-	-	-	-	-	-	-	-
T20s	55	-	-	-	-	-	-	-	-	-	-

RIKKI CLARKE RHB / RMF / R1 / W0 / MVP25

FULL NAME: Rikki Clarke
BORN: September 29, 1981, Orsett, Essex
SQUAD NO: 81
HEIGHT: 6ft 5in
NICKNAME: Clarkey, Crouchy, Rock
EDUCATION: Broadwater Secondary, Surrey; Godalming College
TEAMS: England, Surrey, Derbyshire, Warwickshire
ROLE: Allrounder
DEBUT: Test: 2003; ODI: 2003; First-class: 2002; List A: 2001; T20: 2003

BEST BATTING: 214 Surrey vs Somerset, Guildford, 2006
BEST BOWLING: 7-55 Surrey vs Somerset, The Oval, 2017
COUNTY CAP: 2005 (Surrey); 2011 (Warwickshire)

WHAT WAS YOUR FIRST CRICKET CLUB? Godalming CC, Surrey. Mum did the teas and Dad played. I was nine when I played my first men's game
BEST INNINGS YOU'VE SEEN? I was 12th man when Brian Lara made 400 at Antigua
WHICH RULE WOULD YOU CHANGE ABOUT CRICKET? On the last day of a Championship match the captains can shake hands on a draw an hour after lunch
YOUR BIGGEST CRICKETING REGRET? That I didn't know earlier what I know now. When I was younger I made mistakes. If I was the person I am now when I was 21 then things might have been better
FAVOURITE QUOTE OR SAYING? If not now, when? If not you, who? (Always helps me to stay motivated – if I'm not doing it someone else will be)
TWITTER: @rikkiclarke81

Batting	Mat	Inns	NO	Runs	HS	Ave	SR	100	50	Ct	St
Tests	2	3	0	96	55	32.00	37.94	0	1	1	0
ODIs	20	13	0	144	39	11.07	62.06	0	0	11	0
First-class	253	384	46	11104	214	32.85		17	57	374	0
List A	232	189	27	4087	98*	25.22		0	21	106	0
T20s	167	145	39	2272	79*	21.43	122.74	0	6	84	0
Bowling	**Mat**	**Balls**	**Runs**	**Wkts**	**BBI**	**BBM**	**Ave**	**Econ**	**SR**	**5w**	**10**
Tests	2	174	60	4	2/7	3/11	15.00	2.06	43.5	0	0
ODIs	20	469	415	11	2/28	2/28	37.72	5.30	42.6	0	0
First-class	253	28235	15524	505	7/55		30.74	3.29	55.9	7	0
List A	232	6417	5801	154	5/26	5/26	37.66	5.42	41.6	1	0
T20s	167	2202	2769	112	4/16	4/16	24.72	7.54	19.6	0	0

MITCHELL CLAYDON

LHB / RMF / R0 / W2

FULL NAME: Mitchell Eric Claydon
BORN: November 25, 1982, Fairfield, New South Wales, Australia
SQUAD NO: 4
HEIGHT: 6ft 4in
NICKNAME: Ellen, Precious
EDUCATION: Westfield Sports High School, Sydney
TEAMS: Sussex, Canterbury, Central Districts, Durham, Kent, Yorkshire
ROLE: Bowler
DEBUT: First-class: 2005; List A: 2006; T20: 2006

BEST BATTING: 77 Kent vs Leicestershire, Leicester, 2014
BEST BOWLING: 6-104 Durham vs Somerset, Taunton, 2011
COUNTY CAP: 2016 (Kent)

WHAT WAS YOUR FIRST CRICKET CLUB? St Andrews CC, New South Wales, Australia
HOW WOULD YOU DISMISS STEVE SMITH? Bowl him round his legs
MOST INTERESTING TEAMMATE? Heino Kuhn – far too clean and goes around cleaning up everyone else's gear through the course of a game
CRICKETING HERO? Ricky Ponting
SURPRISING FACT ABOUT YOU? I'm a magician, a keen surfer and I love to play a prank or two
TWITTER: @mitchellclaydon
NOTES: The 37-year-old seamer has signed for Sussex after seven seasons at Kent. "I'm absolutely delighted to be joining Sussex," Claydon said. "It's always a place I've enjoyed playing cricket over my career and I'm looking forward to calling it home. After playing with Dizzy [Jason Gillespie] in my first year in England and spending time with him when he was with Kent, I'm really excited to be playing under him again. I still feel as though I have plenty to offer and look forward to hopefully putting in some match-winning performances for Sussex"

Batting	Mat	Inns	NO	Runs	HS	Ave	SR	100	50	Ct	St
First-class	108	137	32	1611	77	15.34	60.76	0	4	11	0
List A	110	50	17	276	19	8.36	82.88	0	0	9	0
T20s	147	50	30	191	19	9.55	89.25	0	0	26	0
Bowling	**Mat**	**Balls**	**Runs**	**Wkts**	**BBI**	**BBM**	**Ave**	**Econ**	**SR**	**5w**	**10**
First-class	108	16023	9595	299	6/104		32.09	3.59	53.5	9	0
List A	110	4799	4501	138	5/31	5/31	32.61	5.62	34.7	1	0
T20s	147	3037	4289	159	5/26	5/26	26.97	8.47	19.1	2	0

BEN COAD

RHB / RFM / R0 / W1

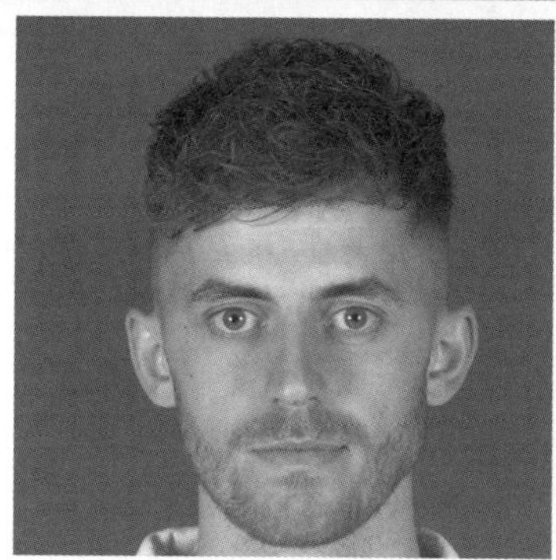

FULL NAME: Benjamin Oliver Coad
BORN: January 10, 1994, Harrogate, Yorkshire
SQUAD NO: 10
HEIGHT: 6ft 3in
NICKNAME: Hench
EDUCATION: Thirsk School and Sixth Form College, North Yorkshire
TEAMS: Yorkshire
ROLE: Bowler
DEBUT: First-class: 2016; List A: 2013; T20: 2015

BEST BATTING: 48 Yorkshire vs Surrey, Scarborough, 2019
BEST BOWLING: 6-25 Yorkshire vs Lancashire, Headingley, 2017
COUNTY CAP: 2018

FAMILY TIES? My brothers played representative cricket at junior levels. My dad played Minor Counties cricket for Suffolk
WHAT WAS YOUR FIRST CRICKET CLUB? Studley Royal CC, Ripon, North Yorkshire
WHAT WERE YOU DOING WHEN ENGLAND WON THE WORLD CUP? Watching it at the pub
HOW WOULD YOU DISMISS STEVE SMITH? Pitch it on leg and hit the top of off
BIGGEST TOPIC OF DISCUSSION IN YOUR DRESSING ROOM? Cricket, football, golf – and sports quizzes
SURPRISING FACT ABOUT YOU? I'm a Newcastle United fan
CRICKET STAR OF THE FUTURE? George Hill (England U19, Yorkshire Second XI)
IF YOU WERE AN ANIMAL, WHICH WOULD IT BE? A cheetah
TWITTER: @bencoad10

Batting	Mat	Inns	NO	Runs	HS	Ave	SR	100	50	Ct	St
First-class	36	48	16	487	48	15.21	65.10	0	0	1	0
List A	17	6	5	15	9	15.00	62.50	0	0	5	0
T20s	7	2	1	3	2*	3.00	60.00	0	0	5	0
Bowling	**Mat**	**Balls**	**Runs**	**Wkts**	**BBI**	**BBM**	**Ave**	**Econ**	**SR**	**5w**	**10**
First-class	36	6476	3043	145	6/25	10/102	20.98	2.81	44.6	8	2
List A	17	764	748	20	4/63	4/63	37.40	5.87	38.2	0	0
T20s	7	109	186	6	2/24	2/24	31.00	10.23	18.1	0	0

JOSH COBB

RHB / LB / R0 / W0

FULL NAME: Joshua James Cobb
BORN: August 17, 1990, Leicester
SQUAD NO: 4
HEIGHT: 6ft
NICKNAME: Cobby, Tuck Shop, Lord
EDUCATION: Oakham School, Rutland
TEAMS: Northamptonshire, Barisal Bulls, Central Districts, Dhaka Gladiators, England U19, Leicestershire, Prime Doleshwar Sporting Club, Sylhet Superstars
ROLE: Batsman
DEBUT: First-class: 2007; List A: 2008; T20: 2008

BEST BATTING: 148* Leicestershire vs Middlesex, Lord's, 2008
BEST BOWLING: 2-11 Leicestershire vs Gloucestershire, Leicester, 2011
COUNTY CAP: 2018 (Northamptonshire)

FAMILY TIES? My dad Russell played for Leicestershire
WHAT WAS YOUR FIRST CRICKET CLUB? Kibworth CC, Leicestershire
BIGGEST TOPIC OF DISCUSSION IN YOUR DRESSING ROOM? Skinfolds
MOST INTERESTING TEAMMATE? Paul Nixon – great stories
BEST INNINGS YOU'VE SEEN? Abdul Razzaq's 62 from 30 balls for Leicestershire at Old Trafford in a T20 match in 2011
CRICKETING HERO? Brad Hodge
SURPRISING FACT ABOUT YOU? At Oakham I was a member of the debating society and took an active interest in historical and modern British politics. I take a number of books and papers with me to away games which keep me busy during rain delays, much to the dismay of my teammates
WHICH BOOK MEANS MOST TO YOU? The Art of Captaincy by Mike Brearley
IF YOU WERE AN ANIMAL, WHICH WOULD IT BE? A lion because I'm a Leo
TWITTER: @Cobby24

Batting	Mat	Inns	NO	Runs	HS	Ave	SR	100	50	Ct	St
First-class	126	216	22	5155	148*	26.57	50.29	4	30	53	0
List A	99	94	7	3330	146*	38.27	91.45	7	21	29	0
T20s	147	139	14	3165	103	25.32	134.11	1	19	65	0
Bowling	**Mat**	**Balls**	**Runs**	**Wkts**	**BBI**	**BBM**	**Ave**	**Econ**	**SR**	**5w**	**10**
First-class	126	2716	1607	18	2/11	2/11	89.27	3.55	150.8	0	0
List A	99	1758	1712	35	3/34	3/34	48.91	5.84	50.2	0	0
T20s	147	1323	1776	56	4/22	4/22	31.71	8.05	23.6	0	0

IAN COCKBAIN RHB / RM / R0 / W0

FULL NAME: Ian Andrew Cockbain
BORN: February 17, 1987, Liverpool
SQUAD NO: 28
HEIGHT: 6ft
NICKNAME: Coey, Bird's Nest, Gramps
EDUCATION: Maghull High School, Sefton; Liverpool John Moores University
TEAMS: Gloucestershire
ROLE: Batsman
DEBUT: First-class: 2011; List A: 2011; T20: 2011

BEST BATTING: 151* Gloucestershire vs Surrey, Bristol, 2014
BEST BOWLING: 1-23 Gloucestershire vs Durham MCCU, Bristol, 2016
COUNTY CAP: 2011; BENEFIT: 2019

FAMILY TIES? My dad Ian played for Lancashire
WHAT WAS YOUR FIRST CRICKET CLUB? Bootle CC, Merseyside. My grandad, dad and uncle all played there when they were kids
WHAT EXCITES YOU ABOUT THE HUNDRED? Seeing how players and teams adapt to the new format
BIGGEST TOPIC OF DISCUSSION IN YOUR DRESSING ROOM? There's a lot of boring coffee chat. Or it's about Gareth Roderick not having a driving license
MOST INTERESTING TEAMMATE? AJ Tye. And by 'interesting', I don't mean it in an intellectual way. He is a man-child
CRICKETING HERO? Andrew Flintoff
WHICH RULE WOULD YOU CHANGE ABOUT CRICKET? Introduce a free hit for a wide or no-ball in red-ball cricket. 'Double play' in white-ball cricket (for example, two wickets can fall when there is a catch and a run-out off the same delivery)
CRICKET STAR OF THE FUTURE? Tom Price (Gloucestershire)
IF YOU WERE AN ANIMAL, WHICH WOULD IT BE? An owl – old and wise!

Batting	Mat	Inns	NO	Runs	HS	Ave	SR	100	50	Ct	St
First-class	51	86	6	2382	151*	29.77	42.81	4	13	35	0
List A	68	59	11	1633	108*	34.02	88.36	2	10	41	0
T20s	111	103	19	2665	123	31.72	126.84	1	13	52	0
Bowling	**Mat**	**Balls**	**Runs**	**Wkts**	**BBI**	**BBM**	**Ave**	**Econ**	**SR**	**5w**	**10**
First-class	51	47	44	1	1/23	1/23	44.00	5.61	47.0	0	0
List A	68	-	-	-	-	-	-	-	-	-	-
T20s	111	-	-	-	-	-	-	-	-	-	-

MICHAEL COHEN LHB / LFM / R0 / W0

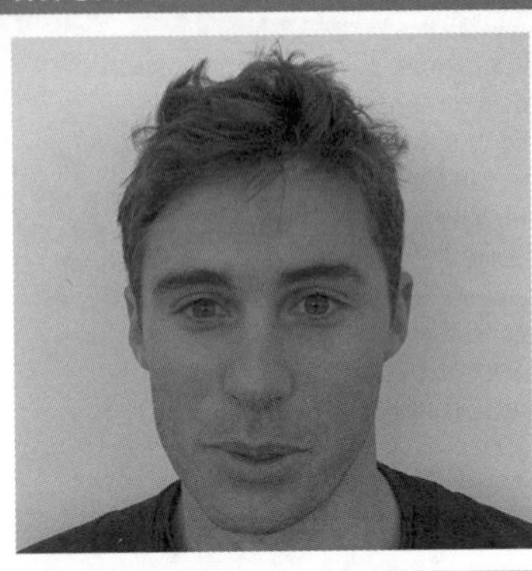

FULL NAME: Michael Alexander Robert Cohen
BORN: August 4, 1998, Cape Town, South Africa
SQUAD NO: 8
HEIGHT: 5ft 10in
NICKNAME: Uncoh
EDUCATION: Reddam House Constantia, Cape Town; University of South Africa, Pretoria
TEAMS: Derbyshire, Cape Cobras, South Africa U19, Western Province
ROLE: Bowler
DEBUT: First-class: 2017; List A: 2018; T20: 2017

BEST BATTING: 23* Western Province vs Northern Cape, Kimberley, 2018
BEST BOWLING: 5-40 Western Province vs South Western Districts, Rondesbosch, 2018

WHAT WAS YOUR FIRST CRICKET CLUB? Western Province CC, Cape Town, South Africa
WHAT WERE YOU DOING WHEN ENGLAND WON THE WORLD CUP? I was recovering from a back injury in Cape Town
HOW WOULD YOU DISMISS STEVE SMITH? Hope that he misses a straight one – he has a tendency to do that after scoring 230 runs
WHAT EXCITES YOU ABOUT THE HUNDRED? The opportunity to showcase the talent of emerging players as well as the various high-calibre contests between bat and ball
BIGGEST TOPIC OF DISCUSSION IN YOUR DRESSING ROOM? I haven't played for Derbyshire yet so I'm not sure – but your ability at FIFA (video game) will always be fiercely debated
MOST INTERESTING TEAMMATE? Mpilo Njoloza. Not only is his comedic timing impeccable, but his wisdom, compassion and his stories from the past are a pleasure to be around
CRICKET STAR OF THE FUTURE? Jono Bird (Western Province)

Batting	Mat	Inns	NO	Runs	HS	Ave	SR	100	50	Ct	St
First-class	15	17	12	88	23*	17.60	28.57	0	0	1	0
List A	4	1	0	16	16	16.00	123.07	0	0	1	0
T20s	4	2	2	1	1*	-	100.00	0	0	0	0
Bowling	**Mat**	**Balls**	**Runs**	**Wkts**	**BBI**	**BBM**	**Ave**	**Econ**	**SR**	**5w**	**10**
First-class	15	1963	1306	50	5/40	9/70	26.12	3.99	39.2	2	0
List A	4	192	160	3	1/17	1/17	53.33	5.00	64.0	0	0
T20s	4	88	98	4	2/17	2/17	24.50	6.68	22.0	0	0

BEN COMPTON LHB / OB / R0 / W0

FULL NAME: Benjamin Garnet Compton
BORN: March 29, 1994, Durban, South Africa
SQUAD NO: 7
HEIGHT: 6ft 1in
NICKNAME: Compo
EDUCATION: Clifton College, Durban; The Open University, Milton Keynes
TEAMS: Nottinghamshire
ROLE: Batsman
DEBUT: First-class: 2019

BEST BATTING: 16* Nottinghamshire vs Surrey, The Oval, 2019

WHAT WAS YOUR FIRST CRICKET CLUB? Wimbledon CC, London
WHAT EXCITES YOU ABOUT THE HUNDRED? Getting more people to watch and support cricket
MOST INTERESTING TEAMMATE? Wasim Akram – it was a fundraising match. Just a pleasure and privilege to play with one of the game's all-time greats
CRICKET STAR OF THE FUTURE? Jack Nelson (Richmond CC U11)
IF YOU WERE AN ANIMAL, WHICH WOULD IT BE? A wolf – I'd have fun howling at the moon
NOTES: The 26-year-old left-hander signed his first professional contract with Notts last October. Grandson of Denis and cousin of Nick, Ben has cricketing genes in the blood. He was born and raised in South Africa before moving to the London in his late teens, playing first for Wimbledon CC and then Richmond CC. Compton made his first-class debut for Notts last summer after hitting five Second XI hundreds last year, four of them for Kent. "His style is well-suited to longer form cricket and we hope his approach will dovetail with the strokemakers we have in the side," said Mick Newell, Nottinghamshire's director of cricket. "He's earned his opportunity in the professional game the hard way, by performing on the second-team circuit for a number of years. He's shown that he has the patience to bat for long periods of time, which is something we certainly value"

Batting	Mat	Inns	NO	Runs	HS	Ave	SR	100	50	Ct	St
First-class	2	3	1	43	16*	21.50	32.08	0	0	1	0
Bowling	**Mat**	**Balls**	**Runs**	**Wkts**	**BBI**	**BBM**	**Ave**	**Econ**	**SR**	**5w**	**10**
First-class	2	-	-	-	-	-	-	-	-	-	-

SAM CONNERS

RHB / RFM / R0 / W0

FULL NAME: Samuel Conners
BORN: February 13, 1999, Nottingham
SQUAD NO: 59
HEIGHT: 6ft
NICKNAME: Sammy
EDUCATION: George Spencer Academy, Nottingham
TEAMS: Derbyshire, England U19
ROLE: Bowler
DEBUT: First-class: 2019; List A: 2019

BEST BATTING: 14 Derbyshire vs Lancashire, Derby, 2019
BEST BOWLING: 2-13 Derbyshire vs Leeds/Bradford MCCU, Derby, 2019

WHAT WAS YOUR FIRST CRICKET CLUB? Attenborough CC, Nottingham
WHAT WERE YOU DOING WHEN ENGLAND WON THE WORLD CUP? I was jumping around in my sitting room
HOW WOULD YOU DISMISS STEVE SMITH? Bouncer with two men out
BIGGEST TOPIC OF DISCUSSION IN YOUR DRESSING ROOM? Who can bowl the fastest
MOST INTERESTING TEAMMATE? Tony Palladino – knowledgeable but also hilarious
WHICH RULE WOULD YOU CHANGE ABOUT CRICKET? It should be 10 runs if you hit the ball out of the ground
CRICKET STAR OF THE FUTURE? Josh Lacey (Derbyshire Academy)
WHICH BOOK MEANS MOST TO YOU? Firestarter – Me, Cricket and the Heat of the Moment by Ben Stokes
IF YOU WERE AN ANIMAL, WHICH WOULD IT BE? A dog – because they're cool
TWITTER: @SamConners7

Batting	Mat	Inns	NO	Runs	HS	Ave	SR	100	50	Ct	St
First-class	3	2	1	20	14	20.00	28.98	0	0	0	0
List A	3	1	0	4	4	4.00	200.00	0	0	2	0
Bowling	**Mat**	**Balls**	**Runs**	**Wkts**	**BBI**	**BBM**	**Ave**	**Econ**	**SR**	**5w**	**10**
First-class	3	222	113	5	2/13	3/36	22.60	3.05	44.4	0	0
List A	3	138	150	2	1/45	1/45	75.00	6.52	69.0	0	0

ALASTAIR COOK LHB / RM / R9 / W0 / MVP77

FULL NAME: Alastair Nathan Cook
BORN: December 25, 1984, Gloucester
SQUAD NO: 26
HEIGHT: 6ft 2in
NICKNAME: Cookie, Chef
EDUCATION: Bedford School
TEAMS: England, Essex
ROLE: Batsman
DEBUT: Test: 2006; ODI: 2006; T20I: 2007; First-class: 2003; List A: 2003; T20: 2005

BEST BATTING: 294 England vs India, Edgbaston, 2011
BEST BOWLING: 3-13 Essex vs Northamptonshire, Chelmsford, 2005
COUNTY CAP: 2005; BENEFIT: 2014

FAMILY TIES? Dad played for the local club side and was a very good opening bat, while my mum made the teas. My brothers played for Maldon Cricket Club
CRICKETING HERO? Graham Gooch – I watched him playing for Essex at Chelmsford
IF YOU WEREN'T A CRICKETER? I'd be a farmer

Batting	Mat	Inns	NO	Runs	HS	Ave	SR	100	50	Ct	St
Tests	161	291	16	12472	294	45.35	46.95	33	57	175	0
ODIs	92	92	4	3204	137	36.40	77.13	5	19	36	0
T20Is	4	4	0	61	26	15.25	112.96	0	0	1	0
First-class	304	538	41	23667	294	47.61	50.68	65	114	323	0
List A	168	166	11	6055	137	39.06	79.97	12	35	68	0
T20s	32	30	2	892	100*	31.85	127.61	1	5	13	0
Bowling	**Mat**	**Balls**	**Runs**	**Wkts**	**BBI**	**BBM**	**Ave**	**Econ**	**SR**	**5w**	**10**
Tests	161	18	7	1	1/6	1/6	7.00	2.33	18.0	0	0
ODIs	92	-	-	-	-	-	-	-	-	-	-
T20Is	4	-	-	-	-	-	-	-	-	-	-
First-class	304	282	211	7	3/13		30.14	4.48	40.2	0	0
List A	168	18	10	0	-	-	-	3.33	-	0	0
T20s	32	-	-	-	-	-	-	-	-	-	-

SAM COOK

RHB / RFM / R0 / W0

FULL NAME: Samuel James Cook
BORN: August 4, 1997, Chelmsford, Essex
SQUAD NO: 16
HEIGHT: 6ft 2in
NICKNAME: Glen, Little Chef
EDUCATION: Great Baddow High School, Chelmsford; Loughborough University
TEAMS: Essex
ROLE: Bowler
DEBUT: First-class: 2016; List A: 2018; T20: 2018

BEST BATTING: 37* Essex vs Yorkshire, Headingley, 2019
BEST BOWLING: 7-23 Essex vs Kent, Canterbury, 2019

WHAT WAS YOUR FIRST CRICKET CLUB? Writtle CC, Essex. The team was made up of kids from the football team who played at the same ground
WHAT EXCITES YOU ABOUT THE HUNDRED? Free crisps for everyone!
BEST INNINGS YOU'VE SEEN? Ben Stokes's 258 at Cape Town in 2016 – an I-was-there moment
CRICKETING HERO? Glenn McGrath
WHICH RULE WOULD YOU CHANGE ABOUT CRICKET? Allow three men out in T20 powerplays (it's a batsman's game)
SURPRISING FACT ABOUT YOU? I don't like cheese
CRICKET STAR OF THE FUTURE? Ben Allison (Essex)
WHICH BOOK MEANS MOST TO YOU? Origin by Dan Brown
IF YOU WERE AN ANIMAL, WHICH WOULD IT BE? A golden eagle
TWITTER: @samcook09

Batting	Mat	Inns	NO	Runs	HS	Ave	SR	100	50	Ct	St
First-class	29	30	14	114	37*	7.12	34.86	0	0	3	0
List A	12	4	2	9	6	4.50	69.23	0	0	1	0
T20s	8	2	1	0	0*	0.00	0.00	0	0	0	0
Bowling	**Mat**	**Balls**	**Runs**	**Wkts**	**BBI**	**BBM**	**Ave**	**Econ**	**SR**	**5w**	**10**
First-class	29	4255	2143	87	7/23	12/65	24.63	3.02	48.9	6	1
List A	12	582	457	11	3/37	3/37	41.54	4.71	52.9	0	0
T20s	8	126	203	4	1/27	1/27	50.75	9.66	31.5	0	0

CHRIS COOKE RHB / WK / R0 / W0

FULL NAME: Christopher Barry Cooke
BORN: May 30, 1986, Johannesburg, South Africa
SQUAD NO: 46
HEIGHT: 5ft 11in
NICKNAME: Chris Jelly, Dough, Beans, Minty, Shapeless, Cookie
EDUCATION: Bishops School, Cape Town; University of Cape Town
TEAMS: Glamorgan, Birmingham Phoenix, Western Province
ROLE: Batsman/wicketkeeper
DEBUT: First-class: 2009; List A: 2009; T20: 2011

BEST BATTING: 171 Glamorgan vs Kent, Canterbury, 2014

COUNTY CAP: 2016

WHAT WAS YOUR FIRST CRICKET CLUB? Cape Town CC, South Africa. Cheap beer and I made lots of friends there
CRICKETING HERO? Hylton Ackerman
WHICH BOWLER WOULD YOU LEAST LIKE TO FACE? Any non-bowler who comes on for an over
BEST INNINGS YOU'VE SEEN? Usman Khawaja's Championship hundred on his Glamorgan debut in 2018, coming up against Jeetan Patel on a turning Edgbaston pitch. I was watching at the other end
WHICH RULE WOULD YOU CHANGE ABOUT CRICKET? No runs allowed off a direct hit
WHICH BOOK MEANS MOST TO YOU? Spud by John van de Ruit
TWITTER: @Cooky_24

Batting	Mat	Inns	NO	Runs	HS	Ave	SR	100	50	Ct	St
First-class	84	143	18	4478	171	35.82	54.09	4	29	141	4
List A	88	81	9	2607	161	36.20	98.34	3	14	54	5
T20s	104	88	18	1659	65*	23.70	141.07	0	4	63	6
Bowling	**Mat**	**Balls**	**Runs**	**Wkts**	**BBI**	**BBM**	**Ave**	**Econ**	**SR**	**5w**	**10**
First-class	84	-	-	-	-	-	-	-	-	-	-
List A	88	-	-	-	-	-	-	-	-	-	-
T20s	104	-	-	-	-	-	-	-	-	-	-

JOE COOKE

LHB / RFM / R0 / W0

FULL NAME: Joe Michael Cooke
BORN: May 30, 1997, Hemel Hempstead, Hertfordshire
SQUAD NO: 57
HEIGHT: 6ft 3in
EDUCATION: Parmiter's School, Watford; Durham University
TEAMS: Glamorgan
ROLE: Allrounder
DEBUT: First-class: 2017

BEST BATTING: 21 Durham MCCU vs Gloucestershire, Bristol, 2017
BEST BOWLING: 1-26 Durham MCCU vs Warwickshire, Edgbaston, 2018

WHAT WAS YOUR FIRST CRICKET CLUB? Kings Langley CC, Hertfordshire
WHAT WERE YOU DOING WHEN ENGLAND WON THE WORLD CUP? Watching it with the family while celebrating my gran's birthday
MOST INTERESTING TEAMMATE? Rob Clements at Radlett CC – he's a bit of a character
CRICKET STAR OF THE FUTURE? Alex Horton (Glamorgan Academy)
IF YOU WERE AN ANIMAL, WHICH WOULD IT BE? A giraffe – I'm a bit clumsy
NOTES: Cooke – no relation to his teammate and captain Chris – is a batting allrounder who topped Glamorgan's run-scoring charts in last summer's Second XI Championship, amassing 465 in total, including a top score of 131 against Sussex. Off the back of those performances he was handed a rookie contract last October. Cooke has played four first-class matches for Durham MCCU but was still waiting to make his first-team debut for Glamorgan ahead of this summer. "We brought Joe in mid-season [in 2019] and he's thrived in a professional environment, impressing everyone with his attitude and wide skill-set," said Mark Wallace, Glamorgan's director of cricket. "He can bat anywhere in the order and bowl seam and is another young player to add to our developing group"

Batting	Mat	Inns	NO	Runs	HS	Ave	SR	100	50	Ct	St
First-class	4	2	0	28	21	14.00	34.56	0	0	6	0
Bowling	**Mat**	**Balls**	**Runs**	**Wkts**	**BBI**	**BBM**	**Ave**	**Econ**	**SR**	**5w**	**10**
First-class	4	468	308	3	1/26	1/26	102.66	3.94	156.0	0	0

MARK COSGROVE

LHB / RM / R3 / W0

FULL NAME: Mark James Cosgrove
BORN: June 14, 1984, Adelaide, Australia
SQUAD NO: 55
HEIGHT: 5ft 9in
NICKNAME: Cozzie
EDUCATION: Trinity College, Adelaide
TEAMS: Australia, Leicestershire, Glamorgan, Hobart Hurricanes, South Australia, Sydney Sixers, Sydney Thunder, Tasmania
ROLE: Batsman
DEBUT: ODI: 2006; First-class: 2002; List A: 2002; T20: 2006

BEST BATTING: 233 Glamorgan vs Derbyshire, Derby, 2006
BEST BOWLING: 3-3 South Australia vs Tasmania, Adelaide, 2007
COUNTY CAP: 2006 (Glamorgan)

WHAT WAS YOUR FIRST CRICKET CLUB? South Gawler, South Australia
WHAT WERE YOU DOING WHEN ENGLAND WON THE WORLD CUP? Sleeping
WHAT EXCITES YOU ABOUT THE HUNDRED? That I'll be playing in the 50-over competition
BIGGEST TOPIC OF DISCUSSION IN YOUR DRESSING ROOM? Harry Swindells's ears
CRICKETING HERO? Brian Lara
SURPRISING FACT ABOUT YOU? I grew up at the same club as Darren Lehmann, Ryan Harris and Graham Manou
CRICKET STAR OF THE FUTURE? Cameron Laird (Northern Districts CC in New South Wales, Australia)
IF YOU WERE AN ANIMAL, WHICH WOULD IT BE? A shark
TWITTER: @Cozzie99

Batting	Mat	Inns	NO	Runs	HS	Ave	SR	100	50	Ct	St
ODIs	3	3	0	112	74	37.33	96.55	0	1	0	0
First-class	221	393	22	14976	233	40.36	61.65	36	87	133	0
List A	160	154	4	4821	121	32.14	88.71	4	39	49	0
T20s	139	135	10	3112	89	24.89	123.19	0	14	26	0
Bowling	**Mat**	**Balls**	**Runs**	**Wkts**	**BBI**	**BBM**	**Ave**	**Econ**	**SR**	**5w**	**10**
ODIs	3	30	13	1	1/1	1/1	13.00	2.60	30.0	0	0
First-class	221	4307	2393	52	3/3		46.01	3.33	82.8	0	0
List A	160	1067	1141	18	2/21	2/21	63.38	6.41	59.2	0	0
T20s	139	197	320	10	2/11	2/11	32.00	9.74	19.7	0	0

JOSH COUGHLIN

LHB / RM / R0 / W0

FULL NAME: Josh Coughlin
BORN: September 29, 1997, Sunderland
SQUAD NO: 29
HEIGHT: 6ft 5in
NICKNAME: Coggers
EDUCATION: St Robert of Newminster Catholic School, Sunderland
TEAMS: Durham, England U19
ROLE: Allrounder
DEBUT: First-class: 2016

BEST BATTING: 24 Durham v Durham MCCU, Chester-le-Street, 2019
BEST BOWLING: 2-31 Durham v Derbyshire, Chester-le-Street, 2018

FAMILY TIES? My uncle played Minor Counties and my older brother Paul plays with me at Durham
WHAT WAS YOUR FIRST CRICKET CLUB? Eppington CC, Sunderland
BEST INNINGS YOU'VE SEEN? Alex Hales's 171 against Pakistan at Trent Bridge in 2016
BIGGEST TOPIC OF DISCUSSION IN YOUR DRESSING ROOM? Anything and everything
MOST INTERESTING TEAMMATE? James Weighell – keeps everyone entertained
WHICH RULE WOULD YOU CHANGE ABOUT CRICKET? Allow more fielders outside the circle in one-day and T20 cricket
BIGGEST CRICKETING REGRET? Getting hit on the head with no helmet
IF YOU WERE AN ANIMAL, WHICH WOULD IT BE? A dog – amazing creatures
TWITTER: @Coughlin97

Batting	Mat	Inns	NO	Runs	HS	Ave	SR	100	50	Ct	St
First-class	4	6	0	66	24	11.00	44.00	0	0	1	0
Bowling	**Mat**	**Balls**	**Runs**	**Wkts**	**BBI**	**BBM**	**Ave**	**Econ**	**SR**	**5w**	**10**
First-class	4	492	251	7	2/31	2/45	35.85	3.06	70.2	0	0

PAUL COUGHLIN RHB / RFM / R0 / W0

FULL NAME: Paul Coughlin
BORN: October 23, 1992, Sunderland
SQUAD NO: 23
HEIGHT: 6ft 2in
NICKNAME: Coggers
EDUCATION: St Robert of Newminster Catholic School, Sunderland
TEAMS: Durham, England Lions, Nottinghamshire
ROLE: Allrounder
DEBUT: First-class: 2012; List A: 2012; T20: 2014

BEST BATTING: 85 Durham vs Lancashire, Chester-le-Street, 2014
BEST BOWLING: 5-49 Durham vs Northamptonshire, Chester-le-Street, 2017

WHAT GOT YOU INTO CRICKET? Playing in my uncle's homemade net in his back garden
FAMILY TIES? A different uncle, Tommy Harland, played for Durham as a Minor County. My younger brother Josh is currently at Durham
BEST MOMENT IN CRICKET? Winning the One-Day Cup at Lord's in 2014
CRICKETING HERO? Andrew Flintoff – amazing to watch. Kept the crowd entertained in all aspects of the game
SURPRISING FACT ABOUT YOU? I started out aiming to be a wicketkeeper. Then I tried myself as a batter. Ended up being more of a bowler
TWITTER: @Coughlin92

Batting	Mat	Inns	NO	Runs	HS	Ave	SR	100	50	Ct	St
First-class	38	60	8	1368	85	26.30	56.88	0	7	20	0
List A	27	18	4	177	22	12.64	95.67	0	0	7	0
T20s	33	22	7	433	53	28.86	137.89	0	1	10	0
Bowling	**Mat**	**Balls**	**Runs**	**Wkts**	**BBI**	**BBM**	**Ave**	**Econ**	**SR**	**5w**	**10**
First-class	38	4819	2826	86	5/49	10/133	32.86	3.51	56.0	2	1
List A	27	977	915	18	3/36	3/36	50.83	5.61	54.2	0	0
T20s	33	493	768	34	5/42	5/42	22.58	9.34	14.5	1	0

NATHAN COULTER-NILE RHB/RFM

FULL NAME: Nathan Mitchell Coulter-Nile
BORN: October 11, 1987, Osborne Park, Western Australia, Australia
SQUAD NO: TBC
HEIGHT: 6ft 3in
EDUCATION: Aquinas College, Perth, Australia
TEAMS: Australia, Trent Rockets, Delhi Daredevils, Kolkata Knight Riders, Melbourne Stars, Mumbai Indians, Perth Scorchers, Royal Challengers Bangalore, Western Australia
ROLE: Bowler
DEBUT: ODI: 2013; T20I: 2013; First-class: 2010; List A: 2009; T20: 2009

BEST BATTING: 42* Perth Scorchers vs Adelaide Strikers, Adelaide, 2013 (T20)
BEST BOWLING: 4-20 Delhi Daredevils vs Kings XI Punjab, Delhi, 2015 (T20)

NOTES: A graduate of the Dennis Lillee Fast Bowling Academy, Coulter-Nile was a member of Perth Scorchers' squad for the inaugural season of the Big Bash League and joined the Melbourne Renegades last year. He has been a regular fixture in the IPL and was signed by Mumbai Indians for the 2020 IPL. The Western Australian, now 32, has been plagued by injury since making his international debut in 2013, although he has played in the last two World Cups. In the 2019 tournament he scored his maiden ODI half-century and made the highest score by a No.8 batsman in a World Cup – 92 from 60 balls against West Indies at Trent Bridge. Two matches later, against Pakistan at Taunton, he claimed his 50th ODI wicket. Coulter-Nile will represent Trent Rockets in The Hundred this summer, having been picked up in the £75k category

Batting	Mat	Inns	NO	Runs	HS	Ave	SR	100	50	Ct	St
ODIs	32	21	6	252	92	16.80	96.18	0	1	7	0
T20Is	28	15	4	150	34	13.63	125.00	0	0	13	0
First-class	37	56	3	994	64	18.75	71.56	0	3	24	0
List A	80	53	13	703	92	17.57	95.12	0	3	28	0
T20s	120	69	27	625	42*	14.88	133.54	0	0	38	0
Bowling	**Mat**	**Balls**	**Runs**	**Wkts**	**BBI**	**BBM**	**Ave**	**Econ**	**SR**	**5w**	**10**
ODIs	32	1678	1555	52	4/48	4/48	29.90	5.56	32.2	0	0
T20Is	28	582	802	34	4/31	4/31	23.58	8.26	17.1	0	0
First-class	37	6861	3557	124	6/84	9/125	28.68	3.11	55.3	2	0
List A	80	4310	3647	146	5/26	5/26	24.97	5.07	29.5	2	0
T20s	120	2530	3274	140	4/20	4/20	23.38	7.76	18.0	0	0

BEN COX RHB / WK / R0 / W0 / MVP95

FULL NAME: Oliver Benjamin Cox
BORN: February 2, 1992, Wordsley, Stourbridge, Worcestershire
SQUAD NO: 10
HEIGHT: 5ft 10in
NICKNAME: Cocko
EDUCATION: Bromsgrove School, Worcestershire
TEAMS: Worcestershire, Trent Rockets, Otago
ROLE: Wicketkeeper
DEBUT: First-class: 2009; List A: 2010; T20: 2010

BEST BATTING: 124 Worcestershire vs Gloucestershire, Cheltenham, 2017

WHAT WAS YOUR FIRST CRICKET CLUB? Belbroughton CC, Worcestershire. Tiny village which I had to leave because I couldn't get in the first team as a wicketkeeper
HOW WOULD YOU DISMISS STEVE SMITH? Negotiate a deal: if he chips one up then I'll take him back to Bushwackers
WHAT EXCITES YOU ABOUT THE HUNDRED? The quality of the teams – some of the best players in the world are involved. It's going to be great viewing I reckon
BIGGEST TOPIC OF DISCUSSION IN YOUR DRESSING ROOM? My Instagram account
MOST INTERESTING TEAMMATE? Jack Shantry
WHICH RULE WOULD YOU CHANGE ABOUT CRICKET? I'd introduce a 'double play': if the batsman nicks it and also gets stumped then the next allocated batsman is out too. Same applies with being caught and run out
CRICKET STAR OF THE FUTURE? Henry Cullen (Worcestershire Academy)
IF YOU WERE AN ANIMAL, WHICH WOULD IT BE? A wild dog
TWITTER: @bencox10

Batting	Mat	Inns	NO	Runs	HS	Ave	SR	100	50	Ct	St
First-class	116	188	24	4539	124	27.67	60.49	4	26	305	13
List A	74	58	9	1371	122*	27.97	97.16	1	5	80	9
T20s	111	96	37	1609	59*	27.27	124.24	0	3	49	27
Bowling	**Mat**	**Balls**	**Runs**	**Wkts**	**BBI**	**BBM**	**Ave**	**Econ**	**SR**	**5w**	**10**
First-class	116	-	-	-	-	-	-	-	-	-	-
List A	74	-	-	-	-	-	-	-	-	-	-
T20s	111	-	-	-	-	-	-	-	-	-	-

JORDAN COX

RHB / WK / R0 / W0

FULL NAME: Jordan Matthew Cox
BORN: October 21, 2000, Portsmouth
SQUAD NO: 22
HEIGHT: 5ft 11in
EDUCATION: Felsted School, Essex
TEAMS: Kent, England U19
ROLE: Wicketkeeper/batsman
DEBUT: First-class: 2019; List A: 2019; T20: 2019

BEST BATTING: 27 Kent vs Hampshire, Southampton, 2019

WHAT WAS YOUR FIRST CRICKET CLUB? Sandwich Town CC, Dover, Kent
WHAT WERE YOU DOING WHEN ENGLAND WON THE WORLD CUP? I was making my first-class debut for Kent at Hampshire
WHAT EXCITES YOU ABOUT THE HUNDRED? The opportunity for more people to play in the 50-over competition
BIGGEST TOPIC OF DISCUSSION IN YOUR DRESSING ROOM? Girls
MOST INTERESTING TEAMMATE? Mitch Claydon – for so many reasons
CRICKET STAR OF THE FUTURE? Blake Cullen (Middlesex)
IF YOU WERE AN ANIMAL, WHICH WOULD IT BE? A panda
NOTES: The top-order batsman/wicketkeeper has been on Kent's books since the age of 10 and signed a three-year contract with Kent in October 2018. Cox has impressed for England U19 since first being selected in 2018, carrying his bat for a hundred in a 50-over game against Bangladesh last summer and making another ton against Sri Lanka in December. His performances were mixed at the U19 World Cup in South Africa over the winter, although he did make a fifty against Zimbabwe. The 19-year-old made his debut in all formats for Kent last summer

Batting	Mat	Inns	NO	Runs	HS	Ave	SR	100	50	Ct	St
First-class	3	4	0	71	27	17.75	36.22	0	0	1	0
List A	1	1	0	21	21	21.00	80.76	0	0	1	0
T20s	7	6	2	58	23*	14.50	100.00	0	0	1	0
Bowling	**Mat**	**Balls**	**Runs**	**Wkts**	**BBI**	**BBM**	**Ave**	**Econ**	**SR**	**5w**	**10**
First-class	3	-	-	-	-	-	-	-	-	-	-
List A	1	-	-	-	-	-	-	-	-	-	-
T20s	7	-	-	-	-	-	-	-	-	-	-

JOE CRACKNELL RHB / RO / WO

FULL NAME: Joseph Benjamin Cracknell
BORN: March 16, 2000, Enfield, London
SQUAD NO: 48
HEIGHT: 5ft 11in
NICKNAME: Crackers
EDUCATION: London Oratory School; Durham University
TEAMS: Middlesex
ROLE: Batsman
DEBUT: T20: 2019

WHAT WAS YOUR FIRST CRICKET CLUB? North Middlesex CC, London
WHAT WERE YOU DOING WHEN ENGLAND WON THE WORLD CUP? Watching it in the pub with people from my local cricket club
HOW WOULD YOU DISMISS STEVE SMITH? Hit his front shin
MOST INTERESTING TEAMMATE? Sam Robson – hilarious guy
CRICKET STAR OF THE FUTURE? Luke Hollman (Middlesex)
IF YOU WERE AN ANIMAL, WHICH WOULD IT BE? A dog – so I can lie on the sofa all day
TWITTER: @cracknell_joe
NOTES: The 20-year-old batsman signed a one-year rookie contract with Middlesex in January after making his first senior T20 appearance for the club last year. Cracknell has played regularly for the Second XI since making his debut in 2017, a year in which he scored 243 against Kent U17 and was named Middlesex Young Player of the Year. But his stand-out performance was last summer when he made an unbeaten 105 at Merchant Taylors' School against a strong Ireland XI who were warming up for their Test match against England at Lord's. Director of cricket Angus Fraser said: "Joe's talents were identified by Middlesex before he was helping North Middlesex win the league and we believe that his strong and dynamic style of batting will come though, especially in white-ball cricket"

Batting	Mat	Inns	NO	Runs	HS	Ave	SR	100	50	Ct	St
T20s	1	1	0	6	6	6.00	75.00	0	0	0	0
Bowling	**Mat**	**Balls**	**Runs**	**Wkts**	**BBI**	**BBM**	**Ave**	**Econ**	**SR**	**5w**	**10**
T20s	1	-	-	-	-	-	-	-	-	-	-

MASON CRANE

RHB / LB / R0 / W0

FULL NAME: Mason Sidney Crane
BORN: February 18, 1997, Shoreham-by-Sea, Sussex
SQUAD NO: 32
HEIGHT: 5ft 9in
EDUCATION: Lancing College, West Sussex
TEAMS: England, Hampshire, London Spirit, New South Wales
ROLE: Bowler
DEBUT: Test: 2018; T20I: 2017; First-class: 2015; List A: 2015; T20: 2015

BEST BATTING: 29 Hampshire vs Somerset, Taunton, 2017
BEST BOWLING: 5-35 Hampshire vs Warwickshire, Southampton, 2015

WHAT WAS YOUR FIRST CRICKET CLUB? Worthing CC, West Sussex
BEST ADVICE RECEIVED? Never leave a birdie putt short
WHAT EXCITES YOU ABOUT THE HUNDRED? Playing with and against the best players in the world
MOST INTERESTING TEAMMATE? Gareth Berg – never a dull moment
CRICKETING HERO? Shane Warne
SURPRISING FACT ABOUT YOU? To walk back to my mark I always go past the stumps the same side I'm bowling and always turn left at my mark
IF YOU WERE AN ANIMAL, WHICH WOULD IT BE? A tortoise – because they're always at home
TWITTER: @masoncrane32

Batting	Mat	Inns	NO	Runs	HS	Ave	SR	100	50	Ct	St
Tests	1	2	0	6	4	3.00	54.54	0	0	0	0
T20Is	2	-	-	-	-	-	-	-	-	0	0
First-class	38	53	18	386	29	11.02	35.09	0	0	9	0
List A	39	16	12	112	28*	28.00	82.96	0	0	14	0
T20s	28	7	6	19	5*	19.00	65.51	0	0	4	0
Bowling	**Mat**	**Balls**	**Runs**	**Wkts**	**BBI**	**BBM**	**Ave**	**Econ**	**SR**	**5w**	**10**
Tests	1	288	193	1	1/193	1/193	193.00	4.02	288.0	0	0
T20Is	2	48	62	1	1/38	1/38	62.00	7.75	48.0	0	0
First-class	38	6204	4146	82	5/35	6/89	50.56	4.00	75.6	2	0
List A	39	1982	2009	67	4/30	4/30	29.98	6.08	29.5	0	0
T20s	28	576	695	33	3/15	3/15	21.06	7.23	17.4	0	0

ZAK CRAWLEY RHB / RM / R0 / W0 / MVP33

FULL NAME: Zak Crawley
BORN: February 3, 1998, Bromley, Kent
SQUAD NO: 16
HEIGHT: 6ft 5in
NICKNAME: Creepy, Raja
EDUCATION: Tonbridge School, Kent
TEAMS: England, Kent, London Spirit
ROLE: Batsman
DEBUT: First-class: 2017; List A: 2017; T20: 2018

KENT / LONDON SPIRIT

BEST BATTING: 168 Kent vs Glamorgan, Canterbury, 2018

COUNTY CAP: 2019

WHAT WAS YOUR FIRST CRICKET CLUB? Holmesdale CC, Sevenoaks, Kent
HOW WOULD YOU DISMISS STEVE SMITH? Caught at leg slip
BIGGEST TOPIC OF DISCUSSION IN YOUR DRESSING ROOM? Cricket – we're all badgers
MOST INTERESTING TEAMMATE? Mitch Claydon – his life revolves around practical jokes
CRICKETING HERO? Ricky Ponting
WHICH RULE WOULD YOU CHANGE ABOUT CRICKET? You should be able to spray the umpire for giving you a bad decision, and the umpire should be allowed to spray you for complaining if it turns out to be plum
BIGGEST CRICKETING REGRET? My last over in the JET Cup U13 semi-final went for 11 runs. Let the side down
CRICKET STAR OF THE FUTURE? Joe Gordon (Kent Second XI)
WHICH BOOK MEANS MOST TO YOU? The Day After Tomorrow by Allan Folsom
IF YOU WERE AN ANIMAL, WHICH WOULD IT BE? An eagle
TWITTER: @zakcrawley

Batting	Mat	Inns	NO	Runs	HS	Ave	SR	100	50	Ct	St
Tests	4	6	0	164	66	27.33	44.93	0	1	3	0
First-class	42	70	1	2205	168	31.95	57.84	4	12	35	0
List A	23	22	1	743	120	35.38	72.77	1	4	11	0
T20s	13	12	0	310	89	25.83	143.51	0	2	5	0
Bowling	**Mat**	**Balls**	**Runs**	**Wkts**	**BBI**	**BBM**	**Ave**	**Econ**	**SR**	**5w**	**10**
Tests	4	-	-	-	-	-	-	-	-	-	-
First-class	42	66	33	0	-	-	-	3.00	-	0	0
List A	23	12	17	0	-	-	-	8.50	-	0	0
T20s	13	-	-	-	-	-	-	-	-	-	-

MATT CRITCHLEY

RHB / LB / R0 / W0 / MVP45

FULL NAME: Matthew James John Critchley
BORN: August 13, 1996, Preston, Lancashire
SQUAD NO: 20
HEIGHT: 6ft 2in
NICKNAME: Critch
EDUCATION: St Michael's CE High School, Chorley; Cardinal Newman College, Preston; University of Derby
TEAMS: Derbyshire, England Lions
ROLE: Allrounder
DEBUT: First-class: 2015; List A: 2015; T20: 2016

BEST BATTING: 137* Derbyshire vs Northamptonshire, Derby, 2015
BEST BOWLING: 6-106 Derbyshire vs Northamptonshire, Chesterfield, 2018
COUNTY CAP: 2019

WHAT WAS YOUR FIRST CRICKET CLUB? Chorley CC, Lancashire
WHICH BOWLER WOULD YOU LEAST LIKE TO FACE? Stuart MacGill. He still gets me out now
BEST INNINGS YOU'VE SEEN? Kevin Pietersen's 158 at The Oval in the 2005 Ashes
WHO WOULD YOU ASK TO BAT FOR YOUR LIFE? Kevin Pietersen – either way, it would be interesting to watch
FAVOURITE QUOTE OR SAYING? I've missed more than 9,000 shots in my career. I've lost almost 300 games. Twenty-six times I've been trusted to take the game-winning shot and missed. I've failed over and over and over again in my life. And that is why I succeed (Michael Jordan)
WHICH BOOK MEANS MOST TO YOU? No Spin by Shane Warne
TWITTER: @mattcritchley96

Batting	Mat	Inns	NO	Runs	HS	Ave	SR	100	50	Ct	St
First-class	48	81	9	2020	137*	28.05	61.36	3	9	30	0
List A	43	34	9	685	64*	27.40	103.47	0	2	6	0
T20s	51	37	7	524	72*	17.46	122.71	0	1	15	0
Bowling	**Mat**	**Balls**	**Runs**	**Wkts**	**BBI**	**BBM**	**Ave**	**Econ**	**SR**	**5w**	**10**
First-class	48	4509	3221	65	6/106	10/194	49.55	4.28	69.3	1	1
List A	43	1530	1674	31	4/48	4/48	54.00	6.56	49.3	0	0
T20s	51	688	896	39	4/36	4/36	22.97	7.81	17.6	0	0

STEVEN CROFT RHB / RM / OB / R0 / W0 / MVP47

FULL NAME: Steven John Croft
BORN: October 11, 1984, Blackpool
SQUAD NO: 15
HEIGHT: 5ft 11in
NICKNAME: Crofty
EDUCATION: Highfield High School, Blackpool; Myerscough College, Lancashire
TEAMS: Lancashire, Auckland, Northern Districts
ROLE: Batsman
DEBUT: First-class: 2005; List A: 2003; T20: 2006

BEST BATTING: 156 Lancashire vs Northamptonshire, Old Trafford, 2014
BEST BOWLING: 6-41 Lancashire vs Worcestershire, Old Trafford, 2012
COUNTY CAP: 2010; BENEFIT: 2018

WHAT WAS YOUR FIRST CRICKET CLUB? Blackpool CC, Lancashire
HOW WOULD YOU DISMISS STEVE SMITH? In the footy warm-ups
BIGGEST TOPIC OF DISCUSSION IN YOUR DRESSING ROOM? Who is making the next brew
MOST INTERESTING TEAMMATE? James Faulkner – he always has a good story, and it's usually about himself
CRICKETING HERO? Andrew Flintoff – he was from around my area and played in the same league as me
SURPRISING FACT ABOUT YOU? I grew up in Sri Lanka and learnt the game there
CRICKET STAR OF THE FUTURE? George Lavelle (Lancashire)
TWITTER: @Stevenjcroft

Batting	Mat	Inns	NO	Runs	HS	Ave	SR	100	50	Ct	St
First-class	176	270	25	8263	156	33.72	50.78	13	48	176	0
List A	157	140	24	4252	127	36.65		3	31	78	0
T20s	185	170	40	3876	94*	29.81	122.73	0	23	111	0
Bowling	**Mat**	**Balls**	**Runs**	**Wkts**	**BBI**	**BBM**	**Ave**	**Econ**	**SR**	**5w**	**10**
First-class	176	5369	2974	72	6/41	9/105	41.30	3.32	74.5	1	0
List A	157	2787	2561	62	4/24	4/24	41.30	5.51	44.9	0	0
T20s	185	1588	1972	69	3/6	3/6	28.57	7.45	23.0	0	0

BLAKE CULLEN RHB / RFM / R0 / W0

FULL NAME: Blake Carlton Cullen
BORN: March 31, 2002, Hounslow, London
SQUAD NO: 19
HEIGHT: 6ft 3in
NICKNAME: Biebs, The Hammer
EDUCATION: Hampton School, London
TEAMS: Middlesex, England U19
ROLE: Bowler

WHAT WAS YOUR FIRST CRICKET CLUB? Wycombe House CC, Middlesex
WHAT WERE YOU DOING WHEN ENGLAND WON THE WORLD CUP? Watching it with the Young Lions team during a training session
HOW WOULD YOU DISMISS STEVE SMITH? Caught down the leg-side
WHAT EXCITES YOU ABOUT THE HUNDRED? Watching the best in the world go up against each other
BIGGEST TOPIC OF DISCUSSION IN YOUR DRESSING ROOM? Football
MOST INTERESTING TEAMMATE? James Harris – because of his avid love of cycling and fitness
CRICKET STAR OF THE FUTURE? Thilan Walallawita (Middlesex)
IF YOU WERE AN ANIMAL, WHICH WOULD IT BE? A dolphin – I'm enthusiastic and friendly
NOTES: A tall seamer who made his Middlesex Second XI debut in 2017 at the age of just 15, Cullen signed a rookie contract with the club in February which will last until at least the end of the 2022 season. The 18-year-old was a regular for England U19 last year and a member of the 2020 World Cup squad. He first represented Middlesex at U10 level and has come through the Academy system. Director of cricket Angus Fraser said: "He may only be [young] but he bowls like a grown man, which is a characteristic you don't see in many teenagers. Blake is tall, aggressive and has a good, strong, easy-to-repeat bowling action, assets which could quickly see him competing for a place in our First XI"

TOM CULLEN

RHB / WK / R0 / W0

FULL NAME: Thomas Nicholas Cullen
BORN: January 4, 1992, Perth, Australia
SQUAD NO: 54
HEIGHT: 5ft 11in
NICKNAME: TC, Culley, Teece
EDUCATION: Aquinas College, Perth; Cardiff Metropolitan University
TEAMS: Glamorgan
ROLE: Wicketkeeper
DEBUT: First-class: 2015

BEST BATTING: 63 Glamorgan vs Northamptonshire, Northampton, 2019

WHAT WAS YOUR FIRST CRICKET CLUB? South Perth CC, Western Australia
BEST ADVICE EVER RECEIVED? Nothing worth experiencing comes easy
HOW WOULD YOU DISMISS STEVE SMITH? Bounce him with five out on the leg-side
BIGGEST TOPIC OF DISCUSSION IN YOUR DRESSING ROOM? How we're going to find the next winner (horse racing)
MOST INTERESTING TEAMMATE? Marnus Labuschagne – the guy has so much energy, all the time!
CRICKETING HERO? Growing up in Australia, I loved watching Ricky Ponting and Adam Gilchrist come to play at the WACA every year
SURPRISING FACT ABOUT YOU? When I was younger I wanted to be a fighter pilot
SURPRISING FACT ABOUT A TEAMMATE? Connor Brown has a lot of stories and will make a great grandad one day
CRICKET STAR OF THE FUTURE? Alex Horton (Glamorgan Academy) – the kid that'll probably end up taking my spot in the team!
IF YOU WERE AN ANIMAL, WHICH WOULD IT BE? A lion – if you're coming at me, I'm not backing down
TWITTER: @thomascullen186

Batting	Mat	Inns	NO	Runs	HS	Ave	SR	100	50	Ct	St
First-class	17	25	3	502	63	22.81	39.65	0	4	44	1
Bowling	**Mat**	**Balls**	**Runs**	**Wkts**	**BBI**	**BBM**	**Ave**	**Econ**	**SR**	**5w**	**10**
First-class	17	-	-	-	-	-	-	-	-	-	-

MIGUEL CUMMINS

LHB / RFM / R0 / W0

FULL NAME: Miguel Lamar Cummins
BORN: September 5, 1990, St Michael, Barbados
SQUAD NO: 41
HEIGHT: 6ft 2in
NICKNAME: Miggy
EDUCATION: Parkinson Memorial School, Bridgetown, Barbados; University of the West Indies, Kingston, Jamaica
TEAMS: West Indies, Middlesex, Barbados, Trinidad & Tobago Red Steel, Worcestershire
ROLE: Bowler
DEBUT: Test: 2016; ODI: 2014; First-class: 2012; List A: 2013; T20: 2013

BEST BATTING: 29* Barbados vs Leeward Islands, Basseterre, 2016
BEST BOWLING: 7-45 Barbados vs Trinidad & Tobago, Port of Spain, 2013

WHAT WAS YOUR FIRST CRICKET CLUB? YMPC CC, Bridgetown, Barbados
BIGGEST TOPIC OF DISCUSSION IN YOUR DRESSING ROOM? Music
CRICKET STAR OF THE FUTURE? Zachary McCaskie (Barbados)
IF YOU WERE AN ANIMAL, WHICH WOULD IT BE? A killer whale – fierce but also gentle
TWITTER: @lamar_pooh
NOTES: The Bajan fast bowler had a brief stint with Middlesex at the end of last summer on the recommendation of head coach Stuart Law, who had worked with Cummins when coaching the West Indies. He took eight wickets in three Championship matches and impressed enough to earn a three-year Kolpak contract with the club in October, effectively terminating his international career. Cummins played the last of his 14 Tests for West Indies last August. Middlesex director of cricket Angus Fraser said: "He has control, is able to move the ball away from a right-handed batsman and, I believe, the ability to bowl fast, aggressive spells when conditions dictate"

Batting	Mat	Inns	NO	Runs	HS	Ave	SR	100	50	Ct	St
Tests	14	22	7	114	24*	7.60	35.51	0	0	2	0
ODIs	11	3	1	10	5	5.00	37.03	0	0	1	0
First-class	79	103	42	408	29*	6.68	36.07	0	0	31	0
List A	35	14	8	62	20	10.33	68.88	0	0	10	0
T20s	9	5	4	14	10	14.00	58.33	0	0	5	0
Bowling	**Mat**	**Balls**	**Runs**	**Wkts**	**BBI**	**BBM**	**Ave**	**Econ**	**SR**	**5w**	**10**
Tests	14	1976	1084	27	6/48	9/102	40.14	3.29	73.1	1	0
ODIs	11	450	474	9	3/82	3/82	52.66	6.32	50.0	0	0
First-class	79	10738	5672	218	7/45	12/166	26.01	3.16	49.2	9	1
List A	35	1578	1256	48	4/27	4/27	26.16	4.77	32.8	0	0
T20s	9	108	150	4	3/19	3/19	37.50	8.33	27.0	0	0

BEN CURRAN

LHB / OB / R0 / W0

FULL NAME: Benjamin Jack Curran
BORN: June 7, 1996, Northampton
SQUAD NO: 57
HEIGHT: 5ft 9in
NICKNAME: Lord, BC
EDUCATION: Wellington College, Berkshire
TEAMS: Northamptonshire
ROLE: Batsman
DEBUT: First-class: 2018; List A: 2019; T20: 2018

BEST BATTING: 83* Northamptonshire vs Sussex, Northampton, 2018

FAMILY TIES? My father Kevin played for Zimbabwe, Gloucestershire and Northamptonshire. My older brother Tom and younger brother Sam both play for Surrey
WHAT WAS YOUR FIRST CRICKET CLUB? Weybridge CC, Surrey
WHAT WERE YOU DOING WHEN ENGLAND WON THE WORLD CUP? I was there!
HOW WOULD YOU DISMISS STEVE SMITH? An away-swinging nip-backer
BIGGEST TOPIC OF DISCUSSION IN YOUR DRESSING ROOM? Winning
BEST INNINGS YOU'VE EVER SEEN? Adam Gilchrist's 149 in the 2007 World Cup final
WHICH RULE WOULD YOU CHANGE ABOUT CRICKET? Make lunch half an hour and tea half an hour
BIGGEST CRICKETING REGRET? Not bowling left-arm
IF YOU WERE AN ANIMAL, WHICH WOULD IT BE? A peacock
TWITTER: @curranjb_57

Batting	Mat	Inns	NO	Runs	HS	Ave	SR	100	50	Ct	St
First-class	13	22	3	619	83*	32.57	52.59	0	4	6	0
List A	3	3	0	102	69	34.00	89.47	0	1	2	0
T20s	5	5	0	54	29	10.80	103.84	0	0	2	0
Bowling	**Mat**	**Balls**	**Runs**	**Wkts**	**BBI**	**BBM**	**Ave**	**Econ**	**SR**	**5w**	**10**
First-class	13	-	-	-	-	-	-	-	-	-	-
List A	3	-	-	-	-	-	-	-	-	-	-
T20s	5	-	-	-	-	-	-	-	-	-	-

SAM CURRAN LHB / LFM / R0 / W0

SURREY / OVAL INVINCIBLES

FULL NAME: Samuel Matthew Curran
BORN: June 3, 1998, Northampton
SQUAD NO: 58
HEIGHT: 5ft 11in
NICKNAME: Junior, Sammy
EDUCATION: Wellington College, Berkshire
TEAMS: England, Surrey, Oval Invincibles, Auckland, Chennai Super Kings, Kings XI Punjab
ROLE: Allrounder
DEBUT: Test: 2018; ODI: 2018; T20I: 2019; First-class: 2015; List A: 2015; T20: 2015

BEST BATTING: 96 Surrey vs Lancashire, The Oval, 2016
BEST BOWLING: 7-58 Surrey vs Durham, Chester-le-Street, 2016
COUNTY CAP: 2018

FAMILY TIES? My father Kevin played for Zimbabwe, and my brother Tom plays with me at Surrey. Ben, my other brother, plays for Northants. We have always been a competitive family
CRICKETING HERO? Brian Lara
TWITTER: @CurranSM

Batting	Mat	Inns	NO	Runs	HS	Ave	SR	100	50	Ct	St
Tests	17	30	4	711	78	27.34	66.20	0	3	3	0
ODIs	4	3	0	24	15	8.00	51.06	0	0	0	0
T20Is	5	3	0	35	24	11.66	152.17	0	0	0	0
First-class	67	105	13	2602	96	28.28	60.69	0	18	17	0
List A	53	35	5	604	57	20.13	83.08	0	1	20	0
T20s	69	55	11	838	55*	19.04	130.93	0	4	18	0
Bowling	**Mat**	**Balls**	**Runs**	**Wkts**	**BBI**	**BBM**	**Ave**	**Econ**	**SR**	**5w**	**10**
Tests	17	2158	1173	37	4/58	5/92	31.70	3.26	58.3	0	0
ODIs	4	114	134	2	2/44	2/44	67.00	7.05	57.0	0	0
T20Is	5	108	153	6	2/22	2/22	25.50	8.50	18.0	0	0
First-class	67	9594	5417	183	7/58	10/101	29.60	3.38	52.4	7	1
List A	53	2334	2173	68	4/32	4/32	31.95	5.58	34.3	0	0
T20s	69	1323	1908	63	4/11	4/11	30.28	8.65	21.0	0	0

TOM CURRAN

RHB / RFM / R0 / W1

FULL NAME: Thomas Kevin Curran
BORN: March 12, 1995, Cape Town, South Africa
SQUAD NO: 59
HEIGHT: 6ft
NICKNAME: TC
EDUCATION: Wellington College, Berkshire
TEAMS: England, Surrey, Oval Invincibles, Kolkata Knight Riders, Rajasthan Royals, Sydney Sixers
ROLE: Allrounder
DEBUT: Test: 2017; ODI: 2017; T20I: 2017; First-class: 2014; List A: 2013; T20: 2014

BEST BATTING: 60 Surrey vs Leicestershire, Leicester, 2015
BEST BOWLING: 7-20 Surrey vs Gloucestershire, The Oval, 2015
COUNTY CAP: 2016

FAMILY TIES? My father Kevin played for Northants and Zimbabwe, my brother Sam also plays for Surrey, and my other younger brother Ben is at Northants
CRICKETING HERO? Hamilton Masakadza
IF YOU WEREN'T A CRICKETER? I would be fishing or playing the guitar in a bar somewhere exotic
SURPRISING FACT ABOUT YOU? I have a degree in Law
TWITTER: @_TC59

Batting	Mat	Inns	NO	Runs	HS	Ave	SR	100	50	Ct	St
Tests	2	3	1	66	39	33.00	55.00	0	0	0	0
ODIs	20	13	8	198	47*	39.60	102.59	0	0	4	0
T20Is	18	8	5	38	14*	12.66	131.03	0	0	4	0
First-class	59	81	11	1241	60	17.72	50.75	0	5	20	0
List A	78	52	20	634	47*	19.81	95.77	0	0	25	0
T20s	120	69	22	873	62	18.57	133.48	0	2	36	0
Bowling	**Mat**	**Balls**	**Runs**	**Wkts**	**BBI**	**BBM**	**Ave**	**Econ**	**SR**	**5w**	**10**
Tests	2	396	200	2	1/65	1/82	100.00	3.03	198.0	0	0
ODIs	20	870	894	27	5/35	5/35	33.11	6.16	32.2	1	0
T20Is	18	354	537	21	4/36	4/36	25.57	9.10	16.8	0	0
First-class	59	10341	5613	195	7/20	10/176	28.78	3.25	53.0	7	1
List A	78	3471	3237	119	5/16	5/16	27.20	5.59	29.1	3	0
T20s	120	2417	3496	149	4/22	4/22	23.46	8.67	16.2	0	0

ANUJ DAL RHB / RM / R0 / W0

FULL NAME: Anuj Kailash Dal
BORN: July 8, 1996, Newcastle-under-Lyme, Staffordshire
SQUAD NO: 65
HEIGHT: 5ft 9in
NICKNAME: Nuj, Nuji
EDUCATION: Nottingham High School
TEAMS: Derbyshire
ROLE: Batsman
DEBUT: First-class: 2018; List A: 2019; T20: 2018

BEST BATTING: 92 Derbyshire vs Middlesex, Derby, 2019
BEST BOWLING: 3-11 Derbyshire vs Sussex, Derby, 2019

WHAT WAS YOUR FIRST CRICKET CLUB? Kimberley Institute CC, Nottinghamshire
WHAT WERE YOU DOING WHEN ENGLAND WON THE WORLD CUP? Watching while listening to Test Match Special
HOW WOULD YOU DISMISS STEVE SMITH? I've already tried when I bowled to him last year. Felt as though I was bowling 50mph, so I asked the skipper to take me off!
BIGGEST TOPIC OF DISCUSSION IN YOUR DRESSING ROOM? The draft for The Hundred
MOST INTERESTING TEAMMATE? Tony Palladino – he's a great story-teller and is full of hilarious impressions of players
WHICH RULE WOULD YOU CHANGE ABOUT CRICKET? Make lunch and tea longer!
CRICKET STAR OF THE FUTURE? An U13 Notts leg-spinner I coach called Adit. He bowls googlies at will
IF YOU WERE AN ANIMAL, WHICH WOULD IT BE? I'm a tragic dog-owner, so definitely a dog
TWITTER: @AnujDal

Batting	Mat	Inns	NO	Runs	HS	Ave	SR	100	50	Ct	St
First-class	15	26	4	402	92	18.27	40.52	0	2	9	0
List A	5	3	1	72	52	36.00	124.13	0	1	1	0
T20s	13	9	2	94	35	13.42	120.51	0	0	5	0
Bowling	**Mat**	**Balls**	**Runs**	**Wkts**	**BBI**	**BBM**	**Ave**	**Econ**	**SR**	**5w**	**10**
First-class	15	382	181	9	3/11	3/11	20.11	2.84	42.4	0	0
List A	5	-	-	-	-	-	-	-	-	-	-
T20s	13	-	-	-	-	-	-	-	-	-	-

JOSH DAVEY

RHB / RMF / RO / WO

FULL NAME: Joshua Henry Davey
BORN: August 3, 1990, Aberdeen, Scotland
SQUAD NO: 38
HEIGHT: 6ft
NICKNAME: JD
EDUCATION: Culford School, Bury St Edmunds; Oxford Brookes University
TEAMS: Scotland, Somerset, Hampshire, Middlesex
ROLE: Allrounder
DEBUT: ODI: 2010; T20I: 2012; First-class: 2010; List A: 2010; T20I: 2010

BEST BATTING: 72 Middlesex vs Oxford MCCU, Oxford, 2010
BEST BOWLING: 5-21 Somerset vs Yorkshire, Taunton, 2019

WHAT WAS YOUR FIRST CRICKET CLUB? Bury St Edmunds CC, Suffolk
BEST INNINGS YOU'VE SEEN? Chris Gayle's 151 not out against Kent at Taunton in 2015
WHO WOULD YOU ASK TO BAT FOR YOUR LIFE? Brian Lara – anyone who can score 500 in an innings has my trust
TWITTER: @JoshDavey38
NOTES: After four years at Middlesex, Davey was released at the end of 2013 and excelled for Somerset Second XI in 2014, which led to a full contract at the county. The seam-bowling allrounder played for Scotland in the 2015 World Cup, finishing as his team's highest wicket-taker. He was a peripheral figure at Somerset for a few seasons until making the breakthrough in 2018 with 34 Championship wickets at 25.35. Injury restricted his appeareances last summer, but he still managed 17 wickets at 17.71 in the Championship and 14 at 27.29 in the One-Day Cup

Batting	Mat	Inns	NO	Runs	HS	Ave	SR	100	50	Ct	St
ODIs	31	28	6	497	64	22.59	66.98	0	2	10	0
T20Is	21	10	5	83	24	16.60	131.74	0	0	12	0
First-class	32	52	9	725	72	16.86	45.45	0	3	12	0
List A	86	68	16	1210	91	23.26	66.92	0	5	27	0
T20s	44	23	12	201	24	18.27	126.41	0	0	24	0
Bowling	**Mat**	**Balls**	**Runs**	**Wkts**	**BBI**	**BBM**	**Ave**	**Econ**	**SR**	**5w**	**10**
ODIs	31	1301	1082	49	6/28	6/28	22.08	4.99	26.5	2	0
T20Is	21	448	610	24	4/34	4/34	25.41	8.16	18.6	0	0
First-class	32	4014	1978	81	5/21	8/51	24.41	2.95	49.5	2	0
List A	86	3164	2811	105	6/28	6/28	26.77	5.33	30.1	2	0
T20s	44	694	1013	41	4/34	4/34	24.70	8.75	16.9	0	0

ALEX DAVIES

RHB / WK / R1 / W0

FULL NAME: Alexander Luke Davies
BORN: August 23, 1994, Darwen, Lancashire
SQUAD NO: 17
HEIGHT: 5ft 8in
NICKNAME: Davo, Warwick
EDUCATION: Queen Elizabeth's Grammar School, Blackburn
TEAMS: Lancashire, Southern Brave, England Lions
ROLE: Batsman/wicketkeeper
DEBUT: First-class: 2012; List A: 2011; T20: 2014

BEST BATTING: 147 Lancashire vs Northamptonshire, Northampton, 2019

COUNTY CAP: 2017

FAMILY TIES? Dad played club cricket all his life
WHAT WAS YOUR FIRST CRICKET CLUB? Darwen CC, Lancashire
WHAT WERE YOU DOING WHEN ENGLAND WON THE WORLD CUP? Watching it in the Lancashire dressing room
WHAT EXCITES YOU ABOUT THE HUNDRED? The free crisps!
BIGGEST TOPIC OF DISCUSSION IN YOUR DRESSING ROOM? Fantasy Football and Liam Livingstone's hairline
CRICKETING HERO? Sachin Tendulkar
SURPRISING FACT ABOUT YOU? Despite being a wicketkeeper, I can bowl with bowl arms
CRICKET STAR OF THE FUTURE? Rocky Flintoff (Lancashire U13)
IF YOU WERE AN ANIMAL, WHICH WOULD IT BE? A penguin
TWITTER: @aldavies23

Batting	Mat	Inns	NO	Runs	HS	Ave	SR	100	50	Ct	St
First-class	75	114	5	3766	147	34.55	56.79	5	23	156	15
List A	49	46	3	1380	147	32.09	90.49	1	7	48	11
T20s	53	49	9	1140	94*	28.50	129.39	0	8	30	4
Bowling	**Mat**	**Balls**	**Runs**	**Wkts**	**BBI**	**BBM**	**Ave**	**Econ**	**SR**	**5w**	**10**
First-class	75	6	6	0	-	-	-	6.00	-	0	0
List A	49	-	-	-	-	-	-	-	-	-	-
T20s	53	-	-	-	-	-	-	-	-	-	-

JACK DAVIES

LHB / WK / R0 / W0

MIDDLESEX

FULL NAME: Jack Leo Benjamin Davies
BORN: March 30, 2000, Reading
SQUAD NO: 23
HEIGHT: 5ft 8in
NICKNAME: Davo
EDUCATION: Wellington College, Berkshire
TEAMS: Middlesex, England U19
ROLE: Wicketkeeper/batsman

WHAT WAS YOUR FIRST CRICKET CLUB? Henley CC, Oxfordshire
BIGGEST TOPIC OF DISCUSSION IN YOUR DRESSING ROOM? How Max Holden and Nick Gubbins are so bad at football
MOST INTERESTING TEAMMATE? James Fuller – he measures how far he hits the ball on Google Maps
BIGGEST CRICKETING REGRET? Plenty of leaves which have blown my pads off
CRICKET STAR OF THE FUTURE? Blake Cullen (England U19, Middlesex Academy)
IF YOU WERE AN ANIMAL, WHICH WOULD IT BE? A shark
TWITTER: @daviesjlb
NOTES: The 20-year-old wicketkeeper-batsman signed his first professional contract in November 2018 when he agreed a two-year deal with Middlesex. Davies inspired Berkshire to the Minor Counties double in 2017, hitting an unbeaten 127 in the one-day final against Lincolnshire. He made his Middlesex Second XI debut that summer and was selected by England for the 2018 U19 World Cup in New Zealand. Last summer he was a regular in the Second XI Championship side, making two fifties in nine matches, but his starring role was for Berkshire in the Minor Counties final against Staffordshire at Bodicote. Chasing just 97 for victory, Berkshire collapsed to 87-9 only for opener Davies (42 not out) to hold firm and see his club to a one-wicket victory and a record-equalling fourth successive Minor Counties crown

STEVEN DAVIES

LHB / WK / R6 / W0

SOMERSET

FULL NAME: Steven Michael Davies
BORN: June 17, 1986, Bromsgrove, Worcestershire
SQUAD NO: 11
HEIGHT: 6ft
NICKNAME: Davos
EDUCATION: King Charles High School, Kidderminster
TEAMS: England, Somerset, Surrey, Worcestershire
ROLE: Batsman/wicketkeeper
DEBUT: ODI: 2009; T20I: 2009; First-class: 2005; List A: 2003; T20: 2006

BEST BATTING: 200* Surrey vs Glamorgan, Cardiff, 2015

COUNTY CAP: 2011 (Surrey); 2017 (Somerset)

WHAT WAS YOUR FIRST CRICKET CLUB? Victoria Carpets CC, Kidderminster, Worcestershire
WHAT WERE YOU DOING WHEN ENGLAND WON THE WORLD CUP? Watching it in a hotel reception area in Leeds
MOST INTERESTING TEAMMATE? Jack Brooks – I didn't know ferrets could talk!
CRICKETING HERO? Adam Gilchrist
WHICH RULE WOULD YOU CHANGE ABOUT CRICKET? Make the stumps taller
SURPRISING FACT ABOUT YOU? I'm a session harp player
BIGGEST CRICKETING REGRET? Getting to Finals Day and not winning
CRICKET STAR OF THE FUTURE? Kasey Aldridge (Somerset)
WHICH BOOK MEANS MOST TO YOU? Open by Andre Agassi
TWITTER: @SteveDavies43

Batting	Mat	Inns	NO	Runs	HS	Ave	SR	100	50	Ct	St
ODIs	8	8	0	244	87	30.50	105.62	0	1	8	0
T20Is	5	5	0	102	33	20.40	124.39	0	0	2	1
First-class	225	374	35	13097	200*	38.63	60.54	24	61	532	33
List A	184	173	14	5645	127*	35.50		9	35	147	42
T20s	142	133	8	2644	99*	21.15	142.15	0	15	65	23
Bowling	**Mat**	**Balls**	**Runs**	**Wkts**	**BBI**	**BBM**	**Ave**	**Econ**	**SR**	**5w**	**10**
ODIs	8	-	-	-	-	-	-	-	-	-	-
T20Is	5	-	-	-	-	-	-	-	-	-	-
First-class	225	-	-	-	-	-	-	-	-	-	-
List A	184	-	-	-	-	-	-	-	-	-	-
T20s	142	-	-	-	-	-	-	-	-	-	-

WILL DAVIS

RHB / RFM / R0 / W0

FULL NAME: William Samuel Davis
BORN: March 6, 1996, Stafford
SQUAD NO: 44
HEIGHT: 6ft 2in
NICKNAME: Thumb, Spaceman
EDUCATION: Stafford Grammar School
TEAMS: Leicestershire, Derbyshire, England U19
ROLE: Bowler
DEBUT: First-class: 2015; List A: 2016; T20: 2019

BEST BATTING: 39* Leicestershire vs Glamorgan, Cardiff, 2019
BEST BOWLING: 7-146 Derbyshire vs Glamorgan, Colwyn Bay, 2016

STRANGEST THING SEEN IN A GAME? Greg Cork's field placements
BEST MOMENT IN CRICKET? Taking my maiden five-wicket haul in first-class cricket against Glamorgan at Colwyn Bay in 2016
SUPERSTITIONS? I have to turn at the end of my bowling mark before running in
CRICKETING HERO? Andrew Flintoff
NON-CRICKETING HERO? Cristiano Ronaldo
IF YOU WEREN'T A CRICKETER? I'd be a professional gamer
TWITTER: @W_Davis44

Batting	Mat	Inns	NO	Runs	HS	Ave	SR	100	50	Ct	St
First-class	24	34	12	254	39*	11.54	46.77	0	0	3	0
List A	4	2	1	17	15*	17.00	70.83	0	0	1	0
T20s	10	3	2	2	2	2.00	66.66	0	0	2	0
Bowling	**Mat**	**Balls**	**Runs**	**Wkts**	**BBI**	**BBM**	**Ave**	**Econ**	**SR**	**5w**	**10**
First-class	24	3576	2217	69	7/146	8/204	32.13	3.71	51.8	1	0
List A	4	135	178	2	1/60	1/60	89.00	7.91	67.5	0	0
T20s	10	159	223	9	3/24	3/24	24.77	8.41	17.6	0	0

LIAM DAWSON RHB / SLA / R1 / W0 / MVP11

FULL NAME: Liam Andrew Dawson
BORN: March 1, 1990, Swindon
SQUAD NO: 8
HEIGHT: 5ft 8in
NICKNAME: Daws, Lemmy, Chav, Stomper
EDUCATION: The John Bentley School, Wiltshire
TEAMS: England, Hampshire, Southern Brave, Comilla Victorians, Essex, Mountaineers, Peshawar Zalmi, Rangpur Riders
ROLE: Allrounder
DEBUT: Test: 2016; ODI: 2016; T20I: 2016; First-class: 2007; List A: 2007; T20: 2008

BEST BATTING: 169 Hampshire vs Somerset, Southampton, 2011
BEST BOWLING: 7-51 Mountaineers vs Mashonaland Eagles, Mutare Sports Club, 2011
COUNTY CAP: 2013 (Hampshire)

WHAT GOT YOU INTO CRICKET? Watching my dad play for Goatacre CC in Wiltshire
FAMILY TIES? My brother Brad has played Minor Counties for Wiltshire
BEST MOMENT IN CRICKET? My England debut in 2016
CRICKETING HERO? Shane Warne
IF YOU WEREN'T A CRICKETER? I'd be an umpire
TWITTER: @daws128

Batting	Mat	Inns	NO	Runs	HS	Ave	SR	100	50	Ct	St
Tests	3	6	2	84	66*	21.00	42.63	0	1	2	0
ODIs	3	2	0	14	10	7.00	82.35	0	0	0	0
T20Is	6	2	1	17	10	17.00	212.50	0	0	2	0
First-class	151	246	26	7320	169	33.27	49.23	9	41	144	0
List A	160	130	23	3529	113*	32.98	95.32	3	18	72	0
T20s	169	126	31	1914	82	20.14	114.06	0	5	75	0
Bowling	**Mat**	**Balls**	**Runs**	**Wkts**	**BBI**	**BBM**	**Ave**	**Econ**	**SR**	**5w**	**10**
Tests	3	526	298	7	2/34	4/101	42.57	3.39	75.1	0	0
ODIs	3	84	96	3	2/70	2/70	32.00	6.85	28.0	0	0
T20Is	6	120	152	5	3/27	3/27	30.40	7.60	24.0	0	0
First-class	151	14440	7181	203	7/51	8/129	35.37	2.98	71.1	3	0
List A	160	6206	4890	162	6/47	6/47	30.18	4.72	38.3	1	0
T20s	169	2699	3278	120	5/17	5/17	27.31	7.28	22.4	1	0

MARCHANT DE LANGE RHB / RF / R0 / W0 / MVP75

FULL NAME: Marchant de Lange
BORN: October 13, 1990, Tzaneen, Transvaal, South Africa
SQUAD NO: 90
HEIGHT: 6ft 7in
NICKNAME: Shanna
TEAMS: South Africa, Glamorgan, Manchester Originals, Barbados Tridents, Durban Heat, Easterns, Free State, Knights, Kolkata Knight Riders, Mumbai Indians, Titans
ROLE: Bowler
DEBUT: Test: 2011; ODI: 2012; T20I: 2012; First-class: 2010; List A: 2010; T20: 2011

BEST BATTING: 90 Glamorgan vs Leicestershire, Leicester, 2018
BEST BOWLING: 7-23 Knights vs Titans, Centurion, 2016

WHAT WAS YOUR FIRST CRICKET CLUB? Tzaneen CC, Limpopo, South Africa
BEST ADVICE EVER RECEIVED? Bowl top of off stump
BIGGEST TOPIC OF DISCUSSION IN YOUR DRESSING ROOM? How to improve performance
MOST INTERESTING TEAMMATE? Jacques Kallis
CRICKETING HERO? Dale Steyn
SURPRISING FACT ABOUT YOU? I love art

Batting	Mat	Inns	NO	Runs	HS	Ave	SR	100	50	Ct	St
Tests	2	2	0	9	9	4.50	47.36	0	0	1	0
ODIs	4	-	-	-	-	-	-	-	-	0	0
T20Is	6	-	-	-	-	-	-	-	-	1	0
First-class	82	109	16	1450	90	15.59	73.67	0	3	34	0
List A	95	66	18	750	58*	15.62	108.06	0	2	25	0
T20s	94	34	15	195	27*	10.26	131.75	0	0	22	0
Bowling	**Mat**	**Balls**	**Runs**	**Wkts**	**BBI**	**BBM**	**Ave**	**Econ**	**SR**	**5w**	**10**
Tests	2	448	277	9	7/81	8/126	30.77	3.70	49.7	1	0
ODIs	4	209	198	10	4/46	4/46	19.80	5.68	20.9	0	0
T20Is	6	140	228	7	2/26	2/26	32.57	9.77	20.0	0	0
First-class	82	15226	9168	305	7/23	11/62	30.05	3.61	49.9	11	2
List A	95	4684	4273	169	5/49	5/49	25.28	5.47	27.7	4	0
T20s	94	1848	2680	106	4/23	4/23	25.28	8.70	17.4	0	0

HARRY DEARDEN

LHB / OB / R0 / W0

FULL NAME: Harry Edward Dearden
BORN: May 7, 1997, Bury, Lancashire
SQUAD NO: 5
HEIGHT: 5ft 8in
NICKNAME: H, Haz, Deards
EDUCATION: Tottington High School, Bury; Bury College
TEAMS: Leicestershire
ROLE: Batsman
DEBUT: First-class: 2016; List A: 2018; T20: 2018

BEST BATTING: 87 Leicestershire vs Glamorgan, Leicester, 2017
BEST BOWLING: 1-0 Leicestershire vs Kent, Leicester, 2017

WHAT GOT YOU INTO CRICKET? The 2005 Ashes. I still have the box set at home and get it out from time to time
FAMILY TIES? Dad played for the Lancashire Cricket Board and still plays now
BEST MOMENT IN CRICKET? My first-class debut for Leicestershire in 2016
STRANGEST THING SEEN IN A GAME? It happened during a T20 on a wet Friday night for my club team. The ball was pretty soggy before an opposition batter hit it out the ground. We gave a replacement ball to the umpire, who proceeded to wipe it along the wet outfield, claiming the substitute ball had to be in the exact same state as the lost one. Madness
SURPRISING FACT ABOUT YOU? I was on a Channel 4 roadshow for the 2001 Ashes series, having a split-screen with Shane Warne
CRICKETING HERO? Brian Lara
NON-CRICKETING HERO? Roy Keane
TWITTER: @HarryDearden97

Batting	Mat	Inns	NO	Runs	HS	Ave	SR	100	50	Ct	St
First-class	37	63	2	1269	87	20.80	41.47	0	6	27	0
List A	10	10	0	341	91	34.10	89.97	0	3	2	0
T20s	14	13	2	228	61	20.72	115.73	0	1	7	0
Bowling	**Mat**	**Balls**	**Runs**	**Wkts**	**BBI**	**BBM**	**Ave**	**Econ**	**SR**	**5w**	**10**
First-class	37	124	108	2	1/0	1/0	54.00	5.22	62.0	0	0
List A	10	-	-	-	-	-	-	-	-	-	-
T20s	14	-	-	-	-	-	-	-	-	-	-

JOSH DELL

RHB / RM / R0 / W0

FULL NAME: Joshua Jamie Dell
BORN: September 26, 1997, Tenbury Wells, Worcestershire
SQUAD NO: 52
HEIGHT: 6ft 2in
NICKNAME: Dellboy
EDUCATION: Abberley Hall School, Worcestershire; Cheltenham College
TEAMS: Worcestershire, England U19
ROLE: Batsman
DEBUT: First-class: 2019; List A: 2018

BEST BATTING: 61 Worcestershire vs Durham, Worcester, 2019

WHAT WAS YOUR FIRST CRICKET CLUB? Ombersley CC, Worcestershire. I've been playing there since I was 11
WHAT EXCITES YOU ABOUT THE HUNDRED? Bigger crowds
BEST INNINGS YOU'VE SEEN? AB de Villiers's 162 not out off 66 balls against West Indies at Sydney in the 2015 World Cup
CRICKET STAR OF THE FUTURE? Jack Haynes (Worcestershire)
WHICH BOOK MEANS MOST TO YOU? Bounce – The Myth of Talent and the Power of Practice by Matthew Syed
IF YOU WERE AN ANIMAL, WHICH WOULD IT BE? A Philippine eagle
NOTES: The former England U19 batsman has come through the Worcestershire Academy and signed his first professional contract in June 2018. Later that month he made an impressive 46 on his List A debut against a strong West Indies A attack at New Road. Dell scored his maiden first-class fifty last summer against Durham at Worcester and signed a new deal which ties him to the county until the end of the 2021 season

Batting	Mat	Inns	NO	Runs	HS	Ave	SR	100	50	Ct	St
First-class	7	12	0	158	61	13.16	31.47	0	1	5	0
List A	1	1	0	46	46	46.00	102.22	0	0	1	0
Bowling	**Mat**	**Balls**	**Runs**	**Wkts**	**BBI**	**BBM**	**Ave**	**Econ**	**SR**	**5w**	**10**
First-class	7	-	-	-	-	-	-	-	-	-	-
List A	1	-	-	-	-	-	-	-	-	-	-

CAMERON DELPORT LHB / RM / R0 / W0

FULL NAME: Cameron Scott Delport
BORN: May 12, 1989, Durban, South Africa
SQUAD NO: 89
HEIGHT: 6ft
NICKNAME: Camo, Delpo, Goose
EDUCATION: Westville Boys' High School, Durban; UCT Graduate School of Business, Cape Town
TEAMS: Essex, Birmingham Phoenix, Dolphins, Guyana Amazon Warriors, Karachi Kings, KwaZulu-Natal, Leicestershire, Rangpur Rangers, Sydney Thunder
ROLE: Batsman
DEBUT: First-class: 2009; List A: 2009; T20: 2010

BEST BATTING: 129 Essex vs Surrey, Chelmsford, 2019 (T20)
BEST BOWLING: 4-17 Dolphins vs Lions, Durban, 2016 (T20)

WHAT WAS YOUR FIRST CRICKET CLUB? Forest Hills CC, Durban, South Africa
BEST ADVICE RECEIVED? See ball, hit ball
WHAT WERE YOU DOING WHEN ENGLAND WON THE WORLD CUP? Riding bikes around London trying to find a fan park to watch the final
WHAT EXCITES YOU ABOUT THE HUNDRED? The new format – I have no clue what to expect but it should be exciting
MOST INTERESTING TEAMMATE? Shane Snater – messy man who takes up all the space, although he does clean up well
SURPRISING FACT ABOUT YOU? I'm a great barbecue chef and entertainer
CRICKET STAR OF THE FUTURE? Jason Biddulph (Pietermaritzburg Spurs in KwaZulu-Natal, South Africa)
TWITTER: @Cam12Delport

Batting	Mat	Inns	NO	Runs	HS	Ave	SR	100	50	Ct	St
First-class	61	106	6	3206	163	32.06	88.29	3	19	36	0
List A	107	97	6	2765	169*	30.38	105.93	3	15	38	0
T20s	236	228	13	5557	129	25.84	139.97	5	28	78	0
Bowling	**Mat**	**Balls**	**Runs**	**Wkts**	**BBI**	**BBM**	**Ave**	**Econ**	**SR**	**5w**	**10**
First-class	61	1183	723	14	2/10	2/10	51.64	3.66	84.5	0	0
List A	107	1572	1596	38	4/42	4/42	42.00	6.09	41.3	0	0
T20s	236	1359	1818	64	4/17	4/17	28.40	8.02	21.2	0	0

JOE DENLY RHB / LB / R4 / W0

FULL NAME: Joseph Liam Denly
BORN: March 16, 1986, Canterbury, Kent
SQUAD NO: 6
HEIGHT: 6ft
NICKNAME: JD, Denners
EDUCATION: Chaucer Technology School, Canterbury
TEAMS: England, Kent, London Spirit, Barisal Burners, Karachi Kings, Kolkata Knight Riders, Middlesex, Sydney Sixers
ROLE: Batsman
DEBUT: Test: 2019; ODI: 2009; T20I: 2009; First-class: 2004; List A: 2004; T20: 2004

BEST BATTING: 227 Kent vs Worcestershire, Worcester, 2017
BEST BOWLING: 4-36 Kent vs Derbyshire, Derby, 2018
COUNTY CAP: 2008 (Kent); 2012 (Middlesex); BENEFIT: 2019 (Kent)

WHAT WAS YOUR FIRST CRICKET CLUB? Whitstable CC, Kent
BIGGEST TOPIC OF DISCUSSION IN YOUR DRESSING ROOM? Football
WHICH RULE WOULD YOU CHANGE ABOUT CRICKET? They should introduce specialist fielders that just field and do nothing else
BIGGEST CRICKETING REGRET? Not got any... yet
CRICKET STAR OF THE FUTURE? Jaydn Denly
TWITTER: @joed1986

Batting	Mat	Inns	NO	Runs	HS	Ave	SR	100	50	Ct	St
Tests	14	26	0	780	94	30.00	39.83	0	6	7	0
ODIs	16	13	0	446	87	34.30	70.90	0	4	7	0
T20Is	12	11	1	96	30	9.60	96.96	0	0	4	0
First-class	211	364	25	12364	227	36.47	55.00	29	62	87	0
List A	159	150	16	4902	150*	36.58	76.83	8	26	54	0
T20s	206	199	17	5057	127	27.78	122.09	4	30	82	0
Bowling	**Mat**	**Balls**	**Runs**	**Wkts**	**BBI**	**BBM**	**Ave**	**Econ**	**SR**	**5w**	**10**
Tests	14	390	219	2	2/42	2/42	109.50	3.36	195.0	0	0
ODIs	16	102	101	1	1/24	1/24	101.00	5.94	102.0	0	0
T20Is	12	66	85	7	4/19	4/19	12.14	7.72	9.4	0	0
First-class	211	5084	2698	68	4/36	6/114	39.67	3.18	74.7	0	0
List A	159	1406	1199	47	4/35	4/35	25.51	5.11	29.9	0	0
T20s	206	481	637	31	4/19	4/19	20.54	7.94	15.5	0	0

CHRIS DENT LHB / SLA / WK / R4 / W0 / MVP83

FULL NAME: Christopher David James Dent
BORN: January 20, 1991, Bristol
SQUAD NO: 15
HEIGHT: 5ft 9in
NICKNAME: Denty
EDUCATION: Backwell School, North Somerset; SGS Filton College, Bristol
TEAMS: Gloucestershire, England U19
ROLE: Batsman
DEBUT: First-class: 2010; List A: 2009; T20: 2010

BEST BATTING: 268 Gloucestershire vs Glamorgan, Bristol, 2015
BEST BOWLING: 2-21 Gloucestershire vs Sussex, Hove, 2016
COUNTY CAP: 2010

WHAT WAS YOUR FIRST CRICKET CLUB? Cleeve CC, Somerset
HOW WOULD YOU DISMISS STEVE SMITH? Bring on Ryan Higgins or Darren Stevens
WHAT EXCITES YOU ABOUT THE HUNDRED? Watching David Payne, Ryan Higgins and Benny Howell
BIGGEST TOPIC OF DISCUSSION IN YOUR DRESSING ROOM? Bats
BEST INNINGS YOU'VE SEEN? Michael Klinger's 137 not out in the 2015 One-Day Cup semi-final at Headingley. I was so nervous but he and Hamish Marshall calmly knocked the runs off
CRICKETING HERO? Brian Lara
WHICH RULE WOULD YOU CHANGE ABOUT CRICKET? If you hit the ball against the stumps at the other end, it's worth five runs (unless the bowler touches it)
BIGGEST CRICKETING REGRET? Every time I was out in the 90s trying to hit a six
WHICH BOOK MEANS MOST TO YOU? Mind Gym – Achieve More by Thinking Differently by Sebastian Bailey and Octavius Black
TWITTER: @cdent15

Batting	Mat	Inns	NO	Runs	HS	Ave	SR	100	50	Ct	St
First-class	143	256	23	8981	268	38.54	51.54	18	51	156	0
List A	70	65	5	1946	151*	32.43	93.15	3	6	24	0
T20s	49	43	7	725	63*	20.13	116.37	0	3	17	0
Bowling	**Mat**	**Balls**	**Runs**	**Wkts**	**BBI**	**BBM**	**Ave**	**Econ**	**SR**	**5w**	**10**
First-class	143	1220	813	9	2/21	2/21	90.33	3.99	135.5	0	0
List A	70	438	412	12	4/43	4/43	34.33	5.64	36.5	0	0
T20s	49	120	168	5	1/4	1/4	33.60	8.40	24.0	0	0

JADE DERNBACH RHB / RFM / R0 / W1

FULL NAME: Jade Winston Dernbach
BORN: March 3, 1986, Johannesburg, South Africa
SQUAD NO: 16
HEIGHT: 6ft 2in
NICKNAME: Doosh
EDUCATION: St John the Baptist School, Woking
TEAMS: England, Surrey, London Spirit, Melbourne Stars, Wellington
ROLE: Bowler
DEBUT: ODI: 2011; T20I: 2011; First-class: 2003; List A: 2005; T20: 2005

BEST BATTING: 56* Surrey vs Northamptonshire, Northampton, 2011
BEST BOWLING: 6-47 Surrey vs Leicestershire, Leicester, 2010
COUNTY CAP: 2011; BENEFIT: 2019

WHAT WAS YOUR FIRST CRICKET CLUB? Old Woking Remnants CC, Surrey. Where dreams are made
WHAT EXCITES YOU ABOUT THE HUNDRED? That it is sponsored by a crisp company
BIGGEST TOPIC OF DISCUSSION IN YOUR DRESSING ROOM? Did we really land on the moon
MOST INTERESTING TEAMMATE? Kumar Sangakkara – most polite, knowledgeable, down-to-earth man around
BIGGEST CRICKETING REGRET? Not being a batsman
WHICH BOOK MEANS MOST TO YOU? ECB Rules and Regulations
IF YOU WERE AN ANIMAL, WHICH WOULD IT BE? Lion – because I like to eat and sleep but can bite you if necessary
TWITTER: @jwd_16

Batting	Mat	Inns	NO	Runs	HS	Ave	SR	100	50	Ct	St
ODIs	24	8	1	19	5	2.71	48.71	0	0	5	0
T20Is	34	7	2	24	12	4.80	114.28	0	0	8	0
First-class	113	139	47	871	56*	9.46		0	1	17	0
List A	144	51	19	242	31	7.56	82.59	0	0	31	0
T20s	160	42	18	178	24*	7.41	102.29	0	0	37	0
Bowling	**Mat**	**Balls**	**Runs**	**Wkts**	**BBI**	**BBM**	**Ave**	**Econ**	**SR**	**5w**	**10**
ODIs	24	1234	1308	31	4/45	4/45	42.19	6.35	39.8	0	0
T20Is	34	702	1020	39	4/22	4/22	26.15	8.71	18.0	0	0
First-class	113	18222	10139	311	6/47		32.60	3.33	58.5	10	0
List A	144	6283	6181	228	6/35	6/35	27.10	5.90	27.5	3	0
T20s	160	3242	4610	173	4/22	4/22	26.64	8.53	18.7	0	0

SEAN DICKSON

RHB / RM / R0 / W0

FULL NAME: Sean Robert Dickson
BORN: September 2, 1991, Johannesburg, South Africa
SQUAD NO: 58
HEIGHT: 5ft 11in
NICKNAME: Dicko
EDUCATION: King Edward VII School, Johannesburg; University of Pretoria
TEAMS: Kent, Northerns
ROLE: Batsman
DEBUT: First-class: 2013; List A: 2013; T20: 2014

BEST BATTING: 318 Kent vs Northamptonshire, Beckenham, 2017
BEST BOWLING: 1-15 Northerns vs Griqualand West, Centurion, 2015

WHAT WAS YOUR FIRST CRICKET CLUB? Old Parks Sports Club, Johannesburg, South Africa
HOW WOULD YOU DISMISS STEVE SMITH? Be relentless outside off stump
WHAT EXCITES YOU ABOUT THE HUNDRED? Exciting for future generations
BIGGEST TOPIC OF DISCUSSION IN YOUR DRESSING ROOM? The weather
MOST INTERESTING TEAMMATE? Mitch Claydon – when he gets bored he becomes a very interesting character. Never a dull moment
BEST INNINGS YOU'VE SEEN? Herschelle Gibbs against Australia in the 438 game
CRICKETING HERO? Hashim Amla
WHICH RULE WOULD YOU CHANGE ABOUT CRICKET? Offer eight runs for hitting the ball out of the ground
WHICH BOOK MEANS MOST TO YOU? Legacy – What the All Blacks Can Teach Us About the Business of Life by James Kerr
IF YOU WERE AN ANIMAL, WHICH WOULD IT BE? A cat – I love to sleep
TWITTER: @Seano_146

Batting	Mat	Inns	NO	Runs	HS	Ave	SR	100	50	Ct	St
First-class	69	117	9	3736	318	34.59	51.10	10	14	59	0
List A	42	38	2	992	99	27.55	75.84	0	8	13	0
T20s	19	14	4	245	53	24.50	121.89	0	1	11	0
Bowling	**Mat**	**Balls**	**Runs**	**Wkts**	**BBI**	**BBM**	**Ave**	**Econ**	**SR**	**5w**	**10**
First-class	69	96	53	2	1/15	2/40	26.50	3.31	48.0	0	0
List A	42	12	20	0	-	-	-	10.00	-	0	0
T20s	19	6	9	1	1/9	1/9	9.00	9.00	6.0	0	0

ANEURIN DONALD

RHB / OB / R1 / W0

FULL NAME: Aneurin Henry Thomas Donald
BORN: December 20, 1996, Swansea, Wales
SQUAD NO: 12
HEIGHT: 6ft 3in
NICKNAME: Sir Don, The Don
EDUCATION: Pontarddulais Comprehensive School, Swansea; Gower College Swansea
TEAMS: Hampshire, England U19, Glamorgan
ROLE: Batsman
DEBUT: First-class: 2014; List A: 2015; T20: 2015

BEST BATTING: 234 Glamorgan vs Derbyshire, Colwyn Bay, 2016

FAMILY TIES? My grand-uncle, Bernard Hedges, scored the first one-day century for Glamorgan. My brother Gafyn played Wales age-group cricket and plays in the Welsh Premier League for Pontarddulais CC
CRICKETING HERO? Kevin Pietersen
SURPRISING FACT? When I used to net with my brother and father on a Saturday morning, rugby international Leigh Halfpenny would be there every week practising his goal-kicking. I never had the courage to ask him to feed the bowling machine
TWITTER: @AneurinDonald12
NOTES: Seen as the brightest of Glamorgan's young Welsh talents, Donald made an extraordinary 234 from 136 balls against Derbyshire at Colwyn Bay in 2016 when he was 19. It equalled the record for the fastest double-century in first-class cricket (123 balls). But he has been unable to live up to those expectations since and turned down a three-year contract renewal in August 2018 to sign a two-year deal with Hampshire in the hope of reviving his career. He had an encouraging first season on the south coast – 554 runs in nine Championship matches – but misfortune struck in December when he tore his anterior cruciate ligament, meaning he is likely to miss most of this season

Batting	Mat	Inns	NO	Runs	HS	Ave	SR	100	50	Ct	St
First-class	48	86	5	2610	234	32.22	73.31	3	15	35	0
List A	30	27	1	424	57	16.30	82.65	0	2	13	0
T20s	54	49	3	927	76	20.15	136.52	0	5	33	0
Bowling	**Mat**	**Balls**	**Runs**	**Wkts**	**BBI**	**BBM**	**Ave**	**Econ**	**SR**	**5w**	**10**
First-class	48	-	-	-	-	-	-	-	-	-	-
List A	30	-	-	-	-	-	-	-	-	-	-
T20s	54	-	-	-	-	-	-	-	-	-	-

DAN DOUTHWAITE

RHB / RMF / R0 / W0

FULL NAME: Daniel Alexander Douthwaite
BORN: February 8, 1997, Kingston-upon-Thames, Surrey
SQUAD NO: 88
HEIGHT: 6ft 1in
NICKNAME: Jugs
EDUCATION: Reed's School, Cobham, Surrey; Cardiff Metropolitan University
TEAMS: Glamorgan, Warwickshire
ROLE: Allrounder
DEBUT: First-class: 2019; List A: 2018; T20: 2018

BEST BATTING: 100* Cardiff MCCU vs Sussex, Hove, 2019
BEST BOWLING: 4-48 Glamorgan vs Derbyshire, Derby, 2019

WHAT WAS YOUR FIRST CRICKET CLUB? Stoke d'Abernon CC, Cobham, Surrey
WHAT EXCITES YOU ABOUT THE HUNDRED? Everything!
MOST INTERESTING TEAMMATE? Fakhar Zaman
IF YOU WERE AN ANIMAL, WHICH WOULD IT BE? A gorilla
TWITTER: @DanDouthwaite
NOTES: Douthwaite signed for Glamorgan in April 2019 after impressing for Cardiff MCCU. The allrounder hit an unbeaten first-class century for the students against Sussex after catching the attention of Glamorgan by scoring 95 and taking the wickets of Marnus Labuschagne and Chris Cooke in a pre-season friendly against the Welsh county. "He's a very dynamic player," said Glamorgan director of cricket Mark Wallace after securing his signature. "He's a very capable batsman and strikes a good ball, and he's also got the ability to bowl with some pace and swing the ball." After completing his studies Douthwaite went on to appear in seven County Championship matches last summer, scoring 298 runs and taking 17 wickets. He also featured in eight T20 Blast and three One-Day Cup matches, hitting his maiden List-A half-century in the latter – a 35-ball 52* against Sussex at Hove

Batting	Mat	Inns	NO	Runs	HS	Ave	SR	100	50	Ct	St
First-class	9	15	1	443	100*	31.64	62.92	1	1	1	0
List A	4	4	2	99	52*	49.50	147.76	0	1	2	0
T20s	10	8	2	64	24	10.66	83.11	0	0	1	0
Bowling	**Mat**	**Balls**	**Runs**	**Wkts**	**BBI**	**BBM**	**Ave**	**Econ**	**SR**	**5w**	**10**
First-class	9	1141	902	21	4/48	6/137	42.95	4.74	54.3	0	0
List A	4	138	126	5	3/43	3/43	25.20	5.47	27.6	0	0
T20s	10	114	178	4	1/7	1/7	44.50	9.36	28.5	0	0

GEORGE DRISSELL RHB / OB / R0 / W0

FULL NAME: George Samuel Drissell
BORN: January 20, 1999, Bristol
SQUAD NO: 20
HEIGHT: 6ft 2in
NICKNAME: Dris, Lemon, Lethal
EDUCATION: Bedminster Down Secondary School, Bristol; SGS Filton College, Bristol
TEAMS: Gloucestershire
ROLE: Allrounder
DEBUT: First-class: 2017; List A: 2018

BEST BATTING: 19 Gloucestershire vs Warwickshire, Edgbaston, 2018
BEST BOWLING: 4-83 Gloucestershire vs Glamorgan, Newport, 2019
COUNTY CAP: 2017

WHAT WAS YOUR FIRST CRICKET CLUB? Bedminster CC, Bristol, where you can see the Clifton Suspension Bridge in the background. I also played football for Bedminster Cricketers FC
WHAT WERE YOU DOING WHEN ENGLAND WON THE WORLD CUP? Down at The Clanage (home of Bedminster CC) with the boys
HOW WOULD YOU DISMISS STEVE SMITH? Just rag one through the gate?
WHAT EXCITES YOU ABOUT THE HUNDRED? All the big names playing in a new competition with nobody knowing how it will go
BIGGEST TOPIC OF DISCUSSION IN YOUR DRESSING ROOM? Coffee – so boring
MOST INTERESTING TEAMMATE? George Hankins – he likes playing with his belly button
CRICKETING HERO? Graeme Swann
SURPRISING FACT ABOUT YOU? I'm a big fan of Bristol City FC
CRICKET STAR OF THE FUTURE? Joseph Armitage (Bedminster U13)
IF YOU WERE AN ANIMAL, WHICH WOULD IT BE? An eagle
TWITTER: @GeorgeDrissell

Batting	Mat	Inns	NO	Runs	HS	Ave	SR	100	50	Ct	St
First-class	7	11	0	77	19	7.00	30.19	0	0	0	0
List A	1	1	0	0	0	0.00	0.00	0	0	0	0
Bowling	**Mat**	**Balls**	**Runs**	**Wkts**	**BBI**	**BBM**	**Ave**	**Econ**	**SR**	**5w**	**10**
First-class	7	817	504	8	4/83	4/174	63.00	3.70	102.1	0	0
List A	1	42	45	0	-	-	-	6.42	-	0	0

LEUS DU PLOOY LHB / SLA / R0 / W0 / MVP93

DERBYSHIRE / WELSH FIRE

FULL NAME: Jacobus Leus du Plooy
BORN: January 12, 1995, Pretoria, South Africa
SQUAD NO: 76
HEIGHT: 5ft 10in
EDUCATION: Afrikaanse Hoër Seunskool (Affies), Pretoria; University of South Africa, Pretoria
TEAMS: Derbyshire, Welsh Fire, Free State, Knights, Northerns, Titans
ROLE: Batsman
DEBUT: First-class: 2015; List A: 2014; T20: 2014

BEST BATTING: 181 Free State vs Namibia, Windhoek, 2015
BEST BOWLING: 3-76 Northerns vs Western Province, Pretoria, 2019

WHAT WAS YOUR FIRST CRICKET CLUB? Tenterden CC, Ashford, Kent
HOW WOULD YOU DISMISS STEVE SMITH? Underarm
MOST INTERESTING TEAMMATE? Logan van Beek – because of all of his life theories
CRICKET STAR OF THE FUTURE? Ximus du Plooy
NOTES: After signing a Kolpak deal in May 2019 the hard-hitting South African left his mark on Derbyshire last season, making a brace of first-class hundreds and three fifties in 11 matches, and averaging 67 from six List A games. But it was in the T20 Blast where he really showed his explosiveness, driving Derbyshire to the quarter-finals with a series of decisive innings at the top of the order. Those numbers, and the combative way in which he made his runs, paved the way for a two-year contract extension last September. The 25-year-old left-hander has been a consistent run-scorer in all formats ever since he made an unbeaten hundred batting at No.9 on his first-class debut for Free State at Durban in 2015. His left-arm spin is another useful string to his bow

Batting	Mat	Inns	NO	Runs	HS	Ave	SR	100	50	Ct	St
First-class	53	84	12	3370	181	46.80	48.62	11	18	46	0
List A	45	42	10	1865	155	58.28	87.51	5	10	23	0
T20s	40	35	12	780	70	33.91	115.04	0	4	13	0
Bowling	**Mat**	**Balls**	**Runs**	**Wkts**	**BBI**	**BBM**	**Ave**	**Econ**	**SR**	**5w**	**10**
First-class	53	1643	1177	23	3/76	3/76	51.17	4.29	71.4	0	0
List A	45	399	389	11	3/19	3/19	35.36	5.84	36.2	0	0
T20s	40	150	171	12	4/15	4/15	14.25	6.84	12.5	0	0

BEN DUCKETT LHB / OB / WK / R2 / W0 / MVP88

FULL NAME: Ben Matthew Duckett
BORN: October 17, 1994, Farnborough, Kent
SQUAD NO: 17
HEIGHT: 5ft 9in
NICKNAME: Ducky, Chode
EDUCATION: Millfield School, Somerset; Winchester House School; Stowe School
TEAMS: England, Nottinghamshire, Welsh Fire, Hobart Hurricanes, Northamptonshire, Islamabad United
ROLE: Batsman
DEBUT: Test: 2016; ODI: 2016; T20I: 2019; First-class: 2013; List A: 2013; T20: 2012

BEST BATTING: 282* Northamptonshire vs Sussex, Northampton, 2016
BEST BOWLING: 1-21 Northamptonshire vs Kent, Beckenham, 2017
COUNTY CAP: 2016 (Northamptonshire)

WHAT WAS YOUR FIRST CRICKET CLUB? Glastonbury CC, Somerset
WHAT WERE YOU DOING WHEN ENGLAND WON THE WORLD CUP? We were playing a T20 match – I got out early and watched it!
MOST INTERESTING TEAMMATE? Ravi Ashwin, my Notts teammate of last season. Great to hear his insights on the game and tales from the Indian dressing room
SURPRISING FACT ABOUT YOU? I have a tattoo of a duck with the number 17 and a cricket bat on one side of my bottom
BIGGEST CRICKETING REGRET? Coming back a few weeks earlier than I should have done after my hand operation in 2018
TWITTER: @benduckett1

Batting	Mat	Inns	NO	Runs	HS	Ave	SR	100	50	Ct	St
Tests	4	7	0	110	56	15.71	57.89	0	1	1	0
ODIs	3	3	0	123	63	41.00	80.92	0	2	0	0
T20Is	1	1	0	9	9	9.00	128.57	0	0	0	0
First-class	90	156	7	5746	282*	38.56	71.95	16	26	67	3
List A	73	68	7	2341	220*	38.37	99.49	3	16	38	3
T20s	96	90	17	2100	96	28.76	131.90	0	10	39	2
Bowling	**Mat**	**Balls**	**Runs**	**Wkts**	**BBI**	**BBM**	**Ave**	**Econ**	**SR**	**5w**	**10**
Tests	4	-	-	-	-	-	-	-	-	-	-
ODIs	3	-	-	-	-	-	-	-	-	-	-
T20Is	1	-	-	-	-	-	-	-	-	-	-
First-class	90	83	65	1	1/21	1/32	65.00	4.69	83.0	0	0
List A	73	-	-	-	-	-	-	-	-	-	-
T20s	96	-	-	-	-	-	-	-	-	-	-

MATT DUNN

LHB / RFM / R0 / W0

FULL NAME: Matthew Peter Dunn
BORN: May 5, 1992, Egham, Surrey
SQUAD NO: 4
HEIGHT: 6ft 1in
NICKNAME: Dunny
EDUCATION: Bishopsgate School; Bearwood College, Wokingham
TEAMS: Surrey, England U19
ROLE: Bowler
DEBUT: First-class: 2010; List A: 2011; T20: 2013

BEST BATTING: 31* Surrey vs Kent, Guildford, 2014
BEST BOWLING: 5-43 Surrey vs Somerset, Guildford, 2019

WHAT WAS YOUR FIRST CRICKET CLUB? Egham CC, Surrey
WHICH BOWLER WOULD YOU LEAST LIKE TO FACE? Fidel Edwards – he has already broken my rib once
BEST INNINGS YOU'VE SEEN? Aaron Finch's hundred against Middlesex at The Oval in the 2018 T20 Blast
YOUR BIGGEST CRICKETING REGRET? Not working on my batting from a younger age
SURPRISING FACT ABOUT YOU? I lived in Norway when I was younger, and I can breakdance. And I absolutely love coffee
FAVOURITE QUOTE OR SAYING? You wouldn't want a warm beer, would you?
TWITTER: @MatthewDunn05

Batting	Mat	Inns	NO	Runs	HS	Ave	SR	100	50	Ct	St
First-class	39	43	21	146	31*	6.63	19.65	0	0	7	0
List A	1	-	-	-	-	-	-	-	-	1	0
T20s	16	2	0	3	2	1.50	60.00	0	0	4	0
Bowling	**Mat**	**Balls**	**Runs**	**Wkts**	**BBI**	**BBM**	**Ave**	**Econ**	**SR**	**5w**	**10**
First-class	39	5871	3853	112	5/43	8/128	34.40	3.93	52.4	4	0
List A	1	36	32	2	2/32	2/32	16.00	5.33	18.0	0	0
T20s	16	300	450	22	3/8	3/8	20.45	9.00	13.6	0	0

BRETT D'OLIVEIRA

RHB / LB / RO / WO

FULL NAME: Brett Louis D'Oliveira
BORN: February 28, 1992, Worcester
SQUAD NO: 15
HEIGHT: 5ft 9in
NICKNAME: Dolly
EDUCATION: Blessed Edward Oldcorne Catholic College, Worcester; Worcester Sixth Form College
TEAMS: Worcestershire, England Lions
ROLE: Allrounder
DEBUT: First-class: 2012; List A: 2011; T20: 2012

BEST BATTING: 202* Worcestershire vs Glamorgan, Cardiff, 2016
BEST BOWLING: 7-92 Worcestershire vs Glamorgan, Cardiff, 2019
COUNTY CAP: 2012

FAMILY TIES? My grandad Basil played for England and Worcestershire and also went on to coach Worcestershire. My dad Damian played for Worcestershire and went on to be assistant coach and Academy director
WHAT WAS YOUR FIRST CRICKET CLUB? Worcester Dominies and Guild CC
HOW WOULD YOU DISMISS STEVE SMITH? Bring on Daryl Mitchell
MOST INTERESTING TEAMMATE? John Hastings
CRICKETING HERO? Shane Warne
SURPRISING FACT ABOUT YOU? I've got a coaching qualification in basketball
SURPRISING FACT ABOUT A TEAMMATE? There are rumours that Joe Leach puts sprinkles in his hair
IF YOU WERE AN ANIMAL, WHICH WOULD IT BE? A lion
TWITTER: @Bdolly09

Batting	Mat	Inns	NO	Runs	HS	Ave	SR	100	50	Ct	St
First-class	59	101	3	2793	202*	28.50	53.73	7	7	28	0
List A	66	56	11	1032	79	22.93	85.57	0	6	29	0
T20s	84	60	18	955	64	22.73	125.00	0	4	17	0
Bowling	**Mat**	**Balls**	**Runs**	**Wkts**	**BBI**	**BBM**	**Ave**	**Econ**	**SR**	**5w**	**10**
First-class	59	4372	2537	51	7/92	9/182	49.74	3.48	85.7	2	0
List A	66	2462	2166	50	3/35	3/35	43.32	5.27	49.2	0	0
T20s	84	1116	1441	42	4/26	4/26	34.30	7.74	26.5	0	0

NED ECKERSLEY RHB / WK / R1 / W0

FULL NAME: Edmund John Holden Eckersley
BORN: August 9, 1989, Oxford
SQUAD NO: 66
HEIGHT: 6ft
NICKNAME: Steady
EDUCATION: St Benedict's School, Ealing, London
TEAMS: Durham, Leicestershire, Mountaineers
ROLE: Batsman/wicketkeeper
DEBUT: First-class: 2011; List A: 2008; T20: 2011

BEST BATTING: 158 Leicestershire vs Derbyshire, Derby, 2017
BEST BOWLING: 2-29 Leicestershire vs Lancashire, Old Trafford, 2013
COUNTY CAP: 2013 (Leicestershire)

WHAT WAS YOUR FIRST CRICKET CLUB? Ealing CC, London
WHAT WERE YOU DOING WHEN ENGLAND WON THE WORLD CUP? Playing for Durham against Worcestershire in the County Championship – but still watching the final on TV because we were batting
BIGGEST TOPIC OF DISCUSSION IN YOUR DRESSING ROOM? Harry Potter
MOST INTERESTING TEAMMATE? Angus Robson – strangest and funniest person I've ever met in my life
CRICKETING HERO? Alec Stewart – he wanted to be a frontline batsman and a wicketkeeper and he was the best when I was a kid
SURPRISING FACT ABOUT YOU? I can play TV theme tunes on the piano
CRICKET STAR OF THE FUTURE? Ollie Gibson
IF YOU WERE AN ANIMAL, WHICH WOULD IT BE? A sloth
TWITTER: @nedeckersley

Batting	Mat	Inns	NO	Runs	HS	Ave	SR	100	50	Ct	St
First-class	121	215	16	6499	158	32.65	50.21	15	23	217	3
List A	44	41	5	1041	108	28.91	86.24	1	5	27	1
T20s	66	56	11	702	43	15.60	108.33	0	0	20	7
Bowling	**Mat**	**Balls**	**Runs**	**Wkts**	**BBI**	**BBM**	**Ave**	**Econ**	**SR**	**5w**	**10**
First-class	121	88	67	2	2/29	2/29	33.50	4.56	44.0	0	0
List A	44	-	-	-	-	-	-	-	-	-	-
T20s	66	-	-	-	-	-	-	-	-	-	-

FIDEL EDWARDS RHB / RF / R0 / W2 / MVP50

FULL NAME: Fidel Henderson Edwards
BORN: February 6, 1982, Gays, Barbados
SQUAD NO: 82
HEIGHT: 5ft 8in
NICKNAME: Castro
TEAMS: West Indies, Hampshire, Barbados, Deccan Chargers, Dolphins, Rajasthan Royals, St Lucia Zouks, Sydney Thunder, Sylhet Superstars, Trinidad & Tobago Red Steel, Warwickshire
ROLE: Bowler
DEBUT: Test: 2003; ODI: 2003; T20I: 2007; First-class: 2001; List A: 2003; T20: 2007

BEST BATTING: 40 Barbados vs Jamaica, Bridgetown, 2008
BEST BOWLING: 7-87 West Indies vs New Zealand, Napier, 2008
COUNTY CAP: 2018 (Hampshire)

TWITTER: @EdwardsFidel
NOTES: The slingy Barbadian fast bowler is entering his sixth season at Hampshire as a Kolpak player after signing a one-year contract extention last August. Edwards took five wickets on Test debut in 2003 after playing just one match for Barbados and being spotted in the nets by Brian Lara. He played the last of his 55 Tests in 2012. The 38-year-old was first drafted into Hampshire's squad in 2015 and took 45 wickets in eight games to help his county stave off relegation. The following year was blighted by injury but he came back to collect 30 Championship wickets in 2017. His previous two seasons have been his best so far, with 54 scalps in 2018 followed by another 48 last summer. His new-ball partnership with Kyle Abbott is arguably the best in the country

Batting	Mat	Inns	NO	Runs	HS	Ave	SR	100	50	Ct	St
Tests	55	88	28	394	30	6.56	28.20	0	0	10	0
ODIs	50	22	14	73	13	9.12	45.62	0	0	4	0
T20Is	20	4	2	10	7*	5.00	111.11	0	0	5	0
First-class	138	190	74	789	40	6.80		0	0	26	0
List A	92	36	20	138	21*	8.62		0	0	11	0
T20s	100	33	15	103	11*	5.72	83.06	0	0	13	0
Bowling	**Mat**	**Balls**	**Runs**	**Wkts**	**BBI**	**BBM**	**Ave**	**Econ**	**SR**	**5w**	**10**
Tests	55	9602	6249	165	7/87	8/132	37.87	3.90	58.1	12	0
ODIs	50	2138	1812	60	6/22	6/22	30.20	5.08	35.6	2	0
T20Is	20	360	497	16	3/23	3/23	31.06	8.28	22.5	0	0
First-class	138	21530	13751	455	7/87		30.22	3.83	47.3	27	2
List A	92	4131	3605	120	6/22	6/22	30.04	5.23	34.4	3	0
T20s	100	2020	2605	96	5/22	5/22	27.13	7.73	21.0	1	0

STEVIE ESKINAZI

RHB / WK / R0 / W0

FULL NAME: Stephen Sean Eskinazi
BORN: March 28, 1994, Johannesburg, South Africa
SQUAD NO: 28
HEIGHT: 6ft 2in
NICKNAME: Eski, Esk, GOAT
EDUCATION: Christ Church Grammar School, Perth; University of Western Australia; University of Hertfordshire
TEAMS: Middlesex
ROLE: Batsman
DEBUT: First-class: 2015; List A: 2018; T20: 2016

BEST BATTING: 179 Middlesex vs Warwickshire, Edgbaston, 2017

COUNTY CAP: 2018

FAMILY TIES? My dad played a good standard of club cricket in South Africa
WHAT WAS YOUR FIRST CRICKET CLUB? Fair Oak CC, Hampshire. I drive past it every time I go to the Ageas Bowl but haven't been back there since I was seven
HOW WOULD YOU DISMISS STEVE SMITH? Offer him 200 bars of chocolate for a loose shot
WHAT EXCITES YOU ABOUT THE HUNDRED? My housemate Tom Helm – who was signed for £75k – getting a round in
SURPRISING FACT ABOUT YOU? I could have four passports (if that was legal)
BIGGEST CRICKETING REGRET? Giving up my medium-pace bowling
CRICKET STAR OF THE FUTURE? Pavel Florin (Romania)
WHICH BOOK MEANS MOST TO YOU? Make Your Bed – Little Things That Can Change Your Life… And Maybe the World by William McRaven
IF YOU WERE AN ANIMAL, WHICH WOULD IT BE? An ibis – big beak
TWITTER: @seskinazi

Batting	Mat	Inns	NO	Runs	HS	Ave	SR	100	50	Ct	St
First-class	51	89	4	2874	179	33.81	55.90	6	12	45	0
List A	17	16	2	496	107*	35.42	90.51	1	1	6	0
T20s	30	27	3	735	57*	30.62	131.48	0	5	13	0
Bowling	**Mat**	**Balls**	**Runs**	**Wkts**	**BBI**	**BBM**	**Ave**	**Econ**	**SR**	**5w**	**10**
First-class	51	12	4	0	-	-	-	2.00	-	0	0
List A	17	-	-	-	-	-	-	-	-	-	-
T20s	30	-	-	-	-	-	-	-	-	-	-

ALEX EVANS

LHB / RFM / R0 / W0

FULL NAME: Huw Alexander Evans
BORN: August 9, 2000, Bedford
SQUAD NO: TBC
HEIGHT: 6ft 2in
NICKNAME: Evo, Baldy
EDUCATION: Bedford Modern School; Loughborough University
TEAMS: Leicestershire
ROLE: Bowler
DEBUT: First-class: 2019

BEST BATTING: 7* Loughborough MCCU vs Kent, Canterbury, 2019
BEST BOWLING: 3-49 Loughborough MCCU vs Kent, Canterbury, 2019

WHAT WAS YOUR FIRST CRICKET CLUB? Ampthill Town CC, Bedfordshire
WHAT WERE YOU DOING WHEN ENGLAND WON THE WORLD CUP? I was watching it with my family at the local cricket club
HOW WOULD YOU DISMISS STEVE SMITH? Hit top of off as much as possible – or try to bowl off-spin instead
WHAT EXCITES YOU ABOUT THE HUNDRED? The opportunities for the players involved, but also for the players who aren't involved and will get a chance in the other county competitions
BIGGEST TOPIC OF DISCUSSION IN YOUR DRESSING ROOM? Football
MOST INTERESTING TEAMMATE? Callum Parkinson – for his many various stories and the fact that he makes me laugh the most
CRICKET STAR OF THE FUTURE? Rehan Ahmed (Leicestershire Academy)
IF YOU WERE AN ANIMAL, WHICH WOULD IT BE? A crafty fox of course
TWITTER: @HuwAlexEvans
NOTES: The 19-year-old seamer signed his first professional contract with Leicestershire in December after taking four wickets on his Championship debut against Northamptonshire at Grace Road earlier in the year. Evans will combine playing for Leicestershire with his studying and playing committments at Loughborough. He was named the club's 2019 Young Player of the Year for his performances for the Second XI

Batting	Mat	Inns	NO	Runs	HS	Ave	SR	100	50	Ct	St
First-class	3	5	3	16	7*	8.00	42.10	0	0	0	0
Bowling	**Mat**	**Balls**	**Runs**	**Wkts**	**BBI**	**BBM**	**Ave**	**Econ**	**SR**	**5w**	**10**
First-class	3	492	229	7	3/49	4/79	32.71	2.79	70.2	0	0

LAURIE EVANS

FULL NAME: Laurie John Evans
BORN: October 12, 1987, Lambeth, London
SQUAD NO: 32
HEIGHT: 6ft
NICKNAME: Loz
EDUCATION: Whitgift School; The John Fisher School, Purley; Durham University
TEAMS: Sussex, Oval Invincibles, Kabul Zwanan, Multan Sultans, Northamptonshire, Rajshahi Kings, Surrey, Warwickshire
ROLE: Batsman
DEBUT: First-class: 2007; List A: 2009; T20: 2009

BEST BATTING: 213* Warwickshire vs Sussex, Edgbaston, 2015
BEST BOWLING: 1-29 Warwickshire vs Sussex, Edgbaston, 2015

WHICH BOWLER WOULD YOU LEAST LIKE TO FACE? Darren Stevens
CRICKETING HERO? Brian Lara
BEST INNINGS YOU'VE SEEN? Brendon McCullum's 158 not out in the first-ever IPL match
WHO WOULD YOU ASK TO BAT FOR YOUR LIFE? Jonathan Trott
WHICH RULE WOULD YOU CHANGE ABOUT CRICKET? The T20 time-restrictions by which the fielding side must have bowled 20 overs
YOUR BIGGEST CRICKETING REGRET? Not batting higher up the order in T20 cricket
FAVOURITE QUOTE OR SAYING? Everything but the kitchen sink
WHICH BOOK MEANS MOST TO YOU? A book about the rules of golf
TWITTER: @laurieevans32

Batting	Mat	Inns	NO	Runs	HS	Ave	SR	100	50	Ct	St
First-class	68	116	6	3302	213*	30.01	45.78	6	17	55	0
List A	63	57	11	1735	134*	37.71	96.98	3	5	25	0
T20s	145	131	31	3261	104*	32.61	129.66	1	22	60	0
Bowling	**Mat**	**Balls**	**Runs**	**Wkts**	**BBI**	**BBM**	**Ave**	**Econ**	**SR**	**5w**	**10**
First-class	68	366	270	2	1/29	1/29	135.00	4.42	183.0	0	0
List A	63	54	82	1	1/29	1/29	82.00	9.11	54.0	0	0
T20s	145	22	35	1	1/5	1/5	35.00	9.54	22.0	0	0

SAM EVANS

RHB / OB / R0 / W0

FULL NAME: Samuel Thomes Evans
BORN: December 20, 1997, Leicester
SQUAD NO: 21
HEIGHT: 5ft 8in
NICKNAME: Smevs
EDUCATION: Lancaster Boys School, Leicester; Wyggeston QE I College; Loughborough University
TEAMS: Leicestershire
ROLE: Batsman
DEBUT: First-class: 2017; List A: 2018

BEST BATTING: 114 Loughborough MCCU vs Northamptonshire, Northampton, 2017

WHAT GOT YOU INTO CRICKET? Playing cricket in the garden with my dad
BEST ADVICE EVER RECEIVED? You'll have more bad days than good so enjoy the good ones
BEST MOMENT IN CRICKET? Making my first-class debut in 2017
BEST THING ABOUT YOUR HOME GROUND? The lovely food
IF YOU WEREN'T A CRICKETER? I'd be a student
SURPRISING FACT ABOUT YOU? I go to Loughborough University and am one of the few who is not studying Sports Science
CRICKETING HERO? Ricky Ponting – he made batting look elegant and easy
NON-CRICKETING HERO? Jamie Vardy – for his tenacity and desire. He started at the bottom and made it to the top
TWITTER: @SamEvans97

Batting	Mat	Inns	NO	Runs	HS	Ave	SR	100	50	Ct	St
First-class	9	13	1	249	114	20.75	42.78	1	0	2	0
List A	1	1	0	20	20	20.00	71.42	0	0	0	0
Bowling	**Mat**	**Balls**	**Runs**	**Wkts**	**BBI**	**BBM**	**Ave**	**Econ**	**SR**	**5w**	**10**
First-class	9	36	24	0	-	-	-	4.00	-	0	0
List A	1	-	-	-	-	-	-	-	-	-	-

JOEY EVISON

RHB / RM / R0 / W0

FULL NAME: Joseph David Michael Evison
BORN: November 14, 2001, Peterborough, Cambridgeshire
SQUAD NO: 90
HEIGHT: 6ft 2in
NICKNAME: Evo
EDUCATION: Stamford School, Lincolnshire
TEAMS: Nottinghamshire, England U19
ROLE: Allrounder
DEBUT: First-class: 2019

BEST BATTING: 45 Nottinghamshire vs Warwickshire, Trent Bridge, 2019

WHAT WAS YOUR FIRST CRICKET CLUB? Bourne CC, Lincolnshire
WHAT WERE YOU DOING WHEN ENGLAND WON THE WORLD CUP? I was at the England U19 camp watching with all the boys
WHAT EXCITES YOU ABOUT THE HUNDRED? Seeing how different the players' mindset is compared to T20
BIGGEST TOPIC OF DISCUSSION IN YOUR DRESSING ROOM? Instagram
MOST INTERESTING TEAMMATE? Luke Fletcher
CRICKET STAR OF THE FUTURE? Chris Gibson (Nottinghamshire Academy)
IF YOU WERE AN ANIMAL, WHICH WOULD IT BE? A cheetah
TWITTER: @EvisonJoey
NOTES: The England U19 allrounder signed a three-year contract with Notts in September, shortly after scoring 45 on his first-class debut for the club against Warwickshire. At 17, Evison was the youngest Notts debutant since Bilal Shafayat in 2001. He has been tipped for the top ever since scoring his first century for Lincolnshire U10. In December he equalled the fastest recorded fifty at U19 level – off just 18 balls – against Sri Lanka U19 in a Youth ODI. "It's exciting for him and for the club because he seems to have that ability to step up to new levels of cricket and adapt," said Notts head coach Peter Moores. "That's a difficult skill for anybody, particularly when stepping into the first-class game as Joey did"

Batting	Mat	Inns	NO	Runs	HS	Ave	SR	100	50	Ct	St
First-class	1	2	0	57	45	28.50	59.37	0	0	1	0
Bowling	**Mat**	**Balls**	**Runs**	**Wkts**	**BBI**	**BBM**	**Ave**	**Econ**	**SR**	**5w**	**10**
First-class	1	54	33	0	-	-	-	3.66	-	0	0

JAMES FAULKNER

RHB / LFM / R0 / W0

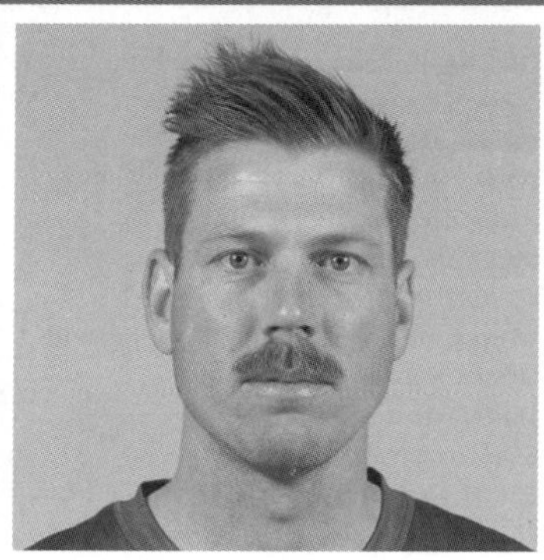

FULL NAME: James Peter Faulkner
BORN: April 29, 1990, Launceston, Tasmania, Australia
SQUAD NO: 44
HEIGHT: 6ft 1in
TEAMS: Australia, Lancashire, Gujarat Lions, Hobart Hurricanes, Kings XI Punjab, Melbourne Stars, Pune Warriors, Rajasthan Royals, Tasmania
ROLE: Allrounder
DEBUT: Test: 2013; ODI: 2013; T20I: 2012; First-class: 2008; List A: 2008; T20: 2009

BEST BATTING: 73 Lancashire vs Northamptonshire, Northampton, 2015 (T20)
BEST BOWLING: 5-16 Rajasthan Royals vs Sunrisers Hyderabad, Jaipur, 2013 (T20)
COUNTY CAP: 2019

TWITTER: @JamesFaulkner44
NOTES: The Australian allrounder, who turns 30 in April, has signed up for his fourth T20 Blast campaign at Lancashire. Faulkner had a starring role in Lancashire's 2015 T20 title win and has played 40 T20 matches for the club, taking 56 wickets at 17.53 with an economy rate of just 7.21, as well as scoring well over 400 runs. A canny left-arm seamer who excels as a death bowler, Faulkner was Player of the Match in the 2015 World Cup final against New Zealand and in 2016 became the first Australian to take a five-for in T20Is. He is no slouch with the bat, hitting 116 from 57 balls in an ODI against India at Bangalore in 2013. Faulkner hasn't played for his country since 2017

Batting	Mat	Inns	NO	Runs	HS	Ave	SR	100	50	Ct	St
Tests	1	2	0	45	23	22.50	104.65	0	0	0	0
ODIs	69	52	22	1032	116	34.40	104.24	1	4	21	0
T20Is	24	18	7	159	41*	14.45	115.21	0	0	11	0
First-class	63	95	12	2566	121	30.91	50.91	2	15	26	0
List A	128	100	32	2026	116	29.79	89.76	1	10	35	0
T20s	206	148	64	1770	73	21.07	122.23	0	1	66	0
Bowling	**Mat**	**Balls**	**Runs**	**Wkts**	**BBI**	**BBM**	**Ave**	**Econ**	**SR**	**5w**	**10**
Tests	1	166	98	6	4/51	6/98	16.33	3.54	27.6	0	0
ODIs	69	3211	2962	96	4/32	4/32	30.85	5.53	33.4	0	0
T20Is	24	515	684	36	5/27	5/27	19.00	7.96	14.3	1	0
First-class	63	9776	4759	192	5/5	8/97	24.78	2.92	50.9	5	0
List A	128	6041	5367	175	4/20	4/20	30.66	5.33	34.5	0	0
T20s	206	4147	5490	235	5/16	5/16	23.36	7.94	17.6	3	0

TOM FELL

RHB / OB / R1 / W0

WORCESTERSHIRE

FULL NAME: Thomas Charles Fell
BORN: October 17, 1993, Hillingdon, Middlesex
SQUAD NO: 29
HEIGHT: 6ft 1in
NICKNAME: Lord, Feltch
EDUCATION: Tettenhall College, Wolverhampton; Oakham School, Rutland; Oxford Brookes University
TEAMS: Worcestershire
ROLE: Batsman
DEBUT: First-class: 2013; List A: 2013; T20: 2018

BEST BATTING: 171 Worcestershire vs Middlesex, Worcester, 2015

COUNTY CAP: 2013

WHAT WAS YOUR FIRST CRICKET CLUB? Wolverhampton CC, West Midlands. Joined when I was nine and still playing there today
WHAT WERE YOU DOING WHEN ENGLAND WON THE WORLD CUP? I was sat at home with my missus, which made for a good atmosphere
HOW WOULD YOU DISMISS STEVE SMITH? Not sure my off-breaks would give him too much trouble
BIGGEST TOPIC OF DISCUSSION IN YOUR DRESSING ROOM? What's spoken about in the dressing room stays in the dressing room
MOST INTERESTING TEAMMATE? Richard Oliver – he lived in a caravan and is simply a very rare individual
IF YOU WERE AN ANIMAL, WHICH WOULD IT BE? A sloth
TWITTER: @TomFell_29

Batting	Mat	Inns	NO	Runs	HS	Ave	SR	100	50	Ct	St
First-class	79	134	5	3808	171	29.51	50.19	5	16	61	0
List A	45	44	5	1369	116*	35.10	80.01	1	11	16	0
T20s	7	5	0	62	28	12.40	101.63	0	0	2	0
Bowling	**Mat**	**Balls**	**Runs**	**Wkts**	**BBI**	**BBM**	**Ave**	**Econ**	**SR**	**5w**	**10**
First-class	79	20	17	0	-	-	-	5.10	-	0	0
List A	45	-	-	-	-	-	-	-	-	-	-
T20s	7	-	-	-	-	-	-	-	-	-	-

AARON FINCH RHB / SLA / R0 / W0

FULL NAME: Aaron James Finch
BORN: November 17, 1986, Colac, Victoria, Australia
SQUAD NO: TBC
HEIGHT: 5ft 8in
TEAMS: Australia, Northern Superchargers, Delhi Daredevils, Gujarat Lions, Kings XI Punjab, Melbourne Renegades, Pune Warriors, RC Bangalore, Sunrisers Hyderabad, Surrey, Victoria, Yorkshire
ROLE: Batsman
DEBUT: Test: 2018; ODI: 2013; T20I: 2011; First-class: 2007; List A: 2007; T20: 2009

BEST BATTING: 172 Australia vs Zimbabwe, Harare, 2018 (T20)
BEST BOWLING: 1-9 Yorkshire vs Lancashire, Old Trafford, 2015 (T20)

TWITTER: @AaronFinch5
NOTES: The hard-hitting Victorian has plenty of experience of English conditions, having played county cricket for Yorkshire and Surrey, including 57 T20 matches since 2014. He signed for Royal Challengers Bangalore ahead of the 2020 Indian Premier League and has represented eight IPL teams in all. Finch made his ODI debut against Sri Lanka in 2013 and he has hit two of the three highest scores in T20I history. His 172 against Zimbabwe in 2018, from 76 balls, is the highest ever in the format. He has previously been ranked as the No.1 batsman in T20I cricket and captained Australia at the 2019 World Cup, when his side reached the semi-finals. Finch will captain Northern Superchargers in The Hundred after being selected in the £125k category

Batting	Mat	Inns	NO	Runs	HS	Ave	SR	100	50	Ct	St
Tests	5	10	0	278	62	27.80	44.98	0	2	7	0
ODIs	126	122	3	4882	153*	41.02	88.71	16	26	60	0
T20Is	61	61	9	1989	172	38.25	155.87	2	12	26	0
First-class	88	143	6	4915	288*	35.87	61.59	7	33	81	0
List A	211	207	9	8180	188*	41.31	88.48	22	46	88	0
T20s	284	279	32	8914	172	36.08	143.75	8	60	127	0
Bowling	**Mat**	**Balls**	**Runs**	**Wkts**	**BBI**	**BBM**	**Ave**	**Econ**	**SR**	**5w**	**10**
Tests	5	12	8	0	-	-	-	4.00	-	0	0
ODIs	126	284	259	4	1/2	1/2	64.75	5.47	71.0	0	0
T20Is	61	12	27	0	-	-	-	13.50	-	0	0
First-class	88	464	318	5	1/0	1/0	63.60	4.11	92.8	0	0
List A	211	479	440	9	2/44	2/44	48.88	5.51	53.2	0	0
T20s	284	233	359	7	1/9	1/9	51.28	9.24	33.2	0	0

ADAM FINCH

RHB / RMF / R0 / W0

FULL NAME: Adam William Finch
BORN: May 28, 2000, Wordsley, Stourbridge, Worcestershire
SQUAD NO: 61
HEIGHT: 6ft 4in
EDUCATION: Kingswinford School, West Midlands; Oldswinford Hospital Sixth Form College, Stourbridge
TEAMS: Worcestershire, England U19
ROLE: Bowler
DEBUT: First-class: 2019

BEST BATTING: 18* Worcestershire vs Australians, Worcester, 2019
BEST BOWLING: 2-23 Worcestershire vs Gloucestershire, Worcester, 2019

WHAT WAS YOUR FIRST CRICKET CLUB? Himley CC, Staffordshire. It has one of the best youth systems in the area
HOW WOULD YOU DISMISS STEVE SMITH? Bowl outside off consistently
BEST INNINGS YOU'VE SEEN? Alastair Cook's final Test innings
BIGGEST TOPIC OF DISCUSSION IN YOUR DRESSING ROOM? Football
MOST INTERESTING TEAMMATE? Moeen Ali – for his vast experience
WHICH RULE WOULD YOU CHANGE ABOUT CRICKET? Overthrows should not be marked down against the bowler
CRICKET STAR OF THE FUTURE? Ollie Walker (Worcestershire Academy)
WHICH BOOK MEANS MOST TO YOU? Harry Potter and the Philosopher's Stone
IF YOU WERE AN ANIMAL, WHICH WOULD IT BE? A lion – king of the Savannah

Batting	Mat	Inns	NO	Runs	HS	Ave	SR	100	50	Ct	St
First-class	8	10	5	61	18*	12.20	26.52	0	0	0	0
Bowling	**Mat**	**Balls**	**Runs**	**Wkts**	**BBI**	**BBM**	**Ave**	**Econ**	**SR**	**5w**	**10**
First-class	8	1064	682	12	2/23	3/126	56.83	3.84	88.6	0	0

HARRY FINCH

RHB / RM / R0 / W0

FULL NAME: Harry Zacariah Finch
BORN: February 10, 1995, Hastings, Sussex
SQUAD NO: 6
HEIGHT: 5ft 9in
NICKNAME: Chozza
EDUCATION: St Richard's Catholic College, Bexhill; Eastbourne College, East Sussex
TEAMS: Sussex, England U19
ROLE: Batsman
DEBUT: First-class: 2013; List A: 2013; T20: 2014

BEST BATTING: 135* Sussex vs Leeds/Bradford MCCU, Hove, 2016
BEST BOWLING: 1-9 Sussex vs Leeds/Bradford MCCU, Hove, 2016

WHAT WAS YOUR FIRST CRICKET CLUB? Hastings & St Leonards Priory CC, East Sussex
WHAT WERE YOU DOING WHEN ENGLAND WON THE WORLD CUP? Hiding behind my sofa
HOW WOULD YOU DISMISS STEVE SMITH? Get Luke Wells to talk him out
BIGGEST TOPIC OF DISCUSSION IN YOUR DRESSING ROOM? Football and Netflix
SURPRISING FACT ABOUT A TEAMMATE? Jofra Archer and George Garton can spend hours playing Call of Duty or Fortnite (video games)
BIGGEST CRICKETING REGRET? Not being 7ft 1in – that would make my seamers useful
CRICKET STAR OF THE FUTURE? Alfie Hunter (Buxted Park CC)
WHICH BOOK MEANS MOST TO YOU? Harry Kane – The Biography by Frank Worrall
IF YOU WERE AN ANIMAL, WHICH WOULD IT BE? A polar bear – it can swim underwater and is top of the food chain
TWITTER: @hfinch72

Batting	Mat	Inns	NO	Runs	HS	Ave	SR	100	50	Ct	St
First-class	48	79	6	1907	135*	26.12	52.21	3	11	62	0
List A	35	33	3	1125	108	37.50	77.58	1	8	8	0
T20s	20	15	3	193	35*	16.08	105.46	0	0	6	0
Bowling	**Mat**	**Balls**	**Runs**	**Wkts**	**BBI**	**BBM**	**Ave**	**Econ**	**SR**	**5w**	**10**
First-class	48	168	118	2	1/9	1/9	59.00	4.21	84.0	0	0
List A	35	16	24	0	-	-	-	9.00	-	0	0
T20s	20	-	-	-	-	-	-	-	-	-	-

STEVEN FINN RHB / RFM / R0 / W2

FULL NAME: Steven Thomas Finn
BORN: April 4, 1989, Watford, Hertfordshire
SQUAD NO: 9
HEIGHT: 6ft 8in
NICKNAME: Finny, Cyril
EDUCATION: Parmiter's School, Watford
TEAMS: England, Middlesex, Islamabad United, Otago
ROLE: Bowler
DEBUT: Test: 2010; ODI: 2011; T20I: 2011; First-class: 2005; List A: 2007; T20: 2008

BEST BATTING: 56 England vs New Zealand, Dunedin, 2013
BEST BOWLING: 9-37 Middlesex vs Worcestershire, Worcester, 2010
COUNTY CAP: 2009

FAMILY TIES? My father, Terry, played Minor Counties cricket for Hertfordshire
WHAT WAS YOUR FIRST CRICKET CLUB? Langlebury CC, Hertfordshire. The slope is more pronounced that it is at Lord's
BIGGEST TOPIC OF DISCUSSION IN YOUR DRESSING ROOM? Who has the worst throwing arm in the team (I'll give you a clue: Nick Gubbins)
MOST INTERESTING TEAMMATE? Sam Robson – very unpredictable
CRICKETING HERO? Glenn McGrath
CRICKET STAR OF THE FUTURE? Blake Cullen (Middlesex Second XI)
TWITTER: @finnysteve

Batting	Mat	Inns	NO	Runs	HS	Ave	SR	100	50	Ct	St
Tests	36	47	22	279	56	11.16	30.96	0	1	8	0
ODIs	69	30	13	136	35	8.00	60.98	0	0	15	0
T20Is	21	3	3	14	8*	-	73.68	0	0	6	0
First-class	157	191	62	1266	56	9.81	40.35	0	2	49	0
List A	144	59	25	411	42*	12.08	67.48	0	0	33	0
T20s	103	21	15	60	8*	10.00	80.00	0	0	27	0
Bowling	**Mat**	**Balls**	**Runs**	**Wkts**	**BBI**	**BBM**	**Ave**	**Econ**	**SR**	**5w**	**10**
Tests	36	6412	3800	125	6/79	9/187	30.40	3.55	51.2	5	0
ODIs	69	3550	2996	102	5/33	5/33	29.37	5.06	34.8	2	0
T20Is	21	480	583	27	3/16	3/16	21.59	7.28	17.7	0	0
First-class	157	27676	15981	551	9/37		29.00	3.46	50.2	14	1
List A	144	6821	5847	201	5/33	5/33	29.08	5.14	33.9	3	0
T20s	103	2138	2815	125	5/16	5/16	22.52	7.89	17.1	1	0

MATTHEW FISHER

RHB / RFM / R0 / W0

FULL NAME: Matthew David Fisher
BORN: November 9, 1997, York
SQUAD NO: 7
HEIGHT: 6ft 2in
NICKNAME: Fish, Nemo, Pup
EDUCATION: Easingwold School, North Yorkshire
TEAMS: Yorkshire, England Lions
ROLE: Bowler
DEBUT: First-class: 2015; List A: 2013; T20: 2015

BEST BATTING: 47* Yorkshire vs Kent, Headingley, 2019
BEST BOWLING: 5-54 Yorkshire vs Warwickshire, Headingley, 2017

WHAT GOT YOU INTO CRICKET? Playing with my brothers at our local club. And the 2005 Ashes
BEST MOMENT IN CRICKET? Taking 5-22 against Derbyshire at Headingley on my T20 Blast debut for Yorkshire in 2015
SURPRISING FACT ABOUT YOU? I'm deaf in one ear
CRICKETING HERO? Andrew Flintoff – he played at his best when under pressure
NON-CRICKETING HERO? My dad – he taught me values and morals
TWITTER: @9M_Fisher

Batting	Mat	Inns	NO	Runs	HS	Ave	SR	100	50	Ct	St
First-class	13	17	3	246	47*	17.57	31.33	0	0	4	0
List A	34	18	10	228	36*	28.50	98.70	0	0	10	0
T20s	23	6	4	33	17*	16.50	137.50	0	0	7	0
Bowling	**Mat**	**Balls**	**Runs**	**Wkts**	**BBI**	**BBM**	**Ave**	**Econ**	**SR**	**5w**	**10**
First-class	13	1922	1077	31	5/54	5/89	34.74	3.36	62.0	1	0
List A	34	1384	1366	32	3/32	3/32	42.68	5.92	43.2	0	0
T20s	23	419	659	23	5/22	5/22	28.65	9.43	18.2	1	0

LUKE FLETCHER RHB / RFM / R0 / W0 / MVP38

FULL NAME: Luke Jack Fletcher
BORN: September 18, 1988, Nottingham
SQUAD NO: 19
HEIGHT: 6ft 6in
NICKNAME: Fletch
EDUCATION: Henry Mellish Comprehensive School, Nottingham
TEAMS: Nottinghamshire, Trent Rockets, Derbyshire, England U19, Surrey, Wellington
ROLE: Bowler
DEBUT: First-class: 2008; List A: 2008; T20: 2009

BEST BATTING: 92 Nottinghamshire vs Hampshire, Southampton, 2009
BEST BOWLING: 5-27 Nottinghamshire vs Worcestershire, Worcester, 2018
COUNTY CAP: 2014 (Nottinghamshire)

WHAT WAS YOUR FIRST CRICKET CLUB? Bulwell CC, Nottinghamshire
WHAT WERE YOU DOING WHEN ENGLAND WON THE WORLD CUP? I was at Eddie Someck's barbecue
HOW WOULD YOU DISMISS STEVE SMITH? Caught behind
MOST INTERESTING TEAMMATE? Rob Ferley – he once made me wrestle him in a baby pool at the gym at 9pm. Top man
BEST INNINGS YOU'VE SEEN? Alex Hales: 187 not out to win the Lord's final in 2017
CRICKETING HERO? Andrew Flintoff
WHICH RULE WOULD YOU CHANGE ABOUT CRICKET? One hour for lunch
BIGGEST CRICKETING REGRET? Getting out on 92 – twice
IF YOU WERE AN ANIMAL, WHICH WOULD IT BE? A rhino
TWITTER: @fletcherluke

Batting	Mat	Inns	NO	Runs	HS	Ave	SR	100	50	Ct	St
First-class	117	174	28	2029	92	13.89	46.80	0	4	28	0
List A	75	40	16	495	53*	20.62	113.01	0	1	13	0
T20s	72	26	10	113	27	7.06	111.88	0	0	9	0
Bowling	**Mat**	**Balls**	**Runs**	**Wkts**	**BBI**	**BBM**	**Ave**	**Econ**	**SR**	**5w**	**10**
First-class	117	19720	9654	343	5/27	9/108	28.14	2.93	57.4	6	0
List A	75	3112	2936	81	5/56	5/56	36.24	5.66	38.4	1	0
T20s	72	1464	1969	79	4/30	4/30	24.92	8.06	18.5	0	0

BEN FOAKES RHB / WK / R0 / W0 / MVP57

FULL NAME: Benjamin Thomas Foakes
BORN: February 15, 1993, Colchester, Essex
SQUAD NO: 7
HEIGHT: 6ft 2in
NICKNAME: Foakesey
EDUCATION: Tendring Technology College, Essex
TEAMS: England, Surrey, Northern Superchargers, Essex
ROLE: Wicketkeeper/batsman
DEBUT: Test: 2018; ODI: 2019; T20I: 2019; First-class: 2011; List A: 2013; T20: 2014

BEST BATTING: 141* Surrey vs Hampshire, Southampton, 2016

COUNTY CAP: 2016 (Surrey)

WHAT GOT YOU INTO CRICKET? Growing up in a small town there wasn't a lot to do so I got involved with all the local sports clubs
FAMILY TIES? My brother plays in the East Anglian Premier League for Frinton-on-Sea
SUPERSTITIONS? I touch my belly button and top and bottom lip between each ball
CRICKETING HERO? James Foster – he made me want to become a keeper when I first started watching Essex play as a kid
IF YOU WEREN'T A CRICKETER? I'd be exploring Asia
SURPRISING FACT ABOUT YOU? After I had a car crash a tooth was glued back together. It came unstuck while I was batting and was dangling, so I tore it out at lunch and batted with no front teeth

Batting	Mat	Inns	NO	Runs	HS	Ave	SR	100	50	Ct	St
Tests	5	10	2	332	107	41.50	53.80	1	1	10	2
ODIs	1	1	1	61	61*	-	80.26	0	1	2	1
T20Is	1	-	-	-	-	-	-	-	-	1	0
First-class	109	172	28	5474	141*	38.01	52.59	9	30	225	23
List A	73	63	11	1941	92	37.32	86.49	0	18	86	11
T20s	66	45	10	764	75*	21.82	125.24	0	3	34	7
Bowling	**Mat**	**Balls**	**Runs**	**Wkts**	**BBI**	**BBM**	**Ave**	**Econ**	**SR**	**5w**	**10**
Tests	5	-	-	-	-	-	-	-	-	-	-
ODIs	1	-	-	-	-	-	-	-	-	-	-
T20Is	1	-	-	-	-	-	-	-	-	-	-
First-class	109	6	6	0	-	-	-	6.00	-	0	0
List A	73	-	-	-	-	-	-	-	-	-	-
T20s	66	-	-	-	-	-	-	-	-	-	-

WILL FRAINE

RHB / RM / R0 / W0

FULL NAME: William Alan Richard Fraine
BORN: June 13, 1996, Huddersfield
SQUAD NO: 31
EDUCATION: Silcoates School, Wakefield, West Yorkshire; Bromsgrove Sixth Form College, Worcestershire; Durham University
TEAMS: Yorkshire, Nottinghamshire
ROLE: Batsman
DEBUT: First-class: 2017; List A: 2018; T20: 2018

BEST BATTING: 106 Yorkshire vs Surrey, Scarborough, 2019

NOTES: Fraine is a top-order batsman who turned down an offer from Nottinghamshire to sign for his home county Yorkshire in October 2018. "There's always that pull of being a Yorkie lad," he said upon joining the White Rose. He was born in Huddersfield and played for Yorkshire's age-group sides up until representing the U19s in 2014. After moving to a boarding school in Bromsgrove, Fraine played Second XI cricket for Worcestershire and in 2016 he made his first-class debut for Durham MCCU against Gloucestershire at Bristol. Nottinghamshire then gave him a run in their Second XI and signed him on a short contract in May 2018. He scored his maiden first-class hundred last summer in the Championship match against Surrey at Scarborough but is unlikely to be fit for the start of this season after undergoing knee surgery in December

Batting	Mat	Inns	NO	Runs	HS	Ave	SR	100	50	Ct	St
First-class	13	20	1	490	106	25.78	49.09	1	0	8	0
List A	4	3	1	27	13	13.50	122.72	0	0	1	0
T20s	11	10	2	79	16	9.87	112.85	0	0	10	0
Bowling	**Mat**	**Balls**	**Runs**	**Wkts**	**BBI**	**BBM**	**Ave**	**Econ**	**SR**	**5w**	**10**
First-class	13	-	-	-	-	-	-	-	-	-	-
List A	4	-	-	-	-	-	-	-	-	-	-
T20s	11	-	-	-	-	-	-	-	-	-	-

JAMES FULLER

RHB / RFM / R0 / W0

FULL NAME: James Kerr Fuller
BORN: January 24, 1990, Cape Town, South Africa
SQUAD NO: 26
HEIGHT: 6ft 2in
NICKNAME: Foz
EDUCATION: Westlake Boys High School, Auckland; University of Otago
TEAMS: Hampshire, Auckland, England Lions, Gloucestershire, Middlesex, Otago
ROLE: Bowler
DEBUT: First-class: 2010; List A: 2011; T20: 2011

BEST BATTING: 93 Middlesex vs Somerset, Taunton, 2016
BEST BOWLING: 6-24 Otago vs Wellington, Dunedin, 2013
COUNTY CAP: 2011 (Gloucestershire)

WHAT WAS YOUR FIRST CRICKET CLUB? North Shore CC, Auckland, New Zealand
WHAT WERE YOU DOING WHEN ENGLAND WON THE WORLD CUP? I was in with the rest of the Hampshire team after a day's play at the Ageas. We were all circled round the TV
HOW WOULD YOU DISMISS STEVE SMITH? New Zealand had success by putting a catcher round the corner and bowling into his ribs
WHAT EXCITES YOU ABOUT THE HUNDRED? Everything that goes with a franchise tournament
BIGGEST TOPIC OF DISCUSSION IN YOUR DRESSING ROOM? The size of boundaries
MOST INTERESTING TEAMMATE? Tom Alsop – he's always got a science book on the go, so we have some good discussions on how the natural world works. Ryan Stevenson has some good stories of growing up in a farm in the south west
CRICKETING HERO? Shane Bond
CRICKET STAR OF THE FUTURE? Ajeet Dale (Hampshire Academy)
IF YOU WERE AN ANIMAL, WHICH WOULD IT BE? A polar bear – very good sense of smell, strong paws, big appetite
TWITTER: @James_Fuller246

Batting	Mat	Inns	NO	Runs	HS	Ave	SR	100	50	Ct	St
First-class	53	69	9	1239	93	20.65	64.06	0	6	21	0
List A	62	49	16	759	55*	23.00	102.15	0	1	21	0
T20s	89	53	19	639	46*	18.79	146.55	0	0	37	0
Bowling	**Mat**	**Balls**	**Runs**	**Wkts**	**BBI**	**BBM**	**Ave**	**Econ**	**SR**	**5w**	**10**
First-class	53	8342	4964	150	6/24	10/79	33.09	3.57	55.6	5	1
List A	62	2449	2422	75	6/35	6/35	32.29	5.93	32.6	1	0
T20s	89	1586	2328	96	6/28	6/28	24.25	8.80	16.5	1	0

GEORGE FURRER

RHB / LFM / R0 / W0

WARWICKSHIRE

FULL NAME: George William Furrer
BORN: October 10, 1998, London
SQUAD NO: TBC
HEIGHT: 6ft 7in
EDUCATION: Barker College, Sydney; University of New South Wales
TEAMS: Warwickshire
ROLE: Bowler

NOTES: The 21-year-old fast bowler signed a two-year contract at Edgbaston last August following a trial with Warwickshire's Second XI. Furrer was born in London and has a British passport but grew up in Australia, representing Eastern Suburbs in Sydney grade cricket. He was also part of the New South Wales Academy and played for their U19 side. A tall and pacy left-armer, Furrer nevertheless describes himself as "not an out-and-out fast bowler… I pride myself on my skills, my ability to swing the ball and deliver it from a good height". On joining up with the first-team squad, Furrer said: "For such a professional set-up, I've been amazed about how relaxed they are and how much they enjoy the game. They've all been very warm and welcoming." He will also be playing club cricket for Birmingham Premier League side Moseley CC this summer

GEORGE GARRETT

RHB / RMF / R0 / W0

FULL NAME: George Anthony Garrett
BORN: March 4, 2000, Harpenden, Hertfordshire
SQUAD NO: 44
HEIGHT: 6ft 4in
NICKNAME: Gazza
EDUCATION: Shrewsbury School; University of Birmingham
TEAMS: Warwickshire
ROLE: Bowler
DEBUT: First-class: 2019; T20: 2019

BEST BATTING: 24 Warwickshire vs Essex, Edgbaston, 2019
BEST BOWLING: 2-53 Warwickshire vs Nottinghamshire, Trent Bridge, 2019

WHAT WAS YOUR FIRST CRICKET CLUB? Harpenden CC, Hertfordshire
WHAT WERE YOU DOING WHEN ENGLAND WON THE WORLD CUP? I was in a pub in Selly Oak (Birmingham) with Ashton Agar
HOW WOULD YOU DISMISS STEVE SMITH? With a wobble seamer
WHAT EXCITES YOU ABOUT THE HUNDRED? Watching Benny Howell play for Birmingham Phoenix
BIGGEST TOPIC OF DISCUSSION IN YOUR DRESSING ROOM? Whether Bristol City will get promoted
MOST INTERESTING TEAMMATE? Matt Lamb – lives in his own world. Only has two pairs of gloves. Stiffest man alive
CRICKET STAR OF THE FUTURE? Jacob Bethell (Warwickshire Academy)
IF YOU WERE AN ANIMAL, WHICH WOULD IT BE? A robin – Bristol City till I die
TWITTER: @Georgegarrett14

GEORGE GARTON LHB / LFM / R0 / W0

SUSSEX / SOUTHERN BRAVE

FULL NAME: George Henry Simmons Garton
BORN: April 15, 1997, Brighton
SQUAD NO: 15
HEIGHT: 6ft 1in
NICKNAME: Garts
EDUCATION: Hurstpierpoint College, West Sussex
TEAMS: Sussex, Southern Brave, England Lions
ROLE: Bowler
DEBUT: First-class: 2016; List A: 2016; T20: 2016

BEST BATTING: 59* Sussex vs Worcestershire, Hove, 2019
BEST BOWLING: 3-20 Sussex vs Durham, Chester-le-Street, 2017

WHAT WAS YOUR FIRST CRICKET CLUB? Preston Nomads CC, West Sussex
HOW WOULD YOU DISMISS STEVE SMITH? Ask Neil Wagner
WHAT EXCITES YOU ABOUT THE HUNDRED? The opportunity to test myself against the best in the world
BEST INNINGS YOU'VE SEEN? Phil Salt's Championship hundred against Derbyshire at Hove in 2018 – that was some serious ball-striking
WHICH RULE WOULD YOU CHANGE ABOUT CRICKET? Remove the limit on bouncers
CRICKET STAR OF THE FUTURE? Tom Clark (Sussex)
TWITTER: @george_garton

Batting	Mat	Inns	NO	Runs	HS	Ave	SR	100	50	Ct	St
First-class	13	15	5	213	59*	21.30	63.01	0	2	6	0
List A	24	11	2	103	38	11.44	86.55	0	0	11	0
T20s	12	1	1	2	2*	-	100.00	0	0	3	0
Bowling	**Mat**	**Balls**	**Runs**	**Wkts**	**BBI**	**BBM**	**Ave**	**Econ**	**SR**	**5w**	**10**
First-class	13	1572	1049	28	3/20	5/109	37.46	4.00	56.1	0	0
List A	24	942	993	29	4/43	4/43	34.24	6.32	32.4	0	0
T20s	12	186	272	11	4/16	4/16	24.72	8.77	16.9	0	0

EMILIO GAY

LHB / RM / R0 / W0

FULL NAME: Emilio Nico Gay
BORN: April 14, 2000, Bedford
SQUAD NO: 19
HEIGHT: 6ft 2in
NICKNAME: Nico, Floyd
EDUCATION: Rushmoor School, Bedford; Bedford School
TEAMS: Northamptonshire
ROLE: Batsman
DEBUT: First-class: 2019

TWITTER: @emilio_nico1
NOTES: A former student at Bedford School, the alma mater of Sir Alastair Cook, Gay signed his first professional contract with Northamptonshire last July after impressing for the county's Second XI. He made his first-class debut in the Championship clash with Gloucestershire at Bristol last September but persistent rain prevented him from batting or bowling. Gay played eight Second XI Championship matches in 2019, scoring 672 runs at an average of 56 and hitting two centuries. The highlight was a matchwinning 186 not out against Warwickshire. "You get a lot of young players who doubt themselves and think, 'Am I good enough?', but Emilio's attitude is very good," said Northants head coach David Ripley. "He's got a real desire to succeed, he's very confident in his ability, which is to be encouraged and welcomed"

Batting	Mat	Inns	NO	Runs	HS	Ave	SR	100	50	Ct	St
First-class	1	-	-	-	-	-	-	-	-	1	0
Bowling	**Mat**	**Balls**	**Runs**	**Wkts**	**BBI**	**BBM**	**Ave**	**Econ**	**SR**	**5w**	**10**
First-class	1	-	-	-	-	-	-	-	-	-	-

OLIVER GIBSON

RHB / RFM / R0 / W0

FULL NAME: Oliver James Gibson
BORN: July 7, 2000, Northallerton, Yorkshire
SQUAD NO: 73
HEIGHT: 5ft 11in
NICKNAME: Gibbo
EDUCATION: Queen Elizabeth Grammar School, Hexham, Northumberland; Derwentside Sixth Form College, Consett, County Durham
TEAMS: Durham
ROLE: Bowler

NOTES: A seamer who has come through the Durham Academy, Gibson featured in matchday squads in last season's County Championship but was still awaiting his first-team debut ahead of the 2020 season. He signed a youth contract with the county in November last year after making three appearances in last season's Second XI Championship, taking five wickets at 38.20. He also played a handful of Second XI Trophy matches in a Durham side which reached the final, where they lost to Kent, and took seven wickets at 16.57 in four second-team T20 games. Gibson plays his club cricket for Shotley Bridge CC in the north-west of County Durham, home of his boyhood hero Paul Collingwood

NATHAN GILCHRIST RHB / RFM / R0 / W0

FULL NAME: Nathan Nicholas Gilchrist
BORN: June 11, 2000, Harare, Zimbabwe
SQUAD NO: 21
HEIGHT: 6ft 5in
NICKNAME: Gilly, Melman
EDUCATION: St Stithians School, Johannesburg; King's College, Taunton
TEAMS: Somerset
ROLE: Bowler

WHAT WAS YOUR FIRST CRICKET CLUB? Staplegrove CC, Somerset. The cricket field was right next to a heard of cows
WHAT WERE YOU DOING WHEN ENGLAND WON THE WORLD CUP? Drinking a cup of tea
HOW WOULD YOU DISMISS STEVE SMITH? Bowl yorkers
BIGGEST TOPIC OF DISCUSSION IN YOUR DRESSING ROOM? Who has the biggest head
MOST INTERESTING TEAMMATE? Marcus Trescothick – for his wealth of experience and 2005 Ashes stories
WHICH RULE WOULD YOU CHANGE ABOUT CRICKET? Allow more bumpers per over
CRICKET STAR OF THE FUTURE? Will Smeed (Somerset Academy)
IF YOU WERE AN ANIMAL, WHICH WOULD IT BE? A leopard
TWITTER: @nathgilchrist
NOTES: A genuinely quick bowler and clean striker of a ball, Gilchrist signed his first professional contract with Somerset in 2018. The tall 19-year-old was born in Harare to an English father and first came to this country when he was involved in a cricket exchange between St Stithians in Johannesburg and King's College Taunton. He represented Somerset at U17 level and has been a regular in the Second XI side for the last two seasons

RICHARD GLEESON RHB / RFM / R0 / W0 / MVP85

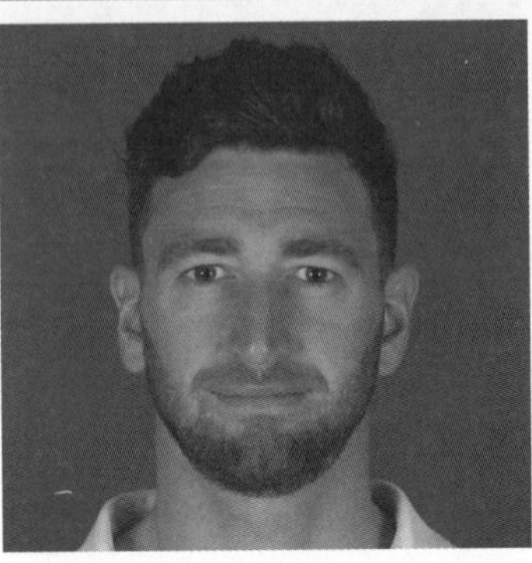

FULL NAME: Richard James Gleeson
BORN: December 2, 1987, Blackpool
SQUAD NO: 11
HEIGHT: 6ft 4in
NICKNAME: Glees, Granddaddy
EDUCATION: Baines High School, Lancashire; University of Cumbria
TEAMS: Lancashire, Northern Superchargers, England Lions, Melbourne Renegades, Northamptonshire, Rangpur Riders
ROLE: Bowler
DEBUT: First-class: 2015; List A: 2016; T20: 2016

BEST BATTING: 31 Northamptonshire vs Gloucestershire, Bristol, 2016
BEST BOWLING: 6-43 Lancashire vs Leicestershire, Leicester, 2019

FAMILY TIES? My father ran the bar at our local cricket club, my sister ran the kitchen, and my brother-in-law was the First XI captain
WHAT WAS YOUR FIRST CRICKET CLUB? Blackpool CC, Lancashire
BEST ADVICE RECEIVED? Just enjoy it maaaate (Steven Crook)
HOW WOULD YOU DISMISS STEVE SMITH? With a googly
BIGGEST TOPIC OF DISCUSSION IN YOUR DRESSING ROOM? Hair transplants
MOST INTERESTING TEAMMATE? Steven Crook
CRICKETING HERO? Allan Donald
SURPRISING FACT ABOUT YOU? I am a published poet
CRICKET STAR OF THE FUTURE? Emilio Gay (Northamptonshire)
TWITTER: @RicGleeson

Batting	Mat	Inns	NO	Runs	HS	Ave	SR	100	50	Ct	St
First-class	33	38	16	253	31	11.50	34.61	0	0	8	0
List A	21	13	5	53	13	6.62	42.06	0	0	3	0
T20s	50	11	6	24	7*	4.80	85.71	0	0	10	0
Bowling	**Mat**	**Balls**	**Runs**	**Wkts**	**BBI**	**BBM**	**Ave**	**Econ**	**SR**	**5w**	**10**
First-class	33	5418	3001	140	6/43	10/113	21.43	3.32	38.7	10	1
List A	21	841	816	28	5/47	5/47	29.14	5.82	30.0	1	0
T20s	50	984	1288	50	3/12	3/12	25.76	7.85	19.6	0	0

BRANDON GLOVER RHB / RFM / R0 / W0

FULL NAME: Brandon Dale Glover
BORN: April 3, 1997, Johannesburg, South Africa
SQUAD NO: 20
HEIGHT: 6ft 2in
NICKNAME: Gloves
EDUCATION: St Stithians College, Johannesburg; Stellenbosch University, Western Province
TEAMS: Netherlands, Northamptonshire, Boland, South Africa U19
ROLE: Bowler
DEBUT: ODI: 2019; T20I: 2019; First-class: 2016; List A: 2017; T20: 2019

BEST BATTING: 12* Boland vs Gauteng, Paarl, 2019
BEST BOWLING: 4-83 Boland vs Free State, Bloemfontein, 2017

WHAT WAS YOUR FIRST CRICKET CLUB? Old Parks Sports Club, Johannesburg, South Africa
MOST INTERESTING TEAMMATE? Netherlands captain Pieter Seelaar – great stories from on and off the field
CRICKET STAR OF THE FUTURE? Netherlands leg-spinner Philippe Boissevain
IF YOU WERE AN ANIMAL, WHICH WOULD IT BE? A honey badger – seems to be able to take on everything
NOTES: Northants have signed the 23-year-old Netherlands fast bowler on a three-year contract. Glover is noted for his pace and was the leading wicket-taker in T20I cricket last year, spearheading the Netherlands side which won the T20 World Cup Qualfier last November. Glover was born in Johannesburg and has represented South Africa U19. He is good friends with Northants batsman Ricardo Vasconcelos, who described his new teammate as "a crazy fast bowler – fiery, competitive, aggressive and a bit awkward at times"

Batting	Mat	Inns	NO	Runs	HS	Ave	SR	100	50	Ct	St
ODIs	1	-	-	-	-	-	-	-	-	1	0
T20Is	19	4	3	2	1*	2.00	25.00	0	0	3	0
First-class	9	13	6	38	12*	5.42	31.93	0	0	1	0
List A	6	5	2	55	27	18.33	67.90	0	0	1	0
T20s	19	4	3	2	1*	2.00	25.00	0	0	3	0
Bowling	**Mat**	**Balls**	**Runs**	**Wkts**	**BBI**	**BBM**	**Ave**	**Econ**	**SR**	**5w**	**10**
ODIs	1	60	37	1	1/37	1/37	37.00	3.70	60.0	0	0
T20Is	19	390	448	28	4/12	4/12	16.00	6.89	13.9	0	0
First-class	9	1176	733	20	4/83	5/104	36.65	3.73	58.8	0	0
List A	6	236	198	4	2/60	2/60	49.50	5.03	59.0	0	0
T20s	19	390	448	28	4/12	4/12	16.00	6.89	13.9	0	0

BILLY GODLEMAN LHB / LB / R2 / W0 / MVP8

FULL NAME: Billy Ashley Godleman
BORN: February 11, 1989, Camden, London
SQUAD NO: 1
HEIGHT: 6ft 2in
NICKNAME: G, Chief
EDUCATION: Islington Green School, London
TEAMS: Derbyshire, England U19, Essex, Middlesex
ROLE: Batsman
DEBUT: First-class: 2005; List A: 2007; T20: 2006

BEST BATTING: 227 Derbyshire vs Glamorgan, Swansea, 2019

COUNTY CAP: 2015 (Derbyshire)

WHAT WAS YOUR FIRST CRICKET CLUB? Brondesbury CC, London
WHAT EXCITES YOU ABOUT THE HUNDRED? That it will give the game broader exposure to children
MOST INTERESTING TEAMMATE? Tom Westley – intelligent, caring and funny
CRICKETING HERO? I admire Hashim Amla. He stands for something more than cricket. He shares his experience and inside knowledge with other players. And he scores runs consistently in all competitions. Top bloke
SURPRISING FACT ABOUT YOU? I don't engage on social media
SURPRISING FACT ABOUT A TEAMMATE? My close friend Tony Palladino wears a Batman skin under his whites – and he has delivered many superhuman spells over the years
WHICH BOOK MEANS MOST TO YOU? Luck – A Fresh Look at Fortune by Ed Smith
IF YOU WERE AN ANIMAL, WHICH WOULD IT BE? Anything that lives on land

Batting	Mat	Inns	NO	Runs	HS	Ave	SR	100	50	Ct	St
First-class	158	285	13	8803	227	32.36	46.96	21	38	98	0
List A	69	67	8	2559	137	43.37	78.47	6	12	23	0
T20s	79	74	7	1654	92	24.68	117.89	0	12	36	0
Bowling	**Mat**	**Balls**	**Runs**	**Wkts**	**BBI**	**BBM**	**Ave**	**Econ**	**SR**	**5w**	**10**
First-class	158	30	35	0	-	-	-	7.00	-	0	0
List A	69	-	-	-	-	-	-	-	-	-	-
T20s	79	-	-	-	-	-	-	-	-	-	-

LEWIS GOLDSWORTHY RHB / SLA / R0 / W0

FULL NAME: Lewis Peter Goldsworthy
BORN: January 8, 2001, Cornwall
SQUAD NO: 44
HEIGHT: 5ft 7in
NICKNAME: Golders
EDUCATION: Cambourne Science & International Academy, Cornwall; Millfield School, Street, Somerset
TEAMS: Somerset, England U19
ROLE: Allrounder

WHAT WAS YOUR FIRST CRICKET CLUB? Troon CC, Cornwall
WHAT WERE YOU DOING WHEN ENGLAND WON THE WORLD CUP? I was at Loughborough meeting up with the England U19 squad
BIGGEST TOPIC OF DISCUSSION IN YOUR DRESSING ROOM? Football
CRICKET STAR OF THE FUTURE? Will Smeed (England U19, Somerset Second XI)
TWITTER: @lewisgoldsworthy
NOTES: The left-arm spinner and middle-order batsman signed his first professional contract with Somerset last September, keeping him at Taunton until the end of the 2021 season. "It's an unreal feeling to have signed for the club that I've grown up watching and supporting," said Goldsworthy. "I was speechless when I was offered the contract by [director of cricket] Andy Hurry. The crowds in Taunton are unbelievable and the club is well known for the support that it gets, so it would mean the world to me to make my debut for the first team." Born and raised in Cornwall, Goldsworthy has been playing Minor Counties since 2017 and scored 178 for Somerset U17 against Surrey U17 two years ago. Impressive performances for the club's Second XI led to a call-up to the England U19 squad last year and he was the team's joint-leading wicket-taker in South Africa during the recent World Cup, taking 12 wickets at 9.58 with an equally impressive economy rate of just 2.34

BEN GREEN

RHB / RFM / R0 / W0

FULL NAME: Benjamin George Frederick Green
BORN: September 28, 1997, Exeter, Devon
SQUAD NO: 54
HEIGHT: 6ft 2in
NICKNAME: Greener, Neil
EDUCATION: St Peter's Preparatory School, Lympstone, Devon; Exeter School
TEAMS: Somerset, England U19
ROLE: Allrounder
DEBUT: First-class: 2018; List A: 2018; T20: 2016

BEST BATTING: 26 Somerset vs Hampshire, Southampton, 2018
BEST BOWLING: 1-8 Somerset vs Hampshire, Southampton, 2018

WHAT WAS YOUR FIRST CRICKET CLUB? Clyst St George CC, East Devon – my local village team. It was a brilliant starting point and I have fond memories of Friday-night training
HOW WOULD YOU DISMISS STEVE SMITH? Try the classic moon ball and hope he chips it up
BIGGEST TOPIC OF DISCUSSION IN YOUR DRESSING ROOM? Who is the best table-tennis player
MOST INTERESTING TEAMMATE? Chris Gayle
WHICH RULE WOULD YOU CHANGE ABOUT CRICKET? Allow more than two fielders behind square on the leg-side
CRICKET STAR OF THE FUTURE? Kasey Aldridge (Somerset)
WHICH BOOK MEANS MOST TO YOU? The Harry Potter books – my parents used to read a chapter to me and my sister every night
IF YOU WERE AN ANIMAL, WHICH WOULD IT BE? A Labrador – loyal, affectionate and easy-going
TWITTER: @Ben_Green28

Batting	Mat	Inns	NO	Runs	HS	Ave	SR	100	50	Ct	St
First-class	2	4	0	43	26	10.75	40.18	0	0	3	0
List A	3	3	2	35	26*	35.00	79.54	0	0	0	0
T20s	1	1	1	12	12*	-	92.30	0	0	0	0
Bowling	**Mat**	**Balls**	**Runs**	**Wkts**	**BBI**	**BBM**	**Ave**	**Econ**	**SR**	**5w**	**10**
First-class	2	42	17	1	1/8	1/17	17.00	2.42	42.0	0	0
List A	3	66	70	1	1/52	1/52	70.00	6.36	66.0	0	0
T20s	1	12	12	0	-	-	-	6.00	-	0	0

CHRIS GREEN

RHB / OB

FULL NAME: Christopher James Green
BORN: October 1, 1993, Durban, South Africa
SQUAD NO: TBC
EDUCATION: Knox Grammar School, Wahroonga, New South Wales
TEAMS: Warwickshire, Guyana Amazon Warriors, Multan Sultans, New South Wales, Sydney Thunder
ROLE: Allrounder
DEBUT: List A: 2014; T20: 2015

BEST BATTING: 49 Sydney Thunder vs Sydney Sixes, Sydney, 2018 (T20)
BEST BOWLING: 4-14 Guyana AW vs Barbados Tridents, Bridgetown, 2019 (T20)

TWITTER: @chrisgreen_93
NOTES: An off-spinning allrounder who has built his reputation in Australia's Big Bash League, Green played six matches for Birmingham Bears in last season's T20 Blast and was set to skipper the side this summer. "It's a huge honour to return to the club as captain," said Green. "There's tremendous potential in this young squad. We have every chance of making the knockout stages and pushing for a home Finals Day." He was also picked up in the 2020 IPL Auction by Kolkata Knight Riders, although his career hit a blip when in January he was given a three-month suspension from bowling after he was reported for an illegal action in the Big Bash. In November last year he signed the longest deal in Big Bash history, with Sydney Thunder securing his services for six seasons

Batting	Mat	Inns	NO	Runs	HS	Ave	SR	100	50	Ct	St
List A	8	6	3	78	24	26.00	71.55	0	0	1	0
T20s	82	53	21	506	49	15.81	127.77	0	0	43	0
Bowling	**Mat**	**Balls**	**Runs**	**Wkts**	**BBI**	**BBM**	**Ave**	**Econ**	**SR**	**5w**	**10**
List A	8	281	230	8	5/53	5/53	28.75	4.91	35.1	1	0
T20s	82	1602	1810	65	4/14	4/14	27.84	6.77	24.6	0	0

LEWIS GREGORY RHB / RFM / R0 / W1 / MVP6

FULL NAME: Lewis Gregory
BORN: May 24, 1992, Plymouth, Devon
SQUAD NO: 24
HEIGHT: 6ft
NICKNAME: Mowgli
EDUCATION: Hele's School, Plymouth
TEAMS: England, Somerset, Trent Rockets, Peshawar Zalmi, Rangpur Rangers
ROLE: Allrounder
DEBUT: T20I: 2019; First-class: 2011; List A: 2010; T20: 2011

BEST BATTING: 137 Somerset vs Middlesex, Lord's, 2017
BEST BOWLING: 6-32 Somerset vs Kent, Canterbury, 2019
COUNTY CAP: 2015

WHAT GOT YOU INTO CRICKET? I saw it on TV and gave it a go
STRANGEST THING SEEN IN A GAME? Ryan Davies going out to bat in a 50-over game in the wrong shirt
BEST MOMENT IN CRICKET? Taking my maiden first-class five-wicket haul at Lord's and scoring my maiden first-class hundred at the same ground
CRICKETING HERO? Michael Vaughan
NON-CRICKETING HERO? Tiger Woods
SURPRISING FACT ABOUT YOU? I'm a black belt in taekwondo
TWITTER: @Lewisgregory23

Batting	Mat	Inns	NO	Runs	HS	Ave	SR	100	50	Ct	St
T20Is	5	3	0	21	15	7.00	110.52	0	0	0	0
First-class	86	127	13	2491	137	21.85	57.80	2	8	48	0
List A	76	57	6	1206	105*	23.64	100.83	1	7	27	0
T20s	103	80	20	1336	76*	22.26	146.17	0	4	39	0
Bowling	**Mat**	**Balls**	**Runs**	**Wkts**	**BBI**	**BBM**	**Ave**	**Econ**	**SR**	**5w**	**10**
T20Is	5	24	29	1	1/10	1/10	29.00	7.25	24.0	0	0
First-class	86	12413	6782	264	6/32	11/53	25.68	3.27	47.0	13	2
List A	76	2948	2941	106	4/23	4/23	27.74	5.98	27.8	0	0
T20s	103	1783	2614	100	4/15	4/15	26.14	8.79	17.8	0	0

GAVIN GRIFFITHS

RHB / RFM / R0 / W0

FULL NAME: Gavin Timothy Griffiths
BORN: November 19, 1993, Ormskirk, Lancashire
SQUAD NO: 93
HEIGHT: 6ft 2in
NICKNAME: Gavlar
EDUCATION: St Michael's CE High School, Chorley; St Mary's College, Crosby
TEAMS: Leicestershire, England U19, Hampshire, Lancashire
ROLE: Bowler
DEBUT: First-class: 2017; List A: 2014; T20: 2015

BEST BATTING: 40 Leicestershire vs Middlesex, Leicester, 2018
BEST BOWLING: 6-49 Leicestershire vs Durham, Chester-le-Street, 2018

WHAT WAS YOUR FIRST CRICKET CLUB? Ormskirk CC, West Lancashire.
WHICH BOWLER WOULD YOU LEAST LIKE TO FACE? Mohammad Abbas – enough pace, line and length, seam movement
BEST INNINGS YOU'VE SEEN? Ben Stokes's 258 at Cape Town in 2016
CRICKETING HERO? Allan Donald
WHICH RULE WOULD YOU CHANGE ABOUT CRICKET? Bowlers don't need to field
YOUR BIGGEST CRICKETING REGRET? Not learning more about my game as a teenager
SURPRISING FACT ABOUT YOU? I have played chess for England
FAVOURITE QUOTE OR SAYING? If you don't risk anything, you risk even more
WHICH BOOK MEANS MOST TO YOU? Bounce – The Myth of Talent and the Power of Practice by Matthew Syed
TWITTER: @Gavvlar

Batting	Mat	Inns	NO	Runs	HS	Ave	SR	100	50	Ct	St
First-class	23	33	11	303	40	13.77	33.59	0	0	3	0
List A	22	10	8	29	15*	14.50	37.66	0	0	11	0
T20s	38	14	13	40	11	40.00	78.43	0	0	8	0
Bowling	**Mat**	**Balls**	**Runs**	**Wkts**	**BBI**	**BBM**	**Ave**	**Econ**	**SR**	**5w**	**10**
First-class	23	3218	1755	55	6/49	10/83	31.90	3.27	58.5	1	1
List A	22	976	978	29	4/30	4/30	33.72	6.01	33.6	0	0
T20s	38	622	871	29	3/14	3/14	30.03	8.40	21.4	0	0

TIM GROENEWALD

RHB / RFM / R0 / W0

FULL NAME: Timothy Duncan Groenewald
BORN: January 10, 1984, Pietermaritzburg, South Africa
SQUAD NO: 36
HEIGHT: 6ft
NICKNAME: TimmyG, Groeners
EDUCATION: Maritzburg College; University of South Africa
TEAMS: Kent, Derbyshire, Somerset, Warwickshire
ROLE: Bowler
DEBUT: First-class: 2006; List A: 2006; T20: 2006

BEST BATTING: 78 Warwickshire vs Bangladesh A, Edgbaston, 2008
BEST BOWLING: 6-50 Derbyshire vs Surrey, Whitgift School, 2009
COUNTY CAP: 2011 (Derbyshire); 2016 (Somerset)

WHAT WAS YOUR FIRST CRICKET CLUB? Sutton Coldfield CC, Birmingham. The slope is twice as bad as at Lord's
WHICH BOWLER WOULD YOU LEAST LIKE TO FACE? Max Waller – love to whack him everywhere but couldn't face getting out to him
BEST INNINGS YOU'VE SEEN? Johann Myburgh's 42-ball hundred for Somerset against Essex in the 2018 T20 Blast
WHO WOULD YOU ASK TO BAT FOR YOUR LIFE? Jack Leach – he can't live without me
YOUR BIGGEST CRICKETING REGRET? Not being an opening bat in white-ball cricket
TWITTER: @timmyg12

Batting	Mat	Inns	NO	Runs	HS	Ave	SR	100	50	Ct	St
First-class	138	200	66	2375	78	17.72	50.52	0	6	45	0
List A	109	64	24	793	57	19.82	111.37	0	2	26	0
T20s	110	46	18	394	41	14.07	125.47	0	0	29	0
Bowling	**Mat**	**Balls**	**Runs**	**Wkts**	**BBI**	**BBM**	**Ave**	**Econ**	**SR**	**5w**	**10**
First-class	138	23011	11785	401	6/50	9/136	29.38	3.07	57.3	16	0
List A	109	4321	4051	123	4/22	4/22	32.93	5.62	35.1	0	0
T20s	110	1975	2710	95	4/21	4/21	28.52	8.23	20.7	0	0

NICK GUBBINS

LHB / LB / R1 / W0

FULL NAME: Nicholas Richard Trail Gubbins
BORN: December 31, 1993, Richmond, Surrey
SQUAD NO: 18
HEIGHT: 6ft
NICKNAME: Cathy
EDUCATION: Radley College, Oxfordshire; University of Leeds
TEAMS: Middlesex, England Lions
ROLE: Batsman
DEBUT: First-class: 2013; List A: 2014; T20: 2015

BEST BATTING: 201* Middlesex vs Lancashire, Lord's, 2016

COUNTY CAP: 2016

FAMILY TIES? My dad played one ODI for Singapore
WHAT WAS YOUR FIRST CRICKET CLUB? Stirlands CC, Chichester, West Sussex. Joe Burns and Saeed Ajmal played as overseas players at the club when I was there
BIGGEST TOPIC OF DISCUSSION IN YOUR DRESSING ROOM? Who is next to propose... Finny, you're up next!
MOST INTERESTING TEAMMATE? Tim Murtagh. Loves shower time
CRICKETING HERO? Marcus Trescothick – I used to get his GM bats when I was younger and I always tried to mimic him in the back garden
WHICH RULE WOULD YOU CHANGE ABOUT CRICKET? For DRS referrals, you can't be out on umpire's call. What happened to the benefit of the doubt?
CRICKET STAR OF THE FUTURE? Tom Wigglesworth – hard-hitting, tenacious keeper-batsman who plays in Hertfordshire and had a breakthrough in 2019. I'd be surprised if a county didn't sign him by 2021
WHICH BOOK MEANS MOST TO YOU? The Forgotten Highlander – My Incredible Story of Survival During the War in the Far East by Alistair Urquhart
TWITTER: @ngubbins18

Batting	Mat	Inns	NO	Runs	HS	Ave	SR	100	50	Ct	St
First-class	73	129	2	4184	201*	32.94	48.28	7	26	28	0
List A	56	55	2	2067	141	39.00	94.12	5	12	11	0
T20s	33	30	0	479	75	15.96	124.41	0	1	14	0
Bowling	**Mat**	**Balls**	**Runs**	**Wkts**	**BBI**	**BBM**	**Ave**	**Econ**	**SR**	**5w**	**10**
First-class	73	66	52	0	-	-	-	4.72	-	0	0
List A	56	-	-	-	-	-	-	-	-	-	-
T20s	33	-	-	-	-	-	-	-	-	-	-

BROOKE GUEST

RHB / WK / R0 / W0

LANCASHIRE

FULL NAME: Brooke David Guest
BORN: May 14, 1997, Whitworth Park, Manchester
SQUAD NO: 29
HEIGHT: 5ft 11in
NICKNAME: Guesty
EDUCATION: Kent Street Senior High School, Perth; Murdoch University, Perth
TEAMS: Lancashire
ROLE: Wicketkeeper
DEBUT: First-class: 2018; List A: 2019

BEST BATTING: 17 Lancashire vs Middlesex, Lord's, 2019

WHAT WAS YOUR FIRST CRICKET CLUB? South Perth CC, Australia. I've played there my whole life
WHAT WERE YOU DOING WHEN ENGLAND WON THE WORLD CUP? I was at the local cricket club
WHAT EXCITES YOU ABOUT THE HUNDRED? The opportunities for the lads playing in the tournament but also for the others who will play in the 50-over competition
BIGGEST TOPIC OF DISCUSSION IN YOUR DRESSING ROOM? The Hundred
BEST INNINGS YOU'VE SEEN? Graeme Smith against Australia in the 2009 Sydney Test – he showed a lot of guts to bat with a broken hand against Mitchell Johnson
CRICKET STAR OF THE FUTURE? Jack Morley (Lancashire)
NOTES: Born in Manchester, Guest moved to Australia as a young boy and made his Australia U19 debut in 2016. The wicketkeeper committed his future to England after returning to the UK in 2016 to play for Lancashire Second XI. In 2018 he scored 256 runs at an average of 53 with 18 dismissals in the Second XI Championship and also made his first-class debut against Hampshire at Southampton. He was rewarded with a new contract which runs until the end of 2020. Guest spent most of last summer in the Second XI, although he did play a Championship match and scored a fluent 36 on his List A debut against Worcestershire

Batting	Mat	Inns	NO	Runs	HS	Ave	SR	100	50	Ct	St
First-class	2	4	0	36	17	9.00	33.64	0	0	5	0
List A	2	2	0	41	36	20.50	78.84	0	0	0	1
Bowling	**Mat**	**Balls**	**Runs**	**Wkts**	**BBI**	**BBM**	**Ave**	**Econ**	**SR**	**5w**	**10**
First-class	2	-	-	-	-	-	-	-	-	-	-
List A	2	-	-	-	-	-	-	-	-	-	-

HARRY GURNEY

RHB / LFM / R0 / W0

FULL NAME: Harry Frederick Gurney
BORN: October 20, 1986, Nottingham
SQUAD NO: 11
HEIGHT: 6ft 2in
NICKNAME: Gramps
EDUCATION: Loughborough Grammar School; University of Leeds
TEAMS: England, Nottinghamshire, Trent Rockets, Kolkata Knight Riders, Leicestershire, Melbourne Renegades
ROLE: Bowler
DEBUT: ODI: 2014; T20I: 2014; First-class: 2007; List A: 2009; T20: 2009

BEST BATTING: 6 Nottinghamshire vs Somerset, Taunton, 2018 (T20)
BEST BOWLING: 5-30 Nottinghamshire vs Derbyshire, Derby, 2019 (T20)
COUNTY CAP: 2014 (Nottinghamshire)

WHAT WAS YOUR FIRST CRICKET CLUB? Loughborough Town CC, Leicestershire
WHAT WERE YOU DOING WHEN ENGLAND WON THE WORLD CUP? Jumping around my local pub
BIGGEST TOPIC OF DISCUSSION IN YOUR DRESSING ROOM? Which flavour of crisps Samit (Patel) will arrive with
MOST INTERESTING TEAMMATE? Dan Christian – he is Siri
BEST INNINGS YOU'VE SEEN? Alex Hales in the 2017 one-day final at Lord's. Pretty much single-handedly won the game for us
WHICH RULE WOULD YOU CHANGE ABOUT CRICKET? The bouncer over head-height should be a wide like it is everywhere else in the world. Why do we have to be different?
CRICKET STAR OF THE FUTURE? Nick Kimber (Surrey)
TWITTER: @gurneyhf
NOTES: Gurney signed a white-ball contract with Notts in March 2019

Batting	Mat	Inns	NO	Runs	HS	Ave	SR	100	50	Ct	St
ODIs	10	6	4	15	6*	7.50	45.45	0	0	1	0
T20Is	2	-	-	-	-	-	-	-	-	0	0
First-class	103	131	63	424	42*	6.23	40.57	0	0	12	0
List A	93	29	18	61	13*	5.54	50.00	0	0	7	0
T20s	156	25	18	27	6	3.85	79.41	0	0	18	0
Bowling	**Mat**	**Balls**	**Runs**	**Wkts**	**BBI**	**BBM**	**Ave**	**Econ**	**SR**	**5w**	**10**
ODIs	10	455	432	11	4/55	4/55	39.27	5.69	41.3	0	0
T20Is	2	48	55	3	2/26	2/26	18.33	6.87	16.0	0	0
First-class	103	16909	9472	310	6/25	9/136	30.55	3.36	54.5	8	0
List A	93	3934	3870	114	5/24	5/24	33.94	5.90	34.5	3	0
T20s	156	3281	4291	190	5/30	5/30	22.58	7.84	17.2	1	0

CALUM HAGGETT

LHB / RM / R0 / W0

FULL NAME: Calum John Haggett
BORN: October 30, 1990, Taunton
SQUAD NO: 25
HEIGHT: 6ft 3in
NICKNAME: Haggs
EDUCATION: Crispin School, Somerset; Millfield School
TEAMS: Kent, Somerset, England U19
ROLE: Bowler
DEBUT: First-class: 2013; List A: 2013; T20: 2011

BEST BATTING: 80 Kent vs Surrey, The Oval, 2015
BEST BOWLING: 4-15 Kent vs Derbyshire, Derby, 2016

FAMILY TIES? My father played village cricket and my brother played for Somerset seconds
WHAT WAS YOUR FIRST CRICKET CLUB? Shapwick & Polden CC, a little village club in the heart of Somerset which formed as a merger between Ashcott & Shapwick CC and Chilton Polden CC
WHAT EXCITES YOU ABOUT THE HUNDRED? Fewer balls to bowl
BIGGEST TOPIC OF DISCUSSION IN YOUR DRESSING ROOM? The county grind
CRICKETING HEROES? Chris March and Phil Hunt from Ashcott & Shapwick CC. They showed me what to do after the game
WHICH RULE WOULD YOU CHANGE ABOUT CRICKET? The minimum distance to the boundary should be bigger
WHICH BOOK MEANS MOST TO YOU? 1984 by George Orwell
IF YOU WERE AN ANIMAL, WHICH WOULD IT BE? A blue whale – nothing else is eating you

Batting	Mat	Inns	NO	Runs	HS	Ave	SR	100	50	Ct	St
First-class	41	54	13	926	80	22.58	39.60	0	2	10	0
List A	38	24	4	337	45	16.85	75.56	0	0	13	0
T20s	32	15	9	98	20	16.33	125.64	0	0	5	0
Bowling	**Mat**	**Balls**	**Runs**	**Wkts**	**BBI**	**BBM**	**Ave**	**Econ**	**SR**	**5w**	**10**
First-class	41	5884	3008	89	4/15	7/97	33.79	3.06	66.1	0	0
List A	38	1682	1662	47	4/59	4/59	35.36	5.92	35.7	0	0
T20s	32	534	824	26	2/12	2/12	31.69	9.25	20.5	0	0

SAM HAIN

RHB / RM / R0 / W0 / MVP21

FULL NAME: Samuel Robert Hain
BORN: July 16, 1995, Hong Kong
SQUAD NO: 16
HEIGHT: 6ft
NICKNAME: Ched, Hainy
EDUCATION: The Southport School, Queensland, Australia
TEAMS: Warwickshire, Australia U19, England Lions
ROLE: Batsman
DEBUT: First-class: 2014; List A: 2013; T20: 2016

BEST BATTING: 208 Warwickshire vs Northamptonshire, Edgbaston, 2014

COUNTY CAP: 2018

WHAT GOT YOU INTO CRICKET? The battles with the brothers in the back yard. Always ended in tears
BEST MOMENT IN CRICKET? Winning the One-Day Cup at Lord's in 2016
IF YOU WEREN'T A CRICKETER? I'd be opening a coffeehouse on the Gold Coast with my best mate
NON-CRICKETING HERO? Bryson DeChambeau – I've tried to copy his golf swing
TWITTER: @Sammiehain

Batting	Mat	Inns	NO	Runs	HS	Ave	SR	100	50	Ct	St
First-class	75	117	12	3897	208	37.11	46.86	10	19	64	0
List A	58	56	9	2810	161*	59.78	86.46	10	15	22	0
T20s	57	55	6	1692	95	34.53	124.41	0	10	37	0
Bowling	**Mat**	**Balls**	**Runs**	**Wkts**	**BBI**	**BBM**	**Ave**	**Econ**	**SR**	**5w**	**10**
First-class	75	42	31	0	-	-	-	4.42	-	0	0
List A	58	-	-	-	-	-	-	-	-	-	-
T20s	57	-	-	-	-	-	-	-	-	-	-

TOM HAINES

LHB / RM / R0 / W0

FULL NAME: Thomas Jacob Haines
BORN: October 28, 1998, Crawley, West Sussex
SQUAD NO: 20
HEIGHT: 5ft 11in
NICKNAME: Hainus
EDUCATION: Tanbridge House School, Horsham; Hurstpierpoint College, West Sussex
TEAMS: Sussex
ROLE: Batsman
DEBUT: First-class: 2016

BEST BATTING: 124 Sussex vs Durham, Arundel, 2018
BEST BOWLING: 1-9 Sussex vs Durham, Chester-le-Street, 2019

WHAT WAS YOUR FIRST CRICKET CLUB? Brockham Green CC, Surrey
BIGGEST TOPIC OF DISCUSSION IN YOUR DRESSING ROOM? Fantasy Football
CRICKETING HERO? Marcus Trescothick
WHICH RULE WOULD YOU CHANGE ABOUT CRICKET? Sixes should be worth 10
BIGGEST CRICKETING REGRET? Not bowling leggies
CRICKET STAR OF THE FUTURE? Alfred Haines (Horsham U13)
IF YOU WERE AN ANIMAL, WHICH WOULD IT BE? A sloth
TWITTER: @tomhaines
NOTES: Haines is a 21-year-old opening batsman from Crawley who has come through the Sussex Academy and also bowls medium-pace. He signed his first professional contract in October 2017 after scoring two hundreds for the Second XI and helping the side win the T20 competition. Haines made his first-class debut in 2016 at the age of 17 and had a breakthrough season two years later, scoring his maiden first-class hundred at Arundel and making 319 runs in 10 Championship innings. He had a tougher time of it last year, with a best score of 39 in six Championship matches

Batting	Mat	Inns	NO	Runs	HS	Ave	SR	100	50	Ct	St
First-class	16	25	0	583	124	23.32	53.98	1	2	5	0
Bowling	**Mat**	**Balls**	**Runs**	**Wkts**	**BBI**	**BBM**	**Ave**	**Econ**	**SR**	**5w**	**10**
First-class	16	654	294	7	1/9	2/73	42.00	2.69	93.4	0	0

ALEX HALES

RHB / RM / R3 / W0

FULL NAME: Alexander Daniel Hales
BORN: January 3, 1989, Hillingdon, London
SQUAD NO: 10
HEIGHT: 6ft 5in
EDUCATION: Chesham High School, Bucks
TEAMS: England, Notts, Trent Rockets, Adelaide Strikers, Hobart Hurricanes, Melbourne Renegades, Sunrisers Hyderabad, Sydney Thunder, Worcestershire
ROLE: Batsman
DEBUT: Test: 2015; ODI: 2014; T20I: 2011; First-class: 2008; List A: 2008; T20: 2009

BEST BATTING: 116* England vs Sri Lanka, Chittagong, 2014 (T20)

COUNTY CAP: 2011 (Nottinghamshire)

WHAT WAS YOUR FIRST CRICKET CLUB? Denham CC, Buckinghamshire. We lived in a bungalow on the cricket ground
WHAT WERE YOU DOING WHEN ENGLAND WON THE WORLD CUP? Multitasking between watching the cricket and the Wimbledon final
WHAT EXCITES YOU ABOUT THE HUNDRED? Getting to share another changing room with Luke Fletcher
CRICKETING HERO? Dominic Cork
WHICH BOOK MEANS MOST TO YOU? Fifty Shades of Grey by EL James
TWITTER: @AlexHales1
NOTES: Hales signed a two-year deal in September to play white-ball cricket for Notts

Batting	Mat	Inns	NO	Runs	HS	Ave	SR	100	50	Ct	St
Tests	11	21	0	573	94	27.28	43.84	0	5	8	0
ODIs	70	67	3	2419	171	37.79	95.72	6	14	27	0
T20Is	60	60	7	1644	116*	31.01	136.65	1	8	32	0
First-class	107	182	6	6655	236	37.81	59.06	13	38	84	0
List A	175	169	6	6260	187*	38.40	99.09	17	32	66	0
T20s	258	255	19	7149	116*	30.29	142.86	3	48	123	0
Bowling	**Mat**	**Balls**	**Runs**	**Wkts**	**BBI**	**BBM**	**Ave**	**Econ**	**SR**	**5w**	**10**
Tests	11	18	2	0	-	-	-	0.66	-	0	0
ODIs	70	-	-	-	-	-	-	-	-	-	-
T20Is	60	-	-	-	-	-	-	-	-	-	-
First-class	107	311	173	3	2/63	2/63	57.66	3.33	103.6	0	0
List A	175	4	10	0	-	-	-	15.00	-	0	0
T20s	258	3	7	0	-	-	-	14.00	-	0	0

HASEEB HAMEED

RHB / LB / R1 / W0

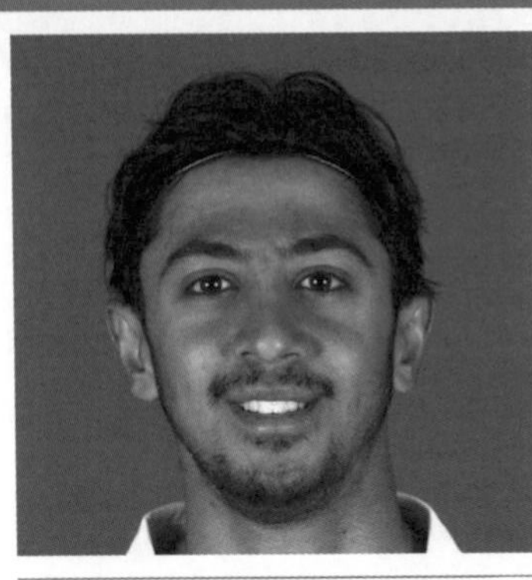

FULL NAME: Haseeb Hameed
BORN: January 17, 1997, Bolton, Lancashire
SQUAD NO: 99
HEIGHT: 6ft
NICKNAME: Has
EDUCATION: Bolton School
TEAMS: England, Nottinghamshire, Lancashire
ROLE: Batsman
DEBUT: Test: 2016; First-class: 2015; List A: 2017

BEST BATTING: 122 Lancashire vs Nottinghamshire, Trent Bridge, 2015

COUNTY CAP: 2016 (Lancashire)

WHAT WAS YOUR FIRST CRICKET CLUB? Tonge CC, Bolton, Greater Manchester
WHAT WERE YOU DOING WHEN ENGLAND WON THE WORLD CUP? We were all together in the Lancashire dressing room
MOST INTERESTING TEAMMATE? Luke Fletcher – because he worked in Hooters
CRICKET STAR OF THE FUTURE? Kundeel Haider (Nottinghamshire Academy)
TWITTER: @HaseebHameed97
NOTES: The 23-year-old opening batsman has signed for Notts in the hope of ressurecting a career that has badly stalled since his extraordinary feats in 2016, when Hameed made 1,000 runs in his first full season at Old Trafford and a fifty on his Test debut at Rajkot later that year. Tipped as one of the hottest batting prospects in England, Hameed hit 389 runs in five matches for England U19 against South Africa U19 in 2014, an international record for a batsman in a youth bilateral one-day series. After a dismal 2018 (170 runs in 11 Championship matches), Hameed scored his first first-class hundred in almost three years for Lancashire against Middlesex at Lord's last April

Batting	Mat	Inns	NO	Runs	HS	Ave	SR	100	50	Ct	St
Tests	3	6	1	219	82	43.80	34.21	0	2	4	0
First-class	63	106	11	2907	122	30.60	37.07	5	15	35	0
List A	19	19	3	556	88	34.75	78.08	0	4	3	0
Bowling	**Mat**	**Balls**	**Runs**	**Wkts**	**BBI**	**BBM**	**Ave**	**Econ**	**SR**	**5w**	**10**
Tests	3	-	-	-	-	-	-	-	-	-	-
First-class	63	42	21	0	-	-	-	3.00	-	0	0
List A	19	-	-	-	-	-	-	-	-	-	-

MILES HAMMOND LHB / OB / R0 / W0

FULL NAME: Miles Arthur Halhead Hammond
BORN: January 11, 1996, Cheltenham, Gloucestershire
SQUAD NO: 88
HEIGHT: 6ft 1in
NICKNAME: Hammo, Hammer, Wally, Rowdy
EDUCATION: St Edward's School, Oxford; University of the Arts London
TEAMS: Gloucestershire, England U19
ROLE: Batsman
DEBUT: First-class: 2013; List A: 2013; T20: 2013

BEST BATTING: 123* Gloucestershire vs Middlesex, Bristol, 2018
BEST BOWLING: 1-29 MCC vs Nepal, Kirtipur, 2019
COUNTY CAP: 2013

WHAT WAS YOUR FIRST CRICKET CLUB? Cumnor CC, Oxford
WHAT EXCITES YOU ABOUT THE HUNDRED? Live cricket back on terrestrial television
BIGGEST TOPIC OF DISCUSSION IN YOUR DRESSING ROOM? Fantasy Football
CRICKETING HERO? Marcus Trescothick
WHICH RULE WOULD YOU CHANGE ABOUT CRICKET? You can be out lbw if the ball pitches outside leg stump
BIGGEST CRICKETING REGRET? Choosing initially to bowl off-spin
IF YOU WERE AN ANIMAL, WHICH WOULD IT BE? A poison dart frog
TWITTER: @hammo125

Batting	Mat	Inns	NO	Runs	HS	Ave	SR	100	50	Ct	St
First-class	26	44	3	991	123*	24.17	42.36	2	5	22	0
List A	8	6	0	185	95	30.83	73.12	0	1	1	0
T20s	29	25	0	635	63	25.40	147.67	0	3	14	0
Bowling	**Mat**	**Balls**	**Runs**	**Wkts**	**BBI**	**BBM**	**Ave**	**Econ**	**SR**	**5w**	**10**
First-class	26	472	368	2	1/29	1/37	184.00	4.67	236.0	0	0
List A	8	114	97	5	2/18	2/18	19.40	5.10	22.8	0	0
T20s	29	12	17	0	-	-	-	8.50	-	0	0

PETER HANDSCOMB

RHB / WK / R0 / W0

FULL NAME: Peter Stephen Patrick Handscomb
BORN: April 26, 1991, Melbourne, Victoria
SQUAD NO: 29
HEIGHT: 6ft 4in
NICKNAME: Hank
EDUCATION: Mount Waverley Secondary College; Deakin University, Melbourne
TEAMS: Australia, Middlesex, Durham, Gloucestershire, Melbourne Stars, Rising Pune Supergiants, Victoria, Yorkshire
ROLE: Batsman/wicketkeeper
DEBUT: Test: 2016; ODI: 2017; T20I: 2019; First-class: 2011; List A: 2011; T20: 2012

BEST BATTING: 215 Victoria vs New South Wales, Sydney, 2016

COUNTY CAP: 2015 (Gloucestershire)

TWITTER: @phandscomb54
NOTES: Handscomb has joined Middlesex on a two-year deal and will captain the side in the County Championship and One-Day Cup, replacing outgoing skipper Dawid Malan, who has joined Yorkshire. "He is a successful captain, a fine middle-order player and the sort of character who will help create a strong, positive environment that will keep moving the club forward," said Middlesex head coach Stuart Law. Born to British parents but raised in Australia, Handscomb passed 50 in each of his first four Test matches, including two centuries, but hasn't played a Test since January 2019. The Victorian, who also captains his state side in the Sheffield Shield, hit his maiden ODI century last year. He has had previous county stints with Gloucestershire (2015), Yorkshire (2017) and Durham (2018)

Batting	Mat	Inns	NO	Runs	HS	Ave	SR	100	50	Ct	St
Tests	16	29	5	934	110	38.91	49.83	2	4	28	0
ODIs	22	20	1	632	117	33.26	97.38	1	4	14	0
T20Is	2	2	1	33	20*	33.00	100.00	0	0	0	0
First-class	111	185	12	6500	215	37.57	54.10	14	38	176	4
List A	108	98	15	3180	140	38.31	89.98	3	20	99	5
T20s	84	73	19	1318	103*	24.40	118.20	1	5	43	13
Bowling	**Mat**	**Balls**	**Runs**	**Wkts**	**BBI**	**BBM**	**Ave**	**Econ**	**SR**	**5w**	**10**
Tests	16	-	-	-	-	-	-	-	-	-	-
ODIs	22	-	-	-	-	-	-	-	-	-	-
T20Is	2	-	-	-	-	-	-	-	-	-	-
First-class	111	66	79	0	-	-	-	7.18	-	0	0
List A	108	-	-	-	-	-	-	-	-	-	-
T20s	84	-	-	-	-	-	-	-	-	-	-

GEORGE HANKINS

RHB / OB / R0 / W0

FULL NAME: George Thomas Hankins
BORN: January 4, 1997, Bath
SQUAD NO: 21
HEIGHT: 6ft 1in
NICKNAME: Hanks, Hanko
EDUCATION: Kingswood School, Bath; Millfield School, Somerset
TEAMS: Gloucestershire, England U19
ROLE: Batsman
DEBUT: First-class: 2016; List A: 2017; T20: 2017

BEST BATTING: 116 Gloucestershire vs Northamptonshire, Northampton, 2016

COUNTY CAP: 2016

WHAT WAS YOUR FIRST CRICKET CLUB? Bath CC, Somerset
WHICH BOWLER WOULD YOU LEAST LIKE TO FACE? Jasprit Bumrah – horrible angle
BEST INNINGS YOU'VE SEEN? Liam Norwell scoring a century as a nightwatchman in 2016 – amazing quality from a No.11
CRICKETING HERO? Joe Root
WHO WOULD YOU ASK TO BAT FOR YOUR LIFE? Rahul Dravid
SURPRISING FACT ABOUT YOU? I have no earlobes
FAVOURITE QUOTE OR SAYING? With great power comes great responsibilty
TWITTER: @hankins1997

Batting	Mat	Inns	NO	Runs	HS	Ave	SR	100	50	Ct	St
First-class	28	45	2	961	116	22.34	51.63	1	6	29	0
List A	15	15	1	535	92	38.21	73.28	0	5	11	0
T20s	7	3	0	17	14	5.66	60.71	0	0	1	0
Bowling	**Mat**	**Balls**	**Runs**	**Wkts**	**BBI**	**BBM**	**Ave**	**Econ**	**SR**	**5w**	**10**
First-class	28	13	13	0	-	-	-	6.00	-	0	0
List A	15	-	-	-	-	-	-	-	-	-	-
T20s	7	-	-	-	-	-	-	-	-	-	-

WARWICKSHIRE

OLIVER HANNON-DALBY LHB / RFM / R0 / W0 / MVP69

FULL NAME: Oliver James Hannon-Dalby
BORN: June 20, 1989, Halifax, Yorkshire
SQUAD NO: 20
HEIGHT: 6ft 8in
NICKNAME: OHD, Owl Face, Dizzle
EDUCATION: Brooksbank School, West Yorkshire; Leeds Metropolitan University
TEAMS: Warwickshire, Yorkshire
ROLE: Bowler
DEBUT: First-class: 2008; List A: 2011; T20: 2012

BEST BATTING: 40 Warwickshire vs Somerset, Taunton, 2014
BEST BOWLING: 5-11 MCC vs Nepal, Kirtipur, 2019

WHAT WAS YOUR FIRST CRICKET CLUB? Copley CC, West Yorkshire. 'The Arches' is one of the most beautiful grounds in the Halifax League, defined by the Copley viaduct which runs along the north side of the ground. Well worth a visit for good cricket, great teas and the expert opinion of groundsman Tommy 'Topsoil' Thorpe on all things cricket
HOW WOULD YOU DISMISS STEVE SMITH? I'd ask Chris Woakes
WHAT EXCITES YOU ABOUT THE HUNDRED? That Ed Pollock can now afford a decent haircut
BIGGEST TOPIC OF DISCUSSION IN YOUR DRESSING ROOM? What's on for breakfast, what soup is on for brunch, lasagna or fish pie for lunch, toasties or sandwiches for tea and hotel burger or Nando's for dinner
MOST INTERESTING TEAMMATE? Sam Hain – he thinks hammering screws into a wall is a good way to hang a picture
WHICH BOOK MEANS MOST TO YOU? Owls by Marianne Taylor
IF YOU WERE AN ANIMAL, WHICH WOULD IT BE? My dog Toby – he lives the life of Riley
TWITTER: @OHD_20

Batting	Mat	Inns	NO	Runs	HS	Ave	SR	100	50	Ct	St
First-class	70	84	28	406	40	7.25	26.10	0	0	7	0
List A	43	15	9	91	21*	15.16	95.78	0	0	14	0
T20s	60	12	7	53	14*	10.60	96.36	0	0	12	0
Bowling	**Mat**	**Balls**	**Runs**	**Wkts**	**BBI**	**BBM**	**Ave**	**Econ**	**SR**	**5w**	**10**
First-class	70	10415	5584	175	5/11	9/137	31.90	3.21	59.5	5	0
List A	43	1978	2075	65	5/27	5/27	31.92	6.29	30.4	1	0
T20s	60	1252	1829	75	4/20	4/20	24.38	8.76	16.6	0	0

SIMON HARMER

RHB / OB / R0 / W3 / MVP1

FULL NAME: Simon Ross Harmer
BORN: February 10, 1989, Pretoria, South Africa
SQUAD NO: 11
HEIGHT: 6ft 2in
NICKNAME: Big Red, Harmy
EDUCATION: Pretoria Boys High School; Nelson Mandela Metropolitan University, Port Elizabeth
TEAMS: South Africa, Essex, Welsh Fire, Border, Eastern Province, Jozi Stars, Warriors
ROLE: Bowler
DEBUT: Test: 2015; First-class: 2009; List A: 2010; T20: 2011

BEST BATTING: 102* Essex vs Surrey, The Oval, 2018
BEST BOWLING: 9-95 Essex vs Middlesex, Chelmsford, 2017
COUNTY CAP: 2018

WHAT WAS YOUR FIRST CRICKET CLUB? Pretoria High School Old Boys CC, South Africa
WHAT WERE YOU DOING WHEN ENGLAND WON THE WORLD CUP? Watching it in the dressing room at the home of cricket (Chelmsford)
BIGGEST TOPIC OF DISCUSSION IN YOUR DRESSING ROOM? Tom Westley's hairline
MOST INTERESTING TEAMMATE? Ravi Bopara – he's part of the Flat Earth Society
CRICKET STAR OF THE FUTURE? Ryan ten Doeschate's twin boys
IF YOU WERE AN ANIMAL, WHICH WOULD IT BE? A killer whale – they rule the ocean and don't take any stick from sharks... and I'm very scared of sharks
TWITTER: @Simon_Harmer_

Batting	Mat	Inns	NO	Runs	HS	Ave	SR	100	50	Ct	St
Tests	5	6	1	58	13	11.60	33.33	0	0	1	0
First-class	145	218	43	4292	102*	24.52	49.54	2	22	140	0
List A	83	70	21	1002	44*	20.44	97.85	0	0	55	0
T20s	97	55	20	666	43	19.02	129.82	0	0	45	0
Bowling	**Mat**	**Balls**	**Runs**	**Wkts**	**BBI**	**BBM**	**Ave**	**Econ**	**SR**	**5w**	**10**
Tests	5	1148	588	20	4/61	7/153	29.40	3.07	57.4	0	0
First-class	145	34602	16905	608	9/95	14/128	27.80	2.93	56.9	34	6
List A	83	3858	3299	78	4/42	4/42	42.29	5.13	49.4	0	0
T20s	97	1735	2222	72	4/19	4/19	30.86	7.68	24.0	0	0

JAMES HARRIS

RHB / RMF / R0 / W3

FULL NAME: James Alexander Russell Harris
BORN: May 16, 1990, Morriston, Swansea
SQUAD NO: 5
HEIGHT: 6ft 1in
NICKNAME: Bones, Harry
EDUCATION: Pontarddulais Comprehensive School, Swansea; Gorseinon College, Swansea
TEAMS: Middlesex, England Lions, Glamorgan, Kent
ROLE: Bowler
DEBUT: First-class: 2007; List A: 2007; T20: 2008

BEST BATTING: 87* Glamorgan vs Nottinghamshire, Swansea, 2007
BEST BOWLING: 9-34 Middlesex vs Durham, Lord's, 2015
COUNTY CAP: 2010 (Glamorgan); 2015 (Middlesex)

WHAT WAS YOUR FIRST CRICKET CLUB? Pontarddulais CC, South Wales. I spent all our summers practising in the nets or playing in the outfield with a dustbin for stumps and a tennis ball covered in tape
WHAT EXCITES YOU ABOUT THE HUNDRED? It'll be really interesting to see how it develops and changes the landscape of the game in this country
BIGGEST TOPIC OF DISCUSSION IN YOUR DRESSING ROOM? My cycling exploits, Ro-Jo's Man United, Tim Murtagh's Liverpool and Steven Finn's cat
MOST INTERESTING TEAMMATE? AB de Villiers, my teammate last summer. The bloke is just a champion at everything
WHICH BOOK MEANS MOST TO YOU? Own the Day, Own Your Life – Optimized Practices for Waking, Working, Learning, Eating, Training, Playing, Sleeping and Sex by Aubrey Marcus
IF YOU WERE AN ANIMAL, WHICH WOULD IT BE? A cheetah – I wouldn't mind being a bit quicker across the turf
TWITTER: @James_Harris9

Batting	Mat	Inns	NO	Runs	HS	Ave	SR	100	50	Ct	St
First-class	144	209	49	3734	87*	23.33		0	18	42	0
List A	64	37	8	417	117	14.37	73.80	1	0	14	0
T20s	53	25	12	150	18	11.53	109.48	0	0	5	0
Bowling	**Mat**	**Balls**	**Runs**	**Wkts**	**BBI**	**BBM**	**Ave**	**Econ**	**SR**	**5w**	**10**
First-class	144	25079	13913	485	9/34	13/103	28.68	3.32	51.7	15	2
List A	64	2726	2648	88	4/38	4/38	30.09	5.82	30.9	0	0
T20s	53	970	1463	47	4/23	4/23	31.12	9.04	20.6	0	0

GARETH HARTE RHB / RM / R0 / W0

FULL NAME: Gareth Jason Harte
BORN: March 15, 1993, Johannesburg, South Africa
SQUAD NO: 93
HEIGHT: 5ft 11in
NICKNAME: Gaz
EDUCATION: King Edward VII School, Johannesburg
TEAMS: Durham
ROLE: Allrounder
DEBUT: First-class: 2018; List A: 2018; T20: 2017

BEST BATTING: 114 Durham vs Derbyshire, Chester-le-Street, 2018
BEST BOWLING: 4-15 Durham vs Derbyshire, Chester-le-Street, 2019

WHAT WAS YOUR FIRST CRICKET CLUB? Old Edwardians CC, Johannesburg, South Africa
HOW WOULD YOU DISMISS STEVE SMITH? Get a fan to hold him down as he comes down the stairs so that he is timed out
WHAT EXCITES YOU ABOUT THE HUNDRED? Watching Brydon Carse bowling 'heat' on TV
MOST INTERESTING TEAMMATE? Cameron Bancroft – he is just a different fish, but in a good way
CRICKETING HERO? Ricky Ponting
WHICH RULE WOULD YOU CHANGE ABOUT CRICKET? The toss rule in the Championship
WHICH BOOK MEANS MOST TO YOU? The Obstacle is the Way – The Timeless Art of Turning Trials into Triumphs by Ryan Holiday
TWITTER: @HarteGareth

Batting	Mat	Inns	NO	Runs	HS	Ave	SR	100	50	Ct	St
First-class	20	38	2	951	114	26.41	40.95	3	3	6	0
List A	9	7	2	205	51*	41.00	87.23	0	1	2	0
T20s	5	4	0	24	11	6.00	96.00	0	0	4	0
Bowling	**Mat**	**Balls**	**Runs**	**Wkts**	**BBI**	**BBM**	**Ave**	**Econ**	**SR**	**5w**	**10**
First-class	20	835	429	13	4/15	4/36	33.00	3.08	64.2	0	0
List A	9	180	172	4	2/35	2/35	43.00	5.73	45.0	0	0
T20s	5	18	20	1	1/11	1/11	20.00	6.66	18.0	0	0

TOM HARTLEY RHB / SLA / R0 / W0

FULL NAME: Tom William Hartley
BORN: May 3, 1998, Ormskirk, Lancashire
SQUAD NO: 2
HEIGHT: 6ft 4in
NICKNAME: Harts, TDF
EDUCATION: Merchant Taylors' School, Crosby, Merseyside
TEAMS: Lancashire
ROLE: Bowler

WHAT WAS YOUR FIRST CRICKET CLUB? Ormskirk CC, West Lancashire
WHAT WERE YOU DOING WHEN ENGLAND WON THE WORLD CUP? Supporting in the pub
HOW WOULD YOU DISMISS STEVE SMITH? Slide one on with the arm
BIGGEST TOPIC OF DISCUSSION IN YOUR DRESSING ROOM? Hair
MOST INTERESTING TEAMMATE? Jimmy Faulkner – he always has a story to tell
CRICKET STAR OF THE FUTURE? Harvey and Rob Rankin (Lancashire U17)
IF YOU WERE AN ANIMAL, WHICH WOULD IT BE? A giraffe – I'm tall and have a long neck
NOTES: Hartley signed his first professional contract with Lancashire in the lead-up to last season and renewed his deal in November. The slow left-armer, who plays his club cricket for Ormskirk CC, was Lancashire's leading wicket-taker in the 2019 Second XI (50-over) Trophy, claiming 10 victims at 19.10 with an impressive economy rate of 4.44. He also made seven appearances in the Second XI Championship, although he was used sparingly, taking six wickets from the 92 overs he bowled. Hartley was a key player in the Lancashire Second XI side which were crowned T20 champions in 2018, returning figures of 3-12 in the final against Essex. He has also shown promise with the bat, scoring a half-century in a Second XI Roses clash against Yorkshire at Scarborough last season

JACK HAYNES

RHB / OB / R0 / W0

FULL NAME: Jack Alexander Haynes
BORN: January 30, 2001, Worcester
SQUAD NO: 17
HEIGHT: 6ft 1in
EDUCATION: Malvern College
TEAMS: Worcestershire, England U19
ROLE: Batsman
DEBUT: First-class: 2019; List A: 2018

BEST BATTING: 31 Worcestershire vs Glamorgan, Worcester, 2019

FAMILY TIES? My father Gavin played more than 200 matches for Worcestershire in the 1990s and my older brother Josh plays for Leeds/Bradford MCCU
WHAT WAS YOUR FIRST CRICKET CLUB? Ombersley CC, Worcestershire
MOST INTERESTING TEAMMATE? Moeen Ali
CRICKET STAR OF THE FUTURE? Josh Dickenson (Worcestershire Academy)
WHICH BOOK MEANS MOST TO YOU? Bounce – The Myth of Talent and the Power of Practice by Matthew Syed
IF YOU WERE AN ANIMAL, WHICH WOULD IT BE? I'd be a racehorse
TWITTER: @jack_haynes1
NOTES: Son of the former Worcestershire allrounder Gavin Haynes, Jack is a top-order batsman who captained the England Schools U16 side and Worcestershire U17 before making his Second XI debut in 2017. Haynes made his England U19 debut the following year, scoring 74 as an opener against South Africa U19 in a Youth ODI at Gosforth, and he made a match-winning 89 against India at Cheltenham last year. The teenager registered a series of tidy scores in the recent U19 World Cup in South Africa, including a fifty against Sri Lanka at Benoni in February. Haynes made his first-class debut last summer in the tour match against the Australians at Worcester, as well as appearing in four Championship matches

Batting	Mat	Inns	NO	Runs	HS	Ave	SR	100	50	Ct	St
First-class	5	7	0	119	31	17.00	46.30	0	0	1	0
List A	1	1	0	33	33	33.00	86.84	0	0	1	0
Bowling	**Mat**	**Balls**	**Runs**	**Wkts**	**BBI**	**BBM**	**Ave**	**Econ**	**SR**	**5w**	**10**
First-class	5	-	-	-	-	-	-	-	-	-	-
List A	1	-	-	-	-	-	-	-	-	-	-

TRAVIS HEAD LHB / OB / RO / WO

FULL NAME: Travis Michael Head
BORN: December 29, 1993, Adelaide, Australia
SQUAD NO: 62
TEAMS: Australia, Sussex, Adelaide Strikers, Delhi Daredevils, Royal Challengers Bangalore, South Australia, Worcestershire Yorkshire
ROLE: Allrounder
DEBUT: Test: 2018; ODI: 2016; T20I: 2016; First-class: 2012; List A: 2013; T20: 2013

BEST BATTING: 192 South Australia vs Tasmania, Adelaide, 2016
BEST BOWLING: 3-42 South Australia vs New South Wales, Adelaide, 2015

TWITTER: @travishead34
NOTES: Head has signed for Sussex for the entirety of the 2020 summer and will be available across all formats. "We wanted a top-four batsman to improve our team and Travis will do that," said Sussex head coach Jason Gillespie. "He's shown his class in his international career so far, he brings some useful off-spin and he will offer good leadership support to our captains from his time leading South Australia and the [Adelaide] Strikers." Head was named South Australia's youngest-ever captain in 2015 at the age of 21. After making his international limited-overs debuts in 2016, he made his Test bow two years later. He has been in and out of the side since and played four Tests in last summer's Ashes, scoring 191 runs at 27.28 before being dropped for the final match at The Oval. But he reconfirmed his Test credentials over the winter with a hundred against New Zealand at the MCG. He had a stint with Worcestershire in 2018 and a short spell with Yorkshire in 2016

Batting	Mat	Inns	NO	Runs	HS	Ave	SR	100	50	Ct	St
Tests	17	28	2	1091	161	41.96	50.41	2	7	10	0
ODIs	42	39	2	1273	128	34.40	90.02	1	10	12	0
T20Is	16	15	3	319	48*	26.58	130.20	0	0	4	0
First-class	105	189	10	7025	192	39.24	59.13	12	46	46	0
List A	94	90	4	3202	202	37.23	93.40	7	17	29	0
T20s	80	77	12	2036	101*	31.32	136.09	1	9	25	0
Bowling	**Mat**	**Balls**	**Runs**	**Wkts**	**BBI**	**BBM**	**Ave**	**Econ**	**SR**	**5w**	**10**
Tests	17	126	76	0	-	-	-	3.61	-	0	0
ODIs	42	765	737	12	2/22	2/22	61.41	5.78	63.7	0	0
T20Is	16	24	39	1	1/16	1/16	39.00	9.75	24.0	0	0
First-class	105	4617	2975	43	3/42	4/64	69.18	3.86	107.3	0	0
List A	94	1290	1268	21	2/9	2/9	60.38	5.89	61.4	0	0
T20s	80	379	545	21	3/16	3/16	25.95	8.62	18.0	0	0

TOM HELM

RHB / RMF / R0 / W0 / MVP53

FULL NAME: Thomas George Helm
BORN: May 7, 1994, Aylesbury, Buckinghamshire
SQUAD NO: 7
HEIGHT: 6ft 4in
NICKNAME: Ched, Zizou
EDUCATION: The Misbourne School, Buckinghamshire
TEAMS: Middlesex, Birmingham Phoenix, England Lions, Glamorgan
ROLE: Bowler
DEBUT: First-class: 2013; List A: 2013; T20: 2016

BEST BATTING: 52 Middlesex vs Derbyshire, Lord's, 2018
BEST BOWLING: 5-36 Middlesex vs Worcestershire, Worcester, 2019

FAMILY TIES? My brother Sam played Minor Counties for Buckinghamshire
WHAT WAS YOUR FIRST CRICKET CLUB? Chesham CC, Buckinghamshire
WHAT WERE YOU DOING WHEN ENGLAND WON THE WORLD CUP? Eating dirt in Cardiff
BIGGEST TOPIC OF DISCUSSION IN YOUR DRESSING ROOM? Weapons
MOST INTERESTING TEAMMATE? Robbie White – he's had a vast amount of work experience
BEST INNINGS YOU'VE SEEN? Tim Murtagh – take your pick
CRICKETING HERO? James Anderson
WHICH RULE WOULD YOU CHANGE ABOUT CRICKET? Make bats smaller
CRICKET STAR OF THE FUTURE? Gary Helm
IF YOU WERE AN ANIMAL, WHICH WOULD IT BE? A koala bear – sleeps all day
TWITTER: @tomhelm7

Batting	Mat	Inns	NO	Runs	HS	Ave	SR	100	50	Ct	St
First-class	29	39	8	530	52	17.09	46.69	0	1	9	0
List A	40	24	8	206	30	12.87	71.28	0	0	15	0
T20s	33	13	8	61	28*	12.20	110.90	0	0	4	0
Bowling	**Mat**	**Balls**	**Runs**	**Wkts**	**BBI**	**BBM**	**Ave**	**Econ**	**SR**	**5w**	**10**
First-class	29	4290	2293	78	5/36	7/140	29.39	3.20	55.0	3	0
List A	40	1816	1742	56	5/33	5/33	31.10	5.75	32.4	2	0
T20s	33	670	966	42	5/11	5/11	23.00	8.65	15.9	1	0

CHARLIE HEMPHREY RHB / OB / R0 / W0

FULL NAME: Charlie Richard Hemphrey
BORN: August 31, 1989, Doncaster, Yorkshire
SQUAD NO: 22
HEIGHT: 6ft 2in
NICKNAME: Bronson, Prince
EDUCATION: Harvey Grammar School, Folkestone, Kent
TEAMS: Glamorgan, Queensland
ROLE: Batsman
DEBUT: First-class: 2015; List A: 2015

BEST BATTING: 118 Queensland vs South Australia, Brisbane, 2015
BEST BOWLING: 2-56 Queensland vs South Australia, Adelaide, 2016

WHAT WAS YOUR FIRST CRICKET CLUB? Hythe CC, Kent. It used to be under the English Channel
WHAT WERE YOU DOING WHEN ENGLAND WON THE WORLD CUP? Drinking a post-match beer after a Championship game and watching Wimbledon
HOW WOULD YOU DISMISS STEVE SMITH? Bowl to him at the Gabba in a Sheffield Shield game...
BIGGEST TOPIC OF DISCUSSION IN YOUR DRESSING ROOM? Marnus Labuschagne's spelling, Nick Selman's tightness, Tom Cullen's skunk, Graham Wagg's hair and Chris Cooke's dad-bod
MOST INTERESTING TEAMMATE? Lukas Carey aka 'The Bont'
CRICKET STAR OF THE FUTURE? Jake Fraser-McGurk (Victoria)
WHICH BOOK MEANS MOST TO YOU? Enemy Number One – The Secrets of the UK's Most Feared Professional Punter by Patrick Veitch
IF YOU WERE AN ANIMAL, WHICH WOULD IT BE? A leopard – shrewd, smart, enjoys the sun, determined when needed and loves a feed
TWITTER: @chemp1989

Batting	Mat	Inns	NO	Runs	HS	Ave	SR	100	50	Ct	St
First-class	48	89	6	2513	118	30.27	41.77	4	16	35	0
List A	22	20	0	430	87	21.50	77.47	0	2	9	0
Bowling	**Mat**	**Balls**	**Runs**	**Wkts**	**BBI**	**BBM**	**Ave**	**Econ**	**SR**	**5w**	**10**
First-class	48	861	603	8	2/56	3/91	75.37	4.20	107.6	0	0
List A	22	156	151	2	1/18	1/18	75.50	5.80	78.0	0	0

MOISES HENRIQUES

RHB/RFM

FULL NAME: Moises Constantino Henriques
BORN: February 1, 1987, Funchal, Portugal
SQUAD NO: 7
HEIGHT: 6ft 1in
NICKNAME: Moey
TEAMS: Australia, Essex, Delhi Daredevils, Glamorgan, Kolkata Knight Riders, New South Wales, Royal Challengers Bangalore, Sunrisers Hyderabad, Surrey, Sydney Sixers
ROLE: Allrounder
DEBUT: Test: 2013; ODI: 2009; T20I: 2009; First-class: 2006; List A: 2006; T20: 2006

BEST BATTING: 77 Sydney Sixers vs Perth Scorchers, Canberra, 2015 (T20)
BEST BOWLING: 3-11 New South Wales vs Victoria, Delhi, 2009 (T20)

TWITTER: @Mozzie21
NOTES: The 33-year-old Australian allrounder signed up for the whole of Essex's T20 Blast campaign in February, just a few weeks after skippering Sydney Sixers to the Big Bash title in Australia. A powerful ball-striker and fast bowler, Henriques has previously played in England for Glamorgan and Surrey, as well as appearing for four IPL franchises. Essex head coach Anthony McGrath said: "I've been following Moises' career for a while now and I think he's exactly what we need going into this year's Blast campaign. He's been excellent in the IPL and was instrumental for Sydney Sixers in their recent Big Bash success. His runs got them over the line on plenty of occasions and it's clear he's an excellent leader too, so I have no doubt he'll be a great fit in our dressing room"

Batting	Mat	Inns	NO	Runs	HS	Ave	SR	100	50	Ct	St
Tests	4	8	1	164	81*	23.42	47.39	0	2	1	0
ODIs	11	10	1	81	18	9.00	68.06	0	0	4	0
T20Is	11	8	3	159	62*	31.80	130.32	0	2	3	0
First-class	100	163	16	5129	265	34.89	55.90	10	22	42	0
List A	105	95	14	2784	164*	34.37	87.82	3	13	41	0
T20s	205	184	42	3775	77	26.58	127.44	0	18	93	0
Bowling	**Mat**	**Balls**	**Runs**	**Wkts**	**BBI**	**BBM**	**Ave**	**Econ**	**SR**	**5w**	**10**
Tests	4	330	164	2	1/48	1/48	82.00	2.98	165.0	0	0
ODIs	11	354	306	7	3/32	3/32	43.71	5.18	50.5	0	0
T20Is	11	102	158	4	2/35	2/35	39.50	9.29	25.5	0	0
First-class	100	6831	3535	114	5/17	6/94	31.00	3.10	59.9	2	0
List A	105	3487	3028	81	4/17	4/17	37.38	5.21	43.0	0	0
T20s	205	2378	3297	108	3/11	3/11	30.52	8.31	22.0	0	0

MATT HENRY

RHB / RFM / R0 / W1

FULL NAME: Matthew James Henry
BORN: December 14, 1991, Christchurch, New Zealand
SQUAD NO: 24
HEIGHT: 6ft 2in
NICKNAME: Henaz
EDUCATION: St Bede's College, Christchurch
TEAMS: New Zealand, Kent, Derbyshire, Canterbury, Kings XI Punjab, Worcestershire
ROLE: Bowler
DEBUT: Test: 2015; ODI: 2014; T20I: 2014; First-class: 2011; List A: 2011; T20: 2011

BEST BATTING: 81 Kent vs Derbyshire, Derby, 2018
BEST BOWLING: 7-42 Kent vs Northamptonshire, Canterbury, 2018
COUNTY CAP: 2018 (Kent)

TWITTER: @Matthenry014
NOTES: The Kiwi seamer returns for a second spell at Kent and will be available for the first seven Championship games of the season. Henry was devastating when he appeared for the county in 2018, taking 75 wickets in 11 Championship matches to help inspire Kent to promotion. He has previously played for Derbyshire and Worcestershire. "Matt's ability to lead the attack and his proven ability to take wickets in English conditions make him a really exciting addition to our squad," said Kent director of cricket Paul Downton. An established international, particularly in the 50-over format, Henry starred in New Zealand's run to the World Cup final last summer, his 14 wickets including a superb spell of 3-37 in the semi-final against India for which he was named Player of the Match after taking out three of India's top five

Batting	Mat	Inns	NO	Runs	HS	Ave	SR	100	50	Ct	St
Tests	12	16	4	224	66	18.66	76.45	0	1	5	0
ODIs	52	21	7	211	48*	15.07	100.00	0	0	17	0
T20Is	6	2	1	10	10	10.00	200.00	0	0	1	0
First-class	68	89	16	1520	81	20.82	77.98	0	5	30	0
List A	118	64	18	569	48*	12.36	103.45	0	0	44	0
T20s	79	45	18	363	42	13.44	161.33	0	0	27	0
Bowling	**Mat**	**Balls**	**Runs**	**Wkts**	**BBI**	**BBM**	**Ave**	**Econ**	**SR**	**5w**	**10**
Tests	12	2761	1505	30	4/93	6/105	50.16	3.27	92.0	0	0
ODIs	52	2703	2437	92	5/30	5/30	26.48	5.40	29.3	2	0
T20Is	6	132	191	7	3/44	3/44	27.28	8.68	18.8	0	0
First-class	68	14030	7315	287	7/42	12/73	25.48	3.12	48.8	14	3
List A	118	5875	5242	190	6/45	6/45	27.58	5.35	30.9	4	0
T20s	79	1529	2238	74	4/43	4/43	30.24	8.78	20.6	0	0

RYAN HIGGINS

RHB / OB / R0 / W1 / MVP5

FULL NAME: Ryan Francis Higgins
BORN: January 6, 1995, Harare, Zimbabwe
SQUAD NO: 29
HEIGHT: 5ft 11in
NICKNAME: Mad Bry, Brian, Higgo
EDUCATION: Peterhouse School, Marondera, Zimbabwe; Bradfield College, Reading
TEAMS: Gloucestershire, Welsh Fire, Middlesex, England U19
ROLE: Allrounder
DEBUT: First-class: 2017; List A: 2014; T20: 2014

BEST BATTING: 199 Gloucestershire vs Leicestershire, Leicester, 2019
BEST BOWLING: 5-21 Gloucestershire vs Sussex, Hove, 2018
COUNTY CAP: 2018 (Gloucestershire)

WHAT WAS YOUR FIRST CRICKET CLUB? Falkland CC, Berkshire. It was only five minutes from home
HOW WOULD YOU DISMISS STEVE SMITH? Bring up the keeper
MOST INTERESTING TEAMMATE? Graeme van Buuren – talks about South Africa and the Titans all the time. And plays pranks on everyone all season long
CRICKETING HERO? Michael Hussey
WHICH RULE WOULD YOU CHANGE ABOUT CRICKET? Have a maximum of 80 overs in a day
BIGGEST CRICKETING REGRET? My time in Sydney – I did not take the game as seriously out there
CRICKET STAR OF THE FUTURE? Ben Charlesworth (Gloucestershire)
IF YOU WERE AN ANIMAL, WHICH WOULD IT BE? A Jack Russell
TWITTER: @ryanhiggins21

Batting	Mat	Inns	NO	Runs	HS	Ave	SR	100	50	Ct	St
First-class	33	53	8	1613	199	35.84	67.94	5	5	10	0
List A	33	29	5	680	81*	28.33	97.00	0	3	5	0
T20s	64	56	14	1021	77*	24.30	132.76	0	4	16	0
Bowling	**Mat**	**Balls**	**Runs**	**Wkts**	**BBI**	**BBM**	**Ave**	**Econ**	**SR**	**5w**	**10**
First-class	33	5469	2355	110	5/21	8/54	21.40	2.58	49.7	4	0
List A	33	915	845	24	4/50	4/50	35.20	5.54	38.1	0	0
T20s	64	600	864	31	5/13	5/13	27.87	8.64	19.3	1	0

JAMES HILDRETH RHB / RM / R7 / W0 / MVP62

FULL NAME: James Charles Hildreth
BORN: September 9, 1984, Milton Keynes, Buckinghamshire
SQUAD NO: 25
HEIGHT: 5ft 10in
NICKNAME: Hildy, Hildz
EDUCATION: Millfield School, Somerset
TEAMS: Somerset, England Lions
ROLE: Batsman
DEBUT: First-class: 2003; List A: 2003; T20: 2004

BEST BATTING: 303* Somerset vs Warwickshire, Taunton, 2009
BEST BOWLING: 2-39 Somerset vs Hampshire, Taunton, 2009
COUNTY CAP: 2007; BENEFIT: 2017

BEST MOMENT IN CRICKET? Winning the T20 in 2005, captaining England Lions and captaining Somerset
CRICKETING HERO? Ricky Ponting
IF YOU WEREN'T A CRICKETER? I'd be travelling
SURPRISING FACT ABOUT YOU? I'm a big MK Dons fan
TWITTER: @dreth25
NOTES: At 35 years of age Hildreth is still one of the classiest batsmen on the circuit yet to play for England. He was in vintage form in 2018, becoming one of only nine batsmen who passed 1,000 first-class runs in the season, as well as being Somerset's top run-scorer in the One-Day Cup and second-highest in the T20 Blast. He had a rare blip in four-day cricket last summer, averaging 23.04 in the Championship, although he was once again the club's chief run-getter in the One-Day Cup with 457 at 45.70

Batting	Mat	Inns	NO	Runs	HS	Ave	SR	100	50	Ct	St
First-class	263	434	31	17158	303*	42.57		46	77	223	0
List A	212	199	36	5781	159	35.46		7	27	79	0
T20s	192	179	31	3575	107*	24.15	123.74	1	16	70	0
Bowling	**Mat**	**Balls**	**Runs**	**Wkts**	**BBI**	**BBM**	**Ave**	**Econ**	**SR**	**5w**	**10**
First-class	263	576	492	6	2/39		82.00	5.12	96.0	0	0
List A	212	150	185	6	2/26	2/26	30.83	7.40	25.0	0	0
T20s	192	169	247	10	3/24	3/24	24.70	8.76	16.9	0	0

LEWIS HILL

RHB / WK / R0 / W0

FULL NAME: Lewis John Hill
BORN: October 5, 1990, Leicester
SQUAD NO: 23
HEIGHT: 5ft 8in
NICKNAME: Lew Show, Lew, Hilly
EDUCATION: Hastings High School, Hinckley; John Cleveland College, Hinckley
TEAMS: Leicestershire
ROLE: Wicketkeeper
DEBUT: First-class: 2015; List A: 2012; T20: 2015

BEST BATTING: 126 Leicestershire vs Surrey, The Oval, 2015

WHAT GOT YOU INTO CRICKET? Friends played it when we were nine years old, so I joined in at their club
FAMILY TIES? My dad and brother both play for Lutterworth CC
BEST MOMENT IN CRICKET? Scoring my maiden first-class century at The Oval and having Kumar Sangakkara and Kevin Pietersen shake my hand at the end of the day
CRICKETING HEROES? Karl Smith, Craig Wilson & Nathan Welham of Lutterworth CC
IF YOU WEREN'T A CRICKETER? I'd be working for my dad in the family sports engineering business
SURPRISING FACT ABOUT YOU? I was targeted by armed robbers twice while working at my local newsagents
TWITTER: @lhjill23

Batting	Mat	Inns	NO	Runs	HS	Ave	SR	100	50	Ct	St
First-class	41	71	9	1459	126	23.53	49.02	1	5	96	3
List A	41	37	2	846	118	24.17	94.41	1	3	24	2
T20s	42	32	7	502	58	20.08	126.13	0	1	16	0
Bowling	**Mat**	**Balls**	**Runs**	**Wkts**	**BBI**	**BBM**	**Ave**	**Econ**	**SR**	**5w**	**10**
First-class	41	12	6	0	-	-	-	3.00	-	0	0
List A	41	-	-	-	-	-	-	-	-	-	-
T20s	42	-	-	-	-	-	-	-	-	-	-

MICHAEL HOGAN

RHB / RFM / R0 / W3

GLAMORGAN

FULL NAME: Michael Garry Hogan
BORN: May 31, 1981, Newcastle, Australia
SQUAD NO: 31
HEIGHT: 6ft 5in
NICKNAME: Hulk, Hoges
TEAMS: Glamorgan, Hobart Hurricanes, Western Australia
ROLE: Bowler
DEBUT: First-class: 2009; List A: 2009; T20: 2010

BEST BATTING: 57 Glamorgan vs Lancashire, Colwyn Bay, 2015
BEST BOWLING: 7-92 Glamorgan vs Gloucestershire, Bristol, 2013
COUNTY CAP: 2013

BEST ADVICE EVER RECEIVED? If the grass looks greener on the other side, there's probably more shit there
SURPRISING FACT ABOUT YOU? I'm very boring
SURPRISING FACT ABOUT A TEAMMATE? Marchant de Lange drinks two litres of Coca-Cola every day
CRICKETING HERO? Glenn McGrath
NON-CRICKETING HERO? Roger Federer
TWITTER: @hoges31

Batting	Mat	Inns	NO	Runs	HS	Ave	SR	100	50	Ct	St
First-class	155	218	85	2170	57	16.31	84.99	0	3	78	0
List A	69	28	18	171	27	17.10	82.60	0	0	25	0
T20s	97	21	13	78	17*	9.75	102.63	0	0	41	0
Bowling	**Mat**	**Balls**	**Runs**	**Wkts**	**BBI**	**BBM**	**Ave**	**Econ**	**SR**	**5w**	**10**
First-class	155	31919	14352	594	7/92	10/87	24.16	2.69	53.7	23	2
List A	69	3556	3017	102	5/44	5/44	29.57	5.09	34.8	1	0
T20s	97	1966	2565	105	5/17	5/17	24.42	7.82	18.7	1	0

MAX HOLDEN LHB / OB / R0 / W0

FULL NAME: Max David Edward Holden
BORN: December 18, 1997, Cambridge
SQUAD NO: 4
HEIGHT: 6ft 1in
NICKNAME: Pepsi, Little Chef
EDUCATION: Sawston Village College, Cambridge; Hills Road Sixth Form College, Cambridge
TEAMS: Middlesex, England Lions, Northamptonshire
ROLE: Batsman
DEBUT: First-class: 2017; List A: 2017; T20: 2018

BEST BATTING: 153 Northamptonshire vs Kent, Beckenham, 2017
BEST BOWLING: 2-59 Northamptonshire vs Kent, Beckenham, 2017

WHAT WAS YOUR FIRST CRICKET CLUB? Cambridge St Giles CC, Cambridgeshire. It had a 20-metre leg-side boundary
WHAT WERE YOU DOING WHEN ENGLAND WON THE WORLD CUP? Watching in the Glamorgan dressing room
HOW WOULD YOU DISMISS STEVE SMITH? Pitch it on leg, hit the top of off
MOST INTERESTING TEAMMATE? Martin Andersson – because he knows everything
BEST INNINGS YOU'VE SEEN? Ben Duckett's hundred before lunch for Northants against Leicestershire in 2017. I watched it from the other end
CRICKETING HERO? Brian Lara
CRICKET STAR OF THE FUTURE? Jack Davies (Middlesex)
WHICH BOOK MEANS MOST TO YOU? Harry Potter and the Goblet of Fire by JK Rowling
IF YOU WERE AN ANIMAL, WHICH WOULD IT BE? A tortoise. I'm pretty slow around the boundary
TWITTER: @maxholden_4

Batting	Mat	Inns	NO	Runs	HS	Ave	SR	100	50	Ct	St
First-class	38	68	4	1732	153	27.06	45.94	3	7	11	0
List A	11	10	1	412	166	45.77	90.74	1	2	2	0
T20s	7	7	1	199	84	33.16	135.37	0	1	4	0
Bowling	**Mat**	**Balls**	**Runs**	**Wkts**	**BBI**	**BBM**	**Ave**	**Econ**	**SR**	**5w**	**10**
First-class	38	636	452	5	2/59	3/94	90.40	4.26	127.2	0	0
List A	11	120	93	1	1/29	1/29	93.00	4.65	120.0	0	0
T20s	7	6	12	0	-	-	-	12.00	-	0	0

IAN HOLLAND

RHB / RMF / R0 / W0

FULL NAME: Ian Gabriel Holland
BORN: October 3, 1990, Wisconsin, USA
SQUAD NO: 22
HEIGHT: 6ft
NICKNAME: Dutchy
EDUCATION: Ringwood Secondary College, Melbourne
TEAMS: USA, Hampshire, Northamptonshire, Victoria
ROLE: Allrounder
DEBUT: First-class: 2016; List A: 2017; T20: 2017

BEST BATTING: 143 Hampshire vs Warwickshire, Southampton, 2019
BEST BOWLING: 4-16 Hampshire vs Somerset, Southampton, 2017

WHAT WAS YOUR FIRST CRICKET CLUB? Ringwood CC, Melbourne, Australia
HOW WOULD YOU DISMISS STEVE SMITH? The logical answer is food poisoning at lunch
BEST INNINGS YOU'VE SEEN? Ricky Ponting's 140 not out against India in the 2003 World Cup final – stood up as captain on the big occasion
CRICKETING HERO? Jacques Kallis
WHICH RULE WOULD YOU CHANGE ABOUT CRICKET? No limit on the number of bouncers allowed per over
CRICKET STAR OF THE FUTURE? Zak Evans (Australia U19)
WHICH BOOK MEANS MOST TO YOU? Green Bay Packers' Playbook
IF YOU WERE AN ANIMAL, WHICH WOULD IT BE? A Labrador
TWITTER: @IanHolland22

Batting	Mat	Inns	NO	Runs	HS	Ave	SR	100	50	Ct	St
ODIs	8	8	0	244	75	30.50	76.48	0	2	3	0
First-class	26	41	6	871	143	24.88	43.52	1	5	9	0
List A	21	20	4	400	75	25.00	83.33	0	3	8	0
T20s	4	2	2	12	11*	-	133.33	0	0	2	0
Bowling	**Mat**	**Balls**	**Runs**	**Wkts**	**BBI**	**BBM**	**Ave**	**Econ**	**SR**	**5w**	**10**
ODIs	8	275	209	7	3/11	3/11	29.85	4.56	39.2	0	0
First-class	26	2785	1196	40	4/16	6/39	29.90	2.57	69.6	0	0
List A	21	729	703	17	3/11	3/11	41.35	5.78	42.8	0	0
T20s	4	36	50	1	1/33	1/33	50.00	8.33	36.0	0	0

LUKE HOLLMAN

LHB / LB / RO / WO

FULL NAME: Luke Barnaby Kurt Hollman
BORN: September 16, 2000, Islington, London
SQUAD NO: 56
HEIGHT: 6ft 3in
NICKNAME: Hollers, Donny, Sid, Hans
EDUCATION: Acland Burghley School, Camden, London
TEAMS: Middlesex, England U19
ROLE: Allrounder

WHAT WAS YOUR FIRST CRICKET CLUB? North Middlesex CC, London
HOW WOULD YOU DISMISS STEVE SMITH? Bowled
BIGGEST TOPIC OF DISCUSSION IN YOUR DRESSING ROOM? Football
MOST INTERESTING TEAMMATE? Steven Finn – class player and a top bloke
CRICKET STAR OF THE FUTURE? Max Harris (Middlesex Academy)
IF YOU WERE AN ANIMAL, WHICH WOULD IT BE? A monkey – so I can be free and have a good time
NOTES: The young leg-spinning allrounder signed a two-year deal with Middlesex last November, having represented the club through the age-groups since he was nine. Hollman said: "I am massively honoured, overwhelmed, and hugely privileged to have been given the opportunity to sign this contract with Middlesex – my boyhood club and the club that I've been a fan of my whole life." The 19-year-old has played for the club's Second XI regularly across all formats since making his debut in 2017, and he also featured for England in the 2018 U19 World Cup as well as playing four Youth Tests. "Luke thoroughly deserves his rookie contract," said Angus Fraser, Middlesex's director of cricket. "It comes on the back of strong performances for Middlesex's Youth sides, our Second XI and for North Middlesex Cricket Club, who he has helped become a major force in the Middlesex Cricket League. His potential as an allrounder excites everyone at Middlesex and we look forward to him developing into a fine cricketer"

PAUL HORTON RHB / RM / R3 / W0

FULL NAME: Paul James Horton
BORN: September 20, 1982, Sydney, Australia
SQUAD NO: 2
HEIGHT: 5ft 10in
NICKNAME: Horts, Torts, Aussie, Custard
EDUCATION: Colo High School, Sydney; St Margaret's High School, Liverpool
TEAMS: Leicestershire, Lancashire, Matabeleland Tuskers
ROLE: Batsman
DEBUT: First-class: 2003; List A: 2003; T20: 2005

BEST BATTING: 209 Matabeleland Tuskers vs Southern Rocks, Masvingo, 2011
BEST BOWLING: 2-6 Leicestershire vs Sussex, Leicester, 2016
COUNTY CAP: 2007 (Lancashire)

STRANGEST THING SEEN IN A GAME? A team refuse to take the field because they weren't being paid enough
BEST MOMENT IN CRICKET? Nothing can top winning the County Championship in 2011 with Lancashire. Back-to-back Logan Cup trophies with Matabeleland Tuskers in 2010/11 and 2011/12 was also special
CRICKETING HERO? Dean Jones
NON-CRICKETING HERO? Robbie Fowler
SURPRISING FACT ABOUT YOU? I was a left-handed batsman as a kid. And I was once detained as an illegal immigrant
TWITTER: @PJHorton20

Batting	Mat	Inns	NO	Runs	HS	Ave	SR	100	50	Ct	St
First-class	218	373	26	12309	209	35.47	48.54	24	67	201	1
List A	121	112	13	2953	111*	29.82	78.28	3	14	50	0
T20s	82	76	14	1477	71*	23.82	108.52	0	5	32	0
Bowling	**Mat**	**Balls**	**Runs**	**Wkts**	**BBI**	**BBM**	**Ave**	**Econ**	**SR**	**5w**	**10**
First-class	218	118	80	2	2/6	2/6	40.00	4.06	59.0	0	0
List A	121	13	8	1	1/7	1/7	8.00	3.69	13.0	0	0
T20s	82	-	-	-	-	-	-	-	-	-	-

ADAM HOSE RHB / RMF / R0 / W0

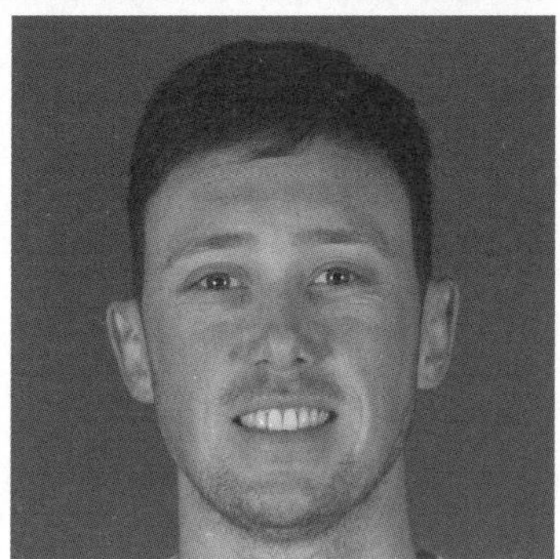

FULL NAME: Adam John Hose
BORN: October 25, 1992, Newport, Isle of Wight
SQUAD NO: 21
HEIGHT: 6ft 5in
NICKNAME: Pipe
EDUCATION: Carisbrooke School, Newport
TEAMS: Warwickshire, Birmingham Phoenix, Somerset, Wellington
ROLE: Batsman
DEBUT: First-class: 2016; List A: 2015; T20: 2015

BEST BATTING: 111 Warwickshire vs Nottinghamshire, Edgbaston, 2019

WHAT WAS YOUR FIRST CRICKET CLUB? Ventnor CC, Isle of Wight. Ever since I can remember I was down at my home club, watching and pestering all the players to throw me balls. The club's ground is a unique bowl
WHICH BOWLER WOULD YOU LEAST LIKE TO FACE? Darren Stevens on an early-season greentop
CRICKETING HERO? Kevin Pietersen
BEST INNINGS YOU'VE SEEN? Roelof van der Merwe's 165 not out to beat Surrey in the 2017 One-Day Cup. We were chasing 291 and it wasn't looking good at 22-5…
WHO WOULD YOU ASK TO BAT FOR YOUR LIFE? Jonathan Trott
TWITTER: @adamhose21

Batting	Mat	Inns	NO	Runs	HS	Ave	SR	100	50	Ct	St
First-class	19	35	1	746	111	21.94	44.99	1	4	5	0
List A	29	24	1	761	101*	33.08	90.27	1	4	16	0
T20s	45	44	5	1189	76	30.48	143.94	0	9	19	0
Bowling	**Mat**	**Balls**	**Runs**	**Wkts**	**BBI**	**BBM**	**Ave**	**Econ**	**SR**	**5w**	**10**
First-class	19	-	-	-	-	-	-	-	-	-	-
List A	29	-	-	-	-	-	-	-	-	-	-
T20s	45	-	-	-	-	-	-	-	-	-	-

HARVEY HOSEIN

RHB / WK / R0 / W0

DERBYSHIRE

FULL NAME: Harvey Richard Hosein
BORN: August 12, 1996, Chesterfield, Derbyshire
SQUAD NO: 16
HEIGHT: 6ft
NICKNAME: General
EDUCATION: Denstone College, Staffordshire
TEAMS: Derbyshire
ROLE: Wicketkeeper
DEBUT: First-class: 2014; List A: 2016; T20: 2016

BEST BATTING: 138* Derbyshire vs Durham, Derby, 2019

WHAT WAS YOUR FIRST CRICKET CLUB? Matlock CC, Peak District, Derbyshire. The club shares just under half the outfield with the football club
BIGGEST TOPIC OF DISCUSSION IN YOUR DRESSING ROOM? Who's on the music
MOST INTERESTING TEAMMATE? Hashim Amla – great to play with one of the greats of the game and tap into his knowledge
CRICKETING HERO? AB de Villiers
SURPRISING FACT ABOUT YOU? I played county-level tennis when I was younger
SURPRISING FACT ABOUT A TEAMMATE? Wayne Madsen was an international hockey player for South Africa before coming to England to play cricket
CRICKET STAR OF THE FUTURE? Ben Hutchinson (Tea Tree Gully CC, South Australia/ Swarkestone CC, South Derbyshire)
WHICH BOOK MEANS MOST TO YOU? The Champion's Mind – How Great Athletes Think, Train, and Thrive by Jim Afremow
IF YOU WERE AN ANIMAL, WHICH WOULD IT BE? A lion – looks cool
TWITTER: @HarveyHosein16

Batting	Mat	Inns	NO	Runs	HS	Ave	SR	100	50	Ct	St
First-class	47	80	14	2042	138*	30.93	45.20	2	14	108	4
List A	13	9	3	139	41*	23.16	106.92	0	0	8	3
T20s	5	2	2	0	0*	-	-	0	0	7	0
Bowling	**Mat**	**Balls**	**Runs**	**Wkts**	**BBI**	**BBM**	**Ave**	**Econ**	**SR**	**5w**	**10**
First-class	47	-	-	-	-	-	-	-	-	-	-
List A	13	-	-	-	-	-	-	-	-	-	-
T20s	5	-	-	-	-	-	-	-	-	-	-

BENNY HOWELL RHB / RM / R0 / W0 / MVP80

FULL NAME: Benny Alexander Cameron Howell
BORN: October 5, 1988, Bordeaux, France
SQUAD NO: 13
HEIGHT: 5ft 11in
NICKNAME: Novak, Howler
EDUCATION: The Oratory School, Reading
TEAMS: Gloucestershire, Birmingham Phoenix, Hampshire, Khulna Titans, Rangpur Riders
ROLE: Allrounder
DEBUT: First-class: 2011; List A: 2010; T20: 2011

BEST BATTING: 163 Gloucestershire vs Glamorgan, Cardiff, 2017
BEST BOWLING: 5-57 Gloucestershire vs Leicestershire, Leicester, 2013
COUNTY CAP: 2012 (Gloucestershire)

WHAT WAS YOUR FIRST CRICKET CLUB? Stoke Row CC, Oxfordshire. Beers were drank before and after the game. My brother Nicky was the best drunk batter I have seen
HOW WOULD YOU DISMISS STEVE SMITH? Bowl 30 different deliveries
WHAT EXCITES YOU ABOUT THE HUNDRED? Playing with and against the best in the world
MOST INTERESTING TEAMMATE? James Fuller – clever guy with interesting and random theories about cricket and life
BEST INNINGS YOU'VE SEEN? Jack Taylor hitting 41 off 14 balls against Derbyshire in the 2015 One-Day Cup. We scored 69 in four overs to chase down the target off the last ball
CRICKETING HERO? Michael Klinger – the ultimate professional and extremely humble. He never gave up on his dream to play for Australia
CRICKET STAR OF THE FUTURE? Alex Russell (Gloucestershire Second XI)
WHICH BOOK MEANS MOST TO YOU? Moneyball – The Art of Winning an Unfair Game by Michael Lewis
TWITTER: @bennyhowell510

Batting	Mat	Inns	NO	Runs	HS	Ave	SR	100	50	Ct	St
First-class	86	136	13	3378	163	27.46	54.35	2	18	52	0
List A	86	72	14	2050	122	35.34	90.70	1	13	27	0
T20s	116	95	27	1509	57	22.19	121.89	0	4	46	0
Bowling	**Mat**	**Balls**	**Runs**	**Wkts**	**BBI**	**BBM**	**Ave**	**Econ**	**SR**	**5w**	**10**
First-class	86	6455	3222	96	5/57	8/96	33.56	2.99	67.2	1	0
List A	86	3043	2640	76	3/37	3/37	34.73	5.20	40.0	0	0
T20s	116	2087	2400	125	5/18	5/18	19.20	6.89	16.6	1	0

FYNN HUDSON-PRENTICE RHB / RMF / R0 / W0

FULL NAME: Fynn Jake Hudson-Prentice
BORN: January 12, 1996, Haywards Heath, Sussex
SQUAD NO: 33
HEIGHT: 6ft
NICKNAME: Jack Sparrow
EDUCATION: Warden Park School, Cuckfield, West Sussex; Bede's Senior School, Hailsham, East Sussex
TEAMS: Derbyshire, Sussex
ROLE: Allrounder
DEBUT: First-class: 2015; List A: 2014; T20: 2019

BEST BATTING: 99 Derbyshire vs Middlesex, Derby, 2019
BEST BOWLING: 3-27 Derbyshire vs Worcestershire, Kidderminster

WHAT WAS YOUR FIRST CRICKET CLUB? St Andrews CC, Burgess Hill, West Sussex
WHAT WERE YOU DOING WHEN ENGLAND WON THE WORLD CUP? Driving home after losing a Championship game against Northants
HOW WOULD YOU DISMISS STEVE SMITH? If I knew, then I would have been playing in the Ashes last summer!
WHAT EXCITES YOU ABOUT THE HUNDRED? The fact that the games will be done and dusted in two hours
BIGGEST TOPIC OF DISCUSSION IN YOUR DRESSING ROOM? Golf Clash (video game)
MOST INTERESTING TEAMMATE? Phil Salt – there's never a lull in the conversation with him around
CRICKET STAR OF THE FUTURE? Oscar Wilson (Lancaster Park CC, Christchurch, New Zealand)
IF YOU WERE AN ANIMAL, WHICH WOULD IT BE? A shark – my name is Fynn
TWITTER: @fynnhudson33

Batting	Mat	Inns	NO	Runs	HS	Ave	SR	100	50	Ct	St
First-class	12	20	2	426	99	23.66	68.48	0	2	1	0
List A	3	2	0	67	48	33.50	95.71	0	0	0	0
T20s	14	7	2	94	31*	18.80	111.90	0	0	3	0
Bowling	**Mat**	**Balls**	**Runs**	**Wkts**	**BBI**	**BBM**	**Ave**	**Econ**	**SR**	**5w**	**10**
First-class	12	936	516	20	3/27	6/69	25.80	3.30	46.8	0	0
List A	3	84	112	0	-	-	-	8.00	-	0	0
T20s	14	222	320	11	2/2	2/2	29.09	8.64	20.1	0	0

ALEX HUGHES RHB / RM / R0 / W0 / MVP97

FULL NAME: Alex Lloyd Hughes
BORN: September 29, 1991, Wordsley, Staffordshire
SQUAD NO: 18
HEIGHT: 6ft
NICKNAME: Yozza, Horse, Megatron, Mini Goggins
EDUCATION: Ounsdale High School, Wolverhampton; University of Worcester
TEAMS: Derbyshire
ROLE: Allrounder
DEBUT: First-class: 2013; List A: 2012; T20: 2011

BEST BATTING: 142 Derbyshire vs Gloucestershire, Bristol, 2017
BEST BOWLING: 4-46 Derbyshire vs Glamorgan, Derby, 2014
COUNTY CAP: 2017

WHAT WAS YOUR FIRST CRICKET CLUB? Wombourne CC, Staffordshire
WHAT WERE YOU DOING WHEN ENGLAND WON THE WORLD CUP? Annoying my wife because I was shouting
WHAT EXCITES YOU ABOUT THE HUNDRED? Money
BIGGEST TOPIC OF DISCUSSION IN YOUR DRESSING ROOM? Matt Critchley
CRICKETING HERO? Mark Ealham
SURPRISING FACT ABOUT YOU? I got to the X Factor bootcamp in 2012
WHICH BOOK MEANS MOST TO YOU? Any of the Mr Men books
IF YOU WERE AN ANIMAL, WHICH WOULD IT BE? A pterodactyl
TWITTER: @Yozza18

Batting	Mat	Inns	NO	Runs	HS	Ave	SR	100	50	Ct	St
First-class	71	125	11	3277	142	28.74	46.35	6	13	53	0
List A	65	44	8	852	96*	23.66	92.70	0	3	27	0
T20s	79	59	16	687	43*	15.97	117.63	0	0	34	0
Bowling	**Mat**	**Balls**	**Runs**	**Wkts**	**BBI**	**BBM**	**Ave**	**Econ**	**SR**	**5w**	**10**
First-class	71	3375	1735	35	4/46	4/75	49.57	3.08	96.4	0	0
List A	65	2027	1898	43	4/44	4/44	44.13	5.61	47.1	0	0
T20s	79	1247	1669	49	4/42	4/42	34.06	8.03	25.4	0	0

LIAM HURT

RHB / RMF / R0 / W0

FULL NAME: Liam Jack Hurt
BORN: March 15, 1994, Preston, Lancashire
SQUAD NO: 22
HEIGHT: 6ft 3in
NICKNAME: Tyrone
EDUCATION: Balshaw's CE High School, Leyland, Lancashire
TEAMS: Lancashire, Leicestershire
ROLE: Bowler
DEBUT: First-class: 2019; List A: 2015; T20: 2019

BEST BATTING: 38 Lancashire vs Leicestershire, Leicester, 2019

WHAT WAS YOUR FIRST CRICKET CLUB? Leyland CC, Lancashire
HOW WOULD YOU DISMISS STEVE SMITH? Beamer-bouncer-yorker
BIGGEST TOPIC OF DISCUSSION IN YOUR DRESSING ROOM? Fantasy Football, Love Island and Netflix
MOST INTERESTING TEAMMATE? Shivnarine Chanderpaul
CRICKETING HERO? Andrew Flintoff
WHICH RULE WOULD YOU CHANGE ABOUT CRICKET? No front-foot no-balls
BIGGEST CRICKETING REGRET? Not being a batter
IF YOU WERE AN ANIMAL, WHICH WOULD IT BE? Silverback gorilla
TWITTER: @LiamHurt

Batting	Mat	Inns	NO	Runs	HS	Ave	SR	100	50	Ct	St
First-class	1	1	0	38	38	38.00	48.71	0	0	0	0
List A	5	3	2	34	15*	34.00	79.06	0	0	1	0
T20s	1	1	0	0	0	0.00	0.00	0	0	0	0
Bowling	**Mat**	**Balls**	**Runs**	**Wkts**	**BBI**	**BBM**	**Ave**	**Econ**	**SR**	**5w**	**10**
First-class	1	150	66	0	-	-	-	2.64	-	0	0
List A	5	198	193	7	2/24	2/24	27.57	5.84	28.2	0	0
T20s	1	12	25	0	-	-	-	12.50	-	0	0

BRETT HUTTON RHB / RMF / R0 / W0

FULL NAME: Brett Alan Hutton
BORN: February 6, 1993, Doncaster, Yorkshire
SQUAD NO: 16
HEIGHT: 6ft 3in
NICKNAME: Bert, Bredge
EDUCATION: Worksop College, Nottinghamshire
TEAMS: Northamptonshire, England U19, Nottinghamshire
ROLE: Bowler
DEBUT: First-class: 2011; List A: 2011; T20: 2016

BEST BATTING: 74 Nottinghamshire vs Durham, Trent Bridge, 2016
BEST BOWLING: 8-57 Northamptonshire vs Gloucestershire, Northampton, 2018

WHAT WAS YOUR FIRST CRICKET CLUB? Worksop CC, Nottinghamshire
WHAT EXCITES YOU ABOUT THE HUNDRED? Something different is always fun
BIGGEST TOPIC OF DISCUSSION IN YOUR DRESSING ROOM? Money
CRICKETING HERO? Paul Franks – he had a very good career. I played cricket with him from a young age, watching him and learning
WHICH RULE WOULD YOU CHANGE ABOUT CRICKET? Bring free hits into red-ball cricket
SURPRISING FACT ABOUT YOU? I have a stamp collection
CRICKET STAR OF THE FUTURE? Emilio Gay (Northamptonshire)
IF YOU WERE AN ANIMAL, WHICH WOULD IT BE? A sloth
TWITTER: @BrettAH26

Batting	Mat	Inns	NO	Runs	HS	Ave	SR	100	50	Ct	St
First-class	56	88	12	1371	74	18.03	43.33	0	4	34	0
List A	15	11	5	173	34*	28.83	93.01	0	0	5	0
T20s	9	7	4	50	18*	16.66	106.38	0	0	3	0
Bowling	**Mat**	**Balls**	**Runs**	**Wkts**	**BBI**	**BBM**	**Ave**	**Econ**	**SR**	**5w**	**10**
First-class	56	9143	5045	187	8/57	10/106	26.97	3.31	48.8	9	2
List A	15	728	776	16	3/72	3/72	48.50	6.39	45.5	0	0
T20s	9	172	255	5	2/28	2/28	51.00	8.89	34.4	0	0

COLIN INGRAM

LHB / LB / R0 / W0

FULL NAME: Colin Alexander Ingram
BORN: July 3, 1985, Port Elizabeth, SA
SQUAD NO: 41
HEIGHT: 5ft 10in
NICKNAME: Bozie, Stingray, Farmer
EDUCATION: Woodbridge College, Eastern Cape, South Africa
TEAMS: South Africa, Glamorgan, Welsh Fire, Adelaide Strikers, Delhi Daredevils, Eastern Province, Somerset, Warriors
ROLE: Allrounder
DEBUT: ODI: 2010; T20I: 2010; First-class: 2004; List A: 2005; T20: 2007

BEST BATTING: 127* Karachi Kings vs Quetta Gladiators, Sharjah, 2019 (T20)
BEST BOWLING: 4-32 Glamorgan vs Yorkshire, Cardiff, 2016 (T20)
COUNTY CAP: 2017 (Glamorgan)

WHAT WAS YOUR FIRST CRICKET CLUB? Old Grey CC, Port Elizabeth, South Africa
BEST ADVICE RECEIVED? Hit them high, make them fly, there ain't no fielders in the sky… sixes!
WHAT WERE YOU DOING WHEN ENGLAND WON THE WORLD CUP? Switching frantically between that game and the Federer-Nadal Wimbledon final
WHAT EXCITES YOU ABOUT THE HUNDRED? A chance to play for a team with "Welsh" in the name
WHICH RULE WOULD YOU CHANGE ABOUT CRICKET? If it's hitting, it must be lbw!
SURPRISING FACT ABOUT YOU? I do a bit of home brewing
SURPRISING FACT ABOUT A TEAMMATE? Andy Salter wants to start a business taking portable Jacuzzis to events with a Land Rover. He's going to call it Salty Tubs
IF YOU WERE AN ANIMAL, WHICH WOULD IT BE? A Golden Retriever – happy with the simple things in life: love, food, sun
TWITTER: @CAIngram41

Batting	Mat	Inns	NO	Runs	HS	Ave	SR	100	50	Ct	St
ODIs	31	29	3	843	124	32.42	82.32	3	3	12	0
T20Is	9	9	1	210	78	26.25	129.62	0	1	2	0
First-class	111	195	17	6641	190	37.30		14	30	75	0
List A	186	178	18	7584	142	47.40	90.13	18	48	65	0
T20s	265	259	38	6658	127*	30.12	140.07	4	40	83	0
Bowling	**Mat**	**Balls**	**Runs**	**Wkts**	**BBI**	**BBM**	**Ave**	**Econ**	**SR**	**5w**	**10**
ODIs	31	6	17	0	-	-	-	17.00	-	0	0
T20Is	9	-	-	-	-	-	-	-	-	-	-
First-class	111	3516	2132	50	4/16	5/50	42.64	3.63	70.3	0	0
List A	186	1482	1345	40	4/39	4/39	33.62	5.44	37.0	0	0
T20s	265	949	1247	38	4/32	4/32	32.81	7.88	24.9	0	0

WILL JACKS

RHB / RM / R0 / W0

FULL NAME: William George Jacks
BORN: November 21, 1998, Chertsey, Surrey
SQUAD NO: 9
HEIGHT: 6ft 2in
NICKNAME: Jacksy, Jacko
EDUCATION: St George's College, Weybridge
TEAMS: Surrey, Oval Invincibles, England Lions
ROLE: Batsman
DEBUT: First-class: 2018; List A: 2018; T20: 2018

BEST BATTING: 120 Surrey vs Kent, Beckenham, 2019

WHAT WAS YOUR FIRST CRICKET CLUB? Valley End CC, Surrey
WHAT WERE YOU DOING WHEN ENGLAND WON THE WORLD CUP? In the Trent Bridge Inn
WHAT EXCITES YOU ABOUT THE HUNDRED? The big crowds
MOST INTERESTING TEAMMATE? Harry Weatherall (Ealing Trailfinders CC) – a great fine-leg-to-fine-leg cricketer
BEST INNINGS YOU'VE SEEN? Aaron Finch's 116 not out for Surrey against Middlesex in the T20 game at The Oval in 2018. Best hitting I've ever seen
CRICKETING HERO? Kevin Pietersen
WHICH RULE WOULD YOU CHANGE ABOUT CRICKET? We should have a separate team for fielding so that batsmen don't have to do it
SURPRISING FACT ABOUT A TEAMMATE? Amir Virdi had a full beard at the age of 14
IF YOU WERE AN ANIMAL, WHICH WOULD IT BE? The great Altior (racehorse)
TWITTER: @Wjacks9

Batting	Mat	Inns	NO	Runs	HS	Ave	SR	100	50	Ct	St
First-class	19	29	2	748	120	27.70	52.05	1	5	22	0
List A	22	21	0	506	121	24.09	95.65	1	2	13	0
T20s	23	18	0	372	63	20.66	149.39	0	2	10	0
Bowling	**Mat**	**Balls**	**Runs**	**Wkts**	**BBI**	**BBM**	**Ave**	**Econ**	**SR**	**5w**	**10**
First-class	19	132	87	0	-	-	-	3.95	-	0	0
List A	22	482	423	11	2/32	2/32	38.45	5.26	43.8	0	0
T20s	23	18	40	0	-	-	-	13.33	-	0	0

LYNDON JAMES

RHB / RMF / R0 / W0

FULL NAME: Lyndon Wallace James
BORN: December 27, 1998, Worksop, Nottinghamshire
SQUAD NO: 45
HEIGHT: 6ft 3in
NICKNAME: LJ
EDUCATION: Oakham School, Rutland
TEAMS: Nottinghamshire
ROLE: Allrounder
DEBUT: First-class: 2018; List A: 2019

BEST BATTING: 13 Nottinghamshire vs Essex, Trent Bridge, 2018
BEST BOWLING: 3-54 Nottinghamshire vs Essex, Trent Bridge, 2018

WHAT WAS YOUR FIRST CRICKET CLUB? Ordsall Bridon CC, Nottinghamshire
WHAT EXCITES YOU ABOUT THE HUNDRED? Playing in the 50-over competition
BIGGEST TOPIC OF DISCUSSION IN YOUR DRESSING ROOM? Call of Duty (video game)
MOST INTERESTING TEAMMATE? Jack Blatherwick – for his constant impressions
CRICKET STAR OF THE FUTURE? Shay Brady – described as "the new Gilly" before a terrible knee injury set him back
TWITTER: @LyndonJames27
NOTES: A genuine allrounder who bowls seamers, James made a successful start to his first-class career by taking 3-54 against Essex at Trent Bridge in 2018 including the wicket of India Test opener Murali Vijay. He captained Notts Second XI for much of last summer, guiding the team to the T20 Finals Day, and he also made his List A debut for the club in the One-Day Cup fixture against Worcestershire at New Road. James has come all the way through the Notts age-groups after attending Oakham School, a nursery for a number of future cricketers including Stuart Broad

Batting	Mat	Inns	NO	Runs	HS	Ave	SR	100	50	Ct	St
First-class	1	2	0	14	13	7.00	51.85	0	0	0	0
List A	1	1	0	0	0	0.00	0.00	0	0	1	0
Bowling	**Mat**	**Balls**	**Runs**	**Wkts**	**BBI**	**BBM**	**Ave**	**Econ**	**SR**	**5w**	**10**
First-class	1	90	68	3	3/54	3/68	22.66	4.53	30.0	0	0
List A	1	-	-	-	-	-	-	-	-	-	-

KEATON JENNINGS LHB / RM / R1 / W0 / MVP100

FULL NAME: Keaton Kent Jennings
BORN: June 19, 1992, Johannesburg, South Africa
SQUAD NO: 1
HEIGHT: 6ft 4in
NICKNAME: Jet, Keats
EDUCATION: King Edward VII School; University of South Africa
TEAMS: England, Lancashire, Durham, Gauteng, South Africa U19
ROLE: Batsman
DEBUT: Test: 2016; First-class: 2011; List A: 2012; T20: 2014

BEST BATTING: 221* Durham vs Yorkshire, Chester-le-Street, 2016
BEST BOWLING: 3-37 Durham vs Sussex, Chester-le-Street, 2017
COUNTY CAP: 2018 (Lancashire)

FAMILY TIES? My brother Dylan, uncle Kenneth and father Ray have all played first-class cricket
WHAT WAS YOUR FIRST CRICKET CLUB? Pirates CC, Johannesburg, South Africa
BIGGEST TOPIC OF DISCUSSION IN YOUR DRESSING ROOM? Graham Onion's age
MOST INTERESTING TEAMMATE? Mark Wood – you've really got to keep your wits about you with him around
CRICKETING HERO? Mike Hussey
CRICKET STAR OF THE FUTURE? Tyla Jennings
IF YOU WERE AN ANIMAL, WHICH WOULD IT BE? A giraffe
TWITTER: @JetJennings

Batting	Mat	Inns	NO	Runs	HS	Ave	SR	100	50	Ct	St
Tests	17	32	1	781	146*	25.19	42.49	2	1	17	0
First-class	133	233	15	7319	221*	33.57	45.48	18	27	105	0
List A	68	67	12	2271	139	41.29	83.27	4	17	31	0
T20s	55	37	14	721	88	31.34	116.47	0	3	11	0
Bowling	**Mat**	**Balls**	**Runs**	**Wkts**	**BBI**	**BBM**	**Ave**	**Econ**	**SR**	**5w**	**10**
Tests	17	73	55	0	-	-	-	4.52	-	0	0
First-class	133	1671	960	29	3/37	4/48	33.10	3.44	57.6	0	0
List A	68	594	614	11	2/19	2/19	55.81	6.20	54.0	0	0
T20s	55	510	628	22	4/37	4/37	28.54	7.38	23.1	0	0

MICHAEL JONES RHB / OB / R0 / W0

FULL NAME: Michael Alexander Jones
BORN: January 5, 1998, Ormskirk, Lancashire
SQUAD NO: 10
HEIGHT: 6ft 3in
NICKNAME: Conquers
EDUCATION: Ormskirk School; Myerscough College, Preston; Edge Hill University, Ormskirk
TEAMS: Scotland, Durham
ROLE: Batsman
DEBUT: ODI: 2018; First-class: 2018; List A: 2018

BEST BATTING: 10 Durham vs Derbyshire, Chester-le-Street, 2018

TWITTER: @mikejones04
NOTES: The Lancashire-born top-order batsman scored 87 on his ODI debut for Scotland against Ireland in January 2018 and notched his third international half-century in a World Cup League 2 encounter with USA last December at Sharjah. Jones was a regular source of runs for Durham's second-team last season, scoring 242 at an average of 34.57 in the Second XI Championship. He made his County Championship debut in the 2018 campaign, scoring 10 and 3 against Derbyshire, and had two outings in Durham's first-team last year without posting a notable score. Jones had been part of the Lancashire Academy and played second XI cricket for Derbyshire and Leicestershire before signing with the Durham Academy ahead of the 2018 season

Batting	Mat	Inns	NO	Runs	HS	Ave	SR	100	50	Ct	St
ODIs	8	8	0	281	87	35.12	70.07	0	3	3	0
First-class	3	5	0	22	10	4.40	24.71	0	0	0	0
List A	8	8	0	281	87	35.12	70.07	0	3	3	0
Bowling	**Mat**	**Balls**	**Runs**	**Wkts**	**BBI**	**BBM**	**Ave**	**Econ**	**SR**	**5w**	**10**
ODIs	8	-	-	-	-	-	-	-	-	-	-
First-class	3	-	-	-	-	-	-	-	-	-	-
List A	8	-	-	-	-	-	-	-	-	-	-

ROB JONES

RHB / LB / R0 / W0

FULL NAME: Robert Peter Jones
BORN: November 3, 1995, Warrington, Cheshire
SQUAD NO: 12
HEIGHT: 5ft 10in
NICKNAME: Jonesy, Jonah, Bobbly
EDUCATION: Bridgewater High School, Warrington; Priestley College
TEAMS: Lancashire, England U19
ROLE: Batsman
DEBUT: First-class: 2016; List A: 2018; T20: 2017

BEST BATTING: 122 Lancashire vs Middlesex, Lord's, 2019
BEST BOWLING: 1-18 Lancashire vs Worcestershire, Worcester, 2018

WHAT WAS YOUR FIRST CRICKET CLUB? Stretton CC, Warrington, Cheshire
HOW WOULD YOU DISMISS STEVE SMITH? With my googly
BIGGEST TOPIC OF DISCUSSION IN YOUR DRESSING ROOM? Food
MOST INTERESTING TEAMMATE? Steven Croft – he was my hero when I was growing up
BEST INNINGS YOU'VE SEEN? Jos Buttler's unbeaten hundred when England beat Australia by one wicket in an ODI at Old Trafford in 2018
CRICKET STAR OF THE FUTURE? Tom Hartley (Lancashire)
WHICH BOOK MEANS MOST TO YOU? The Go-Giver – A Little Story About a Powerful Business Idea by Bob Burg and John David Mann
IF YOU WERE AN ANIMAL, WHICH WOULD IT BE? A mountain goat – because I love being up a mountain
TWITTER: @robpeterjones

Batting	Mat	Inns	NO	Runs	HS	Ave	SR	100	50	Ct	St
First-class	27	40	5	1098	122	31.37	38.40	2	5	24	0
List A	13	10	2	205	65	25.62	79.76	0	1	8	0
T20s	2	-	-	-	-	-	-	-	-	0	0
Bowling	**Mat**	**Balls**	**Runs**	**Wkts**	**BBI**	**BBM**	**Ave**	**Econ**	**SR**	**5w**	**10**
First-class	27	72	38	1	1/18	1/18	38.00	3.16	72.0	0	0
List A	13	122	122	2	1/3	1/3	61.00	6.00	61.0	0	0
T20s	2	-	-	-	-	-	-	-	-	-	-

CHRIS JORDAN

RHB / RFM / R0 / W1

FULL NAME: Christopher James Jordan
BORN: October 4, 1988, Christ Church, Barbados
SQUAD NO: 8
HEIGHT: 6ft
EDUCATION: Combermere School, Barbados; Dulwich College, London
TEAMS: England, Sussex, Southern Brave, Adelaide Strikers, Barbados, Perth Scorchers, RC Bangalore, Sunrisers Hyderabad, Surrey, Sydney Thunder
ROLE: Allrounder
DEBUT: Test: 2014; ODI: 2013; T20I: 2013; First-class: 2007; List A: 2007; T20: 2008

BEST BATTING: 166 Sussex vs Northamptonshire, Northampton, 2019
BEST BOWLING: 7-43 Barbados vs Combined Campuses and Colleges, Bridgetown, 2013
COUNTY CAP: 2014 (Sussex)

WHAT WAS YOUR FIRST CRICKET CLUB? Spartan Juniors CC, Barbados
WHAT WERE YOU DOING WHEN ENGLAND WON THE WORLD CUP? Watching it in the Old Trafford changing room
HOW WOULD YOU DISMISS STEVE SMITH? With patience
WHAT EXCITES YOU ABOUT THE HUNDRED? The new tactics that will be required
BIGGEST TOPIC OF DISCUSSION IN YOUR DRESSING ROOM? Football
MOST INTERESTING TEAMMATE? Jofra Archer – no matter what is going on in his life, whenever gets on that 22 yards of pitch he turns it on
TWITTER: @ChrisJordan94

Batting	Mat	Inns	NO	Runs	HS	Ave	SR	100	50	Ct	St
Tests	8	11	1	180	35	18.00	56.25	0	0	14	0
ODIs	34	23	9	170	38*	12.14	88.08	0	0	19	0
T20Is	46	27	12	223	36	14.86	131.95	0	0	25	0
First-class	114	159	23	3443	166	25.31		3	15	137	0
List A	84	56	15	634	55	15.46		0	1	45	0
T20s	192	115	45	996	45*	14.22	118.99	0	0	112	0
Bowling	**Mat**	**Balls**	**Runs**	**Wkts**	**BBI**	**BBM**	**Ave**	**Econ**	**SR**	**5w**	**10**
Tests	8	1530	752	21	4/18	7/50	35.80	2.94	72.8	0	0
ODIs	34	1618	1611	45	5/29	5/29	35.80	5.97	35.9	1	0
T20Is	46	975	1408	58	4/6	4/6	24.27	8.66	16.8	0	0
First-class	114	18986	10730	335	7/43	9/58	32.02	3.39	56.6	10	0
List A	84	3798	3633	121	5/28	5/28	30.02	5.73	31.3	2	0
T20s	192	3811	5398	206	4/6	4/6	26.20	8.49	18.5	0	0

ROB KEOGH

RHB / OB / R0 / W0 / MVP41

FULL NAME: Robert Ian Keogh
BORN: October 21, 1991, Dunstable, Bedfordshire
SQUAD NO: 14
HEIGHT: 6ft 2in
NICKNAME: Keezy, Key Dog
EDUCATION: Queensbury Upper School, Dunstable; Dunstable College
TEAMS: Northamptonshire
ROLE: Allrounder
DEBUT: First-class: 2012; List A: 2010; T20: 2011

BEST BATTING: 221 Northamptonshire vs Hampshire, Southampton, 2013
BEST BOWLING: 9-52 Northamptonshire vs Glamorgan, Northampton, 2016

WHAT WAS YOUR FIRST CRICKET CLUB? Dunstable Town CC, Bedfordshire. I got into cricket watching my dad play for the club. I owe a lot to DTCC – especially Brian Chapman
WHAT WERE YOU DOING WHEN ENGLAND WON THE WORLD CUP? We had just won a Championship game in three days away at Derby. Then watched it in the pavilion
HOW WOULD YOU DISMISS STEVE SMITH? Caught long-on
WHAT EXCITES YOU ABOUT THE HUNDRED? The wildcard pick
MOST INTERESTING TEAMMATE? Brett Hutton – he never has any clothes on
WHICH RULE WOULD YOU CHANGE ABOUT CRICKET? No slips allowed
BIGGEST CRICKETING REGRET? Choosing a locker next to David Murphy
IF YOU WERE AN ANIMAL, WHICH WOULD IT BE? A monkey – they look like they have fun
TWITTER: @RobKeogh91

Batting	Mat	Inns	NO	Runs	HS	Ave	SR	100	50	Ct	St
First-class	79	129	8	3607	221	29.80	50.17	9	10	23	0
List A	46	42	3	1272	134	32.61	87.42	2	11	9	0
T20s	57	34	10	525	59*	21.87	113.14	0	1	26	0
Bowling	**Mat**	**Balls**	**Runs**	**Wkts**	**BBI**	**BBM**	**Ave**	**Econ**	**SR**	**5w**	**10**
First-class	79	6370	3759	88	9/52	13/125	42.71	3.54	72.3	1	1
List A	46	1002	925	8	2/26	2/26	115.62	5.53	125.2	0	0
T20s	57	300	397	16	3/30	3/30	24.81	7.94	18.7	0	0

RASHID KHAN

RHB / LB / R0 / W0

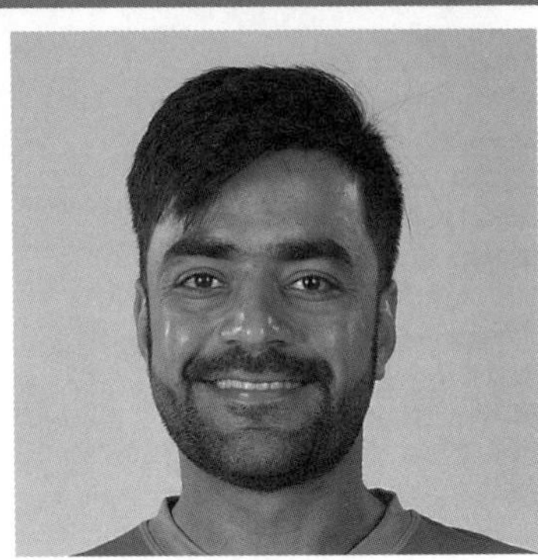

FULL NAME: Rashid Khan Arman
BORN: September 20, 1998, Nangarhar, Afghanistan
SQUAD NO: 1
TEAMS: Afghanistan, Sussex, Trent Rockets, Adelaide Strikers, Durban Heat, Guyana Amazon Warriors, Kabul Zwanan, Quetta Gladiators, Sunrisers Hyderabad
ROLE: Bowler
DEBUT: Test: 2018; ODI: 2015; T20I: 2015; First-class: 2016; List A: 2015; T20: 2015

BEST BATTING: 56* Kabul Zwanan vs Balkh Legends, Sharjah, 2018 (T20)
BEST BOWLING: 5-3 Afghanistan vs Ireland, Greater Noida, 2017 (T20)

TWITTER: @rashidkhan_19

NOTES: Sussex have re-signed the 20-year-old leg-spinner for a third succesive T20 Blast campaign. Rashid was the first Afghan to sign for an English county when he joined Sussex ahead of the 2018 season and he played a huge part in taking the club to the final of the competition, taking 17 wickets at an average of 14.35 with an economy-rate of 6.59. Possessing a lethal googly, Rashid is the biggest talent to emerge from Afghanistan and has played in the major T20 leagues all over the world. As of March 2020, he was the No.1 bowler in the ICC T20I rankings. Sussex head coach Jason Gillespie said: "Everyone knows about his fantastic skills on the field, but he brings so much more to our club behind the scenes. He's a wonderful ambassador for Sussex, for Afghanistan and for the game in general"

Batting	Mat	Inns	NO	Runs	HS	Ave	SR	100	50	Ct	St
Tests	4	7	0	106	51	15.14	79.69	0	1	0	0
ODIs	71	56	9	905	60*	19.25	99.88	0	4	22	0
T20Is	48	23	12	163	33	14.81	125.38	0	0	20	0
First-class	8	11	1	231	52	23.10	77.00	0	2	0	0
List A	73	57	9	926	60*	19.29	100.65	0	4	23	0
T20s	211	109	37	879	56*	12.20	149.48	0	1	67	0
Bowling	**Mat**	**Balls**	**Runs**	**Wkts**	**BBI**	**BBM**	**Ave**	**Econ**	**SR**	**5w**	**10**
Tests	4	938	485	23	6/49	11/104	21.08	3.10	40.7	3	1
ODIs	71	3558	2467	133	7/18	7/18	18.54	4.16	26.7	4	0
T20Is	48	1098	1124	89	5/3	5/3	12.62	6.14	12.3	2	0
First-class	8	2117	1012	58	8/74	12/122	17.44	2.86	36.5	7	2
List A	73	3665	2555	137	7/18	7/18	18.64	4.18	26.7	4	0
T20s	211	4853	5100	296	5/3	5/3	17.22	6.30	16.3	2	0

SHADAB KHAN RHB / LB

FULL NAME: Shadab Khan
BORN: October 4, 1998, Mianwali, Punjab, Pakistan
SQUAD NO: TBC
HEIGHT: 5ft 10in
TEAMS: Pakistan, Surrey, Southern Brave, Brisbane Heat, Dhaka Platoon, Guyana Amazon Warriors, Islamabad United, Rawalpindi, Sui Northern Gas Pipelines Limited, Trinbago Knight Riders
ROLE: Allrounder
DEBUT: Test: 2017; ODI: 2017; T20I: 2017; First-class: 2016; List A: 2016; T20: 2016

BEST BATTING: 77 Islamabad United vs Peshawar Zalmi, Rawalpindi, 2020 (T20)
BEST BOWLING: 4-14 Pakistan vs West Indies, Port of Spain, 2017 (T20)

TWITTER: @76Shadabkhan
NOTES: The Pakistani leg-spinning allrounder will represent Surrey in the T20 Blast this summer. Still only 21, Shadab arrives with an impressive cricketing CV. He made his debut for Pakistan across all formats while in his teens, winning the Player of the Match award in his first two T20I appearances against West Indies in 2017. He took nine wickets in last summer's 50-over World Cup and has starred in T20 leagues across the world, including the Big Bash and the Caribbean Premier League. Known for his ability to extract turn and bowl googlies, Shadab is also a handy batsman down the order, as he showed with a T20 career-best 77 for Islamabad United in the Pakistan Super League earlier this year. He will also line up for Southern Brave in The Hundred this summer, subject to his involvement in Pakistan's Test and T20I series against England

Batting	Mat	Inns	NO	Runs	HS	Ave	SR	100	50	Ct	St
Tests	5	9	2	240	56	34.28	62.99	0	3	1	0
ODIs	43	22	9	337	54	25.92	68.63	0	3	8	0
T20Is	40	14	5	122	29	13.55	127.08	0	0	11	0
First-class	15	21	2	524	132	27.57	68.76	1	3	8	0
List A	56	32	11	549	56	26.14	78.76	0	4	16	0
T20s	123	71	18	829	77	15.64	128.12	0	4	40	0
Bowling	**Mat**	**Balls**	**Runs**	**Wkts**	**BBI**	**BBM**	**Ave**	**Econ**	**SR**	**5w**	**10**
Tests	5	885	466	12	3/31	4/80	38.83	3.15	73.7	0	0
ODIs	43	2088	1750	59	4/28	4/28	29.66	5.02	35.3	0	0
T20Is	40	855	1002	48	4/14	4/14	20.87	7.03	17.8	0	0
First-class	15	3008	1706	66	6/77	10/157	25.84	3.40	45.5	2	1
List A	56	2682	2333	80	4/28	4/28	29.16	5.21	33.5	0	0
T20s	123	2663	3070	144	4/14	4/14	21.31	6.91	18.4	0	0

FEROZE KHUSHI

RHB / OB / R0 / W0

FULL NAME: Feroze Isa Nazir Khushi
BORN: June 23, 1999, Whipps Cross, Essex
SQUAD NO: 23
HEIGHT: 6ft 1in
NICKNAME: Fink
EDUCATION: Kelmscott School, Walthamstow, London
TEAMS: Essex
ROLE: Batsman

WHAT GOT YOU INTO CRICKET? My father introduced me to the sport at the age of three
BEST ADVICE EVER RECEIVED? Work hard and be dedicated
BEST MOMENT IN CRICKET? When I hit six sixes in the last over of a school match when we needed 30 runs to win
IF YOU WEREN'T A CRICKETER? I'd be a professional footballer
SURPRISING FACT ABOUT YOU? I went to the same school as Fabrice Muamba
CRICKETING HERO? Shahid Afridi
NON-CRICKETING HERO? Cristiano Ronaldo – he works very hard at his game and is a great role model of professionalism on and off the field
NOTES: Khushi is a 20-year-old batsman who signed a professional contract with Essex in October 2017 after a number of impressive performances for Essex Second XI. He played regularly for the Second XI last summer, scoring 567 runs at 47.25, including one hundred and three half-centuries. Khushi also compiled an unbeaten 120 for Suffolk in the Minor Counties Championship towards the end of the season. He signed a new one-year deal with Essex in October. Head coach Anthony McGrath said: "Feroze has been exceptional with the bat for the Second XI this year and has scored well in every match I've seen him play. Everyone at the club is excited about his potential and we feel he'll be a big player for us for years to come"

NICK KIMBER RHB / RMF / R0 / W0

FULL NAME: Nicholas John Henry Kimber
BORN: January 16, 2001, Lincoln
SQUAD NO: 12
HEIGHT: 6ft 2in
NICKNAME: Kimbo
EDUCATION: William Farr Church of England School, Lincoln; Oakham School, Rutland
TEAMS: Surrey, England U19
ROLE: Bowler

WHAT WAS YOUR FIRST CRICKET CLUB? Lindum CC, Lincolnshire
WHAT WERE YOU DOING WHEN ENGLAND WON THE WORLD CUP? I was with England U19 watching the tv as a team
BIGGEST TOPIC OF DISCUSSION IN YOUR DRESSING ROOM? Football
CRICKET STAR OF THE FUTURE? Kasey Aldridge (Somerset)
IF YOU WERE AN ANIMAL, WHICH WOULD IT BE? A koala
TWITTER: @NKimber11
NOTES: The England U19 seamer signed a two-year contract with Surrey in October after coming through Nottinghamshire's youth setup. Kimber arrived at The Oval at the same time as his England U19 teammate James Taylor, who joined from Derbyshire. It means that Surrey begin the 2020 season with as many as 15 seamers in their squad. Kimber has represented Notts from U14 level upwards, turning out for the club's Academy side and the Second XI, and he has also played age-group cricket for Lincolnshire. The 19-year-old made his England U19 debut in 2018 and took nine wickets at 26.44 in six Youth ODIs up to the start of this year, including a best of 5-38 against Bangladesh U19 at Billericay last August. Highlighting the credentials of both Kimber and Taylor, Surrey director of cricket Alec Stewart said: "Nick and James have demonstrated their considerable talents for England U19s and within their county set-ups so to have two of the most promising pace bowlers in the country is an exciting prospect"

FRED KLAASSEN RHB / LMF / R0 / W0

FULL NAME: Frederick Jack Klaassen
BORN: November 13, 1992, Haywards Heath, Sussex
SQUAD NO: 18
HEIGHT: 6ft 4in
EDUCATION: University of Otago, Dunedin, New Zealand
TEAMS: Netherlands, Kent
ROLE: Bowler
DEBUT: ODI: 2018; T20I: 2018; First-class: 2019; List A: 2017; T20: 2018

BEST BATTING: 14* Kent vs Loughborough MCCU, Canterbury, 2019
BEST BOWLING: 1-44 Kent vs Yorkshire, Canterbury, 2019

WHAT WAS YOUR FIRST CRICKET CLUB? Cornwall CC, Auckland, New Zealand
WHAT WERE YOU DOING WHEN ENGLAND WON THE WORLD CUP? Watching it with the squad at the Ageas Bowl
HOW WOULD YOU DISMISS STEVE SMITH? Bowl short to a leg-side field
BIGGEST TOPIC OF DISCUSSION IN YOUR DRESSING ROOM? Who is the top goal-scorer in the football warm-ups
MOST INTERESTING TEAMMATE? Zak Crawley – an old man's mind in a young man's body
IF YOU WERE AN ANIMAL, WHICH WOULD IT BE? A kiwi – flightless bird which is practically extinct
TWITTER: @freddieklaassen

Batting	Mat	Inns	NO	Runs	HS	Ave	SR	100	50	Ct	St
ODIs	4	3	1	30	13	15.00	57.69	0	0	2	0
T20Is	21	7	1	33	13	5.50	97.05	0	0	10	0
First-class	2	3	1	37	14*	18.50	19.78	0	0	2	0
List A	21	15	8	87	16*	12.42	63.97	0	0	11	0
T20s	36	10	3	41	13	5.85	102.50	0	0	18	0
Bowling	**Mat**	**Balls**	**Runs**	**Wkts**	**BBI**	**BBM**	**Ave**	**Econ**	**SR**	**5w**	**10**
ODIs	4	240	150	10	3/30	3/30	15.00	3.75	24.0	0	0
T20Is	21	415	581	20	3/31	3/31	29.05	8.40	20.7	0	0
First-class	2	270	170	2	1/44	2/132	85.00	3.77	135.0	0	0
List A	21	1006	865	31	3/30	3/30	27.90	5.15	32.4	0	0
T20s	36	722	1041	34	3/31	3/31	30.61	8.65	21.2	0	0

DIETER KLEIN

RHB / LMF / RO / WO

FULL NAME: Dieter Klein
BORN: October 31, 1988, Lichtenburg, North West Province, South Africa
SQUAD NO: 77
HEIGHT: 5ft 9in
NICKNAME: Diets
EDUCATION: Hoërskool Lichtenburg, South Africa
TEAMS: Germany, Leicestershire, Lions, North West
ROLE: Bowler
DEBUT: First-class: 2008; List A: 2008; T20: 2013

BEST BATTING: 94 Leicestershire vs Glamorgan, Cardiff, 2018
BEST BOWLING: 8-72 North West vs Northerns, Potchefstroom, 2014

WHAT GOT YOU INTO CRICKET? I always had a love for all sports, but something had to give and eventually cricket won through
BEST ADVICE EVER RECEIVED? Nothing comes for free. What you put in is what you get out. Anything is possible
IF YOU WEREN'T A CRICKETER? I'd be a pilot
CRICKETING HERO? Jacques Kallis – very controlled and good at all aspects of the game
NON-CRICKETING HERO? My brother – just a hero. Nothing gets him down. One hell of a fighter

Batting	Mat	Inns	NO	Runs	HS	Ave	SR	100	50	Ct	St
T20Is	2	2	2	48	31*	-	200.00	0	0	0	0
First-class	64	91	18	1390	94	19.04	76.24	0	6	19	0
List A	33	19	4	206	46	13.73	79.53	0	0	1	0
T20s	30	20	9	128	31*	11.63	111.30	0	0	7	0
Bowling	**Mat**	**Balls**	**Runs**	**Wkts**	**BBI**	**BBM**	**Ave**	**Econ**	**SR**	**5w**	**10**
T20Is	2	48	41	2	1/12	1/12	20.50	5.12	24.0	0	0
First-class	64	9251	6039	212	8/72	10/125	28.48	3.91	43.6	10	1
List A	33	1577	1368	49	5/35	5/35	27.91	5.20	32.1	1	0
T20s	30	508	678	24	3/27	3/27	28.25	8.00	21.1	0	0

TOM KOHLER-CADMORE RHB / OB / R1 / W0 / MVP23

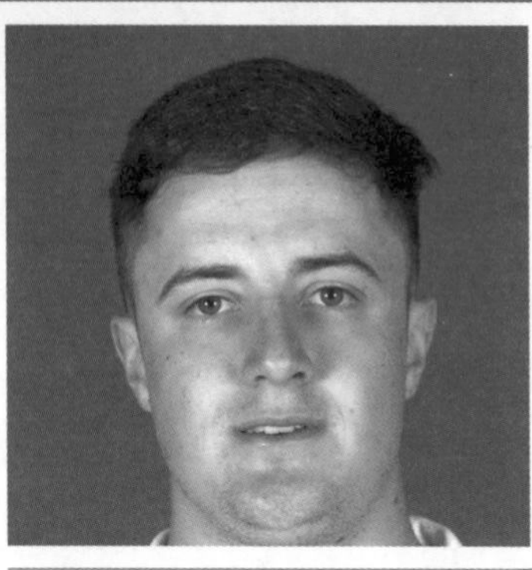

FULL NAME: Tom Kohler-Cadmore
BORN: August 19, 1994, Chatham, Kent
SQUAD NO: 32
HEIGHT: 6ft 2in
NICKNAME: Pepsi, Herbert, Brother Bilo
EDUCATION: Malvern College, Worcestershire
TEAMS: Yorkshire, Northern Superchargers, England Lions, Quetta Gladiators, Worcestershire
ROLE: Batsman
DEBUT: First-class: 2014; List A: 2013; T20: 2014

BEST BATTING: 176 Yorkshire vs Leeds/Bradford MCCU, Weetwood, 2019

COUNTY CAP: 2019 (Yorkshire)

BEST ADVICE EVER RECEIVED? In cricket: hit the sightscreen. In life: never eat yellow snow
CRICKETING HERO? Dwayne Leverock – because of that one-handed screamer
IF YOU WEREN'T A CRICKETER? I'd be an underwater fireman
SURPRISING FACT ABOUT YOU? I've been called the songbird of my generation by people who have heard me sing
SURPRISING FACT ABOUT A TEAMMATE? Ben Coad only eats chicken nuggets. I've never seen someone take down 20 nuggets so quickly and easily and come back for more
TWITTER: @tomkcadmore

Batting	Mat	Inns	NO	Runs	HS	Ave	SR	100	50	Ct	St
First-class	61	100	7	3332	176	35.82	55.15	9	15	85	0
List A	56	54	1	1808	164	34.11	86.79	3	10	29	0
T20s	76	76	5	2015	127	28.38	140.51	1	14	41	0
Bowling	**Mat**	**Balls**	**Runs**	**Wkts**	**BBI**	**BBM**	**Ave**	**Econ**	**SR**	**5w**	**10**
First-class	61	-	-	-	-	-	-	-	-	-	-
List A	56	-	-	-	-	-	-	-	-	-	-
T20s	76	-	-	-	-	-	-	-	-	-	-

HEINO KUHN RHB / WK / R0 / W0

FULL NAME: Heino Gunther Kuhn
BORN: April 1, 1984, Piet Retief, South Africa
SQUAD NO: 4
NICKNAME: H, Koenie
TEAMS: South Africa, Kent, Dhaka Dynamites, Nelson Mandela Bay Giants, Northerns, Titans
ROLE: Batsman
DEBUT: Test: 2017; T20I: 2009; First-class: 2005; List A: 2005; T20: 2007

BEST BATTING: 244* Titans vs Lions, Benoni, 2015

COUNTY CAP: 2018

WHAT WERE YOU DOING WHEN ENGLAND WON THE WORLD CUP? Watching it with the Kent boys after a Championship match
HOW WOULD YOU DISMISS STEVE SMITH? I'd have someone bowl bouncers at him with two guys out on the leg side and a leg gully
WHAT EXCITES YOU ABOUT THE HUNDRED? It's something different
BIGGEST TOPIC OF DISCUSSION IN YOUR DRESSING ROOM? Umpiring
MOST INTERESTING TEAMMATE? Mitchell Claydon – he's extremely funny
IF YOU WERE AN ANIMAL, WHICH WOULD IT BE? An orca – beautiful, majestic, clever and dangerous
TWITTER: @HeinoKuhn

Batting	Mat	Inns	NO	Runs	HS	Ave	SR	100	50	Ct	St
Tests	4	8	0	113	34	14.12	38.04	0	0	1	0
T20Is	7	6	2	49	29	12.25	116.66	0	0	5	0
First-class	173	303	27	11240	244*	40.72		23	58	369	18
List A	174	159	18	4859	141*	34.46	89.69	13	22	179	22
T20s	125	105	17	2321	83*	26.37	126.96	0	13	78	6
Bowling	**Mat**	**Balls**	**Runs**	**Wkts**	**BBI**	**BBM**	**Ave**	**Econ**	**SR**	**5w**	**10**
Tests	4	-	-	-	-	-	-	-	-	-	-
T20Is	7	-	-	-	-	-	-	-	-	-	-
First-class	173	6	12	0	-	-	-	12.00	-	0	0
List A	174	-	-	-	-	-	-	-	-	-	-
T20s	125	-	-	-	-	-	-	-	-	-	-

MARNUS LABUSCHAGNE RHB / LB / R0 / W0

FULL NAME: Marnus Labuschagne
BORN: June 22, 1994, Klerksdorp, North West Province, South Africa
SQUAD NO: 99
TEAMS: Australia, Glamorgan, Brisbane Heat, Queensland
ROLE: Batsman
DEBUT: Test: 2018; ODI: 2020; First-class: 2014; List A: 2015; T20: 2017

BEST BATTING: 215 Australia vs New Zealand, Sydney, 2020
BEST BOWLING: 3-45 Australia vs Pakistan, Abu Dhabi, 2018

TWITTER: @marnus3cricket
NOTES: Labuschagne returns to Glamorgan on a two-year contract after an extraordinary 2019 which saw him start the year ranked No.110 in the ICC Test batting rankings and finish it at No.3. Following a superb first half of the county season in which he scored five centuries and five fifties in 10 Championship matches, he went on to star for Australia in the Ashes after entering the fray at Lord's as the first concussion substitute in Test cricket. He scored 1,104 Test runs in 2019, more than any other batsman, with 896 of those coming in the Australian Test summer – only Ricky Ponting, Matthew Hayden and Wally Hammond have managed more. And Labuschagne began 2020 imperiously, scoring 215 against New Zealand at the SCG. "He reminded me very much of Viv Richards in terms of his drive, his passion and being a real leader on the field," said Glamorgan head coach Matthew Maynard after Labuschagne was re-signed

Batting	Mat	Inns	NO	Runs	HS	Ave	SR	100	50	Ct	St
Tests	14	23	0	1459	215	63.43	56.52	4	8	13	0
ODIs	7	6	0	305	108	50.83	94.42	1	2	1	0
First-class	76	137	9	5524	215	43.15	53.80	13	32	74	0
List A	40	39	2	1478	135	39.94	88.13	2	13	13	0
T20s	10	9	1	97	28	12.12	100.00	0	0	4	0
Bowling	**Mat**	**Balls**	**Runs**	**Wkts**	**BBI**	**BBM**	**Ave**	**Econ**	**SR**	**5w**	**10**
Tests	14	756	464	12	3/45	5/119	38.66	3.68	63.0	0	0
ODIs	7	24	36	0	-	-	-	9.00	-	0	0
First-class	76	3864	2480	58	3/45	5/77	42.75	3.85	66.6	0	0
List A	40	474	497	8	3/46	3/46	62.12	6.29	59.2	0	0
T20s	10	42	81	1	1/25	1/25	81.00	11.57	42.0	0	0

TOM LACE

RHB / WK / R0 / W0

FULL NAME: Thomas Cresswell Lace
BORN: May 27, 1998, Hammersmith
SQUAD NO: 27
HEIGHT: 5ft 9in
NICKNAME: Lacey
EDUCATION: Millfield School, Somerset; Royal Holloway, University of London
TEAMS: Middlesex, Derbyshire
ROLE: Batsman
DEBUT: First-class: 2018; List A: 2019

BEST BATTING: 143 Derbyshire vs Glamorgan, Swansea, 2019

WHAT WAS YOUR FIRST CRICKET CLUB? Sheen Park Colts, Wycombe, Buckinghamshire
WHAT WERE YOU DOING WHEN ENGLAND WON THE WORLD CUP? Carrying on like a wally
HOW WOULD YOU DISMISS STEVE SMITH? Mental warfare
WHAT EXCITES YOU ABOUT THE HUNDRED? The combination of young English talent and overseas superstars
BIGGEST TOPIC OF DISCUSSION IN YOUR DRESSING ROOM? Quotes from The Inbetweeners (sitcom)
MOST INTERESTING TEAMMATE? Tony Palladino – because of his extensive knowledge of FIFA Ultimate Team (from the video game)
CRICKETING HERO? Andrew Flintoff
SURPRISING FACT ABOUT A TEAMMATE? Max Holden has never scored in a game of warm-up football
WHICH BOOK MEANS MOST TO YOU? To Kill a Mockingbird by Harper Lee
TWITTER: @tom_lace

Batting	Mat	Inns	NO	Runs	HS	Ave	SR	100	50	Ct	St
First-class	16	31	1	1084	143	36.13	46.30	3	4	12	0
List A	9	7	0	115	48	16.42	78.76	0	0	2	0
Bowling	**Mat**	**Balls**	**Runs**	**Wkts**	**BBI**	**BBM**	**Ave**	**Econ**	**SR**	**5w**	**10**
First-class	16	-	-	-	-	-	-	-	-	-	-
List A	9	12	20	2	2/20	2/20	10.00	10.00	6.0	0	0

LANCASHIRE

DANIEL LAMB RHB / RFM / R0 / W0

FULL NAME: Daniel John Lamb
BORN: September 7, 1995, Preston, Lancashire
SQUAD NO: 26
HEIGHT: 6ft
NICKNAME: Lamby, Sherman, Wust
EDUCATION: St Michael's CE High School, Chorley; Cardinal Newman College, Preston; Edgehill University
TEAMS: Lancashire
ROLE: Allrounder
DEBUT: First-class: 2018; List A: 2017; T20: 2017

BEST BATTING: 49 Lancashire vs Glamorgan, Colwyn Bay, 2019
BEST BOWLING: 4-70 Lancashire vs Glamorgan, Colwyn Bay, 2019

FAMILY TIES? My younger sister Emma plays for Lancashire and we have played together regularly for Bramhall in the Cheshire Premier League
WHAT WAS YOUR FIRST CRICKET CLUB? Hoghton CC, Lancashire. There's a massive hill on the outfield
CRICKETING HERO? Andrew Flintoff
WHICH BOWLER WOULD YOU LEAST LIKE TO FACE? Shane Warne
WHO WOULD YOU ASK TO BAT FOR YOUR LIFE? Matty Parkinson – I enjoy seeing him get into the battle
SURPRISING FACT ABOUT YOU? I was Blackburn Rovers FC Academy goalkeeper from U9 to U16 level
TWITTER: @lamby236

Batting	Mat	Inns	NO	Runs	HS	Ave	SR	100	50	Ct	St
First-class	5	7	2	106	49	21.20	43.98	0	0	1	0
List A	2	2	2	5	4*	-	83.33	0	0	0	0
T20s	11	4	1	54	24	18.00	93.10	0	0	1	0
Bowling	**Mat**	**Balls**	**Runs**	**Wkts**	**BBI**	**BBM**	**Ave**	**Econ**	**SR**	**5w**	**10**
First-class	5	324	235	6	4/70	6/89	39.16	4.35	54.0	0	0
List A	2	120	108	4	2/51	2/51	27.00	5.40	30.0	0	0
T20s	11	156	210	10	3/30	3/30	21.00	8.07	15.6	0	0

MATT LAMB

RHB / RM / R0 / W0

FULL NAME: Matthew Lamb
BORN: July 19, 1996, Wolverhampton, Staffordshire
SQUAD NO: 7
HEIGHT: 6ft 2in
NICKNAME: Jonny
EDUCATION: North Bromsgrove High School, Worcestershire
TEAMS: Warwickshire
ROLE: Batsman
DEBUT: First-class: 2016; List A: 2017; T20: 2019

BEST BATTING: 173 Warwickshire vs Essex, Edgbaston, 2019
BEST BOWLING: 1-15 Warwickshire vs Essex, Edgbaston, 2019

FAMILY TIES? My grandad and dad didn't have any interest in cricket. It was my brother who was the only one who played and subsequently got me involved
WHAT WAS YOUR FIRST CRICKET CLUB? Barnt Green CC, Worcestershire
BEST INNINGS YOU'VE SEEN? KP's hundred at The Oval in 2005
CRICKETING HERO? Andrew Flintoff
WHICH RULE WOULD YOU CHANGE ABOUT CRICKET? Eight runs if you hit it out the stands
SURPRISING FACT ABOUT YOU? I was about to quit cricket until I was luckily selected for a Second XI game against Worcestershire in September 2015 and managed to score 142
WHICH BOOK MEANS MOST TO YOU? Muhammad Ali's autobiography
TWITTER: @Lamb_Matt

Batting	Mat	Inns	NO	Runs	HS	Ave	SR	100	50	Ct	St
First-class	16	28	2	690	173	26.53	40.82	1	3	5	0
List A	3	3	0	61	47	20.33	89.70	0	0	1	0
T20s	5	5	2	102	35	34.00	130.76	0	0	0	0
Bowling	**Mat**	**Balls**	**Runs**	**Wkts**	**BBI**	**BBM**	**Ave**	**Econ**	**SR**	**5w**	**10**
First-class	16	362	254	6	1/15	1/15	42.33	4.20	60.3	0	0
List A	3	6	9	0	-	-	-	9.00	-	0	0
T20s	5	-	-	-	-	-	-	-	-	-	-

SANDEEP LAMICHHANE RHB / LB

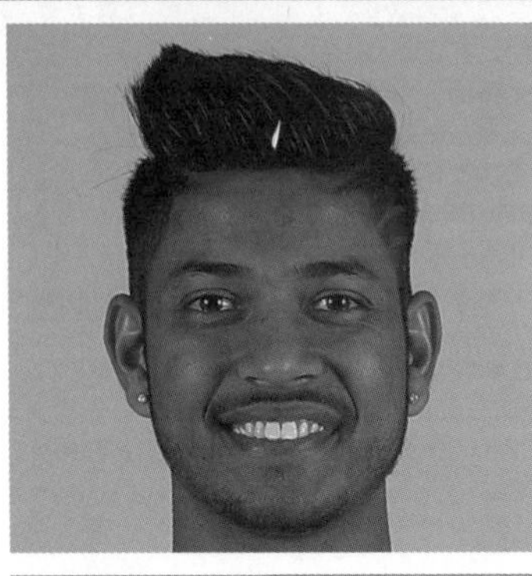

FULL NAME: Sandeep Lamichhane
BORN: August 2, 2000, Aruchaur, Syangja District, Nepal
SQUAD NO: TBC
HEIGHT: 5ft 7in
TEAMS: Nepal, Oval Invincibles, Barbados Tridents, Delhi Capitals, Delhi Daredevils, Lahore Qalandars, Melbourne Stars, Montreal Tigers, St Kitts and Nevis Patriots, Sylhet Sixers
ROLE: Bowler
DEBUT: ODI: 2018; T20I: 2018; First-class: 2019; List A: 2016; T20: 2018

BEST BATTING: 10* Barbados Tridents vs Jamaica Tallawahs, Kingston, 2019 (T20)
BEST BOWLING: 4-10 Lahore Qalanders vs Quetta Gladiators, Dubai, 2019 (T20)

TWITTER: IamSandeep25
NOTES: The Nepal leg-spinner has gone from strength to strength since finishing the 2016 U19 World Cup as the tournament's second-highest wicket-taker. Later that year former Australia captain Michael Clarke invited him to play in Sydney for the Western Suburbs District Cricket Club. In 2018 he became the first Nepalese cricketer to receive a contract in the IPL after he was bought by Delhi Daredevils. He has also played in T20 competitions in Canada, Bangladesh, Afghanistan, Pakistan, Australia and the Caribbean. Lamichhane made his T20I debut against West Indies in 2018 and his first appearance in Australia's Big Bash the following year. In February 2020 he took the second-best figures by an Associate bowler in an ODI – 6-16 as Nepal bowled out USA for 35. Oval Invincibles selected Lamichhane for The Hundred in the £100k salary band

Batting	Mat	Inns	NO	Runs	HS	Ave	SR	100	50	Ct	St
ODIs	10	8	2	78	28	13.00	74.28	0	0	2	0
T20Is	21	10	4	24	9	4.00	70.58	0	0	3	0
First-class	1	2	1	64	39*	64.00	160.00	0	0	0	0
List A	31	19	7	114	28	9.50	51.58	0	0	10	0
T20s	77	24	13	59	10*	5.36	73.75	0	0	13	0
Bowling	**Mat**	**Balls**	**Runs**	**Wkts**	**BBI**	**BBM**	**Ave**	**Econ**	**SR**	**5w**	**10**
ODIs	10	535	375	23	6/16	6/16	16.30	4.20	23.2	1	0
T20Is	21	456	495	34	4/20	4/20	14.55	6.51	13.4	0	0
First-class	1	216	134	3	3/84	3/134	44.66	3.72	72.0	0	0
List A	31	1650	1127	65	6/16	6/16	17.33	4.09	25.3	2	0
T20s	77	1657	1913	105	4/10	4/10	18.21	6.92	15.7	0	0

TOM LAMMONBY LHB / LMF / R0 / W0

FULL NAME: Thomas Alexander Lammonby
BORN: June 2, 2000, Exeter, Devon
SQUAD NO: 15
HEIGHT: 6ft
NICKNAME: Lammers, Bubbles
EDUCATION: Exeter School
TEAMS: Somerset, England U19
ROLE: Allrounder
DEBUT: T20: 2019

WHAT WAS YOUR FIRST CRICKET CLUB? Exeter CC, Devon
WHAT WERE YOU DOING WHEN ENGLAND WON THE WORLD CUP? Watching it down at my local cricket club
BIGGEST TOPIC OF DISCUSSION IN YOUR DRESSING ROOM? Brexit
MOST INTERESTING TEAMMATE? Steve Davies – getting to hear all about the players he's played with but also people outside of cricket. He's always helpful to others, especially the next generation of cricketers
BEST INNINGS YOU'VE SEEN? Chris Rogers hitting his maiden Test century against England at Chester-le-Street in the 2013 Ashes. Gritty and unconventional
WHICH RULE WOULD YOU CHANGE ABOUT CRICKET? Hit it out of the ground = 12 runs
BIGGEST CRICKETING REGRET? Not playing at the 2018 U19 World Cup because of injury
CRICKET STAR OF THE FUTURE? Teague Wyllie (Australia U16)
IF YOU WERE AN ANIMAL, WHICH WOULD IT BE? I'd like to be a tiger but I'm actually more of a goldfish – forgetful, a bit boring, but everyone has wanted one
TWITTER: @TomLammonby

Batting	Mat	Inns	NO	Runs	HS	Ave	SR	100	50	Ct	St
T20s	12	9	3	88	31	14.66	139.68	0	0	5	0
Bowling	**Mat**	**Balls**	**Runs**	**Wkts**	**BBI**	**BBM**	**Ave**	**Econ**	**SR**	**5w**	**10**
T20s	12	120	218	8	2/32	2/32	27.25	10.90	15.0	0	0

GEORGE LAVELLE

LHB / WK / R0 / W0

FULL NAME: George Isaac Davies Lavelle
BORN: March 24, 2000, Lancashire
SQUAD NO: 24
HEIGHT: 5ft 8in
NICKNAME: Spizza
EDUCATION: Merchant Taylors' School, Crosby, Merseyside
TEAMS: Lancashire, England U19
ROLE: Wicketkeeper/batsman

WHAT WAS YOUR FIRST CRICKET CLUB? Ormskirk CC, Lancashire
BIGGEST TOPIC OF DISCUSSION IN YOUR DRESSING ROOM? Hair loss
WHICH RULE WOULD YOU CHANGE ABOUT CRICKET? Byes down the legside shouldn't go down against the wicketkeeper
BEST INNINGS YOU'VE SEEN? Alastair Cook's 294 against India at Edgbaston in 2011. Just to be able to concentrate for nearly 13 hours is incredible
BIGGEST CRICKETING REGRET? Losing the Royal London Club Championship final with Ormskirk against Wanstead and Snaresbrook at Chelmsford in 2017
CRICKET STAR OF THE FUTURE? Jack Morley (Lancashire)
IF YOU WERE AN ANIMAL, WHICH WOULD IT BE? A bear – have to be adaptable
TWITTER: @Glavelle_181
NOTES: The 20-year-old wicket-keeper batsman signed his first professional contract with Lancashire ahead of the 2019 season and had it extended at the end of last summer. Lavelle scored 342 runs in eight Second XI Championship matches in 2019, as well as turning out regularly for his club side Ormskirk in the Liverpool and District Competition. Though yet to make his first-team debut for Lancashire, he played a Youth Test for England U19 in 2018, scoring 25 in the second innings to help beat South Africa U19 by four wickets at Chester-le-Street. This season he will be keen to learn all he can from BJ Watling, the veteran Kiwi wicketkeeper who has joined Lancashire for the first nine Championship games

DANIEL LAWRENCE RHB / OB / R1 / W0

FULL NAME: Daniel William Lawrence
BORN: July 12, 1997, Whipps Cross, Essex
SQUAD NO: 28
EDUCATION: Trinity Catholic High School, Woodford Green, London
TEAMS: Essex, London Spirit, England Lions
ROLE: Batsman
DEBUT: First-class: 2015; List A: 2016; T20: 2015

ESSEX / LONDON SPIRIT

BEST BATTING: 161 Essex vs Surrey, The Oval, 2015
BEST BOWLING: 2-63 Essex vs MCC, Barbados, 2018
COUNTY CAP: 2017

FAMILY TIES? My dad is the groundsman at Chingford Cricket Club. My great uncle played for England
CRICKETING HEROES? Ricky Ponting, Graeme Smith, AB de Villiers
NON-CRICKETING HEROES? Martin Luther King, David Beckham
TWITTER: @Lawrenc28Daniel
NOTES: The top-order batsman has been on England's radar ever since he made 161 as a 17-year-old in 2015 in his second Championship appearance. The following year he passed 1,000 first-class runs in his first full season at Chelmsford and was the Cricket Writers' Young Player of the Year in 2017 after contributing three hundreds to Essex's title-winning campaign. He made his England Lions debut that year. Lawrence came back strongly from a difficult 2018 season by scoring 725 Championship runs last summer and he was in red-hot form during England Lions 2019/20 tour down under, scoring 125 in the first-class match against Australia A at the MCG after a blistering 190 off 194 balls in the tour game against a Cricket Australia XI at Hobart. He also took 11 wickets with his off-spin

Batting	Mat	Inns	NO	Runs	HS	Ave	SR	100	50	Ct	St
First-class	70	111	12	3804	161	38.42	52.03	10	17	55	0
List A	28	25	0	670	115	26.80	89.09	1	4	9	0
T20s	51	46	6	1086	86	27.15	142.33	0	5	16	0
Bowling	**Mat**	**Balls**	**Runs**	**Wkts**	**BBI**	**BBM**	**Ave**	**Econ**	**SR**	**5w**	**10**
First-class	70	642	377	9	2/63	2/8	41.88	3.52	71.3	0	0
List A	28	573	597	11	3/35	3/35	54.27	6.25	52.0	0	0
T20s	51	270	325	17	3/21	3/21	19.11	7.22	15.8	0	0

JACK LEACH

LHB / SLA / R0 / W3

FULL NAME: Matthew Jack Leach
BORN: June 22, 1991, Taunton, Somerset
SQUAD NO: 17
HEIGHT: 6ft
NICKNAME: Nut
EDUCATION: Bishop Fox's Community School; Richard Huish College; Cardiff Metropolitan University
TEAMS: England, Somerset
ROLE: Bowler
DEBUT: Test: 2018; First-class: 2012; List A: 2012

BEST BATTING: 92 England vs Ireland, Lord's, 2019
BEST BOWLING: 8-85 Somerset vs Essex, Taunton, 2018
COUNTY CAP: 2017

WHAT WAS YOUR FIRST CRICKET CLUB? Taunton Deane CC, Somerset
HOW WOULD YOU DISMISS STEVE SMITH? Keep my foot behind the line – see the 2019 Old Trafford Test
WHAT EXCITES YOU ABOUT THE HUNDRED? Cricket on terrestrial TV
BEST INNINGS YOU'VE SEEN? Marcus Trescothick's 13-ball fifty in a T20 in 2010
CRICKETING HERO? Jos Buttler
WHICH RULE WOULD YOU CHANGE ABOUT CRICKET? You can be given lbw even if you are hit outside the line
SURPRISING FACT ABOUT YOU? I wrote a letter to Marcus Trescothick asking for advice when I was about 10 years old. He sent me a long reply and I still have the letter. What a man
CRICKET STAR OF THE FUTURE? Luke Poole (Taunton St Andrews CC)
TWITTER: @jackleach1991

Batting	Mat	Inns	NO	Runs	HS	Ave	SR	100	50	Ct	St
Tests	10	18	6	220	92	18.33	39.71	0	1	5	0
First-class	89	122	32	1123	92	12.47	35.91	0	3	37	0
List A	16	5	2	22	18	7.33	44.00	0	0	9	0
Bowling	**Mat**	**Balls**	**Runs**	**Wkts**	**BBI**	**BBM**	**Ave**	**Econ**	**SR**	**5w**	**10**
Tests	10	2072	987	34	5/83	8/153	29.02	2.85	60.9	1	0
First-class	89	16583	7474	290	8/85	12/102	25.77	2.70	57.1	20	3
List A	16	824	641	21	3/7	3/7	30.52	4.66	39.2	0	0

JOE LEACH

RHB / RFM / R0 / W3

FULL NAME: Joseph Leach
BORN: October 30, 1990, Stafford
SQUAD NO: 23
HEIGHT: 6ft
NICKNAME: Blockers, SSSB
EDUCATION: Shrewsbury School; University of Leeds
TEAMS: Worcestershire
ROLE: Allrounder
DEBUT: First-class: 2012; List A: 2012; T20: 2013

BEST BATTING: 114 Worcestershire vs Gloucestershire, Cheltenham, 2013
BEST BOWLING: 6-73 Worcestershire vs Warwickshire, Edgbaston, 2015
COUNTY CAP: 2012

WHAT WAS YOUR FIRST CRICKET CLUB? Stone CC, Staffordshire. Never play on the back foot at Stone!
HOW WOULD YOU DISMISS STEVE SMITH? Give the ball to Daryl Mitchell
BIGGEST TOPIC OF DISCUSSION IN YOUR DRESSING ROOM? The Hundred
MOST INTERESTING TEAMMATE? Thilan Samaraweera – because of the stories he told about the attack on the Sri Lanka bus in Lahore
WHICH RULE WOULD YOU CHANGE ABOUT CRICKET? It's far too much a batsman's game, so I'd say three play-and-misses in a row and you're out
BIGGEST CRICKETING REGRET? Being injured on T20 Finals Day in 2018
CRICKET STAR OF THE FUTURE? Harry Richardson (Alan's five-year-old)
IF YOU WERE AN ANIMAL, WHICH WOULD IT BE? A bear
TWITTER: @joeleach230

Batting	Mat	Inns	NO	Runs	HS	Ave	SR	100	50	Ct	St
First-class	88	132	16	2872	114	24.75	63.58	2	18	22	0
List A	38	28	8	539	63	26.95	100.00	0	1	13	0
T20s	54	33	8	261	24	10.44	113.47	0	0	10	0
Bowling	**Mat**	**Balls**	**Runs**	**Wkts**	**BBI**	**BBM**	**Ave**	**Econ**	**SR**	**5w**	**10**
First-class	88	14157	8125	311	6/73	10/122	26.12	3.44	45.5	13	1
List A	38	1707	1719	43	4/30	4/30	39.97	6.04	39.6	0	0
T20s	54	849	1355	52	5/33	5/33	26.05	9.57	16.3	1	0

JACK LEANING

RHB / RM / R0 / W0

FULL NAME: Jack Andrew Leaning
BORN: October 18, 1993, Bristol
SQUAD NO: 34
HEIGHT: 6ft
EDUCATION: Archbishop Holgate's School, York; York College
TEAMS: Kent, England U19, Yorkshire
ROLE: Batsman
DEBUT: First-class: 2013; List A: 2012; T20: 2013

BEST BATTING: 123 Yorkshire vs Somerset, Taunton, 2015
BEST BOWLING: 2-20 Yorkshire vs Hampshire, Southampton, 2019
COUNTY CAP: 2016 (Yorkshire)

TWITTER: @JackLeaning1
NOTES: The former Yorkshire batsman signed for Kent last August in a bid to revive a career which started so promisingly. Son of former York City goalkeeper Andy, Leaning wrote himself into the Yorkshire record books when he hit an unbeaten 164 for the county's U14 side against Cheshire. He was Yorkshire's Academy Player of the Year in 2012 and made his List A debut in the same season. Leaning made his first-class debut in 2013 against Surrey at Headingley and played 10 Championship matches in 2014, top-scoring with 99. He scored his maiden Championship century in 2015 and added two more on his way to 922 runs, earning him the Cricket Writers' Club Young Player of the Year award. But the runs have dried up since, and he hasn't scored a first-class hundred since 2017

Batting	Mat	Inns	NO	Runs	HS	Ave	SR	100	50	Ct	St
First-class	68	108	11	2955	123	30.46	41.93	4	16	52	0
List A	50	43	7	1061	131*	29.47	79.29	2	5	24	0
T20s	51	45	11	952	64	28.00	132.96	0	2	24	0
Bowling	**Mat**	**Balls**	**Runs**	**Wkts**	**BBI**	**BBM**	**Ave**	**Econ**	**SR**	**5w**	**10**
First-class	68	700	455	8	2/20	2/25	56.87	3.90	87.5	0	0
List A	50	303	286	9	5/22	5/22	31.77	5.66	33.6	1	0
T20s	51	24	45	1	1/15	1/15	45.00	11.25	24.0	0	0

ALEX LEES

LHB / LB / R2 / W0 / MVP63

FULL NAME: Alexander Zak Lees
BORN: April 14, 1993, Halifax, Yorkshire
SQUAD NO: 19
HEIGHT: 6ft 3in
NICKNAME: Leesy
EDUCATION: Holy Trinity Senior School, Halifax
TEAMS: Durham, England Lions, Yorkshire
ROLE: Batsman
DEBUT: First-class: 2010; List A: 2011; T20: 2013

BEST BATTING: 275* Yorkshire vs Derbyshire, Chesterfield, 2013
BEST BOWLING: 2-51 Yorkshire vs Middlesex, Lord's, 2016
COUNTY CAP: 2014 (Yorkshire)

WHAT WAS YOUR FIRST CRICKET CLUB? Bradshaw & Illingworth CC, Halifax
HOW WOULD YOU DISMISS STEVE SMITH? Round the wicket
BIGGEST TOPIC OF DISCUSSION IN YOUR DRESSING ROOM? The draft for The Hundred
MOST INTERESTING TEAMMATE? Mark Wood
CRICKETING HERO? Brian Lara
SURPRISING FACT ABOUT YOU? I do a bit of magic on the side
IF YOU WERE AN ANIMAL, WHICH WOULD IT BE? A dog
TWITTER: @aleesy14
NOTES: The left-handed opener joined Durham on a three-year permanent deal in August 2018 following a tough couple of seasons at Yorkshire. The former Cricket Writers' Club Young Player of the Year appears to have recovered the form of his early career, falling narrowly short of 1,000 first-class runs last summer and also impressing in 50-over cricket

Batting	Mat	Inns	NO	Runs	HS	Ave	SR	100	50	Ct	St
First-class	110	190	13	6064	275*	34.25	48.25	15	27	77	0
List A	54	49	5	1533	115	34.84	75.48	2	12	18	0
T20s	45	43	4	985	67*	25.25	119.82	0	4	15	0
Bowling	**Mat**	**Balls**	**Runs**	**Wkts**	**BBI**	**BBM**	**Ave**	**Econ**	**SR**	**5w**	**10**
First-class	110	55	77	2	2/51	2/51	38.50	8.40	27.5	0	0
List A	54	-	-	-	-	-	-	-	-	-	-
T20s	45	-	-	-	-	-	-	-	-	-	-

TOBY LESTER

LHB / LFM / R0 / W0

FULL NAME: Toby James Lester
BORN: April 5, 1993, Blackpool
SQUAD NO: 5
HEIGHT: 6ft 4in
NICKNAME: Tobs
EDUCATION: Baines High School, Blackpool; Rossall School, Lancashire; Loughborough University
TEAMS: Lancashire, Warwickshire
ROLE: Bowler
DEBUT: First-class: 2012; T20: 2018

BEST BATTING: 8 Lancashire vs Worcestershire, Southport, 2018
BEST BOWLING: 4-41 Warwickshire vs Surrey, The Oval, 2019

WHAT GOT YOU INTO CRICKET? Playing cricket in the back garden with my brothers
BEST MOMENT IN CRICKET? Making my debut for Lancashire and taking my first wicket
CRICKETING HERO? Andrew Flintoff
NON-CRICKETING HERO? Will Ferrell
TWITTER: @lobylester
NOTES: The left-arm pace bowler made his first-class debut for Loughborough MCCU in 2014. Lester impressed with his performances in the Second XI in 2015, earning a first call-up to the senior side for two matches and a Championship debut against Essex at Old Trafford. He has played only three Championship matches for Lancashire since then but was a regular in the T20 side in 2018, taking 15 wickets at an average of 22.33. Lester had a loan spell at Warwickshire last summer, taking a first-class best of 4-41 against Surrey at The Oval

Batting	Mat	Inns	NO	Runs	HS	Ave	SR	100	50	Ct	St
First-class	13	15	9	22	8	3.66	18.18	0	0	3	0
T20s	13	4	2	8	7*	4.00	88.88	0	0	3	0
Bowling	**Mat**	**Balls**	**Runs**	**Wkts**	**BBI**	**BBM**	**Ave**	**Econ**	**SR**	**5w**	**10**
First-class	13	1771	1132	17	4/41	4/129	66.58	3.83	104.1	0	0
T20s	13	238	350	15	4/25	4/25	23.33	8.82	15.8	0	0

RICHARD LEVI RHB / RM / R0 / W0

FULL NAME: Richard Ernst Levi
BORN: January 14, 1988, Johannesburg
SQUAD NO: 88
HEIGHT: 6ft
NICKNAME: Bear
EDUCATION: Wynberg Boys' High School, Cape Town; University of South Africa
TEAMS: South Africa, Northamptonshire, Cape Cobras, Mumbai Indians, Somerset, Western Province
ROLE: Batsman
DEBUT: T20I: 2012; First-class: 2006; List A: 2005; T20: 2008

BEST BATTING: 168 Northamptonshire vs Essex, Northampton, 2015

COUNTY CAP: 2017 (Northamptonshire)

WHAT WAS YOUR FIRST CRICKET CLUB? Claremont CC, Cape Town, South Africa. Feeder club for Wynberg Boys' and Western Province
HOW WOULD YOU DISMISS STEVE SMITH? In the warm-ups
WHAT EXCITES YOU ABOUT THE HUNDRED? The new strategies that will develop
BIGGEST TOPIC OF DISCUSSION IN YOUR DRESSING ROOM? Who has the best coffee
MOST INTERESTING TEAMMATE? Alistair Gray (Cape Cobras)
CRICKETING HERO? Gary Kirsten
BIGGEST CRICKETING REGRET? Not bowling
CRICKET STAR OF THE FUTURE? My unborn son
IF YOU WERE AN ANIMAL, WHICH WOULD IT BE? A bear. It's pretty self-explanatory, right?
TWITTER: @RichardLevi88

Batting	Mat	Inns	NO	Runs	HS	Ave	SR	100	50	Ct	St
T20Is	13	13	2	236	117*	21.45	141.31	1	1	4	0
First-class	105	174	18	5703	168	36.55	68.17	10	32	88	0
List A	140	132	6	4614	166	36.61	104.53	8	29	44	0
T20s	205	196	13	5226	117*	28.55	144.80	3	33	54	0
Bowling	**Mat**	**Balls**	**Runs**	**Wkts**	**BBI**	**BBM**	**Ave**	**Econ**	**SR**	**5w**	**10**
T20Is	13	-	-	-	-	-	-	-	-	-	-
First-class	105	-	-	-	-	-	-	-	-	-	-
List A	140	-	-	-	-	-	-	-	-	-	-
T20s	205	-	-	-	-	-	-	-	-	-	-

JAKE LIBBY RHB / OB / R0 / W0

FULL NAME: Jacob Daniel Libby
BORN: January 3, 1993, Plymouth, Devon
SQUAD NO: 2
HEIGHT: 5ft 8in
NICKNAME: Libs
EDUCATION: Plymouth College; Truro College, Cornwall; Cardiff Metropolitan University
TEAMS: Worcestershire, Northamptonshire, Nottinghamshire
ROLE: Batsman
DEBUT: First-class: 2014; List A: 2019; T20: 2018

BEST BATTING: 144 Nottinghamshire vs Durham, Chester-le-Street, 2016
BEST BOWLING: 1-13 Northamptonshire vs Leicestershire, Leicester, 2016

FAMILY TIES? My brother captains Callington CC in the Cornish Premier League
WHAT WAS YOUR FIRST CRICKET CLUB? Menheniot & Looe CC, Cornwall – where I used to watch my dad play on Saturday
HOW WOULD YOU DISMISS STEVE SMITH? Not possible, he's an alien
BIGGEST TOPIC OF DISCUSSION IN YOUR DRESSING ROOM? Golf
MOST INTERESTING TEAMMATE? Luke Wood – he's mad
CRICKETING HERO? Marcus Trescothick – I grew up watching him at Taunton
WHICH RULE WOULD YOU CHANGE ABOUT CRICKET? Ban the Dukes ball!
CRICKET STAR OF THE FUTURE? Connor Marshall (Nottinghamshire Academy)
WHICH BOOK MEANS MOST TO YOU? Relentless – From Good to Great to Unstoppable by Tim Grover
TWITTER: @JakeLibby1

Batting	Mat	Inns	NO	Runs	HS	Ave	SR	100	50	Ct	St
First-class	55	96	6	2574	144	28.60	42.20	5	11	19	0
List A	7	5	0	117	66	23.40	101.73	0	1	1	0
T20s	20	14	3	369	58	33.54	134.18	0	1	9	0
Bowling	**Mat**	**Balls**	**Runs**	**Wkts**	**BBI**	**BBM**	**Ave**	**Econ**	**SR**	**5w**	**10**
First-class	55	460	296	4	1/13	1/22	74.00	3.86	115.0	0	0
List A	7	-	-	-	-	-	-	-	-	-	-
T20s	20	6	11	1	1/11	1/11	11.00	11.00	6.0	0	0

ARRON LILLEY

RHB / OB / R0 / W0

FULL NAME: Arron Mark Lilley
BORN: April 1, 1991, Tameside, Lancashire
SQUAD NO: 19
HEIGHT: 6ft 2in
NICKNAME: Bigshow, Lil, Azza
EDUCATION: Mossley Hollins High School, Tameside; Ashton Sixth Form
TEAMS: Leicestershire, Lancashire
ROLE: Bowler
DEBUT: First-class: 2013; List A: 2012; T20: 2013

BEST BATTING: 63 Lancashire vs Derbyshire, Southport, 2015
BEST BOWLING: 5-23 Lancashire vs Derbyshire, Southport, 2015

WHAT WAS YOUR FIRST CRICKET CLUB? Micklehurst CC, Greater Manchester. My grandad and dad played there before me
HOW WOULD YOU DISMISS STEVE SMITH? Pepper him
BIGGEST TOPIC OF DISCUSSION IN YOUR DRESSING ROOM? My hair
CRICKETING HERO? Shane Warne
WHICH RULE WOULD YOU CHANGE ABOUT CRICKET? Ban the bouncer!
SURPRISING FACT ABOUT YOU? I have a didgeridoo at home
BIGGEST CRICKETING REGRET? Not winning the T20 Blast with Lancashire in 2018 after getting to Finals Day
WHICH BOOK MEANS MOST TO YOU? Blessed – The Autobiography by George Best
TWITTER: @Arronlilley20

Batting	Mat	Inns	NO	Runs	HS	Ave	SR	100	50	Ct	St
First-class	15	18	5	426	63	32.76	94.03	0	2	4	0
List A	19	11	1	100	25	10.00	113.63	0	0	10	0
T20s	85	56	9	786	66	16.72	155.33	0	1	43	0
Bowling	**Mat**	**Balls**	**Runs**	**Wkts**	**BBI**	**BBM**	**Ave**	**Econ**	**SR**	**5w**	**10**
First-class	15	2685	1407	40	5/23	6/151	35.17	3.14	67.1	2	0
List A	19	570	530	15	4/30	4/30	35.33	5.57	38.0	0	0
T20s	85	1064	1306	43	3/31	3/31	30.37	7.36	24.7	0	0

MIDDLESEX

DAN LINCOLN RHB / RM / R0 / W0

FULL NAME: Daniel John Lincoln
BORN: May 26, 1995, Frimley, Surrey
SQUAD NO: 43
HEIGHT: 6ft 2in
NICKNAME: Lincs, Abraham
EDUCATION: Edgbarrow School, Crowthorne, Berkshire
TEAMS: Middlesex
ROLE: Batsman
DEBUT: T20: 2019

WHAT WAS YOUR FIRST CRICKET CLUB? Finchampstead CC, Berkshire
MOST INTERESTING TEAMMATE? Jamie Mackie – pro footballer currently playing for Oxford United. I was a young apprentice when he was at Reading FC and to see him torment his teammates and the staff was hilarious. He'd constantly have the room in tears of laughter
IF YOU WERE AN ANIMAL, WHICH WOULD IT BE? A cobra – deadly, short-tempered and extremely fast. And they've got a beer named after them
TWITTER: @Dan1Lincoln
NOTES: The hard-hitting batsman signed a one-year rookie contract with Middlesex in January. Last July Lincoln walloped 118 from only 53 balls for the Second XI and was called up to the senior squad a week later to replace the injured AB de Villiers for the T20 Blast match against Gloucestershire at Cheltenham. Coming in at No.3, the 24-year-old showed no signs of nerves with a cool 24-ball 30 which included four boundaries and one six. "Dan enters our elite environment at an older age than most but his desire to improve and make the most of his opportunities is clear to see," said director of cricket Angus Fraser. "In his own uncomplicated way, he scored more Second XI runs than anybody at the club in 2019 and is one of the best fielders I have seen. This skill is undoubtedly helped by him being a semi-professional goalkeeper for Hampton and Richmond Borough Football Club. His slip catching is almost comparable to that of Ollie Rayner"

Batting	Mat	Inns	NO	Runs	HS	Ave	SR	100	50	Ct	St
T20s	3	3	0	38	30	12.66	108.57	0	0	3	0
Bowling	**Mat**	**Balls**	**Runs**	**Wkts**	**BBI**	**BBM**	**Ave**	**Econ**	**SR**	**5w**	**10**
T20s	3	-	-	-	-	-	-	-	-	-	-

LIAM LIVINGSTONE RHB / LB / R0 / W0 / MVP49

FULL NAME: Liam Stephen Livingstone
BORN: August 4, 1993, Barrow-in-Furness, Cumbria
SQUAD NO: 7
HEIGHT: 6ft 2in
EDUCATION: Chetwynde School, Barrow-in-Furness
TEAMS: England, Lancashire, Birmingham Phoenix, Karachi Kings, Perth Scorchers, Peshawar Zalmi, Rajasthan Royals
ROLE: Allrounder
DEBUT: T20I: 2018; First-class: 2016; List A: 2015; T20: 2015

BEST BATTING: 224 Lancashire vs Warwickshire, Old Trafford, 2017
BEST BOWLING: 6-52 Lancashire vs Surrey, Old Trafford, 2017
COUNTY CAP: 2017

WHAT GOT YOU INTO CRICKET? Playing on the outfield at Barrow CC from a very early age
FAMILY TIES? My father and brother played low-level club cricket
BEST MOMENT IN CRICKET? Winning the T20 Blast in 2015
CRICKETING HEROES? Andrew Flintoff – so good to watch as a young kid. Shane Warne – I was a leg-spinner growing up
NON-CRICKETING HERO? David Beckham
SURPRISING FACT ABOUT YOU? I scored 350 in a club game. I support Blackburn Rovers FC
TWITTER: @liaml4893

Batting	Mat	Inns	NO	Runs	HS	Ave	SR	100	50	Ct	St
T20Is	2	2	0	16	16	8.00	84.21	0	0	0	0
First-class	54	85	14	2955	224	41.61	59.48	7	15	68	0
List A	55	46	3	1552	129	36.09	99.48	1	10	25	0
T20s	107	102	9	2515	100	27.04	140.42	1	14	46	0
Bowling	**Mat**	**Balls**	**Runs**	**Wkts**	**BBI**	**BBM**	**Ave**	**Econ**	**SR**	**5w**	**10**
T20Is	2	-	-	-	-	-	-	-	-	-	-
First-class	54	2700	1214	34	6/52	6/52	35.70	2.69	79.4	1	0
List A	55	1305	1134	23	3/51	3/51	49.30	5.21	56.7	0	0
T20s	107	430	573	33	4/17	4/17	17.36	7.99	13.0	0	0

GLAMORGAN

DAVID LLOYD RHB / OB / R0 / W0 / MVP51

FULL NAME: David Liam Lloyd
BORN: June 15, 1992, St Asaph, Denbighshire, Wales
SQUAD NO: 73
HEIGHT: 5ft 9in
NICKNAME: Dai, Ramos
EDUCATION: Darland High School, Wrexham; Shrewsbury School
TEAMS: Glamorgan
ROLE: Batsman
DEBUT: First-class: 2012; List A: 2014; T20: 2014

BEST BATTING: 119 Glamorgan vs Gloucestershire, Bristol, 2018
BEST BOWLING: 3-36 Glamorgan vs Northamptonshire, Swansea, 2016

FAMILY TIES? My father and both of my uncles played local cricket and represented Wales Minor Counties
WHAT WAS YOUR FIRST CRICKET CLUB? Brymbo CC, Clwyd, Wales
BEST ADVICE RECEIVED? Work hard, play hard
WHAT WERE YOU DOING WHEN ENGLAND WON THE WORLD CUP? Playing golf
BEST INNINGS YOU'VE SEEN? Mitchell Marsh's maiden Test hundred against England at Perth in the 2017/18 Ashes. Never seen anyone hit the ball so clean
CRICKETING HERO? Brendon McCullum
SURPRISING FACT ABOUT YOU? I support Wrexham FC and I have a degree in Economics
BIGGEST CRICKETING REGRET? Getting 97 not out in a T20 against Kent in 2016
WHICH BOOK MEANS MOST TO YOU? From Nowhere – My Story by Jamie Vardy
TWITTER: @lloyddl2010

Batting	Mat	Inns	NO	Runs	HS	Ave	SR	100	50	Ct	St
First-class	69	116	12	2939	119	28.25	59.55	4	11	34	0
List A	46	40	2	942	92	24.78	85.24	0	5	12	0
T20s	48	42	2	939	97*	23.47	126.04	0	5	15	0
Bowling	**Mat**	**Balls**	**Runs**	**Wkts**	**BBI**	**BBM**	**Ave**	**Econ**	**SR**	**5w**	**10**
First-class	69	4345	2812	61	3/36	3/53	46.09	3.88	71.2	0	0
List A	46	745	741	17	5/53	5/53	43.58	5.96	43.8	1	0
T20s	48	54	81	5	2/13	2/13	16.20	9.00	10.8	0	0

JAMES LOGAN

LHB / SLA / R0 / W0

FULL NAME: James Edwin Graham Logan
BORN: October 12, 1997, Wakefield, Yorkshire
SQUAD NO: 11
NICKNAME: Logi
EDUCATION: Normanton Freestone High School, West Yorkshire; Pontefract New College
TEAMS: Yorkshire
ROLE: Bowler
DEBUT: First-class: 2018

BEST BATTING: 20* Yorkshire vs Warwickshire, York, 2019
BEST BOWLING: 4-22 Yorkshire vs Warwickshire, York, 2019

NOTES: A left-arm spinner, Logan made his first-team debut in a Championship win over Worcestershire at New Road in 2018 and impressed in his one four-day appeareance last summer, taking a career-best 4-22 against Warwickshire at York. The Wakefield-born 22-year-old first represented Yorkshire at U13 level in 2011 and has gone on to play for every age-group, making his Second XI debut in 2014. The following summer he took 8-76 in the second innings of a rain-affected win over Leicestershire at Scarborough. He had made over 50 appearances for the Second XI going into the new season and was part of the Academy team that won a historic league-and-cup double in 2014. Last summer was marred by injuries but he has since returned to fitness and spent February in India on a spin-bowling camp organised by former England bowler Peter Such

Batting	Mat	Inns	NO	Runs	HS	Ave	SR	100	50	Ct	St
First-class	2	3	1	33	20*	16.50	19.41	0	0	1	0
Bowling	**Mat**	**Balls**	**Runs**	**Wkts**	**BBI**	**BBM**	**Ave**	**Econ**	**SR**	**5w**	**10**
First-class	2	198	85	4	4/22	4/41	21.25	2.57	49.5	0	0

CHRIS LYNN RHB / SLA

FULL NAME: Christopher Austin Lynn
BORN: April 10, 1990, Brisbane, Australia
SQUAD NO: TBC
HEIGHT: 6ft
NICKNAME: Lynnsanity
TEAMS: Australia, Northern Superchargers, Brisbane Heat, Hobart Hurricanes, Jamaica Tallawahs, Kolkata Knight Riders, Lahore Qalandars, Queensland, Mumbai Indians, Trinbago Knight Riders
ROLE: Batsman
DEBUT: ODI: 2017; T20I: 2014; First-class: 2010; List A: 2010; T20: 2010

BEST BATTING: 101 Brisbane Heat vs Hobart Hurricanes, Brisbane, 2015 (T20)
BEST BOWLING: 2-15 Brisbane Heat vs Melbourne Renegades, Melbourne, 2013 (T20)

TWITTER: @lynny50
NOTES: An aggressive opener in white-ball cricket, Lynn has excelled as captain for Brisbane Heat in the Big Bash League and been part of a number of teams in the IPL, including the Kolkata Knight Riders between 2014 and 2019. He was bought by Mumbai Indians ahead of the 2020 IPL. Lynn made his T20I debut against England in Hobart in 2014 and his ODI bow three years later but is yet to nail down a position in either format for the national team. The Queenslander holds the record for the highest score in the T10 League, hitting 91 runs from 30 balls playing for the Maratha Arabians against Team Abu Dhabi last November. In December he announced that he would only play T20 cricket henceforth. He was selected by the Leeds-based Northern Superchargers for The Hundred in the £100k category

Batting	Mat	Inns	NO	Runs	HS	Ave	SR	100	50	Ct	St
ODIs	4	4	0	75	44	18.75	84.26	0	0	3	0
T20Is	18	16	1	291	44	19.40	131.67	0	0	3	0
First-class	41	71	8	2743	250	43.53	55.87	6	12	26	0
List A	50	50	6	1597	135	36.29	96.55	2	12	24	0
T20s	184	177	21	5096	113*	32.66	144.15	2	34	54	0
Bowling	**Mat**	**Balls**	**Runs**	**Wkts**	**BBI**	**BBM**	**Ave**	**Econ**	**SR**	**5w**	**10**
ODIs	4	-	-	-	-	-	-	-	-	-	-
T20Is	18	-	-	-	-	-	-	-	-	-	-
First-class	41	84	64	0	-	-	-	4.57	-	0	0
List A	50	69	45	1	1/3	1/3	45.00	3.91	69.0	0	0
T20s	184	78	93	3	2/15	2/15	31.00	7.15	26.0	0	0

NATHAN LYON

RHB / OB / R0 / W0

FULL NAME: Nathan Michael Lyon
BORN: November 20, 1987, Young, New South Wales, Australia
SQUAD NO: 67
NICKNAME: Garry, Gazza
TEAMS: Australia, Hampshire, Adelaide Strikers, New South Wales, South Australia, Sydney Sixers, Worcestershire
ROLE: Bowler
DEBUT: Test: 2011; ODI: 2012; T20I: 2016; First-class: 2011; List A: 2011; T20: 2011

BEST BATTING: 75 New South Wales vs Victoria, Alice Springs, 2016
BEST BOWLING: 8-50 Australia vs India, Bengaluru, 2017

TWITTER: @NathLyon421
NOTES: Hampshire's signing of Nathan Lyon for most if not all of next summer's red-ball campaign is an indication that they are serious Championship contenders this year. With the acquisition of a new groundsman in Simon Lee, who learnt his craft on the spin-friendly pitches of Taunton, it's a sound move to pick up perhaps the most potent finger-spinner of the last decade to spearhead their push for the title. As Australia's premier slow bowler in the post-Warne years – in 2018 he became just the sixth Australian to take 300 Test wickets – Lyon brings immense experience to the job. The fact that Warne, a former Hampshire captain, has helped forge such a strong pathway for Australian cricketers to the south coast was a key factor in Lyon's decision. He said: "It is a fabulous opportunity to be involved with a leading county who have had a long and successful relationship with Australian cricketers"

Batting	Mat	Inns	NO	Runs	HS	Ave	SR	100	50	Ct	St
Tests	96	123	39	1031	47	12.27	46.99	0	0	48	0
ODIs	29	14	10	77	30	19.25	92.77	0	0	7	0
T20Is	2	1	1	4	4*	-	100.00	0	0	0	0
First-class	161	206	61	1899	75	13.09	49.93	0	2	74	0
List A	72	35	19	227	37*	14.18	102.25	0	0	31	0
T20s	46	16	7	55	11	6.11	93.22	0	0	14	0
Bowling	**Mat**	**Balls**	**Runs**	**Wkts**	**BBI**	**BBM**	**Ave**	**Econ**	**SR**	**5w**	**10**
Tests	96	24568	12320	390	8/50	13/154	31.58	3.00	62.9	18	3
ODIs	29	1626	1334	29	4/44	4/44	46.00	4.92	56.0	0	0
T20Is	2	30	48	1	1/33	1/33	48.00	9.60	30.0	0	0
First-class	161	38500	19455	572	8/50	13/154	34.01	3.03	67.3	20	3
List A	72	3913	3179	84	4/10	4/10	37.84	4.87	46.5	0	0
T20s	46	922	1108	54	5/23	5/23	20.51	7.21	17.0	1	0

ADAM LYTH

LHB / OB / R3 / W0 / MVP31

FULL NAME: Adam Lyth
BORN: September 25, 1987, Whitby, Yorkshire
SQUAD NO: 9
HEIGHT: 5ft 9in
NICKNAME: Budge, Peanut
EDUCATION: Caedmon School; Whitby Community School
TEAMS: England, Yorkshire, Northern Superchargers, Rangpur Riders
ROLE: Batsman
DEBUT: Test: 2015; First-class: 2007; List A: 2006; T20: 2008

BEST BATTING: 251 Yorkshire vs Lancashire, Old Trafford, 2014
BEST BOWLING: 2-9 Yorkshire vs Middlesex, Scarborough, 2016
COUNTY CAP: 2010

FAMILY TIES? My brother and dad played for Scarborough and my grandad played for Whitby CC
CRICKETING HERO? Graham Thorpe
SURPRISING FACT? I had trials with Manchester City before choosing cricket
TWITTER: @lythy09
NOTES: The dashing left-handed opener has been one of Yorkshire's more consistent run-getters in the Championship over the last few seasons and has set the standard in white-ball cricket. He was the club's leading run-scorer in T20 cricket in 2017 and 2018. A sharp fielder, Lyth scored his maiden Test hundred against New Zealand in 2015 but was dropped after a poor Ashes later that summer and has not been recalled since

Batting	Mat	Inns	NO	Runs	HS	Ave	SR	100	50	Ct	St
Tests	7	13	0	265	107	20.38	50.09	1	0	8	0
First-class	176	296	14	10674	251	37.85		23	57	231	0
List A	122	115	8	3765	144	35.18	93.84	5	18	55	0
T20s	113	104	3	2605	161	25.79	142.58	1	14	58	0
Bowling	**Mat**	**Balls**	**Runs**	**Wkts**	**BBI**	**BBM**	**Ave**	**Econ**	**SR**	**5w**	**10**
Tests	7	6	0	0	-	-	-	0.00	-	0	0
First-class	176	2689	1624	34	2/9	2/9	47.76	3.62	79.0	0	0
List A	122	360	373	6	2/27	2/27	62.16	6.21	60.0	0	0
T20s	113	252	321	17	5/31	5/31	18.88	7.64	14.8	1	0

WAYNE MADSEN RHB / OB / R5 / W0 / MVP13

FULL NAME: Wayne Lee Madsen
BORN: January 2, 1984, Durban, South Africa
SQUAD NO: 77
HEIGHT: 5ft 11in
NICKNAME: Madders, Mads, Psycho
EDUCATION: Highbury Preparatory School; Kearsney College; University of South Africa
TEAMS: Derbyshire, Manchester Originals, Dolphins, KwaZulu-Natal, Multan Sultans, Peshawar Zalmi
ROLE: Batsman
DEBUT: First-class: 2004; List A: 2004; T20: 2010

BEST BATTING: 231* Derbyshire vs Northamptonshire, Northampton, 2012
BEST BOWLING: 3-45 KwaZulu-Natal vs Eastern Province, Port Elizabeth, 2008
COUNTY CAP: 2011; BENEFIT: 2017

FAMILY TIES? My uncles Trevor Madsen and Henry Fotheringham represented South Africa
WHAT WAS YOUR FIRST CRICKET CLUB? Crusaders CC, Durban, South Africa. Got a golden duck in my first game
HOW WOULD YOU DISMISS STEVE SMITH? Lock the opposition's changing-room door
WHAT EXCITES YOU ABOUT THE HUNDRED? Playing at Old Trafford in front of a full house for the Manchester Originals
BIGGEST TOPIC OF DISCUSSION IN YOUR DRESSING ROOM? Aside from the nature of the pitch, probably Fantasy Football
SURPRISING FACT ABOUT YOU? I hold the Guinness World Record for cricket's version of keepy-uppies: the most bat touches in one minute (282)
CRICKET STAR OF THE FUTURE? Anoop Chima (Derbyshire Academy)
WHICH BOOK MEANS MOST TO YOU? The Bible
IF YOU WERE AN ANIMAL, WHICH WOULD IT BE? An elephant – wise, adaptable to conditions, loyal to its herd and family, quick, strong, agile and flexible
TWITTER: @waynemadsen2017

Batting	Mat	Inns	NO	Runs	HS	Ave	SR	100	50	Ct	St
First-class	184	329	23	11964	231*	39.09	51.64	30	61	189	0
List A	105	97	17	3323	138	41.53	89.93	6	19	69	0
T20s	116	113	20	2814	86*	30.25	132.79	0	19	43	0
Bowling	**Mat**	**Balls**	**Runs**	**Wkts**	**BBI**	**BBM**	**Ave**	**Econ**	**SR**	**5w**	**10**
First-class	184	3079	1708	33	3/45		51.75	3.32	93.3	0	0
List A	105	668	573	16	3/27	3/27	35.81	5.14	41.7	0	0
T20s	116	402	532	17	2/20	2/20	31.29	7.94	23.6	0	0

KESHAV MAHARAJ

RHB / SLA / R0 / W0

FULL NAME: Keshav Athmanand Maharaj
BORN: February 7, 1990, Durban, South Africa
SQUAD NO: 27
TEAMS: South Africa, Yorkshire, Dolphins, Durban Heat, KwaZulu-Natal, Lancashire
ROLE: Bowler
DEBUT: Test: 2016; ODI: 2017; First-class: 2006; List A: 2006; T20: 2010

BEST BATTING: 114* KwaZulu-Natal vs Northerns, Pretoria, 2013
BEST BOWLING: 9-129 South Africa vs Sri Lanka, Colombo (SSC), 2018

TWITTER: @keshavmaharaj16
NOTES: The South African left-arm spinner has been signed by Yorkshire for the first two matches of the Championship season before Ravi Ashwin takes over following the latter's IPL stint. Maharaj returns to Headingley after a hugely successful five-match Championship spell last summer in which he took 38 wickets at 18.92. "He won matches for us," said Martyn Moxon, Yorkshire's director of cricket. "He was fantastic on the pitch for us, but also off the field with the way he spoke to our players." The 30-year-old has previously represented Roses rivals Lancashire in 2018. At Colombo in 2018 Maharaj returned the 19th-best Test figures of all time, and the second-best by a South African, taking 9-129 in a losing cause

Batting	Mat	Inns	NO	Runs	HS	Ave	SR	100	50	Ct	St
Tests	30	48	6	643	72	15.30	60.48	0	2	8	0
ODIs	7	3	0	27	17	9.00	96.42	0	0	1	0
First-class	128	185	26	3241	114*	20.38	67.90	2	12	46	0
List A	102	60	17	702	50*	16.32	86.66	0	1	38	0
T20s	98	50	25	521	45*	20.84	123.16	0	0	26	0
Bowling	**Mat**	**Balls**	**Runs**	**Wkts**	**BBI**	**BBM**	**Ave**	**Econ**	**SR**	**5w**	**10**
Tests	30	6678	3651	110	9/129	12/283	33.19	3.28	60.7	6	1
ODIs	7	367	312	7	3/25	3/25	44.57	5.10	52.4	0	0
First-class	128	26501	13416	481	9/129	13/157	27.89	3.03	55.0	27	6
List A	102	4864	3883	131	5/34	5/34	29.64	4.78	37.1	2	0
T20s	98	2022	2283	75	3/7	3/7	30.44	6.77	26.9	0	0

SAQIB MAHMOOD RHB / RFM / R0 / W0 / MVP55

FULL NAME: Saqib Mahmood
BORN: February 25, 1997, Birmingham
SQUAD NO: 25
HEIGHT: 6ft 3in
NICKNAME: Saq
EDUCATION: Matthew Moss High School, Rochdale
TEAMS: England, Lancashire, Manchester Originals
ROLE: Bowler
DEBUT: ODI: 2020; List A: 2019; First-class: 2016; List A: 2016; T20: 2015

BEST BATTING: 34 Lancashire vs Middlesex, Old Trafford, 2019
BEST BOWLING: 4-48 Lancashire vs Bristol, Cheltenham, 2019

TWITTER: @SaqMahmood25
NOTES: The England fast bowler has had a meteoric rise over the last year, culminating in international debuts in both white-ball formats and a call-up to the Test squad. Mahmood made his full Lancashire debut in 2015 and made a big impact at the 2016 U19 World Cup, becoming a regular for England Lions side. Injuries and the tough competition for places initially limited Mahmood's opportunites for his county, but he was exceptional last year – particularly in the One-Day Cup in which he took 28 wickets at 18.50 to be named player of the tournament

Batting	Mat	Inns	NO	Runs	HS	Ave	SR	100	50	Ct	St
ODIs	1	-	-	-	-	-	-	-	-	0	0
T20Is	3	2	1	7	4	7.00	100.00	0	0	1	0
First-class	16	18	7	154	34	14.00	30.67	0	0	1	0
List A	28	12	6	117	45	19.50	89.31	0	0	7	0
T20s	20	3	2	7	4	7.00	87.50	0	0	3	0
Bowling	**Mat**	**Balls**	**Runs**	**Wkts**	**BBI**	**BBM**	**Ave**	**Econ**	**SR**	**5w**	**10**
ODIs	1	30	17	1	1/17	1/17	17.00	3.40	30.0	0	0
T20Is	3	60	115	3	1/20	1/20	38.33	11.50	20.0	0	0
First-class	16	2136	1214	42	4/48	5/120	28.90	3.41	50.8	0	0
List A	28	1332	1283	51	6/37	6/37	25.15	5.77	26.1	3	0
T20s	20	350	491	23	4/14	4/14	21.34	8.41	15.2	0	0

DAWID MALAN LHB / LB / R3 / W0 / MVP17

FULL NAME: Dawid Johannes Malan
BORN: September 3, 1987, Roehampton
SQUAD NO: 29
HEIGHT: 6ft
NICKNAME: Mal, Mala
EDUCATION: Paarl Boys' High School; University of South Africa
TEAMS: England, Yorkshire, Trent Rockets, Comilla Warriors, Boland, Khulna Titans, Middlesex, Islamabad United, Peshawar Zalmi
ROLE: Batsman
DEBUT: Test: 2017; T20I: 2017; First-class: 2006; List A: 2006; T20: 2006

BEST BATTING: 199 Middlesex vs Derbyshire, Derby, 2019
BEST BOWLING: 5-61 Middlesex vs Lancashire, Liverpool, 2012
COUNTY CAP: 2010 (Middlesex); BENEFIT: 2019 (Middlesex)

FAMILY TIES? My dad Dawid played for Transvaal B and Western Province B and my brother Charl played for MCC Young Cricketers and Loughborough MCCU
SUPERSTITIONS? Too many to write down
CRICKETING HERO? Gary Kirsten
IF YOU WEREN'T A CRICKETER? I would like to have gone into sports psychology
SURPRISING FACT ABOUT YOU? I love to go to the cinema by myself
TWITTER: @DJMalan29

Batting	Mat	Inns	NO	Runs	HS	Ave	SR	100	50	Ct	St
Tests	15	26	0	724	140	27.84	41.08	1	6	11	0
ODIs	1	1	0	24	24	24.00	80.00	0	0	0	0
T20Is	10	10	1	469	103*	52.11	153.77	1	5	2	0
First-class	188	321	21	11229	199	37.43	52.29	25	59	198	0
List A	149	145	21	5135	185*	41.41	83.76	10	25	51	0
T20s	200	195	32	5430	117	33.31	128.88	5	30	69	0
Bowling	**Mat**	**Balls**	**Runs**	**Wkts**	**BBI**	**BBM**	**Ave**	**Econ**	**SR**	**5w**	**10**
Tests	15	156	70	0	-	-	-	2.69	-	0	0
ODIs	1	-	-	-	-	-	-	-	-	-	-
T20Is	10	12	27	1	1/27	1/27	27.00	13.50	12.0	0	0
First-class	188	4057	2431	59	5/61	5/61	41.20	3.59	68.7	1	0
List A	149	1347	1310	40	4/25	4/25	32.75	5.83	33.6	0	0
T20s	200	555	706	23	2/10	2/10	30.69	7.63	24.1	0	0

JANNEMAN MALAN

RHB / LB / R0 / W0

FULL NAME: Janneman Nieuwoudt Malan
BORN: April 18, 1996, Neslpruit, Mpumalanga, South Africa
SQUAD NO: TBC
TEAMS: South Africa, Leicestershire, Cape Cobras, Cape Town Blitz, North West
ROLE: Batsman
DEBUT: ODI: 2020; T20I: 2019; First-class: 2015; List A: 2015; T20: 2015

BEST BATTING: 208* North West vs Western Province, Potchefstroom, 2017

TWITTER: @Janneman_Malan
NOTES: The youngest of three talented brothers, Malan has been signed by Leicestershire to be their overseas player for the whole of the club's T20 Blast and One-Day Cup campaigns. The South African batsman will also be available for the first three Championship matches, subject to international committments. Leicestershire head coach Paul Nixon said: "Securing a high-class opening batsman in T20 and the Royal London Cup has been a major priority and Janneman fits the bill for us. His record across all formats is outstanding... Janneman strikes the ball very cleanly and will be an asset to us. He fits the profile of our squad; young, hungry and adaptable." Malan made his T20I debut last year and played his first ODI in February against Australia, setting up a series win with an an unbeaten 129 at Bloemfontein in just his second 50-over match for his country. His eldest brother Pieter made his Test debut against England earlier this year, while Andre is one of the best allrounders in South African domestic cricket

Batting	Mat	Inns	NO	Runs	HS	Ave	SR	100	50	Ct	St
ODIs	3	3	1	152	129*	76.00	91.56	1	0	3	0
T20Is	2	2	0	35	33	17.50	94.59	0	0	2	0
First-class	38	65	5	3022	208*	50.36	64.72	11	9	43	0
List A	51	51	5	2050	170*	44.56	86.90	5	10	30	0
T20s	45	45	3	1369	128*	32.59	135.54	2	6	28	0
Bowling	**Mat**	**Balls**	**Runs**	**Wkts**	**BBI**	**BBM**	**Ave**	**Econ**	**SR**	**5w**	**10**
ODIs	3	-	-	-	-	-	-	-	-	-	-
T20Is	2	-	-	-	-	-	-	-	-	-	-
First-class	38	54	27	0	-	-	-	3.00	-	0	0
List A	51	-	-	-	-	-	-	-	-	-	-
T20s	45	-	-	-	-	-	-	-	-	-	-

MITCHELL MARSH RHB / RM

FULL NAME: Mitchell Ross Marsh
BORN: October 20, 1991, Perth, Australia
SQUAD NO: 8
TEAMS: Australia, Middlesex, Deccan Chargers, Fremantle, Perth Scorchers, Pune Warriors, Rising Pune Supergiants, Sunrisers Hyderabad, Western Australia
ROLE: Allrounder
DEBUT: Test: 2014; ODI: 2011; T20I: 2011; First-class: 2009; List A: 2009; T20: 2009

BEST BATTING: 93* Perth Scorchers vs Brisbane Heat, Perth, 2020 (T20)
BEST BOWLING: 4-10 Western Australia vs New South Wales, Perth, 2010 (T20)

TWITTER: @mitchmarsh235
NOTES: The Australian allrounder has been signed by Middlesex for this summer's T20 Blast campaign. "Mitch is a hard-hitting batsman, steady medium-fast bowler and athletic in the field," said Middlesex head coach Stuart Law. "As a tremendous team man and such a loveable character, I'm sure he'll fit in well with our group." The son of former Test opener Geoff, and brother to fellow international batsman Shaun, Mitchell has racked up more than 100 appearances across all formats for Australia, the highlight of which is his 181 on his home ground at Perth in the third Test against England in 2017, sharing a 301-run partnership with his captain Steve Smith. Marsh is a three-time winner of the Big Bash League with Perth Scorchers and is playing in this year's IPL for Sunrisers Hyderabad, his fourth Indian franchise

Batting	Mat	Inns	NO	Runs	HS	Ave	SR	100	50	Ct	St
Tests	32	55	5	1260	181	25.20	50.68	2	3	16	0
ODIs	57	53	9	1539	102*	34.97	91.99	1	11	27	0
T20Is	14	14	3	219	36	19.90	115.87	0	0	4	0
First-class	102	176	14	5210	211	32.16	55.54	11	21	53	0
List A	113	106	22	3156	124	37.57	91.47	3	21	56	0
T20s	91	84	21	1913	93*	30.36	124.70	0	9	36	0
Bowling	**Mat**	**Balls**	**Runs**	**Wkts**	**BBI**	**BBM**	**Ave**	**Econ**	**SR**	**5w**	**10**
Tests	32	2853	1623	42	5/46	7/86	38.64	3.41	67.9	1	0
ODIs	57	1835	1700	47	5/33	5/33	36.17	5.55	39.0	1	0
T20Is	14	120	159	7	2/6	2/6	22.71	7.95	17.1	0	0
First-class	102	8579	4838	158	6/84	9/156	30.62	3.38	54.2	2	0
List A	113	3221	2911	92	5/33	5/33	31.64	5.42	35.0	2	0
T20s	91	971	1378	49	4/6	4/6	28.12	8.51	19.8	0	0

GLENN MAXWELL RHB / OB

FULL NAME: Glenn James Maxwell
BORN: October 14, 1988, Kew, Melbourne
SQUAD NO: 32
HEIGHT: 5ft 10in
TEAMS: Australia, Lancashire, London Spirit, Delhi Daredevils, Hampshire, Kings XI Punjab, Melbourne Renegades, Melbourne Stars, Mumbai Indians, Surrey, Victoria, Yorkshire
ROLE: Allrounder
DEBUT: Test: 2013; ODI: 2012; T20I: 2012; First-class: 2011; List A: 2010; T20: 2010

BEST BATTING: 145* Australia vs Sri Lanka, Pallekele, 2016 (T20)
BEST BOWLING: 3-10 Australia vs England, Hobart, 2018 (T20)

TWITTER: @Gmaxi_32
NOTES: An inventive shotmaker, spectacular fielder and useful off-spinner, Maxwell is one of the hottest properties in T20 cricket. After scoring the fastest half-century (off 19 balls) in Australian domestic one-day cricket in 2011, he quickly graduated into the international set-up and was bought for $1m by Mumbai Indians in the 2013 IPL auction. The Australia allrounder was named in the Team of the Tournament at the 2014 World T20. Three years later he scored his maiden Test hundred to become only the second Australian to make a century in all three international formats. He took a short break from the game for mental health reasons last October but returned as captain of Melbourne Stars and was a star performer in the 2019/20 Big Bash. Maxwell returns to Lancashire this summer for a second successive T20 stint and was picked up by London Spirit for The Hundred in the £125k salary band

Batting	Mat	Inns	NO	Runs	HS	Ave	SR	100	50	Ct	St
Tests	7	14	1	339	104	26.07	59.47	1	0	5	0
ODIs	110	100	11	2877	102	32.32	123.37	1	19	65	0
T20Is	61	54	9	1576	145*	35.02	160.00	3	7	30	0
First-class	67	112	10	4061	278	39.81	73.35	7	23	55	0
List A	182	164	19	4762	146	32.84	120.43	4	29	110	0
T20s	268	251	34	5983	145*	27.57	154.40	3	33	139	0
Bowling	**Mat**	**Balls**	**Runs**	**Wkts**	**BBI**	**BBM**	**Ave**	**Econ**	**SR**	**5w**	**10**
Tests	7	462	341	8	4/127	4/127	42.62	4.42	57.7	0	0
ODIs	110	2698	2525	50	4/46	4/46	50.50	5.61	53.9	0	0
T20Is	61	564	704	26	3/10	3/10	27.07	7.48	21.6	0	0
First-class	67	5680	3174	77	5/40	6/76	41.22	3.35	73.7	1	0
List A	182	4577	4172	94	4/46	4/46	44.38	5.46	48.6	0	0
T20s	268	2307	2959	95	3/10	3/10	31.14	7.69	24.2	0	0

BEN MCDERMOTT RHB/WK

FULL NAME: Benjamin Reginald McDermott
BORN: December 12, 1994, Brisbane, Australia
SQUAD NO: 47
HEIGHT: 6ft
TEAMS: Australia, Derbyshire, Brisbane Heat, Hobart Hurricanes, Melbourne Renegades, Queensland, Tasmania
ROLE: Wicketkeeper/batsman
DEBUT: T20I: 2018; First-class: 2014; List A: 2014; T20: 2014

BEST BATTING: 114 Hobart Hurricanes vs Melbourne Renegades, Melbourne, 2017 (T20)

TWITTER: @benmcdermott100
NOTES: A hard-hitting keeper-batsman – and son of legendary fast bowler Craig – McDermott was identified as a special talent after scoring a double-century for the Gold Coast Dolphins at U17 level. He made his Big Bash debut for Brisbane Heat in 2014 at the age of 19 before switching to Hobart Hurricanes ahead of the 2016/17 campaign. He made an instant impression at his new home, hitting 114 from 52 balls in his second innings for the franchise to inspire a record chase of 223. McDermott's strokeplay caught the attention of the Australian selectors, who handed him his T20I debut against UAE in October 2018. He will join his compatriot Sean Abbott at Derbyshire this summer, having signed for the Falcons on a white-ball contract which covers the One-Day Cup and the whole of the T20 Blast

Batting	Mat	Inns	NO	Runs	HS	Ave	SR	100	50	Ct	St
T20Is	12	10	3	98	32*	14.00	93.33	0	0	8	0
First-class	33	58	6	1549	104	29.78	42.59	1	11	21	0
List A	21	21	2	936	117	49.26	78.39	3	5	20	0
T20s	61	56	14	1258	114	29.95	128.10	1	4	26	2
Bowling	**Mat**	**Balls**	**Runs**	**Wkts**	**BBI**	**BBM**	**Ave**	**Econ**	**SR**	**5w**	**10**
T20Is	12	-	-	-	-	-	-	-	-	-	-
First-class	33	102	75	0	-	-	-	4.41	-	0	0
List A	21	-	-	-	-	-	-	-	-	-	-
T20s	61	-	-	-	-	-	-	-	-	-	-

JAMIE MCILROY

RHB / LFM / R0 / W0

FULL NAME: Jamie Peter McIlroy
BORN: June 19, 1994, Hereford
SQUAD NO: 35
HEIGHT: 6ft 3in
NICKNAME: Macca
EDUCATION: Builth Wells High School, Powys; Coleg Powys Newtown
TEAMS: Glamorgan
ROLE: Bowler

WHAT WAS YOUR FIRST CRICKET CLUB? Builth Wells CC, Powys
WHAT WERE YOU DOING WHEN ENGLAND WON THE WORLD CUP? Watching from the balcony at Lord's
MOST INTERESTING TEAMMATE? Kashif Ali (MCC Young Cricketers) – he comes out with some comical lines
CRICKET STAR OF THE FUTURE? Billy Mead (MCC Young Cricketers)
IF YOU WERE AN ANIMAL, WHICH WOULD IT BE? A dog – because they live such a luxurious life
TWITTER: @Jamiemcilroy94
NOTES: McIlroy signed his first professional contract with Glamorgan in March 2019 after impressing for the club's Second XI the previous summer. The left-arm seamer earned a dual contract with MCC Young Cricketers after excelling for Brockhampton in Birmingham club cricket, as well as turning out for Herefordshire at Minor Counties level. He has developed his game in Australia, playing for the Doutta Stars Cricket Club in Essendon, Victoria. After a modest 2019 for Glamorgan's seamers, with Michael Hogan the only paceman to pass 30 Championship wickets, McIlroy will be targeting a first-team debut this summer

CONOR MCKERR

RHB / RFM / R0 / W0

FULL NAME: Conor McKerr
BORN: January 19, 1998, Johannesburg, South Africa
SQUAD NO: 83
HEIGHT: 6ft 6in
NICKNAME: Tree
EDUCATION: St John's College, Johannesburg
TEAMS: Surrey, Derbyshire, South Africa U19
ROLE: Bowler
DEBUT: First-class: 2017; List A: 2019

BEST BATTING: 29 Surrey vs Yorkshire, The Oval, 2018
BEST BOWLING: 5-54 Derbyshire vs Northamptonshire, Northampton, 2017

WHAT WAS YOUR FIRST CRICKET CLUB? Randburg CC, Johannesburg, South Africa. I remember the old concrete nets
WHAT WERE YOU DOING WHEN ENGLAND WON THE WORLD CUP? I was on the sofa with a Kiwi
BIGGEST TOPIC OF DISCUSSION IN YOUR DRESSING ROOM? The Hundred
MOST INTERESTING TEAMMATE? Mark Stoneman – incredible family man and a real calming influence on the group
CRICKETING HERO? Dale Steyn
WHICH RULE WOULD YOU CHANGE ABOUT CRICKET? Remove the stump mics
BIGGEST CRICKETING REGRET? Ducking into a short ball in the nets
CRICKET STAR OF THE FUTURE? Jack Lees (South Africa U19)
WHICH BOOK MEANS MOST TO YOU? The Alchemist by Paulo Coelho
IF YOU WERE AN ANIMAL, WHICH WOULD IT BE? A rhino – I'm from Africa and I'm relatively fast
TWITTER: @cemckerr83

Batting	Mat	Inns	NO	Runs	HS	Ave	SR	100	50	Ct	St
First-class	14	15	4	133	29	12.09	41.43	0	0	2	0
List A	6	6	2	56	26*	14.00	88.88	0	0	3	0
Bowling	**Mat**	**Balls**	**Runs**	**Wkts**	**BBI**	**BBM**	**Ave**	**Econ**	**SR**	**5w**	**10**
First-class	14	1705	1054	38	5/54	10/141	27.73	3.70	44.8	2	1
List A	6	311	334	8	3/56	3/56	41.75	6.44	38.8	0	0

MATTIE MCKIERNAN RHB / LB / R0 / W0

FULL NAME: Matthew Henry McKiernan
BORN: June 14, 1994, Lancashire
SQUAD NO: 21
HEIGHT: 6ft 1in
NICKNAME: Macca
EDUCATION: Lowton High School, Leigh, Greater Manchester; St John Rigby College, Wigan; Edge Hill University, Ormskirk, Lancashire
TEAMS: Derbyshire
ROLE: Bowler
DEBUT: First-class: 2019; T20: 2018

BEST BATTING: 7 Derbyshire vs Sussex, Derby, 2019

WHAT WAS YOUR FIRST CRICKET CLUB? Leigh CC, Wigan, Greater Manchester
WHAT WERE YOU DOING WHEN ENGLAND WON THE WORLD CUP? Watching it at Leigh CC
BIGGEST TOPIC OF DISCUSSION IN YOUR DRESSING ROOM? There's a variety of topics, most of them generated by our coach Steve Kirby
BEST INNINGS YOU'VE SEEN? George Bailey's 202 for South Hobart Sandy Bay vs North Hobart in the 2015/16 Cricket Tasmania Premier League. Manipulated the field effortlessly and made it look easy
WHICH RULE WOULD YOU CHANGE ABOUT CRICKET? It should be five runs if the ball bounces once on its way to the boundary
BIGGEST CRICKETING REGRET? Missing the South Hobart Sandy Bay grand final week in 2015/16
CRICKET STAR OF THE FUTURE? Mitchell Wagstaff (Derbyshire Academy)
WHICH BOOK MEANS MOST TO YOU? What's a book?!
IF YOU WERE AN ANIMAL, WHICH WOULD IT BE? A cat
TWITTER: @MattieMcKiernan

Batting	Mat	Inns	NO	Runs	HS	Ave	SR	100	50	Ct	St
First-class	1	2	0	7	7	3.50	25.92	0	0	3	0
T20s	1	1	1	1	1*	-	100.00	0	0	0	0
Bowling	**Mat**	**Balls**	**Runs**	**Wkts**	**BBI**	**BBM**	**Ave**	**Econ**	**SR**	**5w**	**10**
First-class	1	-	-	-	-	-	-	-	-	-	-
T20s	1	24	27	0	-	-	-	6.75	-	0	0

LEWIS MCMANUS

RHB / WK / R0 / W0

FULL NAME: Lewis David McManus
BORN: October 9, 1994, Poole, Dorset
SQUAD NO: 18
HEIGHT: 5ft 8in
NICKNAME: Lewy, King
EDUCATION: Clayesmore School, Bournemouth; University of Exeter
TEAMS: Hampshire, England U19
ROLE: Wicketkeeper/batsman
DEBUT: First-class: 2015; List A: 2016; T20: 2016

BEST BATTING: 132* Hampshire vs Surrey, Southampton, 2016

WHAT GOT YOU INTO CRICKET? It was a sport to play during the football off-season
STRANGEST THING SEEN IN A GAME? James Tomlinson's one-handed catch at fine-leg while holding a banana in the other hand during a first-class game
BEST MOMENT IN CRICKET? My maiden first-class century in 2016
CRICKETING HERO? Ricky Ponting
NON-CRICKETING HERO? Floyd Mayweather
IF YOU WEREN'T A CRICKETER? I'd be a gym junkie
SURPRISING FACT ABOUT YOU? I play in the same team as Batman
TWITTER: @lewis_mcmanus

Batting	Mat	Inns	NO	Runs	HS	Ave	SR	100	50	Ct	St
First-class	39	56	6	1414	132*	28.28	48.64	1	6	83	10
List A	32	25	5	430	47	21.50	88.47	0	0	24	8
T20s	40	30	8	396	59	18.00	135.61	0	1	13	8
Bowling	**Mat**	**Balls**	**Runs**	**Wkts**	**BBI**	**BBM**	**Ave**	**Econ**	**SR**	**5w**	**10**
First-class	39	-	-	-	-	-	-	-	-	-	-
List A	32	-	-	-	-	-	-	-	-	-	-
T20s	40	-	-	-	-	-	-	-	-	-	-

STUART MEAKER

RHB / RF / R0 / W1

FULL NAME: Stuart Christopher Meaker
BORN: January 21, 1989, Pietermaritzburg, South Africa
SQUAD NO: 12
HEIGHT: 5ft 11in
NICKNAME: Meaks, Ten Bears
EDUCATION: Cranleigh Senior School, Surrey
TEAMS: England, Sussex, Auckland, Surrey
ROLE: Bowler
DEBUT: ODI: 2011; T20I: 2012; First-class: 2008; List A: 2008; T20: 2010

BEST BATTING: 94 Surrey vs Bangladeshis, The Oval, 2010
BEST BOWLING: 8-52 Surrey vs Somerset, The Oval, 2012
COUNTY CAP: 2012 (Surrey)

WHAT WAS YOUR FIRST CRICKET CLUB? Normandy CC, Guildford, Surrey
WHAT WERE YOU DOING WHEN ENGLAND WON THE WORLD CUP? Watching at a mate's with a hangover
BIGGEST TOPIC OF DISCUSSION IN YOUR DRESSING ROOM? Why Laurie Evans gets a new kit sponsor every season
MOST INTERESTING TEAMMATE? Kevin Piersersen – never met such a genius
CRICKETING HERO? Allan Donald
SURPRISING FACT ABOUT YOU? I have a certificate in corporate governance but still don't know what it means
IF YOU WERE AN ANIMAL, WHICH WOULD IT BE? A drop bear (predatory koala) – they're lethal
TWITTER: @SMeaker18

Batting	Mat	Inns	NO	Runs	HS	Ave	SR	100	50	Ct	St
ODIs	2	2	0	2	1	1.00	12.50	0	0	0	0
T20Is	2	-	-	-	-	-	-	-	-	1	0
First-class	89	117	24	1445	94	15.53	37.43	0	6	20	0
List A	73	38	18	198	50	9.90	63.46	0	1	21	0
T20s	32	11	6	46	17	9.20	121.05	0	0	13	0
Bowling	**Mat**	**Balls**	**Runs**	**Wkts**	**BBI**	**BBM**	**Ave**	**Econ**	**SR**	**5w**	**10**
ODIs	2	114	110	2	1/45	1/45	55.00	5.78	57.0	0	0
T20Is	2	47	70	2	1/28	1/28	35.00	8.93	23.5	0	0
First-class	89	13762	8701	279	8/52	11/167	31.18	3.79	49.3	11	2
List A	73	2762	2842	80	4/37	4/37	35.52	6.17	34.5	0	0
T20s	32	519	774	26	4/30	4/30	29.76	8.94	19.9	0	0

DUSTIN MELTON

RHB / RFM / R0 / W0

FULL NAME: Dustin Renton Melton
BORN: April 11, 1995, Harare, Zimbabwe
SQUAD NO: 13
HEIGHT: 6ft 4in
NICKNAME: Dusty
EDUCATION: Pretoria Boys High School; University of Pretoria
TEAMS: Derbyshire
ROLE: Bowler

BEST BATTING: 1* Derbyshire vs Sussex, Derby, 2019
BEST BOWLING: 1-24 Derbyshire vs Sussex, Derby, 2019

WHAT WAS YOUR FIRST CRICKET CLUB? Tuks CC, Pretoria, South Africa
HOW WOULD YOU DISMISS STEVE SMITH? With a 95mph bumper to the head
BIGGEST TOPIC OF DISCUSSION IN YOUR DRESSING ROOM? Getting through the winter
MOST INTERESTING TEAMMATE? Andre Nel
CRICKET STAR OF THE FUTURE? Alex Oxley (Suffolk CCC)
IF YOU WERE AN ANIMAL, WHICH WOULD IT BE? A wild dog – for its unrelenting tenacity to never give up chasing its next meal
TWITTER: @Dusty_Melts
NOTES: The Zimbabwe-born fast bowler made his first-class debut last August against the touring Australians, having impressed for Derbyshire's Second XI. Melton signed a one-year deal with the club a week later and took two wickets on his Championship bow against Sussex in September. "It's good for us to have such depth and quality in our bowling ranks, and he will add another element of pace and bounce," said Dave Houghton, Derbyshire's head of cricket. Melton, who was educated in South Africa but moved to the UK in 2016, has previously played Second XI cricket for Essex and Leicestershire

Batting	Mat	Inns	NO	Runs	HS	Ave	SR	100	50	Ct	St
First-class	3	4	2	1	1*	0.50	4.76	0	0	1	0
Bowling	**Mat**	**Balls**	**Runs**	**Wkts**	**BBI**	**BBM**	**Ave**	**Econ**	**SR**	**5w**	**10**
First-class	3	191	149	2	1/24	2/54	74.50	4.68	95.5	0	0

CRAIG MESCHEDE RHB / RMF / R0 / W0

FULL NAME: Craig Anthony Joseph Meschede
BORN: November 21, 1991, Johannesburg, South Africa
SQUAD NO: 44
HEIGHT: 6ft 2in
NICKNAME: Mesh, Meshy
EDUCATION: King's College, Taunton
TEAMS: Germany, Glamorgan, Somerset
ROLE: Allrounder
DEBUT: First-class: 2011; List A: 2011; T20: 2011

BEST BATTING: 107 Glamorgan vs Northamptonshire, Cardiff, 2015
BEST BOWLING: 5-84 Glamorgan vs Essex, Chelmsford, 2016

WHAT WAS YOUR FIRST CRICKET CLUB? Old Edwardians CC, Johannesburg
WHICH BOWLER WOULD YOU LEAST LIKE TO FACE? Shoaib Akhtar
BEST INNINGS YOU'VE SEEN? Herschelle Gibbs' 175 against Australia at Joburg when South Africa scored 438-9 to beat Australia's 434-4 in 2006. I was very fortunate to be there
YOUR BIGGEST CRICKETING REGRET? Not giving it my all at the start of my career as a pro
FAVOURITE QUOTE OR SAYING? Dream as if you will live forever, live as if you will for today (LeBron James)
WHICH BOOK MEANS MOST TO YOU? Rich Dad Poor Dad by Robert Kiyosaki
TWITTER: @cmeschy

Batting	Mat	Inns	NO	Runs	HS	Ave	SR	100	50	Ct	St
T20Is	5	5	1	179	67	44.75	155.65	0	1	1	0
First-class	70	101	13	2250	107	25.56	64.04	2	13	23	0
List A	55	39	5	472	45	13.88	90.59	0	0	12	0
T20s	96	71	17	1011	77*	18.72	134.08	0	3	17	0
Bowling	**Mat**	**Balls**	**Runs**	**Wkts**	**BBI**	**BBM**	**Ave**	**Econ**	**SR**	**5w**	**10**
T20Is	5	120	115	6	2/11	2/11	19.16	5.75	20.0	0	0
First-class	70	8866	5310	142	5/84	7/80	37.39	3.59	62.4	1	0
List A	55	1995	1852	52	4/5	4/5	35.61	5.56	38.3	0	0
T20s	96	1190	1664	60	3/9	3/9	27.73	8.38	19.8	0	0

BEN MIKE

RHB / RFM / R0 / W0

FULL NAME: Benjamin Wentworth Munro Mike
BORN: August 24, 1998, Nottingham
SQUAD NO: 8
HEIGHT: 6ft 1in
NICKNAME: Benny, Mike, Mikey
EDUCATION: Loughborough Grammar School
TEAMS: Leicestershire, Warwickshire
ROLE: Bowler
DEBUT: First-class: 2018; List A: 2018; T20: 2019

BEST BATTING: 72 Warwickshire vs Hampshire, Southampton, 2019
BEST BOWLING: 5-37 Leicestershire vs Sussex, Hove, 2018

WHAT WAS YOUR FIRST CRICKET CLUB? Radcliffe-On-Trent CC, Nottingham. Runners-up in the U13 national cup – lost on net run-rate
MOST INTERESTING TEAMMATE? Mohammad Abbas – very knowledgeable and caring
BEST INNINGS YOU'VE SEEN? Chris Gayle's 175 not out off 66 balls for Royal Challengers Bangalore in the 2013 IPL. Universe boss
WHICH RULE WOULD YOU CHANGE ABOUT CRICKET? Be kinder to bowlers when calling leg-side wides
BIGGEST CRICKETING REGRET? Trying to be perfect
CRICKET STAR OF THE FUTURE? Nat Bowley (Leicestershire)
WHICH BOOK MEANS MOST TO YOU? Jamie's 30-Minute Meals – A Revolutionary Approach to Cooking Good Food Fast by Jamie Oliver
TWITTER: @benmike_

Batting	Mat	Inns	NO	Runs	HS	Ave	SR	100	50	Ct	St
First-class	11	18	2	293	72	18.31	36.94	0	1	2	0
List A	4	4	0	80	41	20.00	79.20	0	0	0	0
T20s	7	5	1	70	37	17.50	112.90	0	0	1	0
Bowling	**Mat**	**Balls**	**Runs**	**Wkts**	**BBI**	**BBM**	**Ave**	**Econ**	**SR**	**5w**	**10**
First-class	11	1367	1034	31	5/37	9/94	33.35	4.53	44.0	1	0
List A	4	90	145	1	1/47	1/47	145.00	9.66	90.0	0	0
T20s	7	95	183	5	3/38	3/38	36.60	11.55	19.0	0	0

CRAIG MILES RHB / RMF / R0 / W3

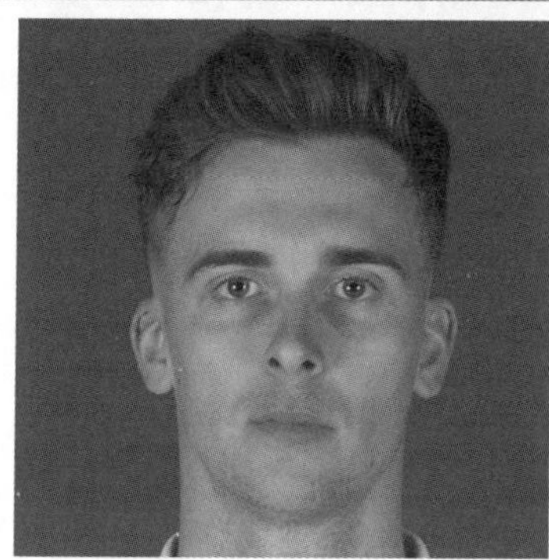

FULL NAME: Craig Neil Miles
BORN: July 20, 1994, Swindon, Wiltshire
SQUAD NO: 18
HEIGHT: 6ft 4in
NICKNAME: Milo, Miler
EDUCATION: Bradon Forest School, Purton, Wiltshire; SGS Filton College, Bristol
TEAMS: Warwickshire, Gloucestershire
ROLE: Bowler
DEBUT: First-class: 2011; List A: 2011; T20: 2013

BEST BATTING: 62* Gloucestershire vs Worcestershire, Cheltenham, 2014
BEST BOWLING: 6-63 Gloucestershire vs Northamptonshire, Northampton, 2015
COUNTY CAP: 2011 (Gloucestershire)

FAMILY TIES? My older brother Adam has played for Cardiff MCCU and for New Zealand side Otago in first-class cricket
WHAT WAS YOUR FIRST CRICKET CLUB? Purton CC, Swindon. The oldest club in Wiltshire
WHAT EXCITES YOU ABOUT THE HUNDRED? That I get to play some 50-over cricket
MOST INTERESTING TEAMMATE? Let's just say that a documentary called A Day in the Life of Benny Howell would be a big hit
BEST INNINGS YOU'VE SEEN? Jack Taylor and Benny Howell scoring 69 off four overs to beat Derbyshire in the 2015 One-Day Cup. Every game that year was a thriller, especially the final
WHICH RULE WOULD YOU CHANGE ABOUT CRICKET? Something to make T20 more bowler-friendly
SURPRISING FACT ABOUT YOU? I played football for Swindon Town Academy until I was 13
CRICKET STAR OF THE FUTURE? Hamza Shaikh (Warwickshire Academy)
IF YOU WERE AN ANIMAL, WHICH WOULD IT BE? A giraffe – long limbs
TWITTER: @cmiles34

Batting	Mat	Inns	NO	Runs	HS	Ave	SR	100	50	Ct	St
First-class	73	102	15	1420	62*	16.32	46.07	0	5	19	0
List A	37	15	3	115	31	9.58	76.15	0	0	5	0
T20s	13	5	2	13	8	4.33	92.85	0	0	4	0
Bowling	**Mat**	**Balls**	**Runs**	**Wkts**	**BBI**	**BBM**	**Ave**	**Econ**	**SR**	**5w**	**10**
First-class	73	11717	7347	272	6/63	10/121	27.01	3.76	43.0	14	1
List A	37	1553	1632	44	4/29	4/29	37.09	6.30	35.2	0	0
T20s	13	265	351	15	3/25	3/25	23.40	7.94	17.6	0	0

TYMAL MILLS RHB / LF / R0 / W0

FULL NAME: Tymal Solomon Mills
BORN: August 12, 1992, Dewsbury, Yorkshire
SQUAD NO: 7
HEIGHT: 6ft 1in
NICKNAME: T, Tyrone
EDUCATION: Mildenhall College of Technology, Suffolk; University of East London
TEAMS: England, Sussex, Southern Brave, Brisbane Heat, Essex, Hobart Hurricanes, Peshawar Zalmi, RC Bangalore
ROLE: Bowler
DEBUT: T20I: 2016; First-class: 2011; List A: 2011; T20: 2012

BEST BATTING: 8* Essex vs Middlesex, Chelmsford, 2013 (T20)
BEST BOWLING: 4-22 Sussex vs Middlesex, Lord's, 2015 (T20)

WHAT WAS YOUR FIRST CRICKET CLUB? Tuddenham CC and then Mildenhall CC, both in Suffolk. Both clubs helped me a lot on and off the field
HOW WOULD YOU DISMISS STEVE SMITH? I only play T20 cricket, so I'd hope he'd hit one to a fielder
BIGGEST TOPIC OF DISCUSSION IN YOUR DRESSING ROOM? Why every pitch in the country isn't a flat road
MOST INTERESTING TEAMMATE? Kieron Pollard
BEST INNINGS YOU'VE SEEN? Mohammad Shahzad's 74 from 16 balls during the 2018/19 T10 League in the UAE
WHICH RULE WOULD YOU CHANGE ABOUT CRICKET? Allow two bouncers per over in T20 cricket
SURPRISING FACT ABOUT YOU? I've got a tattoo on my arm which says: "It's not the cards that you're dealt in life, it's how you play the hand"
IF YOU WERE AN ANIMAL, WHICH WOULD IT BE? A bald eagle – no natural predators
TWITTER: @tmills15

Batting	Mat	Inns	NO	Runs	HS	Ave	SR	100	50	Ct	St
T20Is	5	1	0	0	0	0.00	0.00	0	0	1	0
First-class	32	38	15	260	31*	11.30	57.77	0	0	9	0
List A	23	9	5	7	3*	1.75	31.81	0	0	3	0
T20s	114	23	11	55	8*	4.58	87.30	0	0	19	0
Bowling	**Mat**	**Balls**	**Runs**	**Wkts**	**BBI**	**BBM**	**Ave**	**Econ**	**SR**	**5w**	**10**
T20Is	5	114	129	3	1/27	1/27	43.00	6.78	38.0	0	0
First-class	32	3531	2008	55	4/25	5/79	36.50	3.41	64.2	0	0
List A	23	790	787	22	3/23	3/23	35.77	5.97	35.9	0	0
T20s	114	2363	3085	120	4/22	4/22	25.70	7.83	19.6	0	0

MATT MILNES RHB / RFM / R0 / W1 / MVP24

FULL NAME: Matthew Edward Milnes
BORN: July 29, 1994, Nottingham
SQUAD NO: 8
HEIGHT: 6ft 1in
NICKNAME: Milnesy, Milner
EDUCATION: West Bridgford School; Durham University
TEAMS: Kent, England Lions, Nottinghamshire
ROLE: Bowler
DEBUT: First-class: 2014; List A: 2019; T20: 2019

BEST BATTING: 43 Nottinghamshire vs Yorkshire, Trent Bridge, 2018
BEST BOWLING: 5-68 Kent vs Nottinghamshire, Tunbridge Wells, 2019

WHAT WAS YOUR FIRST CRICKET CLUB? Plumtree CC, Nottinghamshire
WHAT WERE YOU DOING WHEN ENGLAND WON THE WORLD CUP? Thankfully we'd just got off the field at Hampshire in time to see the carnage unfold in the pavilion
HOW WOULD YOU DISMISS STEVE SMITH? Bring on Darren Stevens
WHAT EXCITES YOU ABOUT THE HUNDRED? Bigger crowds
BIGGEST TOPIC OF DISCUSSION IN YOUR DRESSING ROOM? Nomination Whist (the card game)
MOST INTERESTING TEAMMATE? Mitchell Claydon – one of a kind
CRICKETING HERO? Jimmy Anderson
SURPRISING FACT ABOUT YOU? I once scored a goal for Manchester United. It was a horror own goal when I was playing against them at U14 level, but I'm counting it
SURPRISING FACT ABOUT A TEAMMATE? Ivan Thomas has a quote from The Office (tv series) for every situation
CRICKET STAR OF THE FUTURE? Joey Evison (Nottinghamshire) – I played with him in the Notts Second XI when he was around 15 and he could be a proper player
IF YOU WERE AN ANIMAL, WHICH WOULD IT BE? A badger
TWITTER: @mmilnes84

Batting	Mat	Inns	NO	Runs	HS	Ave	SR	100	50	Ct	St
First-class	23	32	11	292	43	13.90	38.42	0	0	12	0
List A	8	5	0	77	26	15.40	140.00	0	0	4	0
T20s	1	-	-	-	-	-	-	-	-	1	0
Bowling	**Mat**	**Balls**	**Runs**	**Wkts**	**BBI**	**BBM**	**Ave**	**Econ**	**SR**	**5w**	**10**
First-class	23	3608	2113	72	5/68	7/111	29.34	3.51	50.1	2	0
List A	8	431	494	16	5/79	5/79	30.87	6.87	26.9	1	0
T20s	1	12	25	0	-	-	-	12.50	-	0	0

ALEX MILTON

RHB / WK / R0 / W0

FULL NAME: Alexander Geoffrey Milton
BORN: May 19, 1996, Redhill, Surrey
SQUAD NO: 12
HEIGHT: 5ft 6in
NICKNAME: Milts
EDUCATION: Malvern College; Cardiff Metropolitan University
TEAMS: Worcestershire
ROLE: Wicketkeeper/batsman
DEBUT: First-class: 2016; List A: 2018

BEST BATTING: 104* Worcestershire vs Somerset, Worcester, 2018

WHAT WAS YOUR FIRST CRICKET CLUB? Dormansland CC, Sussex. Played my first U12s match as an eight-year-old
WHAT WERE YOU DOING WHEN ENGLAND WON THE WORLD CUP? Watching it at Repton School after playing in an old boys game
HOW WOULD YOU DISMISS STEVE SMITH? Let him get to 140 first
BIGGEST TOPIC OF DISCUSSION IN YOUR DRESSING ROOM? 'Twiggy' (Ben Twohig) leaving his car at New Road when it flooded
WHICH RULE WOULD YOU CHANGE ABOUT CRICKET? Give free hits for no-balls in Championship cricket
SURPRISING FACT ABOUT YOU? I played a drum solo blindfolded in my school unplugged concert
BIGGEST CRICKETING REGRET? Getting to 60 at Lord's in the MCCU final and not going on to score a hundred
WHICH BOOK MEANS MOST TO YOU? Who Wants to be a Batsman? by Simon Hughes
IF YOU WERE AN ANIMAL, WHICH WOULD IT BE? An owl – I've been told I look wise
TWITTER: @alex_milton12

Batting	Mat	Inns	NO	Runs	HS	Ave	SR	100	50	Ct	St
First-class	14	22	2	358	104*	17.90	46.92	1	1	12	1
List A	1	1	0	0	0	0.00	-	0	0	0	0
Bowling	**Mat**	**Balls**	**Runs**	**Wkts**	**BBI**	**BBM**	**Ave**	**Econ**	**SR**	**5w**	**10**
First-class	14	-	-	-	-	-	-	-	-	-	-
List A	1	-	-	-	-	-	-	-	-	-	-

DARYL MITCHELL RHB / RM / R6 / W0 / MVP82

FULL NAME: Daryl Keith Henry Mitchell
BORN: November 25, 1983, Badsey, Worcestershire
SQUAD NO: 27
HEIGHT: 6ft
NICKNAME: Mitch
EDUCATION: Prince Henry's High School, Evesham; University of Worcester
TEAMS: Worcestershire, Mountaineers
ROLE: Allrounder
DEBUT: First-class: 2005; List A: 2005; T20: 2005

BEST BATTING: 298 Worcestershire vs Somerset, Taunton, 2009
BEST BOWLING: 4-49 Worcestershire vs Yorkshire, Headingley, 2009
COUNTY CAP: BENEFIT: 2016

WHAT WAS YOUR FIRST CRICKET CLUB? Bretforton CC (aka The Bughut), Worcestershire
HOW WOULD YOU DISMISS STEVE SMITH? Drag him across with my exceptional out-swing for a couple of overs before nipping one back and trapping him lbw
BIGGEST TOPIC OF DISCUSSION IN YOUR DRESSING ROOM? Ben Cox's Instagram
MOST INTERESTING TEAMMATE? Dillon Pennington – never know what is going to come out of his mouth
CRICKETING HERO? Ian Botham and Graeme Hick – Worcester legends I grew up watching at New Road
SURPRISING FACT ABOUT YOU? I was in the Aston Villa Academy
BIGGEST CRICKETING REGRET? Getting bowled slogging on 298
IF YOU WERE AN ANIMAL, WHICH WOULD IT BE? A cheetah – I'd be nearly as quick between the wickets as I am now
TWITTER: @mitchwccc

Batting	Mat	Inns	NO	Runs	HS	Ave	SR	100	50	Ct	St
First-class	206	371	39	13066	298	39.35	46.08	37	50	281	0
List A	135	120	17	3466	107	33.65	81.95	4	22	56	0
T20s	162	125	29	2193	68*	22.84	117.90	0	7	66	0
Bowling	**Mat**	**Balls**	**Runs**	**Wkts**	**BBI**	**BBM**	**Ave**	**Econ**	**SR**	**5w**	**10**
First-class	206	2540	1295	28	4/49		46.25	3.05	90.7	0	0
List A	135	3181	2925	81	4/19	4/19	36.11	5.51	39.2	0	0
T20s	162	2095	2674	92	5/28	5/28	29.06	7.65	22.7	1	0

TOM MOORES LHB / WK / R0 / W0 / MVP86

FULL NAME: Thomas James Moores
BORN: September 4, 1996, Brighton, Sussex
SQUAD NO: 23
HEIGHT: 5ft 9in
NICKNAME: Mooresy
EDUCATION: Loughborough Grammar School; Millfield School, Somerset
TEAMS: Nottinghamshire, Trent Rockets, England Lions, Lancashire, Multan Sultans
ROLE: Wicketkeeper
DEBUT: First-class: 2016; List A: 2016; T20: 2016

BEST BATTING: 103 Nottinghamshire vs Somerset, Taunton, 2018

FAMILY TIES? My father Peter played for Sussex and was England head coach. He's now my coach at Nottinghamshire
WHAT WAS YOUR FIRST CRICKET CLUB? Barrow Town CC, Leicestershire. The club gave me my first opportunity to play men's cricket
CRICKETING HERO? Adam Gilchrist
WHICH BOWLER WOULD YOU LEAST LIKE TO FACE? Jimmy Anderson
WHO WOULD YOU ASK TO BAT FOR YOUR LIFE? Virat Kohli
WHICH RULE WOULD YOU CHANGE ABOUT CRICKET? A batsman should have more than one life
TWITTER: @tommoores23

Batting	Mat	Inns	NO	Runs	HS	Ave	SR	100	50	Ct	St
First-class	34	59	1	1165	103	20.08	46.23	1	2	77	1
List A	21	19	3	566	76	35.37	113.65	0	5	18	5
T20s	52	46	12	926	80*	27.23	139.66	0	5	29	5
Bowling	**Mat**	**Balls**	**Runs**	**Wkts**	**BBI**	**BBM**	**Ave**	**Econ**	**SR**	**5w**	**10**
First-class	34	-	-	-	-	-	-	-	-	-	-
List A	21	-	-	-	-	-	-	-	-	-	-
T20s	52	-	-	-	-	-	-	-	-	-	-

EOIN MORGAN

LHB / RM / R1 / W0

FULL NAME: Eoin Joseph Gerard Morgan
BORN: September 10, 1986, Dublin
SQUAD NO: 16
HEIGHT: 5ft 9in
NICKNAME: Moggie, Morgs, Iceman
EDUCATION: Catholic University School, Dublin; Dulwich College, London
TEAMS: England, Ireland, Middlesex, London Spirit, Karachi Kings, Kolkata Knight Riders, RC Bangalore, Sunrisers, Sydney Thunder
ROLE: Batsman
DEBUT: Test: 2010; ODI: 2006; T20I: 2009; First-class: 2004; List A: 2003; T20: 2006

BEST BATTING: 209* Ireland vs UAE, Abu Dhabi, 2007
BEST BOWLING: 2-24 Middlesex vs Nottinghamshire, Lord's, 2007
COUNTY CAP: 2008

TWITTER: @Eoin16
NOTES: An Irishman by birth, Morgan switched his allegiance to England after he was named in England's provisional squad for the 2009 World T20. He made his Test debut in 2010 and scored two hundreds, but ultimately his unorthodox technique was exposed in the longer form of the game and he played the last of his 16 Tests in 2012. He was handed the ODI captaincy in 2014 and has transformed England's limited-overs cricket, leading the side to a euphoric victory in last year's World Cup. Morgan also leads the T20I side and will captain Middlesex in the T20 Blast this summer, as well as turning out for London Spirit in The Hundred. He is very rarely seen in four-day cricket and was re-signed by Kolkata Knight Riders for this year's IPL

Batting	Mat	Inns	NO	Runs	HS	Ave	SR	100	50	Ct	St
Tests	16	24	1	700	130	30.43	54.77	2	3	11	0
ODIs	236	219	32	7368	148	39.40	91.13	13	46	83	0
T20Is	89	87	18	2138	91	30.98	137.49	0	13	37	0
First-class	102	169	18	5042	209*	33.39	51.02	11	24	76	1
List A	367	338	47	11321	161	38.90	90.94	21	67	123	0
T20s	285	271	38	6321	91	27.12	132.01	0	35	129	0
Bowling	**Mat**	**Balls**	**Runs**	**Wkts**	**BBI**	**BBM**	**Ave**	**Econ**	**SR**	**5w**	**10**
Tests	16	-	-	-	-	-	-	-	-	-	-
ODIs	236	-	-	-	-	-	-	-	-	-	-
T20Is	89	-	-	-	-	-	-	-	-	-	-
First-class	102	120	94	2	2/24	2/24	47.00	4.70	60.0	0	0
List A	367	42	49	0	-	-	-	7.00	-	0	0
T20s	285	-	-	-	-	-	-	-	-	-	-

OWEN MORGAN RHB / SLA / R0 / W0

FULL NAME: Alan Owen Morgan
BORN: April 14, 1994, Swansea
SQUAD NO: 29
HEIGHT: 5ft 11in
NICKNAME: Morgs, Pewts, Strawbs
EDUCATION: Ysgol Gyfun Y Strade, Llanelli; Cardiff University
TEAMS: Glamorgan
ROLE: Allrounder
DEBUT: First-class: 2014; List A: 2016; T20: 2019

BEST BATTING: 103* Glamorgan vs Worcestershire, Worcester, 2016
BEST BOWLING: 2-37 Glamorgan vs Northamptonshire, Northampton, 2016

WHAT WAS YOUR FIRST CRICKET CLUB? Llangennech CC, Carmarthenshire
WHAT WERE YOU DOING WHEN ENGLAND WON THE WORLD CUP? I was 12th man for Glamorgan, hiding behind the TV in the changing room and hoping that nobody would call for a drink
HOW WOULD YOU DISMISS STEVE SMITH? Bring on Connor Brown to bowl his leggies from round the wicket
BIGGEST TOPIC OF DISCUSSION IN YOUR DRESSING ROOM? Who is the worst "changing-room player"
MOST INTERESTING TEAMMATE? Connor Brown – he says he can name every player's squad number
CRICKETING HERO? Ricky Ponting
SURPRISING FACT ABOUT YOU? I'm fluent in Welsh, grew up on a farm, and have a degree in Accounting and Finance
IF YOU WERE AN ANIMAL, WHICH WOULD IT BE? A cheetah – I'm lacking some fast-twitch fibres so being a cheetah would help – especially to keep the strength-and-conditioning coach happy
TWITTER: @owenmorgan14

Batting	Mat	Inns	NO	Runs	HS	Ave	SR	100	50	Ct	St
First-class	21	37	6	638	103*	20.58	38.50	1	1	6	0
List A	3	2	0	32	29	16.00	76.19	0	0	0	0
T20s	5	4	1	15	11	5.00	62.50	0	0	0	0
Bowling	**Mat**	**Balls**	**Runs**	**Wkts**	**BBI**	**BBM**	**Ave**	**Econ**	**SR**	**5w**	**10**
First-class	21	1885	1003	15	2/37	3/57	66.86	3.19	125.6	0	0
List A	3	84	81	2	2/49	2/49	40.50	5.78	42.0	0	0
T20s	5	30	38	0	-	-	-	7.60	-	0	0

DANIEL MORIARTY

LHB / SLA / R0 / W0

FULL NAME: Daniel Thornhill Moriarty
BORN: December 2, 1999, Reigate, Surrey
SQUAD NO: 21
HEIGHT: 6ft 2in
NICKNAME: Mozza
EDUCATION: Rondesbosch Boy's High School, Cape Town
TEAMS: Surrey, South Africa U19
ROLE: Bowler

WHAT WAS YOUR FIRST CRICKET CLUB? Western Province CC, Cape Town, South Africa
HOW WOULD YOU DISMISS STEVE SMITH? Left-arm spin, set straight fields, lbw or bowled
BIGGEST TOPIC OF DISCUSSION IN YOUR DRESSING ROOM? Football
MOST INTERESTING TEAMMATE? Gareth Batty – put simply, experience equals stories and many a laugh
CRICKET STAR OF THE FUTURE? Justin Broad (MCC Young Cricketers)
IF YOU WERE AN ANIMAL, WHICH WOULD IT BE? Psychrolutes marcidus (blobfish) – to explore the unknowns of the deep sea
NOTES: The 21-year-old left-arm spinner signed his first professional contract with Surrey last October to last through until the end of the 2021 season. Moriarty played one Youth Test and ODI for South Africa U19 in 2016 and has also represented Western Province at various age-groups. The South African is a former pupil of Rondesbosch Boys' High School in Cape Town, which has a history of producing professional cricketers, among them Jonathan Trott and Gary Kirsten. Moriarty, who was born in Reigate and holds a British passport, has since played for an eclectic band of clubs across the UK including Bury St Edmunds, Aston Rowant and MCC Young Cricketers. He featured for the second teams of both Essex and Surrey last year, taking figures of 6-71 for Surrey Second XI against Yorkshire Second XI at York

MORNE MORKEL LHB / RFM / R0 / W1 / MVP60

FULL NAME: Morne Morkel
BORN: October 6, 1984, Vereeniging, Transvaal, South Africa
SQUAD NO: 65
HEIGHT: 6ft 5in
TEAMS: South Africa, Surrey, Delhi Daredevils, Easterns, Kent, Kolkata Knight Riders, Perth Scorchers, Rajasthan Royals, St Lucia Zouks, Titans, Tshwane Spartans, Yorkshire
ROLE: Bowler
DEBUT: Test: 2006; ODI: 2007; T20I: 2007; First-class: 2004; List A: 2005; T20: 2005

BEST BATTING: 82* Titans vs Warriors, East London, 2008
BEST BOWLING: 6-23 South Africa vs New Zealand, Wellington, 2012
COUNTY CAP: 2018 (Surrey)

TWITTER: @mornemorkel65
NOTES: The South Africa fast bowler signed for Surrey on a two-year Kolpak contract in April 2018 and was hugely influential in the county winning their first Championship title for 16 years last summer, claiming 59 wickets at an exceptional average of 14.32. He signed a new deal in March 2019 to run until the end of this season. Morkel announced he would be retiring from international duty in February 2018 and finished his Test career with 309 wickets, putting him fifth on South Africa's all-time list. He is also his country's seventh-highest wicket-taker in ODIs, with 180 victims

Batting	Mat	Inns	NO	Runs	HS	Ave	SR	100	50	Ct	St
Tests	86	104	23	944	40	11.65	50.80	0	0	25	0
ODIs	117	47	18	268	32*	9.24	75.70	0	0	31	0
T20Is	44	8	5	22	8*	7.33	122.22	0	0	5	0
First-class	152	190	35	2029	82*	13.09	50.52	0	4	51	0
List A	156	65	25	378	35	9.45	81.64	0	0	41	0
T20s	184	49	26	209	23*	9.08	112.97	0	0	27	0
Bowling	**Mat**	**Balls**	**Runs**	**Wkts**	**BBI**	**BBM**	**Ave**	**Econ**	**SR**	**5w**	**10**
Tests	86	16498	8550	309	6/23	9/110	27.66	3.10	53.3	8	0
ODIs	117	5760	4761	188	5/21	5/21	25.32	4.95	30.6	2	0
T20Is	44	952	1191	47	4/17	4/17	25.34	7.50	20.2	0	0
First-class	152	27801	14388	566	6/23		25.42	3.10	49.1	20	2
List A	156	7490	6145	239	5/21	5/21	25.71	4.92	31.3	3	0
T20s	184	4034	5061	202	4/17	4/17	25.05	7.52	19.9	0	0

JACK MORLEY

LHB / SLA / R0 / W0

FULL NAME: Jack Peter Morley
BORN: June 25, 2001, Rochdale, Lancashire
SQUAD NO: 18
HEIGHT: 5ft 11in
NICKNAME: Morles
EDUCATION: Siddal Moor Sports College, Heywood, Greater Manchester; Myerscough College, Preston, Lancashire
TEAMS: Lancashire, England U19
ROLE: Bowler

WHAT WAS YOUR FIRST CRICKET CLUB? Heywood CC, Rochdale, Greater Manchester
WHAT WERE YOU DOING WHEN ENGLAND WON THE WORLD CUP? Watching it at the ECB Performance Centre in Loughborough
BIGGEST TOPIC OF DISCUSSION IN YOUR DRESSING ROOM? Brexit
MOST INTERESTING TEAMMATE? Ed Fluck (Lancashire Academy) – doesn't stop talking
CRICKET STAR OF THE FUTURE? Keshana Fonseka (Lancashire U13)
IF YOU WERE AN ANIMAL, WHICH WOULD IT BE? A lion
TWITTER: @jackmorley196
NOTES: An emerging left-arm spinner who is highly thought of at Old Trafford, Morley made his England U19 debut last year, taking 2-46 in a Youth ODI against Bangladesh at Cox's Bazar. He played in the U19 Test which followed at Chittagong against the same opposition and then returned figures of 1-44 in a Youth ODI at Worcester when Bangladesh toured England last summer, although he missed out on selection for the 2020 U19 World Cup. Morley joined the Lancashire Academy in 2018 and signed a professional contract at the end of last season. "It is a dream come true to sign professional terms with Lancashire," said Morley. "After coming through the age-group pathway and joining the Academy, this is the next step for me and I hope that I can repay the faith that the club have put in me"

CHARLIE MORRIS

RHB / RMF / R0 / W2 / MVP89

FULL NAME: Charles Andrew John Morris
BORN: July 6, 1992, Hereford
SQUAD NO: 31
HEIGHT: 6ft
NICKNAME: Moz, Bish
EDUCATION: Kingswood School, Bath; King's College, Taunton; Oxford Brookes University
TEAMS: Worcestershire
ROLE: Bowler
DEBUT: First-class: 2012; List A: 2013; T20: 2013

BEST BATTING: 53* Worcestershire vs Australians, Worcester, 2019
BEST BOWLING: 7-45 Worcestershire vs Leicestershire, Leicester, 2019

WHAT WAS YOUR FIRST CRICKET CLUB? Yelverton CC, Devon, on the edge of Dartmoor between Tavistock and Plymouth. Played from the U10s to the first XI
MOST INTERESTING TEAMMATE? Daryl Mitchell – great stories from his career and seems to have good knowledge about most things
BIGGEST CRICKETING REGRET? Not backing myself 100 per cent in certain match scenarios. Take the risk and seize the opportunity
WHICH BOOK MEANS MOST TO YOU? Hard to choose one. I enjoy military reading. It puts perspective into daily life and is humbling to read the sacrifices made by individuals
IF YOU WERE AN ANIMAL, WHICH WOULD IT BE? An ant. My teammates would probably agree. Boring and has thin arms and legs. Hardworking, love doing jobs, determined and can lift more weight than their tiny build would suggest
TWITTER: @morris_9

Batting	Mat	Inns	NO	Runs	HS	Ave	SR	100	50	Ct	St
First-class	60	83	47	454	53*	12.61	29.92	0	1	12	0
List A	34	18	12	58	16*	9.66	59.18	0	0	6	0
T20s	7	3	2	5	3	5.00	83.33	0	0	1	0
Bowling	**Mat**	**Balls**	**Runs**	**Wkts**	**BBI**	**BBM**	**Ave**	**Econ**	**SR**	**5w**	**10**
First-class	60	10496	5464	183	7/45	9/109	29.85	3.12	57.3	5	0
List A	34	1403	1379	40	4/33	4/33	34.47	5.89	35.0	0	0
T20s	7	132	199	5	2/30	2/30	39.80	9.04	26.4	0	0

ED MOULTON

RHB / RMF / R0 / W0

FULL NAME: Edwin Henry Taylor Moulton
BORN: April 18, 1999, Preston, Lancashire
SQUAD NO: 27
EDUCATION: Bishop Rawstone Church of England Academy; Myerscough College, Preston
TEAMS: Lancashire
ROLE: Bowler

TWITTER: @EdwinMoulton
NOTES: The seam bowler, who turns 21 in April, signed his first professional contract with Lancashire in November. Moulton featured regularly for the Second XI last year, claiming 18 wickets across both the Championship and One-Day competitions at an average of 25. He is one of three of the club's Academy graduates who are former pupils at Myerscough College, alongside Jack Morley and Owais Shah. The Preston-based college has a history of producing professional cricketers, including current Lancashire players Tom Bailey and Steven Croft. Moulton, who has also represented Leicestershire Second XI, plays in the Northern Premier League for Chorley CC, for whom he took 39 wickets at 16 last summer

DAN MOUSLEY

LHB / OB / R0 / W0

FULL NAME: Daniel Richard Mousley
BORN: July 8, 2001, Birmingham
SQUAD NO: TBC
HEIGHT: 6ft 2in
NICKNAME: Mouse
EDUCATION: Bablake School, Coventry
TEAMS: Warwickshire, England U19
ROLE: Batsman
DEBUT: First-class: 2019

BEST BATTING: 3 Warwickshire vs Essex, Chelmsford, 2019

WHAT WAS YOUR FIRST CRICKET CLUB? Nether Whitacre CC, Coleshill, Warwickshire
WHAT EXCITES YOU ABOUT THE HUNDRED? The opportunities to play with the best players in the world
MOST INTERESTING TEAMMATE? George Garrett – very funny lad who loves talking cricket or football
CRICKET STAR OF THE FUTURE? Jacob Bethell (Warwickshire Academy)
TWITTER: @danmousley80
NOTES: Having made his Championship debut last season, the up-and-coming left-hander will be pushing for more first-team opportunities across all formats this summer after starring for England at the 2020 U19 World Cup in South Africa. Mousley was comfortably England's most impressive batsman at the tournament, scoring 241 runs at an average of 80.33 including a sparkling century against Sri Lanka in the Plate final. He recently featured in Wisden Cricket Monthly's list of the 19 most exciting teenagers in the UK. "Dan has got a bit of x-factor about him," says Paul Greetham, Warwickshire's elite cricket development manager. "He's had equal success with bat and ball through our pathway system but his batting has really started to flourish. He has shown flair but also the ability to bat for long periods. He's a genuine all-format player"

Batting	Mat	Inns	NO	Runs	HS	Ave	SR	100	50	Ct	St
First-class	1	2	0	3	3	1.50	14.28	0	0	0	0
Bowling	**Mat**	**Balls**	**Runs**	**Wkts**	**BBI**	**BBM**	**Ave**	**Econ**	**SR**	**5w**	**10**
First-class	1	-	-	-	-	-	-	-	-	-	-

STEVEN MULLANEY RHB / RM / R1 / W0 / MVP48

FULL NAME: Steven John Mullaney
BORN: November 19, 1986, Warrington, Cheshire
SQUAD NO: 5
HEIGHT: 5ft 8in
NICKNAME: Mull
EDUCATION: St Mary's Catholic High School, Greater Manchester
TEAMS: Nottinghamshire, Trent Rockets, England Lions, Lancashire
ROLE: Allrounder
DEBUT: First-class: 2006; List A: 2006; T20: 2006

BEST BATTING: 179 Nottinghamshire vs Warwickshire, Trent Bridge, 2019
BEST BOWLING: 5-32 Nottinghamshire vs Gloucestershire, Trent Bridge, 2017
COUNTY CAP: 2013 (Nottinghamshire)

WHAT WAS YOUR FIRST CRICKET CLUB? Golborne CC, Cheshire
BEST ADVICE EVER RECEIVED? Fear has two meanings – Forget Everything And Run or Face Everything And Rise. The choice is yours (Zig Ziglar)
WHAT EXCITES YOU ABOUT THE HUNDRED? Working with the best coaches in the world
CRICKETING HERO? Luke Fletcher
WHICH RULE WOULD YOU CHANGE ABOUT CRICKET? No-balls should be free hits in any format
SURPRISING FACT ABOUT YOU? I played England schools rugby league
CRICKET STAR OF THE FUTURE? Kundeel Haider (Nottinghamshire Academy)
WHICH BOOK MEANS MOST TO YOU? Legacy – What the All Blacks Can Teach Us About The Business of Life by James Kerr
TWITTER: @mull05

Batting	Mat	Inns	NO	Runs	HS	Ave	SR	100	50	Ct	St
First-class	138	234	9	7492	179	33.29	57.91	15	40	132	0
List A	123	91	17	2611	124	35.28	103.32	2	19	57	0
T20s	126	89	22	1150	55	17.16	141.80	0	2	57	0
Bowling	**Mat**	**Balls**	**Runs**	**Wkts**	**BBI**	**BBM**	**Ave**	**Econ**	**SR**	**5w**	**10**
First-class	138	7497	3901	109	5/32	7/46	35.78	3.12	68.7	1	0
List A	123	3981	3458	100	4/29	4/29	34.58	5.21	39.8	0	0
T20s	126	2060	2734	92	4/19	4/19	29.71	7.96	22.3	0	0

TIM MURTAGH

LHB / RFM / R0 / W8 / MVP79

MIDDLESEX

FULL NAME: Timothy James Murtagh
BORN: August 2, 1981, Lambeth, London
SQUAD NO: 34
HEIGHT: 6ft
NICKNAME: Murts, Jack, Brow
EDUCATION: The John Fisher School, London; St Mary's College, Twickenham
TEAMS: Ireland, Middlesex, England U19, Surrey
ROLE: Bowler
DEBUT: Test: 2018; ODI: 2012; T20I: 2012; First-class: 2000; List A: 2000; T20: 2003

BEST BATTING: 74* Surrey vs Middlesex, The Oval, 2004
BEST BOWLING: 7-82 Middlesex vs Derbyshire, Derby, 2009
COUNTY CAP: 2008 (Middlesex); BENEFIT: 2015 (Middlesex)

FAMILY TIES? My brother Chris played for Surrey and uncle Andrew played for Hampshire
WHAT WAS YOUR FIRST CRICKET CLUB? Purley CC, London
HOW WOULD YOU DISMISS STEVE SMITH? How I always get him out: lbw to a nip-backer
WHAT EXCITES YOU ABOUT THE HUNDRED? That I'll be watching it in a bar while on holiday somewhere warm
BIGGEST TOPIC OF DISCUSSION IN YOUR DRESSING ROOM? The size of guys' equipment
WHICH RULE WOULD YOU CHANGE ABOUT CRICKET? No play past 6pm
BIGGEST CRICKETING REGRET? Missing the 2015 World Cup through injury
WHICH BOOK MEANS MOST TO YOU? Shoe Dog – A Memoir by the Creator of Nike by Phil Knight
IF YOU WERE AN ANIMAL, WHICH WOULD IT BE? A goat – it's bleatingly obvious why
TWITTER: @tjmurtagh

Batting	Mat	Inns	NO	Runs	HS	Ave	SR	100	50	Ct	St
Tests	3	6	2	109	54*	27.25	82.57	0	1	0	0
ODIs	58	36	12	188	23*	7.83	63.08	0	0	16	0
T20Is	14	5	3	26	12*	13.00	104.00	0	0	3	0
First-class	232	308	88	4171	74*	18.95		0	11	64	0
List A	211	127	45	820	35*	10.00		0	0	55	0
T20s	102	38	14	227	40*	9.45	106.57	0	0	22	0
Bowling	**Mat**	**Balls**	**Runs**	**Wkts**	**BBI**	**BBM**	**Ave**	**Econ**	**SR**	**5w**	**10**
Tests	3	570	213	13	5/13	6/65	16.38	2.24	43.8	1	0
ODIs	58	3020	2290	74	5/21	5/21	30.94	4.54	40.8	1	0
T20Is	14	268	324	13	3/23	3/23	24.92	7.25	20.6	0	0
First-class	232	40561	20518	816	7/82		25.14	3.03	49.7	35	4
List A	211	9772	8133	275	5/21	5/21	29.57	4.99	35.5	1	0
T20s	102	1984	2727	106	6/24	6/24	25.72	8.24	18.7	1	0

BLESSING MUZARABANI RHB / RFM / R0 / W0

FULL NAME: Blessing Muzarabani
BORN: October 2, 1996, Harare, Zimbabwe
SQUAD NO: 40
HEIGHT: 6ft 6in
EDUCATION: Churchill School, Harare
TEAMS: Zimbabwe, Northamptonshire, Eagles, Rising Stars
ROLE: Bowler
DEBUT: Test: 2017; ODI: 2017; T20I: 2018; First-class: 2017; List A: 2017; T20: 2018

BEST BATTING: 52* Eagles vs Rhinos, Harare, 2019
BEST BOWLING: 5-32 Rising Stars vs Bulawayo Metropolitan Tuskers, Kwekwe, 2017

WHAT WAS YOUR FIRST CRICKET CLUB? Takashinga CC, Harare, Zimbabwe
IF YOU WERE AN ANIMAL, WHICH WOULD IT BE? A lion – aggressive
TWITTER: @BMuzarabani
NOTES: Northants signed the tall, young Zimbabwean fast bowler on a three-year Kolpak deal in September 2018. "I've come here to chase my dreams," said Muzarabani upon joining the county. He has represented his country on 25 occasions but decided to put his international career on hold by joining Northants, for whom he played 11 times across all formats last season. Because of his Kolpak status, the 23-year-old featured as an overseas player for Eagles in Zimbabwean domestic cricket over the winter

Batting	Mat	Inns	NO	Runs	HS	Ave	SR	100	50	Ct	St
Tests	1	2	1	14	10	14.00	100.00	0	0	0	0
ODIs	18	15	7	16	7	2.00	17.97	0	0	7	0
T20Is	6	3	2	1	1*	1.00	20.00	0	0	2	0
First-class	12	18	5	211	52*	16.23	53.41	0	1	5	0
List A	24	20	10	39	18	3.90	33.05	0	0	7	0
T20s	10	5	3	10	9	5.00	55.55	0	0	3	0
Bowling	**Mat**	**Balls**	**Runs**	**Wkts**	**BBI**	**BBM**	**Ave**	**Econ**	**SR**	**5w**	**10**
Tests	1	78	48	0	-	-	-	3.69	-	0	0
ODIs	18	786	733	18	4/47	4/47	40.72	5.59	43.6	0	0
T20Is	6	144	220	9	3/21	3/21	24.44	9.16	16.0	0	0
First-class	12	1296	726	31	5/32	6/48	23.41	3.36	41.8	1	0
List A	24	1060	957	25	4/47	4/47	38.28	5.41	42.4	0	0
T20s	10	192	296	10	3/21	3/21	29.60	9.25	19.2	0	0

MOHAMMAD NABI RHB / OB

FULL NAME: Mohammad Nabi
BORN: January 1, 1985, Loger, Afghanistan
SQUAD NO: 77
NICKNAME: Mr President
TEAMS: Afghanistan, Kent, London Spirit, Balkh Legends, Chittagong Vikings, Comilla Victorians, Leicestershire, Melbourne Renegades, Quetta Gladiators, St Kitts and Nevis Patriots, Rangpur Riders, Sunrisers Hyderabad, Sylhet Royals
ROLE: Allrounder
DEBUT: Test: 2018; ODI: 2009; T20I: 2010; First-class: 2007; List A: 2008; T20: 2010

BEST BATTING: 89 Afghanistan vs Ireland, Greater Noida, 2017 (T20)
BEST BOWLING: 4-10 Afghanistan vs Ireland, Dubai, 2017 (T20)

TWITTER: @MohammadNabi007
NOTES: The veteran off-spinning allrounder has signed up for a second successive T20 campaign with Kent and will be available for the entire group phase. Nabi was among the first wave of Afghan cricketers to play county cricket in 2018, scoring 246 runs and taking nine wickets in 13 T20s for Leicestershire. He fared less well with the bat last year, scoring 147 runs in nine innings, but he was the meanest of Kent's frontline bowlers with an economy rate of 7.23 and showed off his athleticism with a brilliant boundary catch on his Kent debut. A leading member of the Afghanistan side which has shot to prominence over the last decade, Nabi has played in the IPL and the Big Bash League. He was top of the ICC's ODI rankings for allrounders earlier this year. Nabi will also line up for London Spirit in The Hundred

Batting	Mat	Inns	NO	Runs	HS	Ave	SR	100	50	Ct	St
Tests	3	6	0	33	24	5.50	48.52	0	0	2	0
ODIs	124	112	12	2782	116	27.82	85.54	1	15	55	0
T20Is	78	72	11	1347	89	22.08	145.30	0	4	44	0
First-class	35	57	4	1284	117	24.22	51.71	2	5	20	0
List A	159	145	15	3786	146	29.12	88.41	3	18	71	0
T20s	258	216	42	3951	89	22.70	142.07	0	11	120	0
Bowling	**Mat**	**Balls**	**Runs**	**Wkts**	**BBI**	**BBM**	**Ave**	**Econ**	**SR**	**5w**	**10**
Tests	3	546	254	8	3/36	4/95	31.75	2.79	68.2	0	0
ODIs	124	5919	4231	130	4/30	4/30	32.54	4.28	45.5	0	0
T20Is	78	1564	1871	69	4/10	4/10	27.11	7.17	22.6	0	0
First-class	35	4848	2178	94	6/33	8/85	23.17	2.69	51.5	3	0
List A	159	7720	5471	178	5/12	5/12	30.73	4.25	43.3	1	0
T20s	258	5157	6007	255	4/10	4/10	23.55	6.98	20.2	0	0

SUNIL NARINE RHB/OB

FULL NAME: Sunil Philip Narine
BORN: May 26, 1988, Arima, Trinidad & Tobago
SQUAD NO: TBC
HEIGHT: 5ft 10in
TEAMS: West Indies, Oval Invincibles, Comilla Victorians, Dhaka Dynamites, Guyana Amazon Warriors, Kolkata Knight Riders, Lahore Qalandars, Melbourne Renegades, Sydney Sixers, Trinbago Knight Riders, Trinidad & Tobago
ROLE: Bowler
DEBUT: Test: 2012; ODI: 2011; T20I: 2012; First-class: 2009; List A: 2011; T20: 2011

BEST BATTING: 79 Trinbago Knight Riders vs Babados Tridents, Port of Spain, 2017 (T20)
BEST BOWLING: 5-19 Kolkata Knight Riders vs Kings XI Punjab, Kolkata, 2012 (T20)

NOTES: A mystery spinner and useful pinch-hitter in T20 cricket, Narine burst onto the scene in 2009 when he took 10 wickets in an innings in a trial match and was selected by Trinidad & Tobago. He is a familiar face on the global T20 circuit but has featured only sporadically for West Indies in the shortest format in recent years and hasn't played ODI cricket since 2016. He played the last of six Test matches in 2013, instead focusing on white-ball cricket. Narine has excelled in the Indian Premier League, helping Kolkata Knight Riders to the title in 2012 and 2014. Few batsmen have got to grips with his bowling, as shown by a T20 economy rate of a shade over six runs an over. He will represent Oval Invincibles in The Hundred after being selected in the £125k salary band

Batting	Mat	Inns	NO	Runs	HS	Ave	SR	100	50	Ct	St
Tests	6	7	2	40	22*	8.00	43.47	0	0	2	0
ODIs	65	45	12	363	36	11.00	82.31	0	0	14	0
T20Is	51	23	8	155	30	10.33	112.31	0	0	7	0
First-class	13	18	6	213	40*	17.75		0	0	10	0
List A	96	67	16	606	51	11.88		0	1	22	0
T20s	336	191	40	2241	79	14.84	146.95	0	6	71	0
Bowling	**Mat**	**Balls**	**Runs**	**Wkts**	**BBI**	**BBM**	**Ave**	**Econ**	**SR**	**5w**	**10**
Tests	6	1650	851	21	6/91	8/223	40.52	3.09	78.5	2	0
ODIs	65	3540	2435	92	6/27	6/27	26.46	4.12	38.4	2	0
T20Is	51	1102	1105	52	4/12	4/12	21.25	6.01	21.1	0	0
First-class	13	3023	1398	65	8/17	13/39	21.50	2.77	46.5	8	3
List A	96	5241	3253	160	6/9	6/9	20.33	3.72	32.7	6	0
T20s	336	7682	7720	379	5/19	5/19	20.36	6.02	20.2	1	0

CHRIS NASH

RHB / OB / R4 / W0

FULL NAME: Christopher David Nash
BORN: May 19, 1983, Cuckfield, Sussex
SQUAD NO: 3
HEIGHT: 6ft
NICKNAME: Nashy, Fossil
EDUCATION: Collyer's Sixth Form College; Loughborough University
TEAMS: Nottinghamshire, Auckland, England Lions, Otago, Sussex
ROLE: Allrounder
DEBUT: First-class: 2002; List A: 2006; T20: 2006

BEST BATTING: 184 Sussex vs Leicestershire, Leicester, 2010
BEST BOWLING: 4-12 Sussex vs Glamorgan, Cardiff, 2010
COUNTY CAP: 2008 (Sussex); BENEFIT: 2017 (Sussex)

WHAT WAS YOUR FIRST CRICKET CLUB? Horsham CC, West Sussex. Venue of the legendary Beer Olympics, played annually after the last home game and soon to gain IOC status
WHAT WERE YOU DOING WHEN ENGLAND WON THE WORLD CUP? Watching the Wimbledon final on the iPad (jokes)
HOW WOULD YOU DISMISS STEVE SMITH? Lbw? Bowled? Caught? Is this a quiz?
WHAT EXCITES YOU ABOUT THE HUNDRED? Free prawn-cocktail Skips
BIGGEST TOPIC OF DISCUSSION IN YOUR DRESSING ROOM? How I've still got so much hair and look so youthful
MOST INTERESTING TEAMMATE? Luke Wright – he's so intelligent and is always thinking of new and exciting topics to talk about
BEST INNINGS YOU'VE SEEN? Harry Gurney's 42 not out against Sussex in 2017 – purity in an innings
CRICKETING HERO? Michael Slater
IF YOU WERE AN ANIMAL, WHICH WOULD IT BE? A goldfish – every three seconds I would forget the previous two
TWITTER: @chrisnash23

Batting	Mat	Inns	NO	Runs	HS	Ave	SR	100	50	Ct	St
First-class	206	355	20	12474	184	37.23	57.30	24	67	122	0
List A	129	120	5	3548	124*	30.85	88.52	2	24	28	0
T20s	157	149	20	3494	112*	27.08	125.77	1	21	48	0
Bowling	**Mat**	**Balls**	**Runs**	**Wkts**	**BBI**	**BBM**	**Ave**	**Econ**	**SR**	**5w**	**10**
First-class	206	5797	3271	78	4/12		41.93	3.38	74.3	0	0
List A	129	1603	1477	45	4/40	4/40	32.82	5.52	35.6	0	0
T20s	157	1022	1222	49	4/7	4/7	24.93	7.17	20.8	0	0

MICHAEL NESER RHB / RMF / R0 / W0

FULL NAME: Michael Gertges Neser
BORN: March 29, 1990, Pretoria, South Africa
SQUAD NO: 18
TEAMS: Australia, Surrey, Adelaide Strikers, Brisbane Heat, Kings XI Punjab, Queensland
ROLE: Bowler
DEBUT: ODI: 2018; First-class: 2010; List A: 2010; T20: 2011

BEST BATTING: 77 Queensland vs Western Australia, Perth, 2013
BEST BOWLING: 6-57 Queensland vs Tasmania, Hobart, 2017

NOTES: An experienced Australian seamer who was part of Australia's Ashes squad last summer, Neser returns to the UK this summer as Surrey's overseas player for the first half of their Championship campaign. It will be his third consecutive summer on these shores, having made his two ODI appearances against England in 2018. Neser, who was born in South Africa but relocated to Australia's Gold Coast aged 10, has been a prolific wicket-taker in the Sheffield Shield across the last three seasons for Queensland, taking well over 100 wickets. Surrey director of cricket Alec Stewart said: "What I have seen of him, plus strong recommendations from former Australian players whose opinions I greatly respect, means I am very pleased Michael will join us for the first half of the County Championship"

Batting	Mat	Inns	NO	Runs	HS	Ave	SR	100	50	Ct	St
ODIs	2	2	0	8	6	4.00	50.00	0	0	0	0
First-class	55	83	11	1758	77	24.41	52.11	0	11	23	0
List A	54	40	12	631	122	22.53	85.50	1	1	18	0
T20s	71	44	15	417	40*	14.37	117.13	0	0	32	0
Bowling	**Mat**	**Balls**	**Runs**	**Wkts**	**BBI**	**BBM**	**Ave**	**Econ**	**SR**	**5w**	**10**
ODIs	2	100	120	2	2/46	2/46	60.00	7.20	50.0	0	0
First-class	55	9582	4680	181	6/57	8/76	25.85	2.93	52.9	3	0
List A	54	2515	2217	61	4/41	4/41	36.34	5.28	41.2	0	0
T20s	71	1382	1955	71	3/24	3/24	27.53	8.48	19.4	0	0

ROB NEWTON

RHB / LB / R1 / W0

FULL NAME: Robert Irving Newton
BORN: January 18, 1990, Taunton
SQUAD NO: 10
HEIGHT: 5ft 8in
NICKNAME: Newts
EDUCATION: Framlingham College, Suffolk
TEAMS: Northamptonshire
ROLE: Batsman
DEBUT: First-class: 2010; List A: 2009; T20: 2010

BEST BATTING: 202* Northamptonshire vs Leicestershire, Northampton, 2016
BEST BOWLING: 1-82 Northamptonshire vs Derbyshire, Derby, 2017
COUNTY CAP: 2017

WHAT WAS YOUR FIRST CRICKET CLUB? Swardeston CC, Norfolk
BEST ADVICE RECEIVED? Don't touch that – it's hot!
WHAT WERE YOU DOING WHEN ENGLAND WON THE WORLD CUP? I was playing a Championship game at Chesterfield
HOW WOULD YOU DISMISS STEVE SMITH? Get him drunk
MOST INTERESTING TEAMMATE? Paul Best – once ate microwave pizza for Christmas dinner
CRICKETING HERO? Ajaz Akhtar
SURPRISING FACT ABOUT YOU? I once won the 'stump game' at Northamptonshire's end-of-season celebrations
CRICKET STAR OF THE FUTURE? Emilio Gay
IF YOU WERE AN ANIMAL, WHICH WOULD IT BE? Anything that gets to hibernate
TWITTER: @robbienewts77

Batting	Mat	Inns	NO	Runs	HS	Ave	SR	100	50	Ct	St
First-class	98	172	13	5675	202*	35.69	56.80	15	24	28	0
List A	45	41	2	1148	107	29.43	90.18	1	6	8	0
T20s	21	18	1	214	38	12.58	102.88	0	0	0	0
Bowling	**Mat**	**Balls**	**Runs**	**Wkts**	**BBI**	**BBM**	**Ave**	**Econ**	**SR**	**5w**	**10**
First-class	98	73	107	1	1/82	1/82	107.00	8.79	73.0	0	0
List A	45	-	-	-	-	-	-	-	-	-	-
T20s	21	-	-	-	-	-	-	-	-	-	-

ARON NIJJAR

LHB / SLA / R0 / W0

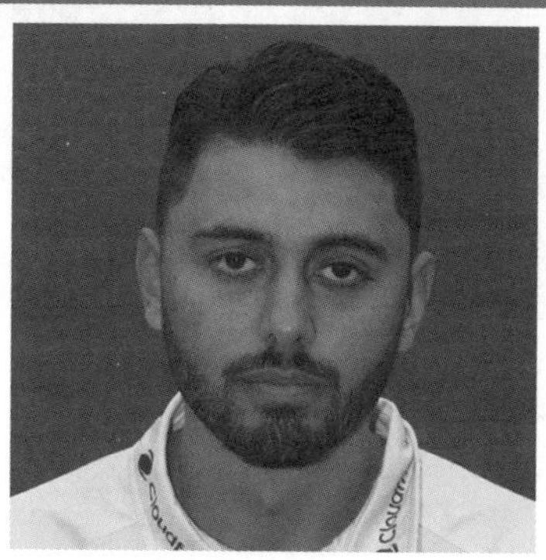

FULL NAME: Aron Stuart Singh Nijjar
BORN: September 24, 1994, Goodmayes, Essex
SQUAD NO: 24
EDUCATION: Ilford County High School
TEAMS: Essex
ROLE: Bowler
DEBUT: First-class: 2015; List A: 2015; T20: 2018

BEST BATTING: 53 Essex vs Northamptonshire, Chelmsford, 2015
BEST BOWLING: 2-28 Essex vs Cambridge MCCU, Cambridge, 2019

TWITTER: @aronnijjar
NOTES: A left-arm orthodox spinner and a fluent left-handed strokemaker, Nijjar has yet to establish himself at his hometown club despite playing a handful of Championship matches in 2015. He played only three first-team matches last summer, although two of these were on T20 Finals Day at Edgbaston, where he responded to the tough task of replacing Adam Zampa by holding his nerve admirably to help Essex lift the trophy. Nijjar, who plays for the hugely successful Wanstead & Snaresbrook club, is highly regarded at Chelmsford and is expected to have more opportunities soon – although it won't be easy to break into such a successful side

Batting	Mat	Inns	NO	Runs	HS	Ave	SR	100	50	Ct	St
First-class	13	15	5	237	53	23.70	45.22	0	1	3	0
List A	3	1	0	21	21	21.00	70.00	0	0	4	0
T20s	3	-	-	-	-	-	-	-	-	1	0
Bowling	**Mat**	**Balls**	**Runs**	**Wkts**	**BBI**	**BBM**	**Ave**	**Econ**	**SR**	**5w**	**10**
First-class	13	1175	785	19	2/28	3/48	41.31	4.00	61.8	0	0
List A	3	126	107	1	1/39	1/39	107.00	5.09	126.0	0	0
T20s	3	66	87	4	3/26	3/26	21.75	7.90	16.5	0	0

SAM NORTHEAST RHB / OB / R4 / W0 / MVP35

FULL NAME: Sam Alexander Northeast
BORN: October 16, 1989, Ashford, Kent
SQUAD NO: 17
HEIGHT: 5ft 11in
NICKNAME: North, Bam, Nick Knight
EDUCATION: Harrow School, London
TEAMS: Hampshire, England Lions, Kent
ROLE: Batsman
DEBUT: First-class: 2007; List A: 2007; T20: 2010

BEST BATTING: 191 Kent vs Derbyshire, Canterbury, 2016
BEST BOWLING: 1-60 Kent vs Gloucestershire, Cheltenham, 2013
COUNTY CAP: 2012 (Kent)

TWITTER: @sanortheast
NOTES: Northeast made a much publicised move to Hampshire in February 2018 after 10 seasons at Canterbury. He suffered a finger injury at the beginning of his first season with his new club and wasn't able to find form when he returned to the side. His most significant innings was an unbeaten 75 in Hampshire's victory over his old club in the Lord's one-day final, an innings which began with Kent fans booing him to the crease. The 30-year-old was back to his best last summer, passing 1,000 first-class runs for the fourth time in five seasons. Tipped for England from his early teens, Northeast scored his maiden first-class hundred for Kent in 2009 and went on to score more than 13,000 runs for the club. He has also been a prolific scorer in T20 cricket, although a recent dip in form led to him being overlooked for The Hundred this summer

Batting	Mat	Inns	NO	Runs	HS	Ave	SR	100	50	Ct	St
First-class	165	281	21	10184	191	39.16	55.99	24	51	85	0
List A	106	98	10	2986	132	33.93	77.13	4	17	38	0
T20s	116	106	12	2811	114	29.90	130.25	1	20	31	0
Bowling	**Mat**	**Balls**	**Runs**	**Wkts**	**BBI**	**BBM**	**Ave**	**Econ**	**SR**	**5w**	**10**
First-class	165	178	147	1	1/60	1/60	147.00	4.95	178.0	0	0
List A	106	-	-	-	-	-	-	-	-	-	-
T20s	116	-	-	-	-	-	-	-	-	-	-

LIAM NORWELL RHB / RM / R0 / W2

FULL NAME: Liam Connor Norwell
BORN: December 27, 1991, Bournemouth
SQUAD NO: 24
HEIGHT: 6ft 3in
NICKNAME: Pasty
EDUCATION: Redruth School, Cornwall
TEAMS: Warwickshire, Gloucestershire
ROLE: Bowler
DEBUT: First-class: 2011; List A: 2012; T20: 2012

BEST BATTING: 102 Gloucestershire vs Derbyshire, Bristol, 2016
BEST BOWLING: 8-43 Gloucestershire vs Leicestershire, Leicester, 2017
COUNTY CAP: 2011 (Gloucestershire)

WHAT WAS YOUR FIRST CRICKET CLUB? Redruth CC, Cornwall
WHAT WERE YOU DOING WHEN ENGLAND WON THE WORLD CUP? Packing up the house
WHAT EXCITES YOU ABOUT THE HUNDRED? That I might get to play some 50-over cricket
BIGGEST TOPIC OF DISCUSSION IN YOUR DRESSING ROOM? Spikeball (sport)
BEST INNINGS YOU'VE SEEN? Michael Klinger's match-winning hundred for Gloucestershire at Headingley in the 2015 One-Day Cup semi-final. That was a special win
WHICH RULE WOULD YOU CHANGE ABOUT CRICKET? Let each team make one tactical sub at the interval in T20 cricket
SURPRISING FACT ABOUT YOU? I was born in Bournemouth but everyone thinks I was born in Cornwall because that's where I grew up
BIGGEST CRICKETING REGRET? Not learning enough from the senior players in the first years of my career
CRICKET STAR OF THE FUTURE? Lewis Goldsworthy (Somerset)
TWITTER: @icnorwell24

Batting	Mat	Inns	NO	Runs	HS	Ave	SR	100	50	Ct	St
First-class	72	92	36	823	102	14.69	44.60	1	2	16	0
List A	17	10	2	47	16	5.87	69.11	0	0	2	0
T20s	24	5	5	5	2*	-	71.42	0	0	10	0
Bowling	**Mat**	**Balls**	**Runs**	**Wkts**	**BBI**	**BBM**	**Ave**	**Econ**	**SR**	**5w**	**10**
First-class	72	12587	7050	262	8/43	10/65	26.90	3.36	48.0	11	3
List A	17	780	716	23	6/52	6/52	31.13	5.50	33.9	2	0
T20s	24	422	653	12	3/27	3/27	54.41	9.28	35.1	0	0

MARCUS O'RIORDAN

RHB / OB / R0 / W0

FULL NAME: Marcus Kevin O'Riordan
BORN: January 25, 1998, Pembury, Kent
SQUAD NO: 55
HEIGHT: 5ft 10in
NICKNAME: Cus
EDUCATION: Holmewood House School, Tunbridge Wells; Tonbridge School
TEAMS: Kent
ROLE: Allrounder
DEBUT: First-class: 2019; T20: 2019

BEST BATTING: 12 Kent vs Nottinghamshire, Trent Bridge, 2019

WHAT WAS YOUR FIRST CRICKET CLUB? Tunbridge Wells CC, Kent
WHAT WERE YOU DOING WHEN ENGLAND WON THE WORLD CUP? Playing for Old Tonbridgians in the Cricketer Cup
WHAT EXCITES YOU ABOUT THE HUNDRED? The different tactics used by each team and watching the best short-format players in the world
BIGGEST TOPIC OF DISCUSSION IN YOUR DRESSING ROOM? I haven't been in the dressing room long enough yet, but the poor standard of the "young" team in the footy warm-ups has featured regularly
MOST INTERESTING TEAMMATE? Mitchell Claydon – good card tricks
CRICKET STAR OF THE FUTURE? Artie Paice (Western Rhinos CC, Kent)
NOTES: The off-spinning allrounder made his first-class and T20 debuts for Kent last season after signing his first professional contract in August. "He is a three-dimensional cricketer in both red- and white-ball cricket," said Kent director of cricket Paul Downton. O'Riordan joined the Kent Cricket Academy as a 16-year-old in 2014 and was a star performer in Kent's triumphant Second XI Trophy campaign last year, taking 4-43 in the final against Durham. He claimed 11 wickets at 21.63 across the competition and averaged 36 with the bat. He also excelled in the Second XI Championship, taking 21 wickets at 28.95 and contributing 223 runs

Batting	Mat	Inns	NO	Runs	HS	Ave	SR	100	50	Ct	St
First-class	1	2	0	21	12	10.50	26.58	0	0	0	0
T20s	1	-	-	-	-	-	-	-	-	0	0
Bowling	**Mat**	**Balls**	**Runs**	**Wkts**	**BBI**	**BBM**	**Ave**	**Econ**	**SR**	**5w**	**10**
First-class	1	42	33	0	-	-	-	4.71	-	0	0
T20s	1	12	13	0	-	-	-	6.50	-	0	0

DUANNE OLIVIER RHB / RFM / R0 / W0 / MVP76

FULL NAME: Duanne Olivier
BORN: May 9, 1992, Groblersdal, South Africa
SQUAD NO: 74
TEAMS: South Africa, Yorkshire, Derbyshire, Free State, Jozi Stars, Knights
ROLE: Bowler
DEBUT: Test: 2017; ODI: 2019; First-class: 2011; List A: 2011; T20: 2011

BEST BATTING: 72 Free State vs Namibia, Bloemfontein, 2014
BEST BOWLING: 6-37 South Africa vs Pakistan, Centurion, 2018

TWITTER: @Duanne992
NOTES: Olivier caused a shock in February 2018 when Yorkshire announced that they had signed the rib-tickling fast bowler on a three-year Kolpak deal, making him ineligible to play for South Africa. He had been playing Test cricket just three days earlier. Olivier, who turns 28 in May, had become a key member of a new generation of hostile South African quicks, having taken 48 wickets at an average of just 19.25 in 10 Tests. He had a successful spell with Derbyshire in 2018 and in his first summer at Headingley took 43 wickets at 32.33 in the County Championship

Batting	Mat	Inns	NO	Runs	HS	Ave	SR	100	50	Ct	St
Tests	10	12	5	26	10*	3.71	27.95	0	0	2	0
ODIs	2	-	-	-	-	-	-	-	-	0	0
First-class	110	143	47	1230	72	12.81	43.15	0	3	30	0
List A	49	25	10	201	25*	13.40	65.68	0	0	7	0
T20s	44	15	10	73	15*	14.60	85.88	0	0	5	0
Bowling	**Mat**	**Balls**	**Runs**	**Wkts**	**BBI**	**BBM**	**Ave**	**Econ**	**SR**	**5w**	**10**
Tests	10	1440	924	48	6/37	11/96	19.25	3.85	30.0	3	1
ODIs	2	114	124	3	2/73	2/73	41.33	6.52	38.0	0	0
First-class	110	19088	10180	446	6/37	11/96	22.82	3.19	42.7	24	4
List A	49	2013	1777	63	4/34	4/34	28.20	5.29	31.9	0	0
T20s	44	869	1230	51	4/28	4/28	24.11	8.49	17.0	0	0

GRAHAM ONIONS

RHB / RMF / R0 / W8

FULL NAME: Graham Onions
BORN: September 9, 1982, Gateshead, County Durham
SQUAD NO: 99
HEIGHT: 6ft 2in
NICKNAME: Bunny, Wills
EDUCATION: St Thomas More Roman Catholic School, Blaydon, Gateshead
TEAMS: England, Lancashire, Dolphins, Durham
ROLE: Bowler
DEBUT: Test: 2009; ODI: 2009; First-class: 2004; List A: 2003; T20: 2004

BEST BATTING: 65 Durham vs Nottinghamshire, Chester-le-Street, 2016
BEST BOWLING: 9-67 Durham vs Nottinghamshire, Trent Bridge, 2012
COUNTY CAP: 2018 (Lancashire); BENEFIT: 2015 (Durham)

BEST MOMENT IN CRICKET? My Test debut, taking nine wickets against Nottinghamshire and returning to Test cricket against West Indies in 2012 after my serious back injury
SUPERSTITIONS? I lick my fingers before I bowl
CRICKETING HERO? Darren Gough
IF YOU WEREN'T A CRICKETER? I'd be struggling! Maybe a PE teacher
TWITTER: @BunnyOnions
NOTES: The veteran former England fast bowler, plagued by injury throughout his career, returned to form at the end of the 2017 season with 32 Championship wickets at 22.66. After 14 seasons at Durham, Onions moved to Lancashire in September 2017 and immediately formed a deadly new-ball pairing with Tom Bailey, taking 57 wickets at 21.77 in 2018. He was in rich form again last summer, with 45 Championship wickets at 19.58, and signed a new one-year contract in November

Batting	Mat	Inns	NO	Runs	HS	Ave	SR	100	50	Ct	St
Tests	9	10	7	30	17*	10.00	30.92	0	0	0	0
ODIs	4	1	0	1	1	1.00	50.00	0	0	1	0
First-class	192	248	86	2100	65	12.96	52.08	0	1	35	0
List A	99	38	15	185	30*	8.04	82.22	0	0	13	0
T20s	47	14	7	62	31	8.85	103.33	0	0	10	0
Bowling	**Mat**	**Balls**	**Runs**	**Wkts**	**BBI**	**BBM**	**Ave**	**Econ**	**SR**	**5w**	**10**
Tests	9	1606	957	32	5/38	7/102	29.90	3.57	50.1	1	0
ODIs	4	204	185	4	2/58	2/58	46.25	5.44	51.0	0	0
First-class	192	33474	18583	723	9/67		25.70	3.33	46.2	31	3
List A	99	4218	3658	113	4/45	4/45	32.37	5.20	37.3	0	0
T20s	47	990	1133	38	3/15	3/15	29.81	6.86	26.0	0	0

FELIX ORGAN

RHB / OB / R0 / W0

FULL NAME: Felix Spencer Organ
BORN: June 2, 1999, Sydney, Australia
SQUAD NO: 3
HEIGHT: 5ft 10in
EDUCATION: Canford School, Dorset
TEAMS: Hampshire, England U19
ROLE: Batsman
DEBUT: First-class: 2017; List A: 2018

BEST BATTING: 100 Hampshire vs Kent, Southampton, 2019
BEST BOWLING: 5-25 Hampshire vs Surrey, Southampton, 2019

NOTES: The 20-year-old top-order batsman signed his first professional contract with Hampshire in early 2018 and made a strong impression last summer, scoring his maiden first-class hundred against Kent in July. He followed this up two months later with his first five-wicket haul, proving that he is more than a handy off-spinner. Born in Sydney, Organ has come through the Hampshire youth system and was vice-captain of the side which won the U17 County Championship in 2015. In 2018 he averaged nearly 50 in the Second XI Championship and scored 843 runs at an average of 56.20 for the Hampshire Academy in the Southern Premier League. Organ signed a contract extension in February, although Hampshire have not disclosed its length

Batting	Mat	Inns	NO	Runs	HS	Ave	SR	100	50	Ct	St
First-class	7	12	0	316	100	26.33	45.66	1	2	4	0
List A	4	2	0	0	0	0.00	0.00	0	0	2	0
Bowling	**Mat**	**Balls**	**Runs**	**Wkts**	**BBI**	**BBM**	**Ave**	**Econ**	**SR**	**5w**	**10**
First-class	7	275	125	8	5/25	5/25	15.62	2.72	34.3	1	0
List A	4	63	33	2	1/6	1/6	16.50	3.14	31.5	0	0

CRAIG OVERTON

RHB / RFM / R0 / W0 / MVP7

SOMERSET / SOUTHERN BRAVE

FULL NAME: Craig Overton
BORN: April 10, 1994, Barnstaple, Devon
SQUAD NO: 12
HEIGHT: 6ft 5in
NICKNAME: Goober
EDUCATION: West Buckland School, Devon
TEAMS: England, Somerset, Southern Brave
ROLE: Allrounder
DEBUT: Test: 2017; ODI: 2018; First-class: 2012; List A: 2012; T20: 2014

BEST BATTING: 138 Somerset vs Hampshire, Taunton, 2016
BEST BOWLING: 6-24 Somerset vs Cardiff MCCU, Taunton, 2019
COUNTY CAP: 2016

FAMILY TIES? My father played Minor Counties and my twin Jamie also plays for Somerset
WHAT WAS YOUR FIRST CRICKET CLUB? North Devon CC, Bideford
HOW WOULD YOU DISMISS STEVE SMITH? Nip one back through the gate
WHAT EXCITES YOU ABOUT THE HUNDRED? Playing with different players
MOST INTERESTING TEAMMATE? Peter Trego – so many stories
BEST INNINGS YOU'VE SEEN? Chris Gayle's 151 not out for Somerset against Kent in the 2015 T20 Blast
WHICH RULE WOULD YOU CHANGE ABOUT CRICKET? If the batsman edges it through the slips then they can't score any runs
BIGGEST CRICKETING REGRET? Not winning the Championship
CRICKET STAR OF THE FUTURE? Will Smeed (England U19, Somerset Second XI)
TWITTER: @craigoverton12

Batting	Mat	Inns	NO	Runs	HS	Ave	SR	100	50	Ct	St
Tests	4	8	2	124	41*	20.66	40.78	0	0	1	0
ODIs	1	-	-	-	-	-	-	-	-	2	0
First-class	89	130	16	2392	138	20.98	63.92	1	9	60	0
List A	69	50	16	756	66*	22.23	116.84	0	2	31	0
T20s	44	24	9	241	35*	16.06	118.13	0	0	20	0
Bowling	**Mat**	**Balls**	**Runs**	**Wkts**	**BBI**	**BBM**	**Ave**	**Econ**	**SR**	**5w**	**10**
Tests	4	707	403	9	3/105	4/116	44.77	3.42	78.5	0	0
ODIs	1	42	55	0	-	-	-	7.85	-	0	0
First-class	89	14481	7459	292	6/24	9/134	25.54	3.09	49.5	7	0
List A	69	3178	2820	90	5/18	5/18	31.33	5.32	35.3	1	0
T20s	44	817	1289	36	3/17	3/17	35.80	9.46	22.6	0	0

JAMIE OVERTON RHB / RFM / R0 / W0 / MVP73

FULL NAME: Jamie Overton
BORN: April 10, 1994, Barnstaple, Devon
SQUAD NO: 8
HEIGHT: 6ft 5in
NICKNAME: J
EDUCATION: West Buckland School, Devon
TEAMS: Somerset, England Lions, Northamptonshire
ROLE: Bowler
DEBUT: First-class: 2012; List A: 2012; T20: 2015

BEST BATTING: 56 Somerset vs Warwickshire, Edgbaston, 2014
BEST BOWLING: 6-95 Somerset vs Middlesex, Taunton, 2013

FAMILY TIES? My dad played for Devon and my twin brother Craig plays for Somerset too
WHAT WAS YOUR FIRST CRICKET CLUB? North Devon CC, situated on the splitting of the Taw-Torridge Estuary
BEST INNINGS YOU'VE SEEN? Matt Renshaw's hundred before lunch against Yorkshire at Taunton in 2018
CRICKETING HERO? James Anderson
SURPRISING FACT ABOUT YOU? I was in a film when I was younger
CRICKET STAR OF THE FUTURE? Kasey Aldridge (Somerset CC)
IF YOU WERE AN ANIMAL, WHICH WOULD IT BE? A horse – fascinating animal
TWITTER: @JamieOverton

Batting	Mat	Inns	NO	Runs	HS	Ave	SR	100	50	Ct	St
First-class	64	92	21	1245	56	17.53	79.85	0	6	29	0
List A	42	31	8	399	40*	17.34	114.65	0	0	19	0
T20s	48	23	11	164	31	13.66	156.19	0	0	24	0
Bowling	**Mat**	**Balls**	**Runs**	**Wkts**	**BBI**	**BBM**	**Ave**	**Econ**	**SR**	**5w**	**10**
First-class	64	8439	5063	164	6/95	8/143	30.87	3.59	51.4	3	0
List A	42	1662	1742	57	4/42	4/42	30.56	6.28	29.1	0	0
T20s	48	937	1490	56	5/47	5/47	26.60	9.54	16.7	1	0

TONY PALLADINO

RHB / RMF / R0 / W3

FULL NAME: Antonio Paul Palladino
BORN: June 29, 1983, Tower Hamlets, London
SQUAD NO: 28
HEIGHT: 6ft
NICKNAME: Battler, Pallas, Dino
EDUCATION: Cardinal Pole Sixth Form, London; Anglia Polytechnic University
TEAMS: Namibia, Derbyshire, Essex
ROLE: Bowler
DEBUT: First-class: 2003; List A: 2003; T20: 2005

BEST BATTING: 106 Derbyshire vs Australia A, Derby, 2012
BEST BOWLING: 7-53 Derbyshire vs Kent, Derby, 2012
COUNTY CAP: 2012 (Derbyshire); BENEFIT: 2018 (Derbyshire)

WHAT WAS YOUR FIRST CRICKET CLUB? Wanstead CC, London
HOW WOULD YOU DISMISS STEVE SMITH? Sniff him off with some back-of-a-length gas
WHAT EXCITES YOU ABOUT THE HUNDRED? That I might get to play in the 50-over competition
BIGGEST TOPIC OF DISCUSSION IN YOUR DRESSING ROOM? Depends on the ground. At Derby: how much the ball is nipping. At Durham: how much the Russian (Chris Rushworth) is nipping it. At Lord's: how much Murts (Tim Murtagh) is nipping it. Otherwise, some Love Island chat
MOST INTERESTING TEAMMATE? He wasn't a teammate, but our old kit man and good friend Ted McMinn – who played football for Rangers and Derby County – used to tell some amazing stories
CRICKETING HERO? Ian Botham
SURPRISING FACT ABOUT YOU? I like classical music and I sometimes wear a Batman underarmour when I bowl
BIGGEST CRICKETING REGRET? Not moving to Derbyshire earlier
TWITTER: @apalladino28

Batting	Mat	Inns	NO	Runs	HS	Ave	SR	100	50	Ct	St
First-class	166	239	50	2915	106	15.42	47.99	1	8	40	0
List A	57	33	8	268	31	10.72	92.09	0	0	6	0
T20s	26	12	5	48	14*	6.85	81.35	0	0	5	0
Bowling	**Mat**	**Balls**	**Runs**	**Wkts**	**BBI**	**BBM**	**Ave**	**Econ**	**SR**	**5w**	**10**
First-class	166	27369	13255	464	7/53		28.56	2.90	58.9	17	1
List A	57	2273	2036	54	5/49	5/49	37.70	5.37	42.0	1	0
T20s	26	490	614	28	4/21	4/21	21.92	7.51	17.5	0	0

CALLUM PARKINSON RHB / SLA / R0 / W0

FULL NAME: Callum Francis Parkinson
BORN: October 24, 1996, Bolton, Lancashire
SQUAD NO: 10
HEIGHT: 5ft 7in
NICKNAME: Parky
EDUCATION: Bolton School; Canon Slade, Bolton
TEAMS: Leicestershire, Derbyshire
ROLE: Bowler
DEBUT: First-class: 2016; List A: 2017; T20: 2017

BEST BATTING: 75 Leicestershire vs Kent, Canterbury, 2017
BEST BOWLING: 8-148 Leicestershire vs Worcestershire, Worcester, 2017

FAMILY TIES? My dad played in the Bolton League. My twin brother Matt is at Lancashire and made his England debut at the end of last year
WHAT WAS YOUR FIRST CRICKET CLUB? Heaton CC, Bolton
WHAT WERE YOU DOING WHEN ENGLAND WON THE WORLD CUP? I was with a few of the lads at a pub in a lovely little spot of Cheltenham on the eve of a Championship game
HOW WOULD YOU DISMISS STEVE SMITH? Underarm?
BIGGEST TOPIC OF DISCUSSION IN YOUR DRESSING ROOM? Harry Swindell's ears
WHICH RULE WOULD YOU CHANGE ABOUT CRICKET? Five men outside the ring in List A cricket. Having only four is killing spinners!
CRICKET STAR OF THE FUTURE? JJ Fielding (Lancashire Academy). He's got a bit of ticker about him
WHICH BOOK MEANS MOST TO YOU? The Bolton Wanderers Season Review 2005
IF YOU WERE AN ANIMAL, WHICH WOULD IT BE? Woodpecker – so that I could consistently annoy some of the lads in the dressing room
TWITTER: @cal_parky

Batting	Mat	Inns	NO	Runs	HS	Ave	SR	100	50	Ct	St
First-class	25	39	7	593	75	18.53	41.26	0	1	4	0
List A	13	11	3	222	52*	27.75	87.40	0	1	2	0
T20s	43	22	10	146	27*	12.16	95.42	0	0	6	0
Bowling	**Mat**	**Balls**	**Runs**	**Wkts**	**BBI**	**BBM**	**Ave**	**Econ**	**SR**	**5w**	**10**
First-class	25	3730	2148	46	8/148	10/185	46.69	3.45	81.0	1	1
List A	13	552	589	4	1/34	1/34	147.25	6.40	138.0	0	0
T20s	43	804	1048	42	4/20	4/20	24.95	7.82	19.1	0	0

MATTHEW PARKINSON RHB / LB / R0 / W0 / MVP90

FULL NAME: Matthew William Parkinson
BORN: October 24, 1996, Bolton, Lancashire
SQUAD NO: 28
HEIGHT: 5ft 9in
NICKNAME: Daddy, Parky
EDUCATION: Canon Slade School, Bolton
TEAMS: England, Lancashire, Manchester Originals
ROLE: Bowler
DEBUT: ODI: 2020; T20I: 2019; First-class: 2016; List A: 2018; T20: 2017

BEST BATTING: 14 Lancashire vs Middlesex, Lord's, 2017
BEST BOWLING: 6-23 Lancashire vs Sussex, Old Trafford, 2019
COUNTY CAP: 2019

FAMILY TIES? Dad played for Lancashire Federation U19 and league cricket in Bolton. My twin Callum plays for Leicestershire
WHAT WAS YOUR FIRST CRICKET CLUB? Heaton CC, Bolton, Greater Manchester
BIGGEST TOPIC OF DISCUSSION IN YOUR DRESSING ROOM? Instagram choices
MOST INTERESTING TEAMMATE? Shivnarine Chanderpaul – so many stories and funny traits. He wore a box when fielding
CRICKETING HERO? Stuart MacGill
CRICKET STAR OF THE FUTURE? England U19 captain George Balderson
IF YOU WERE AN ANIMAL, WHICH WOULD IT BE? Winnie the Pooh – slow, tubby and I like honey
TWITTER: @mattypark96

Batting	Mat	Inns	NO	Runs	HS	Ave	SR	100	50	Ct	St
ODIs	2	-	-	-	-	-	-	-	-	0	0
T20Is	2	-	-	-	-	-	-	-	-	0	0
First-class	21	27	9	112	22	6.22	29.78	0	0	6	0
List A	27	11	8	43	15*	14.33	52.43	0	0	4	0
T20s	38	7	4	14	7*	4.66	87.50	0	0	5	0
Bowling	**Mat**	**Balls**	**Runs**	**Wkts**	**BBI**	**BBM**	**Ave**	**Econ**	**SR**	**5w**	**10**
ODIs	2	64	63	0	-	-	-	5.90	-	0	0
T20Is	2	36	61	5	4/47	4/47	12.20	10.16	7.2	0	0
First-class	21	3071	1583	63	6/23	10/165	25.12	3.09	48.7	3	1
List A	27	1366	1178	42	5/51	5/51	28.04	5.17	32.5	2	0
T20s	38	814	977	65	4/23	4/23	15.03	7.20	12.5	0	0

WAYNE PARNELL LFM / LHB / R0 / W0 / MVP29

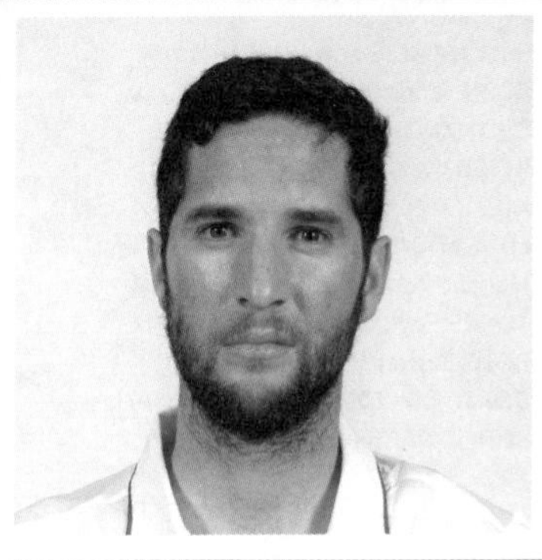

FULL NAME: Wayne Dillon Parnell
BORN: July 30, 1989, Port Elizabeth, SA
SQUAD NO: 7
HEIGHT: 6ft 2in
NICKNAME: Parny, Parnygram
EDUCATION: Nelson Mandela University
TEAMS: South Africa, Worcestershire, Manchester Originals, Delhi Daredevils, Eastern Province, Glamorgan, Kent, Pune Warriors, Sussex, Warriors, Western Province
ROLE: Allrounder
DEBUT: Test: 2010; ODI: 2009; T20I: 2009; First-class: 2006; List A: 2007; T20: 2008

BEST BATTING: 111* Cape Cobras vs Warriors, Paarl, 2016
BEST BOWLING: 7-51 Cape Cobras vs Dolphins, Cape Town, 2016

WHAT WAS YOUR FIRST CRICKET CLUB? Northville CC, Port Elizabeth, South Africa. I was recruited aged 14 to play in the first XI and that's where I learned to be mentally tough. The older guys really helped me cope with the pressure
HOW WOULD YOU DISMISS STEVE SMITH? I'd send him an invitation
BIGGEST TOPIC OF DISCUSSION IN YOUR DRESSING ROOM? Who is getting the next round of coffee
MOST INTERESTING TEAMMATE? Charlie Morris – the neatest cricketer I've ever met
WHICH BOOK MEANS MOST TO YOU? The Quran
IF YOU WERE AN ANIMAL, WHICH WOULD IT BE? A lion – king of the jungle
TWITTER: @WayneParnell

Batting	Mat	Inns	NO	Runs	HS	Ave	SR	100	50	Ct	St
Tests	6	4	0	67	23	16.75	37.22	0	0	3	0
ODIs	65	38	14	508	56	21.16	78.39	0	1	12	0
T20Is	40	13	9	114	29*	28.50	118.75	0	0	5	0
First-class	75	101	11	2502	111*	27.80	52.68	2	15	23	0
List A	165	115	32	2087	129	25.14	87.72	2	6	31	0
T20s	206	120	46	1460	99	19.72	123.93	0	4	36	0
Bowling	**Mat**	**Balls**	**Runs**	**Wkts**	**BBI**	**BBM**	**Ave**	**Econ**	**SR**	**5w**	**10**
Tests	6	556	414	15	4/51	6/89	27.60	4.46	37.0	0	0
ODIs	65	2911	2738	94	5/48	5/48	29.12	5.64	30.9	2	0
T20Is	40	749	1038	41	4/13	4/13	25.31	8.31	18.2	0	0
First-class	75	11431	6542	220	7/51	12/105	29.73	3.43	51.9	7	1
List A	165	7431	6750	233	6/51	6/51	28.96	5.45	31.8	5	0
T20s	206	4054	5282	209	4/13	4/13	25.27	7.81	19.3	0	0

STEPHEN PARRY

RHB / SLA / R0 / W0

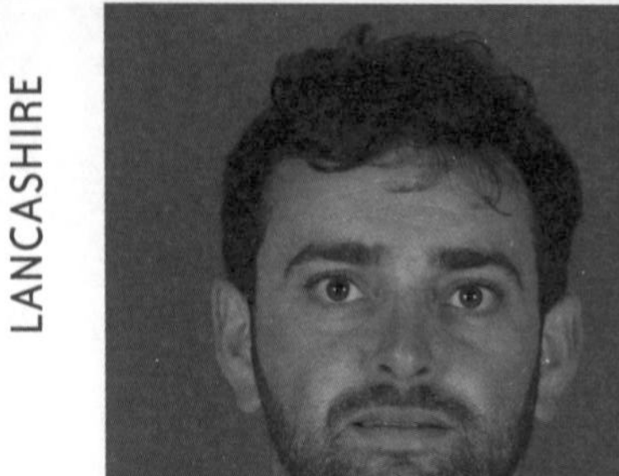

FULL NAME: Stephen David Parry
BORN: January 12, 1986, Manchester
SQUAD NO: 4
HEIGHT: 6ft
NICKNAME: Pazza
EDUCATION: Audenshaw High School, Manchester
TEAMS: England, Lancashire, Brisbane Heat
ROLE: Bowler
DEBUT: ODI: 2014; T20I: 2014; First-class: 2007; List A: 2009; T20: 2009

BEST BATTING: 44 Lancashire vs Somerset, Old Trafford, 2017
BEST BOWLING: 5-23 Lancashire vs Durham UCCE, Durham University, 2007
COUNTY CAP: 2015; BENEFIT: 2020

WHAT WAS YOUR FIRST CRICKET CLUB? Denton CC, Tameside, Greater Manchester
WHAT WERE YOU DOING WHEN ENGLAND WON THE WORLD CUP? Cheering on the boys in the pub
BIGGEST TOPIC OF DISCUSSION IN YOUR DRESSING ROOM? Lancashire winning trophies
SURPRISING FACT ABOUT YOU? I'm an elite table-tennis player
IF YOU WERE AN ANIMAL, WHICH WOULD IT BE? A crocodile – very patient
TWITTER: @SDParry86

Batting	Mat	Inns	NO	Runs	HS	Ave	SR	100	50	Ct	St
ODIs	2	-	-	-	-	-	-	-	-	0	0
T20Is	5	1	0	1	1	1.00	100.00	0	0	2	0
First-class	28	34	2	456	44	14.25	44.66	0	0	7	0
List A	96	49	21	342	31	12.21	77.37	0	0	32	0
T20s	125	35	22	140	15*	10.76	106.87	0	0	27	0
Bowling	**Mat**	**Balls**	**Runs**	**Wkts**	**BBI**	**BBM**	**Ave**	**Econ**	**SR**	**5w**	**10**
ODIs	2	114	92	4	3/32	3/32	23.00	4.84	28.5	0	0
T20Is	5	96	138	3	2/33	2/33	46.00	8.62	32.0	0	0
First-class	28	4301	1926	58	5/23	6/101	33.20	2.68	74.1	2	0
List A	96	4162	3485	116	5/17	5/17	30.04	5.02	35.8	1	0
T20s	125	2598	3135	122	5/13	5/13	25.69	7.24	21.2	1	0

JEETAN PATEL

RHB / OB / R0 / W7 / MVP3

FULL NAME: Jeetan Shashi Patel
BORN: May 7, 1980, Wellington, New Zealand
SQUAD NO: 5
HEIGHT: 5ft 8in
NICKNAME: Dave
TEAMS: New Zealand, Warwickshire, North Island, Wellington
ROLE: Bowler
DEBUT: Test: 2006; ODI: 2005; T20I: 2005; First-class: 1999; List A: 1999; T20: 2005

BEST BATTING: 120 Warwickshire vs Yorkshire, Edgbaston, 2014
BEST BOWLING: 8-36 Warwickshire vs Surrey, Edgbaston, 2019
COUNTY CAP: 2012

WHAT GOT YOU INTO CRICKET? My old man – he's a cricket badger
WHAT WAS YOUR FIRST CRICKET CLUB? Eastern Suburbs CC, Wellington, New Zealand
BEST THING ABOUT YOUR HOME GROUND? Edgbaston has the best dressing rooms in the country
WHICH BOWLER WOULD YOU LEAST LIKE TO FACE? Courtney Walsh
CRICKETING HERO? Saqlain Mushtaq
NON-CRICKETING HERO? Tiger Woods

Batting	Mat	Inns	NO	Runs	HS	Ave	SR	100	50	Ct	St
Tests	24	38	8	381	47	12.70	51.62	0	0	13	0
ODIs	43	15	8	95	34	13.57	58.64	0	0	13	0
T20Is	11	4	1	9	5	3.00	64.28	0	0	4	0
First-class	293	392	79	6695	120	21.38		3	28	156	0
List A	231	121	37	836	50	9.95		0	1	96	0
T20s	232	94	30	434	34*	6.78	125.43	0	0	80	0
Bowling	**Mat**	**Balls**	**Runs**	**Wkts**	**BBI**	**BBM**	**Ave**	**Econ**	**SR**	**5w**	**10**
Tests	24	5833	3078	65	5/110	6/151	47.35	3.16	89.7	1	0
ODIs	43	2014	1691	49	3/11	3/11	34.51	5.03	41.1	0	0
T20Is	11	199	269	16	3/20	3/20	16.81	8.11	12.4	0	0
First-class	293	61003	29239	892	8/36		32.77	2.87	68.3	38	7
List A	231	11229	8748	288	5/43	5/43	30.37	4.67	38.9	2	0
T20s	232	4811	5601	234	4/11	4/11	23.93	6.98	20.5	0	0

RISHI PATEL

RHB / LB / R0 / W0

FULL NAME: Rishi Ketan Patel
BORN: July 26, 1998, Chigwell, Essex
SQUAD NO: 12
HEIGHT: 6ft 2in
NICKNAME: Yogi
EDUCATION: Brentwood School, Essex
TEAMS: Essex
ROLE: Batsman
DEBUT: First-class: 2019; List A: 2019

BEST BATTING: 35 Essex vs Yorkshire, Chelmsford, 2019

WHAT WAS YOUR FIRST CRICKET CLUB? Ilford CC, London
BIGGEST TOPIC OF DISCUSSION IN YOUR DRESSING ROOM? Golf
MOST INTERESTING TEAMMATE? Matt Quinn – he is a unique character to have in the dressing room
CRICKET STAR OF THE FUTURE? Robin Das (Essex Academy)
IF YOU WERE AN ANIMAL, WHICH WOULD IT BE? A dolphin – they're so relaxed
TWITTER: @rp2426
NOTES: The 21-year-old batsman signed his first professional contract in September 2018 running until the end of this season. Patel equalled the club record of five centuries in a Second XI Championship in 2018 and played against the Indians in a tour match that summer. Breaking into a powerful Essex side will not be easy, but Patel did make seven senior appearances for the club last season, four of them in the Championship, while also turning out for Cambridge MCCU

Batting	Mat	Inns	NO	Runs	HS	Ave	SR	100	50	Ct	St
First-class	6	8	0	146	35	18.25	48.82	0	0	6	0
List A	3	3	0	65	35	21.66	91.54	0	0	0	0
Bowling	**Mat**	**Balls**	**Runs**	**Wkts**	**BBI**	**BBM**	**Ave**	**Econ**	**SR**	**5w**	**10**
First-class	6	-	-	-	-	-	-	-	-	-	-
List A	3	-	-	-	-	-	-	-	-	-	-

RYAN PATEL

LHB / RFM / R0 / W0

FULL NAME: Ryan Patel
BORN: October 26, 1997, Sutton, Surrey
SQUAD NO: 26
HEIGHT: 5ft 10in
NICKNAME: FP
EDUCATION: Whitgift School, Croydon
TEAMS: Surrey, England U19
ROLE: Allrounder
DEBUT: First-class: 2017; List A: 2019; T20: 2019

BEST BATTING: 100* Surrey vs Essex, The Oval, 2019
BEST BOWLING: 6-5 Surrey vs Somerset, Guildford, 2018

WHAT WAS YOUR FIRST CRICKET CLUB? Old Rutlishians CC, London
CRICKETING HERO? Jacques Kallis
WHICH BOWLER WOULD YOU LEAST LIKE TO FACE? Pat Cummins
BEST INNINGS YOU'VE SEEN? Kumar Sangakkara's double hundred against Essex at Chelmsford in 2017
WHICH RULE WOULD YOU CHANGE ABOUT CRICKET? Make the stumps bigger
YOUR BIGGEST CRICKETING REGRET? Realising that hair-loss treatment doesn't work
SURPRISING FACT ABOUT YOU? I was an opening bowler who batted down the order until I was 15 but have since become an opening batsman who bowls
SURPRISING FACT ABOUT A TEAMMATE? Matt Dunn used to live in Norway
FAVOURITE QUOTE OR SAYING? I am the master of my fate: I am the captain of my soul (William Ernest Henley)
WHICH BOOK MEANS MOST TO YOU? The Obstacle is the Way – The Timeless Art of Turning Trials into Triumph by Ryan Holiday

Batting	Mat	Inns	NO	Runs	HS	Ave	SR	100	50	Ct	St
First-class	23	36	4	848	100*	26.50	39.44	1	2	9	0
List A	3	3	1	57	41*	28.50	95.00	0	0	1	0
T20s	7	3	1	7	5*	3.50	70.00	0	0	1	0
Bowling	**Mat**	**Balls**	**Runs**	**Wkts**	**BBI**	**BBM**	**Ave**	**Econ**	**SR**	**5w**	**10**
First-class	23	1263	701	15	6/5	6/12	46.73	3.33	84.2	1	0
List A	3	72	82	2	2/65	2/65	41.00	6.83	36.0	0	0
T20s	7	21	36	0	-	-	-	10.28	-	0	0

SAMIT PATEL RHB / SLA / R4 / W0 / MVP52

FULL NAME: Samit Rohit Patel
BORN: November 30, 1984, Leicester
SQUAD NO: 21
HEIGHT: 5ft 8in
NICKNAME: Sarnie, Slippery
EDUCATION: Worksop College, Nottinghamshire
TEAMS: England, Nottinghamshire, Islamabad United, Lahore Qalandars, Melbourne Renegades, Rajshahi Kings, Wellington
ROLE: Allrounder
DEBUT: Test: 2012; ODI: 2008; T20I: 2011; First-class: 2002; List A: 2002; T20: 2003

BEST BATTING: 257* Nottinghamshire vs Gloucestershire, Bristol, 2017
BEST BOWLING: 7-68 Nottinghamshire vs Hampshire, Southampton, 2011
COUNTY CAP: 2008; BENEFIT: 2017

FAMILY TIES? My brother Akhil played for Nottinghamshire for two years
WHAT WAS YOUR FIRST CRICKET CLUB? Kimberley Institute CC, Nottinghamshire
BEST INNINGS YOU'VE SEEN? Sachin Tendulkar's double century in the 2004 Sydney Test – for the mental strength he showed in not playing a cover-drive
CRICKETING HERO? Stephen Fleming
WHICH RULE WOULD YOU CHANGE ABOUT CRICKET? Being run out backing up
TWITTER: @Samitpatel21

Batting	Mat	Inns	NO	Runs	HS	Ave	SR	100	50	Ct	St
Tests	6	9	0	151	42	16.77	44.67	0	0	3	0
ODIs	36	22	7	482	70*	32.13	93.23	0	1	7	0
T20Is	18	14	2	189	67	15.75	109.24	0	1	3	0
First-class	226	369	20	12482	257*	35.76	62.58	26	62	138	0
List A	245	212	34	6270	136*	35.22	85.38	8	33	70	0
T20s	278	237	49	4921	90*	26.17	125.40	0	29	85	0
Bowling	**Mat**	**Balls**	**Runs**	**Wkts**	**BBI**	**BBM**	**Ave**	**Econ**	**SR**	**5w**	**10**
Tests	6	858	421	7	2/27	3/164	60.14	2.94	122.5	0	0
ODIs	36	1187	1091	24	5/41	5/41	45.45	5.51	49.4	1	0
T20Is	18	252	321	7	2/6	2/6	45.85	7.64	36.0	0	0
First-class	226	25971	13262	344	7/68		38.55	3.06	75.4	5	1
List A	245	8319	7491	225	6/13	6/13	33.29	5.40	36.9	2	0
T20s	278	5043	6114	226	4/5	4/5	27.05	7.27	22.3	0	0

STEVEN PATTERSON RHB / RMF / R0 / W2 / MVP59

FULL NAME: Steven Andrew Patterson
BORN: October 3, 1983, Beverley, Yorkshire
SQUAD NO: 17
HEIGHT: 6ft 4in
NICKNAME: Dead Man, Patto
EDUCATION: Malet Lambert School, Hull; St Mary's Sixth Form College, Hull; University of Leeds
TEAMS: Yorkshire
ROLE: Bowler
DEBUT: First-class: 2005; List A: 2003; T20: 2009

BEST BATTING: 63* Yorkshire vs Warwickshire, Edgbaston, 2016
BEST BOWLING: 6-40 Yorkshire vs Essex, Chelmsford, 2018
COUNTY CAP: 2012; BENEFIT: 2017

FAMILY TIES? My grandad played for Durham before World War II
BEST MOMENT IN CRICKET? Making my Championship debut at Scarborough, receiving my first XI cap, and winning the County Championship
CRICKETING HERO? Shaun Pollock
NON-CRICKETING HERO? My grandad
IF YOU WEREN'T A CRICKETER? I'd be working in finance

Batting	Mat	Inns	NO	Runs	HS	Ave	SR	100	50	Ct	St
First-class	155	186	43	2354	63*	16.46	39.43	0	4	31	0
List A	96	40	21	249	25*	13.10		0	0	17	0
T20s	63	9	4	9	3*	1.80	42.85	0	0	10	0
Bowling	**Mat**	**Balls**	**Runs**	**Wkts**	**BBI**	**BBM**	**Ave**	**Econ**	**SR**	**5w**	**10**
First-class	155	25047	11454	409	6/40	8/94	28.00	2.74	61.2	8	0
List A	96	4116	3524	122	6/32	6/32	28.88	5.13	33.7	2	0
T20s	63	1290	1811	61	4/30	4/30	29.68	8.42	21.1	0	0

LIAM PATTERSON-WHITE LHB / SLA / R0 / W0

FULL NAME: Liam Anthony Patterson-White
BORN: November 8, 1998, Sunderland, County Durham
SQUAD NO: 87
HEIGHT: 6ft
NICKNAME: LPW, Patto
EDUCATION: Worksop College, Nottinghamshire
TEAMS: Nottinghamshire, England U19
ROLE: Allrounder
DEBUT: First-class: 2019

BEST BATTING: 58* Nottinghamshire vs Yorkshire, Scarborough, 2019
BEST BOWLING: 5-73 Nottinghamshire vs Somerset, Taunton, 2019

WHAT WAS YOUR FIRST CRICKET CLUB? Basford Mill CC, Nottingham
WHAT WERE YOU DOING WHEN ENGLAND WON THE WORLD CUP? Celebrating in the changing room at Trent Bridge
BIGGEST TOPIC OF DISCUSSION IN YOUR DRESSING ROOM? Performance
MOST INTERESTING TEAMMATE? Ravi Ashwin – an infinite source of wisdom
CRICKET STAR OF THE FUTURE? Chris Gibson (Nottinghamshire Academy)
IF YOU WERE AN ANIMAL, WHICH WOULD IT BE? A lion
TWITTER: @LiamPattersonW2
NOTES: The left-arm spinner and middle-order batsman signed a three year contract with Notts last September after breaking into the first team with a series of stellar performances in the County Championship. A former England U19 allrounder who has come through the Notts Academy, Patterson-White's first-class career got off to an unfortunate start when he made his Championship debut against Somerset at Taunton last July. He had to leave the field after an hour of play because of tonsillitis and was out for a duck when he returned to action the next day. But his first five-wicket haul followed in Somerset's second innings and he went on to take 20 wickets at 21.00 in five Championship matches last summer, also notching a maiden first-class fifty

Batting	Mat	Inns	NO	Runs	HS	Ave	SR	100	50	Ct	St
First-class	5	8	2	91	58*	15.16	29.35	0	1	3	0
Bowling	**Mat**	**Balls**	**Runs**	**Wkts**	**BBI**	**BBM**	**Ave**	**Econ**	**SR**	**5w**	**10**
First-class	5	809	420	20	5/73	6/107	21.00	3.11	40.4	1	0

DAVID PAYNE RHB / LFM / R0 / W0 / MVP46

FULL NAME: David Alan Payne
BORN: February 15, 1991, Poole, Dorset
SQUAD NO: 14
HEIGHT: 6ft 3in
NICKNAME: Sid, Payney
EDUCATION: Lytchett Minster Secondary and Sixth Form, Poole, Dorset
TEAMS: Gloucestershire, Welsh Fire, England U19
ROLE: Bowler
DEBUT: First-class: 2011; List A: 2009; T20: 2010

BEST BATTING: 67* Gloucestershire vs Glamorgan, Cardiff, 2016
BEST BOWLING: 6-26 Gloucestershire vs Leicestershire, Bristol, 2011
COUNTY CAP: 2011

WHAT WAS YOUR FIRST CRICKET CLUB? Parley CC, Dorset
HOW WOULD YOU DISMISS STEVE SMITH? Left arm over, swing some in, cross my fingers
MOST INTERESTING TEAMMATE? David Wade – he served in the army before becoming a cricketer
BEST INNINGS YOU'VE SEEN? Michael Klinger and Jack Taylor scoring hundreds to chase down 320 in 50-odd overs in a Championship match at New Road in 2016
CRICKETING HERO? Andrew Flintoff
WHICH RULE WOULD YOU CHANGE ABOUT CRICKET? Set a maximum of 75 overs per day for four-day cricket
SURPRISING FACT ABOUT YOU? I cut my own hair
TWITTER: @sidpayne7

Batting	Mat	Inns	NO	Runs	HS	Ave	SR	100	50	Ct	St
First-class	95	117	38	1628	67*	20.60	47.29	0	6	31	0
List A	66	27	17	171	36*	17.10	76.68	0	0	19	0
T20s	82	21	13	49	10	6.12	90.74	0	0	15	0
Bowling	**Mat**	**Balls**	**Runs**	**Wkts**	**BBI**	**BBM**	**Ave**	**Econ**	**SR**	**5w**	**10**
First-class	95	15593	8214	263	6/26	9/96	31.23	3.16	59.2	3	0
List A	66	2867	2746	110	7/29	7/29	24.96	5.74	26.0	3	0
T20s	82	1610	2252	99	5/24	5/24	22.74	8.39	16.2	1	0

DILLON PENNINGTON RHB / RMF / R0 / W0

FULL NAME: Dillon Young Pennington
BORN: February 26, 1999, Shrewsbury, Shropshire
SQUAD NO: 22
HEIGHT: 6ft 4in
NICKNAME: Dill
EDUCATION: Wrekin College, Shropshire; University of Worcester
TEAMS: Worcestershire, England U19
ROLE: Bowler
DEBUT: First-class: 2018; List A: 2018; T20: 2018

BEST BATTING: 37 Worcestershire vs Somerset, Worcester, 2018
BEST BOWLING: 4-53 Worcestershire vs Yorkshire, Scarborough, 2018

WHAT WAS YOUR FIRST CRICKET CLUB? Shrewsbury CC, Shropshire
WHAT EXCITES YOU ABOUT THE HUNDRED? Bigger crowds and a bigger fanbase
MOST INTERESTING TEAMMATE? Adam Finch – tends to do very odd things
WHICH RULE WOULD YOU CHANGE ABOUT CRICKET? Outlaw the lbw rule! I get hit on the front pad quite a lot
BIGGEST CRICKETING REGRET? Being injured a lot of the time and causing the Worcestershire staff hell
CRICKET STAR OF THE FUTURE? Josh Dickenson (Worcestershire Academy)
IF YOU WERE AN ANIMAL, WHICH WOULD IT BE? A dog – they're chilled and don't have to think about a lot
TWITTER: @DillonPenning14

Batting	Mat	Inns	NO	Runs	HS	Ave	SR	100	50	Ct	St
First-class	12	22	3	138	37	7.26	36.80	0	0	4	0
List A	3	2	1	7	4*	7.00	28.00	0	0	2	0
T20s	16	5	3	15	6*	7.50	75.00	0	0	3	0
Bowling	**Mat**	**Balls**	**Runs**	**Wkts**	**BBI**	**BBM**	**Ave**	**Econ**	**SR**	**5w**	**10**
First-class	12	1812	1079	30	4/53	6/80	35.96	3.57	60.4	0	0
List A	3	156	178	8	5/67	5/67	22.25	6.84	19.5	1	0
T20s	16	264	383	16	4/9	4/9	23.93	8.70	16.5	0	0

MICHAEL PEPPER

RHB / WK / R0 / W0

FULL NAME: Michael-Kyle Steven Pepper
BORN: June 25, 1998, Harlow, Essex
SQUAD NO: 19
HEIGHT: 6ft 2in
NICKNAME: Peps
EDUCATION: The Perse School, Cambridge
TEAMS: Essex
ROLE: Wicketkeeper/batsman
DEBUT: First-class: 2018; T20: 2018

BEST BATTING: 22 Essex vs Somerset, Chelmsford, 2018

WHAT WAS YOUR FIRST CRICKET CLUB? Wendens Ambo CC, Saffron Walden
HOW WOULD YOU DISMISS STEVE SMITH? Get one to swing in, nip away, and roll along the ground
BIGGEST TOPIC OF DISCUSSION IN YOUR DRESSING ROOM? When we're going to play the next game of four-ball golf
MOST INTERESTING TEAMMATE? Feroze Khushi – he watches from inside the downstairs changing room
CRICKET STAR OF THE FUTURE? Jack Plom (Essex)
NOTES: The 21-year-old wicketkeeper/batsman signed his first two-year deal with the club in September 2018 after making his Championship and T20 debuts earlier that summer. As understudy to Adam Wheater, he was sidelined after appendix surgery in the early part of last season and made just one Championship appereance in 2019. Pepper has also played for Cambridgeshire in Minor Counties cricket and for Cambridge Granta in the East Anglian Premier League

Batting	Mat	Inns	NO	Runs	HS	Ave	SR	100	50	Ct	St
First-class	3	6	0	61	22	10.16	39.35	0	0	6	0
T20s	4	3	2	53	27	53.00	98.14	0	0	1	0
Bowling	**Mat**	**Balls**	**Runs**	**Wkts**	**BBI**	**BBM**	**Ave**	**Econ**	**SR**	**5w**	**10**
First-class	3	-	-	-	-	-	-	-	-	-	-
T20s	4	-	-	-	-	-	-	-	-	-	-

VERNON PHILANDER RHB / RFM / R0 / W0

FULL NAME: Vernon Darryl Philander
BORN: June 24, 1985, Bellville, South Africa
SQUAD NO: 1
NICKNAME: Pro
EDUCATION: Ravensmead High School, Cape Town
TEAMS: South Africa, Somerset, Cape Cobras, Cape Town Blitz, Durban Heat, Jamaica Tallawahs, Kent, Middlesex, Nottinghamshire, South Western Districts, Western Province
ROLE: Bowler
DEBUT: Test: 2011; ODI: 2007; T20I: 2007; First-class: 2004; List A: 2004; T20: 2005

BEST BATTING: 168 Western Province vs Griqualand West, Kimberley, 2004
BEST BOWLING: 7-61 Cape Cobras vs Knights, Cape Town, 2012
COUNTY CAP: 2015 (Nottinghamshire)

TWITTER: @VDP_24
NOTES: The prolific South African seamer has signed for Somerset on a two-year Kolpak deal having retired from international cricket at the conclusion of the home Test series against England in January. He will be available across all formats. Philander's haul of 224 Test wickets puts him seventh on South Africa's all-time list and his average of 22.32 is bettered by only seven bowlers in the history of the game who have taken 200 wickets or more. He is also a dangerous batsman in the lower order, with a healthy first-class average in the mid-20s and three hundreds. He played five Championship matches for Somerset in 2012, taking 23 wickets at 21.34, and has also had successful spells at Middlesex, Kent and Nottinghamshire

Batting	Mat	Inns	NO	Runs	HS	Ave	SR	100	50	Ct	St
Tests	64	94	20	1779	74	24.04	44.53	0	8	17	0
ODIs	30	19	7	151	30*	12.58	70.89	0	0	6	0
T20Is	7	4	0	14	6	3.50	50.00	0	0	1	0
First-class	168	234	45	4941	168	26.14	46.94	3	17	41	0
List A	129	89	29	1418	79*	23.63	75.06	0	5	12	0
T20s	123	89	45	1211	56*	27.52	137.30	0	1	28	0
Bowling	**Mat**	**Balls**	**Runs**	**Wkts**	**BBI**	**BBM**	**Ave**	**Econ**	**SR**	**5w**	**10**
Tests	64	11391	5000	224	6/21	10/102	22.32	2.63	50.8	13	2
ODIs	30	1279	986	41	4/12	4/12	24.04	4.62	31.1	0	0
T20Is	7	83	114	4	2/23	2/23	28.50	8.24	20.7	0	0
First-class	168	29108	12661	580	7/61		21.82	2.60	50.1	24	2
List A	129	5419	4207	129	4/12	4/12	32.61	4.65	42.0	0	0
T20s	123	2164	2868	92	5/17	5/17	31.17	7.95	23.5	2	0

MATHEW PILLANS

RHB / RF / RO / WO

FULL NAME: Mathew William Pillans
BORN: July 4, 1991, Pretoria, South Africa
SQUAD NO: 47
HEIGHT: 6ft 4in
EDUCATION: Pretoria Boys High School
TEAMS: Yorkshire, Dolphins, KwaZulu-Natal, Leicestershire, Northerns, Surrey
ROLE: Bowler
DEBUT: First-class: 2012; List A: 2013; T20: 2014

BEST BATTING: 56 Leicestershire vs Northamptonshire, Northampton, 2017
BEST BOWLING: 6-67 Dolphins vs Knights, Durban, 2015

FAMILY TIES? My mum played for the Springbok hockey team for 13 years and my dad played rugby in Zimbabwe and represented the World XV
BEST MOMENT IN CRICKET? Bowling the final over for Leicestershire against Notts in the 2017 T20 Blast and defending eight runs
CRICKETING HERO? Brett Lee. He is an amazingly dedicated cricketer and a great man both on and off the field to anyone he meets
IF YOU WEREN'T A CRICKETER? I'd be a fly-fisherman
SURPRISING FACT ABOUT YOU? I had open-heart surgery when I was 12
NON-CRICKETING HERO? Nelson Mandela
TWITTER: @matwilpil

Batting	Mat	Inns	NO	Runs	HS	Ave	SR	100	50	Ct	St
First-class	42	59	5	730	56	13.51	64.71	0	1	20	0
List A	19	13	5	133	31	16.62	91.09	0	0	5	0
T20s	39	18	9	174	34*	19.33	108.07	0	0	8	0
Bowling	**Mat**	**Balls**	**Runs**	**Wkts**	**BBI**	**BBM**	**Ave**	**Econ**	**SR**	**5w**	**10**
First-class	42	6505	3710	131	6/67	10/129	28.32	3.42	49.6	3	1
List A	19	734	688	32	5/29	5/29	21.50	5.62	22.9	1	0
T20s	39	715	1022	38	3/15	3/15	26.89	8.57	18.8	0	0

JACK PLOM

LHB / RFM / R0 / W0

ESSEX

FULL NAME: Jack Henry Plom
BORN: August 27, 1999, Basildon, Essex
SQUAD NO: 77
HEIGHT: 6ft 3in
NICKNAME: Plommy
EDUCATION: Gable Hall School, Corringham; South Essex College, Southend-on-Sea
TEAMS: Essex, England U19
ROLE: Bowler
DEBUT: First-class: 2018

WHAT WAS YOUR FIRST CRICKET CLUB? Shenfield CC, Brentwood
WHAT WERE YOU DOING WHEN ENGLAND WON THE WORLD CUP? Watching in the changing room – we had just beaten Notts in a Championship game inside three days and started watching with about a dozen overs left of England's chase
HOW WOULD YOU DISMISS STEVE SMITH? Slow full toss about thigh high
WHAT EXCITES YOU ABOUT THE HUNDRED? The players from each county being mixed up into new teams
BIGGEST TOPIC OF DISCUSSION IN YOUR DRESSING ROOM? What's for lunch
MOST INTERESTING TEAMMATE? Ravi Bopara – down to earth, good banter, and some okay stories
WHICH RULE WOULD YOU CHANGE ABOUT CRICKET? In T20, allow a 'last-man-stands' rule so that the not-out batsman can bat on his own
CRICKET STAR OF THE FUTURE? Robin Das (Essex Academy)
WHICH BOOK MEANS MOST TO YOU? Thinking Out Loud – Love, Grief and Being Mum and Dad by Rio Ferdinand
IF YOU WERE AN ANIMAL, WHICH WOULD IT BE? A giraffe – I've got a long neck

Batting	Mat	Inns	NO	Runs	HS	Ave	SR	100	50	Ct	St
First-class	1	-	-	-	-	-	-	-	-	-	-
Bowling	**Mat**	**Balls**	**Runs**	**Wkts**	**BBI**	**BBM**	**Ave**	**Econ**	**SR**	**5w**	**10**
First-class	1	-	-	-	-	-	-	-	-	-	-

LIAM PLUNKETT RHB / RFM / R0 / W3

FULL NAME: Liam Edward Plunkett
BORN: April 6, 1985, Middlesbrough
SQUAD NO: 28
HEIGHT: 6ft 4in
NICKNAME: Pudsy
EDUCATION: Nunthorpe Comprehensive School; Teesside Tertiary College
TEAMS: England, Surrey, Welsh Fire, Chattogram Challengers, Delhi Daredevils, Durham, Melbourne Stars, Sylhet Sixers, Yorkshire
ROLE: Bowler
DEBUT: Test: 2005; ODI: 2005; T20I: 2006; First-class: 2003; List A: 2003; T20: 2003

BEST BATTING: 126 Yorkshire vs Hampshire, Headingley, 2016
BEST BOWLING: 6-33 Durham vs Leeds/Bradford MCCU, Headingley, 2013
COUNTY CAP: 2013 (Yorkshire)

WHAT WAS YOUR FIRST CRICKET CLUB? Marske CC, North Yorkshire
WHAT WERE YOU DOING WHEN ENGLAND WON THE WORLD CUP? I was playing in the final!
HOW WOULD YOU DISMISS STEVE SMITH? With a 100mph leg-stump yorker
WHAT EXCITES YOU ABOUT THE HUNDRED? The unknown
MOST INTERESTING TEAMMATE? Mark Wood – funny and annoying at the same time
CRICKET STAR OF THE FUTURE? Charlie Hudson (Marton CC, Middlesbrough)
IF YOU WERE AN ANIMAL, WHICH WOULD IT BE? A bear – links in with my nickname
TWITTER: @Liam628

Batting	Mat	Inns	NO	Runs	HS	Ave	SR	100	50	Ct	St
Tests	13	20	5	238	55*	15.86	46.75	0	1	3	0
ODIs	89	50	19	646	56	20.83	102.70	0	1	26	0
T20Is	22	11	4	42	18	6.00	123.52	0	0	7	0
First-class	158	216	39	4378	126	24.73		3	22	86	0
List A	215	133	50	1677	72	20.20	100.78	0	3	64	0
T20s	152	91	35	821	41	14.66	130.94	0	0	41	0
Bowling	**Mat**	**Balls**	**Runs**	**Wkts**	**BBI**	**BBM**	**Ave**	**Econ**	**SR**	**5w**	**10**
Tests	13	2659	1536	41	5/64	9/176	37.46	3.46	64.8	1	0
ODIs	89	4137	4010	135	5/52	5/52	29.70	5.81	30.6	1	0
T20Is	22	476	627	25	3/21	3/21	25.08	7.90	19.0	0	0
First-class	158	23909	14433	453	6/33		31.86	3.62	52.7	11	1
List A	215	9275	8592	283	5/52	5/52	30.36	5.55	32.7	1	0
T20s	152	2896	3905	139	5/31	5/31	28.09	8.09	20.8	1	0

HARRY PODMORE RHB / RM / R0 / W1 / MVP27

KENT

FULL NAME: Harry William Podmore
BORN: July 23, 1994, Hammersmith, Middlesex
SQUAD NO: 1
HEIGHT: 6ft 3in
NICKNAME: Podders, Pongo, Nu-Nu
EDUCATION: Twyford CE High School, London
TEAMS: Kent, Derbyshire, Glamorgan, Middlesex
ROLE: Bowler
DEBUT: First-class: 2016; List A: 2014; T20: 2014

BEST BATTING: 66* Derbyshire vs Sussex, Hove, 2017
BEST BOWLING: 6-36 Kent vs Middlesex, Canterbury, 2018
COUNTY CAP: 2019 (Kent)

WHAT WAS YOUR FIRST CRICKET CLUB? Ealing CC, Middlesex
HOW WOULD YOU DISMISS STEVE SMITH? Inswinger which then nips away and takes off stump
WHAT EXCITES YOU ABOUT THE HUNDRED? Bowling in the nets
BIGGEST TOPIC OF DISCUSSION IN YOUR DRESSING ROOM? Love Island
MOST INTERESTING TEAMMATE? He wasn't exactly a teammate, but it was special to share a dressing room with our former assistant coach Allan Donald
CRICKETING HERO? Ian Botham
SURPRISING FACT ABOUT YOU? I have my family crest tattooed on my chest
IF YOU WERE AN ANIMAL, WHICH WOULD IT BE? A dog – playful, loving, loyal and easily pleased
TWITTER: @harrypod16

Batting	Mat	Inns	NO	Runs	HS	Ave	SR	100	50	Ct	St
First-class	42	62	17	773	66*	17.17	46.87	0	3	10	0
List A	18	8	2	111	40	18.50	94.87	0	0	6	0
T20s	21	8	3	32	9	6.40	57.14	0	0	9	0
Bowling	**Mat**	**Balls**	**Runs**	**Wkts**	**BBI**	**BBM**	**Ave**	**Econ**	**SR**	**5w**	**10**
First-class	42	6812	3449	130	6/36	8/110	26.53	3.03	52.4	3	0
List A	18	866	910	18	4/57	4/57	50.55	6.30	48.1	0	0
T20s	21	367	572	18	3/13	3/13	31.77	9.35	20.3	0	0

KIERON POLLARD RHB / RM

FULL NAME: Kieron Adrian Pollard
BORN: May 12, 1987, Tacarigua, Trinidad
SQUAD NO: TBC
TEAMS: West Indies, Northamptonshire, Adelaide Strikers, Barbados Tridents, Dhaka Dynamites, Karachi Kings, Melbourne Renegades, Multan Sultans, Mumbai Indians, Peshawar Zalmi, Somerset, St Lucia Stars, Trinbago Knight Riders, Trinidad & Tobago
ROLE: Allrounder
DEBUT: ODI: 2007; T20I: 2008; First-class: 2007; List A: 2007; T20: 2006

BEST BATTING: 104 St Lucia Stars vs Barbados Tridents, Gros Islet, 2018 (T20)
BEST BOWLING: 4-15 Somerset vs Kent, Beckenham, 2010 (T20)

TWITTER: @KieronPollard55
NOTES: Northants pulled off a major coup by signing the West Indies' limited-overs captain for the middle section of this summer's T20 Blast. Pollard has previous experience in the competition having represented Somerset in 2010 and 2011, scoring 588 runs at 34.58 with two half-centuries. "I've spoken to many people about Kieron and the biggest factor you get from everyone is that he's a winner," said Northants head coach David Ripley. "He's got a fantastic record in winning T20 comps and is just an absolute competitor. He can bowl the big overs, field in key positions and whack it out of any cricket ground in the world." Pollard was part of the Mumbai Indians side which won the 2019 Indian Premier League, the Trinidadian scoring a crucial 41 not out from 25 balls in the final

Batting	Mat	Inns	NO	Runs	HS	Ave	SR	100	50	Ct	St
ODIs	113	104	8	2496	119	26.00	94.65	3	10	61	0
T20Is	73	60	12	1123	68	23.39	132.27	0	4	36	0
First-class	27	44	2	1584	174	37.71		4	7	42	0
List A	151	137	12	3341	119	26.72		3	16	87	0
T20s	501	450	126	10000	104	30.86	150.57	1	49	288	0
Bowling	**Mat**	**Balls**	**Runs**	**Wkts**	**BBI**	**BBM**	**Ave**	**Econ**	**SR**	**5w**	**10**
ODIs	113	2188	2105	53	3/27	3/27	39.71	5.77	41.2	0	0
T20Is	73	654	919	35	4/25	4/25	26.25	8.43	18.6	0	0
First-class	27	811	436	14	5/36	5/40	31.14	3.22	57.9	1	0
List A	151	2817	2610	88	4/32	4/32	29.65	5.55	32.0	0	0
T20s	501	4974	6798	279	4/15	4/15	24.36	8.20	17.8	0	0

ED POLLOCK

LHB / OB / R0 / W0

FULL NAME: Edward John Pollock
BORN: July 10, 1995, High Wycombe, Buckinghamshire
SQUAD NO: 28
HEIGHT: 5ft 10in
EDUCATION: Royal Grammar School, Worcester; Shrewsbury School; Durham University
TEAMS: Warwickshire, Manchester Originals
ROLE: Batsman
DEBUT: First-class: 2015; List A: 2018; T20: 2017

BEST BATTING: 52 Durham MCCU vs Gloucestershire, Bristol, 2017

FAMILY TIES? My dad and brother have both captained Cambridge University
WHAT WAS YOUR FIRST CRICKET CLUB? Barnt Green CC, Worcestershire. Andy and Grant Flower have both played for the club
BIGGEST TOPIC OF DISCUSSION IN YOUR DRESSING ROOM? Will the batters beat the bowlers in the Amiss/Hollies golf competition for the fifth year in a row?
MOST INTERESTING TEAMMATE? Michael Burgess – he owns a black cab
CRICKETING HERO? Brian Lara
WHICH RULE WOULD YOU CHANGE ABOUT CRICKET? Hitting the ball out the ground should be worth 10 runs
SURPRISING FACT ABOUT YOU? I am a published poet
BIGGEST CRICKETING REGRET? Letting my bowling decline
IF YOU WERE AN ANIMAL, WHICH WOULD IT BE? A mayfly – they have a lifespan of 24 hours, so it's over almost before it's begun, much like most of my innings
TWITTER: @kcollopde

Batting	Mat	Inns	NO	Runs	HS	Ave	SR	100	50	Ct	St
First-class	5	7	1	184	52	30.66	50.13	0	1	1	0
List A	17	15	0	362	57	24.13	128.36	0	2	4	0
T20s	29	29	0	663	77	22.86	174.93	0	4	8	0
Bowling	**Mat**	**Balls**	**Runs**	**Wkts**	**BBI**	**BBM**	**Ave**	**Econ**	**SR**	**5w**	**10**
First-class	5	-	-	-	-	-	-	-	-	-	-
List A	17	-	-	-	-	-	-	-	-	-	-
T20s	29	-	-	-	-	-	-	-	-	-	-

NICHOLAS POORAN LHB / WK

FULL NAME: Nicholas Pooran
BORN: October 2, 1995, Couva, Trinidad
SQUAD NO: 39
TEAMS: West Indies, Yorkshire, Barbados Tridents, Guyana Amazon Warriors, Islamabad United, Khulna Titans, Kings XI Punjab, Sylhet Sixers, Trinidad & Tobabgo
ROLE: Wicketkeeper/batsman
DEBUT: ODI: 2019; T20I: 2016; First-class: 2014; List A: 2013; T20: 2013

BEST BATTING: 81 Barbados Tridents vs St Lucia Zouks, Bridgetown, 2016 (T20)

TWITTER: @nicholas_47
NOTES: The Trinidadian left-hander has been signed by Yorkshire Vikings for "the majority" of the T20 Blast campaign after a brief spell at Headingley last summer which included a match-winning innings of 67 from 28 balls against Leicestershire. Identified as a rare talent in his teens, Pooran was involved in a road accident five years ago which left him with career-threatening injuries. But he still managed to establish himself on the T20 global circuit and impressed for West Indies at last summer's World Cup, scoring 367 runs at 52.42 including a maiden hundred against Sri Lanka at Chester-le-Street. A white-ball specialist who has represented Kings XI Punjab in the IPL, Pooran is a good enough keeper to have taken the gloves at international level

Batting	Mat	Inns	NO	Runs	HS	Ave	SR	100	50	Ct	St
ODIs	25	23	4	932	118	49.05	106.51	1	7	8	1
T20Is	21	19	4	353	58	23.53	124.73	0	2	13	0
First-class	3	6	0	143	55	23.83	58.60	0	1	2	2
List A	43	40	7	1424	118	43.15		1	10	19	1
T20s	127	115	18	2381	81	24.54	143.78	0	12	70	11
Bowling	**Mat**	**Balls**	**Runs**	**Wkts**	**BBI**	**BBM**	**Ave**	**Econ**	**SR**	**5w**	**10**
ODIs	25	-	-	-	-	-	-	-	-	-	-
T20Is	21	-	-	-	-	-	-	-	-	-	-
First-class	3	-	-	-	-	-	-	-	-	-	-
List A	43	-	-	-	-	-	-	-	-	-	-
T20s	127	-	-	-	-	-	-	-	-	-	-

OLLIE POPE RHB / WK / R1 / W0

FULL NAME: Oliver John Douglas Pope
BORN: January 2, 1998, Chelsea, Middlesex
SQUAD NO: 32
HEIGHT: 5ft 10in
NICKNAME: Pope-dog
EDUCATION: Cranleigh School, Surrey
TEAMS: England, Surrey, Southern Brave
ROLE: Batsman/wicketkeeper
DEBUT: Test: 2018; First-class: 2017; List A: 2016; T20: 2017

BEST BATTING: 251 Surrey vs MCC, Dubai, 2019

COUNTY CAP: 2018

WHAT WAS YOUR FIRST CRICKET CLUB? Grayshott CC, Hampshire
WHICH BOWLER WOULD YOU LEAST LIKE TO FACE? Morne Morkel
CRICKETING HERO? My former teammate Kumar Sangakkara – he just didn't stop scoring runs and was amazing to watch
BEST INNINGS YOU'VE SEEN? Aaron Finch's hundred against Middlesex in the 2018 T20 Blast. Made the boundaries look 30 yards away
WHICH RULE WOULD YOU CHANGE ABOUT CRICKET? First ball: free hit
SURPRISING FACT ABOUT A TEAMMATE? Sam Curran is a useless footballer
TWITTER: @opope32

Batting	Mat	Inns	NO	Runs	HS	Ave	SR	100	50	Ct	St
Tests	7	11	2	430	135*	47.77	50.58	1	3	12	0
First-class	38	56	9	2852	251	60.68	61.95	9	11	48	0
List A	28	25	5	751	93*	37.55	80.40	0	5	8	0
T20s	36	34	8	736	48	28.30	134.06	0	0	15	0
Bowling	**Mat**	**Balls**	**Runs**	**Wkts**	**BBI**	**BBM**	**Ave**	**Econ**	**SR**	**5w**	**10**
Tests	7	-	-	-	-	-	-	-	-	-	-
First-class	38	-	-	-	-	-	-	-	-	-	-
List A	28	-	-	-	-	-	-	-	-	-	-
T20s	36	-	-	-	-	-	-	-	-	-	-

JAMIE PORTER RHB / RMF / R0 / W5 / MVP56

FULL NAME: James Alexander Porter
BORN: May 25, 1993, Leytonstone, Essex
SQUAD NO: 44
HEIGHT: 6ft 1in
NICKNAME: Ports
EDUCATION: Oaks Park High School, Ilford; Epping Forest College, Essex
TEAMS: Essex, England Lions
ROLE: Bowler
DEBUT: First-class: 2014; List A: 2015; T20: 2017

BEST BATTING: 34 Essex vs Glamorgan, Cardiff, 2015
BEST BOWLING: 7-41 Essex vs Worcestershire, Chelmsford, 2018
COUNTY CAP: 2015

WHAT WAS YOUR FIRST CRICKET CLUB? Chingford CC, London
WHAT WERE YOU DOING WHEN ENGLAND WON THE WORLD CUP? Watching it in the dressing room during an England Lions game
WHAT EXCITES YOU ABOUT THE HUNDRED? Supporting the Chelmsford Cactuses…
BIGGEST TOPIC OF DISCUSSION IN YOUR DRESSING ROOM? Ryan ten Doeschate's questionable golf handicap
BEST INNINGS YOU'VE SEEN? Dan Lawrence's 161 against Surrey in 2015. It was only his second first-class match and Surrey were coming at him hard, but he got the last laugh
CRICKETING HERO? James Anderson
CRICKET STAR OF THE FUTURE? Ben Allison (Essex)
WHICH BOOK MEANS MOST TO YOU? The Cat in the Hat by Dr. Seuss
IF YOU WERE AN ANIMAL, WHICH WOULD IT BE? A giraffe – then I could look Paul Weaver in the eye
TWITTER: @jamieporter93

Batting	Mat	Inns	NO	Runs	HS	Ave	SR	100	50	Ct	St
First-class	84	97	34	357	34	5.66	24.74	0	0	24	0
List A	31	12	8	35	7*	8.75	52.23	0	0	7	0
T20s	19	5	4	5	1*	5.00	71.42	0	0	5	0
Bowling	**Mat**	**Balls**	**Runs**	**Wkts**	**BBI**	**BBM**	**Ave**	**Econ**	**SR**	**5w**	**10**
First-class	84	14418	8001	329	7/41	12/95	24.31	3.32	43.8	12	2
List A	31	1378	1193	33	4/29	4/29	36.15	5.19	41.7	0	0
T20s	19	325	476	17	4/20	4/20	28.00	8.78	19.1	0	0

MATTY POTTS RHB / RFM / R0 / W0

FULL NAME: Matthew James Potts
BORN: October 29, 1998, Sunderland, County Durham
SQUAD NO: 35
HEIGHT: 6ft 2in
NICKNAME: Harry, Junior, Pottsy
EDUCATION: St Robert of Newminster Catholic School, Sunderland
TEAMS: Durham, England U19
ROLE: Allrounder
DEBUT: First-class: 2017; List A: 2018; T20: 2019

BEST BATTING: 53* Durham vs Derbyshire, Chester-le-Street, 2017
BEST BOWLING: 3-48 Durham vs Glamorgan, Chester-le-Street, 2017

WHAT WAS YOUR FIRST CRICKET CLUB? Philadelphia CC, Tyne and Wear
BEST ADVICE RECEIVED? Bowl at three wooden things
WHAT EXCITES YOU ABOUT THE HUNDRED? Having a mainstream competition in the UK to rival the IPL and the Big Bash
CRICKETING HERO? Kevin Pietersen
WHICH RULE WOULD YOU CHANGE ABOUT CRICKET? DRS: if it's hitting the stumps, it's out
BIGGEST CRICKETING REGRET? Bottling a double hundred playing a reverse-sweep
CRICKET STAR OF THE FUTURE? Jonny Bushnell (Durham Academy)
WHICH BOOK MEANS MOST TO YOU? Bravo Two Zero – The Harrowing True Story of a Special Forces Patrol Behind the Lines in Iraq by Andy McNab
IF YOU WERE AN ANIMAL, WHICH WOULD IT BE? A silverback gorilla
TWITTER: @mattyjpotts

Batting	Mat	Inns	NO	Runs	HS	Ave	SR	100	50	Ct	St
First-class	9	13	4	166	53*	18.44	47.02	0	1	1	0
List A	9	3	0	53	30	17.66	72.60	0	0	2	0
T20s	12	5	3	8	3*	4.00	88.88	0	0	4	0
Bowling	**Mat**	**Balls**	**Runs**	**Wkts**	**BBI**	**BBM**	**Ave**	**Econ**	**SR**	**5w**	**10**
First-class	9	1416	715	17	3/48	5/106	42.05	3.02	83.2	0	0
List A	9	324	319	13	4/62	4/62	24.53	5.90	24.9	0	0
T20s	12	239	332	17	3/22	3/22	19.52	8.33	14.0	0	0

STUART POYNTER RHB / WK / R0 / W0

FULL NAME: Stuart William Poynter
BORN: October 18, 1990, Hammersmith, London
SQUAD NO: 90
HEIGHT: 5ft 7in
NICKNAME: Stuey, Poynts
EDUCATION: Teddington School, London
TEAMS: Ireland, Durham, Middlesex, Warwickshire
ROLE: Wicketkeeper
DEBUT: Test: 2019; ODI: 2014; T20I: 2015; First-class: 2010; List A: 2012; T20: 2015

BEST BATTING: 170 Durham vs Derbyshire, Derby, 2018

FAMILY TIES? My uncle Deryck and Andrew both played for Ireland
WHAT WAS YOUR FIRST CRICKET CLUB? Sunbury CC, Surrey
WHAT EXCITES YOU ABOUT THE HUNDRED? It's on the BBC
BIGGEST TOPIC OF DISCUSSION IN YOUR DRESSING ROOM? Love Island
MOST INTERESTING TEAMMATE? Phil Mustard – every day is a complete lottery: anything can happen
CRICKETING HERO? Jack Russell – the best keeper I have ever seen and one of the first I saw standing up to pace bowling
SURPRISING FACT ABOUT YOU? I'm a massive Westlife fan and play the ukulele
IF YOU WERE AN ANIMAL, WHICH WOULD IT BE? Giraffe – I'd love to be tall
TWITTER: @spoynter_90

Batting	Mat	Inns	NO	Runs	HS	Ave	SR	100	50	Ct	St
Tests	1	2	0	1	1	0.50	9.09	0	0	2	1
ODIs	21	19	5	185	36	13.21	66.54	0	0	22	1
T20Is	25	21	6	240	39	16.00	112.67	0	0	13	2
First-class	39	62	2	1379	170	22.98	65.88	2	4	117	4
List A	47	40	9	581	109	18.74	85.94	1	0	42	3
T20s	64	49	20	694	61*	23.93	125.04	0	1	35	10
Bowling	**Mat**	**Balls**	**Runs**	**Wkts**	**BBI**	**BBM**	**Ave**	**Econ**	**SR**	**5w**	**10**
Tests	1	-	-	-	-	-	-	-	-	-	-
ODIs	21	-	-	-	-	-	-	-	-	-	-
T20Is	25	-	-	-	-	-	-	-	-	-	-
First-class	39	-	-	-	-	-	-	-	-	-	-
List A	47	-	-	-	-	-	-	-	-	-	-
T20s	64	-	-	-	-	-	-	-	-	-	-

JOSH POYSDEN LHB / LB / R0 / W0

FULL NAME: Joshua Edward Poysden
BORN: August 8, 1991, Shoreham-by-Sea, Sussex
SQUAD NO: 14
HEIGHT: 5ft 10in
NICKNAME: Dobby, Bendicii
EDUCATION: Cardinal Newman School, Hove; Anglia Ruskin University
TEAMS: Yorkshire, England Lions, Warwickshire
ROLE: Bowler
DEBUT: First-class: 2011; List A: 2013; T20: 2014

BEST BATTING: 47 Cambridge MCCU vs Surrey, Cambridge, 2011
BEST BOWLING: 5-29 Warwickshire vs Glamorgan, Edgbaston, 2018

WHAT WAS YOUR FIRST CRICKET CLUB? Brighton and Hove CC, coached by the great man Dick Roberts
CRICKETING HERO? Shane Warne
BEST INNINGS YOU'VE SEEN? Brendon McCullum's 158 not out off 64 balls for Warwickshire against Derbyshire at Edgbaston in the 2015 T20 Blast
WHO WOULD YOU ASK TO BAT FOR YOUR LIFE? Matt Fisher – lovely defence
WHICH RULE WOULD YOU CHANGE ABOUT CRICKET? Set a minimum temperature that it is acceptable to play at
YOUR BIGGEST CRICKETING REGRET? Deciding to bat left-handed
SURPRISING FACT ABOUT YOU? I have a mild obsession with sausage dogs – I can't walk past one in the street without stroking it, and one day I hope to have one called Frank
WHICH BOOK MEANS MOST TO YOU? The Alchemist by Paulo Coelho
TWITTER: @JoshPoysden14

Batting	Mat	Inns	NO	Runs	HS	Ave	SR	100	50	Ct	St
First-class	14	14	4	96	47	9.60	36.22	0	0	2	0
List A	32	16	6	35	10*	3.50	52.23	0	0	7	0
T20s	27	10	8	13	9*	6.50	118.18	0	0	6	0
Bowling	**Mat**	**Balls**	**Runs**	**Wkts**	**BBI**	**BBM**	**Ave**	**Econ**	**SR**	**5w**	**10**
First-class	14	1549	1084	33	5/29	8/133	32.84	4.19	46.9	2	0
List A	32	1281	1248	30	3/33	3/33	41.60	5.84	42.7	0	0
T20s	27	492	615	20	4/51	4/51	30.75	7.50	24.6	0	0

TOM PRICE RHB / RFM / R0 / W0

FULL NAME: Thomas James Price
BORN: January 2, 2000, Oxford
SQUAD NO: TBC
EDUCATION: Magdalen College School, Oxford
TEAMS: Gloucestershire
ROLE: Allrounder
DEBUT: List A: 2019

TWITTER: @_tomprice_
NOTES: An emerging seam-bowling allrounder currently studying at the University of Durham, Price was handed his first professional contract by Gloucestershire in January, putting pen to paper on a two-year deal. He received the Academy Player of the Year award at the end of last season after finishing as Gloucestershire's second-highest wicket-taker in the Second XI Championship, with a haul of 14 at 30.57. "Tom has developed his game after playing in our second team in 2019 and has shown huge potential," said Gloucestershire head coach Richard Dawson. "Everybody at the club is excited to be working with Tom over the next two seasons in helping him become a quality Gloucestershire cricketer." The 20-year-old made his List A debut against Australia A at Bristol last August

Batting	Mat	Inns	NO	Runs	HS	Ave	SR	100	50	Ct	St
List A	1	1	0	0	0	0.00	-	0	0	0	0
Bowling	**Mat**	**Balls**	**Runs**	**Wkts**	**BBI**	**BBM**	**Ave**	**Econ**	**SR**	**5w**	**10**
List A	1	36	52	0	-	-	-	8.66	-	0	0

NILS PRIESTLEY LHB / SLA / R0 / W0

FULL NAME: Nils Oscar Priestley
BORN: September 18, 2000, Sutton Coldfield, Warwickshire
SQUAD NO: 53
HEIGHT: 6ft 3in
NICKNAME: Nee-Lo-Green, Breadstick
EDUCATION: Blessed Robert Sutton School, Burton-upon-Trent, Staffordshire; Loughborough University
TEAMS: Derbyshire
ROLE: Batsman

WHAT WAS YOUR FIRST CRICKET CLUB? Lullington Park CC, Derbyshire
WHAT WERE YOU DOING WHEN ENGLAND WON THE WORLD CUP? I was 12th man for the Derbyshire first XI at Chesterfield
WHAT EXCITES YOU ABOUT THE HUNDRED? The new tactics
BIGGEST TOPIC OF DISCUSSION IN YOUR DRESSING ROOM? Who has the best bat
IF YOU WERE AN ANIMAL, WHICH WOULD IT BE? A giraffe – I'm tall and lanky
TWITTER: @nilspriestley
NOTES: The tall 19-year-old left-hander has come through the Derbyshire Academy and signed a one-year contract in January. Priestley, who has impressed mainly as a batsman, used to bowl seamers until injuries forced him to adopt left-arm spin. He was a regular in Derbyshire's Second XI last summer and is enrolled on the Loughborough MCCU programme. He has played Derbyshire Premier League cricket for Rolleston and Swarkestone, and represented the county at all age levels from U10 up. "I'm really pleased to have signed but the hard work does not stop here, I know that I've got to keep driving myself forward and take my chances," he said. "This club means a lot to me, I'm really proud to represent Derbyshire, and I can't wait to get started again next season"

LUKE PROCTER

LHB / RMF / R0 / W0

FULL NAME: Luke Anthony Procter
BORN: June 24, 1988, Oldham, Lancashire
SQUAD NO: 2
HEIGHT: 5ft 11in
NICKNAME: Dicky
EDUCATION: Counthill School, Oldham
TEAMS: Northamptonshire, Lancashire
ROLE: Allrounder
DEBUT: First-class: 2010; List A: 2009; T20: 2011

BEST BATTING: 137 Lancashire vs Hampshire, Old Trafford, 2016
BEST BOWLING: 7-71 Lancashire vs Surrey, Liverpool, 2012

WHAT WAS YOUR FIRST CRICKET CLUB? Oldham CC, Greater Manchester
BEST ADVICE RECEIVED? Never settle for second-best
HOW WOULD YOU DISMISS STEVE SMITH? I would nick him off (tooooo easy)
WHAT EXCITES YOU ABOUT THE HUNDRED? The money it brings into the game
BIGGEST TOPIC OF DISCUSSION IN YOUR DRESSING ROOM? Chippy tea
CRICKETING HERO? Shivnarine Chanderpaul
SURPRISING FACT ABOUT YOU? I'm a level-two umpire
IF YOU WERE AN ANIMAL, WHICH WOULD IT BE? A bird
TWITTER: @vvsprocter

Batting	Mat	Inns	NO	Runs	HS	Ave	SR	100	50	Ct	St
First-class	94	149	15	4108	137	30.65	44.22	3	22	23	0
List A	45	35	12	710	97	30.86	88.75	0	5	7	0
T20s	32	19	6	171	25*	13.15	98.27	0	0	10	0
Bowling	**Mat**	**Balls**	**Runs**	**Wkts**	**BBI**	**BBM**	**Ave**	**Econ**	**SR**	**5w**	**10**
First-class	94	6662	3819	106	7/71	8/79	36.02	3.43	62.8	3	0
List A	45	1090	1042	23	3/29	3/29	45.30	5.73	47.3	0	0
T20s	32	236	374	12	3/22	3/22	31.16	9.50	19.6	0	0

CHETESHWAR PUJARA

RHB / LB / R0 / W0

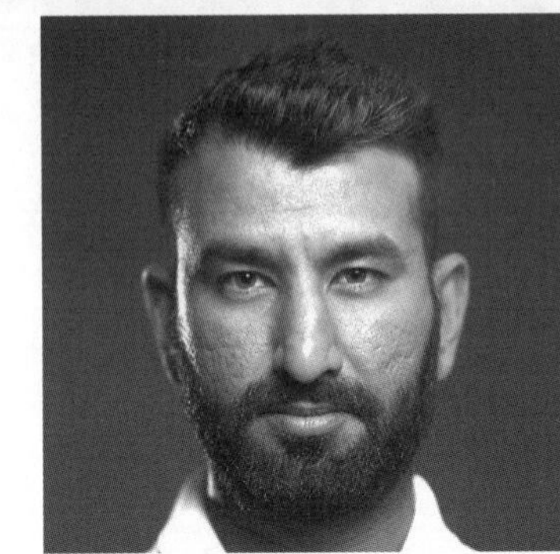

FULL NAME: Cheteshwar Arvind Pujara
BORN: January 25, 1988, Rajkot, Gujarat, India
SQUAD NO: TBC
TEAMS: India, Gloucestershire, Derbyshire, India Green, Kings XI Punjab, Kolkata Knight Riders, Nottinghamshire, Royal Challengers Bangalore, Saurashtra, Yorkshire
ROLE: Batsman
DEBUT: Test: 2010; ODI: 2013; First-class: 2005; List A: 2006; T20: 2007

BEST BATTING: 352 Saurashtra vs Karnataka, Rajkot, 2013
BEST BOWLING: 2-4 Saurashtra vs Rajasthan, Jaipur, 2007
COUNTY CAP: 2017 (Nottinghamshire)

TWITTER: @cheteshwar1
NOTES: Gloucestershire will be Pujara's fourth English county in six years after the club signed the Indian batsman for the first six Championship matches of the season. Known for his patient batting style – in contrast to many of his national teammates – Pujara has been a fixture in the top-order of the Indian Test team for a decade, scoring 18 hundreds in 77 matches. He has found it harder going in county cricket, where he averages less than 30 in 21 Championship matches for Derbyshire, Nottinghamshire and Yorkshire. But he seems to relish playing in this country. He said: "I have really enjoyed the experience of coming over to the UK and playing county cricket over the last few years and I am looking forward to building on that while continuing to improve my game"

Batting	Mat	Inns	NO	Runs	HS	Ave	SR	100	50	Ct	St
Tests	77	128	8	5840	206*	48.66	46.18	18	25	51	0
ODIs	5	5	0	51	27	10.20	39.23	0	0	0	0
First-class	203	331	37	15771	352	53.64		50	60	133	0
List A	103	101	19	4445	158*	54.20		11	29	39	0
T20s	64	56	10	1356	100*	29.47	109.35	1	7	32	0
Bowling	**Mat**	**Balls**	**Runs**	**Wkts**	**BBI**	**BBM**	**Ave**	**Econ**	**SR**	**5w**	**10**
Tests	77	6	2	0	-	-	-	2.00	-	0	0
ODIs	5	-	-	-	-	-	-	-	-	-	-
First-class	203	251	157	6	2/4	2/4	26.16	3.75	41.8	0	0
List A	103	6	8	0	-	-	-	8.00	-	0	0
T20s	64	-	-	-	-	-	-	-	-	-	-

HAMIDULLAH QADRI

RHB / OB / R0 / W0

FULL NAME: Hamidullah Qadri
BORN: December 5, 2000, Kandahar, Afghanistan
SQUAD NO: 75
HEIGHT: 5ft 7in
NICKNAME: Hammy
EDUCATION: Chellaston Academy, Derby; Derby Moor Academy
TEAMS: Kent, Derbyshire, England U19
ROLE: Bowler
DEBUT: First-class: 2017; List A: 2017; T20: 2017

BEST BATTING: 17* Derbyshire vs Lancashire, Old Trafford, 2019
BEST BOWLING: 5-60 Derbyshire vs Glamorgan, Cardiff, 2017

WHAT WAS YOUR FIRST CRICKET CLUB? Alvaston & Boulton CC, Derbyshire
BEST ADVICE RECEIVED? Keep practising until you get it right
WHAT EXCITES YOU ABOUT THE HUNDRED? That young local players with be sharing a dressing room with star players. And that the game will be quicker
MOST INTERESTING TEAMMATE? Wayne Madsen – very knowledgeable and a nice bloke
BEST INNINGS YOU'VE SEEN? Kevin Pietersen's 186 in Mumbai in 2012
CRICKETING HERO? Saqlain Mushtaq – inventor of the doosra
WHICH RULE WOULD YOU CHANGE ABOUT CRICKET? Hitting the ball out the ground should be worth eight runs
SURPRISING FACT ABOUT YOU? I learnt the art of off-spin by watching YouTube clips
TWITTER: @Hamid_Qadri2000

Batting	Mat	Inns	NO	Runs	HS	Ave	SR	100	50	Ct	St
First-class	10	20	8	81	17*	6.75	32.66	0	0	6	0
List A	3	1	0	4	4	4.00	50.00	0	0	1	0
T20s	1	-	-	-	-	-	-	-	-	0	0
Bowling	**Mat**	**Balls**	**Runs**	**Wkts**	**BBI**	**BBM**	**Ave**	**Econ**	**SR**	**5w**	**10**
First-class	10	1399	826	23	5/60	6/76	35.91	3.54	60.8	1	0
List A	3	61	61	1	1/31	1/31	61.00	6.00	61.0	0	0
T20s	1	6	12	0	-	-	-	12.00	-	0	0

IMRAN QAYYUM RHB / SLA / R0 / W0

FULL NAME: Imran Qayyum
BORN: May 23, 1993, Ealing, Middlesex
SQUAD NO: 11
HEIGHT: 5ft 11in
NICKNAME: Imy, Ish
EDUCATION: Villiers High School, Ealing; Greenford High School, Ealing; City University of London
TEAMS: Kent
ROLE: Bowler
DEBUT: First-class: 2016; List A: 2017; T20: 2017

BEST BATTING: 39 Kent vs Leicestershire, Canterbury, 2017
BEST BOWLING: 3-158 Kent vs Northamptonshire, Northampton, 2016

FAMILY TIES? Dad played in Pakistan, my brother plays club cricket in Hertfordshire
WHAT WAS YOUR FIRST CRICKET CLUB? Perivale Phoenicians CC, Ealing, Middlesex
BEST ADVICE RECEIVED? Try coffee
HOW WOULD YOU DISMISS STEVE SMITH? Bowl left-arm spin
WHAT EXCITES YOU ABOUT THE HUNDRED? The colourful kits
BIGGEST TOPIC OF DISCUSSION IN YOUR DRESSING ROOM? Brexit
CRICKETING HERO? Virat Kohli
SURPRISING FACT ABOUT YOU? I hate sleeping because it makes me feel that I am missing out on life. I also talk in my sleep
SURPRISING FACT ABOUT A TEAMMATE? Ivan Thomas eats two dinners every night
IF YOU WERE AN ANIMAL, WHICH WOULD IT BE? A cheetah
TWITTER: @ImranQC

Batting	Mat	Inns	NO	Runs	HS	Ave	SR	100	50	Ct	St
First-class	6	9	4	55	39	11.00	36.42	0	0	3	0
List A	29	19	6	99	26*	7.61	64.70	0	0	5	0
T20s	34	8	5	43	21*	14.33	143.33	0	0	6	0
Bowling	**Mat**	**Balls**	**Runs**	**Wkts**	**BBI**	**BBM**	**Ave**	**Econ**	**SR**	**5w**	**10**
First-class	6	823	524	12	3/158	3/46	43.66	3.82	68.5	0	0
List A	29	1368	1178	29	4/33	4/33	40.62	5.16	47.1	0	0
T20s	34	614	829	34	5/21	5/21	24.38	8.10	18.0	1	0

MATT QUINN RHB / RMF / R0 / W0

FULL NAME: Matthew Richard Quinn
BORN: February 28, 1993, Auckland, New Zealand
SQUAD NO: 94
HEIGHT: 6ft 5in
NICKNAME: Quinny
EDUCATION: Sacred Heart College, Auckland; Auckland University of Technology
TEAMS: Essex, Auckland, New Zealand U19
ROLE: Bowler
DEBUT: First-class: 2013; List A: 2013; T20: 2012

BEST BATTING: 50 Auckland vs Canterbury, Auckland, 2013
BEST BOWLING: 7-76 Essex vs Gloucestershire, Cheltenham, 2016

FAMILY TIES? My great grandad played social cricket in Yorkshire
WHAT WAS YOUR FIRST CRICKET CLUB? Cornwall CC, Auckland – the largest cricket club in New Zealand
BEST INNINGS YOU'VE SEEN? Colin Munro scoring 281 from 167 balls for Auckland against Central Districts in 2015 – including 23 sixes, a record for a first-class innings
CRICKETING HERO? Martin Crowe – a fantastic cricketer and even better man
WHICH RULE WOULD YOU CHANGE ABOUT CRICKET? The one which says you can only have two fielders behind square on the leg-side
SURPRISING FACT ABOUT YOU? I was once attacked by a goose
TWITTER: @quinny_cricket

Batting	Mat	Inns	NO	Runs	HS	Ave	SR	100	50	Ct	St
First-class	34	44	11	347	50	10.51	46.76	0	1	7	0
List A	34	19	11	128	36	16.00	73.14	0	0	4	0
T20s	57	11	9	28	8*	14.00	107.69	0	0	11	0
Bowling	**Mat**	**Balls**	**Runs**	**Wkts**	**BBI**	**BBM**	**Ave**	**Econ**	**SR**	**5w**	**10**
First-class	34	6438	3559	120	7/76	11/163	29.65	3.31	53.6	1	1
List A	34	1714	1682	46	4/71	4/71	36.56	5.88	37.2	0	0
T20s	57	1115	1666	60	4/20	4/20	27.76	8.96	18.5	0	0

BEN RAINE LHB / RMF / R0 / W3 / MVP32

FULL NAME: Benjamin Alexander Raine
BORN: September 14, 1991, Sunderland
SQUAD NO: 44
HEIGHT: 6ft
NICKNAME: Ranger, Reindeer, Slush Puppy
EDUCATION: St Aidan's Catholic Academy, Sunderland
TEAMS: Durham, Leicestershire, Otago
ROLE: Bowler
DEBUT: First-class: 2011; List A: 2011; T20: 2014

BEST BATTING: 82 Durham vs Northamptonshire, Chester-le-Street, 2019
BEST BOWLING: 6-27 Durham vs Sussex, Hove, 2019
COUNTY CAP: 2018 (Leicestershire)

WHAT WAS YOUR FIRST CRICKET CLUB? Murton CC, County Durham. They drew lots for the batting order in the second team and as a nine-year-old I drew No.4 so that's where I batted
HOW WOULD YOU DISMISS STEVE SMITH? Top of off, with the odd bouncer
BEST INNINGS YOU'VE SEEN? Charlie Shreck's maiden fifty in the 2014 Championship match between Surrey and Leicestershire. He bludgeoned it all around The Oval. It delayed our departure from London until the rush hour but was worth every second of traffic
BIGGEST TOPIC OF DISCUSSION IN YOUR DRESSING ROOM? The tactics and gamesmanship of cricket
MOST INTERESTING TEAMMATE? Mark Wood – he loves shower time
BIGGEST CRICKETING REGRET? Taking far too long to realise that it doesn't really matter if I have a bad game
IF YOU WERE AN ANIMAL, WHICH WOULD IT BE? A dog: eat, walkies, sleep, repeat
TWITTER: @BenRaine88

Batting	Mat	Inns	NO	Runs	HS	Ave	SR	100	50	Ct	St
First-class	79	129	11	2465	82	20.88	48.68	0	10	16	0
List A	28	20	2	392	83	21.77	107.10	0	1	9	0
T20s	60	46	10	709	113	19.69	132.27	1	1	15	0
Bowling	**Mat**	**Balls**	**Runs**	**Wkts**	**BBI**	**BBM**	**Ave**	**Econ**	**SR**	**5w**	**10**
First-class	79	13863	6971	267	6/27	9/96	26.10	3.01	51.9	8	0
List A	28	1226	1161	27	3/31	3/31	43.00	5.68	45.4	0	0
T20s	60	1029	1561	55	3/7	3/7	28.38	9.10	18.7	0	0

RAVI RAMPAUL LHB / RFM / R0 / W0 / MVP26

FULL NAME: Ravindranath Rampaul
BORN: October 15, 1984, Preysal, Trinidad
SQUAD NO: 14
HEIGHT: 5ft 9in
NICKNAME: Frisco Kid, Hawk
EDUCATION: Presentation College, Trinidad
TEAMS: West Indies, Derbyshire, Welsh Fire, Barbados Tridents, Ireland, Royal Challengers Bangalore, Surrey, Trinidad & Tobago
ROLE: Bowler
DEBUT: Test: 2009; ODI: 2003; T20I: 2007; First-class: 2002; List A: 2003; T20: 2007

BEST BATTING: 64* West Indies A vs Sri Lanka A, Basseterre, 2006
BEST BOWLING: 7-51 Trinidad & Tobago vs Barbados, Point-a-Pierre, 2007
COUNTY CAP: 2019 (Derbyshire)

WHAT WAS YOUR FIRST CRICKET CLUB? Preysal Sports Club, Trinidad and Tobago
WHAT EXCITES YOU ABOUT THE HUNDRED? The 10-ball over
BIGGEST TOPIC OF DISCUSSION IN YOUR DRESSING ROOM? Rain
IF YOU WERE AN ANIMAL, WHICH WOULD IT BE? A hawk – that's my nickname
TWITTER: @RaviRampaul14
NOTES: Veteran West Indies seamer who joined Derbyshire on a three-year deal in October 2017 after spending two seasons at Surrey as a Kolpak player. Rampaul was in vintage form across all formats last season, finishing as the top wicket-taker in the T20 Blast (23 victims). The 35-year-old also had his best season in Championship cricket with 44 wickets at 25.89

Batting	Mat	Inns	NO	Runs	HS	Ave	SR	100	50	Ct	St
Tests	18	31	8	335	40*	14.56	53.25	0	0	3	0
ODIs	92	40	11	362	86*	12.48	76.69	0	1	14	0
T20Is	23	6	5	12	8	12.00	57.14	0	0	2	0
First-class	92	135	33	1317	64*	12.91		0	2	25	0
List A	189	87	31	637	86*	11.37		0	1	33	0
T20s	153	47	27	188	23*	9.40	101.07	0	0	26	0
Bowling	**Mat**	**Balls**	**Runs**	**Wkts**	**BBI**	**BBM**	**Ave**	**Econ**	**SR**	**5w**	**10**
Tests	18	3440	1705	49	4/48	7/75	34.79	2.97	70.2	0	0
ODIs	92	4033	3434	117	5/49	5/49	29.35	5.10	34.4	2	0
T20Is	23	497	705	29	3/16	3/16	24.31	8.51	17.1	0	0
First-class	92	14800	8160	274	7/51		29.78	3.30	54.0	11	1
List A	189	8624	7035	285	5/48	5/48	24.68	4.89	30.2	3	0
T20s	153	3274	4135	192	5/9	5/9	21.53	7.57	17.0	1	0

ADIL RASHID

RHB / LB / RO / W2

FULL NAME: Adil Usman Rashid
BORN: February 17, 1988, Bradford, Yorkshire
SQUAD NO: 3
HEIGHT: 5ft 8in
NICKNAME: Dilly, Dilo, Rash
EDUCATION: Heaton School, Bradford; Bellevue Sixth Form College, Bradford
TEAMS: England, Yorkshire, Northern Superchargers, Adelaide Strikers, South Australia
ROLE: Bowler
DEBUT: Test: 2015; ODI: 2009; T20I: 2009; First-class: 2006; List A: 2006; T20: 2008

BEST BATTING: 36* Yorkshire vs Uva Next, Johannesburg, 2012 (T20)
BEST BOWLING: 4-19 Yorkshire vs Durham, Headingley, 2017 (T20)
COUNTY CAP: 2008; BENEFIT: 2018

CRICKETING HEROES? Sachin Tendulkar, Shane Warne
NON-CRICKETING HERO? Muhammad Ali
IF YOU WEREN'T A CRICKETER? I'd be a taxi driver
SURPRISING FACT? I have a big FIFA (video game) rivalry with Moeen Ali
TWITTER: @AdilRashid03
NOTES: Rashid has signed a new deal to play white-ball cricket for Yorkshire this summer. He said: "I have decided to concentrate on white-ball cricket this summer in the lead up to the T20 World Cup. This is due to an ongoing shoulder injury, so it is important for me to manage my workload to give me the best chance of remaining fit. Although I won't be playing red-ball cricket this summer, I still have ambitions of playing Test cricket in the future"

Batting	Mat	Inns	NO	Runs	HS	Ave	SR	100	50	Ct	St
Tests	19	33	5	540	61	19.28	42.51	0	2	4	0
ODIs	100	44	12	590	69	18.43	101.02	0	1	30	0
T20Is	43	16	8	52	9*	6.50	83.87	0	0	11	0
First-class	175	251	41	6822	180	32.48		10	37	79	0
List A	218	127	37	1711	71	19.01	91.05	0	2	69	0
T20s	170	87	32	687	36*	12.49	104.88	0	0	48	0
Bowling	**Mat**	**Balls**	**Runs**	**Wkts**	**BBI**	**BBM**	**Ave**	**Econ**	**SR**	**5w**	**10**
Tests	19	3816	2390	60	5/49	7/178	39.83	3.75	63.6	2	0
ODIs	100	4911	4598	146	5/27	5/27	31.49	5.61	33.6	2	0
T20Is	43	864	1099	41	3/11	3/11	26.80	7.63	21.0	0	0
First-class	175	29901	17949	512	7/107	11/114	35.05	3.60	58.4	20	1
List A	218	10028	9091	292	5/27	5/27	31.13	5.43	34.3	3	0
T20s	170	3477	4322	191	4/19	4/19	22.62	7.45	18.2	0	0

DELRAY RAWLINS LHB / SLA / R0 / W0

FULL NAME: Delray Millard Wendell Rawlins
BORN: September 14, 1997, Bermuda
SQUAD NO: 9
HEIGHT: 6ft 2in
NICKNAME: Del
EDUCATION: St Bede's School, East Sussex
TEAMS: Bermuda, Sussex, Southern Brave, England U19
ROLE: Allrounder
DEBUT: T20I: 2019; First-class: 2017; List A: 2017; T20: 2018

BEST BATTING: 100 Sussex vs Lancashire, Old Trafford, 2019
BEST BOWLING: 3-19 Sussex vs Durham, Hove, 2019

WHAT WAS YOUR FIRST CRICKET CLUB? Warwick Workmen's Club, Bermuda. Helped me grow a love for the sport
BEST ADVICE EVER RECEIVED? If it's in the arc, it's out the park!
WHAT WERE YOU DOING WHEN ENGLAND WON THE WORLD CUP? Watching with the Sussex lads at Old Trafford after a day's play
WHAT EXCITES YOU ABOUT THE HUNDRED? The free Pom-Bear
BIGGEST TOPIC OF DISCUSSION IN YOUR DRESSING ROOM? Fantasy Football
CRICKETING HERO? Brian Lara
SURPRISING FACT ABOUT YOU? I eat pineapple slices out of the tin
IF YOU WERE AN ANIMAL, WHICH WOULD IT BE? A cheetah
TWITTER: @Delraw90

Batting	Mat	Inns	NO	Runs	HS	Ave	SR	100	50	Ct	St
T20Is	11	11	0	261	63	23.72	129.85	0	1	9	0
First-class	14	24	1	642	100	27.91	51.60	1	5	5	0
List A	11	11	0	285	53	25.90	109.61	0	2	7	0
T20s	32	29	3	619	69	23.80	141.64	0	2	23	0
Bowling	**Mat**	**Balls**	**Runs**	**Wkts**	**BBI**	**BBM**	**Ave**	**Econ**	**SR**	**5w**	**10**
T20Is	11	222	285	5	2/22	2/22	57.00	7.70	44.4	0	0
First-class	14	894	557	11	3/19	3/52	50.63	3.73	81.2	0	0
List A	11	300	269	3	1/27	1/27	89.66	5.38	100.0	0	0
T20s	32	252	312	7	2/19	2/19	44.57	7.42	36.0	0	0

LUIS REECE LHB / LM / R0 / W1 / MVP4

FULL NAME: Luis Michael Reece
BORN: August 4, 1990, Taunton
SQUAD NO: 10
HEIGHT: 6ft 2in
NICKNAME: Reecey, Rexy
EDUCATION: St Michael's School; Myerscough College; Leeds Metropolitan University
TEAMS: Derbyshire, London Spirit, Chittagong Vikings, Dhaka Platoon, Lancashire
ROLE: Allrounder
DEBUT: First-class: 2012; List A: 2011; T20: 2016

BEST BATTING: 184 Derbyshire vs Sussex, Derby, 2019
BEST BOWLING: 7-20 Derbyshire vs Gloucestershire, Derby, 2018
COUNTY CAP: 2019 (Derbyshire)

WHAT WAS YOUR FIRST CRICKET CLUB? Vernon Carus CC, Lancashire
BIGGEST TOPIC OF DISCUSSION IN YOUR DRESSING ROOM? Cricket
MOST INTERESTING TEAMMATE? Alex Hughes – you get to see his every emotion and usually also half his kit as he's messy!
CRICKETING HERO? AB de Villiers
WHICH RULE WOULD YOU CHANGE ABOUT CRICKET? It should be a no-ball if the bowler hits the bails at the non-striker's end with his hand
SURPRISING FACT ABOUT YOU? As a kid I played chess at national level
SURPRISING FACT ABOUT A TEAMMATE? Matt Critchley went to the same school as me
WHICH BOOK MEANS MOST TO YOU? Of Mice and Men by John Steinbeck
TWITTER: @lreece17

Batting	Mat	Inns	NO	Runs	HS	Ave	SR	100	50	Ct	St
First-class	63	113	7	3528	184	33.28	49.96	6	20	29	0
List A	40	36	5	908	128	29.29	87.98	1	5	11	0
T20s	42	40	4	956	97*	26.55	128.15	0	8	16	0
Bowling	**Mat**	**Balls**	**Runs**	**Wkts**	**BBI**	**BBM**	**Ave**	**Econ**	**SR**	**5w**	**10**
First-class	63	4354	2272	88	7/20	7/38	25.81	3.13	49.4	4	0
List A	40	938	964	19	4/35	4/35	50.73	6.16	49.3	0	0
T20s	42	420	546	21	3/33	3/33	26.00	7.80	20.0	0	0

NICO REIFER RHB / RM / R0 / W0

FULL NAME: Nico Reifer
BORN: November 11, 2000, Bridgetown, Barbados
SQUAD NO: 27
HEIGHT: 6ft 4in
EDUCATION: Queen's College, Bridgetown; Whitgift School, Croydon
TEAMS: Surrey
ROLE: Allrounder

WHAT WAS YOUR FIRST CRICKET CLUB? Wanderers CC, Christ Church, Barbados
WHAT EXCITES YOU ABOUT THE HUNDRED? That it could be a great opportunity for me in a couple of years' time
CRICKET STAR OF THE FUTURE? Max John (Middlesex Academy)
IF YOU WERE AN ANIMAL, WHICH WOULD IT BE? A wolf
TWITTER: @reifzzzz
NOTES: The Barbados-born batting allrounder signed a one-year rookie contract with Surrey last October, having been on the county's books since the age of 15. Reifer said: "I'm proud to have signed this contract with Surrey and I'm excited to have the opportunity to show what I can do. I'll be working hard over the winter to make sure I'm ready for pre-season and the start of the 2020 season in England." Reifer was educated at Queen's College in Barbados and has played for the country's U19 team, as well as being a member of the U15 West Indies team which toured England five years ago. The 19-year-old has attended Whitgift School for the previous four years and has made 10 appeareances for Surrey Second XI since his debut in 2018. Reifer spent the winter playing grade cricket in Australia for Perth-based club Midland-Guildford alongside his Surrey teammate Scott Borthwick

GEORGE RHODES

RHB / OB / R0 / W0

FULL NAME: George Harry Rhodes
BORN: October 26, 1993, Birmingham
SQUAD NO: TBC
HEIGHT: 6ft
NICKNAME: Sherlock, Gnomey
EDUCATION: The Chase School, Malvern; University of Worcester
TEAMS: Leicestershire, Worcestershire
ROLE: Allrounder
DEBUT: First-class: 2016; List A: 2016; T20: 2016

BEST BATTING: 61* Leicestershire vs Northamptonshire, Leicester, 2019
BEST BOWLING: 2-83 Worcestershire vs Kent, Canterbury, 2016

FAMILY TIES? My father Steve played for England, and Worcestershire for 20 years, and my grandfather William played first-class cricket for Nottinghamshire
WHAT WAS YOUR FIRST CRICKET CLUB? Rushwick CC, Worcestershire. Grass is long, the walk-off much longer
BIGGEST TOPIC OF DISCUSSION IN YOUR DRESSING ROOM? Whether Arron Lilley's hairstyle looks more like a pad thai or a bird's nest
MOST INTERESTING TEAMMATE? Dillon Pennington – he's like a big Labrador: clumsy, unpredictable, but you can't not love him
BIGGEST CRICKETING REGRET? Not persevering with my raw pace
CRICKET STAR OF THE FUTURE? Gabriel D'Oliveira
WHICH BOOK MEANS MOST TO YOU? Sapiens – A Brief History of Humankind by Yuval Noah Harari
TWITTER: @Ghrhodes

Batting	Mat	Inns	NO	Runs	HS	Ave	SR	100	50	Ct	St
First-class	24	45	6	873	61*	22.38	38.97	0	5	10	0
List A	10	7	1	228	106	38.00	89.41	1	1	6	0
T20s	15	10	4	62	17*	10.33	101.63	0	0	7	0
Bowling	**Mat**	**Balls**	**Runs**	**Wkts**	**BBI**	**BBM**	**Ave**	**Econ**	**SR**	**5w**	**10**
First-class	24	869	631	6	2/83	2/83	105.16	4.35	144.8	0	0
List A	10	240	252	5	2/34	2/34	50.40	6.30	48.0	0	0
T20s	15	114	164	10	4/13	4/13	16.40	8.63	11.4	0	0

WILL RHODES LHB / RMF / R0 / W0 / MVP39

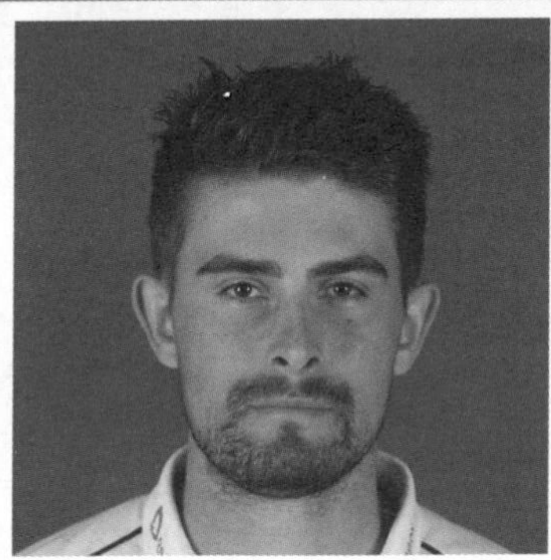

FULL NAME: William Michael Harry Rhodes
BORN: March 2, 1995, Nottingham
SQUAD NO: 35
HEIGHT: 6ft 1in
NICKNAME: Codhead
EDUCATION: Cottingham High School, Hull
TEAMS: Warwickshire, England U19, Essex, Yorkshire
ROLE: Allrounder
DEBUT: First-class: 2015; List A: 2013; T20: 2013

BEST BATTING: 137 Warwickshire vs Gloucestershire, Edgbaston, 2018
BEST BOWLING: 5-17 Warwickshire vs Essex, Chelmsford, 2019

FAMILY TIES? My dad played a bit of Nottinghamshire junior cricket
WHAT WAS YOUR FIRST CRICKET CLUB? Cottingham CC, East Riding of Yorkshire
MOST INTERESTING TEAMMATE? Jonathan Trott – he did some strange things
BEST INNINGS YOU'VE SEEN? Adam Lyth's 161 from 73 balls against Northamptonshire at Headingley in the 2017 T20 Blast
WHICH RULE WOULD YOU CHANGE ABOUT CRICKET? If it pitches outside leg stump then it can still be given out lbw
TWITTER: @willrhodes_152
NOTES: The former Yorkshire allrounder, who turned 25 in March, took over from Jeetan Patel as Warwickshire club captain last November and will look after both the Championship and 50-over sides this summer. Warwickshire sport director Paul Farbrace said: "Will has quickly become recognised as a senior member of the dressing room and he has demonstrated excellent leadership qualities that have impressed the cricket management team"

Batting	Mat	Inns	NO	Runs	HS	Ave	SR	100	50	Ct	St
First-class	50	79	3	2674	137	35.18	50.26	5	14	31	0
List A	32	28	2	569	69	21.88	77.83	0	2	12	0
T20s	33	29	6	281	45	12.21	114.22	0	0	5	0
Bowling	**Mat**	**Balls**	**Runs**	**Wkts**	**BBI**	**BBM**	**Ave**	**Econ**	**SR**	**5w**	**10**
First-class	50	2904	1508	43	5/17	9/55	35.06	3.11	67.5	1	0
List A	32	629	612	13	2/22	2/22	47.07	5.83	48.3	0	0
T20s	33	331	498	22	3/27	3/27	22.63	9.02	15.0	0	0

NATHAN RIMMINGTON RHB / RFM / R0 / W0

FULL NAME: Nathan John Rimmington
BORN: November 11, 1982, Redcliffe, Queensland, Australia
SQUAD NO: 11
HEIGHT: 5ft 11in
EDUCATION: Queensland University of Technology, Brisbane
TEAMS: Durham, Northern Superchargers, Derbyshire, Hampshire, Kings XI Punjab, Melbourne Renegades, Perth Scorchers, Queensland, Western Australia
ROLE: Bowler
DEBUT: First-class: 2006; List A: 2006; T20: 2006

BEST BATTING: 102* Western Australia vs New South Wales, Sydney, 2011
BEST BOWLING: 5-27 Western Australia vs Queensland, Perth, 2014

WHAT WAS YOUR FIRST CRICKET CLUB? Wamuran CC, Queensland, Australia. Tiny country town with only two junior teams
HOW WOULD YOU DISMISS STEVE SMITH? He'd be caught slip
WHAT EXCITES YOU ABOUT THE HUNDRED? I'm playing in it!
BIGGEST TOPIC OF DISCUSSION IN YOUR DRESSING ROOM? Harry Potter
MOST INTERESTING TEAMMATE? Ned Eckersley for his Harry Potter knowledge
WHICH RULE WOULD YOU CHANGE ABOUT CRICKET? No leg byes
BIGGEST CRICKETING REGRET? Not being taller
WHICH BOOK MEANS MOST TO YOU? The God Delusion by Richard Dawkins
IF YOU WERE AN ANIMAL, WHICH WOULD IT BE? An arctic fox – adapts brilliantly to its environment
TWITTER: @nrimmo11

Batting	Mat	Inns	NO	Runs	HS	Ave	SR	100	50	Ct	St
First-class	53	76	16	1221	102*	20.35	54.02	1	4	15	0
List A	56	39	9	534	55	17.80	91.28	0	1	10	0
T20s	108	40	20	206	26	10.30	104.04	0	0	24	0
Bowling	**Mat**	**Balls**	**Runs**	**Wkts**	**BBI**	**BBM**	**Ave**	**Econ**	**SR**	**5w**	**10**
First-class	53	8432	4235	134	5/27	8/116	31.60	3.01	62.9	3	0
List A	56	2970	2337	74	4/34	4/34	31.58	4.72	40.1	0	0
T20s	108	2168	2878	126	5/27	5/27	22.84	7.96	17.2	1	0

OLLIE ROBINSON RHB / WK / R0 / W0 / MVP58

FULL NAME: Oliver Graham Robinson
BORN: December 1, 1998, Sidcup, Kent
SQUAD NO: 21
HEIGHT: 5ft 8in
NICKNAME: Robbo, Bob
EDUCATION: Hurstmere School; Chislehurst and Sidcup Grammar
TEAMS: Kent, England Lions
ROLE: Wicketkeeper/batsman
DEBUT: First-class: 2018; List A: 2017; T20: 2019

BEST BATTING: 143 Kent vs Warwickshire, Edgbaston, 2019

WHAT WAS YOUR FIRST CRICKET CLUB? Sidcup CC, London. Played with my dad for two seasons in the first team
WHAT WERE YOU DOING WHEN ENGLAND WON THE WORLD CUP? Watching it after a day in the dirt at Hampshire
BIGGEST TOPIC OF DISCUSSION IN YOUR DRESSING ROOM? Fantasy Football
MOST INTERESTING TEAMMATE? Mitchell Claydon – he's just a clown
CRICKETING HERO? AB de Villiers
SURPRISING FACT ABOUT YOU? I have to put on everything on the left first – including my contact lenses
BIGGEST CRICKETING REGRET? Not bowling fast
WHICH BOOK MEANS MOST TO YOU? Any of the Harry Potter books
IF YOU WERE AN ANIMAL, WHICH WOULD IT BE? An African hunting dog – class animals to watch
TWITTER: @ollierobinson7

Batting	Mat	Inns	NO	Runs	HS	Ave	SR	100	50	Ct	St
First-class	18	30	2	845	143	30.17	58.80	2	3	55	0
List A	8	5	0	132	49	26.40	75.00	0	0	4	0
T20s	12	10	0	139	53	13.90	104.51	0	1	6	2
Bowling	**Mat**	**Balls**	**Runs**	**Wkts**	**BBI**	**BBM**	**Ave**	**Econ**	**SR**	**5w**	**10**
First-class	18	-	-	-	-	-	-	-	-	-	-
List A	8	-	-	-	-	-	-	-	-	-	-
T20s	12	-	-	-	-	-	-	-	-	-	-

OLLIE ROBINSON RHB / RFM / R0 / W2 / MVP34

FULL NAME: Oliver Edward Robinson
BORN: December 1, 1993, Margate, Kent
SQUAD NO: 25
HEIGHT: 6ft 5in
NICKNAME: The Rig
EDUCATION: King's School, Canterbury
TEAMS: Sussex, England Lions, Hampshire, Yorkshire
ROLE: Bowler
DEBUT: First-class: 2015; List A: 2013; T20: 2014

BEST BATTING: 110 Sussex vs Durham, Chester-le-Street, 2015
BEST BOWLING: 8-34 Sussex vs Middlesex, Hove, 2019
COUNTY CAP: 2019 (Sussex)

WHAT WAS YOUR FIRST CRICKET CLUB? Margate CC, Kent
WHAT WERE YOU DOING WHEN ENGLAND WON THE WORLD CUP? Watching it in the dressing room during a match for England Lions at Canterbury
HOW WOULD YOU DISMISS STEVE SMITH? Nip back the ole Duke ball – lbw/bowled
WHAT EXCITES YOU ABOUT THE HUNDRED? Nothing – I'll be playing in the One-Day Cup instead
BIGGEST TOPIC OF DISCUSSION IN YOUR DRESSING ROOM? Cricket gossip, crosswords, hair, trainers, food
MOST INTERESTING TEAMMATE? Michael Burgess – watching him when he's waiting to bat is like nothing you've ever seen
SURPRISING FACT ABOUT YOU? I was county champion at discus and shot put at the age of 13 and came fourth at the nationals
IF YOU WERE AN ANIMAL, WHICH WOULD IT BE? A sloth
TWITTER: @ollierobinson25

Batting	Mat	Inns	NO	Runs	HS	Ave	SR	100	50	Ct	St
First-class	56	81	16	1382	110	21.26	61.80	1	5	19	0
List A	14	10	3	122	30	17.42	89.70	0	0	6	0
T20s	34	15	7	56	18*	7.00	82.35	0	0	12	0
Bowling	**Mat**	**Balls**	**Runs**	**Wkts**	**BBI**	**BBM**	**Ave**	**Econ**	**SR**	**5w**	**10**
First-class	56	10344	5270	236	8/34	14/135	22.33	3.05	43.8	13	4
List A	14	576	568	14	3/31	3/31	40.57	5.91	41.1	0	0
T20s	34	588	853	31	4/15	4/15	27.51	8.70	18.9	0	0

SAM ROBSON

RHB / LB / R2 / W0

FULL NAME: Samuel David Robson
BORN: July 1, 1989, Sydney, Australia
SQUAD NO: 12
HEIGHT: 6ft
NICKNAME: Bronco
EDUCATION: Marcellin College, Sydney
TEAMS: England, Middlesex, Australia U19
ROLE: Batsman
DEBUT: Test: 2014; First-class: 2009; List A: 2008; T20: 2011

BEST BATTING: 231 Middlesex vs Warwickshire, Lord's, 2016
BEST BOWLING: 2-4 Middlesex vs Lancashire, Lord's, 2019
COUNTY CAP: 2013

WHAT WAS YOUR FIRST CRICKET CLUB? Randwick Junior CC, New South Wales, Australia
BIGGEST TOPIC OF DISCUSSION IN YOUR DRESSING ROOM? Tim Murtagh's dress sense and James Harris's diet fads
MOST INTERESTING TEAMMATE? Tim Murtagh – 38 and still behaving like he is 17
BEST INNINGS YOU'VE SEEN? Hashim Amla scoring 80-odd against us at The Oval in 2013 on a disgraceful pitch which was turning square and going up and down. The best innings I have seen up close
BIGGEST CRICKETING REGRET? Not learning to bowl slow left-arm – very handy bowlers for any team even if they are rarely champion bowlers
CRICKET STAR OF THE FUTURE? Josh de Caires (Middlesex Second XI)
WHICH BOOK MEANS MOST TO YOU? Harry Potter and the Goblet of Fire by JK Rowling
IF YOU WERE AN ANIMAL, WHICH WOULD IT BE? A Great White – many adventures across the sea and top of the food chain

Batting	Mat	Inns	NO	Runs	HS	Ave	SR	100	50	Ct	St
Tests	7	11	0	336	127	30.54	44.50	1	1	5	0
First-class	157	276	18	9750	231	37.79	51.49	23	39	144	0
List A	20	18	0	603	106	33.50	73.35	1	3	8	0
T20s	5	5	2	75	28*	25.00	115.38	0	0	3	0
Bowling	**Mat**	**Balls**	**Runs**	**Wkts**	**BBI**	**BBM**	**Ave**	**Econ**	**SR**	**5w**	**10**
Tests	7	-	-	-	-	-	-	-	-	-	-
First-class	157	253	199	4	2/4	2/4	49.75	4.71	63.2	0	0
List A	20	36	43	1	1/27	1/27	43.00	7.16	36.0	0	0
T20s	5	24	31	3	3/31	3/31	10.33	7.75	8.0	0	0

GARETH RODERICK

RHB / WK / R0 / W0

GLOUCESTERSHIRE

FULL NAME: Gareth Hugh Roderick
BORN: August 29, 1991, Durban, South Africa
SQUAD NO: 27
HEIGHT: 6ft
NICKNAME: Rodders, Pear
EDUCATION: Maritzburg College, South Africa
TEAMS: Gloucestershire, KwaZulu-Natal
ROLE: Batsman/wicketkeeper
DEBUT: First-class: 2011; List A: 2011; T20: 2011

BEST BATTING: 171 Gloucestershire vs Leicestershire, Bristol, 2014

COUNTY CAP: 2013

WHAT WAS YOUR FIRST CRICKET CLUB? Northwood Crusaders CC, Durban, South Africa
BIGGEST TOPIC OF DISCUSSION IN YOUR DRESSING ROOM? Fantasy Football
BEST INNINGS YOU'VE SEEN? Hashim Amla's triple century against England at The Oval in 2012. Pretty much a chanceless innings
CRICKETING HERO? Steve Waugh – best Test captain and played cricket the way it should be played. Ruthless
SURPRISING FACT ABOUT YOU? I played in a club game in South Africa when two gun shots went off in the field next to us
TWITTER: @Roders369

Batting	Mat	Inns	NO	Runs	HS	Ave	SR	100	50	Ct	St
First-class	96	156	20	4801	171	35.30	50.94	6	32	265	5
List A	51	41	6	1184	104	33.82	83.08	2	8	50	4
T20s	41	24	8	213	32	13.31	119.66	0	0	20	1
Bowling	**Mat**	**Balls**	**Runs**	**Wkts**	**BBI**	**BBM**	**Ave**	**Econ**	**SR**	**5w**	**10**
First-class	96	-	-	-	-	-	-	-	-	-	-
List A	51	-	-	-	-	-	-	-	-	-	-
T20s	41	-	-	-	-	-	-	-	-	-	-

TOBY ROLAND-JONES RHB / RMF / R0 / W2 / MVP20

FULL NAME: Tobias Skelton Roland-Jones
BORN: January 29, 1988, Ashford, Middlesex
SQUAD NO: 21
HEIGHT: 6ft 3in
NICKNAME: Rojo, TRJ
EDUCATION: Hampton School, Greater London; University of Leeds
TEAMS: England, Middlesex
ROLE: Bowler
DEBUT: Test: 2017; ODI: 2017; First-class: 2010; List A: 2010; T20: 2011

BEST BATTING: 103* Middlesex vs Yorkshire, Lord's, 2015
BEST BOWLING: 7-52 Middlesex vs Gloucestershire, Northwood, 2019
COUNTY CAP: 2012

FAMILY TIES? My older brother Olly played for Leeds/Bradford MCCU and Middlesex Second XI. My dad is a coach
BEST MOMENT IN CRICKET? Winning the 2016 County Championship in the final session of the season will take some beating
CRICKETING HERO? Ian Botham
IF YOU WEREN'T A CRICKETER? I'd be working in my friends' wine investment company
SURPRISING FACT ABOUT YOU? I actually live in Surrey
TWITTER: @tobyrj21

Batting	Mat	Inns	NO	Runs	HS	Ave	SR	100	50	Ct	St
Tests	4	6	2	82	25	20.50	69.49	0	0	0	0
ODIs	1	1	1	37	37*	-	100.00	0	0	0	0
First-class	114	159	30	2824	103*	21.89	58.14	1	11	33	0
List A	79	47	15	684	65	21.37	95.13	0	1	13	0
T20s	54	31	12	317	40	16.68	128.34	0	0	15	0
Bowling	**Mat**	**Balls**	**Runs**	**Wkts**	**BBI**	**BBM**	**Ave**	**Econ**	**SR**	**5w**	**10**
Tests	4	536	334	17	5/57	8/129	19.64	3.73	31.5	1	0
ODIs	1	42	34	1	1/34	1/34	34.00	4.85	42.0	0	0
First-class	114	19597	10387	403	7/52	12/105	25.77	3.18	48.6	19	4
List A	79	3671	3181	126	4/10	4/10	25.24	5.19	29.1	0	0
T20s	54	1065	1549	64	5/21	5/21	24.20	8.72	16.6	1	0

BILLY ROOT

LHB / OB / R0 / W0

GLAMORGAN

FULL NAME: William Thomas Root
BORN: August 5, 1992, Sheffield
SQUAD NO: 7
HEIGHT: 5ft 11in
NICKNAME: Rooty, Rootfish, Ferret
EDUCATION: Worksop College, Nottinghamshire; Leeds Metropolitan University
TEAMS: Glamorgan, Nottinghamshire
ROLE: Batsman
DEBUT: First-class: 2015; List A: 2017; T20: 2017

BEST BATTING: 229 Glamorgan vs Northamptonshire, Northampton, 2019
BEST BOWLING: 3-29 Nottinghamshire vs Sussex, Hove, 2017

FAMILY TIES? My dad was a good cricketer and my brother plays the occasional game
WHAT WAS YOUR FIRST CRICKET CLUB? Sheffield Collegiate CC. It's got exactly the same slope as the one at Lord's
WHAT WERE YOU DOING WHEN ENGLAND WON THE WORLD CUP? I was watching it still in my short-leg pads after too may overs in the dirt
BIGGEST TOPIC OF DISCUSSION IN YOUR DRESSING ROOM? Winding up Marnus Labuschagne
CRICKET STAR OF THE FUTURE? Isaac Parkin (Sheffield Collegiate CC, Notts Cricket Board U15)
WHICH BOOK MEANS MOST TO YOU? Jamie's 30-Minute Meals – A Revolutionary Approach to Cooking Good Food Fast by Jamie Oliver
IF YOU WERE AN ANIMAL, WHICH WOULD IT BE? A ferret
TWITTER: @Rootdog22

Batting	Mat	Inns	NO	Runs	HS	Ave	SR	100	50	Ct	St
First-class	28	46	2	1465	229	33.29	59.69	4	3	7	0
List A	24	20	4	773	113*	48.31	92.57	2	3	7	0
T20s	29	21	6	337	40	22.46	110.85	0	0	10	0
Bowling	**Mat**	**Balls**	**Runs**	**Wkts**	**BBI**	**BBM**	**Ave**	**Econ**	**SR**	**5w**	**10**
First-class	28	269	176	8	3/29	3/29	22.00	3.92	33.6	0	0
List A	24	292	310	6	2/36	2/36	51.66	6.36	48.6	0	0
T20s	29	18	37	0	-	-	-	12.33	-	0	0

JOE ROOT

RHB / OB / R3 / W0

FULL NAME: Joseph Edward Root
BORN: December 30, 1990, Sheffield
SQUAD NO: 66
HEIGHT: 6ft
NICKNAME: Roota, Rootfish
EDUCATION: King Ecgbert School, Sheffield; Worksop College, Nottinghamshire
TEAMS: England, Yorkshire, Trent Rockets, Sydney Thunder
ROLE: Batsman
DEBUT: Test: 2012; ODI: 2013; T20I: 2012; First-class: 2010; List A: 2009; T20: 2011

BEST BATTING: 254 England vs Pakistan, Old Trafford, 2016
BEST BOWLING: 4-5 Yorkshire vs Lancashire, Old Trafford, 2018
COUNTY CAP: 2012

FAMILY TIES? My dad played club cricket and represented Nottinghamshire Second XI and Colts. My brother Billy has played for Notts and is currently at Glamorgan
CRICKETING HERO? Michael Vaughan
NON-CRICKETING HEROES? Seve Ballesteros, Alan Shearer
IF YOU WEREN'T A CRICKETER? I'd be studying Art and Design at college
SURPRISING FACT ABOUT YOU? I taught myself to play the ukulele on tour with England
TWITTER: @root66

Batting	Mat	Inns	NO	Runs	HS	Ave	SR	100	50	Ct	St
Tests	92	169	12	7599	254	48.40	54.54	17	48	114	0
ODIs	146	137	21	5922	133*	51.05	87.40	16	33	74	0
T20Is	32	30	5	893	90*	35.72	126.30	0	5	18	0
First-class	153	266	23	11789	254	48.51	55.73	28	65	153	0
List A	185	175	27	7206	133*	48.68	86.03	17	42	86	0
T20s	72	66	13	1619	92*	30.54	125.69	0	9	32	0
Bowling	**Mat**	**Balls**	**Runs**	**Wkts**	**BBI**	**BBM**	**Ave**	**Econ**	**SR**	**5w**	**10**
Tests	92	2646	1402	28	4/87	4/112	50.07	3.17	94.5	0	0
ODIs	146	1504	1445	24	3/52	3/52	60.20	5.76	62.6	0	0
T20Is	32	84	139	6	2/9	2/9	23.16	9.92	14.0	0	0
First-class	153	4579	2419	48	4/5	4/5	50.39	3.16	95.3	0	0
List A	185	2091	1944	38	3/52	3/52	51.15	5.57	55.0	0	0
T20s	72	264	415	10	2/9	2/9	41.50	9.43	26.4	0	0

ADAM ROSSINGTON RHB / WK / R0 / W0 / MVP68

FULL NAME: Adam Matthew Rossington
BORN: May 5, 1993, Edgware, Middlesex
SQUAD NO: 7
HEIGHT: 6ft
NICKNAME: Rosso
EDUCATION: Belmont Preparatory School, Surrey; Mill Hill School, London
TEAMS: Northamptonshire, London Spirit, England U19, Middlesex
ROLE: Wicketkeeper/batsman
DEBUT: First-class: 2010; List A: 2012; T20: 2011

BEST BATTING: 138* Northamptonshire vs Sussex, Arundel, 2016

WHAT WAS YOUR FIRST CRICKET CLUB? Barnet CC, London
BEST ADVICE RECEIVED? Watch the ball
MOST INTERESTING TEAMMATE? Richard Levi – gets more deliveries than the post office
CRICKETING HERO? Alec Stewart
WHICH RULE WOULD YOU CHANGE ABOUT CRICKET? Introduce a free hit for a no-ball in all forms of the game
SURPRISING FACT ABOUT YOU? I can't ride a bicycle
BIGGEST CRICKETING REGRET? That I've never played in the Hong Kong Sixes
CRICKET STAR OF THE FUTURE? Emilio Gay (Northamptonshire)
IF YOU WERE AN ANIMAL, WHICH WOULD IT BE? A horse – so that I could go up the Cheltenham hill
TWITTER: @rossington17

Batting	Mat	Inns	NO	Runs	HS	Ave	SR	100	50	Ct	St
First-class	77	123	12	3903	138*	35.16	68.48	6	28	167	11
List A	49	44	7	1381	97	37.32	99.42	0	11	34	5
T20s	76	72	6	1392	85	21.09	142.04	0	8	37	13
Bowling	**Mat**	**Balls**	**Runs**	**Wkts**	**BBI**	**BBM**	**Ave**	**Econ**	**SR**	**5w**	**10**
First-class	77	120	86	0	-	-	-	4.30	-	0	0
List A	49	-	-	-	-	-	-	-	-	-	-
T20s	76	-	-	-	-	-	-	-	-	-	-

RILEE ROSSOUW LHB / OB / R0 / W0 / MVP81

FULL NAME: Rilee Roscoe Rossouw
BORN: October 9, 1989, Bloemfontein, South Africa
SQUAD NO: 30
NICKNAME: Rudi
EDUCATION: Grey College, Bloemfontein
TEAMS: South Africa, Hampshire, Oval Invincibles, Eagles, Free State, Knights, Multan Sultans, Quetta Gladiators, Rangpur Riders, RC Bangalore
ROLE: Batsman
DEBUT: ODI: 2014; T20I: 2014; First-class: 2007; List A: 2007; T20: 2008

BEST BATTING: 319 Eagles vs Titans, Centurion, 2010
BEST BOWLING: 1-1 Knights vs Cape Cobras, Cape Town, 2013

TWITTER: @Rileerr
NOTES: A top-order batsman, Rossouw quit international cricket ahead of the 2017 season to take up a three-year Kolpak deal with Hampshire to play in all formats. He scored just one fifty from 13 Championship innings in his first season at the club, although a one-day hundred served notice of his talent. The left-hander scored his first Championship century in 2018 but his starring role came in the One-Day Cup, making three figures in the final at Lord's to help Hampshire lift the trophy. He was a solid presence across all formats last summer and was signed by Oval Invincibles for The Hundred. Rossouw's South Africa career got off to a shaky start in 2014, with ducks in four of his first six ODI innings, but he soon established himself as one of his country's most consistent white-ball performers. His highest first-class score, a 291-ball innings of 319 which included 47 fours, is indicative of his pedigree in the longer format

Batting	Mat	Inns	NO	Runs	HS	Ave	SR	100	50	Ct	St
ODIs	36	35	3	1239	132	38.71	94.36	3	7	22	0
T20Is	15	14	3	327	78	29.72	137.97	0	2	9	0
First-class	108	190	10	7363	319	40.90	63.89	19	33	119	0
List A	152	149	8	5646	156	40.04	96.26	12	34	76	0
T20s	199	191	25	4934	100*	29.72	135.99	2	27	86	0
Bowling	**Mat**	**Balls**	**Runs**	**Wkts**	**BBI**	**BBM**	**Ave**	**Econ**	**SR**	**5w**	**10**
ODIs	36	45	44	1	1/17	1/17	44.00	5.86	45.0	0	0
T20Is	15	-	-	-	-	-	-	-	-	-	-
First-class	108	78	70	3	1/1	1/1	23.33	5.38	26.0	0	0
List A	152	45	44	1	1/17	1/17	44.00	5.86	45.0	0	0
T20s	199	28	29	2	1/3	1/3	14.50	6.21	14.0	0	0

ADAM ROUSE

RHB / WK / R0 / W0

FULL NAME: Adam Paul Rouse
BORN: June 30, 1992, Harare, Zimbabwe
SQUAD NO: 12
HEIGHT: 5ft 10in
NICKNAME: Rousie
EDUCATION: Perins Community Sports College, Hampshire; Peter Symonds College, Winchester
TEAMS: Kent, England U19, Gloucestershire, Hampshire, Surrey, Sussex
ROLE: Wicketkeeper/batsman
DEBUT: First-class: 2013; List A: 2013; T20: 2014

BEST BATTING: 95* Kent vs Derbyshire, Canterbury, 2017

COUNTY CAP: 2014 (Gloucestershire)

WHAT WAS YOUR FIRST CRICKET CLUB? Basingstoke & North Hants CC, Hampshire
WHAT WERE YOU DOING WHEN ENGLAND WON THE WORLD CUP? Watching it at home. I'm pretty sure I was standing on the sofa for most of the super over
HOW WOULD YOU DISMISS STEVE SMITH? I'd just bowl some of my offies at him and probably get one through the gate
WHAT EXCITES YOU ABOUT THE HUNDRED? I think it helps at grassroots level, allowing kids to watch cricket on terrestrial TV. I also hope it will allow some of England's young talent to shine and potentially become household names
BIGGEST TOPIC OF DISCUSSION IN YOUR DRESSING ROOM? Who is the top goal-scorer in the footy warm-ups
MOST INTERESTING TEAMMATE? Mitchell Claydon – a dangerous guy because he's just a big kid, always looking for the next gag to play on some unsuspecting teammate. But in other ways he adds a lot to the changing room, always keeping everyone pretty relaxed
TWITTER: @Rousie20

Batting	Mat	Inns	NO	Runs	HS	Ave	SR	100	50	Ct	St
First-class	36	51	4	1103	95*	23.46	51.88	0	5	112	4
List A	40	34	9	682	75*	27.28	73.25	0	3	37	3
T20s	8	7	2	61	35*	12.20	117.30	0	0	4	4
Bowling	**Mat**	**Balls**	**Runs**	**Wkts**	**BBI**	**BBM**	**Ave**	**Econ**	**SR**	**5w**	**10**
First-class	36	-	-	-	-	-	-	-	-	-	-
List A	40	-	-	-	-	-	-	-	-	-	-
T20s	8	-	-	-	-	-	-	-	-	-	-

JASON ROY

RHB / RM / R1 / W0

FULL NAME: Jason Jonathan Roy
BORN: July 21, 1990, Durban, South Africa
SQUAD NO: 20
HEIGHT: 6ft
NICKNAME: JRoy, Roy the Boy
EDUCATION: Whitgift School, Croydon
TEAMS: England, Surrey, Oval Invincibles, Delhi Capitals, Gujarat Lions, Lahore Qalanders, Quetta Gladiators, Sydney Sixers, Sylhet Sixers
ROLE: Batsman
DEBUT: Test: 2019; ODI: 2015; T20I: 2014; First-class: 2010; List A: 2008; T20: 2008

BEST BATTING: 143 Surrey vs Lancashire, The Oval, 2015
BEST BOWLING: 3-9 Surrey vs Gloucestershire, Bristol, 2014
COUNTY CAP: 2014

BEST MOMENTS IN CRICKET? Winning the Championship with Surrey, my England T20, ODI and Test debuts, my first century for England in ODI cricket and winning the World Cup last summer
CRICKETING HERO? Jacques Kallis
NON-CRICKETING HERO? Superman
IF YOU WEREN'T A CRICKETER? I'd be a professional surfer and living on a beach
TWITTER: @JasonRoy20

Batting	Mat	Inns	NO	Runs	HS	Ave	SR	100	50	Ct	St
Tests	5	10	0	187	72	18.70	58.80	0	1	1	0
ODIs	87	83	2	3434	180	42.39	107.27	9	18	31	0
T20Is	35	35	0	860	78	24.57	147.51	0	5	5	0
First-class	86	142	11	4832	143	36.88	80.87	9	23	74	0
List A	183	174	8	6494	180	39.12	107.26	16	34	69	0
T20s	210	205	10	5350	122*	27.43	144.67	4	35	96	0
Bowling	**Mat**	**Balls**	**Runs**	**Wkts**	**BBI**	**BBM**	**Ave**	**Econ**	**SR**	**5w**	**10**
Tests	5	-	-	-	-	-	-	-	-	-	-
ODIs	87	-	-	-	-	-	-	-	-	-	-
T20Is	35	-	-	-	-	-	-	-	-	-	-
First-class	86	712	495	14	3/9	4/47	35.35	4.17	50.8	0	0
List A	183	6	12	0	-	-	-	12.00	-	0	0
T20s	210	18	39	1	1/23	1/23	39.00	13.00	18.0	0	0

CHRIS RUSHWORTH RHB / RFM / R0 / W5 / MVP61

FULL NAME: Christopher Rushworth
BORN: July 11, 1986, Sunderland
SQUAD NO: 22
HEIGHT: 6ft 2in
NICKNAME: Russian, Sponge, Pilko
EDUCATION: Castle View Comprehensive School, Sunderland
TEAMS: Durham
ROLE: Bowler
DEBUT: First-class: 2010; List A: 2004; T20: 2011

BEST BATTING: 57 Durham vs Kent, Canterbury, 2017
BEST BOWLING: 9-52 Durham vs Northamptonshire, Chester-le-Street, 2014
BENEFIT: 2019

FAMILY TIES? My brother Lee represented England U19 and my cousin Phil Mustard played for England, Durham and Gloucestershire
WHAT WAS YOUR FIRST CRICKET CLUB? Hylton Colliery CC, Sunderland
HOW WOULD YOU DISMISS STEVE SMITH? Ask him to bat at the Riverside in April
BIGGEST TOPIC OF DISCUSSION IN YOUR DRESSING ROOM? This season it is likely to be about how good Gareth Harte's new hair looks
MOST INTERESTING TEAMMATE? I had the pleasure of sharing a dressing room with Angus Robson for a few games last year. His outlook on life is different and interesting
WHICH RULE WOULD YOU CHANGE ABOUT CRICKET? At least one extra fielder outside the circle in the first six overs of T20
BIGGEST CRICKETING REGRET? Trying to sweep Liam Dawson while my partner was on 99 at the other end. I was the last man. Oops
CRICKET STAR OF THE FUTURE? Young leg-spinner Luke Husband (Sacriston CC, County Durham)
TWITTER: @ChrisRush22

Batting	Mat	Inns	NO	Runs	HS	Ave	SR	100	50	Ct	St
First-class	127	179	57	1460	57	11.96	62.41	0	1	28	0
List A	72	30	15	188	38*	12.53	87.85	0	0	18	0
T20s	85	15	9	20	5	3.33	50.00	0	0	18	0
Bowling	**Mat**	**Balls**	**Runs**	**Wkts**	**BBI**	**BBM**	**Ave**	**Econ**	**SR**	**5w**	**10**
First-class	127	22697	11276	494	9/52	15/95	22.82	2.98	45.9	25	4
List A	72	3139	2765	111	5/31	5/31	24.90	5.28	28.2	2	0
T20s	85	1623	2121	78	3/14	3/14	27.19	7.84	20.8	0	0

ANDRE RUSSELL RHB/RFM

FULL NAME: Andre Dwayne Russell
BORN: April 29, 1988, Kingston, Jamaica
SQUAD NO: TBC
HEIGHT: 6ft 1in
NICKNAME: Dre Russ
TEAMS: West Indies, Southern Brave, Delhi Daredevils, Dhaka Dynamites, Jamaica Tallawahs, Kolkata KR, Melbourne Renegades, Multan Sultans, Nottinghamshire, Rajshahi Royals, Sydney Thunder, Worcestershire
ROLE: Allrounder
DEBUT: Test: 2010; ODI: 2011; T20I: 2011; First-class: 2007; List A: 2008; T20: 2010

BEST BATTING: 121* Jamaica Tallawahs vs Trinbago Knight Riders, Port of Spain, 2018 (T20)
BEST BOWLING: 4-11 Knights vs Titans, Benoni, 2015 (T20)

NOTES: An explosive allrounder who hits the ball as hard as any batsman in the game, Russell made his ODI debut at the 2011 World Cup, against Ireland at Mohali, and was subsequently signed by Delhi Daredevils ahead of the 2012 IPL. In 2013, playing for West Indies A, he became the first bowler to take four wickets in successive deliveries in T20 cricket. He was named in the team of the tournament at the 2016 World T20 and that same year scored the second-fastest century in the Caribbean Premier League, off 42 deliveries. In the 2019 IPL Russell recorded the highest strike rate (205) in the tournament's history. He has won titles in five global franchise leagues. The Jamaican has had two spells in the T20 Blast, for Worcestershire in 2013 and Nottinghamshire in 2016. He will play for Southern Brave in The Hundred after being signed in the £125k category

Batting	Mat	Inns	NO	Runs	HS	Ave	SR	100	50	Ct	St
Tests	1	1	0	2	2	2.00	22.22	0	0	1	0
ODIs	56	47	9	1034	92*	27.21	130.22	0	4	11	0
T20Is	49	41	14	540	47	20.00	151.26	0	0	12	0
First-class	17	24	1	609	128	26.47		2	0	6	0
List A	93	78	18	1953	132*	32.55		2	8	22	0
T20s	321	270	71	5365	121*	26.95	171.29	2	18	151	0
Bowling	**Mat**	**Balls**	**Runs**	**Wkts**	**BBI**	**BBM**	**Ave**	**Econ**	**SR**	**5w**	**10**
Tests	1	138	104	1	1/73	1/104	104.00	4.52	138.0	0	0
ODIs	56	2290	2229	70	4/35	4/35	31.84	5.84	32.7	0	0
T20Is	49	643	974	26	2/10	2/10	37.46	9.08	24.7	0	0
First-class	17	2083	1104	54	5/36	9/78	20.44	3.18	38.5	3	0
List A	93	3777	3418	131	6/28	6/28	26.09	5.42	28.8	4	0
T20s	321	5460	7532	291	4/11	4/11	25.88	8.27	18.7	0	0

HAMISH RUTHERFORD

LHB / SLA / R0 / W0

FULL NAME: Hamish Duncan Rutherford
BORN: April 27, 1989, Dunedin, New Zealand
SQUAD NO: TBC
HEIGHT: 5ft 11in
NICKNAME: Ruds
EDUCATION: Otago Boys' High School, Dunedin
TEAMS: New Zealand, Worcestershire, Derbyshire, Essex, Otago
ROLE: Batsman
DEBUT: Test: 2013; ODI: 2013; T20I: 2013; First-class: 2008; List A: 2008; T20: 2009

BEST BATTING: 239 Otago vs Wellington, Dunedin, 2012

WHAT WAS YOUR FIRST CRICKET CLUB? Albion CC, Dunedin, New Zealand
HOW WOULD YOU DISMISS STEVE SMITH? Thankfully I don't have to
BIGGEST TOPIC OF DISCUSSION IN YOUR DRESSING ROOM? Ben Cox's kit
MOST INTERESTING TEAMMATE? Grant Elliott
TWITTER: @HDRutherford17
NOTES: The Kiwi opening batsman has re-signed with Worcestershire for the duration of the season after making 14 appearances for the county last summer in which he hit three centuries. He is available to play in all three formats. He has previously had two successful spells with Derbyshire, in 2015 and 2016. The son of former New Zealand captain Ken Rutherford, the left-hander scored 171 on his Test debut against England at Dunedin in 2013 but hasn't represented his country in the longer format since 2015

Batting	Mat	Inns	NO	Runs	HS	Ave	SR	100	50	Ct	St
Tests	16	29	1	755	171	26.96	56.42	1	1	11	0
ODIs	4	4	0	15	11	3.75	26.78	0	0	2	0
T20Is	8	7	0	151	62	21.57	143.80	0	1	1	0
First-class	103	177	3	6242	239	35.87	61.41	14	29	69	0
List A	91	88	3	3175	155	37.35	94.38	11	9	30	0
T20s	137	132	5	3191	106	25.12	143.35	1	14	39	0
Bowling	**Mat**	**Balls**	**Runs**	**Wkts**	**BBI**	**BBM**	**Ave**	**Econ**	**SR**	**5w**	**10**
Tests	16	6	2	0	-	-	-	2.00	-	0	0
ODIs	4	-	-	-	-	-	-	-	-	-	-
T20Is	8	-	-	-	-	-	-	-	-	-	-
First-class	103	162	81	0	-	-	-	3.00	-	0	0
List A	91	42	33	1	1/4	1/4	33.00	4.71	42.0	0	0
T20s	137	6	11	0	-	-	-	11.00	-	0	0

JOSH RYMELL RHB / RO / WO

FULL NAME: Joshua Sean Rymell
BORN: April 4, 2001, Ipswich, Suffolk
SQUAD NO: 49
EDUCATION: Ipswich School; Colchester Sixth Form College
TEAMS: Essex
ROLE: Batsman

TWITTER: @josh_rymell
NOTES: Rymell has come through the player pathway system at Essex and in January signed a rookie contract which runs until the end of the summer. "I'm absolutely over the moon to sign my first contract with Essex," he said. "It really means a lot to me and my family and I'm really looking forward to getting stuck in and learning from some of the best around." Rymell served notice of his talent in May 2017 when he scored 114 off 107 balls on his debut for Colchester and East Essex in the Essex League Cup. He made 19 appearances for Essex Second XI last season, with a high score of 87 against Durham in a 50-over match at Chelmsford. He spent much of the winter recovering from an interior cruciate ligament injury he suffered last season but was due to join the Essex first team on their pre-season tour of Abu Dhabi in March

OLLIE SALE

RHB / RFM / R0 / W0

FULL NAME: Oliver Richard Trethowan Sale
BORN: September 30, 1995, Newcastle-under-Lyme, Staffordshire
SQUAD NO: 82
HEIGHT: 6ft 2in
NICKNAME: Saler, Snail, Salestorm
EDUCATION: Sherborne School, Dorset; Newcastle University
TEAMS: Somerset
ROLE: Allrounder
DEBUT: T20: 2016

WHAT WAS YOUR FIRST CRICKET CLUB? Tavistock CC, Devon. The pitch is in the middle of Dartmoor and play is often interrupted by ponies and sheep
BEST ADVICE EVER RECEIVED? Don't sweat on the small stuff
WHAT WERE YOU DOING WHEN ENGLAND WON THE WORLD CUP? I was having a quiet beverage
HOW WOULD YOU DISMISS STEVE SMITH? Bowl the Gatting Ball
BIGGEST TOPIC OF DISCUSSION IN YOUR DRESSING ROOM? Eddie Byrom's love life
MOST INTERESTING TEAMMATE? Jack Brooks – he has an uncanny resemblance to a ferret
SURPRISING FACT ABOUT YOU? I'm scared of sponges… when I say "scared" I mean I literally cannot deal with the feel of them
WHICH BOOK MEANS MOST TO YOU? I Am Pilgrim – A Thriller by Terry Hayes
IF YOU WERE AN ANIMAL, WHICH WOULD IT BE? A slow loris – I have a tendency to be slow in day-to-day life
TWITTER: @olliesale1

Batting	Mat	Inns	NO	Runs	HS	Ave	SR	100	50	Ct	St
T20s	1	1	0	1	1	1.00	33.33	0	0	0	0
Bowling	**Mat**	**Balls**	**Runs**	**Wkts**	**BBI**	**BBM**	**Ave**	**Econ**	**SR**	**5w**	**10**
T20s	1	18	40	0	-	-	-	13.33	-	0	0

MATT SALISBURY

RHB / RMF / R0 / W0

FULL NAME: Matthew Edward Thomas Salisbury
BORN: April 18, 1993, Chelmsford, Essex
SQUAD NO: 32
HEIGHT: 6ft 2in
NICKNAME: Sals, Great Wall
EDUCATION: Shenfield High School, Essex; Anglia Ruskin University, Cambridge
TEAMS: Durham, Essex, Hampshire
ROLE: Bowler
DEBUT: First-class: 2012; List A: 2014; T20: 2014

BEST BATTING: 37 Durham vs Warwickshire, Edgbaston, 2018
BEST BOWLING: 6-37 Durham vs Middlesex, Chester-le-Street, 2018

WHAT WAS YOUR FIRST CRICKET CLUB? Shenfield CC, Essex
WHICH BOWLER WOULD YOU LEAST LIKE TO FACE? Mitchell Johnson
WHO WOULD YOU ASK TO BAT FOR YOUR LIFE? Kane Williamson
FAVOURITE QUOTE OR SAYING? He's thrown a kettle over a pub, what have you done? (Gareth from The Office)
WHICH BOOK MEANS MOST TO YOU? The dictionary
TWITTER: @mattsalisbury10

Batting	Mat	Inns	NO	Runs	HS	Ave	SR	100	50	Ct	St
First-class	31	53	11	374	37	8.90	31.85	0	0	4	0
List A	13	3	2	8	5*	8.00	32.00	0	0	2	0
T20s	8	2	2	2	1*	-	100.00	0	0	2	0
Bowling	**Mat**	**Balls**	**Runs**	**Wkts**	**BBI**	**BBM**	**Ave**	**Econ**	**SR**	**5w**	**10**
First-class	31	4595	2804	90	6/37	7/107	31.15	3.66	51.0	1	0
List A	13	510	492	14	4/55	4/55	35.14	5.78	36.4	0	0
T20s	8	172	256	10	2/19	2/19	25.60	8.93	17.2	0	0

PHIL SALT RHB / OB / R0 / W0 / MVP44

FULL NAME: Philip Dean Salt
BORN: August 28, 1996, Bodelwyddan, Denbighshire, Wales
SQUAD NO: 28
HEIGHT: 6ft
NICKNAME: Salty, Hotdog
EDUCATION: Harrison College, Barbados; Reed's School, Surrey
TEAMS: Sussex, Manchester Originals, Adelaide Strikers, Barbados Tridents, Islamabad United, Lahore Qalandars
ROLE: Batsman
DEBUT: First-class: 2016; List A: 2015; T20: 2016

BEST BATTING: 148 Sussex vs Derbyshire, Hove, 2018
BEST BOWLING: 1-32 Sussex vs Warwickshire, Hove, 2018

WHAT WAS YOUR FIRST CRICKET CLUB? St Asaph CC, North Wales
CRICKETING HERO? Growing up in Barbados, I didn't look past Sir Garry Sobers
WHICH BOWLER WOULD YOU LEAST LIKE TO FACE? Jofra Archer – because he bowls off 17 yards in the nets
BEST INNINGS YOU'VE SEEN? My favourite shot was the huge six by Tymal Mills against Gloucestershire at Arundel in the 2016 T20 Blast. I'm pretty sure the ball is still going up
SURPRISING FACT ABOUT YOU? I once picked up Sir Garry Sobers' Indian takeaway by accident
FAVOURITE QUOTE OR SAYING? If it ain't gone in three, it ain't meant to be
WHICH BOOK MEANS MOST TO YOU? Cats Galore – A Compendium of Cultured Cats by Susan Herbert
TWITTER: @PhilSalt1

Batting	Mat	Inns	NO	Runs	HS	Ave	SR	100	50	Ct	St
First-class	34	58	2	1677	148	29.94	74.00	4	7	27	0
List A	16	16	1	494	137*	32.93	104.66	1	2	5	0
T20s	66	63	6	1498	78*	26.28	156.04	0	12	33	1
Bowling	**Mat**	**Balls**	**Runs**	**Wkts**	**BBI**	**BBM**	**Ave**	**Econ**	**SR**	**5w**	**10**
First-class	34	54	32	1	1/32	1/32	32.00	3.55	54.0	0	0
List A	16	-	-	-	-	-	-	-	-	-	-
T20s	66	-	-	-	-	-	-	-	-	-	-

ANDREW SALTER

RHB / OB / R0 / W0

FULL NAME: Andrew Graham Salter
BORN: June 1, 1993, Haverfordwest, Pembrokeshire, Wales
SQUAD NO: 21
HEIGHT: 5ft 9in
NICKNAME: Beak, Salts
EDUCATION: Milford Haven School, Pembrokeshire; Cardiff Metropolitan University
TEAMS: Glamorgan, England U19
ROLE: Bowler
DEBUT: First-class: 2012; List A: 2012; T20: 2014

BEST BATTING: 88 Glamorgan vs Gloucestershire, Cardiff, 2017
BEST BOWLING: 4-80 Glamorgan vs Warwickshire, Edgbaston, 2018

FAMILY TIES? My father and brother both played, my mum made teas and score
WHAT WAS YOUR FIRST CRICKET CLUB? St Ishmaels CC, Pembrokeshire
WHAT WERE YOU DOING WHEN ENGLAND WON THE WORLD CUP? Riding my motorbike around the Brecon Beacons (caught the last hour)
HOW WOULD YOU DISMISS STEVE SMITH? A couple of doorknobs should do the trick
WHAT EXCITES YOU ABOUT THE HUNDRED? The new tactics
BIGGEST TOPIC OF DISCUSSION IN YOUR DRESSING ROOM? Haircuts and dress sense
MOST INTERESTING TEAMMATE? Dale Steyn – because of his love for fishing, surfing and motorcycling
CRICKETING HERO? Nathan Lyon
SURPRISING FACT ABOUT YOU? I co-manage a motorcycle initiative called Baffle Culture which aims at "seizing the opportunity to bring like-minded riders together"
CRICKET STAR OF THE FUTURE? Jack Pritchard (Lisvane CC, Cardiff)
IF YOU WERE AN ANIMAL, WHICH WOULD IT BE? Eagle – big beak
TWITTER: @AndySalts

Batting	Mat	Inns	NO	Runs	HS	Ave	SR	100	50	Ct	St
First-class	56	87	17	1629	88	23.27	42.64	0	8	28	0
List A	36	28	10	371	51	20.61	88.12	0	1	9	0
T20s	68	39	19	292	39*	14.60	116.33	0	0	19	0
Bowling	**Mat**	**Balls**	**Runs**	**Wkts**	**BBI**	**BBM**	**Ave**	**Econ**	**SR**	**5w**	**10**
First-class	56	7177	4130	86	4/80	6/69	48.02	3.45	83.4	0	0
List A	36	1288	1155	17	2/41	2/41	67.94	5.38	75.7	0	0
T20s	68	906	1225	43	4/12	4/12	28.48	8.11	21.0	0	0

BEN SANDERSON RHB / RMF / R0 / W3 / MVP18

FULL NAME: Ben William Sanderson
BORN: January 3, 1989, Sheffield
SQUAD NO: 26
HEIGHT: 6ft
NICKNAME: Sandoooo
EDUCATION: Ecclesfield School, Sheffield; Sheffield College
TEAMS: Northamptonshire, England U19, Yorkshire
ROLE: Bowler
DEBUT: First-class: 2008; List A: 2010; T20: 2010

BEST BATTING: 42 Northamptonshire vs Kent, Canterbury, 2015
BEST BOWLING: 8-73 Northamptonshire vs Gloucestershire, Northampton, 2016
COUNTY CAP: 2018 (Northamptonshire)

WHAT WAS YOUR FIRST CRICKET CLUB? Whitley Hall CC, Sheffield. Very good drinkers
BEST ADVICE RECEIVED? Bite the apple and brush your ear when bowling
WHAT WERE YOU DOING WHEN ENGLAND WON THE WORLD CUP? Watching it on an iPad in the Chesterfield CC changing room
BIGGEST TOPIC OF DISCUSSION IN YOUR DRESSING ROOM? Love Island
MOST INTERESTING TEAMMATE? Nathan Buck – tells some interesting jokes
BIGGEST CRICKETING REGRET? Being a bowler
CRICKET STAR OF THE FUTURE? Emilio Gay – just signed his first professional contract with Northants
WHICH BOOK MEANS MOST TO YOU? My chequebook
IF YOU WERE AN ANIMAL, WHICH WOULD IT BE? Any animal that sleeps a lot
TWITTER: @sando567

Batting	Mat	Inns	NO	Runs	HS	Ave	SR	100	50	Ct	St
First-class	60	77	30	421	42	8.95	44.50	0	0	9	0
List A	33	15	6	99	31	11.00	69.71	0	0	9	0
T20s	35	12	9	33	12*	11.00	100.00	0	0	0	0
Bowling	**Mat**	**Balls**	**Runs**	**Wkts**	**BBI**	**BBM**	**Ave**	**Econ**	**SR**	**5w**	**10**
First-class	60	10622	4676	233	8/73	10/55	20.06	2.64	45.5	12	2
List A	33	1317	1306	37	3/36	3/36	35.29	5.94	35.5	0	0
T20s	35	659	973	39	4/21	4/21	24.94	8.85	16.8	0	0

MITCHELL SANTNER LHB / SLA

FULL NAME: Mitchell Josef Santner
BORN: February 5, 1992, Hamilton, NZ
SQUAD NO: TBC
HEIGHT: 6ft
NICKNAME: Flatline
EDUCATION: Hamilton Boys' High School, New Zealand
TEAMS: New Zealand, Manchester Originals, Chennai Super Kings, Northern Districts, Worcestershire
ROLE: Allrounder
DEBUT: Test: 2015; ODI: 2015; T20I: 2015; First-class: 2011; List A: 2014; T20: 2014

BEST BATTING: 45* Northern Districts vs Central Districts, Hamilton, 2016 (T20)
BEST BOWLING: 4-11 New Zealand vs India, Nagpur, 2016 (T20)

TWITTER: @MitchellSantner
NOTES: A canny left-arm spinner and hard-hitting lower-order batsman, Santner was ranked No.3 in the T20I rankings in January of this year. He was initially elevated into the New Zealand team in 2015 to fill the void left by the retiring Daniel Vettori. Santner was named in the Team of the Tournament at the 2016 World T20, when his figures of 4-11 against India were the best by a Kiwi in a short-format World Cup. He hit his maiden Test century last November, against England at Mount Maunganui, sharing a stand of 261 with BJ Watling – a New Zealand record for the seventh wicket. He took 15 wickets at 24.50 and scored 240 runs for Worcestershire in last summer's T20 Blast and was retained by Chennai Super Kings for the 2020 IPL. Santner was selected by Manchester Originals for The Hundred in the £50k band

Batting	Mat	Inns	NO	Runs	HS	Ave	SR	100	50	Ct	St
Tests	22	29	0	741	126	25.55	42.36	1	2	14	0
ODIs	72	56	22	924	67	27.17	88.33	0	2	27	0
T20Is	44	32	12	282	37	14.10	124.22	0	0	19	0
First-class	52	78	4	2127	126	28.74	48.00	3	12	43	0
List A	96	78	23	1551	86	28.20	87.77	0	6	41	0
T20s	82	65	21	856	45*	19.45	127.57	0	0	35	0
Bowling	**Mat**	**Balls**	**Runs**	**Wkts**	**BBI**	**BBM**	**Ave**	**Econ**	**SR**	**5w**	**10**
Tests	22	3746	1744	39	3/53	5/173	44.71	2.79	96.0	0	0
ODIs	72	3259	2661	71	5/50	5/50	37.47	4.89	45.9	1	0
T20Is	44	893	1096	52	4/11	4/11	21.07	7.36	17.1	0	0
First-class	52	7760	3854	82	4/111	5/75	47.00	2.97	94.6	0	0
List A	96	4389	3465	101	5/50	5/50	34.30	4.73	43.4	1	0
T20s	82	1703	2022	87	4/11	4/11	23.24	7.12	19.5	0	0

GEORGE SCOTT

RHB / RM / R0 / W0

FULL NAME: George Frederick Buchan Scott
BORN: November 6, 1995, Hemel Hempstead, Hertfordshire
SQUAD NO: 17
HEIGHT: 6ft 2in
NICKNAME: Scotty
EDUCATION: Beechwood Park School, St Albans; St Albans School; University of Leeds
TEAMS: Gloucestershire, Middlesex
ROLE: Allrounder
DEBUT: First-class: 2015; List A: 2015; T20: 2015

BEST BATTING: 55 Middlesex vs Leicestershire, Lord's, 2019
BEST BOWLING: 2-49 Middlesex vs Derbyshire, Derby, 2019

FAMILY TIES? I have three brothers, all of whom have played Minor Counties cricket for Hertfordshire
WHAT WAS YOUR FIRST CRICKET CLUB? Potters Bar CC, Hertfordshire
BEST ADVICE EVER RECEIVED? The stiller you are, the easier it is to see
WHAT EXCITES YOU ABOUT THE HUNDRED? Watching my mates tear it up
BIGGEST TOPIC OF DISCUSSION IN YOUR DRESSING ROOM? Coffee
MOST INTERESTING TEAMMATE? AB de Villiers
CRICKETING HERO? Kumar Sangakarra – having a degree in Law and being one of the best cricketers ever shows he must be a very intelligent and well-rounded individual
SURPRISING FACT ABOUT YOU? I was a music scholar at St Albans School, playing the piano and the bassoon
TWITTER: @georgefbscott

Batting	Mat	Inns	NO	Runs	HS	Ave	SR	100	50	Ct	St
First-class	12	18	3	257	55	17.13	44.08	0	1	5	0
List A	11	10	3	194	63	27.71	123.56	0	1	5	0
T20s	24	20	9	278	38*	25.27	100.72	0	0	10	0
Bowling	**Mat**	**Balls**	**Runs**	**Wkts**	**BBI**	**BBM**	**Ave**	**Econ**	**SR**	**5w**	**10**
First-class	12	432	267	5	2/49	2/49	53.40	3.70	86.4	0	0
List A	11	216	239	1	1/65	1/65	239.00	6.63	216.0	0	0
T20s	24	48	83	2	1/14	1/14	41.50	10.37	24.0	0	0

GEORGE SCRIMSHAW RHB / RMF / R0 / W0

FULL NAME: George Louis Sheridan Scrimshaw
BORN: February 10, 1998, Burton-on-Trent, Staffordshire
SQUAD NO: 9
HEIGHT: 6ft 6in
NICKNAME: Scrim, Scrimmy, Tank
EDUCATION: Thomas Russel Junior School; John Taylor High School, Burton-on-Trent
TEAMS: Worcestershire
ROLE: Bowler
DEBUT: T20: 2017

FAMILY TIES? My dad and grandad both played county age-group cricket
WHAT WAS YOUR FIRST CRICKET CLUB? Dunstall CC, Burton-upon-Trent, Staffordshire – aka Deer Park, home of the Stags
WHAT WERE YOU DOING WHEN ENGLAND WON THE WORLD CUP? Lying in bed watching it
HOW WOULD YOU DISMISS STEVE SMITH? Would have to test him in lots of different ways, but above all bowl outside off stump
MOST INTERESTING TEAMMATE? Dillon Pennington – very funny and clueless individual
CRICKETING HERO? Dale Steyn – I love his aggression. For a fast bowler like myself, he's a role model
SURPRISING FACT ABOUT YOU? I once hit 16 sixes in a row in Kwik Cricket
TWITTER: @Gscrimshaw98

Batting	Mat	Inns	NO	Runs	HS	Ave	SR	100	50	Ct	St
T20s	4	1	1	1	1*	-	50.00	0	0	0	0
Bowling	**Mat**	**Balls**	**Runs**	**Wkts**	**BBI**	**BBM**	**Ave**	**Econ**	**SR**	**5w**	**10**
T20s	4	60	90	3	1/20	1/20	30.00	9.00	20.0	0	0

NICK SELMAN

RHB / RM / R0 / W0

GLAMORGAN

FULL NAME: Nicholas James Selman
BORN: October 18, 1995, Brisbane, Australia
SQUAD NO: 9
HEIGHT: 6ft 2in
NICKNAME: Sellers
EDUCATION: Matthew Flinders Anglican College, Queensland, Australia
TEAMS: Glamorgan
ROLE: Batsman
DEBUT: First-class: 2016; List A: 2016; T20: 2016

BEST BATTING: 150 Glamorgan vs Gloucestershire, Newport, 2019
BEST BOWLING: 1-22 Glamorgan vs Northamptonshire, Cardiff, 2019

WHAT WAS YOUR FIRST CRICKET CLUB? Maleny CC, Queensland, Australia
HOW WOULD YOU DISMISS STEVE SMITH? Lbw with a googly
WHAT EXCITES YOU ABOUT THE HUNDRED? Watching Chris Cooke whack 'em
BIGGEST TOPIC OF DISCUSSION IN YOUR DRESSING ROOM? Punting
MOST INTERESTING TEAMMATE? Charlie Hemphrey – he cannot pick a winner when it comes to horses
CRICKETING HERO? Virat Kohli
SURPRISING FACT ABOUT YOU? I name my bats after greyhounds
CRICKET STAR OF THE FUTURE? Angus Lovell (Middlesex Second XI)
IF YOU WERE AN ANIMAL, WHICH WOULD IT BE? A horse – I'd run a quick six-furlong
TWITTER: @nickselman22

Batting	Mat	Inns	NO	Runs	HS	Ave	SR	100	50	Ct	St
First-class	51	93	6	2527	150	29.04	46.58	7	11	54	0
List A	9	9	0	242	92	26.88	67.78	0	1	3	0
T20s	12	9	1	220	66	27.50	136.64	0	1	4	0
Bowling	**Mat**	**Balls**	**Runs**	**Wkts**	**BBI**	**BBM**	**Ave**	**Econ**	**SR**	**5w**	**10**
First-class	51	45	36	1	1/22	1/22	36.00	4.80	45.0	0	0
List A	9	-	-	-	-	-	-	-	-	-	-
T20s	12	-	-	-	-	-	-	-	-	-	-

OWAIS SHAH

LHB / LB / R0 / W0

FULL NAME: Syed Mohammed Owais Shah
BORN: October 1, 1998, Glasgow
SQUAD NO: 19
EDUCATION: Bellahouston Academy, Glasgow; Myerscough College, Preston, Lancashire
TEAMS: Lancashire, Scotland U19
ROLE: Batsman

TWITTER: @OwaisShah
NOTES: Not to be confused with the former England and Middlesex batsman, Shah is a 21-year-old left-handed opening batsman who was one of seven Lancashire Academy cricketers to pen deals ahead of the 2020 season. A former Scotland U19 international, Shah impressed for Lancashire in the Second XI Championship last summer, averaging 50.60 from six innings which included a hundred against Nottinghamshire at Trent Bridge and a half-century against Leicestershire at Kibworth. He was born in Glasgow but moved to Lancashire in 2017 to further his career and has played club cricket for Highfield CC in the Liverpool and District Competition

JOSH SHAW

RHB / RMF / R0 / W0

FULL NAME: Joshua Shaw
BORN: January 3, 1996, Wakefield, Yorkshire
SQUAD NO: 5
HEIGHT: 6ft 1in
NICKNAME: Shawy
EDUCATION: Crofton Academy, West Yorkshire; Skills Exchange College, Wakefield
TEAMS: Gloucestershire, England U19, Yorkshire
ROLE: Bowler
DEBUT: First-class: 2016; List A: 2019; T20: 2015

BEST BATTING: 42 Yorkshire vs Somerset, Headingley, 2018
BEST BOWLING: 5-79 Gloucestershire vs Sussex, Bristol, 2016
COUNTY CAP: 2016 (Gloucestershire)

FAMILY TIES? My father Chris played for Yorkshire. We lived on the back of Streethouse CC so I was always around cricket from a young age
WHAT WAS YOUR FIRST CRICKET CLUB? Wakefield Thornes CC, West Yorkshire
WHAT WERE YOU DOING WHEN ENGLAND WON THE WORLD CUP? I was out for a meal on my girlfriend's birthday – watch the game on my phone at the table
WHAT EXCITES YOU ABOUT THE HUNDRED? Seriously good players
MOST INTERESTING TEAMMATE? Ryan Higgins – he's always got an opinion on something
CRICKETING HERO? Andrew Flintoff
CRICKET STAR OF THE FUTURE? James Wharton (Yorkshire Academy)
IF YOU WERE AN ANIMAL, WHICH WOULD IT BE? A dog – you are loved no matter what
TWITTER: @joshuashaw1

Batting	Mat	Inns	NO	Runs	HS	Ave	SR	100	50	Ct	St
First-class	34	45	9	411	42	11.41	38.37	0	0	8	0
List A	1	-	-	-	-	-	-	-	-	0	0
T20s	5	2	1	1	1	1.00	50.00	0	0	1	0
Bowling	**Mat**	**Balls**	**Runs**	**Wkts**	**BBI**	**BBM**	**Ave**	**Econ**	**SR**	**5w**	**10**
First-class	34	5069	3157	89	5/79	6/102	35.47	3.73	56.9	2	0
List A	1	42	52	0	-	-	-	7.42	-	0	0
T20s	5	84	141	1	1/42	1/42	141.00	10.07	84.0	0	0

WILL SHEFFIELD LHB / LMF / RO / WO

FULL NAME: William Arthur Sheffield
BORN: August 26, 2000, Haywards Heath, Sussex
SQUAD NO: 29
HEIGHT: 6ft 4in
NICKNAME: Sheff
EDUCATION: Uckfield College, East Sussex; Aldridge Academy, Saltdean, Brighton
TEAMS: Sussex
ROLE: Bowler

WHAT WAS YOUR FIRST CRICKET CLUB? Buxted Park CC, East Sussex
WHAT WERE YOU DOING WHEN ENGLAND WON THE WORLD CUP? In my front room watching it with the family
HOW WOULD YOU DISMISS STEVE SMITH? Run him out
BIGGEST TOPIC OF DISCUSSION IN YOUR DRESSING ROOM? Football
MOST INTERESTING TEAMMATE? Phil Salt – he livens up the dressing room
CRICKET STAR OF THE FUTURE? Oli Carter (Sussex Academy)
IF YOU WERE AN ANIMAL, WHICH WOULD IT BE? A falcon – I have a big wingspan
TWITTER: @WillSheff1
NOTES: The 19-year-old left-arm seamer signed his first professional contract last April. Sheffield has come through the Aldridge Cricket Academy – a scheme set up between Sussex CCC and Brighton & Portslade Aldridge Community Academies which allows youngsters to combine their studies with a cricket development programme. He is also the first contracted Sussex player to benefit from the support of the Matthew Hobden Trust, set up in memory of the county's former fast bowler who died in in 2016 at the age of 22. Injury ruled him out for almost all of the 2019 season but he will be hoping to make his first-team debut this summer after undergoing successful knee surgery and being handed a contract extension at the end of last summer. "I was very pleased when I was told that I would be getting re-signed," he said. "After a tough year with injury ruling me out for the season, it is nice to know that I can have a chance to prove myself on the pitch"

D'ARCY SHORT

LHB / SLW / R0 / W0

FULL NAME: D'Arcy John Matthew Short
BORN: August 9, 1990, Katherine, Northern Territory, Australia
SQUAD NO: TBC
TEAMS: Australia, Surrey, Trent Rockets, Durham, Hobart Hurricanes, Rajasthan Royals, Western Australia
ROLE: Allrounder
DEBUT: ODI: 2018; T20I: 2018; First-class: 2016; List A: 2011; T20: 2016

BEST BATTING: 122* Hobart Hurricanes vs Brisbane Heat, Brisbane, 2018 (T20)
BEST BOWLING: 5-21 Hobart Hurricanes vs Sydney Thunder, Hobart, 2020 (T20)

TWITTER: @ShortDarcy
NOTES: Surrey have signed the Australian top-order batsman and left-arm wrist-spinner for the 2019 T20 Blast. Short was outstanding in his first county stint last summer, smashing 483 runs (strike rate of 139.60) and taking 13 wickets in 12 T20 matches for Durham. He made his ODI debut against England at Cardiff in 2018 and has featured frequently for Australia in white-ball cricket over the last two years. Known for his early-order aggression with the bat and unusual bowling style, the 29-year-old was voted Player of the Tournament in the 2017/18 and 2018/19 editions of the Big Bash. In January he took a T20 career-best 5-21 for Hobart Hurricanes against Sydney Thunder at Hobart

Batting	Mat	Inns	NO	Runs	HS	Ave	SR	100	50	Ct	St
ODIs	8	8	1	211	69	30.14	78.43	0	1	2	0
T20Is	20	20	2	592	76	32.88	120.81	0	4	8	0
First-class	14	26	1	654	66	26.16	51.49	0	4	11	0
List A	42	38	3	1291	257	36.88	102.70	3	4	14	0
T20s	83	83	8	2954	122*	39.38	136.12	2	23	33	0
Bowling	**Mat**	**Balls**	**Runs**	**Wkts**	**BBI**	**BBM**	**Ave**	**Econ**	**SR**	**5w**	**10**
ODIs	8	90	114	0	-	-	-	7.60	-	0	0
T20Is	20	114	151	3	1/13	1/13	50.33	7.94	38.0	0	0
First-class	14	987	682	20	3/78	4/43	34.10	4.14	49.3	0	0
List A	42	886	884	19	3/53	3/53	46.52	5.98	46.6	0	0
T20s	83	862	1193	40	5/21	5/21	29.82	8.30	21.5	1	0

JACK SHUTT

RHB / OB / R0 / W0

FULL NAME: Jack William Shutt
BORN: June 24, 1997, Barnsley
SQUAD NO: 24
EDUCATION: Kirk Balk School, Barnsley; Thomas Rotherham College, South Yorkshire
TEAMS: Yorkshire
ROLE: Bowler
DEBUT: T20: 2019

NOTES: The Barnsley-born off-spinner made a strong impression for Yorkshire in the T20 Blast last summer, taking 10 wickets at 16.40 in seven matches and conceding runs at a miserly 6.83 per over. This included a remarkable spell of 5-11 against Durham at Chester-le-Street in the group phase of the competion, the second-best figures in Yorkshire's T20 history behind Tim Bresnan's 6-19 against Lancashire at Headingley in 2017. He has yet to make his debut in first-class or List A cricket. Over the winter Shutt went on a month-long spin bowling camp to Mumbai run by former England spinner Peter Such. To date he has taken 61 wickets for Yorkshire Second XI

Batting	Mat	Inns	NO	Runs	HS	Ave	SR	100	50	Ct	St
T20s	7	2	1	0	0*	0.00	0.00	0	0	2	0
Bowling	**Mat**	**Balls**	**Runs**	**Wkts**	**BBI**	**BBM**	**Ave**	**Econ**	**SR**	**5w**	**10**
T20s	7	144	164	10	5/11	5/11	16.40	6.83	14.4	1	0

DOMINIC SIBLEY

RHB / OB / R1 / W0 / MVP28

FULL NAME: Dominic Peter Sibley
BORN: September 5, 1995, Epsom, Surrey
SQUAD NO: 45
HEIGHT: 6ft 3in
NICKNAME: Frocko, Big Tree
EDUCATION: Whitgift School, Croydon
TEAMS: England, Warwickshire, Surrey
ROLE: Batsman
DEBUT: Test: 2019; First-class: 2013; List A: 2013; T20: 2016

BEST BATTING: 244 Warwickshire vs Kent, Canterbury, 2019
BEST BOWLING: 2-103 Surrey vs Hampshire, Southampton, 2016

WHAT WAS YOUR FIRST CRICKET CLUB? Ashtead CC, Surrey
WHICH BOWLER WOULD YOU LEAST LIKE TO FACE? Shoaib Akhtar
CRICKETING HERO? Virat Kohli
BEST INNINGS YOU'VE SEEN? Kevin Pietersen's hundred against South Africa in the 2012 Headingley Test
WHICH RULE WOULD YOU CHANGE ABOUT CRICKET? Introduce free hits for no-balls in four-day cricket
YOUR BIGGEST CRICKETING REGRET? Playing while I did my A-Levels
SURPRISING FACT ABOUT YOU? I am half-French
WHICH BOOK MEANS MOST TO YOU? The Alchemist by Paulo Coelho
TWITTER: @DomSibley

Batting	Mat	Inns	NO	Runs	HS	Ave	SR	100	50	Ct	St
Tests	6	10	1	362	133*	40.22	38.96	1	0	4	0
First-class	75	126	12	4729	244	41.48	41.62	14	20	59	0
List A	22	20	2	416	115	23.11	78.19	1	0	10	0
T20s	32	29	3	855	74*	32.88	122.14	0	7	13	0
Bowling	**Mat**	**Balls**	**Runs**	**Wkts**	**BBI**	**BBM**	**Ave**	**Econ**	**SR**	**5w**	**10**
Tests	6	-	-	-	-	-	-	-	-	-	-
First-class	75	374	264	4	2/103	2/117	66.00	4.23	93.5	0	0
List A	22	54	62	1	1/20	1/20	62.00	6.88	54.0	0	0
T20s	32	228	338	5	2/33	2/33	67.60	8.89	45.6	0	0

PETER SIDDLE RHB / RFM / R0 / W0 / MVP78

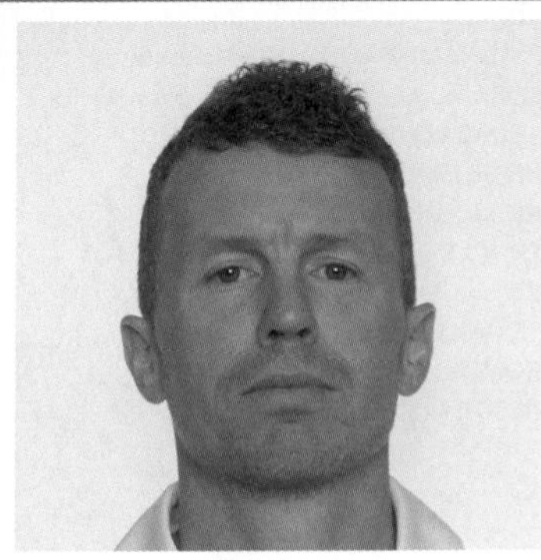

FULL NAME: Peter Matthew Siddle
BORN: November 25, 1984, Traralgon, Victoria, Australia
SQUAD NO: 64
HEIGHT: 6ft 2in
NICKNAME: Vicious, Dermie
TEAMS: Australia, Essex, Adelaide Strikers, Lancashire, Melbourne Renegades, Nottinghamshire, Victoria
ROLE: Bowler
DEBUT: Test: 2008; ODI: 2009; T20I: 2009; First-class: 2005; List A: 2005; T20: 2006

BEST BATTING: 103* Australia A vs Scotland, Edinburgh, 2013
BEST BOWLING: 8-54 Victoria vs South Australia, Adelaide, 2015
COUNTY CAP: 2014 (Nottinghamshire)

TWITTER: @petersiddle403
NOTES: Essex first signed the combative Australian seamer for their 2012 T20 campaign but he pulled out with injury, before agreeing a two-year deal in September 2018 to be the club's overseas player across all formats, after impressing for them in two spells that season. In between he played county cricket for Nottinghamshire and Lancashire. Siddle had a devastating impact for Essex in 2018, taking 37 wickets at 16.41 in seven Championship matches, and followed it up last summer with 34 at 20.09 in eight matches to help Essex to the four-day crown. After 221 wickets in 67 Tests, he retired from international cricket at the end of last year. In February Siddle was named in the Big Bash League's Team of the Tournament after playing a starring role for Adelaide Strikers

Batting	Mat	Inns	NO	Runs	HS	Ave	SR	100	50	Ct	St
Tests	67	94	15	1164	51	14.73	47.16	0	2	19	0
ODIs	20	6	3	31	10*	10.33	103.33	0	0	1	0
T20Is	2	1	1	1	1*	-	100.00	0	0	0	0
First-class	179	239	43	3331	103*	16.99	50.74	1	6	57	0
List A	63	33	11	251	62	11.40	97.28	0	1	6	0
T20s	60	19	11	48	11	6.00	77.41	0	0	12	0
Bowling	**Mat**	**Balls**	**Runs**	**Wkts**	**BBI**	**BBM**	**Ave**	**Econ**	**SR**	**5w**	**10**
Tests	67	13907	6777	221	6/54	9/104	30.66	2.92	62.9	8	0
ODIs	20	901	743	17	3/55	3/55	43.70	4.94	53.0	0	0
T20Is	2	48	58	3	2/24	2/24	19.33	7.25	16.0	0	0
First-class	179	34502	16573	617	8/54	9/77	26.86	2.88	55.9	24	0
List A	63	3178	2520	74	4/27	4/27	34.05	4.75	42.9	0	0
T20s	60	1225	1489	59	4/29	4/29	25.23	7.29	20.7	0	0

RYAN SIDEBOTTOM RHB / RMF / R0 / W0

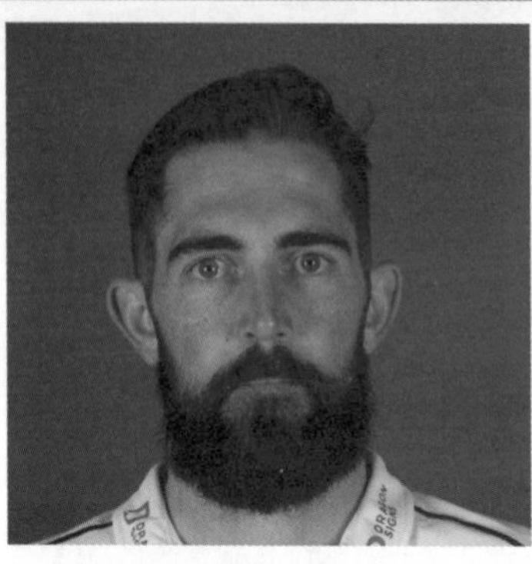

FULL NAME: Ryan Nathan Sidebottom
BORN: August 14, 1989, Shepparton, Victoria
SQUAD NO: 22
HEIGHT: 6ft 2in
NICKNAME: Siddy
EDUCATION: Wanganui Park Secondary College, Victoria, Australia
TEAMS: Warwickshire, Victoria
ROLE: Bowler
DEBUT: First-class: 2013

BEST BATTING: 27* Warwickshire vs Kent, Edgbaston, 2019
BEST BOWLING: 6-35 Warwickshire vs Northamptonshire, Northampton, 2018

WHAT WAS YOUR FIRST CRICKET CLUB? Northerners CC, Victoria, Australia. Formed after a merger of two clubs called Tallygaroopna and Congupna in the early 2000s
FAVOURITE CRICKET BAT? My Kookaburra Kahuna. First bat I owned and I basically carried it everywhere
CRICKETING HERO? Glenn McGrath
WHICH BOWLER WOULD YOU LEAST LIKE TO FACE? Olly Stone – he's quick!
BEST INNINGS YOU'VE SEEN? Ian Bell's double hundred against Glamorgan in 2018. It was a pleasure to watch
WHO WOULD YOU ASK TO BAT FOR YOUR LIFE? Mike Hussey
WHICH RULE WOULD YOU CHANGE ABOUT CRICKET? The one that says only two bouncers are allowed per over
SURPRISING FACT ABOUT YOU? I've got four brothers, one of whom plays Aussie rules for Collingwood. We grew up in Tallygaroopna near Melbourne, but I have a British passport because my mum moved to Devon
WHAT WILL YOU BE DOING IN THE YEAR 2040? Living back home in Australia
TWITTER: @ryansidebottom2

Batting	Mat	Inns	NO	Runs	HS	Ave	SR	100	50	Ct	St
First-class	18	28	14	87	27*	6.21	27.61	0	0	5	0
Bowling	**Mat**	**Balls**	**Runs**	**Wkts**	**BBI**	**BBM**	**Ave**	**Econ**	**SR**	**5w**	**10**
First-class	18	2255	1366	51	6/35	10/96	26.78	3.63	44.2	1	1

JOHN SIMPSON LHB / WK / R0 / W0 / MVP65

FULL NAME: John Andrew Simpson
BORN: July 13, 1988, Bury, Lancashire
SQUAD NO: 20
HEIGHT: 5ft 11in
NICKNAME: Simmo
EDUCATION: St Gabriel's RC High School, Bury; Holy Cross College, Bury
TEAMS: Middlesex, Northern Superchargers, England U19
ROLE: Wicketkeeper/batsman
DEBUT: First-class: 2009; List A: 2009; T20: 2009

BEST BATTING: 167* Middlesex vs Lancashire, Old Trafford, 2019

COUNTY CAP: 2011

FAMILY TIES? Dad played for England Amateurs and Lancashire Cricket Board and holds club and league records in the Lancashire/Central Lancashire leagues. Grandad captained the Army XI
WHAT WAS YOUR FIRST CRICKET CLUB? Ramsbottom CC, Greater Manchester. One of the most picturesque grounds in the UK
BIGGEST TOPIC OF DISCUSSION IN YOUR DRESSING ROOM? Tim Murtagh's liposuction
MOST INTERESTING TEAMMATE? David English – for the comedy and the stories
SURPRISING FACT ABOUT YOU? I don't drink tea or coffee
WHICH BOOK MEANS MOST TO YOU? The Exhaustive Guide to Club Cricket by Dan Whiting. I wrote the foreword to it
IF YOU WERE AN ANIMAL, WHICH WOULD IT BE? A camel
TWITTER: @johnsimpson_88

Batting	Mat	Inns	NO	Runs	HS	Ave	SR	100	50	Ct	St
First-class	155	245	37	6680	167*	32.11	47.53	7	38	467	24
List A	93	72	11	1587	82*	26.01	86.76	0	8	81	19
T20s	109	94	17	1775	84*	23.05	129.75	0	7	52	20
Bowling	**Mat**	**Balls**	**Runs**	**Wkts**	**BBI**	**BBM**	**Ave**	**Econ**	**SR**	**5w**	**10**
First-class	155	18	23	0	-	-	-	7.66	-	0	0
List A	93	-	-	-	-	-	-	-	-	-	-
T20s	109	-	-	-	-	-	-	-	-	-	-

PREM SISODIYA RHB/SLA/R0/W0

GLAMORGAN

FULL NAME: Prem Sisodiya
BORN: September 21, 1998, Cardiff
SQUAD NO: 32
HEIGHT: 5ft 11in
NICKNAME: P-man
EDUCATION: Clifton College, Bristol; Cardiff Metropolitan University
TEAMS: Glamorgan, England U19
ROLE: Bowler
DEBUT: First-class: 2018; T20: 2019

BEST BATTING: 38 Glamorgan vs Derbyshire, Swansea, 2018
BEST BOWLING: 4-79 Cardiff MCCU vs Somerset, Taunton, 2019

WHAT WAS YOUR FIRST CRICKET CLUB? Cardiff CC. In 2014 we won the league-and-cup double with a team whose average age was 19
HOW WOULD YOU DISMISS STEVE SMITH? Run him out
BEST INNINGS YOU'VE SEEN? MS Dhoni's match-winning 91 not out against Sri Lanka in the 2011 World Cup final. He's an unbelievable finisher
BIGGEST TOPIC OF DISCUSSION IN YOUR DRESSING ROOM? Messiness
WHICH RULE WOULD YOU CHANGE ABOUT CRICKET? I would introduce free hits in Tests
BIGGEST CRICKETING REGRET? Trying to switch-hit when I was on 97
WHICH BOOK MEANS MOST TO YOU? Playing It My Way by Sachin Tendulkar
IF YOU WERE AN ANIMAL, WHICH WOULD IT BE? A snow leopard
TWITTER: @PremSisodiya

Batting	Mat	Inns	NO	Runs	HS	Ave	SR	100	50	Ct	St
First-class	4	7	1	83	38	13.83	48.82	0	0	2	0
T20s	2	-	-	-	-	-	-	-	-	0	0
Bowling	**Mat**	**Balls**	**Runs**	**Wkts**	**BBI**	**BBM**	**Ave**	**Econ**	**SR**	**5w**	**10**
First-class	4	731	369	15	4/79	5/73	24.60	3.02	48.7	0	0
T20s	2	48	70	1	1/45	1/45	70.00	8.75	48.0	0	0

BEN SLATER

LHB / OB / R1 / W0

FULL NAME: Benjamin Thomas Slater
BORN: August 26, 1991, Chesterfield, Derbyshire
SQUAD NO: 26
HEIGHT: 5ft 11in
NICKNAME: BennySlats, Slats
EDUCATION: Netherthorpe School, Staveley; Leeds Metropolitan University
TEAMS: Nottinghamshire, Derbyshire, Southern Rocks
ROLE: Batsman
DEBUT: First-class: 2012; List A: 2012; T20: 2012

BEST BATTING: 130 Nottinghamshire vs Cambridge MCCU, Cambridge, 2019

WHAT WAS YOUR FIRST CRICKET CLUB? Chesterfield CC, Derbyshire. They play at Queen's Park – nicest outground in the country
WHAT EXCITES YOU ABOUT THE HUNDRED? Playing in the 50-over competition
MOST INTERESTING TEAMMATE? Zak Chappell – one of a kind
CRICKETING HEROES? Brian Lara, Marcus Trescothick, Matthew Hayden, my grandad (all left-handed batsmen)
WHICH RULE WOULD YOU CHANGE ABOUT CRICKET? Tea should be longer than 20 minutes
BIGGEST CRICKETING REGRET? Getting out for 99 against Middlesex in the first game of 2018
CRICKET STAR OF THE FUTURE? Sol Budinger (Nottinghamshire)
IF YOU WERE AN ANIMAL, WHICH WOULD IT BE? An elephant
TWITTER: @BennySlats

Batting	Mat	Inns	NO	Runs	HS	Ave	SR	100	50	Ct	St
First-class	83	154	7	4604	130	31.31	45.39	5	25	30	0
List A	36	33	4	1611	148*	55.55	86.98	5	9	3	0
T20s	11	11	0	236	57	21.45	105.82	0	1	0	0
Bowling	**Mat**	**Balls**	**Runs**	**Wkts**	**BBI**	**BBM**	**Ave**	**Econ**	**SR**	**5w**	**10**
First-class	83	105	113	0	-	-	-	6.45	-	0	0
List A	36	-	-	-	-	-	-	-	-	-	-
T20s	11	-	-	-	-	-	-	-	-	-	-

JAMIE SMITH RHB / WK / R0 / W0

FULL NAME: Jamie Luke Smith
BORN: July 12, 2000, Epsom, Surrey
SQUAD NO: 11
HEIGHT: 6ft 2in
NICKNAME: Smudger
EDUCATION: Whitgift School, Croydon
TEAMS: Surrey
ROLE: Wicketkeeper
DEBUT: First-class: 2019; List A: 2019; T20: 2018

BEST BATTING: 127 Surrey vs MCC, Dubai, 2019

WHAT WAS YOUR FIRST CRICKET CLUB? Sutton CC, Surrey
WHAT WERE YOU DOING WHEN ENGLAND WON THE WORLD CUP? Watching it in the Trent Bridge Inn
BIGGEST TOPIC OF DISCUSSION IN YOUR DRESSING ROOM? Fantasy Football
MOST INTERESTING TEAMMATE? Gareth Batty – for his experience and knowledge
WHICH RULE WOULD YOU CHANGE ABOUT CRICKET? Longer lunch, longer tea
CRICKET STAR OF THE FUTURE? Nick Kimber (Surrey)
WHICH BOOK MEANS MOST TO YOU? Legacy – What the All Blacks Can Teach Us About the Business of Life by James Kerr
IF YOU WERE AN ANIMAL, WHICH WOULD IT BE? A dolphin
TWITTER: @jamiesm148

Batting	Mat	Inns	NO	Runs	HS	Ave	SR	100	50	Ct	St
First-class	9	15	1	465	127	33.21	49.46	1	2	5	2
List A	5	5	0	110	40	22.00	88.70	0	0	2	0
T20s	3	2	1	7	7*	7.00	70.00	0	0	2	0
Bowling	**Mat**	**Balls**	**Runs**	**Wkts**	**BBI**	**BBM**	**Ave**	**Econ**	**SR**	**5w**	**10**
First-class	9	-	-	-	-	-	-	-	-	-	-
List A	5	-	-	-	-	-	-	-	-	-	-
T20s	3	-	-	-	-	-	-	-	-	-	-

RUAIDHRI SMITH

RHB / RM / R0 / W0

FULL NAME: Ruaidhri Alexander James Smith
BORN: August 5, 1994, Glasgow
SQUAD NO: 20
HEIGHT: 6ft 2in
NICKNAME: Trotts
EDUCATION: The Cathedral School, Llandaff; Shrewsbury School; University of Bristol
TEAMS: Scotland, Glamorgan
ROLE: Allrounder
DEBUT: ODI: 2016; T20I: 2019; First-class: 2013; List A: 2013; T20: 2014

BEST BATTING: 57* Glamorgan vs Gloucestershire, Bristol, 2014
BEST BOWLING: 5-87 Glamorgan vs Durham, Cardiff, 2018

WHAT WAS YOUR FIRST CRICKET CLUB? St Fagans CC, Cardiff. Provides the best teas in south Wales
HOW WOULD YOU DISMISS STEVE SMITH? Try to get the other 10
BEST INNINGS YOU'VE SEEN? AB de Villiers's 169 in the 2012 Perth Test
BIGGEST TOPIC OF DISCUSSION IN YOUR DRESSING ROOM? The weather
MOST INTERESTING TEAMMATE? Andrew Salter – always has something on the go
WHICH RULE WOULD YOU CHANGE ABOUT CRICKET? Lbws can be given if it pitches outside leg stump
SURPRISING FACT ABOUT YOU? Born in Scotland, Irish mother, English father, raised in Wales
CRICKET STAR OF THE FUTURE? Alex Horton (Glamorgan Academy)
IF YOU WERE AN ANIMAL, WHICH WOULD IT BE? An eagle. Who wouldn't want to fly?
TWITTER: @ruaidhrismith

Batting	Mat	Inns	NO	Runs	HS	Ave	SR	100	50	Ct	St
ODIs	2	1	0	10	10	10.00	166.66	0	0	0	0
T20Is	2	1	1	9	9*	-	128.57	0	0	0	0
First-class	29	42	6	655	57*	18.19	59.92	0	2	4	0
List A	18	11	3	71	14	8.87	92.20	0	0	4	0
T20s	19	11	7	87	22*	21.75	124.28	0	0	6	0
Bowling	**Mat**	**Balls**	**Runs**	**Wkts**	**BBI**	**BBM**	**Ave**	**Econ**	**SR**	**5w**	**10**
ODIs	2	90	97	1	1/34	1/34	97.00	6.46	90.0	0	0
T20Is	2	41	66	0	-	-	-	9.65	-	0	0
First-class	29	3492	2288	65	5/87	7/148	35.20	3.93	53.7	1	0
List A	18	572	591	18	4/7	4/7	32.83	6.19	31.7	0	0
T20s	19	297	417	15	4/6	4/6	27.80	8.42	19.8	0	0

STEVE SMITH RHB/LB

FULL NAME: Steven Peter Devereux Smith
BORN: June 2, 1989, Sydney, Australia
SQUAD NO: TBC
HEIGHT: 5ft 8in
EDUCATION: Menai High School, Sydney
TEAMS: Australia, Welsh Fire, Barbados Tridents, Comilla Victorians, New South Wales, Pune Warriors, Rajasthan Royals, Rising Pune Supergiant, Royal Challengers Bangalore, Sydney Sixers, Worcestershire
ROLE: Batsman
DEBUT: Test: 2010; ODI: 2010; T20I: 2010; First-class: 2008; List A: 2007; T20: 2008

BEST BATTING: 101 Rising Pune Supergiant vs Gujarat Lions, Hyderabad, 2016 (T20)
BEST BOWLING: 4-13 New South Wales vs Tasmania, Hobart, 2019 (T20)

TWITTER: @stevesmith49
NOTES: Initially selected by Australia as a leg-spinning allrounder, Smith has developed into statistically the finest Test batsman of the modern era. Last November he became the fastest batsman to 7,000 Test runs, breaking Wally Hammond's record which had stood since 1946. That landmark came after a sensational 2019 Ashes series – his first Test cricket since a 12-month ban for his part in the 2018 ball-tampering scandal – in which he scored 774 runs in seven innings. He is the only player to win the ICC Test Cricketer of the Year twice, in 2015 and 2017. Smith has also forged a successful T20 career and been a regular in the IPL since 2012, skippering Rajasthan Royals in this year's tournament. He will captain Welsh Fire in The Hundred after being picked in the £125k category

Batting	Mat	Inns	NO	Runs	HS	Ave	SR	100	50	Ct	St
Tests	73	131	16	7227	239	62.84	55.30	26	29	117	0
ODIs	125	110	12	4162	164	42.46	86.67	9	25	67	0
T20Is	39	31	8	681	90	29.60	130.71	0	4	21	0
First-class	131	228	26	11707	239	57.95	56.54	42	49	200	0
List A	172	155	23	5966	164	45.19	87.38	11	38	96	0
T20s	189	165	38	4014	101	31.60	126.14	1	18	101	0
Bowling	**Mat**	**Balls**	**Runs**	**Wkts**	**BBI**	**BBM**	**Ave**	**Econ**	**SR**	**5w**	**10**
Tests	73	1381	960	17	3/18	4/83	56.47	4.17	81.2	0	0
ODIs	125	1076	971	28	3/16	3/16	34.67	5.41	38.4	0	0
T20Is	39	291	377	17	3/20	3/20	22.17	7.77	17.1	0	0
First-class	131	5189	3603	68	7/64	8/169	52.98	4.16	76.3	1	0
List A	172	2018	1824	47	3/16	3/16	38.80	5.42	42.9	0	0
T20s	189	824	1056	54	4/13	4/13	19.55	7.68	15.2	0	0

TOM SMITH

RHB / SLA / R0 / W0

FULL NAME: Thomas Michael John Smith
BORN: August 29, 1987, Eastbourne, Sussex
SQUAD NO: 6
HEIGHT: 5ft 9in
NICKNAME: Smudge
EDUCATION: Seaford Head Community College, East Sussex; Sussex Downs College
TEAMS: Gloucestershire, Middlesex, Surrey, Sussex
ROLE: Bowler
DEBUT: First-class: 2007; List A: 2006; T20: 2007

BEST BATTING: 84 Gloucestershire vs Leicestershire, Cheltenham, 2019
BEST BOWLING: 4-35 Gloucestershire vs Kent, Canterbury, 2014
COUNTY CAP: 2013 (Gloucestershire)

WHAT WAS YOUR FIRST CRICKET CLUB? Eastbourne CC, East Sussex. I started aged four on Sunday mornings and went on to captain the club and play a professional match there (Gloucestershire against Sussex)
BEST ADVICE EVER RECEIVED? Peel ginger with a teaspoon
MOST INTERESTING TEAMMATE? Chris Rogers – there's always entertainment when he's around!
BEST INNINGS YOU'VE SEEN? A last-wicket stand of 137 between Liam Norwell and Craig Miles at Cheltenham in 2014. We still lost but it was amazing to watch
CRICKETING HERO? Daniel Vettori
SURPRISING FACT ABOUT YOU? I'm a qualified plumber
CRICKET STAR OF THE FUTURE? Alex Russell (Gloucestershire Second XI) – very talented leg-spinner
WHICH BOOK MEANS MOST TO YOU? Outliers – The Story of Success by Malcolm Gladwell
IF YOU WERE AN ANIMAL, WHICH WOULD IT BE? An owl – as a father of two kids, I am very much nocturnal

Batting	Mat	Inns	NO	Runs	HS	Ave	SR	100	50	Ct	St
First-class	48	67	12	1316	84	23.92	38.20	0	4	15	0
List A	83	42	19	513	65	22.30	74.78	0	1	36	0
T20s	127	48	33	289	36*	19.26	113.33	0	0	40	0
Bowling	**Mat**	**Balls**	**Runs**	**Wkts**	**BBI**	**BBM**	**Ave**	**Econ**	**SR**	**5w**	**10**
First-class	48	6815	3858	78	4/35	6/155	49.46	3.39	87.3	0	0
List A	83	3070	2766	68	4/26	4/26	40.67	5.40	45.1	0	0
T20s	127	2352	2924	123	5/24	5/24	23.77	7.45	19.1	2	0

SHANE SNATER

RHB / RM / R0 / W0

FULL NAME: Shane Snater
BORN: March 24, 1996, Harare, Zimbabwe
SQUAD NO: 29
EDUCATION: St John's College, Harare
TEAMS: Netherlands, Essex, Kent
ROLE: Bowler
DEBUT: ODI: 2018; T20I: 2018; First-class: 2016; List A: 2017; T20: 2018

BEST BATTING: 50* Netherlands vs Namibia, Dubai, 2017
BEST BOWLING: 5-88 Netherlands vs Namibia, Dubai, 2017

TWITTER: @ShaneSnater
NOTES: Essex signed the 24-year-old Netherlands seamer in September following a successful trial period at the club in 2018. He took five wickets in three One-Day Cup matches for the club that year and played five times in the club's successful T20 Blast campaign last summer. Snater signed a one-year contract extension last October. Head coach Anthony McGrath said: "Shane is a skilled and trustworthy bowler and during the first half of our T20 Blast campaign, he performed well. Hopefully he pushes on from here and can play more for us next season." Snater grew up in Harare and played for Zimbabwe U17 back in 2014. He holds a Dutch passport and made his ODI and T20I debut for Netherlands in 2018

Batting	Mat	Inns	NO	Runs	HS	Ave	SR	100	50	Ct	St
ODIs	2	2	0	12	12	6.00	85.71	0	0	3	0
T20Is	13	6	1	18	10	3.60	112.50	0	0	2	0
First-class	3	4	1	73	50*	24.33	90.12	0	1	1	0
List A	16	11	3	68	23*	8.50	76.40	0	0	10	0
T20s	19	8	2	21	10	3.50	100.00	0	0	5	0
Bowling	**Mat**	**Balls**	**Runs**	**Wkts**	**BBI**	**BBM**	**Ave**	**Econ**	**SR**	**5w**	**10**
ODIs	2	71	63	1	1/41	1/41	63.00	5.32	71.0	0	0
T20Is	13	209	337	13	3/42	3/42	25.92	9.67	16.0	0	0
First-class	3	550	324	12	5/88	7/129	27.00	3.53	45.8	2	0
List A	16	627	561	14	5/60	5/60	40.07	5.36	44.7	1	0
T20s	19	305	536	18	3/42	3/42	29.77	10.54	16.9	0	0

OLI SOAMES

RHB / RM / R0 / W0

FULL NAME: Oliver Courtney Soames
BORN: October 27, 1995, Kingston upon Thames, Surrey
SQUAD NO: 27
HEIGHT: 5ft 9in
NICKNAME: Soamsey
EDUCATION: Cheltenham College; Loughborough University
TEAMS: Hampshire
ROLE: Batsman
DEBUT: First-class: 2018

BEST BATTING: 62 Hampshire vs Warwickshire, Southampton, 2019

WHAT WAS YOUR FIRST CRICKET CLUB? Yateley CC, Hampshire. I joined when I was 12 and we made it to the club national finals three times in four years
WHAT WERE YOU DOING WHEN ENGLAND WON THE WORLD CUP? I was in the crowd at Lord's
HOW WOULD YOU DISMISS STEVE SMITH? In-swinger pitching on middle, nips away, takes top of off
BIGGEST TOPIC OF DISCUSSION IN YOUR DRESSING ROOM? What's the best tactics on Call of Duty: Modern Warfare
MOST INTERESTING TEAMMATE? James Fuller. His consumption of food is rivalled only by the bloke in Man v Food (reality tv show)
BIGGEST CRICKETING REGRET? Not winning the club national finals, despite having the best team on the day
CRICKET STAR OF THE FUTURE? James Seymour (Essendon CC, Victoria, Australia)
WHICH BOOK MEANS MOST TO YOU? Mind Gym – An Athlete's Guide to Inner Excellence by Gary Mack
IF YOU WERE AN ANIMAL, WHICH WOULD IT BE? A Pitbull – all bark and no bite
TWITTER: @ozza50

Batting	Mat	Inns	NO	Runs	HS	Ave	SR	100	50	Ct	St
First-class	12	20	0	238	62	11.90	34.14	0	1	3	0
Bowling	**Mat**	**Balls**	**Runs**	**Wkts**	**BBI**	**BBM**	**Ave**	**Econ**	**SR**	**5w**	**10**
First-class	12	-	-	-	-	-	-	-	-	-	-

TOM SOLE

RHB / OB / R0 / W0

FULL NAME: Thomas Barclay Sole
BORN: June 21, 1996, Edinburgh
SQUAD NO: 90
HEIGHT: 5ft 11in
NICKNAME: Soley, Stollers
EDUCATION: Merchiston Castle School, Edinburgh
TEAMS: Scotland, Northamptonshire
ROLE: Allrounder
DEBUT: ODI: 2018; T20I: 2019; List A: 2017; T20: 2018

WHAT WAS YOUR FIRST CRICKET CLUB? Grange CC, Edinburgh – where Scotland beat England for the first time in the summer of 2018!
HOW WOULD YOU DISMISS STEVE SMITH? Bowl at sixth stump
BIGGEST TOPIC OF DISCUSSION IN YOUR DRESSING ROOM? Pre-season
MOST INTERESTING TEAMMATE? Michael Leask – you never know what's going through his head
WHICH RULE WOULD YOU CHANGE ABOUT CRICKET? Free hits for no-balls in all cricket
BIGGEST CRICKETING REGRET? Not getting Northants over the line on my county debut in 2017 against South Africa in a tour match
CRICKET STAR OF THE FUTURE? Tom Mackintosh (Durham Academy, Scotland U19)
WHICH BOOK MEANS MOST TO YOU? My dad's autobiography about his rugby union career for Scotland, even though I wasn't born when he wrote it so didn't get a dedication
IF YOU WERE AN ANIMAL, WHICH WOULD IT BE? A stag
TWITTER: @TomSole1

Batting	Mat	Inns	NO	Runs	HS	Ave	SR	100	50	Ct	St
ODIs	10	7	1	46	20	7.66	106.97	0	0	7	0
T20Is	9	6	2	69	33*	17.25	160.46	0	0	5	0
List A	15	11	1	130	54	13.00	106.55	0	1	8	0
T20s	16	11	5	127	41*	21.16	128.28	0	0	11	0
Bowling	**Mat**	**Balls**	**Runs**	**Wkts**	**BBI**	**BBM**	**Ave**	**Econ**	**SR**	**5w**	**10**
ODIs	10	504	387	10	4/15	4/15	38.70	4.60	50.4	0	0
T20Is	9	126	137	6	2/15	2/15	22.83	6.52	21.0	0	0
List A	15	708	579	14	4/15	4/15	41.35	4.90	50.5	0	0
T20s	16	174	198	6	2/15	2/15	33.00	6.82	29.0	0	0

NATHAN SOWTER RHB / LB / R0 / W0 / MVP67

FULL NAME: Nathan Adam Sowter
BORN: October 12, 1992, Penrith, New South Wales, Australia
SQUAD NO: 72
HEIGHT: 5ft 11in
NICKNAME: Sowts, Racing Snake
EDUCATION: Hills Sport High School, New South Wales
TEAMS: Middlesex, Oval Invincibles
ROLE: Bowler
DEBUT: First-class: 2017; List A: 2016; T20: 2015

BEST BATTING: 57* Middlesex vs Glamorgan, Cardiff, 2019
BEST BOWLING: 3-42 Middlesex vs Lancashire, Old Trafford, 2019

WHAT WAS YOUR FIRST CRICKET CLUB? Rooty Hill RSL CC – a small club not far from where I grew up in western Sydney
WHAT EXCITES YOU ABOUT THE HUNDRED? Playing for Oval Invincibles against the biggest stars in the game
BIGGEST TOPIC OF DISCUSSION IN YOUR DRESSING ROOM? Crosswords
CRICKETING HERO? Shane Warne
SURPRISING FACT ABOUT YOU? I'm a glazier by trade
SURPRISING FACT ABOUT A TEAMMATE? Steve Eskinazi doesn't wash his bedsheets – he just buys new ones when needed
CRICKET STAR OF THE FUTURE? Luke Hollman (Middlesex)
IF YOU WERE AN ANIMAL, WHICH WOULD IT BE? A sea turtle – they roam the ocean and see things we never will
TWITTER: @nsowter

Batting	Mat	Inns	NO	Runs	HS	Ave	SR	100	50	Ct	St
First-class	8	13	1	221	57*	18.41	80.36	0	2	4	0
List A	19	12	3	134	31	14.88	76.13	0	0	17	0
T20s	54	17	7	69	13*	6.90	107.81	0	0	21	0
Bowling	**Mat**	**Balls**	**Runs**	**Wkts**	**BBI**	**BBM**	**Ave**	**Econ**	**SR**	**5w**	**10**
First-class	8	1145	675	15	3/42	4/100	45.00	3.53	76.3	0	0
List A	19	1008	928	36	6/62	6/62	25.77	5.52	28.0	1	0
T20s	54	1012	1393	46	4/23	4/23	30.28	8.25	22.0	0	0

MITCHELL STARC LHB / LF

FULL NAME: Mitchell Aaron Starc
BORN: January 30, 1990, Baulkham Hills, Sydney, Australia
SQUAD NO: TBC
HEIGHT: 6ft 5in
TEAMS: Australia, Welsh Fire, New South Wales, Royal Challengers Bangalore, Sydney Sixers, Western Suburbs, Yorkshire
ROLE: Bowler
DEBUT: Test: 2011; ODI: 2010; T20I: 2012; First-class: 2009; List A: 2009; T20: 2009

BEST BATTING: 29 Royal Challengers Bangalore vs Kings XI Punjab, Bangalore, 2014 (T20)
BEST BOWLING: 4-15 Royal Challengers Bangalore vs Kings XI Punjab, Bengaluru, 2015 (T20)

NOTES: The fearsome left-armer debuted for his home state New South Wales in 2009 at the age of 19 and was called up to the Australian ODI side a year later, before making his Test debut in 2011. He has since become one of the most lethal white-ball bowlers in the game. Starc was awarded Player of the Tournament after taking 22 wickets in the 2015 World Cup, won by Australia. He bettered that by taking 27 during Australia's run to the semi-finals of last year's tournament. No bowler has ever taken more in a single World Cup. Starc had one T20 summer with Yorkshire in 2012. He has also featured for Royal Challengers Bangalore although hasn't appeared in the IPL since 2015, largely due to fitness. He was selected by Welsh Fire for The Hundred in the £125k category

Batting	Mat	Inns	NO	Runs	HS	Ave	SR	100	50	Ct	St
Tests	57	85	17	1515	99	22.27	68.58	0	10	29	0
ODIs	91	51	19	371	52*	11.59	87.50	0	1	27	0
T20Is	31	8	4	21	7*	5.25	91.30	0	0	10	0
First-class	101	127	32	2119	99	22.30	66.61	0	11	49	0
List A	120	66	26	537	52*	13.42	85.37	0	1	33	0
T20s	94	30	15	133	29	8.86	90.47	0	0	32	0
Bowling	**Mat**	**Balls**	**Runs**	**Wkts**	**BBI**	**BBM**	**Ave**	**Econ**	**SR**	**5w**	**10**
Tests	57	11753	6583	244	6/50	11/94	26.97	3.36	48.1	13	2
ODIs	91	4648	3956	178	6/28	6/28	22.22	5.10	26.1	7	0
T20Is	31	696	802	43	3/11	3/11	18.65	6.91	16.1	0	0
First-class	101	18754	10317	404	8/73	11/94	25.53	3.30	46.4	20	4
List A	120	6231	5216	249	6/25	6/25	20.94	5.02	25.0	10	0
T20s	94	2055	2451	140	4/15	4/15	17.50	7.15	14.6	0	0

CAMERON STEEL RHB / LB / R0 / W0

FULL NAME: Cameron Tate Steel
BORN: September 13, 1995, Greenbrae, California, USA
SQUAD NO: 14
HEIGHT: 5ft 10in
NICKNAME: Moggy, Peter, Lex
EDUCATION: Millfield Prep School, Somerset; Scotch College, Perth, Australia; Durham University
TEAMS: Durham
ROLE: Batsman
DEBUT: First-class: 2014; List A: 2017; T20: 2017

BEST BATTING: 224 Durham vs Leicestershire, Leicester, 2017
BEST BOWLING: 2-7 Durham vs Glamorgan, Cardiff, 2018

FAMILY TIES? My sister played youth cricket for Somerset and Western Australia
WHAT WAS YOUR FIRST CRICKET CLUB? Glastonbury CC, Somerset
WHAT WERE YOU DOING WHEN ENGLAND WON THE WORLD CUP? Going crazy on my own in the flat
HOW WOULD YOU DISMISS STEVE SMITH? The same way as everyone else – full toss or long-hop with the field spread
WHAT EXCITES YOU ABOUT THE HUNDRED? Getting some time off
BIGGEST TOPIC OF DISCUSSION IN YOUR DRESSING ROOM? Shower time
MOST INTERESTING TEAMMATE? Mark Wood and his pet horse
WHICH RULE WOULD YOU CHANGE ABOUT CRICKET? Umpires should not rule that leg-spinners must be taken out of the attack for bowling waist-high no-balls – sadly it's happened to me twice
BIGGEST CRICKETING REGRET? Not learning to bowl slow left-arm as a kid
IF YOU WERE AN ANIMAL, WHICH WOULD IT BE? A moggy cat
TWITTER: @CameronSteel2

Batting	Mat	Inns	NO	Runs	HS	Ave	SR	100	50	Ct	St
First-class	37	65	2	1985	224	31.50	40.94	3	11	18	0
List A	11	10	1	181	77	20.11	67.03	0	1	1	0
T20s	6	6	0	93	37	15.50	125.67	0	0	2	0
Bowling	**Mat**	**Balls**	**Runs**	**Wkts**	**BBI**	**BBM**	**Ave**	**Econ**	**SR**	**5w**	**10**
First-class	37	844	630	20	2/7	4/99	31.50	4.47	42.2	0	0
List A	11	30	47	0	-	-	-	9.40	-	0	0
T20s	6	48	88	2	2/60	2/60	44.00	11.00	24.0	0	0

SCOTT STEEL

RHB / OB / R0 / W0

FULL NAME: Scott Steel
BORN: April 20, 1999, Durham
SQUAD NO: 55
HEIGHT: 6ft
NICKNAME: Steely
EDUCATION: Belmont Community School, Durham, New College Durham
TEAMS: Durham
ROLE: Batsman
DEBUT: First-class: 2019; List A: 2019; T20: 2019

BEST BATTING: 39 Durham vs Middlesex, Lord's, 2019

WHAT WAS YOUR FIRST CRICKET CLUB? Durham City CC
HOW WOULD YOU DISMISS STEVE SMITH? Get him caught on the line
BIGGEST TOPIC OF DISCUSSION IN YOUR DRESSING ROOM? Golf
BEST INNINGS YOU'VE SEEN? AB de Villers: 149 off 44 balls vs West Indies at Johannesburg in 2015
MOST INTERESTING TEAMMATE? D'Arcy Short
WHICH RULE WOULD YOU CHANGE ABOUT CRICKET? Remove the stumping rule (I always get stumped)
CRICKET STAR OF THE FUTURE? Jonny Bushnell (Durham Academy)
IF YOU WERE AN ANIMAL, WHICH WOULD IT BE? A seal – chubby and lazy like me
TWITTER: @scottsteel102

Batting	Mat	Inns	NO	Runs	HS	Ave	SR	100	50	Ct	St
First-class	2	4	0	48	39	12.00	71.64	0	0	1	0
List A	8	7	0	227	68	32.42	80.78	0	2	3	0
T20s	11	11	0	369	70	33.54	136.66	0	2	1	0
Bowling	**Mat**	**Balls**	**Runs**	**Wkts**	**BBI**	**BBM**	**Ave**	**Econ**	**SR**	**5w**	**10**
First-class	2	42	16	0	-	-	-	2.28	-	0	0
List A	8	54	53	1	1/38	1/38	53.00	5.88	54.0	0	0
T20s	11	96	99	5	1/6	1/6	19.80	6.18	19.2	0	0

DARREN STEVENS RHB / RM / R3 / W4 / MVP10

FULL NAME: Darren Ian Stevens
BORN: April 30, 1976, Leicester
SQUAD NO: 3
HEIGHT: 5ft 11in
NICKNAME: Stevo
EDUCATION: John Cleveland College, Hinckley; Charles Keene College, Leicester
TEAMS: Kent, Comilla Victorians, Derbyshire, Dhaka Gladiators, Leicestershire, Mid West Rhinos, Otago
ROLE: Allrounder
DEBUT: First-class: 1997; List A: 1997; T20: 2003

BEST BATTING: 237 Kent vs Yorkshire, Headingley, 2019
BEST BOWLING: 8-75 Kent vs Leicestershire, Canterbury, 2017
COUNTY CAP: 2002 (Leicestershire); 2005 (Kent); BENEFIT: 2016 (Kent)

WHAT WAS YOUR FIRST CRICKET CLUB? Swallows Green CC, Hinckley, Leicestershire
HOW WOULD YOU DISMISS STEVE SMITH? With a lack of pace!
BIGGEST TOPIC OF DISCUSSION IN YOUR DRESSING ROOM? Changing 50-over cricket back to 40 overs
MOST INTERESTING TEAMMATE? Mitchell Claydon – too many reasons
CRICKETING HERO? Viv Richards
SURPRISING FACT ABOUT YOU? I am colour blind with browns, reds and greens. I struggled when I was with Otago in New Zealand because there were no sightscreens!
IF YOU WERE AN ANIMAL, WHICH WOULD IT BE? A leopard – so agile!
TWITTER: @Stevo208

Batting	Mat	Inns	NO	Runs	HS	Ave	SR	100	50	Ct	St
First-class	303	476	30	15633	237	35.05		34	79	197	0
List A	314	289	31	7612	147	29.50		7	46	127	0
T20s	212	191	40	4001	90	26.49	136.41	0	17	66	0
Bowling	**Mat**	**Balls**	**Runs**	**Wkts**	**BBI**	**BBM**	**Ave**	**Econ**	**SR**	**5w**	**10**
First-class	303	27725	13020	517	8/75		25.18	2.81	53.6	26	2
List A	314	6383	5114	160	6/25	6/25	31.96	4.80	39.8	3	0
T20s	212	2248	2968	114	4/14	4/14	26.03	7.92	19.7	0	0

RYAN STEVENSON

RHB / RFM / R0 / W0

FULL NAME: Ryan Anthony Stevenson
BORN: April 2, 1992, Torquay
SQUAD NO: 47
HEIGHT: 6ft 2in
NICKNAME: Raz, Stevo
EDUCATION: King Edward VI Community College, Devon
TEAMS: Hampshire
ROLE: Bowler
DEBUT: First-class: 2015; List A: 2016; T20: 2016

BEST BATTING: 51 Hampshire vs Surrey, The Oval, 2019
BEST BOWLING: 1-15 Hampshire vs Nottinghamshire, Trent Bridge, 2015

FAMILY TIES? My dad has played for Devon Over-50s
WHAT WAS YOUR FIRST CRICKET CLUB? Dartington & Totnes CC, Devon
WHAT WERE YOU DOING WHEN ENGLAND WON THE WORLD CUP? Driving to a second-team game trying to keep up with it on Brad Taylor's phone
HOW WOULD YOU DISMISS STEVE SMITH? Give the ball to someone else
BIGGEST TOPIC OF DISCUSSION IN YOUR DRESSING ROOM? End-of-season football
MOST INTERESTING TEAMMATE? Dale Steyn
CRICKETING HERO? Shaun Pollock
CRICKET STAR OF THE FUTURE? AJ Dale (Hampshire). Great lad with unreal variations in white-ball cricket
IF YOU WERE AN ANIMAL, WHICH WOULD IT BE? A snow leopard or a cow. My two favourite animals
TWITTER: @ryanstevenson47

Batting	Mat	Inns	NO	Runs	HS	Ave	SR	100	50	Ct	St
First-class	5	6	1	124	51	24.80	54.86	0	1	1	0
List A	3	1	0	0	0	0.00	0.00	0	0	0	0
T20s	12	7	3	15	4*	3.75	88.23	0	0	2	0
Bowling	**Mat**	**Balls**	**Runs**	**Wkts**	**BBI**	**BBM**	**Ave**	**Econ**	**SR**	**5w**	**10**
First-class	5	581	357	4	1/15	1/46	89.25	3.68	145.2	0	0
List A	3	120	142	2	1/28	1/28	71.00	7.10	60.0	0	0
T20s	12	221	354	11	2/28	2/28	32.18	9.61	20.0	0	0

GRANT STEWART

RHB / RFM / R0 / W0

FULL NAME: Grant Stewart
BORN: February 19, 1994, Kalgoorlie, Western Australia
SQUAD NO: 9
HEIGHT: 6ft 3in
NICKNAME: Stewie
EDUCATION: All Saints College, New South Wales; University of Newcastle, NSW
TEAMS: Kent
ROLE: Allrounder
DEBUT: First-class: 2017; List A: 2018; T20: 2018

BEST BATTING: 103 Kent vs Middlesex, Canterbury, 2018
BEST BOWLING: 6-22 Kent vs Middlesex, Canterbury, 2018

WHAT GOT YOU INTO CRICKET? My older brothers
BEST MOMENT IN CRICKET? My first-class debut for Kent against Glamorgan at Canterbury in 2017
IF YOU WEREN'T A CRICKETER? I'd be a civil engineer
SURPRISING FACT ABOUT YOU? I was a wicketkeeper until I was 16
CRICKETING HERO? Steve Waugh
NON-CRICKETING HERO? Hugh Jackman
TWITTER: @GStewart195

Batting	Mat	Inns	NO	Runs	HS	Ave	SR	100	50	Ct	St
First-class	17	26	4	542	103	24.63	67.16	1	3	3	0
List A	5	4	1	69	44	23.00	62.72	0	0	1	0
T20s	4	3	2	7	5*	7.00	116.66	0	0	3	0
Bowling	**Mat**	**Balls**	**Runs**	**Wkts**	**BBI**	**BBM**	**Ave**	**Econ**	**SR**	**5w**	**10**
First-class	17	1922	1108	39	6/22	8/58	28.41	3.45	49.2	1	0
List A	5	242	152	8	3/17	3/17	19.00	3.76	30.2	0	0
T20s	4	56	91	3	2/23	2/23	30.33	9.75	18.6	0	0

PAUL STIRLING RHB / OB

FULL NAME: Paul Robert Stirling
BORN: September 3, 1990, Belfast, Northern Ireland
SQUAD NO: TBC
HEIGHT: 5ft 9in
NICKNAME: Stirlo
EDUCATION: Belfast High School
TEAMS: Ireland, Northamptonshire, Khulna Titans, Middlesex, Sylhet Royals
ROLE: Allrounder
DEBUT: Test: 2018; ODI: 2008; T20I: 2009; First-class: 2008; List A: 2008; T20: 2008

BEST BATTING: 109 Middlesex vs Surrey, The Oval, 2018 (T20)
BEST BOWLING: 4-10 Ireland vs Hong Kong, Abu Dhabi, 2013 (T20)
COUNTY CAP: 2016 (Middlesex)

FAMILY TIES? My brother Richard represented Ireland in the U19 World Cup in Sri Lanka
CRICKETING HERO? Damien Martyn – pleasing to watch
SURPRISING FACT ABOUT YOU? My father is an ex-international rugby referee
TWITTER: @stirlo90
NOTES: Northants have signed the 29-year-old Ireland allrounder for this summer's T20 Blast. Stirling left Middlesex last September after a decade at the club because new regulations meant that he would have to register as an overseas player or give up his international career. He becomes the second Irishman to join a county as an overseas player following Boyd Rankin's brief spell at Derbyshire last year. Stirling is known for his destructive hitting at the top of the order and smacked a 47-ball 95 to help Ireland beat West Indies in a T20I at St George's in January

Batting	Mat	Inns	NO	Runs	HS	Ave	SR	100	50	Ct	St
Tests	3	6	0	104	36	17.33	58.75	0	0	4	0
ODIs	117	114	2	4121	177	36.79	86.75	8	24	45	0
T20Is	78	77	6	2124	95	29.91	139.27	0	18	22	0
First-class	70	110	5	2932	146	27.92	61.94	6	14	40	0
List A	203	197	8	6845	177	36.21	90.03	16	33	80	0
T20s	217	216	9	5473	109	26.43	142.19	1	39	62	0
Bowling	**Mat**	**Balls**	**Runs**	**Wkts**	**BBI**	**BBM**	**Ave**	**Econ**	**SR**	**5w**	**10**
Tests	3	12	11	0	-	-	-	5.50	-	0	0
ODIs	117	2392	1902	43	6/55	6/55	44.23	4.77	55.6	1	0
T20Is	78	486	615	17	3/21	3/21	36.17	7.59	28.5	0	0
First-class	70	2338	1118	27	2/21	3/31	41.40	2.86	86.5	0	0
List A	203	3440	2865	70	6/55	6/55	40.92	4.99	49.1	1	0
T20s	217	1481	1810	69	4/10	4/10	26.23	7.33	21.4	0	0

BEN STOKES

LHB / RFM / R0 / W0

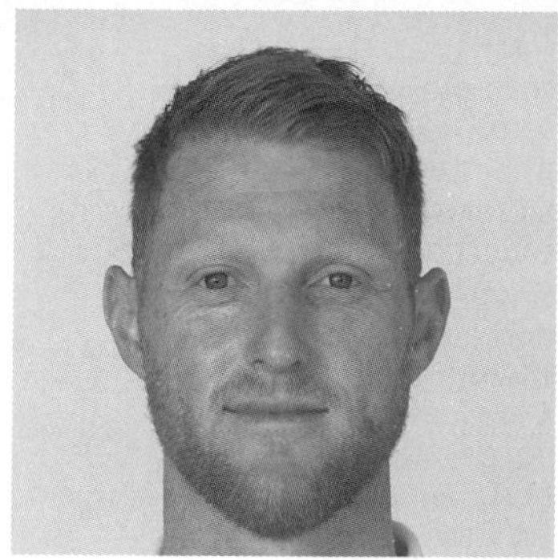

FULL NAME: Benjamin Andrew Stokes
BORN: June 4, 1991, Christchurch, New Zealand
SQUAD NO: 38
HEIGHT: 6ft 2in
NICKNAME: Benji, Stoker
EDUCATION: Cockermouth School, Cumbria
TEAMS: England, Durham, Northern Superchargers, Melbourne Renegades, Rajasthan Royals, Rising Pune Supergiant
ROLE: Allrounder
DEBUT: Test: 2013; ODI: 2011; T20I: 2011; First-class: 2010; List A: 2009; T20: 2010

BEST BATTING: 258 England vs South Africa, Cape Town, 2016
BEST BOWLING: 7-67 Durham vs Sussex, Chester-le-Street, 2014

SUPERSTITIONS? Swiping my bat across the crease at the end of every over
CRICKETING HERO? Herschelle Gibbs
SURPRISING FACT ABOUT YOU? My father played one Test match for New Zealand at rugby league. I was a right-handed batsman when I was younger
TWITTER: @benstokes38

Batting	Mat	Inns	NO	Runs	HS	Ave	SR	100	50	Ct	St
Tests	63	115	4	4056	258	36.54	58.74	9	21	72	0
ODIs	95	81	15	2682	102*	40.63	93.94	3	20	45	0
T20Is	26	23	6	305	47*	17.94	134.36	0	0	13	0
First-class	139	236	12	7849	258	35.04		17	40	113	0
List A	166	145	24	4583	164	37.87	96.56	7	27	76	0
T20s	123	113	19	2330	103*	24.78	135.46	1	8	52	0
Bowling	**Mat**	**Balls**	**Runs**	**Wkts**	**BBI**	**BBM**	**Ave**	**Econ**	**SR**	**5w**	**10**
Tests	63	8683	4804	147	6/22	8/161	32.68	3.31	59.0	4	0
ODIs	95	2912	2920	70	5/61	5/61	41.71	6.01	41.6	1	0
T20Is	26	388	571	14	3/26	3/26	40.78	8.82	27.7	0	0
First-class	139	16570	9553	319	7/67	10/121	29.94	3.45	51.9	7	1
List A	166	4587	4407	134	5/61	5/61	32.88	5.76	34.2	1	0
T20s	123	1537	2156	68	4/16	4/16	31.70	8.41	22.6	0	0

OLLY STONE

RHB / RF / R0 / W0

FULL NAME: Oliver Peter Stone
BORN: October 9, 1993, Norwich
SQUAD NO: 6
HEIGHT: 6ft 2in
NICKNAME: Stoney
EDUCATION: Thorpe St Andrew High School, Norwich; Moulton College, Northamptonshire
TEAMS: England, Warwickshire, Northamptonshire
ROLE: Bowler
DEBUT: Test: 2019; ODI: 2018; First-class: 2012; List A: 2012; T20: 2011

BEST BATTING: 60 Northamptonshire vs Kent, Northampton, 2016
BEST BOWLING: 8-80 Warwickshire vs Sussex, Edgbaston, 2018

WHAT WAS YOUR FIRST CRICKET CLUB? Vauxhall Mallards CC, Norfolk. Home of the ducks
BEST ADVICE EVER RECEIVED? Don't celebrate your wickets
MOST INTERESTING TEAMMATE? Keith Barker – you just never know what he is going to do next
BEST INNINGS YOU'VE SEEN? David Willey's 27-ball 60 for my former county Northants in the 2013 final of the T20 Blast
WHICH RULE WOULD YOU CHANGE ABOUT CRICKET? Allow bowlers to put their feet up after a spell
SURPRISING FACT ABOUT YOU? My great-grandad created the Twix chocolate bar
TWITTER: @ollystone2

Batting	Mat	Inns	NO	Runs	HS	Ave	SR	100	50	Ct	St
Tests	1	2	0	19	19	9.50	65.51	0	0	0	0
ODIs	4	1	1	9	9*	-	128.57	0	0	0	0
First-class	37	48	10	573	60	15.07	47.00	0	1	15	0
List A	30	14	9	122	24*	24.40	70.93	0	0	13	0
T20s	43	12	8	25	8*	6.25	96.15	0	0	10	0
Bowling	**Mat**	**Balls**	**Runs**	**Wkts**	**BBI**	**BBM**	**Ave**	**Econ**	**SR**	**5w**	**10**
Tests	1	72	29	3	3/29	3/29	9.66	2.41	24.0	0	0
ODIs	4	96	97	1	1/23	1/23	97.00	6.06	96.0	0	0
First-class	37	5596	3108	126	8/80	11/96	24.66	3.33	44.4	6	1
List A	30	1125	1023	24	4/71	4/71	42.62	5.45	46.8	0	0
T20s	43	780	1160	34	3/22	3/22	34.11	8.92	22.9	0	0

MARK STONEMAN LHB / OB / R5 / W0

FULL NAME: Mark Daniel Stoneman
BORN: June 26, 1987, Newcastle
SQUAD NO: 23
HEIGHT: 5ft 10in
NICKNAME: Rocky
EDUCATION: Whickham Comprehensive School, Newcastle Upon Tyne
TEAMS: England, Surrey, Durham
ROLE: Batsman
DEBUT: Test: 2017; First-class: 2007; List A: 2008; T20: 2010

BEST BATTING: 197 Surrey vs Sussex, Guildford, 2017

COUNTY CAP: 2018 (Surrey)

WHAT GOT YOU INTO CRICKET? Following my dad everywhere as soon as I could, carrying my little plastic bat along with me
FAMILY TIES? Grandfather played and umpired locally for many years. Dad played all over the north-east as a local pro
SUPERSTITIONS? Nervous wee, box goes on first
CRICKETING HEROES? Dad – he got me into the game and gave me every opportunity to be successful. Michael Di Venuto – the best role model a young county cricketer could have
IF YOU WEREN'T A CRICKETER? I'd be a fisherman
SURPRISING FACT ABOUT YOU? The Lion King makes me cry
TWITTER: @mark23stone

Batting	Mat	Inns	NO	Runs	HS	Ave	SR	100	50	Ct	St
Tests	11	20	1	526	60	27.68	44.27	0	5	1	0
First-class	190	331	8	11180	197	34.61	57.82	23	58	88	0
List A	82	78	5	2763	144*	37.84	92.74	6	17	23	0
T20s	72	67	4	1284	89*	20.38	118.01	0	7	28	0
Bowling	**Mat**	**Balls**	**Runs**	**Wkts**	**BBI**	**BBM**	**Ave**	**Econ**	**SR**	**5w**	**10**
Tests	11	-	-	-	-	-	-	-	-	-	-
First-class	190	216	165	0	-	-	-	4.58	-	0	0
List A	82	4	8	1	1/8	1/8	8.00	12.00	4.0	0	0
T20s	72	-	-	-	-	-	-	-	-	-	-

HARRY SWINDELLS

RHB / WK / R0 / W0

FULL NAME: Harry John Swindells
BORN: February 21, 1999, Leicester
SQUAD NO: 28
HEIGHT: 5ft 8in
NICKNAME: Dumbo
EDUCATION: Brockington College, Leicestershire; Lutterworth College; Loughborough College
TEAMS: Leicestershire, England U19
ROLE: Wicketkeeper
DEBUT: First-class: 2019; List A: 2018; T20: 2018

BEST BATTING: 37 Leicestershire vs Lancashire, Liverpool, 2019

WHAT WAS YOUR FIRST CRICKET CLUB? Narborough & Littlethorpe CC, Leicestershire
WHAT WERE YOU DOING WHEN ENGLAND WON THE WORLD CUP? I was in a pub in Cheltenham
HOW WOULD YOU DISMISS STEVE SMITH? My leggies would do the trick
BIGGEST TOPIC OF DISCUSSION IN YOUR DRESSING ROOM? Who's the baldest (there are a few contenders)
MOST INTERESTING TEAMMATE? Neil Dexter – always trying to play a practical joke at my expense
CRICKETING HERO? Adam Gilchrist
SURPRISING FACT ABOUT YOU? I'm a Leicester City FC supporter and go to both the home and away matches
CRICKET STAR OF THE FUTURE? Alex Evans (Leicestershire)
IF YOU WERE AN ANIMAL, WHICH WOULD IT BE? An elephant – I have huge ears
TWITTER: @harryswindells1

Batting	Mat	Inns	NO	Runs	HS	Ave	SR	100	50	Ct	St
First-class	7	10	0	168	37	16.80	35.14	0	0	12	1
List A	4	2	0	43	28	21.50	79.62	0	0	2	0
T20s	15	13	0	213	63	16.38	105.97	0	2	5	0
Bowling	**Mat**	**Balls**	**Runs**	**Wkts**	**BBI**	**BBM**	**Ave**	**Econ**	**SR**	**5w**	**10**
First-class	7	-	-	-	-	-	-	-	-	-	-
List A	4	-	-	-	-	-	-	-	-	-	-
T20s	15	-	-	-	-	-	-	-	-	-	-

IMRAN TAHIR RHB / LB

FULL NAME: Mohammad Imran Tahir
BORN: March 27, 1979, Lahore, Pakistan
SQUAD NO: 99
HEIGHT: 5ft 8in
TEAMS: South Africa, Manchester Originals, Chennai SK, Delhi Daredevils, Derbyshire, Dolphins, Durham, GA Warriors, Hampshire, Middlesex, Multan Sultans, Notts, Pakistan A, Rising Pune Supergiant, Surrey, Titans, Warwickshire, Yorkshire
ROLE: Bowler
DEBUT: Test: 2011; ODI: 2011; T20I: 2013; First-class: 1996; List A: 1998; T20: 2006

BEST BATTING: 23 Derbyshire vs Hampshire, Derby, 2017 (T20)
BEST BOWLING: 5-23 South Africa vs Zimbabwe, East London, 2018 (T20)
COUNTY CAP: 2009 (Hampshire); 2010 (Warwickshire)

NOTES: The 41-year-old leg-spinner has vast experience of English domestic cricket, having featured for eight different counties since 2003. Tahir first played for Pakistan U19 before moving to South Africa in search of regular international cricket. He made his ODI debut for South Africa during the 2011 World Cup and his Test debut came in the same year. In 2016 he became the fastest South African to reach 100 ODI wickets and the following year he became the No.1-ranked T20I bowler. He retired from ODI cricket after last summer's World Cup. Tahir was retained by Chennai Super Kings for the 2020 IPL after finishing as the previous tournament's highest wicket-taker (26). He will represent Manchester Originals in The Hundred after being selected in the £125k salary band

Batting	Mat	Inns	NO	Runs	HS	Ave	SR	100	50	Ct	St
Tests	20	23	9	130	29*	9.28	55.31	0	0	8	0
ODIs	107	36	16	157	29	7.85	69.77	0	0	25	0
T20Is	38	4	3	19	9*	19.00	105.55	0	0	7	0
First-class	194	246	62	2617	77*	14.22		0	4	82	0
List A	239	79	27	494	41*	9.50		0	0	57	0
T20s	290	54	32	230	23	10.45	105.99	0	0	66	0
Bowling	**Mat**	**Balls**	**Runs**	**Wkts**	**BBI**	**BBM**	**Ave**	**Econ**	**SR**	**5w**	**10**
Tests	20	3925	2294	57	5/32	8/130	40.24	3.50	68.8	2	0
ODIs	107	5541	4297	173	7/45	7/45	24.83	4.65	32.0	3	0
T20Is	38	845	948	63	5/23	5/23	15.04	6.73	13.4	2	0
First-class	194	38291	20882	784	8/42		26.63	3.27	48.8	53	11
List A	239	11434	8860	369	7/45	7/45	24.01	4.64	30.9	7	0
T20s	290	6203	7246	365	5/23	5/23	19.85	7.00	16.9	2	0

JONATHAN TATTERSALL RHB / WK / R0 / W0

FULL NAME: Jonathan Andrew Tattersall
BORN: December 15, 1994, Harrogate, Yorkshire
SQUAD NO: 12
HEIGHT: 5ft 8in
NICKNAME: Tatts
EDUCATION: King James's School, Knaresborough
TEAMS: Yorkshire, England U19
ROLE: Wicketkeeper/batsman
DEBUT: First-class: 2018; List A: 2013; T20: 2018

BEST BATTING: 135 Yorkshire vs Leeds/Bradford MCCU, Weetwood, 2019

BEST ADVICE EVER RECEIVED? Always remember why you played the game in the first place
BEST MOMENT IN CRICKET? Being released from Yorkshire and then getting another contract with Yorkshire
SURPRISING FACT ABOUT YOU? I have a handicap of nine in golf
SURPRISING FACT ABOUT A TEAMMATE? Ed Barnes loves a glass of rosé
CRICKETING HERO? Rahul Dravid – for his temperament
NON-CRICKETING HERO? Steve Coogan – for being Alan Partridge
TWITTER: @JonnyTatts

Batting	Mat	Inns	NO	Runs	HS	Ave	SR	100	50	Ct	St
First-class	22	34	3	1008	135*	32.51	42.01	1	5	55	4
List A	15	11	2	375	89	41.66	112.95	0	4	16	3
T20s	23	17	5	301	53*	25.08	129.74	0	1	14	2
Bowling	**Mat**	**Balls**	**Runs**	**Wkts**	**BBI**	**BBM**	**Ave**	**Econ**	**SR**	**5w**	**10**
First-class	22	-	-	-	-	-	-	-	-	-	-
List A	15	-	-	-	-	-	-	-	-	-	-
T20s	23	-	-	-	-	-	-	-	-	-	-

BRAD TAYLOR RHB / OB / R0 / W0

FULL NAME: Bradley Jacob Taylor
BORN: March 14, 1997, Winchester, Hampshire
SQUAD NO: 93
HEIGHT: 6ft
NICKNAME: Tails, Techno
EDUCATION: Eggar's School, Alton, Hampshire; Alton College
TEAMS: Hampshire, England U19
ROLE: Bowler
DEBUT: First-class: 2013; List A: 2013; T20: 2014

BEST BATTING: 36 Hampshire vs Cardiff MCCU, Southampton, 2016
BEST BOWLING: 4-64 Hampshire vs Lancashire, Southport, 2013

WHAT WAS YOUR FIRST CRICKET CLUB? Holybourne CC, Hampshire
CRICKETING HERO? Daniel Vettori
SURPRISING FACT ABOUT YOU? I'm a massive Southampton fan and I go to the home games whenever I can
TWITTER: @bradtay93
NOTES: A former England U19 captain, in 2013 Taylor became the youngest player to represent Hampshire since 1867 – aged 16 years and 154 days – but he has struggled to establish himself as a first-team regular at the Ageas Bowl. He only made three appearances last summer – two in the T20 Blast and a solitary outing in the One-Day Cup – but signed a new two-year contract last October. "We're really pleased Brad has committed his future to Hampshire," said Giles White, the club's director of cricket. "He is a promising allrounder who has come through the ranks and contributed in all three disciplines in recent years. We feel he fits really well with the make-up of the group and if he continues to develop, I'm confident he will play a big part over the coming seasons"

Batting	Mat	Inns	NO	Runs	HS	Ave	SR	100	50	Ct	St
First-class	6	10	3	133	36	19.00	44.63	0	0	2	0
List A	18	15	5	355	69	35.50	65.74	0	3	7	0
T20s	8	4	1	23	9*	7.66	82.14	0	0	3	0
Bowling	**Mat**	**Balls**	**Runs**	**Wkts**	**BBI**	**BBM**	**Ave**	**Econ**	**SR**	**5w**	**10**
First-class	6	798	544	13	4/64	4/106	41.84	4.09	61.3	0	0
List A	18	852	661	15	4/26	4/26	44.06	4.65	56.8	0	0
T20s	8	104	128	4	2/20	2/20	32.00	7.38	26.0	0	0

CALLUM TAYLOR

RHB / OB / R0 / W0

FULL NAME: Callum Zinzan Taylor
BORN: June 19, 1998, Newport, Monmouthshire
SQUAD NO: 4
HEIGHT: 6ft
EDUCATION: The Southport School
TEAMS: Glamorgan
ROLE: Allrounder
DEBUT: T20: 2019

WHAT WAS YOUR FIRST CRICKET CLUB? Surfers Paradise CC, Queensland, Australia
WHAT WERE YOU DOING WHEN ENGLAND WON THE WORLD CUP? Thinking that they never should have had a chance of winning that World Cup final
HOW WOULD YOU DISMISS STEVE SMITH? Find Neil Wagner
BIGGEST TOPIC OF DISCUSSION IN YOUR DRESSING ROOM? Bats
MOST INTERESTING TEAMMATE? Owen Morgan – he's a space cadet
CRICKET STAR OF THE FUTURE? Alex Horton (Glamorgan Academy)
IF YOU WERE AN ANIMAL, WHICH WOULD IT BE? A seagull – so that I could watch the cricket
TWITTER: @CallumZTaylor
NOTES: Born in Newport but raised in Queensland, Taylor returned to Wales in his late teens and signed his first professional contract with Glamorgan in March 2019. A middle-order batsman and useful off-spinner, he impressed in the county's Second XI last summer, scoring 649 runs across all formats including an unbeaten century against Kent at Newport. Off the back of those performances he forced his way into Glamorgan's T20 side, making four appearances in the Blast. Taylor hit the first ball he faced in professional cricket for four, reverse-sweeping Somerset's Roelof van der Merwe to the ropes. He will hope for further white-ball opportunities this season, particularly given Glamorgan's struggles in both short formats last year

Batting	Mat	Inns	NO	Runs	HS	Ave	SR	100	50	Ct	St
T20s	4	3	2	23	16*	23.00	121.05	0	0	1	0
Bowling	**Mat**	**Balls**	**Runs**	**Wkts**	**BBI**	**BBM**	**Ave**	**Econ**	**SR**	**5w**	**10**
T20s	4	12	14	0	-	-	-	7.00	-	0	0

JACK TAYLOR

RHB / LB / R0 / W0

FULL NAME: Jack Martin Robert Taylor
BORN: November 12, 1991, Banbury, Oxfordshire
SQUAD NO: 10
HEIGHT: 6ft
NICKNAME: JT, Jacko
EDUCATION: Chipping Norton School, Oxfordshire
TEAMS: Gloucestershire
ROLE: Allrounder
DEBUT: First-class: 2010; List A: 2011; T20: 2011

BEST BATTING: 156 Gloucestershire vs Northamptonshire, Cheltenham, 2015
BEST BOWLING: 4-16 Gloucestershire vs Glamorgan, Bristol, 2016
COUNTY CAP: 2010

WHAT WAS YOUR FIRST CRICKET CLUB? Great and Little Tew CC, Oxfordshire. My family have always played there
WHAT WERE YOU DOING WHEN ENGLAND WON THE WORLD CUP? I was walking the dog
HOW WOULD YOU DISMISS STEVE SMITH? With a thigh-high full bunger
BIGGEST TOPIC OF DISCUSSION IN YOUR DRESSING ROOM? Fantasy Football
MOST INTERESTING TEAMMATE? James Fuller – eats like a horse. Picks and chooses his running events
WHICH RULE WOULD YOU CHANGE ABOUT CRICKET? You can be out if the ball pitches outside leg stump
BIGGEST CRICKETING REGRET? Not turning to leg-spin sooner
CRICKET STAR OF THE FUTURE? Tom Price – just signed his first professional contract with Gloucestershire
IF YOU WERE AN ANIMAL, WHICH WOULD IT BE? A dog – sleep, eat, chase a ball
TWITTER: @jacktaylor141

Batting	Mat	Inns	NO	Runs	HS	Ave	SR	100	50	Ct	St
First-class	77	118	9	3229	156	29.62	64.18	7	9	39	0
List A	51	41	8	1100	75	33.33	118.27	0	9	22	0
T20s	80	62	17	928	80	20.62	148.48	0	2	23	0
Bowling	**Mat**	**Balls**	**Runs**	**Wkts**	**BBI**	**BBM**	**Ave**	**Econ**	**SR**	**5w**	**10**
First-class	77	5715	3341	75	4/16	5/140	44.54	3.50	76.2	0	0
List A	51	1185	1027	29	4/38	4/38	35.41	5.20	40.8	0	0
T20s	80	634	862	26	4/16	4/16	33.15	8.15	24.3	0	0

JAMES TAYLOR

RHB / RM / R0 / W0

FULL NAME: James Philip Arthur Taylor
BORN: January 19, 2001, Stoke-on-Trent, Staffordshire
SQUAD NO: 25
HEIGHT: 6ft 3in
NICKNAME: JT
EDUCATION: Trentham High School, Stoke-on-Trent; Newcastle-under-Lyme College, Staffordshire
TEAMS: Surrey, Derbyshire, England U19
ROLE: Bowler
DEBUT: First-class: 2017; List A: 2019

BEST BATTING: 11* Derbyshire vs Leeds/Bradford MCCU, Derby, 2019
BEST BOWLING: 3-26 Derbyshire vs Leeds/Bradford MCCU, Derby, 2019

WHAT WAS YOUR FIRST CRICKET CLUB? Barlaston CC, Staffordshire. Always stay on the front foot because the wicket is slow and low at Barlaston
BEST ADVICE EVER RECEIVED? Play late and straight, be great
HOW WOULD YOU DISMISS STEVE SMITH? Shorten the wicket to 10 yards
MOST INTERESTING TEAMMATE? Dan Moriarty – cricket badger
BEST INNINGS YOU'VE SEEN? Wayne Madsen's Championship hundred against Northants at Chesterfield in 2018. On a turning wicket, he made it look easy
CRICKETING HERO? Andrew Flintoff
BIGGEST CRICKETING REGRET? Being a bowler. It hurts
CRICKET STAR OF THE FUTURE? My mum's a mean backyard cricketer
WHICH BOOK MEANS MOST TO YOU? Biff, Chip and Kipper by Roderick Hunt and Alex Brychta
TWITTER: @_Jamestaylor19

Batting	Mat	Inns	NO	Runs	HS	Ave	SR	100	50	Ct	St
First-class	2	2	2	11	11*	-	42.30	0	0	0	0
List A	1	1	1	6	6*	-	100.00	0	0	0	0
Bowling	**Mat**	**Balls**	**Runs**	**Wkts**	**BBI**	**BBM**	**Ave**	**Econ**	**SR**	**5w**	**10**
First-class	2	240	151	7	3/26	6/74	21.57	3.77	34.2	0	0
List A	1	42	66	2	2/66	2/66	33.00	9.42	21.0	0	0

JEROME TAYLOR RHB / RFM / R0 / W0

FULL NAME: Jerome Everton Taylor
BORN: June 22, 1984, St Elizabeth, Jamaica
SQUAD NO: 74
TEAMS: West Indies, Gloucestershire, Hobart Hurricanes, Jamaica, Leicestershire, Pune Warriors, Rahuna Royals, Somerset, St Lucia Zouks, Sussex
ROLE: Bowler
DEBUT: Test: 2003; ODI: 2003; T20I: 2006; First-class: 2003; List A: 2003; T20: 2006

BEST BATTING: 106 West Indies vs New Zealand, Dunedin, 2008
BEST BOWLING: 8-59 Jamaica vs Trinidad and Tobago, Trinidad, 2003

NOTES: The experienced Jamaican fast bowler moves across the West Country to join Gloucestershire after two T20 Blast campaigns with Somerset. Taylor has signed a three-year deal to play across all formats. He will be registed as a Kolpak this summer but will become an overseas player next year if regulations change because of Brexit. "I am grateful for the opportunity as I really enjoy playing county cricket and I am hopeful that my experience can help on and off the field," he said. Taylor called time on an injury-blighted Test career in 2016, his finest hour coming against England on his home ground of Sabina Park in 2009 when he returned figures of 9-4-11-5. Gloucestershire will be Taylor's fourth English county, and he has also appeared in the IPL and the Big Bash League. In 2018 he helped propel Somerset to T20 Finals Day, taking 22 wickets at 16.63

Batting	Mat	Inns	NO	Runs	HS	Ave	SR	100	50	Ct	St
Tests	46	73	7	856	106	12.96	62.57	1	1	8	0
ODIs	90	42	9	278	43*	8.42	86.06	0	0	20	0
T20Is	30	15	6	118	21	13.11	128.26	0	0	9	0
First-class	103	161	25	1595	106	11.72		1	1	25	0
List A	135	68	17	518	43*	10.15		0	0	27	0
T20s	119	46	23	266	21	11.56	120.90	0	0	21	0
Bowling	**Mat**	**Balls**	**Runs**	**Wkts**	**BBI**	**BBM**	**Ave**	**Econ**	**SR**	**5w**	**10**
Tests	46	7757	4480	130	6/47	9/95	34.46	3.46	59.6	4	0
ODIs	90	4341	3780	128	5/48	5/48	29.53	5.22	33.9	1	0
T20Is	30	600	863	33	3/6	3/6	26.15	8.63	18.1	0	0
First-class	103	15824	8401	326	8/59		25.76	3.18	48.5	16	2
List A	135	6431	5414	203	5/40	5/40	26.66	5.05	31.6	2	0
T20s	119	2503	3560	140	5/10	5/10	25.42	8.53	17.8	2	0

MATT TAYLOR

RHB / LMF / R0 / W1

GLOUCESTERSHIRE

FULL NAME: Matthew David Taylor
BORN: July 8, 1994, Banbury, Oxfordshire
SQUAD NO: 36
HEIGHT: 6ft 2in
NICKNAME: MT, Bomber, Swede
EDUCATION: Chipping Norton Secondary School, Oxfordshire
TEAMS: Gloucestershire
ROLE: Bowler
DEBUT: First-class: 2013; List A: 2011; T20: 2015

BEST BATTING: 48 Gloucestershire vs Glamorgan, Bristol, 2018
BEST BOWLING: 5-15 Gloucestershire vs Cardiff MCCU, Bristol, 2018
COUNTY CAP: 2013

FAMILY TIES? My older brother Jack also plays for Gloucestershire. My dad and grandad played Minor Counties for Oxfordshire
WHAT WAS YOUR FIRST CRICKET CLUB? Great and Little Tew CC, Oxfordshire
BEST ADVICE EVER RECEIVED? When all is said and done, more is always said than done
BIGGEST TOPIC OF DISCUSSION IN YOUR DRESSING ROOM? Fantasy Football
CRICKETING HERO? Darren Gough
WHICH RULE WOULD YOU CHANGE ABOUT CRICKET? No extra balls to be bowled
BIGGEST CRICKETING REGRET? Not being a batsman
TWITTER: @matt_taylor94

Batting	Mat	Inns	NO	Runs	HS	Ave	SR	100	50	Ct	St
First-class	52	67	28	514	48	13.17	40.79	0	0	7	0
List A	28	9	6	41	16	13.66	87.23	0	0	5	0
T20s	31	8	5	28	9*	9.33	84.84	0	0	6	0
Bowling	**Mat**	**Balls**	**Runs**	**Wkts**	**BBI**	**BBM**	**Ave**	**Econ**	**SR**	**5w**	**10**
First-class	52	8025	4734	142	5/15	7/133	33.33	3.53	56.5	5	0
List A	28	1251	1174	20	3/39	3/39	58.70	5.63	62.5	0	0
T20s	31	544	774	26	3/16	3/16	29.76	8.53	20.9	0	0

TOM TAYLOR

RHB / RMF / R0 / W0

FULL NAME: Thomas Alexander Ian Taylor
BORN: December 21, 1994, Stoke-on-Trent, Staffordshire
SQUAD NO: 16
HEIGHT: 6ft 3in
NICKNAME: Audi, Anne Robinson
EDUCATION: Trentham High School, Stoke-on-Trent; Newcastle-under-Lyme College; Leeds Metropolitan University
TEAMS: Leicestershire, Derbyshire
ROLE: Allrounder
DEBUT: First-class: 2014; List A 2014

BEST BATTING: 80 Derbyshire vs Kent, Derby, 2016
BEST BOWLING: 6-47 Leicestershire vs Sussex, Hove, 2019

FAMILY TIES? Father, cousins, uncles all play cricket; other family members used to run my home club. My brother James has just left Derbyshire to join Surrey
WHAT WAS YOUR FIRST CRICKET CLUB? Barlaston CC, Stoke-on-Trent, Staffordshire
WHAT EXCITES YOU ABOUT THE HUNDRED? The money and the opportunities
BIGGEST TOPIC OF DISCUSSION IN YOUR DRESSING ROOM? Anything that involves taking the mickey out of each other
MOST INTERESTING TEAMMATE? Hashim Amla
CRICKETING HERO? Brett Lee
SURPRISING FACT ABOUT YOU? I drink a lot of milk
CRICKET STAR OF THE FUTURE? James Taylor (Surrey)
IF YOU WERE AN ANIMAL, WHICH WOULD IT BE? A lion
TWITTER: @TomTaylor43

Batting	Mat	Inns	NO	Runs	HS	Ave	SR	100	50	Ct	St
First-class	30	46	7	743	80	19.05	43.29	0	3	7	0
List A	12	7	2	242	98*	48.40	113.61	0	2	6	0
Bowling	**Mat**	**Balls**	**Runs**	**Wkts**	**BBI**	**BBM**	**Ave**	**Econ**	**SR**	**5w**	**10**
First-class	30	4684	2837	90	6/47	10/122	31.52	3.63	52.0	3	1
List A	12	602	602	13	3/48	3/48	46.30	6.00	46.3	0	0

RYAN TEN DOESCHATE RHB / RMF / R1 / W0 / MVP99

ESSEX / WELSH FIRE

FULL NAME: Ryan Neil ten Doeschate
BORN: June 30, 1980, Port Elizabeth, SA
SQUAD NO: 27
HEIGHT: 5ft 11in
EDUCATION: University of Cape Town
TEAMS: Netherlands, Essex, Welsh Fire, Adelaide Strikers, Canterbury, Comilla Victorians, Dhaka Dynamites, Kolkata Knight Riders, Lahore Qalandars, Otago, Rajshahi Kings, Western Province
ROLE: Allrounder
DEBUT: ODI: 2006; T20I: 2008; First-class: 2003; List A: 2003; T20: 2003

BEST BATTING: 259* Netherlands vs Canada, Pretoria, 2006
BEST BOWLING: 6-20 Netherlands vs Canada, Pretoria, 2006
COUNTY CAP: 2006

TWITTER: @rtendo27
NOTES: The veteran Netherlands allrounder became Essex skipper in 2016 and immediately led the club to Championship promotion and then the title in successive seasons. After winning a second Championship trophy last year, the 39-year-old handed over the four-day and 50-over captaincy to Tom Westley. This will be his 18th season at Chelmsford. He has played T20 cricket all over the globe, including for Kolkata Knight Riders in the IPL. For Netherlands he scored 686 runs at an average of 228.66 in the ICC Intercontinental Cup in 2006, recording four consecutive hundreds, including a competition record 259* vs Canada in Pretoria. He made a century (119) against England at Nagpur in the 2011 World Cup, becoming the first batsman from the Netherlands to make a hundred in the World Cup finals, and scored a second hundred against Ireland at Kolkata

Batting	Mat	Inns	NO	Runs	HS	Ave	SR	100	50	Ct	St
ODIs	33	32	9	1541	119	67.00	87.70	5	9	13	0
T20Is	22	22	10	533	59	44.41	133.25	0	3	4	0
First-class	188	275	39	10766	259*	45.61		29	49	118	0
List A	225	189	55	6053	180	45.17		11	31	68	0
T20s	360	321	75	7269	121*	29.54	133.96	2	33	128	0
Bowling	**Mat**	**Balls**	**Runs**	**Wkts**	**BBI**	**BBM**	**Ave**	**Econ**	**SR**	**5w**	**10**
ODIs	33	1580	1327	55	4/31	4/31	24.12	5.03	28.7	0	0
T20Is	22	210	245	13	3/23	3/23	18.84	7.00	16.1	0	0
First-class	188	10952	7193	212	6/20		33.92	3.94	51.6	7	0
List A	225	5469	5257	174	5/50	5/50	30.21	5.76	31.4	1	0
T20s	360	2147	2922	114	4/24	4/24	25.63	8.16	18.8	0	0

IVAN THOMAS

RHB / RMF / R0 / W0

FULL NAME: Ivan Alfred Astley Thomas
BORN: September 25, 1991, Greenwich, Kent
SQUAD NO: 5
HEIGHT: 6ft 5in
NICKNAME: Big Red, The Viking
EDUCATION: The John Roan School, Greenwich; University of Leeds
TEAMS: Kent
ROLE: Bowler
DEBUT: First-class: 2012; List A: 2014; T20: 2015

BEST BATTING: 13 Kent vs Australians, Canterbury, 2015
BEST BOWLING: 5-91 Kent vs Leicestershire, Leicester, 2018

WHAT WAS YOUR FIRST CRICKET CLUB? Blackheath CC, Kent
WHAT WERE YOU DOING WHEN ENGLAND WON THE WORLD CUP? Watching Grace Jones perform live
WHAT EXCITES YOU ABOUT THE HUNDRED? The money
BIGGEST TOPIC OF DISCUSSION IN YOUR DRESSING ROOM? Dostoyevsky
MOST INTERESTING TEAMMATE? Matt Milnes – I've never met a northerner so desperate to be from south London!
CRICKETING HERO? Andrew Flintoff
SURPRISING FACT ABOUT YOU? I can tear an apple in half
BIGGEST CRICKETING REGRET? Not being a spinner
CRICKET STAR OF THE FUTURE? AJ Isherwood (Western Suburbs CC, Sydney, Australia; North Devon CC)
WHICH BOOK MEANS MOST TO YOU? The Lord of the Rings by JRR Tolkien
TWITTER: @ivanthomas_5

Batting	Mat	Inns	NO	Runs	HS	Ave	SR	100	50	Ct	St
First-class	33	44	22	114	13	5.18	22.52	0	0	9	0
List A	21	8	5	18	6	6.00	37.50	0	0	8	0
T20s	12	3	2	3	3*	3.00	60.00	0	0	4	0
Bowling	**Mat**	**Balls**	**Runs**	**Wkts**	**BBI**	**BBM**	**Ave**	**Econ**	**SR**	**5w**	**10**
First-class	33	4159	2124	70	5/91	9/126	30.34	3.06	59.4	1	0
List A	21	1036	964	31	4/30	4/30	31.09	5.58	33.4	0	0
T20s	12	210	320	9	2/42	2/42	35.55	9.14	23.3	0	0

SUSSEX

AARON THOMASON RHB / RFM / R0 / W0

FULL NAME: Aaron Dean Thomason
BORN: June 26, 1997, Birmingham
SQUAD NO: 24
HEIGHT: 5ft 10in
NICKNAME: Thomo
EDUCATION: Barr Beacon School, Walsall
TEAMS: Sussex, England U19, Warwickshire
ROLE: Allrounder
DEBUT: First-class: 2019; List A: 2014; T20: 2016

BEST BATTING: 90 Sussex vs Worcestershire, Kidderminster, 2019
BEST BOWLING: 2-107 Sussex vs Australia A, Arundel, 2019

FAMILY TIES? We are members of Sutton Coldfield CC, where my brother plays and my whole family go and watch each Saturday
BEST MOMENT IN CRICKET? Making my Warwickshire debut at Lord's
CRICKETING HERO? Andrew Flintoff
NON-CRICKETING HERO? My great-grandad watched us play all the time. He left me some medals he was awarded for service in the war which I treasure
IF YOU WEREN'T A CRICKETER? I'd be window-cleaning with my dad
SURPRISING FACT ABOUT YOU? Me and Chris Woakes went to the same school – it was a non-cricket-playing school

Batting	Mat	Inns	NO	Runs	HS	Ave	SR	100	50	Ct	St
First-class	4	8	0	129	90	16.12	57.07	0	1	1	0
List A	17	13	6	176	28	25.14	98.32	0	0	6	0
T20s	28	20	5	236	42	15.73	129.67	0	0	13	0
Bowling	**Mat**	**Balls**	**Runs**	**Wkts**	**BBI**	**BBM**	**Ave**	**Econ**	**SR**	**5w**	**10**
First-class	4	451	358	4	2/107	2/119	89.50	4.76	112.7	0	0
List A	17	388	460	14	4/45	4/45	32.85	7.11	27.7	0	0
T20s	28	372	670	24	3/33	3/33	27.91	10.80	15.5	0	0

JORDAN THOMPSON

LHB / RM / R0 / W0

FULL NAME: Jordan Aaron Thompson
BORN: October 9, 1996, Leeds, Yorkshire
SQUAD NO: 44
HEIGHT: 6ft 1in
NICKNAME: Tommo, Lizard
EDUCATION: Benton Park School, Leeds
TEAMS: Yorkshire
ROLE: Allrounder
DEBUT: First-class: 2019; List A: 2019; T20: 2018

BEST BATTING: 34 Yorkshire vs Surrey, Guildford, 2019
BEST BOWLING: 2-28 Yorkshire vs Warwickshire, York, 2019

BEST MOMENT IN CRICKET? Scoring 146 not out in a Second XI Championship match for Yorkshire against Worcestershire at Scarborough in 2016
IF YOU WEREN'T A CRICKETER? I'd be a professional goalkeeper
SURPRISING FACT ABOUT YOU? I'm a Type 1 diabetic
SURPRISING FACT ABOUT A TEAMMATE? Matthew Waite has the nickname 'Pingu' because we all think he walks like a penguin
CRICKETING HERO? Ben Stokes – because of his aggressive style on the field
NON-CRICKETING HERO? Pontus Jansson – Leeds United footballer. Love his aggression and passion on the football field
TWITTER: @Tommo455

Batting	Mat	Inns	NO	Runs	HS	Ave	SR	100	50	Ct	St
First-class	2	3	0	36	34	12.00	64.28	0	0	0	0
List A	1	-	-	-	-	-	-	-	-	0	0
T20s	18	13	7	113	50	18.83	154.79	0	1	4	0
Bowling	**Mat**	**Balls**	**Runs**	**Wkts**	**BBI**	**BBM**	**Ave**	**Econ**	**SR**	**5w**	**10**
First-class	2	240	105	5	2/28	3/64	21.00	2.62	48.0	0	0
List A	1	30	43	0	-	-	-	8.60	-	0	0
T20s	18	294	436	12	3/23	3/23	36.33	8.89	24.5	0	0

ALEX THOMSON

RHB / OB / R0 / W0

FULL NAME: Alexander Thomas Thomson
BORN: October 30, 1993, Stoke-on-Trent, Staffordshire
SQUAD NO: 29
HEIGHT: 6ft 5in
NICKNAME: Sarge, Big Al
EDUCATION: Denstone College, Uttoxeter, Staffordshire; Cardiff Metropolitan University
TEAMS: Warwickshire
ROLE: Allrounder
DEBUT: First-class: 2014; List A: 2018; T20: 2018

BEST BATTING: 30 MCC vs Nepal, Kirtipur, 2019
BEST BOWLING: 6-138 Cardiff MCCU vs Hampshire, Southampton, 2017

WHAT WAS YOUR FIRST CRICKET CLUB? Leek CC, Staffordshire
BEST ADVICE RECEIVED? Leave nothing in the tank
HOW WOULD YOU DISMISS STEVE SMITH? Ask him to kick them over
WHAT EXCITES YOU ABOUT THE HUNDRED? Everything about it
BEST INNINGS YOU'VE SEEN? Alastair Cook's final Test innings at The Oval
CRICKETING HERO? Jacques Kallis
WHICH RULE WOULD YOU CHANGE ABOUT CRICKET? You should be allowed to play in shorts
SURPRISING FACT ABOUT YOU? I'm an avid angler
CRICKET STAR OF THE FUTURE? Ebony Tweats (Leek CC)
WHICH BOOK MEANS MOST TO YOU? The Story of Cricket – A Ladybird Easy-Reading Book by Vera Southgate and Jack Matthew
IF YOU WERE AN ANIMAL, WHICH WOULD IT BE? An elephant – presence and thought while also fostering great knowledge
TWITTER: @tommo1039

Batting	Mat	Inns	NO	Runs	HS	Ave	SR	100	50	Ct	St
First-class	9	10	0	170	30	17.00	44.61	0	0	4	0
List A	9	8	2	258	68*	43.00	92.47	0	2	3	0
T20s	11	6	3	39	14	13.00	108.33	0	0	3	0
Bowling	**Mat**	**Balls**	**Runs**	**Wkts**	**BBI**	**BBM**	**Ave**	**Econ**	**SR**	**5w**	**10**
First-class	9	661	495	16	6/138	7/176	30.93	4.49	41.3	1	0
List A	9	450	379	13	3/27	3/27	29.15	5.05	34.6	0	0
T20s	11	204	277	10	4/35	4/35	27.70	8.14	20.4	0	0

CHARLIE THURSTON RHB / RM / R0 / W0

FULL NAME: Charlie Oliver Thurston
BORN: August 17, 1996, Cambridge
SQUAD NO: 96
HEIGHT: 6ft
NICKNAME: Chazzy, Deano, Baloo
EDUCATION: Bedford School; Loughborough University
TEAMS: Northamptonshire
ROLE: Batsman
DEBUT: First-class: 2016; List A: 2018; T20: 2018

BEST BATTING: 126 Loughborough MCCU vs Northamptonshire, Northampton, 2017

WHAT WAS YOUR FIRST CRICKET CLUB? Shenley Village CC, Hertfordshire. I can just about remember meeting Brian Lara when West Indies and Pakistan once played a warm-up there
WHAT EXCITES YOU ABOUT THE HUNDRED? The new tactics
BIGGEST TOPIC OF DISCUSSION IN YOUR DRESSING ROOM? Why Arsenal are rubbish
MOST INTERESTING TEAMMATE? David Sales (not a teammate but a coach) – he has endless funny tales
BEST INNINGS YOU'VE SEEN? Alastair Cook's 244 not out at the MCG in the 2017/18 Ashes
CRICKET STAR OF THE FUTURE? Lloyd Willingham (Shenley Village CC)
WHICH BOOK MEANS MOST TO YOU? To Kill a Mockingbird by Harper Lee
IF YOU WERE AN ANIMAL, WHICH WOULD IT BE? A horse – very friendly, easy-going and a hard worker
TWITTER: @ThurstonCharlie

Batting	Mat	Inns	NO	Runs	HS	Ave	SR	100	50	Ct	St
First-class	8	10	0	236	126	23.60	59.14	1	0	2	0
List A	4	4	0	128	53	32.00	90.78	0	1	1	0
T20s	8	7	0	98	41	14.00	102.08	0	0	5	0
Bowling	**Mat**	**Balls**	**Runs**	**Wkts**	**BBI**	**BBM**	**Ave**	**Econ**	**SR**	**5w**	**10**
First-class	8	18	16	0	-	-	-	5.33	-	0	0
List A	4	-	-	-	-	-	-	-	-	-	-
T20s	8	-	-	-	-	-	-	-	-	-	-

JOSH TONGUE

RHB / RMF / R0 / W0

WORCESTERSHIRE

FULL NAME: Joshua Charles Tongue
BORN: November 15, 1997, Redditch, Worcestershire
SQUAD NO: 24
HEIGHT: 6ft 5in
NICKNAME: Tonguey
EDUCATION: King's School, Worcester; Christopher Whitehead Language College, Worcester
TEAMS: Worcestershire, England U19
ROLE: Bowler
DEBUT: First-class: 2016; List A: 2017; T20: 2017

BEST BATTING: 41 Worcestershire vs Glamorgan, Worcester, 2017
BEST BOWLING: 6-97 Worcestershire vs Glamorgan, Worcester, 2017

FAMILY TIES? My dad is a coach and my mum used to be manager for different age-groups in Worcester
WHAT WAS YOUR FIRST CRICKET CLUB? Redditch CC, Worcestershire. I started out by watching my dad play for the club
BIGGEST TOPIC OF DISCUSSION IN YOUR DRESSING ROOM? Dillon Pennington's university degree
CRICKETING HERO? Andrew Flintoff
CRICKET STAR OF THE FUTURE? Josh Dickenson (Worcestershire Academy)
IF YOU WERE AN ANIMAL, WHICH WOULD IT BE? A giraffe
TWITTER: @JoshTongue

Batting	Mat	Inns	NO	Runs	HS	Ave	SR	100	50	Ct	St
First-class	31	43	7	392	41	10.88	45.58	0	0	4	0
List A	13	7	3	76	34	19.00	95.00	0	0	2	0
T20s	5	2	2	3	2*	-	150.00	0	0	2	0
Bowling	**Mat**	**Balls**	**Runs**	**Wkts**	**BBI**	**BBM**	**Ave**	**Econ**	**SR**	**5w**	**10**
First-class	31	4805	2674	110	6/97	9/98	24.30	3.33	43.6	5	0
List A	13	529	600	14	2/35	2/35	42.85	6.80	37.7	0	0
T20s	5	84	122	3	2/32	2/32	40.66	8.71	28.0	0	0

REECE TOPLEY RHB / LFM / R0 / W0

FULL NAME: Reece James William Topley
BORN: February 21, 1994, Ipswich
SQUAD NO: 24
HEIGHT: 6ft 6in
NICKNAME: Toppers, Smash, Neil, Zlatan
EDUCATION: Royal Hospital School, Suffolk
TEAMS: England, Surrey, Oval Invincibles, Essex, Hampshire
ROLE: Bowler
DEBUT: ODI: 2015; T20I: 2015; First-class: 2011; List A: 2011; T20: 2012

BEST BATTING: 5* Essex vs Middlesex, Richmond, 2015 (T20)
BEST BOWLING: 4-26 Essex vs Sussex, Hove, 2013 (T20)
COUNTY CAP: 2013 (Essex)

FAMILY TIES? My father Don played for Essex and Surrey and also coached Zimbabwe. My uncle Peter played for Kent
BEST MOMENT IN CRICKET? Taking 4-50 for England in an ODI against South Africa in Port Elizabeth
CRICKETING HERO? Wasim Akram – best left-arm bowler ever
IF YOU WEREN'T A CRICKETER? I'd be an actor
SURPRISING FACT ABOUT YOU? I speak Spanish to a very good standard
TWITTER: @reece_topley
NOTES: Topley signed a two-year contract with Surrey to play white-ball cricket in October 2019

Batting	Mat	Inns	NO	Runs	HS	Ave	SR	100	50	Ct	St
ODIs	10	5	4	7	6	7.00	17.50	0	0	2	0
T20Is	6	1	1	1	1*	-	50.00	0	0	1	0
First-class	36	43	20	100	16	4.34	19.45	0	0	8	0
List A	55	17	11	54	19	9.00	47.78	0	0	13	0
T20s	74	15	10	22	5*	4.40	56.41	0	0	16	0
Bowling	**Mat**	**Balls**	**Runs**	**Wkts**	**BBI**	**BBM**	**Ave**	**Econ**	**SR**	**5w**	**10**
ODIs	10	463	410	16	4/50	4/50	25.62	5.31	28.9	0	0
T20Is	6	103	173	5	3/24	3/24	34.60	10.07	20.6	0	0
First-class	36	6101	3482	133	6/29	11/85	26.18	3.42	45.8	7	2
List A	55	2558	2366	93	4/16	4/16	25.44	5.54	27.5	0	0
T20s	74	1539	2132	101	4/26	4/26	21.10	8.31	15.2	0	0

PETER TREGO

RHB / RM / R1 / W1

NOTTINGHAMSHIRE

FULL NAME: Peter David Trego
BORN: June 12, 1981, Weston-super-Mare
SQUAD NO: 77
HEIGHT: 6ft
NICKNAME: Tregs, Pirate, Tony Dorigo
EDUCATION: Wyvern School, Weston-super-Mare
TEAMS: Nottinghamshire, Central Districts, England Lions, Kent, Mashonaland Eagles, Middlesex, Somerset, Sylhet Royals
ROLE: Allrounder
DEBUT: First-class: 2000; List A: 1999; T20: 2003

BEST BATTING: 154* Somerset vs Lancashire, Old Trafford, 2016
BEST BOWLING: 7-84 Somerset vs Yorkshire, Headingley, 2014
COUNTY CAP: 2007 (Somerset); BENEFIT: 2015 (Somerset)

WHAT WAS YOUR FIRST CRICKET CLUB? Two clubs: Weston-super-Mare CC and Uphill Castle CC. I played juniors in the morning for WSM and then walked over the road in the afternoon to play men's cricket for Uphill
WHAT WERE YOU DOING WHEN ENGLAND WON THE WORLD CUP? Jumping around the house with the family
HOW WOULD YOU DISMISS STEVE SMITH? With an away-swinging nip-backer that keeps a fraction low
WHAT EXCITES YOU ABOUT THE HUNDRED? Watching it on tv after playing another 50-over game!
BIGGEST TOPIC OF DISCUSSION IN YOUR DRESSING ROOM? I'm the new kid at Notts so don't know yet. But really hoping it's not Love Island or some other garbage!
MOST INTERESTING TEAMMATE? There are three: Ian Blackwell, James Hildreth and Steve Davies. Probably because they all laughed at my jokes
IF YOU WERE AN ANIMAL, WHICH WOULD IT BE? My French bulldog Hulk. He lives the dream
TWITTER: @tregs140

Batting	Mat	Inns	NO	Runs	HS	Ave	SR	100	50	Ct	St
First-class	218	324	38	9528	154*	33.31		15	54	89	0
List A	198	176	25	4962	147	32.86		10	26	55	0
T20s	201	186	22	3971	94*	24.21	125.70	0	21	54	0
Bowling	**Mat**	**Balls**	**Runs**	**Wkts**	**BBI**	**BBM**	**Ave**	**Econ**	**SR**	**5w**	**10**
First-class	218	24391	14017	383	7/84		36.59	3.44	63.6	5	1
List A	198	6007	5574	171	5/40	5/40	32.59	5.56	35.1	2	0
T20s	201	1728	2451	78	4/27	4/27	31.42	8.51	22.1	0	0

LIAM TREVASKIS

RHB / SLA / R0 / W0

FULL NAME: Liam Trevaskis
BORN: April 18, 1999, Carlisle, Cumberland
SQUAD NO: 80
HEIGHT: 5ft 10in
NICKNAME: T-rev, Trevor
EDUCATION: Queen Elizabeth Grammar School, Penrith, Cumbria
TEAMS: Durham
ROLE: Allrounder
DEBUT: First-class: 2017; List A: 2019; T20: 2017

BEST BATTING: 64 Durham vs Leicestershire, Leicester, 2019
BEST BOWLING: 2-96 Durham vs Leicestershire, Chester-le-Street, 2019

WHAT WAS YOUR FIRST CRICKET CLUB? Penrith CC, Cumbria
WHAT WERE YOU DOING WHEN ENGLAND WON THE WORLD CUP? Drinking a cold one
BIGGEST TOPIC OF DISCUSSION IN YOUR DRESSING ROOM? Golf
MOST INTERESTING TEAMMATE? Mark Wood – there is never a dull moment
CRICKETING HERO? Steve Waugh
WHICH RULE WOULD YOU CHANGE ABOUT CRICKET? You should get more than six runs for hitting it out the ground
CRICKET STAR OF THE FUTURE? Jonny Bushnell (Durham Academy)
WHICH BOOK MEANS MOST TO YOU? Fantastic Mr Fox by Roald Dahl
IF YOU WERE AN ANIMAL, WHICH WOULD IT BE? A brown bear – I'd be warm all the time and could go fishing a lot
TWITTER: @LiamTrevaskis

Batting	Mat	Inns	NO	Runs	HS	Ave	SR	100	50	Ct	St
First-class	11	19	1	406	64	22.55	36.15	0	2	2	0
List A	8	3	0	16	16	5.33	84.21	0	0	0	0
T20s	21	16	4	97	26	8.08	94.17	0	0	13	0
Bowling	**Mat**	**Balls**	**Runs**	**Wkts**	**BBI**	**BBM**	**Ave**	**Econ**	**SR**	**5w**	**10**
First-class	11	1053	536	7	2/96	3/116	76.57	3.05	150.4	0	0
List A	8	252	187	7	2/37	2/37	26.71	4.45	36.0	0	0
T20s	21	307	351	17	4/16	4/16	20.64	6.85	18.0	0	0

ASHTON TURNER RHB/OB

FULL NAME: Ashton James Turner
BORN: January 25, 1993, Perth, Australia
SQUAD NO: TBC
TEAMS: Australia, Worcestershire, Perth Scorchers, Rajasthan Royals, Western Australia
ROLE: Batsman
DEBUT: ODI: 2019; T20I: 2017; First-class: 2013; List A: 2013; T20: 2013

BEST BATTING: 73* Cricket Australia XI vs South Africans, Sydney, 2014 (T20)
BEST BOWLING: 2-3 Perth Scorchers vs Sydney Sixers, Sydney, 2014 (T20)

TWITTER: @Ashtonturner_70
NOTES: The hard-hitting batsman has joined Worcestershire for the duration of the T20 Blast, supplementing a group which won the title in 2018 and finished as runners-up last year. Turner featured alongside Ian Bell and Tim Bresnan to help Perth Scorchers win the Big Bash in 2016/17 and made his international debut in February 2017 in a T20I against Sri Lanka at the MCG. His most notable achievement so far for Australia was a blistering 84 not out from 43 balls to help his side chase down 359 in an ODI against India at Mohali last March, although it wasn't enough to earn him selection for the 2019 World Cup. Turner represented Rajasthan Royals in last year's IPL but was released ahead of the 2020 auction after struggling for form

Batting	Mat	Inns	NO	Runs	HS	Ave	SR	100	50	Ct	St
ODIs	6	5	1	142	84*	35.50	127.92	0	1	2	0
T20Is	11	7	3	57	22*	14.25	100.00	0	0	5	0
First-class	41	68	6	2119	110	34.17	53.24	3	10	42	0
List A	41	39	8	1019	84*	32.87	95.86	0	6	15	0
T20s	91	78	18	1252	73	20.86	133.33	0	7	32	0
Bowling	**Mat**	**Balls**	**Runs**	**Wkts**	**BBI**	**BBM**	**Ave**	**Econ**	**SR**	**5w**	**10**
ODIs	6	-	-	-	-	-	-	-	-	-	-
T20Is	11	36	42	3	2/12	2/12	14.00	7.00	12.0	0	0
First-class	41	924	507	11	6/111	6/160	46.09	3.29	84.0	1	0
List A	41	354	343	6	2/26	2/26	57.16	5.81	59.0	0	0
T20s	91	246	285	17	2/3	2/3	16.76	6.95	14.4	0	0

BEN TWOHIG RHB / SLA / R0 / W0

FULL NAME: Benjamin Jake Twohig
BORN: April 13, 1998, Dewsbury, Yorkshire
SQUAD NO: 42
HEIGHT: 5ft 8in
NICKNAME: Twiggy, The Owl, Twiglet
EDUCATION: Malvern College
TEAMS: Worcestershire, England U19
ROLE: Bowler
DEBUT: First-class: 2018; List A: 2018

BEST BATTING: 35 Worcestershire vs Nottinghamshire, Trent Bridge, 2018
BEST BOWLING: 2-47 Worcestershire vs Yorkshire, Worcester, 2018

WHAT WAS YOUR FIRST CRICKET CLUB? Birstall CC, West Yorkshire. Best cuppa in the north
BEST ADVICE EVER RECEIVED? Fours and sixes, and don't get out
BIGGEST TOPIC OF DISCUSSION IN YOUR DRESSING ROOM? Brexit
CRICKETING HERO? Daniel Vettori – someone I look up to as a fellow slow left-armer
SURPRISING FACT ABOUT YOU? I played Dorothy in a school production of The Wizard of Oz
CRICKET STAR OF THE FUTURE? Josh Dickenson (Worcestershire Academy)
WHICH BOOK MEANS MOST TO YOU? 1984 by George Orwell
IF YOU WERE AN ANIMAL, WHICH WOULD IT BE? An elephant – because they're very loyal
TWITTER: @Ben_Twohig

Batting	Mat	Inns	NO	Runs	HS	Ave	SR	100	50	Ct	St
First-class	7	13	2	145	35	13.18	36.89	0	0	3	0
List A	1	1	0	1	1	1.00	50.00	0	0	1	0
Bowling	**Mat**	**Balls**	**Runs**	**Wkts**	**BBI**	**BBM**	**Ave**	**Econ**	**SR**	**5w**	**10**
First-class	7	966	598	10	2/47	3/84	59.80	3.71	96.6	0	0
List A	1	60	55	0	-	-	-	5.50	-	0	0

MUJEEB UR RAHMAN RHB / OB / R0 / W0

FULL NAME: Mujeeb Ur Rahman
BORN: March 28, 2001, Khost, Afghanistan
SQUAD NO: 88
TEAMS: Afghanistan, Middlesex, Northern Superchargers, Boost Defenders, Brisbane Heat, Comilla Victorians, Hampshire, Kings XI Punjab, Nangarhar Leopards
ROLE: Bowler
DEBUT: Test: 2018; ODI: 2017; T20I: 2018; First-class: 2018; List A: 2017; T20: 2017

BEST BATTING: 27 Brisbane Heat vs Adelaide Strikers, Brisbane, 2018 (T20)
BEST BOWLING: 4-12 Comilla Victorians vs Sylhet Thunder, Sylhet, 2020 (T20)

TWITTER: @MujeebR99
NOTES: The Afghan teenager returns for his second T20 Blast campaign with Middlesex after taking seven wickets in 2019 at the miserly economy rate of 7.23 runs per over. Mujeeb previously played for Hampshire in 2018 and has also impressed in the IPL and Big Bash League for Kings XI Punjab and Brisbane Heat respectively. An off-spinner with a leg-break and googly in his locker, he burst onto the scene at the 2018 U19 World Cup and has since been a regular at senior level. In February 2018 he became the youngest player to take an ODI five-wicket haul and later that year played in Afghanistan's inaugural Test match – to date his only first-class appearance. Mujeeb will also feature as an overseas player for Northern Superchargers in The Hundred

Batting	Mat	Inns	NO	Runs	HS	Ave	SR	100	50	Ct	St
Tests	1	2	0	18	15	9.00	105.88	0	0	0	0
ODIs	40	21	10	69	15	6.27	87.34	0	0	6	0
T20Is	19	3	3	8	8*	-	100.00	0	0	4	0
First-class	1	2	0	18	15	9.00	105.88	0	0	0	0
List A	47	23	12	73	15	6.63	90.12	0	0	7	0
T20s	111	31	19	116	27	9.66	95.08	0	0	18	0
Bowling	**Mat**	**Balls**	**Runs**	**Wkts**	**BBI**	**BBM**	**Ave**	**Econ**	**SR**	**5w**	**10**
Tests	1	90	75	1	1/75	1/75	75.00	5.00	90.0	0	0
ODIs	40	2153	1414	63	5/50	5/50	22.44	3.94	34.1	1	0
T20Is	19	432	443	25	4/15	4/15	17.72	6.15	17.2	0	0
First-class	1	90	75	1	1/75	1/75	75.00	5.00	90.0	0	0
List A	47	2537	1661	71	5/50	5/50	23.39	3.92	35.7	1	0
T20s	111	2520	2828	115	4/12	4/12	24.59	6.73	21.9	0	0

GRAEME VAN BUUREN RHB / SLA / RO / WO

FULL NAME: Graeme Lourens van Buuren
BORN: August 22, 1990, Pretoria, South Africa
SQUAD NO: 12
HEIGHT: 5ft 7in
NICKNAME: GVB, Buggers
EDUCATION: Pretoria Boys High School, South Africa
TEAMS: Gloucestershire, Northerns, Titans, South Africa U19
ROLE: Allrounder
DEBUT: First-class: 2010; List A: 2010; T20: 2011

BEST BATTING: 235 Northerns vs Eastern Province, Centurion, 2015
BEST BOWLING: 4-12 Northerns vs South Western Districts, Oudtshoorn, 2013
COUNTY CAP: 2016

WHAT WAS YOUR FIRST CRICKET CLUB? Tuks CC, University of Pretoria, South Africa. It's both a public club and university team
BEST ADVICE EVER RECEIVED? Work hard in silence and let the success make the noise
MOST INTERESTING TEAMMATE? Ryan Higgins – because his energy and hunger is infectious
CRICKETING HERO? AB de Villiers
WHICH RULE WOULD YOU CHANGE ABOUT CRICKET? Make the tea break longer
CRICKET STAR OF THE FUTURE? Tom Price (Gloucestershire)
WHICH BOOK MEANS MOST TO YOU? The Bible
IF YOU WERE AN ANIMAL, WHICH WOULD IT BE? A honey badger – fearless
TWITTER: @GraemeGVB

Batting	Mat	Inns	NO	Runs	HS	Ave	SR	100	50	Ct	St
First-class	85	132	21	4711	235	42.44	62.32	10	28	46	0
List A	70	62	12	1454	119*	29.08	81.09	1	7	18	0
T20s	56	41	13	619	64	22.10	113.57	0	3	28	0
Bowling	**Mat**	**Balls**	**Runs**	**Wkts**	**BBI**	**BBM**	**Ave**	**Econ**	**SR**	**5w**	**10**
First-class	85	5885	2812	87	4/12	6/87	32.32	2.86	67.6	0	0
List A	70	2208	1754	52	5/35	5/35	33.73	4.76	42.4	1	0
T20s	56	763	875	33	5/8	5/8	26.51	6.88	23.1	1	0

TIMM VAN DER GUGTEN — RHB / RFM / R0 / W1

FULL NAME: Timm van der Gugten
BORN: February 25, 1991, Sydney, Australia
SQUAD NO: 64
HEIGHT: 6ft 2in
NICKNAME: Vander, Sock
EDUCATION: St Pius X College, Sydney; Swinburn University
TEAMS: Netherlands, Glamorgan, Hobart Hurricanes, New South Wales, Northern Districts, Tasmania
ROLE: Bowler
DEBUT: ODI: 2012; T20I: 2012; First-class: 2011; List A: 2011; T20: 2012

BEST BATTING: 60* Glamorgan vs Gloucestershire, Cardiff, 2018
BEST BOWLING: 7-42 Glamorgan vs Kent, Cardiff, 2018
COUNTY CAP: 2018

WHAT WAS YOUR FIRST CRICKET CLUB? University of New South Wales CC, Australia. Same club where Geoff Lawson played
WHAT EXCITES YOU ABOUT THE HUNDRED? Speaking as a bowler, there are fewer balls that could get hit for six
BIGGEST TOPIC OF DISCUSSION IN YOUR DRESSING ROOM? Veganism
BEST INNINGS YOU'VE SEEN? Watching records tumble as Netherlands chased down 193 in 13.5 overs against Ireland in the 2014 World T20
CRICKETING HERO? Brett Lee
WHICH RULE WOULD YOU CHANGE ABOUT CRICKET? I would love an hour for lunch and half an hour for tea
WHICH BOOK MEANS MOST TO YOU? My passport
IF YOU WERE AN ANIMAL, WHICH WOULD IT BE? One of the Queen's 'dorgis' (corgi-dachshund cross)

Batting	Mat	Inns	NO	Runs	HS	Ave	SR	100	50	Ct	St
ODIs	4	2	0	4	2	2.00	66.66	0	0	0	0
T20Is	39	11	4	109	40*	15.57	134.56	0	0	9	0
First-class	43	62	18	652	60*	14.81	50.34	0	3	8	0
List A	58	33	12	350	36	16.66	92.10	0	0	8	0
T20s	88	31	11	218	40*	10.90	123.86	0	0	22	0
Bowling	**Mat**	**Balls**	**Runs**	**Wkts**	**BBI**	**BBM**	**Ave**	**Econ**	**SR**	**5w**	**10**
ODIs	4	126	85	8	5/24	5/24	10.62	4.04	15.7	1	0
T20Is	39	713	847	40	3/9	3/9	21.17	7.12	17.8	0	0
First-class	43	7525	4104	153	7/42	10/121	26.82	3.27	49.1	10	1
List A	58	2566	2381	68	5/24	5/24	35.01	5.56	37.7	1	0
T20s	88	1595	2081	100	5/21	5/21	20.81	7.82	15.9	1	0

ROELOF VAN DER MERWE RHB / SLA / R0 / W0 / MVP72

FULL NAME: Roelof Erasmus van der Merwe
BORN: December 31, 1984, Johannesburg, SA
SQUAD NO: 52
HEIGHT: 5ft 8in
NICKNAME: Bulldog
EDUCATION: Pretoria High School; University of Hertfordshire
TEAMS: Netherlands, South Africa, Somerset, London Spirit, Brisbane Heat, Delhi Daredevils, Northerns, RC Bangalore, Titans
ROLE: Allrounder
DEBUT: ODIs: 2009; T20I: 2009; First-class: 2006; List A: 2006; T20: 2008

BEST BATTING: 205* Titans vs Warriors, Benoni, 2014
BEST BOWLING: 4-22 Somerset vs Middlesex, Taunton, 2017
COUNTY CAP: 2018

WHAT WAS YOUR FIRST CRICKET CLUB? Pretoria CC, South Africa. Worst pitch in the league
WHAT EXCITES YOU ABOUT THE HUNDRED? The 10-ball overs
MOST INTERESTING TEAMMATE? Eddie Byrom – he thinks the world is flat
CRICKETING HERO? Jonty Rhodes
SURPRISING FACT ABOUT YOU? I hate vegetables
BIGGEST CRICKETING REGRET? Dropping Kumar Sangakkara when he was on 20 at The Oval in 2017. Let's just say he made us field for a long time
CRICKET STAR OF THE FUTURE? Lewis Goldsworthy (Somerset)
TWITTER: @Roela52

Batting	Mat	Inns	NO	Runs	HS	Ave	SR	100	50	Ct	St
ODIs	15	8	3	96	57	19.20	101.05	0	1	4	0
T20Is	43	29	12	454	75*	26.70	131.59	0	2	19	0
First-class	67	108	15	3185	205*	34.24	70.34	6	19	53	0
List A	187	152	44	2901	165*	26.86	98.94	1	11	79	0
T20s	232	167	55	2443	89*	21.81	130.36	0	10	95	0
Bowling	**Mat**	**Balls**	**Runs**	**Wkts**	**BBI**	**BBM**	**Ave**	**Econ**	**SR**	**5w**	**10**
ODIs	15	789	658	18	3/27	3/27	36.55	5.00	43.8	0	0
T20Is	43	895	938	54	4/35	4/35	17.37	6.28	16.5	0	0
First-class	67	9139	4519	133	4/22	8/104	33.97	2.96	68.7	0	0
List A	187	8191	6654	249	5/26	5/26	26.72	4.87	32.8	4	0
T20s	232	4568	5410	223	5/32	5/32	24.26	7.10	20.4	1	0

STIAAN VAN ZYL

LHB / RM / R1 / W0

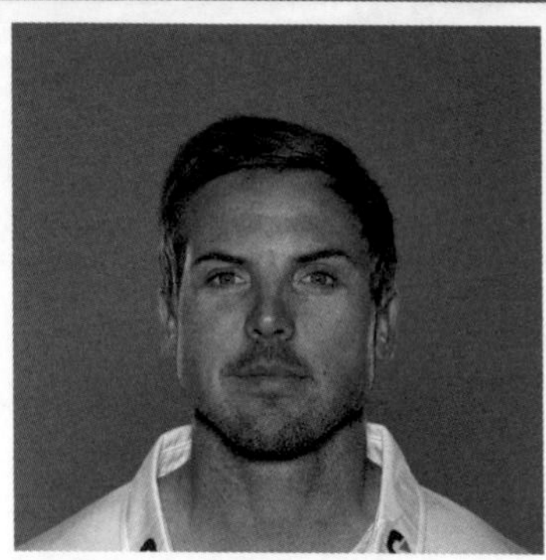

FULL NAME: Stiaan van Zyl
BORN: September 19, 1987, Cape Town, South Africa
SQUAD NO: 74
NICKNAME: Stigo
EDUCATION: Kenridge Primary School, Western Cape; Boland Agricultural School, Paarl
TEAMS: South Africa, Sussex, Boland, Cape Cobras, Chittagong Vikings, Comilla Warriors, Western Province
ROLE: Allrounder
DEBUT: Test: 2014; First-class: 2006; List A: 2006; T20: 2008

BEST BATTING: 228 Cape Cobras vs Lions, Paarl, 2018
BEST BOWLING: 5-32 Boland vs Northerns, Paarl, 2011

WHAT WAS YOUR FIRST CRICKET CLUB? Wellington CC, Western Cape, South Africa
BEST ADVICE EVER RECEIVED? Play with a smile on your face
BIGGEST TOPIC OF DISCUSSION IN YOUR DRESSING ROOM? Anything but cricket!
MOST INTERESTING TEAMMATE? Phil Salt
CRICKETING HERO? Kumar Sangakkara – a legend and a leftie
IF YOU WERE AN ANIMAL, WHICH WOULD IT BE? An eagle – because I could fly wherever I want to go
TWITTER: @laggies74

Batting	Mat	Inns	NO	Runs	HS	Ave	SR	100	50	Ct	St
Tests	12	17	2	395	101*	26.33	50.77	1	0	6	0
First-class	175	293	42	11132	228	44.35	52.18	27	50	99	0
List A	120	110	12	3400	114*	34.69	74.39	5	18	34	0
T20s	73	66	7	1509	86*	25.57	118.63	0	9	21	0
Bowling	**Mat**	**Balls**	**Runs**	**Wkts**	**BBI**	**BBM**	**Ave**	**Econ**	**SR**	**5w**	**10**
Tests	12	403	148	6	3/20	3/22	24.66	2.20	67.1	0	0
First-class	175	5564	2535	68	5/32	7/82	37.27	2.73	81.8	1	0
List A	120	1056	927	20	4/24	4/24	46.35	5.26	52.8	0	0
T20s	73	132	191	7	2/14	2/14	27.28	8.68	18.8	0	0

RICARDO VASCONCELOS LHB / WK / R0 / W0

FULL NAME: Ricardo Surrador Vasconcelos
BORN: October 27, 1997, Johannesburg, South Africa
SQUAD NO: 27
HEIGHT: 5ft 5in
NICKNAME: Vasco, Dave
EDUCATION: St Stithians College, Johannesburg; Stellenbosch University, Western Cape
TEAMS: Northamptonshire, Boland, South Africa U19
ROLE: Batsman/wicketkeeper
DEBUT: First-class: 2016; List A: 2016; T20: 2017

BEST BATTING: 184 Northamptonshire vs Glamorgan, Cardiff, 2019

WHAT WAS YOUR FIRST CRICKET CLUB? Old Edwardians CC, Johannesburg, South Africa. Graeme Smith, Quinton de Kock, Stephen Cook and Neil McKenzie all played there
WHAT WERE YOU DOING WHEN ENGLAND WON THE WORLD CUP? Icing my ankle
HOW WOULD YOU DISMISS STEVE SMITH? Run him out
BEST INNINGS YOU'VE SEEN? Herschelle Gibbs in the 438 game between South Africa and Australia at Johannesburg in 2006
BIGGEST TOPIC OF DISCUSSION IN YOUR DRESSING ROOM? Football
MOST INTERESTING TEAMMATE? Luke Procter – he tries to send me back to South Africa
WHICH RULE WOULD YOU CHANGE ABOUT CRICKET? Batsmen shouldn't have to field
WHICH BOOK MEANS MOST TO YOU? Any of the Harry Potter books
TWITTER: @RicardoVasco27

Batting	Mat	Inns	NO	Runs	HS	Ave	SR	100	50	Ct	St
First-class	33	61	5	2057	184	36.73	55.74	5	11	44	4
List A	26	25	1	713	112	29.70	80.20	1	4	19	2
T20s	10	9	3	126	45*	21.00	122.33	0	0	6	0
Bowling	**Mat**	**Balls**	**Runs**	**Wkts**	**BBI**	**BBM**	**Ave**	**Econ**	**SR**	**5w**	**10**
First-class	33	9	9	0	-	-	-	6.00	-	0	0
List A	26	-	-	-	-	-	-	-	-	-	-
T20s	10	-	-	-	-	-	-	-	-	-	-

DANE VILAS RHB / WK / R1 / W0 / MVP9

FULL NAME: Dane James Vilas
BORN: June 10, 1985, Johannesburg, SA
SQUAD NO: 33
HEIGHT: 6ft
NICKNAME: Vili
EDUCATION: King Edward VII School, Johannesburg
TEAMS: South Africa, Lancashire, Manchester Originals, Dolphins, Gauteng, Lahore Qalandars, Lions, Western Province
ROLE: Batsman/wicketkeeper
DEBUT: Test: 2015; T20I: 2012; First-class: 2006; List A: 2006; T20: 2009

BEST BATTING: 266 Lancashire vs Glamorgan, Colwyn Bay, 2019

COUNTY CAP: 2018

TWITTER: @DaneVilas
NOTES: The former Test wicketkeeper was another South African to announce his international retirement in early 2017 and take up a two-year Kolpak deal with Lancashire to play across all formats. The highlights of his first season at Old Trafford were a career-best 244 against Hampshire in the Championship and a brace of hundreds in the One-Day Cup. After taking over the Lancashire captaincy from Liam Livingstone at the end of the 2018 season, Vilas was at his scintillating best last summer, passing 1,000 runs in the Championship and 400 in the One-Day Cup

Batting	Mat	Inns	NO	Runs	HS	Ave	SR	100	50	Ct	St
Tests	6	9	0	94	26	10.44	44.76	0	0	13	0
T20Is	1	-	-	-	-	-	-	-	-	0	0
First-class	156	239	29	8872	266	42.24	66.44	21	41	429	20
List A	172	157	25	4888	166	37.03	98.80	9	24	172	30
T20s	155	126	28	2868	75*	29.26	127.52	0	12	84	28
Bowling	**Mat**	**Balls**	**Runs**	**Wkts**	**BBI**	**BBM**	**Ave**	**Econ**	**SR**	**5w**	**10**
Tests	6	-	-	-	-	-	-	-	-	-	-
T20Is	1	-	-	-	-	-	-	-	-	-	-
First-class	156	6	3	0	-	-	-	3.00	-	0	0
List A	172	-	-	-	-	-	-	-	-	-	-
T20s	155	-	-	-	-	-	-	-	-	-	-

HARDUS VILJOEN RHB / RF

FULL NAME: GC Viljoen
BORN: March 6, 1989, Witbank, South Africa
SQUAD NO: TBC
HEIGHT: 6ft 2in
EDUCATION: Waterkloof High School, Pretoria, South Africa
TEAMS: South Africa, Oval Invincibles, Chittagong Vikings, Derbyshire, Easterns, Kent, Kings XI Punjab, Lions, Multan Sultans, Paarl Rocks, St Lucia Zouks, Titans
ROLE: Bowler
DEBUT: Test: 2016; First-class: 2008; List A: 2009; T20: 2011

BEST BATTING: 41* Lions vs Titans, Johannesburg, 2016 (T20)
BEST BOWLING: 5-16 Easterns vs Nambia, Benoni, 2012 (T20)

BEST ADVICE EVER RECEIVED? Do what got you to where you are – don't change to please people
BEST MOMENT IN CRICKET? Taking 15 wickets in a Championship match for Derbyshire at Hove in 2017
IF YOU WEREN'T A CRICKETER? I'd be a lawyer. Or a Navy Seal
SURPRISING FACT ABOUT YOU? I love big, fast cars
CRICKETING HERO? I look up to Andrew Flintoff and Malcolm Marshall – I have a similar action to both of them. They never backed down
NON-CRICKETING HERO? Tiger Woods – as a non-white golfer, he faced some considerable challenges early in his career and went on to dominate the game for so long
TWITTER: @Hardus_Vijl

Batting	Mat	Inns	NO	Runs	HS	Ave	SR	100	50	Ct	St
Tests	1	2	1	26	20*	26.00	83.87	0	0	0	0
First-class	115	162	19	2257	132	15.78	60.72	1	7	33	0
List A	95	59	20	629	54*	16.12	83.53	0	3	24	0
T20s	125	71	30	590	41*	14.39	122.40	0	0	23	0
Bowling	**Mat**	**Balls**	**Runs**	**Wkts**	**BBI**	**BBM**	**Ave**	**Econ**	**SR**	**5w**	**10**
Tests	1	114	94	1	1/79	1/94	94.00	4.94	114.0	0	0
First-class	115	20199	12007	445	8/90	15/170	26.98	3.56	45.3	25	5
List A	95	4298	4241	131	6/19	6/19	32.37	5.92	32.8	1	0
T20s	125	2649	3579	140	5/16	5/16	25.56	8.10	18.9	1	0

JAMES VINCE RHB / RM / R2 / W0 / MVP30

FULL NAME: James Michael Vince
BORN: March 14, 1991, Cuckfield, Sussex
SQUAD NO: 14
HEIGHT: 6ft 2in
NICKNAME: JV, Vincey
EDUCATION: Warminster School, Wiltshire
TEAMS: England, Hampshire, Southern Brave, Auckland, Karachi Kings, Multan Sultans, Sydney Sixers, Sydney Thunder
ROLE: Batsman
DEBUT: Test: 2016; ODI: 2015; T20I: 2015; First-class: 2009; List A: 2009; T20: 2010

BEST BATTING: 240 Hampshire vs Essex, Southampton, 2014
BEST BOWLING: 5-41 Hampshire vs Loughborough MCCU, Southampton, 2013
COUNTY CAP: 2013

WHAT WAS YOUR FIRST CRICKET CLUB? Erlestoke CC, Wiltshire. A very small village club
WHAT WERE YOU DOING WHEN ENGLAND WON THE WORLD CUP? I was at long-off
HOW WOULD YOU DISMISS STEVE SMITH? Away, away, away, away, bumper, yorker
BIGGEST TOPIC OF DISCUSSION IN YOUR DRESSING ROOM? How to play Tom Westley's doosra
CRICKETING HERO? Andrew Flintoff
WHICH RULE WOULD YOU CHANGE ABOUT CRICKET? Instead of the coin toss, have a catching competition between two nominated players from each team
TWITTER: @vincey14

Batting	Mat	Inns	NO	Runs	HS	Ave	SR	100	50	Ct	St
Tests	13	22	0	548	83	24.90	49.81	0	3	8	0
ODIs	13	11	0	265	51	24.09	88.62	0	1	4	0
T20Is	12	12	0	340	59	28.33	123.63	0	1	5	0
First-class	162	269	20	9692	240	38.92	62.19	25	36	137	0
List A	136	127	7	4848	190	40.40	98.05	9	23	51	0
T20s	219	212	22	5740	107*	30.21	133.58	1	36	112	0
Bowling	**Mat**	**Balls**	**Runs**	**Wkts**	**BBI**	**BBM**	**Ave**	**Econ**	**SR**	**5w**	**10**
Tests	13	24	13	0	-	-	-	3.25	-	0	0
ODIs	13	-	-	-	-	-	-	-	-	-	-
T20Is	12	-	-	-	-	-	-	-	-	-	-
First-class	162	1669	1031	22	5/41	6/56	46.86	3.70	75.8	1	0
List A	136	132	124	2	1/18	1/18	62.00	5.63	66.0	0	0
T20s	219	72	81	3	1/5	1/5	27.00	6.75	24.0	0	0

AMAR VIRDI

RHB / OB / R0 / W0

FULL NAME: Guramar Singh Virdi
BORN: July 19, 1998, Chiswick, Middlesex
SQUAD NO: 19
HEIGHT: 5ft 10in
NICKNAME: Virds
EDUCATION: Guru Nanak Sikh Academy, Hayes, London
TEAMS: Surrey, England Lions
ROLE: Bowler
DEBUT: First-class: 2017

BEST BATTING: 21* Surrey vs Somerset, Taunton, 2018
BEST BOWLING: 8-61 Surrey vs Nottinghamshire, Trent Bridge, 2019

WHAT WAS YOUR FIRST CRICKET CLUB? Indian Gymkhana CC, London. It's the oldest South Asian cricket club in the UK
BEST ADVICE EVER RECEIVED? Treat everyone the way you wish to be treated
HOW WOULD YOU DISMISS STEVE SMITH? Through the gate
MOST INTERESTING TEAMMATE? Ryan Patel – he has the strangest twitches
CRICKETING HERO? Saqlain Mushtaq
WHICH RULE WOULD YOU CHANGE ABOUT CRICKET? Make boundaries longer
BIGGEST CRICKETING REGRET? Dropping a catch in a club cricket final
CRICKET STAR OF THE FUTURE? Nico Reifer (Surrey)
WHICH BOOK MEANS MOST TO YOU? The Alchemist by Paulo Coelho
IF YOU WERE AN ANIMAL, WHICH WOULD IT BE? A lion – because that's what Sikhs are!
TWITTER: @amarsinghvirdi

Batting	Mat	Inns	NO	Runs	HS	Ave	SR	100	50	Ct	St
First-class	23	27	14	125	21*	9.61	57.87	0	0	5	0
Bowling	**Mat**	**Balls**	**Runs**	**Wkts**	**BBI**	**BBM**	**Ave**	**Econ**	**SR**	**5w**	**10**
First-class	23	3669	1986	69	8/61	14/139	28.78	3.24	53.1	3	1

GRAHAM WAGG RHB / LM / R0 / W2

FULL NAME: Graham Grant Wagg
BORN: April 28, 1983, Rugby, Warwickshire
SQUAD NO: 8
HEIGHT: 6ft
NICKNAME: Waggy
EDUCATION: Ashlawn School, Rugby
TEAMS: Glamorgan, Derbyshire, England U19, Warwickshire
ROLE: Allrounder
DEBUT: First-class: 2002; List A: 2000; T20: 2003

BEST BATTING: 200 Glamorgan vs Surrey, Guildford, 2015
BEST BOWLING: 6-29 Glamorgan vs Surrey, The Oval, 2014
COUNTY CAP: 2007 (Derbyshire); 2013 (Glamorgan); BENEFIT: 2019 (Glamorgan)

FAMILY TIES? My dad played Second XI cricket and Minor Counties – he could bowl a heavy ball and hit a long one. Watch out for my little man Brayden Wagg
WHAT WAS YOUR FIRST CRICKET CLUB? GEC CC, Rugby, Warwickshire
CRICKETING HERO? Allan Donald
WHICH BOWLER WOULD YOU LEAST LIKE TO FACE? Mitchell Johnson. Talking to guys who have faced him, they say he was very quick and could hit you at will. Not for me, thank you. I'll stick to facing Stevo on a flat one
WHICH RULE WOULD YOU CHANGE ABOUT CRICKET? Bowlers can decide to bowl with either arm without telling the umpire. After all, batsmen are allowed to switch hands without saying anything
TWITTER: @GGWagg

Batting	Mat	Inns	NO	Runs	HS	Ave	SR	100	50	Ct	St
First-class	161	240	25	5804	200	26.99	64.44	5	32	51	0
List A	140	116	15	2060	68	20.39		0	5	45	0
T20s	138	103	32	1329	62	18.71	124.67	0	4	35	0
Bowling	**Mat**	**Balls**	**Runs**	**Wkts**	**BBI**	**BBM**	**Ave**	**Econ**	**SR**	**5w**	**10**
First-class	161	27156	15764	454	6/29		34.72	3.48	59.8	12	1
List A	140	5453	5381	156	4/35	4/35	34.49	5.92	34.9	0	0
T20s	138	2319	3211	126	5/14	5/14	25.48	8.30	18.4	1	0

MATTHEW WAITE RHB / RFM / R0 / W0

FULL NAME: Matthew James Waite
BORN: December 24, 1995, Leeds
SQUAD NO: 6
NICKNAME: Pingu
EDUCATION: Brigshaw High School, West Yorkshire
TEAMS: Yorkshire
ROLE: Allrounder
DEBUT: First-class: 2017; List A: 2014; T20: 2015

BEST BATTING: 42 Yorkshire vs Nottinghamshire, Trent Bridge, 2018
BEST BOWLING: 5-16 Yorkshire vs Leeds/Bradford MCCU, Weetwood, 2019

TWITTER: @mat_waite
NOTES: A seam-bowling allrounder, Waite signed a two-year junior professional contract with Yorkshire at the end of 2015. He made his senior debut in the One-Day Cup in 2014 and played his first T20 Blast game the following year. In 2016 he made two appearances for Yorkshire in white-ball cricket, doing well on both occasions. First he hit 19 not out and took 1-6 from two overs in the T20 quarter-final against Glamorgan at Cardiff, and then he made 38 and took 3-48 from 10 overs in the One-Day Cup semi-final against Surrey at Headingley. Waite made his Championship debut against Somerset at Taunton in 2017 but his brief career has been hampered by a recurring ankle injury. He impressed in 2018 with eight wickets at an average of 27.62 in a handful of four-day matches and made his List A debut last summer

Batting	Mat	Inns	NO	Runs	HS	Ave	SR	100	50	Ct	St
First-class	8	11	1	160	42	16.00	52.45	0	0	1	0
List A	13	11	3	278	71	34.75	90.55	0	1	0	0
T20s	5	3	3	34	19*	-	147.82	0	0	3	0
Bowling	**Mat**	**Balls**	**Runs**	**Wkts**	**BBI**	**BBM**	**Ave**	**Econ**	**SR**	**5w**	**10**
First-class	8	966	583	23	5/16	6/57	25.34	3.62	42.0	1	0
List A	13	486	522	16	4/65	4/65	32.62	6.44	30.3	0	0
T20s	5	48	67	2	1/6	1/6	33.50	8.37	24.0	0	0

ALEX WAKELY RHB / RM / R0 / W0

FULL NAME: Alex George Wakely
BORN: November 3, 1988, London
SQUAD NO: 8
HEIGHT: 6ft 2in
NICKNAME: Wakers, Baby Seal
EDUCATION: Bedford School
TEAMS: Northamptonshire, England U19
ROLE: Batsman
DEBUT: First-class: 2007; List A: 2005; T20: 2009

BEST BATTING: 123 Northamptonshire vs Leicestershire, Northampton, 2015
BEST BOWLING: 2-62 Northamptonshire vs Somerset, Taunton, 2007
COUNTY CAP: 2012

WHAT WAS YOUR FIRST CRICKET CLUB? Ampthill Town CC, Bedfordshire
WHAT WERE YOU DOING WHEN ENGLAND WON THE WORLD CUP? I was at Lord's
HOW WOULD YOU DISMISS STEVE SMITH? Bribery
WHAT EXCITES YOU ABOUT THE HUNDRED? It's a great chance for players to raise their profiles
BIGGEST TOPIC OF DISCUSSION IN YOUR DRESSING ROOM? Horses, football, cash
MOST INTERESTING TEAMMATE? Ian Harvey. He's also my favourite human being
CRICKETING HERO? David Sales – he was captain when I made my debut and took me under his wing. Best batsman I have watched
SURPRISING FACT ABOUT YOU? I play the piano
CRICKET STAR OF THE FUTURE? Emilio Gay (Northamptonshire)
IF YOU WERE AN ANIMAL, WHICH WOULD IT BE? Panther – stealthy
TWITTER: @AlexWakely1

Batting	Mat	Inns	NO	Runs	HS	Ave	SR	100	50	Ct	St
First-class	146	233	16	6865	123	31.63	48.11	9	37	96	0
List A	90	85	8	2532	109*	32.88	86.06	2	18	32	0
T20s	125	117	24	2506	64	26.94	119.39	0	14	41	0
Bowling	**Mat**	**Balls**	**Runs**	**Wkts**	**BBI**	**BBM**	**Ave**	**Econ**	**SR**	**5w**	**10**
First-class	146	509	426	6	2/62	2/62	71.00	5.02	84.8	0	0
List A	90	136	131	5	2/14	2/14	26.20	5.77	27.2	0	0
T20s	125	12	29	0	-	-	-	14.50	-	0	0

ROMAN WALKER RHB / RFM / R0 / W0

FULL NAME: Roman Isaac Walker
BORN: August 6, 2000, Wrexham, Clwyd
SQUAD NO: 37
HEIGHT: 6ft 3in
NICKNAME: Stroller
EDUCATION: Ysgol Bryn Alyn, Wrexham
TEAMS: Glamorgan, England U19
ROLE: Bowler
DEBUT: List A: 2019; T20: 2019

WHAT WAS YOUR FIRST CRICKET CLUB? Bersham CC, Wrexham
WHAT WERE YOU DOING WHEN ENGLAND WON THE WORLD CUP? Jumping on my bed screaming!
WHAT EXCITES YOU ABOUT THE HUNDRED? Watching and potentially learning from the world's best players
BIGGEST TOPIC OF DISCUSSION IN YOUR DRESSING ROOM? Golf
MOST INTERESTING TEAMMATE? Jacques Rudolph – for his sheer wisdom
IF YOU WERE AN ANIMAL, WHICH WOULD IT BE? An eagle – no traffic when travelling
TWITTER: @RomanWalker17
NOTES: The tall seamer signed a two-year contract with Glamorgan last December following a breakthrough season with the Welsh county which included hitting the match-sealing six on his first-team debut, against Sussex at Hove in the One-Day Cup. Director of cricket Mark Wallace, said: "We've seen what Roman can do in the Royal London One-Day Cup and Vitality Blast, where he showed a cool head under pressure in some difficult situations. He's got an impressive skillset and if he keeps developing as he is he will enjoy a successful career in the game"

Batting	Mat	Inns	NO	Runs	HS	Ave	SR	100	50	Ct	St
List A	1	1	1	7	7*	-	233.33	0	0	0	0
T20s	3	1	0	1	1	1.00	33.33	0	0	0	0
Bowling	**Mat**	**Balls**	**Runs**	**Wkts**	**BBI**	**BBM**	**Ave**	**Econ**	**SR**	**5w**	**10**
List A	1	24	21	0	-	-	-	5.25	-	0	0
T20s	3	71	119	5	3/39	3/39	23.80	10.05	14.2	0	0

MAX WALLER RHB / LB / RO / WO

FULL NAME: Maximilian Thomas Charles Waller
BORN: March 3, 1988, Salisbury, Wiltshire
SQUAD NO: 10
HEIGHT: 6ft
NICKNAME: Goose, Maxy
EDUCATION: Millfield School, Somerset; Bournemouth University
TEAMS: Somerset, Southern Brave
ROLE: Bowler
DEBUT: First-class: 2009; List A: 2009; T20: 2009

BEST BATTING: 17 Somerset vs Gloucestershire, Bristol, 2017 (T20)
BEST BOWLING: 4-16 Somerset vs Warwickshire, Taunton, 2012 (T20)

WHAT WAS YOUR FIRST CRICKET CLUB? Bashley Rydal CC, Hampshire – great village club based in the New Forest
HOW WOULD YOU DISMISS STEVE SMITH? With a couple of beers and some persuasion
BIGGEST TOPIC OF DISCUSSION IN YOUR DRESSING ROOM? Where's Carl?
MOST INTERESTING TEAMMATE? Peter Trego – non-stop 'trying' to be funny
CRICKETING HERO? Shane Warne
WHICH RULE WOULD YOU CHANGE ABOUT CRICKET? Make the boundaries bigger in Twenty20
SURPRISING FACT ABOUT YOU? I've sold art paintings in an art shop
BIGGEST CRICKETING REGRET? Not yet winning a T20 final for Somerset
CRICKET STAR OF THE FUTURE? Kasey Aldridge (Somerset)
IF YOU WERE AN ANIMAL, WHICH WOULD IT BE? A leopard
TWITTER: @MaxTCWaller
NOTES: Waller signed a two-year contract to play white-ball cricket in October 2018

Batting	Mat	Inns	NO	Runs	HS	Ave	SR	100	50	Ct	St
First-class	9	10	1	91	28	10.11	42.32	0	0	5	0
List A	58	22	15	109	25*	15.57	70.77	0	0	32	0
T20s	124	32	19	96	17	7.38	78.68	0	0	75	0
Bowling	**Mat**	**Balls**	**Runs**	**Wkts**	**BBI**	**BBM**	**Ave**	**Econ**	**SR**	**5w**	**10**
First-class	9	840	493	10	3/33	3/57	49.30	3.52	84.0	0	0
List A	58	1801	1696	45	3/37	3/37	37.68	5.65	40.0	0	0
T20s	124	2384	2930	124	4/16	4/16	23.62	7.37	19.2	0	0

PAUL WALTER

LHB / LM / R0 / W0

FULL NAME: Paul Ian Walter
BORN: May 28, 1994, Basildon, Essex
SQUAD NO: 22
HEIGHT: 6ft 7in
EDUCATION: Billericay School, Essex
TEAMS: Essex
ROLE: Allrounder
DEBUT: First-class: 2016; List A: 2017; T20: 2016

BEST BATTING: 68* Essex vs West Indians, Chelmsford, 2017
BEST BOWLING: 3-44 Essex vs Derbyshire, Derby, 2016

TWITTER: @PWalter_22
NOTES: Walter signed a professional contract with his hometown club midway through the 2016 season after impressing in club cricket for Hornchurch and for Essex Second XI. An allrounder with Premier League hundreds under his belt allied to a series of thrusting spells of high-quality pace bowling, Walter offers Essex options, especially in one-day cricket. At 6ft 7in, he brings considerable physical presence to the Essex attack. He played five Championship matches as Essex romped to the Championship title in 2017, and took 15 wickets in 13 games in the T20 Blast. He has played just one Championship match over the last two seasons but has been a regular face in the the T20 Blast side

Batting	Mat	Inns	NO	Runs	HS	Ave	SR	100	50	Ct	St
First-class	10	10	3	240	68*	34.28	55.29	0	1	0	0
List A	10	8	3	96	25	19.20	90.56	0	0	4	0
T20s	38	27	12	314	40	20.93	134.18	0	0	13	0
Bowling	**Mat**	**Balls**	**Runs**	**Wkts**	**BBI**	**BBM**	**Ave**	**Econ**	**SR**	**5w**	**10**
First-class	10	924	540	13	3/44	4/68	41.53	3.50	71.0	0	0
List A	10	328	375	13	4/37	4/37	28.84	6.85	25.2	0	0
T20s	38	450	727	21	3/24	3/24	34.61	9.69	21.4	0	0

JARED WARNER

RHB / RFM / R0 / W0

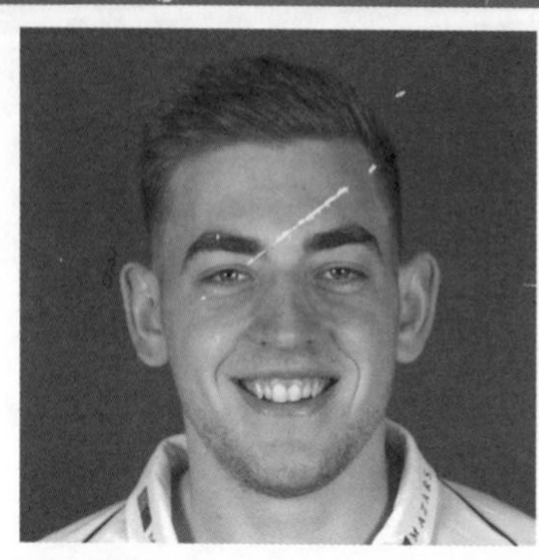

FULL NAME: Jared David Warner
BORN: November 14, 1996, Wakefield, Yorkshire
SQUAD NO: 45
HEIGHT: 6ft 1in
NICKNAME: Jazz
EDUCATION: Silcoates School, West Yorkshire; Kettlethorpe High School, Wakefield
TEAMS: Yorkshire, England U19, Sussex
ROLE: Bowler
DEBUT: First-class: 2019; List A: 2019

BEST BATTING: 13* Sussex vs Middlesex, Hove, 2019
BEST BOWLING: 3-35 Sussex vs Glamorgan, Hove, 2019

WHAT WAS YOUR FIRST CRICKET CLUB? Wakefield Thornes CC, West Yorkshire
BEST ADVICE EVER RECEIVED? Have no fear
BEST MOMENT IN CRICKET? Winning the double with Yorkshire Academy. Taking figures of 9-19 from 10.2 overs for Yorkshire Academy against Castleford in a Yorkshire Premier League North match in 2016. Representing England U19
IF YOU WEREN'T A CRICKETER? I'd be involved in sport in some capacity
SURPRISING FACT ABOUT YOU? I'm a big Sheffield United fan
CRICKETING HERO? Andrew Flintoff – my first memories of watching cricket are of him winning the Ashes in 2005
NON-CRICKETING HERO? Michael Owen – he got me into football
TWITTER: @JaredWarner96

Batting	Mat	Inns	NO	Runs	HS	Ave	SR	100	50	Ct	St
First-class	2	2	2	14	13*	-	36.84	0	0	0	0
List A	1	-	-	-	-	-	-	-	-	0	0
Bowling	**Mat**	**Balls**	**Runs**	**Wkts**	**BBI**	**BBM**	**Ave**	**Econ**	**SR**	**5w**	**10**
First-class	2	182	141	4	3/35	3/79	35.25	4.64	45.5	0	0
List A	1	30	32	0	-	-	-	6.40	-	0	0

BJ WATLING

RHB / WK / R0 / W0

FULL NAME: Bradley-John Watling
BORN: July 9, 1985, Durban, South Africa
SQUAD NO: 47
TEAMS: New Zealand, Lancashire, Durham, Northern Districts
ROLE: Wicketkeeper/batsman
DEBUT: Test: 2009; ODI: 2010; T20I: 2009; First-class: 2004; List A: 2004; T20: 2008

BEST BATTING: 205 New Zealand vs England, Mount Maunganui, 2019

TWITTER: @B_Jwatling
NOTES: The Kiwi arrives at Lancashire for the first nine matches of the Championship season having had a two-match stint with Durham last year. Watling is one of the best keeper-batsmen in the world and he enjoyed an excellent 2019 in which he scored 559 Test runs at 55.90, including a career-best 205 against England at Mount Maunganui. His performances led to him being selected in Wisden Cricket Monthly's Test Team of the Year. After making his Test debut in 2009, he has gone on to score more Test runs and effect more dismissals than any New Zealand keeper before him. "We identified a top-order batsman as a priority in the overseas player market and BJ fits the bill perfectly," said Paul Allott, Lancashire's director of cricket. "He adds valuable experience to the batting line-up"

Batting	Mat	Inns	NO	Runs	HS	Ave	SR	100	50	Ct	St
Tests	70	110	15	3658	205	38.50	42.35	8	18	241	8
ODIs	28	25	2	573	96*	24.91	68.37	0	5	20	0
T20Is	5	4	0	38	22	9.50	65.51	0	0	3	0
First-class	166	278	33	9617	205	39.25	44.32	18	56	413	10
List A	126	118	12	3982	145*	37.56	73.55	8	27	99	3
T20s	67	60	9	1255	75	24.60	108.94	0	6	36	3
Bowling	**Mat**	**Balls**	**Runs**	**Wkts**	**BBI**	**BBM**	**Ave**	**Econ**	**SR**	**5w**	**10**
Tests	70	-	-	-	-	-	-	-	-	-	-
ODIs	28	-	-	-	-	-	-	-	-	-	-
T20Is	5	-	-	-	-	-	-	-	-	-	-
First-class	166	53	39	2	2/31	2/31	19.50	4.41	26.5	0	0
List A	126	-	-	-	-	-	-	-	-	-	-
T20s	67	-	-	-	-	-	-	-	-	-	-

JOE WEATHERLEY

RHB / OB / R0 / W0

FULL NAME: Joe James Weatherley
BORN: January 19, 1997, Winchester, Hampshire
SQUAD NO: 5
HEIGHT: 6ft 2in
NICKNAME: Lord, Weathers
EDUCATION: King Edward VI School, Southampton; The Open University, Milton Keynes
TEAMS: Hampshire, England U19, Kent
ROLE: Batsman
DEBUT: First-class: 2016; List A: 2016; T20: 2016

BEST BATTING: 126* Hampshire vs Lancashire, Old Trafford, 2018
BEST BOWLING: 1-2 Hampshire vs Nottinghamshire, Southampton, 2018

WHAT WAS YOUR FIRST CRICKET CLUB? St Cross Symondians CC, Hampshire. Still play for them every now and again
WHAT WERE YOU DOING WHEN ENGLAND WON THE WORLD CUP? Had my feet up recovering from ankle surgery
HOW WOULD YOU DISMISS STEVE SMITH? Mankad him
BIGGEST TOPIC OF DISCUSSION IN YOUR DRESSING ROOM? That's an easy one – the football warm-ups
CRICKETING HERO? Marcus Trescothick
WHICH RULE WOULD YOU CHANGE ABOUT CRICKET? You are allowed to come off the field if temperatures dip below 10 degrees
SURPRISING FACT ABOUT YOU? My dad played at Wimbledon in the 1972 Championships
SURPRISING FACT ABOUT A TEAMMATE? Mason Crane has pet tortoises
CRICKET STAR OF THE FUTURE? Fletcha Middleton (Hampshire Academy)
IF YOU WERE AN ANIMAL, WHICH WOULD IT BE? A tiger
TWITTER: @Joe_Weatherley

Batting	Mat	Inns	NO	Runs	HS	Ave	SR	100	50	Ct	St
First-class	32	52	3	1158	126*	23.63	44.16	1	5	14	0
List A	20	20	4	509	105*	31.81	72.61	1	3	5	0
T20s	11	9	0	117	43	13.00	112.50	0	0	4	0
Bowling	**Mat**	**Balls**	**Runs**	**Wkts**	**BBI**	**BBM**	**Ave**	**Econ**	**SR**	**5w**	**10**
First-class	32	300	228	4	1/2	1/2	57.00	4.56	75.0	0	0
List A	20	327	221	8	4/25	4/25	27.62	4.05	40.8	0	0
T20s	11	6	9	0	-	-	-	9.00	-	0	0

JAMES WEIGHELL LHB / RMF / R0 / W0

FULL NAME: William James Weighell
BORN: January 28, 1994, Middlesbrough, Yorkshire
SQUAD NO: 28
HEIGHT: 6ft 4in
NICKNAME: Weighelly
EDUCATION: Stokesley School, North Yorkshire
TEAMS: Durham
ROLE: Allrounder
DEBUT: First-class: 2015; List A: 2017; T20: 2017

BEST BATTING: 84 Durham vs Kent, Chester-le-Street, 2018
BEST BOWLING: 7-32 Durham vs Leicestershire, Chester-le-Street, 2018

WHAT WAS YOUR FIRST CRICKET CLUB? Stokesley CC, North Yorkshire
WHAT WERE YOU DOING WHEN ENGLAND WON THE WORLD CUP? Watching it at my local cricket club
BIGGEST TOPIC OF DISCUSSION IN YOUR DRESSING ROOM? Ben Raine's passion for mashed potato
CRICKETING HERO? Andrew Flintoff
WHICH RULE WOULD YOU CHANGE ABOUT CRICKET? Make boundaries shorter
SURPRISING FACT ABOUT A TEAMMATE? Graham Clark can fit 26 grapes into his mouth at once
CRICKET STAR OF THE FUTURE? Jonny Bushnell (Durham Academy)
WHICH BOOK MEANS MOST TO YOU? My Story by Steven Gerrard
IF YOU WERE AN ANIMAL, WHICH WOULD IT BE? Darla the Goldendoodle – I'd like to be stroked by Ryan Pringle every day
TWITTER: @jamesweighell

Batting	Mat	Inns	NO	Runs	HS	Ave	SR	100	50	Ct	St
First-class	15	25	4	506	84	24.09	69.22	0	3	4	0
List A	12	6	1	49	23	9.80	74.24	0	0	3	0
T20s	27	16	9	101	28	14.42	131.16	0	0	16	0
Bowling	**Mat**	**Balls**	**Runs**	**Wkts**	**BBI**	**BBM**	**Ave**	**Econ**	**SR**	**5w**	**10**
First-class	15	2567	1472	52	7/32	9/130	28.30	3.44	49.3	2	0
List A	12	612	632	22	5/57	5/57	28.72	6.19	27.8	1	0
T20s	27	453	707	22	3/28	3/28	32.13	9.36	20.5	0	0

LUKE WELLS

LHB / OB / R2 / W0

SUSSEX

FULL NAME: Luke William Peter Wells
BORN: December 29, 1990, Eastbourne, Sussex
SQUAD NO: 31
HEIGHT: 6ft 4in
NICKNAME: Dave, Rinser
EDUCATION: St Bede's, Hailsham, East Sussex; Loughborough University
TEAMS: Sussex, Colombo, England U19
ROLE: Batsman
DEBUT: First-class: 2010; List A: 2010; T20: 2011

BEST BATTING: 258 Sussex vs Durham, Hove, 2017
BEST BOWLING: 5-63 Sussex vs Glamorgan, Hove, 2019
COUNTY CAP: 2016

FAMILY TIES? My dad Alan played for Sussex, Kent and England. My uncle Colin played for Sussex, Derbyshire and England
WHAT WAS YOUR FIRST CRICKET CLUB? Glynde & Beddingham CC, Sussex
WHAT WERE YOU DOING WHEN ENGLAND WON THE WORLD CUP? Watching it at Old Trafford with my teammates, including Chris Jordan, who was very emotional
WHAT EXCITES YOU ABOUT THE HUNDRED? Watching my Sussex teammates dominate
BIGGEST TOPIC OF DISCUSSION IN YOUR DRESSING ROOM? Unfortunately Fantasy Football, closely followed by what time to go for lunch and which cafe to choose
MOST INTERESTING TEAMMATE? Phil Salt – he's mad as a hatter
CRICKETING HERO? Matthew Hayden
WHICH RULE WOULD YOU CHANGE ABOUT CRICKET? Allow more than two fielders behind square on the leg side
CRICKET STAR OF THE FUTURE? My boy Jonny – he might be the first Wells who's a fast bowler
WHICH BOOK MEANS MOST TO YOU? The Harry Potter books by JK Rowling
TWITTER: @luke_wells07

Batting	Mat	Inns	NO	Runs	HS	Ave	SR	100	50	Ct	St
First-class	141	237	16	7779	258	35.19	46.41	18	33	63	0
List A	26	20	0	232	62	11.60	63.21	0	1	5	0
T20s	5	5	0	18	11	3.60	66.66	0	0	1	0
Bowling	**Mat**	**Balls**	**Runs**	**Wkts**	**BBI**	**BBM**	**Ave**	**Econ**	**SR**	**5w**	**10**
First-class	141	5398	3172	69	5/63	5/63	45.97	3.52	78.2	1	0
List A	26	437	384	10	3/19	3/19	38.40	5.27	43.7	0	0
T20s	5	1	4	0	-	-	-	24.00	-	0	0

RIKI WESSELS RHB / WK / R2 / W0 / MVP37

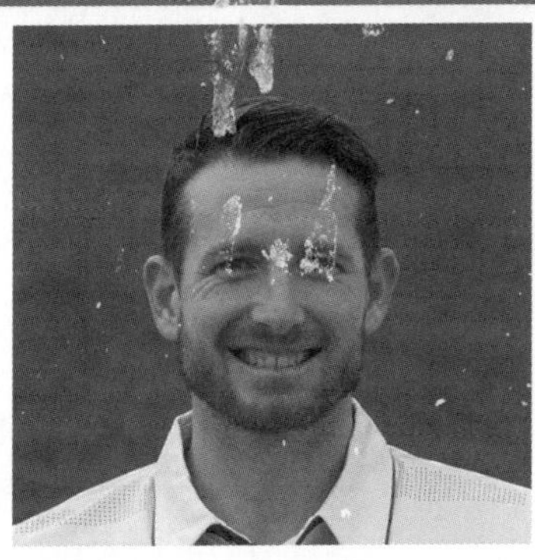

FULL NAME: Mattheus Hendrik Wessels
BORN: November 12, 1985, Australia
SQUAD NO: 9
HEIGHT: 5ft 11in
NICKNAME: Weaz, Blood
EDUCATION: Woodridge College, Port Elizabeth; University of Northampton
TEAMS: Worcestershire, Birmingham Phoenix, Mid West Rhinos, Nondescripts, Northants, Notts, Sydney Sixers
ROLE: Batsman
DEBUT: First-class: 2004; List A: 2005; T20: 2005

BEST BATTING: 202* Nottinghamshire vs Sussex, Trent Bridge, 2017
BEST BOWLING: 1-10 Mid West Rhinos vs Matabeleland Tuskers, Bulawayo, 2009
COUNTY CAP: 2014 (Nottinghamshire)

WHAT WAS YOUR FIRST CRICKET CLUB? United Brothers CC, Eastern Cape, South Africa – a township-based club with some serious talent
BEST INNINGS YOU'VE SEEN? Alex Hales's 187 not out in the 2017 One-Day Cup final
CRICKETING HERO? Justin Langer
WHICH RULE WOULD YOU CHANGE ABOUT CRICKET? Lunch and tea should each be an hour
SURPRISING FACT ABOUT YOU? I've bungee-jumped at Victoria Falls, I lived in Colombo for six months and I love hunting
TWITTER: @rikiwessels

Batting	Mat	Inns	NO	Runs	HS	Ave	SR	100	50	Ct	St
First-class	212	351	31	11342	202*	35.44	64.05	23	58	332	16
List A	179	168	14	4765	146	30.94	101.08	5	26	121	0
T20s	220	207	27	5305	110	29.47	136.72	1	25	85	16
Bowling	**Mat**	**Balls**	**Runs**	**Wkts**	**BBI**	**BBM**	**Ave**	**Econ**	**SR**	**5w**	**10**
First-class	212	240	130	3	1/10	1/10	43.33	3.25	80.0	0	0
List A	179	49	48	1	1/0	1/0	48.00	5.87	49.0	0	0
T20s	220	-	-	-	-	-	-	-	-	-	-

OLLY WESTBURY

RHB / OB / R0 / W0

FULL NAME: Oliver Edward Westbury
BORN: July 2, 1997, Dudley, West Midlands
SQUAD NO: 19
HEIGHT: 5ft 11in
NICKNAME: Wes
EDUCATION: Ellowes Hall Sports College, Dudley; Shrewsbury School
TEAMS: Worcestershire, England U19
ROLE: Batsman
DEBUT: First-class: 2018; List A: 2018; T20: 2018

BEST BATTING: 22 Worcestershire vs Surrey, Worcester, 2018

WHAT WAS YOUR FIRST CRICKET CLUB? Himley CC, Staffordshire
BIGGEST TOPIC OF DISCUSSION IN YOUR DRESSING ROOM? Football
MOST INTERESTING TEAMMATE? Jack Haynes
CRICKETING HERO? Andrew Flintoff
WHICH RULE WOULD YOU CHANGE ABOUT CRICKET? Have a longer tea break
SURPRISING FACT ABOUT YOU? I know all the lyrics to Billy Joel's 'We Didn't Start The Fire'
IF YOU WERE AN ANIMAL, WHICH WOULD IT BE? A cheetah. I'm incredibly slow, so it would be nice to be fast for a change
TWITTER: @ollywestbury

Batting	Mat	Inns	NO	Runs	HS	Ave	SR	100	50	Ct	St
First-class	2	4	0	49	22	12.25	32.66	0	0	1	0
List A	1	1	0	8	8	8.00	34.78	0	0	0	0
T20s	1	1	0	24	24	24.00	150.00	0	0	0	0
Bowling	**Mat**	**Balls**	**Runs**	**Wkts**	**BBI**	**BBM**	**Ave**	**Econ**	**SR**	**5w**	**10**
First-class	2	6	6	0	-	-	-	6.00	-	0	0
List A	1	-	-	-	-	-	-	-	-	-	-
T20s	1	-	-	-	-	-	-	-	-	-	-

TOM WESTLEY RHB / OB / R1 / W0 / MVP36

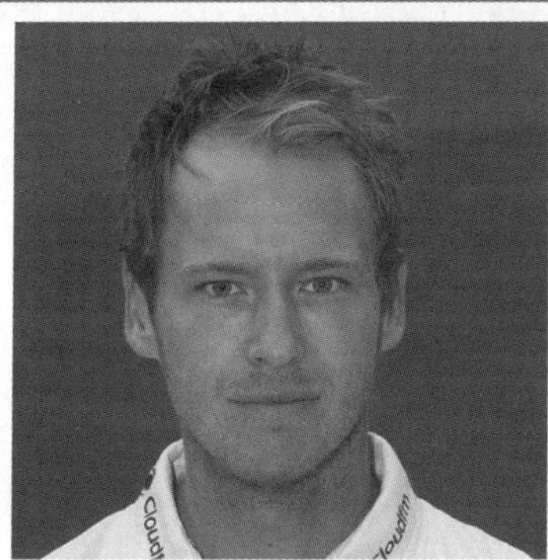

FULL NAME: Thomas Westley
BORN: March 13, 1989, Cambridge
SQUAD NO: 21
HEIGHT: 6ft 2in
NICKNAME: Westie, Shellsy, Wezzo
EDUCATION: Linton Valley College, South Cambridgeshire; Hills Road College, Cambridge; Durham University
TEAMS: England, Essex, Bloomfield Cricket & Athletic Club
ROLE: Batsman
DEBUT: Test: 2017; First-class: 2007; List A: 2006; T20: 2010

BEST BATTING: 254 Essex vs Worcestershire, Chelmsford, 2016
BEST BOWLING: 4-55 Durham MCCU vs Durham, Durham University, 2010
COUNTY CAP: 2013

FAMILY TIES? My dad, uncle and brother all play for Weston Colville CC. My dad also harbours ambitions to play for England Over-50s
CRICKETING HERO? Jacques Kallis
NON-CRICKETING HERO? Giovanni Colussi
SURPRISING FACT ABOUT YOU? I was one of the first students to study Harry Potter academically
TWITTER: @Westley21
NOTES: Westley has replaced Ryan ten Doeschate as Essex captain for the County Championship and the One-Day Cup. He said: "It's a huge honour to captain a county like Essex, with all the success they've had over the years, it's a very special feeling"

Batting	Mat	Inns	NO	Runs	HS	Ave	SR	100	50	Ct	St
Tests	5	9	1	193	59	24.12	42.60	0	1	1	0
First-class	180	299	21	10046	254	36.13	51.78	21	47	115	0
List A	88	82	4	2853	134	36.57	88.68	5	22	19	0
T20s	79	73	8	1974	109*	30.36	129.69	2	6	30	0
Bowling	**Mat**	**Balls**	**Runs**	**Wkts**	**BBI**	**BBM**	**Ave**	**Econ**	**SR**	**5w**	**10**
Tests	5	24	12	0	-	-	-	3.00	-	0	0
First-class	180	5083	2693	59	4/55	5/122	45.64	3.17	86.1	0	0
List A	88	1036	861	21	4/60	4/60	41.00	4.98	49.3	0	0
T20s	79	246	311	7	2/27	2/27	44.42	7.58	35.1	0	0

BRAD WHEAL

RHB / RFM / R0 / W0

FULL NAME: Bradley Thomas James Wheal
BORN: August 28, 1996, Durban, South Africa
SQUAD NO: 58
HEIGHT: 5ft 11in
EDUCATION: Clifton School, Durban
TEAMS: Scotland, Hampshire
ROLE: Bowler
DEBUT: ODI: 2016; T20I: 2016; First-class: 2015; List A: 2016; T20: 2016

BEST BATTING: 25* Hampshire vs Somerset, Taunton, 2018
BEST BOWLING: 6-51 Hampshire vs Nottinghamshire, Trent Bridge, 2016

WHAT WAS YOUR FIRST CRICKET CLUB? Berea Rovers CC, Durban, South Africa
MOST INTERESTING TEAMMATE? Hashim Amla – one of the hardest workers I've ever seen, no matter how well he is playing
IF YOU WERE AN ANIMAL, WHICH WOULD IT BE? A dolphin – who doesn't want to spend their day cruising around the ocean?
TWITTER: @Brad_wheal
NOTES: Born in South Africa, Wheal's mother is Scottish and he holds a British passport. He made his Hampshire debut in 2015 and his Scotland debut the following year aged 19. In 2018 the fast bowler took 11 wickets in five Championship matches before a stress fracture of the back ended his season in mid-summer. Last year he was restricted to just three One-Day Cup appearances and it will be tough again this year to break into Hampshire's star-studded bowling attack

Batting	Mat	Inns	NO	Runs	HS	Ave	SR	100	50	Ct	St
ODIs	13	7	3	16	14	4.00	51.61	0	0	3	0
T20Is	5	2	2	2	2*	-	100.00	0	0	1	0
First-class	25	29	8	157	25*	7.47	24.37	0	0	11	0
List A	28	16	7	63	18*	7.00	66.31	0	0	6	0
T20s	12	5	3	22	16	11.00	95.65	0	0	1	0
Bowling	**Mat**	**Balls**	**Runs**	**Wkts**	**BBI**	**BBM**	**Ave**	**Econ**	**SR**	**5w**	**10**
ODIs	13	687	508	23	3/34	3/34	22.08	4.43	29.8	0	0
T20Is	5	104	143	5	3/20	3/20	28.60	8.25	20.8	0	0
First-class	25	3352	2080	56	6/51	7/71	37.14	3.72	59.8	1	0
List A	28	1319	1154	45	4/38	4/38	25.64	5.24	29.3	0	0
T20s	12	224	317	11	3/20	3/20	28.81	8.49	20.3	0	0

ADAM WHEATER RHB / WK / RO / WO

FULL NAME: Adam Jack Aubrey Wheater
BORN: February 13, 1990, Whipps Cross Hospital, London
SQUAD NO: 31
EDUCATION: Millfield School, Somerset; Anglia Ruskin University
TEAMS: Essex, Badureliya Sports Club, England U19, Hampshire, Matabeleland Tuskers
ROLE: Batsman/wicketkeeper
DEBUT: First-class: 2008; List A: 2010; T20: 2009

BEST BATTING: 204* Hampshire vs Warwickshire, Edgbaston, 2016
BEST BOWLING: 1-86 Essex vs Leicestershire, Leicester, 2012
COUNTY CAP: 2016 (Hampshire)

BEST MOMENT IN CRICKET? On a broader scale, having the opportunity to see the world through cricket
CRICKETING HERO? Alec Stewart
IF YOU WEREN'T A CRICKETER? I'd find myself a very wealthy girlfriend I could sponge off
NOTES: The hard-hitting wicketkeeper signed an extension to his contract in October 2018, keeping him at Essex until the end of this season. Wheater was part of the side which won the County Championship in 2017 and again last summer, having re-joined his old club after a spell at Hampshire. He struggled with the bat last year, averaging less than 20 in both the Championship and the T20 Blast

Batting	Mat	Inns	NO	Runs	HS	Ave	SR	100	50	Ct	St
First-class	138	202	24	6373	204*	35.80	65.55	12	35	237	14
List A	80	65	5	1713	135	28.55	97.38	2	9	41	12
T20s	113	91	15	1392	78	18.31	123.51	0	3	44	24
Bowling	**Mat**	**Balls**	**Runs**	**Wkts**	**BBI**	**BBM**	**Ave**	**Econ**	**SR**	**5w**	**10**
First-class	138	24	86	1	1/86	1/86	86.00	21.50	24.0	0	0
List A	80	-	-	-	-	-	-	-	-	-	-
T20s	113	-	-	-	-	-	-	-	-	-	-

GRAEME WHITE RHB / SLA / R0 / W0

FULL NAME: Graeme Geoffrey White
BORN: April 18, 1987, Milton Keynes, Buckinghamshire
SQUAD NO: 87
HEIGHT: 5ft 11in
NICKNAME: Whitey, G
EDUCATION: Royal Latin School, Buckinghamshire; Stowe School
TEAMS: Northamptonshire, England Lions, Nottinghamshire
ROLE: Bowler
DEBUT: First-class: 2006; List A: 2007; T20: 2007

BEST BATTING: 34 Northamptonshire vs Warwickshire, Northampton, 2014 (T20)
BEST BOWLING: 5-22 Nottinghamshire vs Lancashire, Trent Bridge, 2013 (T20)

WHAT WAS YOUR FIRST CRICKET CLUB? Milton Keynes CC, Buckinghamshire. My sister was my age-group captain
BEST ADVICE EVER RECEIVED? You need a steak and a Guinness to fill out lad (told to me by Nick Cook when I was 13)
WHAT EXCITES YOU ABOUT THE HUNDRED? The sixes
BIGGEST TOPIC OF DISCUSSION IN YOUR DRESSING ROOM? The weather
MOST INTERESTING TEAMMATE? Paul Franks – hilarious, what a man
BEST INNINGS YOU'VE SEEN? David Sales hitting 161 for Northants in a one-day match against Yorkshire at Northampton in 2006. I was 12th man
WHICH RULE WOULD YOU CHANGE ABOUT CRICKET? The distance of the boundary should be set at 120 metres
SURPRISING FACT ABOUT YOU? I have 35 tattoos
WHICH BOOK MEANS MOST TO YOU? Leading – Learning from Life and My Years at Manchester United by Alex Ferguson and Michael Moritz
IF YOU WERE AN ANIMAL, WHICH WOULD IT BE? A sloth
NOTES: White signed a one-year extension to his white-ball contract last September

Batting	Mat	Inns	NO	Runs	HS	Ave	SR	100	50	Ct	St
First-class	39	55	5	659	65	13.18	48.85	0	2	12	0
List A	85	52	16	543	41*	15.08	86.32	0	0	29	0
T20s	106	39	18	284	34	13.52	133.33	0	0	39	0
Bowling	**Mat**	**Balls**	**Runs**	**Wkts**	**BBI**	**BBM**	**Ave**	**Econ**	**SR**	**5w**	**10**
First-class	39	4776	2730	65	6/44	7/89	42.00	3.42	73.4	1	0
List A	85	3216	2709	92	6/37	6/37	29.44	5.05	34.9	2	0
T20s	106	1601	2156	80	5/22	5/22	26.95	8.07	20.0	1	0

JACK WHITE LHB / RFM / R0 / W0

FULL NAME: Curtley-Jack White
BORN: February 19, 1992, Kendal, Cumberland
SQUAD NO: 9
HEIGHT: 6ft 2in
NICKNAME: Whitey
EDUCATION: Ullswater Community College, Penrith, Cumbria; Queen Elizabeth Grammar School, Penrith
TEAMS: Northamptonshire
ROLE: Bowler

WHAT WAS YOUR FIRST CRICKET CLUB? Penrith CC, Cumbria
WHAT EXCITES YOU ABOUT THE HUNDRED? The concept of 10-ball overs
BIGGEST TOPIC OF DISCUSSION IN YOUR DRESSING ROOM? Brexit
NOTES: White was described by Northants head coach David Ripley as "a very English-style seam bowler" after signing a one-year contract with the club last November. "He's a little bit similar to Ben Sanderson in many ways, very skilful and hits the seam," Ripley said. The 28-year-old is trying to follow in the footsteps of fellow Cumbrian seamer Richard Gleeson, who was the same age when he had his breakthrough season at Northants four years ago. White, who has played Minor Counties for Cumberland and Cheshire, was scouted by Northants while playing grade cricket in Australia and joined up with the squad last summer. Niggling injuries restricted him to a handful of appeareances for the club's Second XI last year but he is now back to full fitness after a winter playing club cricket in New Zealand. White said: "I've always been stronger in white-ball cricket but that's in Australia where the ball doesn't move as much. Obviously, it's a bit different over here, ideally I'd like to play all three formats. I'm not going to get carried away though, just work real hard and see what happens"

ROBBIE WHITE

RHB / WK / R0 / W0

FULL NAME: Robert George White
BORN: September 15, 1995, Ealing, London
SQUAD NO: 14
HEIGHT: 5ft 10in
NICKNAME: Whitey, Chalky
EDUCATION: Harrow School, London; Loughborough University
TEAMS: Middlesex, Essex
ROLE: Batsman/wicketkeeper
DEBUT: First-class: 2015; List A: 2018; T20: 2018

BEST BATTING: 69 Loughborough MCCU vs Northamptonshire, Northampton, 2017

WHAT WAS YOUR FIRST CRICKET CLUB? Ealing CC, London
WHAT EXCITES YOU ABOUT THE HUNDRED? Watching it on TV
BIGGEST TOPIC OF DISCUSSION IN YOUR DRESSING ROOM? The poor music taste of most of my teammates
MOST INTERESTING TEAMMATE? Alastair Cook (when I was on loan at Essex last season). Legend
BEST INNINGS YOU'VE SEEN? Aaron Finch's 117 not out off 52 balls against us at The Oval in 2018 – best hitting I've seen close up
CRICKETING HERO? AB de Villiers
WHICH RULE WOULD YOU CHANGE ABOUT CRICKET? If you are caught off a free hit then the ball should be called dead and no runs scored
SURPRISING FACT ABOUT YOU? I like my custard cold
BIGGEST CRICKETING REGRET? Leaving my first Championship ball at Lord's
CRICKET STAR OF THE FUTURE? Josh de Caires (Middlesex Second XI)
IF YOU WERE AN ANIMAL, WHICH WOULD IT BE? A snail – small and slow-moving
TWITTER: @rwhitey15

Batting	Mat	Inns	NO	Runs	HS	Ave	SR	100	50	Ct	St
First-class	16	23	1	274	69	12.45	42.54	0	1	24	2
List A	9	9	4	99	21*	19.80	106.45	0	0	15	2
T20s	3	2	1	11	11*	11.00	100.00	0	0	1	0
Bowling	**Mat**	**Balls**	**Runs**	**Wkts**	**BBI**	**BBM**	**Ave**	**Econ**	**SR**	**5w**	**10**
First-class	16	-	-	-	-	-	-	-	-	-	-
List A	9	-	-	-	-	-	-	-	-	-	-
T20s	3	-	-	-	-	-	-	-	-	-	-

BEN WHITEHEAD RHB / LB / R0 / W0

FULL NAME: Benjamin Guy Whitehead
BORN: April 28, 1997, Sunderland
SQUAD NO: 97
HEIGHT: 6ft 1in
NICKNAME: Benji
EDUCATION: Hetton School, Sunderland
TEAMS: Durham
ROLE: Bowler
DEBUT: T20: 2018

WHAT WAS YOUR FIRST CRICKET CLUB? Hetton Lyons CC, Sunderland. It had the best tuckshop in the league
WHAT WERE YOU DOING WHEN ENGLAND WON THE WORLD CUP? Drinking beers in the hot tub
HOW WOULD YOU DISMISS STEVE SMITH? Bowl straight – he might miss one
BEST INNINGS YOU'VE SEEN? Ben Stokes's 258 at Cape Town in 2016
WHICH RULE WOULD YOU CHANGE ABOUT CRICKET? Give bowlers a chance: have a fourth stump
BIGGEST CRICKETING REGRET? Messing around in my younger years and not taking the game seriously enough
CRICKET STAR OF THE FUTURE? Luke Husband (Durham U15)
WHICH BOOK MEANS MOST TO YOU? No Spin by Shane Warne. So much information on how to bowl leg-spin
IF YOU WERE AN ANIMAL, WHICH WOULD IT BE? A Toy Poodle – cutest dog ever
TWITTER: @Benwhitehead97

Batting	Mat	Inns	NO	Runs	HS	Ave	SR	100	50	Ct	St
T20s	6	1	1	2	2*	-	66.66	0	0	3	0
Bowling	**Mat**	**Balls**	**Runs**	**Wkts**	**BBI**	**BBM**	**Ave**	**Econ**	**SR**	**5w**	**10**
T20s	6	120	144	5	2/23	2/23	28.80	7.20	24.0	0	0

ROSS WHITELEY LHB / LM / R0 / W0

FULL NAME: Ross Andrew Whiteley
BORN: September 13, 1988, Sheffield
SQUAD NO: 44
HEIGHT: 6ft 2in
NICKNAME: Rossco
EDUCATION: Repton School, Derbyshire; Leeds Metropolitan University
TEAMS: Worcestershire, Southern Brave, Derbyshire, England Lions, Multan Sultans, Sylhet Sixers
ROLE: Batsman
DEBUT: First-class: 2008; List A: 2008; T20: 2011

BEST BATTING: 130* Derbyshire vs Kent, Derby, 2011
BEST BOWLING: 2-6 Derbyshire vs Hampshire, Derby, 2012
COUNTY CAP: 2013 (Worcestershire)

WHAT WAS YOUR FIRST CRICKET CLUB? Eckington CC, South Yorkshire
WHAT EXCITES YOU ABOUT THE HUNDRED? Well, I'll tell you what doesn't excite me: the prospect of my Southern Brave net sessions facing Archer, Mills, Jordan, Russell and Garton
BIGGEST TOPIC OF DISCUSSION IN YOUR DRESSING ROOM? Who is worse on Instagram: Ben Cox or Tom Moores
MOST INTERESTING TEAMMATE? Martin Guptill – because of his blow-ups after getting out
BEST INNINGS YOU'VE SEEN? Martin Guptill's 35-ball hundred for Worcestershire in a T20 match at Northampton last summer. Some of the cleanest hitting I have ever seen
SURPRISING FACT ABOUT YOU? I have 11 sheep with each squad number of the 2012 Derbyshire side which won Division Two shaved onto them
TWITTER: @RossWhiteley44

Batting	Mat	Inns	NO	Runs	HS	Ave	SR	100	50	Ct	St
First-class	87	142	13	3543	130*	27.46	49.63	3	19	59	0
List A	81	71	11	1660	131	27.66	99.81	1	10	23	0
T20s	122	111	29	2109	91*	25.71	144.15	0	5	45	0
Bowling	**Mat**	**Balls**	**Runs**	**Wkts**	**BBI**	**BBM**	**Ave**	**Econ**	**SR**	**5w**	**10**
First-class	87	2953	2064	40	2/6	4/43	51.60	4.19	73.8	0	0
List A	81	507	563	14	4/58	4/58	40.21	6.66	36.2	0	0
T20s	122	96	168	4	1/10	1/10	42.00	10.50	24.0	0	0

STUART WHITTINGHAM RHB / RFM / R0 / W0

FULL NAME: Stuart Gordon Whittingham
BORN: February 10, 1994, Derby
SQUAD NO: 19
HEIGHT: 6ft 2in
NICKNAME: The Jug
EDUCATION: Christ's Hospital, Horsham; Loughborough University
TEAMS: Scotland, Gloucestershire, Sussex
ROLE: Bowler
DEBUT: ODI: 2017; T20I: 2018; First-class: 2015; List A: 2017; T20: 2018

BEST BATTING: 22 Sussex vs Nottinghamshire, Hove, 2017
BEST BOWLING: 5-70 Scotland vs Ireland, Dubai, 2017

BEST ADVICE EVER RECEIVED? Respect the game and it will look after you (Russell Cobb)
BEST MOMENT IN CRICKET? My first Championship five-for
IF YOU WEREN'T A CRICKETER? I'd be a scientist
SURPRISING FACT ABOUT YOU? I have a brother who is a celebrity in South Korea
CRICKETING HERO? Dale Steyn
NON-CRICKETING HERO? Bradley Wiggins
TWITTER: @Stuartwhitt10

Batting	Mat	Inns	NO	Runs	HS	Ave	SR	100	50	Ct	St
ODIs	5	4	2	7	3*	3.50	41.17	0	0	3	0
T20Is	3	-	-	-	-	-	-	-	-	0	0
First-class	15	16	6	68	22	6.80	35.23	0	0	3	0
List A	6	4	2	7	3*	3.50	41.17	0	0	3	0
T20s	3	-	-	-	-	-	-	-	-	0	0
Bowling	**Mat**	**Balls**	**Runs**	**Wkts**	**BBI**	**BBM**	**Ave**	**Econ**	**SR**	**5w**	**10**
ODIs	5	251	224	8	3/58	3/58	28.00	5.35	31.3	0	0
T20Is	3	60	79	3	2/33	2/33	26.33	7.90	20.0	0	0
First-class	15	1993	1389	46	5/70	8/93	30.19	4.18	43.3	2	0
List A	6	311	259	11	3/35	3/35	23.54	4.99	28.2	0	0
T20s	3	60	79	3	2/33	2/33	26.33	7.90	20.0	0	0

SUSSEX / NORTHERN SUPERCHARGERS

DAVID WIESE RHB / RMF / R0 / W0 / MVP16

FULL NAME: David Wiese
BORN: May 18, 1985, Roodepoort, Transvaal, South Africa
SQUAD NO: 96
HEIGHT: 6ft 3in
NICKNAME: Weez, Spanish Dave
EDUCATION: University of Pretoria, SA
TEAMS: South Africa, Sussex, Northern Superchargers, Barbados Tridents, Easterns, Paarl Rocks, RC Bangalore, Titans
ROLE: Allrounder
DEBUT: ODI: 2015; T20I: 2013; First-class: 2005; List A: 2005; T20: 2008

BEST BATTING: 208 Easterns vs Griqualand West, Benoni, 2008
BEST BOWLING: 6-58 Titans vs Knights, Centurion, 2015
COUNTY CAP: 2016

WHAT WAS YOUR FIRST CRICKET CLUB? SACE CC, Mpumalanga, South Africa
BEST ADVICE EVER RECEIVED? Your performance on the field doesn't dictate the person you are off the field
CRICKETING HERO? Hansie Cronje – he was an amazing competitor and leader and really knew how to get the best out of his players
WHICH RULE WOULD YOU CHANGE ABOUT CRICKET? No switch-hits allowed
SURPRISING FACT ABOUT YOU? I'm a huge fan of the theatre and musicals
BIGGEST CRICKETING REGRET? Not taking cricket seriously and not backing myself when I started playing
IF YOU WERE AN ANIMAL, WHICH WOULD IT BE? A lion – protects the family
TWITTER: @David_Wiese

Batting	Mat	Inns	NO	Runs	HS	Ave	SR	100	50	Ct	St
ODIs	6	6	1	102	41*	20.40	88.69	0	0	0	0
T20Is	20	11	4	92	28	13.14	122.66	0	0	9	0
First-class	123	192	20	5753	208	33.44	70.83	11	31	69	0
List A	148	125	27	3579	171	36.52	115.63	2	21	46	0
T20s	227	157	57	2265	71*	22.65	144.17	0	5	73	0
Bowling	**Mat**	**Balls**	**Runs**	**Wkts**	**BBI**	**BBM**	**Ave**	**Econ**	**SR**	**5w**	**10**
ODIs	6	294	316	9	3/50	3/50	35.11	6.44	32.6	0	0
T20Is	20	392	497	24	5/23	5/23	20.70	7.60	16.3	1	0
First-class	123	17993	9611	343	6/58	10/111	28.02	3.20	52.4	10	1
List A	148	5508	4937	133	5/25	5/25	37.12	5.37	41.4	1	0
T20s	227	3348	4702	175	5/19	5/19	26.86	8.42	19.1	4	0

DAVID WILLEY LHB / LFM / R0 / W0

FULL NAME: David Jonathan Willey
BORN: February 28, 1990, Northampton
SQUAD NO: 72
HEIGHT: 6ft 1in
NICKNAME: Will Mildman
EDUCATION: Northampton School for Boys
TEAMS: England, Yorkshire, Northen Superchargers, Chennai Super Kings, Northamptonshire, Perth Scorchers
ROLE: Allrounder
DEBUT: ODI: 2015; T20I: 2015; First-class: 2009; List A: 2009; T20: 2009

BEST BATTING: 104* Northamptonshire vs Gloucestershire, Northampton, 2015
BEST BOWLING: 5-29 Northamptonshire vs Gloucestershire, Northampton, 2011
COUNTY CAP: 2013 (Northamptonshire); 2016 (Yorkshire)

FAMILY TIES? My dad Peter played for England, Northamptonshire and Leicestershire
WHAT WAS YOUR FIRST CRICKET CLUB? Old Northamptonians CC, Northampton
BEST ADVICE EVER RECEIVED? Hard to pick one, but most of it came from my dad
WHAT WERE YOU DOING WHEN ENGLAND WON THE WORLD CUP? Playing with my kids
BIGGEST TOPIC OF DISCUSSION IN YOUR DRESSING ROOM? Who's going for coffee
CRICKETING HERO? My dad – I always wanted to follow in his footsteps
SURPRISING FACT ABOUT YOU? My wife Carolyn is a country singer and was a two-time X Factor contestant
IF YOU WERE AN ANIMAL, WHICH WOULD IT BE? A lion
TWITTER: @david_willey

Batting	Mat	Inns	NO	Runs	HS	Ave	SR	100	50	Ct	St
ODIs	46	27	12	279	50	18.60	82.30	0	1	21	0
T20Is	28	19	7	166	29*	13.83	131.74	0	0	12	0
First-class	71	100	12	2350	104*	26.70	64.70	2	14	17	0
List A	129	92	20	1761	167	24.45	94.88	3	6	47	0
T20s	185	139	25	2695	118	23.64	139.78	2	11	72	0
Bowling	**Mat**	**Balls**	**Runs**	**Wkts**	**BBI**	**BBM**	**Ave**	**Econ**	**SR**	**5w**	**10**
ODIs	46	1971	1889	52	4/34	4/34	36.32	5.75	37.9	0	0
T20Is	28	557	761	34	4/7	4/7	22.38	8.19	16.3	0	0
First-class	71	9854	5416	178	5/29	10/75	30.42	3.29	55.3	5	1
List A	129	4762	4531	140	5/62	5/62	32.36	5.70	34.0	1	0
T20s	185	3106	4071	175	4/7	4/7	23.26	7.86	17.7	0	0

KANE WILLIAMSON RHB/OB

FULL NAME: Kane Stuart Williamson
BORN: August 8, 1990, Tauranga, New Zealand
SQUAD NO: TBC
HEIGHT: 5ft 8in
EDUCATION: Tauranga Boys College, Bay of Plenty, New Zealand
TEAMS: New Zealand, Birmingham Phoenix, Barbados Tridents, Gloucestershire, Northern Districts, Sunrisers Hyderabad, Yorkshire
ROLE: Batsman
DEBUT: Test: 2010; ODI: 2010; T20I: 2011; First-class: 2007; List A: 2007: T20: 2009

BEST BATTING: 101* Northern Knights vs Cape Cobras, Raipur, 2014 (T20)
BEST BOWLING: 3-33 Northern Districts vs Wellington, Wellington, 2012 (T20)

NOTES: A prodigious talent from an early age, Williamson played senior representative cricket at the age of 14 and reportedly scored 40 centuries before he left school. In 2008 he captained New Zealand at the U19 World Cup. Aged 20 he became the eighth Kiwi to score a century on Test debut, against India at Ahmedabad. He replaced Brendon McCullum as national captain in 2016, guiding his team to the final of the 2019 World Cup and winning the Player of the Tournament award in the process. He has already scored more Test centuries than any other New Zealander and was leading run-scorer at the 2018 IPL when he captained Sunrisers Hyderabad to the final. Williamson has had county spells with Gloucestershire and latterly Yorkshire. He was signed by Birmingham Phoenix for The Hundred in the £100k category

Batting	Mat	Inns	NO	Runs	HS	Ave	SR	100	50	Ct	St
Tests	80	140	13	6476	242*	50.99	51.63	21	32	71	0
ODIs	151	144	14	6173	148	47.48	81.75	13	39	60	0
T20Is	60	58	7	1665	95	32.64	125.18	0	11	27	0
First-class	148	253	20	11287	284*	48.44	52.11	31	59	135	0
List A	212	201	22	8294	148	46.33	81.36	17	51	87	0
T20s	181	173	21	4593	101*	30.21	124.77	1	31	71	0
Bowling	**Mat**	**Balls**	**Runs**	**Wkts**	**BBI**	**BBM**	**Ave**	**Econ**	**SR**	**5w**	**10**
Tests	80	2103	1178	29	4/44	4/44	40.62	3.36	72.5	0	0
ODIs	151	1467	1310	37	4/22	4/22	35.40	5.35	39.6	0	0
T20Is	60	118	164	6	2/16	2/16	27.33	8.33	19.6	0	0
First-class	148	6576	3692	85	5/75	5/59	43.43	3.36	77.3	1	0
List A	212	2756	2383	67	5/51	5/51	35.56	5.18	41.1	1	0
T20s	181	758	885	30	3/33	3/33	29.50	7.00	25.2	0	0

CHRIS WOAKES

RHB / RFM / R0 / W3

FULL NAME: Christopher Roger Woakes
BORN: March 2, 1989, Birmingham
SQUAD NO: 19
HEIGHT: 6ft 1in
NICKNAME: Wiz, GB
EDUCATION: Barr Beacon Language College, Walsall
TEAMS: England, Warwickshire, Birmingham Phoenix, Kolkata Knight Riders, RC Bangalore, Sydney Thunder, Wellington
ROLE: Allrounder
DEBUT: Test: 2013; ODI: 2011; T20I: 2011; First-class: 2006; List A: 2007; T20: 2008

BEST BATTING: 152* Warwickshire vs Derbyshire, Derby, 2013
BEST BOWLING: 9-36 Warwickshire vs Durham, Edgbaston, 2016
COUNTY CAP: 2009

FAMILY TIES? My brothers played Birmingham League cricket
STRANGEST THING SEEN IN A GAME? Jonathan Trott catching a ball in his pocket (though not on purpose)
SUPERSTITIONS? Only one: always turn off my left shoulder at the end of my run-up
CRICKETING HERO? Jacques Kallis
NON-CRICKETING HERO? Paul 'God' McGrath
SURPRISING FACT ABOUT YOU? I won a keep-uppy competition when I was 10 (70 keepy-ups)
TWITTER: @chriswoakes

Batting	Mat	Inns	NO	Runs	HS	Ave	SR	100	50	Ct	St
Tests	33	55	11	1177	137*	26.75	50.25	1	4	15	0
ODIs	101	69	20	1226	95*	25.02	90.27	0	4	44	0
T20Is	8	7	4	91	37	30.33	144.44	0	0	1	0
First-class	148	220	49	5797	152*	33.90		10	23	63	0
List A	183	122	36	1967	95*	22.87	90.31	0	5	61	0
T20s	111	69	36	803	57*	24.33	136.10	0	2	41	0
Bowling	**Mat**	**Balls**	**Runs**	**Wkts**	**BBI**	**BBM**	**Ave**	**Econ**	**SR**	**5w**	**10**
Tests	33	5714	2934	95	6/17	11/102	30.88	3.08	60.1	3	1
ODIs	101	4716	4384	143	6/45	6/45	30.65	5.57	32.9	3	0
T20Is	8	162	253	7	2/40	2/40	36.14	9.37	23.1	0	0
First-class	148	24801	12754	499	9/36	11/97	25.55	3.08	49.7	20	4
List A	183	7984	7360	221	6/45	6/45	33.30	5.53	36.1	3	0
T20s	111	2175	3040	121	4/21	4/21	25.12	8.38	17.9	0	0

WARWICKSHIRE / BIRMINGHAM PHOENIX

CHRIS WOOD RHB / LMF / R0 / W0

FULL NAME: Christopher Philip Wood
BORN: June 27, 1990, Basingstoke, Hampshire
SQUAD NO: 25
HEIGHT: 6ft 3in
NICKNAME: Woody, Nuts
EDUCATION: St Lawrence CE Primary School; Amery Hill School; Alton College, Hampshire
TEAMS: Hampshire, Oval Invincibles, England U19
ROLE: Bowler
DEBUT: First-class: 2010; List A: 2010; T20: 2010

BEST BATTING: 27 Hampshire vs Surrey, The Oval, 2014 (T20)
BEST BOWLING: 5-32 Hampshire vs Somerset, Taunton, 2018 (T20)
COUNTY CAP: 2018

WHAT WAS YOUR FIRST CRICKET CLUB? Liphook & Ripsley CC, West Sussex
HOW WOULD YOU DISMISS STEVE SMITH? Caught in the stands
CRICKETING HERO? Nathan Bracken
SURPRISING FACT ABOUT YOU? I played football at semi-professional level
CRICKET STAR OF THE FUTURE? Kamran Khanna (Hampshire Academy)
TWITTER: @CWoody27
NOTES: The left-armer signed a contract with Hampshire in October 2018 to keep him at the Ageas Bowl until the end of the 2020 season. Wood's career has been complicated by a knee injury which required surgery and meant that he missed nearly all of the 2016 and 2017 seasons. His first-class appeareances have diminished as a result – Wood announced his retirement from red-ball cricket in March – but he is still one of the canniest short-format bowlers on the circuit

Batting	Mat	Inns	NO	Runs	HS	Ave	SR	100	50	Ct	St
First-class	43	62	6	1326	105*	23.67	64.65	1	6	14	0
List A	79	45	14	400	41	12.90	96.85	0	0	24	0
T20s	121	43	16	289	27	10.70	105.86	0	0	34	0
Bowling	**Mat**	**Balls**	**Runs**	**Wkts**	**BBI**	**BBM**	**Ave**	**Econ**	**SR**	**5w**	**10**
First-class	43	6169	3174	105	5/39	7/49	30.22	3.08	58.7	3	0
List A	79	3304	2964	105	5/22	5/22	28.22	5.38	31.4	2	0
T20s	121	2460	3403	131	5/32	5/32	25.97	8.30	18.7	1	0

LUKE WOOD

LHB / LM / R0 / W0

FULL NAME: Luke Wood
BORN: August 2, 1995, Sheffield
SQUAD NO: 14
HEIGHT: 5ft 9in
NICKNAME: Biscuit
EDUCATION: Portland Comprehensive School, Worksop; Outwood Post 16 Centre Worksop
TEAMS: Lancashire, Trent Rockets, England U19, Nottinghamshire, Worcestershire
ROLE: Bowler
DEBUT: First-class: 2014; List A: 2016; T20: 2016

BEST BATTING: 100 Nottinghamshire vs Sussex, Trent Bridge, 2015
BEST BOWLING: 5-40 Nottinghamshire vs Cambridge MCCU, Cambridge, 2016

WHAT WAS YOUR FIRST CRICKET CLUB? Cuckney CC, Nottinghamshire
WHICH BOWLER WOULD YOU LEAST LIKE TO FACE? Rashid Khan
BEST INNINGS YOU'VE SEEN? Alex Hales's 187 not out against Surrey in the 2017 One-Day Cup final at Lord's
CRICKETING HERO? Ryan Sidebottom
WHICH BOOK MEANS MOST TO YOU? Believe and Achieve – The World's Most Motivational Quotes by Chris Naylor
TWITTER: @lwood_95

Batting	Mat	Inns	NO	Runs	HS	Ave	SR	100	50	Ct	St
First-class	40	63	14	1211	100	24.71	63.13	1	5	14	0
List A	4	3	2	73	52	73.00	119.67	0	1	0	0
T20s	30	9	3	38	11	6.33	92.68	0	0	11	0
Bowling	**Mat**	**Balls**	**Runs**	**Wkts**	**BBI**	**BBM**	**Ave**	**Econ**	**SR**	**5w**	**10**
First-class	40	5297	3208	96	5/40	8/83	33.41	3.63	55.1	3	0
List A	4	126	125	5	2/36	2/36	25.00	5.95	25.2	0	0
T20s	30	499	689	24	3/16	3/16	28.70	8.28	20.7	0	0

MARK WOOD RHB / RF / R0 / W0

FULL NAME: Mark Andrew Wood
BORN: January 11, 1990, Ashington, Northumberland
SQUAD NO: 33
HEIGHT: 6ft
NICKNAME: Woody
EDUCATION: Ashington High School; Newcastle College
TEAMS: England, Durham, London Spirit, Chennai Super Kings
ROLE: Bowler
DEBUT: Test: 2015; ODI: 2015; T20I: 2015; First-class: 2011; List A: 2011; T20: 2013

BEST BATTING: 72* Durham vs Kent, Chester-le-Street, 2017
BEST BOWLING: 6-46 Durham vs Derbyshire, Derby, 2018

FAMILY TIES? My dad Derek and uncle Neil played for Ashington CC and Minor Counties for Northumberland
CRICKETING HEROES? Graham Onions, Stephen Harmison, Ben Harmison, Michael Holding, Ian Botham
NON-CRICKETING HERO? Lennox Lewis
SURPRISING FACT? I was in the Newcastle United FC Academy
TWITTER: @MAWood33

Batting	Mat	Inns	NO	Runs	HS	Ave	SR	100	50	Ct	St
Tests	15	26	6	392	52	19.60	69.13	0	1	7	0
ODIs	51	17	10	56	13	8.00	88.88	0	0	11	0
T20Is	8	2	2	10	5*	-	83.33	0	0	0	0
First-class	53	87	18	1528	72*	22.14	57.72	0	5	16	0
List A	85	33	15	118	24	6.55	80.82	0	0	21	0
T20s	28	12	6	100	27*	16.66	100.00	0	0	4	0
Bowling	**Mat**	**Balls**	**Runs**	**Wkts**	**BBI**	**BBM**	**Ave**	**Econ**	**SR**	**5w**	**10**
Tests	15	2759	1508	48	5/41	9/100	31.41	3.27	57.4	2	0
ODIs	51	2585	2385	61	4/33	4/33	39.09	5.53	42.3	0	0
T20Is	8	165	266	15	3/9	3/9	17.73	9.67	11.0	0	0
First-class	53	8403	4598	174	6/46	9/100	26.42	3.28	48.2	10	0
List A	85	3964	3525	107	4/33	4/33	32.94	5.33	37.0	0	0
T20s	28	561	789	34	4/25	4/25	23.20	8.43	16.5	0	0

TOM WOOD RHB / RO / WO

FULL NAME: Thomas Anthony Wood
BORN: May 11, 1994, Derby
SQUAD NO: 24
HEIGHT: 6ft
NICKNAME: Woody
EDUCATION: Heanor Gate Science College, Derbyshire
TEAMS: Derbyshire
ROLE: Batsman
DEBUT: First-class: 2016; List A: 2016; T20: 2017

BEST BATTING: 15 Derbyshire vs West Indians, Derby, 2017

WHAT WAS YOUR FIRST CRICKET CLUB? Stainsby Hall CC, Derbyshire
WHAT WERE YOU DOING WHEN ENGLAND WON THE WORLD CUP? At home shouting at the tv
HOW WOULD YOU DISMISS STEVE SMITH? Bodyline
CRICKETING HERO? Kevin Pietersen
SURPRISING FACT ABOUT YOU? I was born and bred in Derby but support Newcastle
TWITTER: @tom_wood
NOTES: Wood was released by Derbyshire at the end of the 2017 season but has been re-signed for this summer's 50-over campaign after impressing in Second XI cricket in 2019. The top-order batsman, who has been involved with the club since the age of 10, will join up with his teammates for the whole of July and August, taking in the entire One-Day Cup competition. He will be also available for up to three Championship matches. "There have been a lot of ups and downs over the years," said Wood. "I have worked hard to get back to this point and I feel like I'm ready to take my chance"

Batting	Mat	Inns	NO	Runs	HS	Ave	SR	100	50	Ct	St
First-class	3	5	0	47	15	9.40	34.81	0	0	3	0
List A	2	1	0	44	44	44.00	107.31	0	0	0	0
T20s	2	2	0	33	24	16.50	106.45	0	0	0	0
Bowling	**Mat**	**Balls**	**Runs**	**Wkts**	**BBI**	**BBM**	**Ave**	**Econ**	**SR**	**5w**	**10**
First-class	3	-	-	-	-	-	-	-	-	-	-
List A	2	-	-	-	-	-	-	-	-	-	-
T20s	2	-	-	-	-	-	-	-	-	-	-

CHRIS WRIGHT

RHB / RFM / R0 / W2

FULL NAME: Christopher Julian Clement Wright
BORN: July 14, 1985, Chipping Norton, Oxfordshire
SQUAD NO: 31
HEIGHT: 6ft 3in
NICKNAME: Wrighty, Dog, Wrightdog
EDUCATION: Eggars Grammar School, Alton
TEAMS: Leicestershire, England Lions, Essex, Middlesex, Tamil Union, Warwickshire
ROLE: Bowler
DEBUT: First-class: 2004; List A: 2004; T20: 2004

BEST BATTING: 77 Essex vs Cambridge MCCU, Cambridge, 2011
BEST BOWLING: 6-22 Essex vs Leicestershire, Leicester, 2008
COUNTY CAP: 2013 (Warwickshire)

WHAT GOT YOU INTO CRICKET? Watching my father play for Liphook & Ripsley CC
STRANGEST THING SEEN IN A GAME? Instead of a traditional coin toss, two coach/captains played a game of tossing objects closest to the stumps at the other end. It lasted 15 minutes
BEST MOMENT IN CRICKET? Bowling out Worcestershire in a morning session in 2012. Keith Barker and I each got five wickets and effectively sealed the title for Warwickshire
CRICKETING HEROES? Jason Gillespie – amazing action, quick, moved it away, long hair. Mark Ramprakash – my favourite batter to watch as a boy. Great technique
NON-CRICKETING HERO? James Richardson – former presenter of Gazzetta Football Italia
SURPRISING FACT? I once (a long time ago but as a professional) missed a pre-season game to play in the Irish Open Poker tournament. I got knocked out early on and as a result got very drunk! I then overslept and missed my flight home. I was £10,000 poorer and very ill but a good life experience. The captain and coach of the club didn't think so
TWITTER: @chriswright1985

Batting	Mat	Inns	NO	Runs	HS	Ave	SR	100	50	Ct	St
First-class	162	209	45	2998	77	18.28	48.51	0	12	29	0
List A	103	43	20	263	42	11.43	73.25	0	0	17	0
T20s	62	16	9	30	6*	4.28	90.90	0	0	13	0
Bowling	**Mat**	**Balls**	**Runs**	**Wkts**	**BBI**	**BBM**	**Ave**	**Econ**	**SR**	**5w**	**10**
First-class	162	25974	15153	459	6/22		33.01	3.50	56.5	13	0
List A	103	4025	3766	102	4/20	4/20	36.92	5.61	39.4	0	0
T20s	62	1222	1834	53	4/24	4/24	34.60	9.00	23.0	0	0

LUKE WRIGHT

RHB / RMF / R1 / W0

FULL NAME: Luke James Wright
BORN: March 7, 1985, Grantham, Lincolnshire
SQUAD NO: 10
NICKNAME: Bam Bam
EDUCATION: Loughborough University; Manchester Metropolitan University
TEAMS: England, Sussex, Trent Rockets, Leicestershire, Melbourne Stars, Pune Warriors, Rajshahi Kings
ROLE: Allrounder
DEBUT: ODI: 2007; T20I: 2007; First-class: 2003; List A 2002; T20: 2004

SUSSEX / TRENT ROCKETS

BEST BATTING: 153* Sussex vs Essex, Chelmsford, 2014 (T20)
BEST BOWLING: 3-17 Sussex vs Surrey, The Oval, 2006 (T20)
COUNTY CAP: 2007 (Sussex); BENEFIT: 2017 (Sussex)

FAMILY TIES? My brother Ashley was a pro at Leicestershire
WHAT WAS YOUR FIRST CRICKET CLUB? Bottesford CC, Leicestershire. I played men's cricket at a really young age, which helped me develop. Lots of great memories
BEST ADVICE EVER RECEIVED? Don't get too down on the bad days – everything can change with your next innings
WHAT WERE YOU DOING WHEN ENGLAND WON THE WORLD CUP? Watching with my Kiwi wife
WHAT EXCITES YOU ABOUT THE HUNDRED? The standard of the cricket
MOST INTERESTING TEAMMATE? Chris Nash – still playing at the age of 50...
BEST INNINGS YOU'VE SEEN? I played in the IPL match when Chris Gayle hit 175 not out
WHICH BOOK MEANS MOST TO YOU? Where's Wally? by Martin Handford
TWITTER: @lukewright204
NOTES: Wright retired from red-ball cricket in April 2019

Batting	Mat	Inns	NO	Runs	HS	Ave	SR	100	50	Ct	St
ODIs	50	39	4	707	52	20.20	86.21	0	2	18	0
T20Is	51	45	5	759	99*	18.97	137.00	0	4	14	0
First-class	144	223	23	7622	226*	38.11	65.54	17	38	58	0
List A	211	176	21	5126	166	33.07		11	19	66	0
T20s	314	291	27	7587	153*	28.73	143.04	7	40	95	0
Bowling	**Mat**	**Balls**	**Runs**	**Wkts**	**BBI**	**BBM**	**Ave**	**Econ**	**SR**	**5w**	**10**
ODIs	50	1038	884	15	2/34	2/34	58.93	5.10	69.2	0	0
T20Is	51	330	465	18	2/24	2/24	25.83	8.45	18.3	0	0
First-class	144	8264	4862	120	5/65		40.51	3.53	68.8	3	0
List A	211	4752	4231	111	4/12	4/12	38.11	5.34	42.8	0	0
T20s	314	1799	2563	79	3/17	3/17	32.44	8.54	22.7	0	0

ROB YATES

LHB / OB / R0 / W0

FULL NAME: Robert Michael Yates
BORN: September 19, 1999, Solihull, Warwickshire
SQUAD NO: 17
HEIGHT: 6ft 1in
NICKNAME: Robot, VC
EDUCATION: Warwick School; University of Birmingham
TEAMS: Warwickshire
ROLE: Batsman
DEBUT: First-class: 2019; List A: 2019

BEST BATTING: 141 Warwickshire vs Somerset, Edgbaston, 2019

WHAT WAS YOUR FIRST CRICKET CLUB? Moseley CC, Solihull, West Midlands. I've been there since I was eight years old
WHAT EXCITES YOU ABOUT THE HUNDRED? Watching Ed Pollock's slog sweep
BIGGEST TOPIC OF DISCUSSION IN YOUR DRESSING ROOM? Spikeball
BEST INNINGS YOU'VE SEEN? AB de Villiers breaking the record for the fastest ODI hundred of all time (31 balls), against West Indies at Johannesburg in 2015. Every ball was going for four or six
BIGGEST CRICKETING REGRET? Dropping someone on 10 who went on to make 190. The match would have been over a day earlier if I'd taken that catch
CRICKET STAR OF THE FUTURE? Jacob Bethell (Warwickshire U17)
WHICH BOOK MEANS MOST TO YOU? The Inner Game of Tennis by W Timothy Gallwey
IF YOU WERE AN ANIMAL, WHICH WOULD IT BE? A cat – because I'm boring and love to sleep
TWITTER: @robert_yates99

Batting	Mat	Inns	NO	Runs	HS	Ave	SR	100	50	Ct	St
First-class	12	19	0	570	141	30.00	40.31	1	2	10	0
List A	1	1	0	66	66	66.00	89.18	0	1	0	0
Bowling	**Mat**	**Balls**	**Runs**	**Wkts**	**BBI**	**BBM**	**Ave**	**Econ**	**SR**	**5w**	**10**
First-class	12	-	-	-	-	-	-	-	-	-	-
List A	1	-	-	-	-	-	-	-	-	-	-

SAM YOUNG

RHB / OB / R0 / W0

FULL NAME: Sam Jack Young
BORN: July 30, 2000, Plymouth, Devon
SQUAD NO: 77
HEIGHT: 6ft
NICKNAME: Youngy
EDUCATION: Millfield School, Street, Somerset
TEAMS: Somerset, England U19
ROLE: removeme

WHAT WAS YOUR FIRST CRICKET CLUB? Bath CC, Somerset
WHAT EXCITES YOU ABOUT THE HUNDRED? A new format demanding new skills
CRICKET STAR OF THE FUTURE? Will Smeed (England U19, Somerset Second XI)
IF YOU WERE AN ANIMAL, WHICH WOULD IT BE? An elephant – because I'm peaceful
TWITTER: @sam_y0ung

NOTES: The top-order batsman signed a two-year deal with Somerset last September after coming up all the way through the club's age-group system. Young missed the whole of the 2017 with injury but has played Minor Counties for Cheshire and Devon over the last couple of seasons, while also turning out for Somerset Second XI and Bath CC. The 19-year-old is one of three former Millfield School pupils who have joined the senior playing staff since the end of last season, joining Lewis Goldsworthy and Kasey Aldridge. Like his schoolmates, Young was a member of the England U19 World Cup squad in South Africa over the winter. "It's been a pleasure to work with Sam over the last eight years," said Mark Garraway, Millfield School's director of cricket coaching. "He has always been a fantastic ball-striker who is wonderfully level-headed. He has had some speed bumps along the way and coped with each one in such a mature and admirable way. Sam has developed a number of leadership traits and all these skills will give him a good chance of success as he heads into his professional career with Somerset CCC"

SAIF ZAIB

LHB / SLA / RO / WO

FULL NAME: Saif Ali Zaib
BORN: May 22, 1998, High Wycombe, Buckinghamshire
SQUAD NO: 5
HEIGHT: 5ft 8in
NICKNAME: Danger
EDUCATION: Royal Grammar School, High Wycombe
TEAMS: Northamptonshire
ROLE: Bowler
DEBUT: First-class: 2015; List A: 2014; T20: 2017

BEST BATTING: 65* Northamptonshire vs Glamorgan, Swansea, 2016
BEST BOWLING: 6-115 Northamptonshire vs Loughborough MCCU, Northampton, 2017

WHAT WAS YOUR FIRST CRICKET CLUB? High Wycombe CC, Buckinghamshire
WHAT WERE YOU DOING WHEN ENGLAND WON THE WORLD CUP? I was playing a first-class game against Derbyshire. Tea was extended
WHAT EXCITES YOU ABOUT THE HUNDRED? The opportunity for young players to play with the world's best
BIGGEST TOPIC OF DISCUSSION IN YOUR DRESSING ROOM? Cars and watches
MOST INTERESTING TEAMMATE? Alex Wakely – he's very tidy
CRICKETING HERO? Brian Lara
SURPRISING FACT ABOUT YOU? I'm scared of swimming in open water due to my fear of sharks and crocodiles
CRICKET STAR OF THE FUTURE? My two-year-old cousin – he has a good eye!
IF YOU WERE AN ANIMAL, WHICH WOULD IT BE? A crocodile
TWITTER: @zaib_05

Batting	Mat	Inns	NO	Runs	HS	Ave	SR	100	50	Ct	St
First-class	16	24	3	494	65*	23.52	47.18	0	3	3	0
List A	10	7	0	73	17	10.42	78.49	0	0	0	0
T20s	5	2	0	7	6	3.50	50.00	0	0	2	0
Bowling	**Mat**	**Balls**	**Runs**	**Wkts**	**BBI**	**BBM**	**Ave**	**Econ**	**SR**	**5w**	**10**
First-class	16	661	413	13	6/115	6/115	31.76	3.74	50.8	2	0
List A	10	174	202	3	2/22	2/22	67.33	6.96	58.0	0	0
T20s	5	48	76	0	-	-	-	9.50	-	0	0

ADAM ZAMPA RHB / LB / R0 / W0

FULL NAME: Adam Zampa
BORN: March 31, 1992, Shellharbour, New South Wales, Australia
SQUAD NO: 88
TEAMS: Australia, Essex, Birmingham Phoenix, Adelaide Strikers, Guyana Amazon Warriors, Jamaica Tallawahs, Melbourne Stars, New South Wales, Rising Pune Supergiant, South Australia, Sydney Thunder
ROLE: Bowler
DEBUT: ODI: 2016; T20I: 2016; First-class: 2012; List A: 2012; T20: 2012

BEST BATTING: 17* Melbourne Stars vs Melbourne Renegades, Docklands (Melbourne), 2019 (T20)
BEST BOWLING: 6-19 Rising Pune Supergiant vs Sunrisers Hyderabad, Visakhapatnam, 2016 (T20)

NOTES: The Australian leg-spinner has played in multiple T20 leagues around the world including the IPL, the Caribbean Premier League and the Big Bash League. In 2016 he claimed the second-best figures in IPL history – 6-19 for Rising Pune Supergiant against Sunrisers Hyderabad. He made his T20 international debut against South Africa that same year and has become a regular in Australia's limited-over sides. He was outstanding for Melbourne Stars in the 2019/20 BBL, taking 20 wickets with an economy rate of 7.20. Zampa was a key member of the Essex side that won the 2019 T20 Blast and returns this summer for his third T20 campaign in a row at Chelmsford. He will also appear for Birmingham Phoenix in The Hundred after being selected in the £40k salary band

Batting	Mat	Inns	NO	Runs	HS	Ave	SR	100	50	Ct	St
ODIs	55	24	7	117	22	6.88	65.36	0	0	11	0
T20Is	30	6	4	23	9	11.50	88.46	0	0	4	0
First-class	38	61	7	1177	74	21.79	72.34	0	6	9	0
List A	96	55	14	626	66	15.26	98.27	0	3	20	0
T20s	147	48	21	168	17*	6.22	86.15	0	0	22	0
Bowling	**Mat**	**Balls**	**Runs**	**Wkts**	**BBI**	**BBM**	**Ave**	**Econ**	**SR**	**5w**	**10**
ODIs	55	2888	2701	75	4/43	4/43	36.01	5.61	38.5	0	0
T20Is	30	615	628	33	3/14	3/14	19.03	6.12	18.6	0	0
First-class	38	7697	5068	105	6/62	10/119	48.26	3.95	73.3	2	1
List A	96	5185	4684	137	4/18	4/18	34.18	5.42	37.8	0	0
T20s	147	3018	3632	169	6/19	6/19	21.49	7.22	17.8	1	0

England
Women

ENGLAND WOMEN

CAPTAIN: Heather Knight
COACH: Lisa Keightley

2020 SUMMER FIXTURES

June 25
England vs India
1st T20I
Taunton

June 27
England vs India
2nd T20I
Bristol

July 1
England vs India
1st ODI
Worcester

July 4
England vs India
2nd ODI
Chelmsford

July 6
England vs India
3rd ODI
Canterbury

July 9
England vs India
4th ODI
Hove

September 1
England vs South Africa
1st T20I
Hove

September 4
England vs South Africa
2nd T20I
Chelmsford

September 8
England vs South Africa
1st ODI
Canterbury

September 11
England vs South Africa
2nd ODI
Derby

September 13
England vs South Africa
3rd ODI
Headingley

September 16
England vs South Africa
4th ODI
Leicester

TAMMY BEAUMONT RHB / WK

FULL NAME: Tamsin Tilley Beaumont
BORN: March 11, 1991, Dover, Kent
SQUAD NO: 12
HEIGHT: 5ft 2in
NICKNAME: Tambeau, Beau, Little Mitts
EDUCATION: Sir Roger Manwood's School, Kent; Loughborough University
TEAMS: England, Kent, London Spirit, Adelaide Strikers, Melbourne Renegades, Surrey Stars, Southern Vipers
ROLE: Batsman
DEBUT: Test: 2013; ODI: 2009; T20I: 2009

BEST ODI BATTING: 168* England vs Pakistan, Taunton, 2016

WHAT WAS YOUR FIRST CRICKET CLUB? Sandwich Town CC, Kent. Played in the U11 boys' team when I was eight and a few years later I opened the batting with Sam Northeast in age-group cricket
HOW WOULD YOU DISMISS STEVE SMITH? Mankad (joking)
BIGGEST TOPIC OF DISCUSSION IN YOUR DRESSING ROOM? The environment, veganism
MOST INTERESTING TEAMMATE? Stafanie Taylor (WI) – it was great to have the opportunity to learn about Jamaica and her love of reggae
WHICH RULE WOULD YOU CHANGE ABOUT CRICKET? No Mankading
BIGGEST CRICKETING REGRET? Letting nerves get the better of me in the early part of my career
CRICKET STAR OF THE FUTURE? Grace Scrivens (Kent)
WHICH BOOK MEANS MOST TO YOU? My scrapbook with family photos
IF YOU WERE AN ANIMAL, WHICH WOULD IT BE? A monkey – I'd like to hang out in the trees, and I have a mischievous side to me
TWITTER: @Tammy_Beaumont

Batting	Mat	Inns	NO	Runs	HS	Ave	SR	100	50	Ct	St
Tests	4	6	0	132	70	22.00	40.36	0	1	3	0
ODIs	71	63	6	2387	168*	41.87	73.28	7	9	15	4
T20Is	83	67	10	1262	116	22.14	107.77	1	6	14	4
Bowling	**Mat**	**Balls**	**Runs**	**Wkts**	**BBI**	**BBM**	**Ave**	**Econ**	**SR**	**5w**	**10**
Tests	4	-	-	-	-	-	-	-	-	-	-
ODIs	71	-	-	-	-	-	-	-	-	-	-
T20Is	83	-	-	-	-	-	-	-	-	-	-

KATHERINE BRUNT RHB / RFM

FULL NAME: Katherine Helen Brunt
BORN: July 2, 1985, Barnsley
SQUAD NO: 26
HEIGHT: 5ft 5in
NICKNAME: Baby Rhino, Nunny, Ethel
EDUCATION: Penistone Grammar School, South Yorkshire
TEAMS: England, Yorkshire, Trent Rockets, Perth Scorchers, Yorkshire Diamonds
ROLE: Allrounder
DEBUT: Test: 2004; ODI: 2005; T20I: 2005

BEST ODI BATTING: 72* England vs South Africa, Worcester, 2018
BEST ODI BOWLING: 5-18 England vs Australia, Wormsley, 2011

WHAT WAS YOUR FIRST CRICKET CLUB? Barnsley CC, South Yorkshire. Same club where Darren Gough and Arnie Sidebottom played
WHAT WERE YOU DOING WHEN ENGLAND WON THE WORLD CUP? After an early finish in a friendly game against Australia A, me and the girls watched the end of the final on the projector in the pavilion. Crazy atmosphere – chairs flying everywhere!
BIGGEST TOPIC OF DISCUSSION IN YOUR DRESSING ROOM? Netflix
MOST INTERESTING TEAMMATE? Danielle Wyatt – but I can't say why...
SURPRISING FACT ABOUT YOU? I have dates of all my major career achievements tattooed on my ribs. The last one was "23rd July 2017" to mark the day we won the World Cup
BIGGEST CRICKETING REGRET? Being born in the wrong era. I would have had a safer bowling action earlier because I would have had a proper coach in this day and age. Then I wouldn't have had a chronic back issue
WHICH BOOK MEANS MOST TO YOU? The Hobbit by JRR Tolkien
IF YOU WERE AN ANIMAL, WHICH WOULD IT BE? A rhinoceros
TWITTER: @KBrunt26

Batting	Mat	Inns	NO	Runs	HS	Ave	SR	100	50	Ct	St
Tests	12	15	4	171	52	15.54	29.43	0	1	3	0
ODIs	123	69	18	844	72*	16.54	77.14	0	2	37	0
T20Is	82	49	24	444	42*	17.76	112.12	0	0	24	0
Bowling	**Mat**	**Balls**	**Runs**	**Wkts**	**BBI**	**BBM**	**Ave**	**Econ**	**SR**	**5w**	**10**
Tests	12	2238	923	41	6/69	9/111	22.51	2.47	54.5	2	0
ODIs	123	5976	3480	150	5/18	5/18	23.20	3.49	39.8	5	0
T20Is	82	1783	1646	83	3/6	3/6	19.83	5.53	21.4	0	0

KATE CROSS RHB / RMF

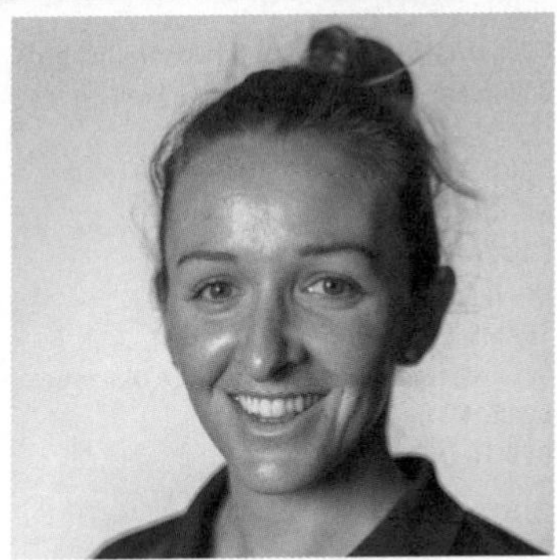

FULL NAME: Kathryn Laura Cross
BORN: October 3, 1991, Manchester
SQUAD NO: 16
HEIGHT: 5ft 7in
NICKNAME: Crossy, Sunny
EDUCATION: Bury Grammar School; University of Leeds
TEAMS: England, Lancashire, Manchester Originals, Brisbane Heat, Lancashire Thunder, Perth Scorchers, Western Australia
ROLE: Bowler
DEBUT: Test: 2014; ODI: 2013; T20I: 2013

BEST ODI BATTING: 8* England vs Australia, Canterbury, 2019
BEST ODI BOWLING: 5-24 England vs New Zealand, Lincoln, 2015

WHAT WAS YOUR FIRST CRICKET CLUB? Heywood CC, Greater Manchester. Andy Flower played a few seasons at the club
WHAT WERE YOU DOING WHEN ENGLAND WON THE WORLD CUP? I was playing a three-day warm-up game for the women's Ashes Test and had to watch the final on my phone
WHAT EXCITES YOU ABOUT THE HUNDRED? The fact that the competition has been set up on level footing for the men and women
BIGGEST TOPIC OF DISCUSSION IN YOUR DRESSING ROOM? Veganism
MOST INTERESTING TEAMMATE? Harmanpreet Kaur – learning about her culture in India is really interesting. And she comes alive when you put some Punjab music on!
CRICKET STAR OF THE FUTURE? Libby Heap (Lowerhouse CC, Burnley)
WHICH BOOK MEANS MOST TO YOU? My sister made me a scrapbook of my first year in international cricket which took her a long time to create and has some amazing memories
IF YOU WERE AN ANIMAL, WHICH WOULD IT BE? A panda – they sit around all day and eat. And they fall over a lot
TWITTER: @katecross16

Batting	Mat	Inns	NO	Runs	HS	Ave	SR	100	50	Ct	St
Tests	3	6	3	15	4*	5.00	24.19	0	0	0	0
ODIs	26	9	6	22	8*	7.33	31.88	0	0	6	0
T20Is	13	1	1	0	0*	-	0.00	0	0	3	0
Bowling	**Mat**	**Balls**	**Runs**	**Wkts**	**BBI**	**BBM**	**Ave**	**Econ**	**SR**	**5w**	**10**
Tests	3	554	209	14	3/29	6/70	14.92	2.26	39.5	0	0
ODIs	26	1128	798	33	5/24	5/24	24.18	4.24	34.1	1	0
T20Is	13	264	296	11	2/18	2/18	26.90	6.72	24.0	0	0

ALICE DAVIDSON-RICHARDS RHB / RFM

ENGLAND WOMEN

FULL NAME: Alice Natica Davidson-Richards
BORN: May 29, 1994, Tunbridge Wells, Kent
SQUAD NO: 36
HEIGHT: 5ft 8in
NICKNAME: ADR, AD
EDUCATION: Epsom College, Surrey; University of Leeds
TEAMS: England, Kent, Northern Superchargers, Otago, Yorkshire Diamonds
ROLE: Allrounder
DEBUT: ODI: 2018; T20I: 2018

BEST ODI BATTING: 9 England vs India, Nagpur, 2018

WHAT WAS YOUR FIRST CRICKET CLUB? Tunbridge Wells CC, Kent, where I grew up
WHAT WERE YOU DOING WHEN ENGLAND WON THE WORLD CUP? Pacing up and down
BIGGEST TOPIC OF DISCUSSION IN YOUR DRESSING ROOM? Food
BEST INNINGS YOU'VE SEEN? For sentimental value, Alastair Cook's final Test innings
WHICH RULE WOULD YOU CHANGE ABOUT CRICKET? Every club has to have a brew ready at the end of an innings. I'd also like to see some rule changes which will help the bowlers a bit more
CRICKET STAR OF THE FUTURE? Issy Wong (Warwickshire) – she likes to bowl fast!
WHICH BOOK MEANS MOST TO YOU? Any of the Harry Potter series
IF YOU WERE AN ANIMAL, WHICH WOULD IT BE? A monkey – smiling, eating, hanging around
TWITTER: @alicedr24

Batting	Mat	Inns	NO	Runs	HS	Ave	SR	100	50	Ct	St
ODIs	1	1	0	9	9	9.00	28.12	0	0	0	0
T20Is	5	3	0	28	24	9.33	82.35	0	0	2	0
Bowling	**Mat**	**Balls**	**Runs**	**Wkts**	**BBI**	**BBM**	**Ave**	**Econ**	**SR**	**5w**	**10**
ODIs	1	-	-	-	-	-	-	-	-	-	-
T20Is	5	24	44	0	-	-	-	11.00	-	0	0

FREYA DAVIES RHB / RFM

FULL NAME: Freya Ruth Davies
BORN: October 27, 1995, Chichester, Sussex
SQUAD NO: 61
HEIGHT: 5ft 9in
NICKNAME: Frey-Frey
EDUCATION: Brighton College; Exeter University
TEAMS: England, Sussex, London Spirit, Western Storm
ROLE: Bowler
DEBUT: ODI: 2019; T20I: 2019

WHAT WAS YOUR FIRST CRICKET CLUB? Singleton CC, West Sussex. A small village club where I started aged seven with my dad. Known as one of the prettiest grounds around – not that I noticed this aged seven
WHAT EXCITES YOU ABOUT THE HUNDRED? Getting to play at Lord's
BIGGEST TOPIC OF DISCUSSION IN YOUR DRESSING ROOM? Climate change
BEST INNINGS YOU'VE SEEN? Smriti Mandhana smashing 52 off 19 balls for Western Storm against Loughborough Lightning in the Kia Super League in 2018
BIGGEST CRICKETING REGRET? That neither of my grandfathers got to see me play
CRICKET STAR OF THE FUTURE? Freya Kemp (Sussex)
WHICH BOOK MEANS MOST TO YOU? To Kill a Mockingbird by Harper Lee
IF YOU WERE AN ANIMAL, WHICH WOULD IT BE? A koala
TWITTER: @FreyaRuth

Batting	Mat	Inns	NO	Runs	HS	Ave	SR	100	50	Ct	St
ODIs	1	-	-	-	-	-	-	-	-	0	0
T20Is	7	-	-	-	-	-	-	-	-	1	0
Bowling	**Mat**	**Balls**	**Runs**	**Wkts**	**BBI**	**BBM**	**Ave**	**Econ**	**SR**	**5w**	**10**
ODIs	1	42	19	0	-	-	-	2.71	-	0	0
T20Is	7	150	147	7	2/18	2/18	21.00	5.88	21.4	0	0

SOPHIA DUNKLEY RHB / LB

FULL NAME: Sophia Ivy Dunkley
BORN: July 16, 1998, Lambeth, Surrey
SQUAD NO: 47
HEIGHT: 5ft 6in
NICKNAME: Dunks, Dunkers, Flippers
EDUCATION: Mill Hill School, London; Loughborough University
TEAMS: England, Middlesex, Southern Brave, Lancashire Thunder, Surrey Stars
ROLE: Allrounder
DEBUT: T20I: 2018

WHAT WAS YOUR FIRST CRICKET CLUB? Finchley CC, London. Couldn't wait to get there after school, and they did great ham-and-cheese toasties
WHAT EXCITES YOU ABOUT THE HUNDRED? Whacking bombs
BIGGEST TOPIC OF DISCUSSION IN YOUR DRESSING ROOM? Love Island
BEST INNINGS YOU'VE SEEN? Alastair Cook's final Test innings at The Oval in 2018. What a special day that was
WHICH RULE WOULD YOU CHANGE ABOUT CRICKET? You should get more runs if you hit a boundary in a certain area
BIGGEST CRICKETING REGRET? Not going to watch more games live – there's still time!
CRICKET STAR OF THE FUTURE? Lauren Bell (Berkshire)
WHICH BOOK MEANS MOST TO YOU? Private Peaceful by Michael Morpurgo
IF YOU WERE AN ANIMAL, WHICH WOULD IT BE? A koala – I like hugs
TWITTER: @dunkleysophia

Batting	Mat	Inns	NO	Runs	HS	Ave	SR	100	50	Ct	St
T20Is	10	3	1	49	35	24.50	100.00	0	0	4	0
Bowling	**Mat**	**Balls**	**Runs**	**Wkts**	**BBI**	**BBM**	**Ave**	**Econ**	**SR**	**5w**	**10**
T20Is	10	24	13	1	1/6	1/6	13.00	3.25	24.0	0	0

SOPHIE ECCLESTONE RHB / SLA

FULL NAME: Sophie Ecclestone
BORN: May 6, 1999, Chester, Cheshire
SQUAD NO: 71
HEIGHT: 5ft 10in
NICKNAME: Eccles
EDUCATION: Helsby High School, Cheshire
TEAMS: England, Lancashire, Manchester Originals, Cheshire, Lancashire Thunder
ROLE: Bowler
DEBUT: Test: 2017; ODI: 2016; T20I: 2016

BEST ODI BATTING: 27 England vs Australia, Leicester, 2019
BEST ODI BOWLING: 4-14 England vs India, Nagpur, 2018

WHAT WAS YOUR FIRST CRICKET CLUB? Alvanley CC, Cheshire. That's my favourite ground too – great view of the surroundings
WHAT WERE YOU DOING WHEN ENGLAND WON THE WORLD CUP? Watching it with a couple of the girls on an iPhone while having tea on tour
WHAT EXCITES YOU ABOUT THE HUNDRED? Playing in double-headers with the men at the big grounds
BIGGEST TOPIC OF DISCUSSION IN YOUR DRESSING ROOM? Love Island in the summer, Netflix in the winter
SURPRISING FACT ABOUT YOU? I love playing crown green bowls competitively
CRICKET STAR OF THE FUTURE? Ellie Threlkeld (Lancashire)
WHICH BOOK MEANS MOST TO YOU? I don't have the concentration to be able to read!
IF YOU WERE AN ANIMAL, WHICH WOULD IT BE? A koala
TWITTER: @sophecc19

Batting	Mat	Inns	NO	Runs	HS	Ave	SR	100	50	Ct	St
Tests	2	2	2	17	9*	-	44.73	0	0	0	0
ODIs	24	16	5	76	27	6.90	64.95	0	0	5	0
T20Is	34	9	4	48	17*	9.60	104.34	0	0	10	0
Bowling	**Mat**	**Balls**	**Runs**	**Wkts**	**BBI**	**BBM**	**Ave**	**Econ**	**SR**	**5w**	**10**
Tests	2	524	234	6	3/107	3/107	39.00	2.67	87.3	0	0
ODIs	24	1249	792	37	4/14	4/14	21.40	3.80	33.7	0	0
T20Is	34	765	769	50	4/18	4/18	15.38	6.03	15.3	0	0

GEORGIA ELWISS RHB / RM

FULL NAME: Georgia Amanda Elwiss
BORN: May 31, 1991, Wolverhampton
SQUAD NO: 34
HEIGHT: 5ft 7in
NICKNAME: G, George, G Dog
EDUCATION: Wolverhampton Girls' High School; Loughborough University
TEAMS: England, Sussex, Birmingham Phoenix, Loughborough Lightning, Melbourne Stars, Staffordshire
ROLE: Allrounder
DEBUT: Test: 2015; ODI: 2011; T20I: 2011

BEST ODI BATTING: 77 England vs Pakistan, Taunton, 2016
BEST ODI BOWLING: 3-17 England vs India, Wormsley, 2012

WHAT WAS YOUR FIRST CRICKET CLUB? Wolverhampton CC, West Midlands. The same club where Rachael Heyhoe Flint played
WHAT EXCITES YOU ABOUT THE HUNDRED? The new tactics for a new format
BIGGEST TOPIC OF DISCUSSION IN YOUR DRESSING ROOM? Wedding guestlists
CRICKETING HERO? AB de Villiers
WHICH RULE WOULD YOU CHANGE ABOUT CRICKET? Do the warm-up after the toss
SURPRISING FACT ABOUT YOU? I learnt Russian at school
BIGGEST CRICKETING REGRET? Not trying to hit bigger sixes
CRICKET STAR OF THE FUTURE? Freya Kemp (Sussex)
WHICH BOOK MEANS MOST TO YOU? Lean in 15 – 15 Minute Meals and Workouts to Keep You Lean and Healthy by Joe Wicks
IF YOU WERE AN ANIMAL, WHICH WOULD IT BE? A cute dog
TWITTER: @gelwiss

Batting	Mat	Inns	NO	Runs	HS	Ave	SR	100	50	Ct	St
Tests	3	5	1	140	46	35.00	28.16	0	0	1	0
ODIs	36	24	5	388	77	20.42	73.20	0	2	11	0
T20Is	14	5	2	29	18	9.66	96.66	0	0	3	0
Bowling	**Mat**	**Balls**	**Runs**	**Wkts**	**BBI**	**BBM**	**Ave**	**Econ**	**SR**	**5w**	**10**
Tests	3	156	83	1	1/40	1/40	83.00	3.19	156.0	0	0
ODIs	36	1097	679	26	3/17	3/17	26.11	3.71	42.1	0	0
T20Is	14	163	161	8	2/9	2/9	20.12	5.92	20.3	0	0

KATIE GEORGE LHB / LFM

FULL NAME: Katie Louise George
BORN: April 7, 1999, Haywards Heath, Sussex
SQUAD NO: 46
HEIGHT: 5ft 5in
NICKNAME: KG
EDUCATION: The Mountbatten School, Hampshire; Richard Taunton Sixth Form, Southampton
TEAMS: England, Hampshire, Welsh Fire, Southern Vipers, Yorkshire Diamonds
ROLE: Bowler
DEBUT: ODI: 2018; T20I: 2018

BEST ODI BATTING: 9 England vs New Zealand, Derby, 2018
BEST ODI BOWLING: 3-36 England vs New Zealand, Derby, 2018

WHAT WAS YOUR FIRST CRICKET CLUB? Cove CC, Hampshire. I'd go along with my dad and brother and play football along the boundary. Then one day I joined in
HOW WOULD YOU DISMISS STEVE SMITH? Go across him and then the inswinger with catchers on the leg-side
WHAT EXCITES YOU ABOUT THE HUNDRED? Being on the big stage alongside the men
BIGGEST TOPIC OF DISCUSSION IN YOUR DRESSING ROOM? A lot of nonsense!
BEST INNINGS YOU'VE SEEN? Jos Buttler dismantling the Aussies in Sydney during the 2017/18 tour
BIGGEST CRICKETING REGRET? Concentrating too much on football and not enough on cricket when I was younger
CRICKET STAR OF THE FUTURE? Lucia Kendall – if she can be prised away from football
IF YOU WERE AN ANIMAL, WHICH WOULD IT BE? A dolphin
TWITTER: @KaTie_George46

Batting	Mat	Inns	NO	Runs	HS	Ave	SR	100	50	Ct	St
ODIs	2	1	0	9	9	9.00	47.36	0	0	1	0
T20Is	5	1	0	0	0	0.00	0.00	0	0	0	0
Bowling	**Mat**	**Balls**	**Runs**	**Wkts**	**BBI**	**BBM**	**Ave**	**Econ**	**SR**	**5w**	**10**
ODIs	2	75	70	4	3/36	3/36	17.50	5.60	18.7	0	0
T20Is	5	78	117	2	1/22	1/22	58.50	9.00	39.0	0	0

SARAH GLENN RHB / LB

FULL NAME: Sarah Glenn
BORN: August 27, 1999, Derby
SQUAD NO: TBC
HEIGHT: 5ft 10in
NICKNAME: Glenny
EDUCATION: Trent College, Long Eaton; Open University
TEAMS: England, Worcestershire, Trent Rockets, Derbyshire, Loughborough Lightning
ROLE: Bowler
DEBUT: ODI: 2019; T20I: 2019

BEST ODI BOWLING: 4-18 England vs Pakistan, Kuala Lumpur, 2019

WHAT WAS YOUR FIRST CRICKET CLUB? Denby CC, Ripley, Derbyshire
WHAT WERE YOU DOING WHEN ENGLAND WON THE WORLD CUP? I was playing at Trent Bridge in the Kia Super League
HOW WOULD YOU DISMISS STEVE SMITH? Hopefully he hasn't seen my googly yet...
WHAT EXCITES YOU ABOUT THE HUNDRED? Being lined up with the men
BIGGEST TOPIC OF DISCUSSION IN YOUR DRESSING ROOM? Love Island
CRICKET STAR OF THE FUTURE? Hannah Baker (Worcestershire)
IF YOU WERE AN ANIMAL, WHICH WOULD IT BE? A bird – so that I can fly anywhere and see a lot of the world
TWITTER: @Lg3Sarah
NOTES: The 21-year-old leg-spinner was an instant hit after making her England debut against Pakistan last December, taking eight wickets in three ODIs. Glenn also impressed in the T20 leg of the tour and in the subsequent tri-series in Australia. In January she was chosen in the squad for the T20 World Cup in Australia, where she took six wickets at 11.33. Glenn attracted the attention of the selectors after an excellent summer for Loughborough Lightning in the 2019 Kia Super League, with 11 wickets and a miserly economy-rate of 6.05

Batting	Mat	Inns	NO	Runs	HS	Ave	SR	100	50	Ct	St
ODIs	3	-	-	-	-	-	-	-	-	2	0
T20Is	10	-	-	-	-	-	-	-	-	3	0
Bowling	**Mat**	**Balls**	**Runs**	**Wkts**	**BBI**	**BBM**	**Ave**	**Econ**	**SR**	**5w**	**10**
ODIs	3	166	93	8	4/18	4/18	11.62	3.36	20.7	0	0
T20Is	10	222	194	15	3/15	3/15	12.93	5.24	14.8	0	0

KIRSTIE GORDON RHB / SLA

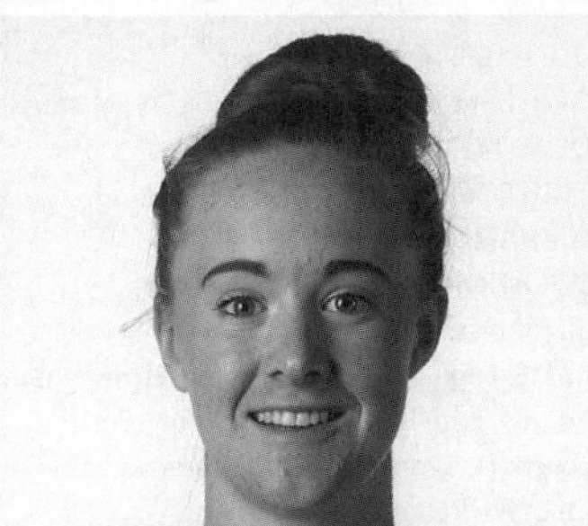

FULL NAME: Kirstie Louise Gordon
BORN: October 20, 1997, Huntly, Aberdeenshire, Scotland
SQUAD NO: 48
HEIGHT: 5ft 5in
NICKNAME: Gordo, Scotty
EDUCATION: Loughborough University
TEAMS: England, Nottinghamshire, Birmingham Phoenix, Loughborough Lightning, Scotland
ROLE: Bowler
DEBUT: Test: 2019; T20I: 2018

WHAT WAS YOUR FIRST CRICKET CLUB? Huntly CC, Aberdeenshire. Formed in 1854 and one of the oldest cricket clubs in Scotland
WHAT WERE YOU DOING WHEN ENGLAND WON THE WORLD CUP? I was running around Fran Wilson's living room, screaming and jumping up and down!
HOW WOULD YOU DISMISS STEVE SMITH? Bowl a moon ball which he'll whack down midwicket's throat
BIGGEST TOPIC OF DISCUSSION IN YOUR DRESSING ROOM? Brexit – love a political debate
BIGGEST CRICKETING REGRET? Not working hard enough through my first year at university
CRICKET STAR OF THE FUTURE? Issy Wong (Warwickshire) – she bowls gas! And she's my new Birmingham Phoenix teammate
WHICH BOOK MEANS MOST TO YOU? Unbelievable by Jessica Ennis-Hill
IF YOU WERE AN ANIMAL, WHICH WOULD IT BE? A leopard – fast and cute, which I can't relate to
TWITTER: @kirstiegordon97

Batting	Mat	Inns	NO	Runs	HS	Ave	SR	100	50	Ct	St
Tests	1	-	-	-	-	-	-	-	-	0	0
T20Is	5	1	1	1	1*	-	100.00	0	0	0	0
Bowling	**Mat**	**Balls**	**Runs**	**Wkts**	**BBI**	**BBM**	**Ave**	**Econ**	**SR**	**5w**	**10**
Tests	1	220	119	3	2/50	3/119	39.66	3.24	73.3	0	0
T20Is	5	114	98	8	3/16	3/16	12.25	5.15	14.2	0	0

AMY JONES RHB / WK

ENGLAND WOMEN

FULL NAME: Amy Ellen Jones
BORN: June 13, 1993, Solihull, Warwickshire
SQUAD NO: 40
HEIGHT: 5ft 9in
NICKNAME: Jonesy
EDUCATION: John Willmott School; Loughborough College
TEAMS: England, Warwickshire, Birmingham Phoenix, Loughborough Lightning, Perth Scorchers, Sydney Sixers, Western Australia
ROLE: Wicketkeeper/batsman
DEBUT: Test: 2019; ODI: 2013; T20I: 2013

BEST ODI BATTING: 94 England vs India, Nagpur, 2018

FAMILY TIES? My younger sister played for Warwickshire U13. My mum played two games for Walmley when we were short
WHAT WAS YOUR FIRST CRICKET CLUB? Walmley CC, West Midlands
WHAT EXCITES YOU ABOUT THE HUNDRED? Playing on free-to-air TV
BIGGEST TOPIC OF DISCUSSION IN YOUR DRESSING ROOM? What we're having for dinner
BEST INNINGS YOU'VE SEEN? Danni Wyatt's 52-ball hundred in a T20 against India in 2018
CRICKETING HERO? AB de Villiers
SURPRISING FACT ABOUT YOU? I used to play football for Aston Villa
BIGGEST CRICKETING REGRET? Not being a left-arm spinner
CRICKET STAR OF THE FUTURE? Issy Wong (Warwickshire)
TWITTER: @amyjones313

Batting	Mat	Inns	NO	Runs	HS	Ave	SR	100	50	Ct	St
Tests	1	1	0	64	64	64.00	45.71	0	1	1	0
ODIs	44	37	2	956	94	27.31	82.77	0	8	28	6
T20Is	49	39	5	668	89	19.64	113.79	0	4	22	12
Bowling	**Mat**	**Balls**	**Runs**	**Wkts**	**BBI**	**BBM**	**Ave**	**Econ**	**SR**	**5w**	**10**
Tests	1	-	-	-	-	-	-	-	-	-	-
ODIs	44	-	-	-	-	-	-	-	-	-	-
T20Is	49	-	-	-	-	-	-	-	-	-	-

HEATHER KNIGHT RHB / OB

FULL NAME: Heather Clare Knight
BORN: December 26, 1990, Plymouth
SQUAD NO: 5
HEIGHT: 5ft 7in
NICKNAME: Trev
EDUCATION: Plymstock School, Plymouth; Cardiff University
TEAMS: England, Berkshire, London Spirit, Devon, Hobart Hurricanes, Tasmania, Western Storm
ROLE: Batsman
DEBUT: Test: 2011; ODI: 2010; T20I: 2010

BEST ODI BATTING: 106 England vs Pakistan, Leicester, 2017
BEST ODI BOWLING: 5-26 England vs Pakistan, Leicester, 2016

WHAT WAS YOUR FIRST CRICKET CLUB? Plymstock CC, Plymouth. Played there with my brother. It was an uncovered wicket which played better when it was wet!
BEST ADVICE RECEIVED? Fashion advice from Kate Cross
HOW WOULD YOU DISMISS STEVE SMITH? With a leg-stump yorker. Or failing that, a voodoo doll
BIGGEST TOPIC OF DISCUSSION IN YOUR DRESSING ROOM? Love Island (unfortunately)
CRICKETING HERO? Marcus Trescothick
WHICH RULE WOULD YOU CHANGE ABOUT CRICKET? You're not allowed to bowl in a hat
SURPRISING FACT ABOUT YOU? I played in the match which set the record for the highest-altitude game of cricket (Mount Kilimanjaro, Tanzania, 2014)
BIGGEST CRICKETING REGRET? The 2015 Ashes
CRICKET STAR OF THE FUTURE? Hannah Baker (Worcestershire)
IF YOU WERE AN ANIMAL, WHICH WOULD IT BE? An eagle – for the views
TWITTER: @heatherknight55

Batting	Mat	Inns	NO	Runs	HS	Ave	SR	100	50	Ct	St
Tests	7	13	1	386	157	32.16	41.50	1	2	7	0
ODIs	101	96	22	2800	106	37.83	71.12	1	19	32	0
T20Is	74	64	14	1139	108*	22.78	119.26	1	4	25	0
Bowling	**Mat**	**Balls**	**Runs**	**Wkts**	**BBI**	**BBM**	**Ave**	**Econ**	**SR**	**5w**	**10**
Tests	7	227	105	4	2/25	2/25	26.25	2.77	56.7	0	0
ODIs	101	1641	1205	48	5/26	5/26	25.10	4.40	34.1	1	0
T20Is	74	519	496	20	3/9	3/9	24.80	5.73	25.9	0	0

NATALIE SCIVER RHB / RM

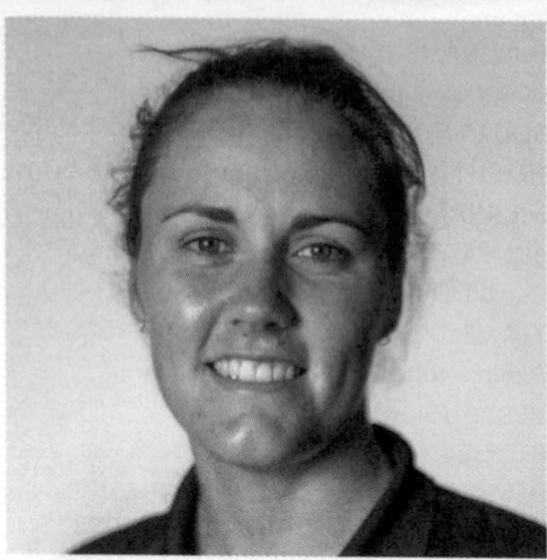

FULL NAME: Natalie Ruth Sciver
BORN: August 20, 1992, Tokyo, Japan
SQUAD NO: 39
HEIGHT: 5ft 10in
NICKNAME: Sciv
EDUCATION: Epsom College; Loughborough University
TEAMS: England, Surrey, Trent Rockets, Melbourne Stars, Perth Scorchers, Surrey Stars
ROLE: Allrounder
DEBUT: Test: 2014; ODI: 2013; T20I: 2013

BEST ODI BATTING: 137 England vs Pakistan, Leicester, 2017
BEST ODI BOWLING: 3-3 England vs West Indies, Bristol, 2017

WHAT WAS YOUR FIRST CRICKET CLUB? Stoke d'Abernon CC, Surrey. I made my sister join for the first year so that I would have a friend
WHAT EXCITES YOU ABOUT THE HUNDRED? Bowling fewer than six balls an over
BIGGEST TOPIC OF DISCUSSION IN YOUR DRESSING ROOM? The schedule
WHICH RULE WOULD YOU CHANGE ABOUT CRICKET? When there's a free hit, the batter gets to nominate who bowls it
SURPRISING FACT ABOUT YOU? I played rugby 7s when I was at school
BIGGEST CRICKETING REGRET? Being right-handed
CRICKET STAR OF THE FUTURE? Issy Wong (Warwickshire)
WHICH BOOK MEANS MOST TO YOU? Any of the Harry Potter books
IF YOU WERE AN ANIMAL, WHICH WOULD IT BE? A dog – you get pampered and if you're lucky you get extra food!
TWITTER: @natsciver

Batting	Mat	Inns	NO	Runs	HS	Ave	SR	100	50	Ct	St
Tests	5	8	0	228	88	28.50	36.07	0	1	4	0
ODIs	67	58	10	1885	137	39.27	97.21	3	13	28	0
T20Is	75	72	17	1425	68*	25.90	111.76	0	8	40	0
Bowling	**Mat**	**Balls**	**Runs**	**Wkts**	**BBI**	**BBM**	**Ave**	**Econ**	**SR**	**5w**	**10**
Tests	5	351	174	2	1/30	1/30	87.00	2.97	175.5	0	0
ODIs	67	1661	1228	44	3/3	3/3	27.90	4.43	37.7	0	0
T20Is	75	1062	1131	58	4/15	4/15	19.50	6.38	18.3	0	0

ANYA SHRUBSOLE RHB / RFM

FULL NAME: Anya Shrubsole
BORN: December 7, 1991, Bath
SQUAD NO: 41
HEIGHT: 5ft 10in
NICKNAME: Hoof
EDUCATION: Hayesfield School, Bath; Loughborough University
TEAMS: England, Berkshire, Southern Brave, Perth Scorchers, Somerset, Western Storm
ROLE: Bowler
DEBUT: Test: 2013; ODI: 2008; T20I: 2008

BEST ODI BATTING: 32* England vs West Indies, Worcester, 2019
BEST ODI BOWLING: 6-46 England vs India, Lord's, 2017

FAMILY TIES? Dad played for Bath CC for many years and a bit of Minor Counties
WHAT WAS YOUR FIRST CRICKET CLUB? Bath CC, which is located in the city centre opposite The Rec where Bath Rugby play their home games
WHAT EXCITES YOU ABOUT THE HUNDRED? That there are fewer balls to bowl (and get whacked out the park)
BIGGEST TOPIC OF DISCUSSION IN YOUR DRESSING ROOM? Reality TV
MOST INTERESTING TEAMMATE? Smriti Mandhana (India) – she just wants to sleep the whole time
CRICKETING HERO? Michael Holding – for the way he bowled with seemingly minimal effort
BIGGEST CRICKETING REGRET? Not being fit enough early in my career
CRICKET STAR OF THE FUTURE? Lauren Filer (Somerset) – quick bowler with a lot of potential
WHICH BOOK MEANS MOST TO YOU? I Love You to the Moon and Back – had it since I was a child
IF YOU WERE AN ANIMAL, WHICH WOULD IT BE? A polar bear – solitary animal
TWITTER: @anya_shrubsole

Batting	Mat	Inns	NO	Runs	HS	Ave	SR	100	50	Ct	St
Tests	6	9	0	62	20	6.88	24.03	0	0	3	0
ODIs	70	31	10	258	32*	12.28	86.00	0	0	17	0
T20Is	75	19	10	104	29	11.55	105.05	0	0	19	0
Bowling	**Mat**	**Balls**	**Runs**	**Wkts**	**BBI**	**BBM**	**Ave**	**Econ**	**SR**	**5w**	**10**
Tests	6	1260	497	17	4/51	7/99	29.23	2.36	74.1	0	0
ODIs	70	3318	2306	90	6/46	6/46	25.62	4.16	36.8	2	0
T20Is	75	1508	1483	101	5/11	5/11	14.68	5.90	14.9	1	0

BRYONY SMITH RHB / OB

ENGLAND WOMEN

FULL NAME: Bryony Frances Smith
BORN: December 12, 1997, Sutton, Surrey
SQUAD NO: 43
HEIGHT: 5ft 5in
NICKNAME: Bry, Smithy
EDUCATION: St Andrews High School, London; Archbishop Tenison's Sixth Form, London
TEAMS: England, Surrey, Welsh Fire, Surrey Stars
ROLE: Batsman
DEBUT: ODI: 2019; T20I: 2018

BEST ODI BOWLING: 1-20 England vs West Indies, Chelmsford, 2019

WHAT WAS YOUR FIRST CRICKET CLUB? Wallington CC, London. I was the only girl in the league throughout age-group cricket and I captained the boys' teams in every age group
WHAT WERE YOU DOING WHEN ENGLAND WON THE WORLD CUP? Secretly watching on my phone at a birthday party
BIGGEST TOPIC OF DISCUSSION IN YOUR DRESSING ROOM? Tactics, or something food-based
MOST INTERESTING TEAMMATE? Marizanne Kapp (South Africa) – very quiet but very knowledgeable about the game, and quite funny when she does speak! Good person to go to for tactical advice
CRICKET STAR OF THE FUTURE? Grace Scrivens (Kent) – left-handed batter who plays 360 degrees around the ground and brings a lot of energy
WHICH BOOK MEANS MOST TO YOU? Bounce – The Myth of Talent and the Power of Practice by Matthew Syed
IF YOU WERE AN ANIMAL, WHICH WOULD IT BE? A bird
TWITTER: @BrySmith97

Batting	Mat	Inns	NO	Runs	HS	Ave	SR	100	50	Ct	St
ODIs	1	-	-	-	-	-	-	-	-	0	0
T20Is	3	3	0	16	15	5.33	100.00	0	0	0	0
Bowling	**Mat**	**Balls**	**Runs**	**Wkts**	**BBI**	**BBM**	**Ave**	**Econ**	**SR**	**5w**	**10**
ODIs	1	48	20	1	1/20	1/20	20.00	2.50	48.0	0	0
T20Is	3	-	-	-	-	-	-	-	-	-	-

LINSEY SMITH LHB / SLA

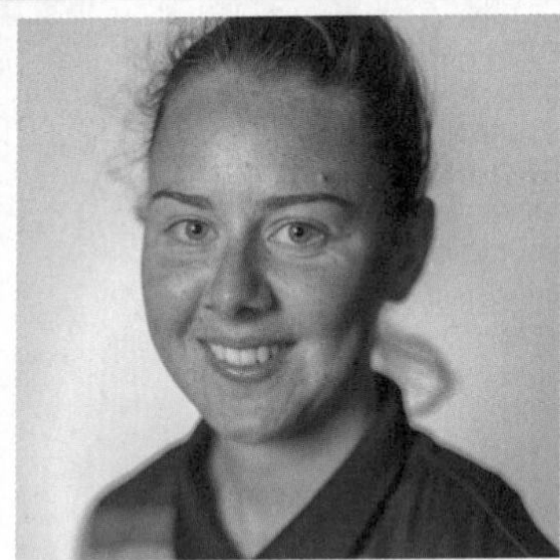

FULL NAME: Linsey Claire Neale Smith
BORN: March 10, 1995, Hillingdon, Middlesex
SQUAD NO: 50
HEIGHT: 5ft 2in
NICKNAME: Smithy, Neal
EDUCATION: Loughborough University
TEAMS: England, Sussex, Northern Superchargers, Berkshire, Loughborough Lightning, Southern Vipers, Yorkshire Diamonds
ROLE: Bowler
DEBUT: T20I: 2018

WHAT WAS YOUR FIRST CRICKET CLUB? Aston Rowant CC, Oxfordshire. They have supported me since I first went there aged 12
HOW WOULD YOU DISMISS STEVE SMITH? Full toss caught at cow
WHAT EXCITES YOU ABOUT THE HUNDRED? It's a new format with some big players
BIGGEST TOPIC OF DISCUSSION IN YOUR DRESSING ROOM? Dinner
MOST INTERESTING TEAMMATE? Anya Shrubsole – she's a genius
WHICH RULE WOULD YOU CHANGE ABOUT CRICKET? The players should come off if it's cold or windy
BIGGEST CRICKETING REGRET? No regrets – everything's a learning curve
CRICKET STAR OF THE FUTURE? Hollie Armitage (Yorkshire)
IF YOU WERE AN ANIMAL, WHICH WOULD IT BE? A monkey – we have similar traits
TWITTER: @LinseySmith95

Batting	Mat	Inns	NO	Runs	HS	Ave	SR	100	50	Ct	St
T20Is	9	-	-	-	-	-	-	-	-	0	0
Bowling	**Mat**	**Balls**	**Runs**	**Wkts**	**BBI**	**BBM**	**Ave**	**Econ**	**SR**	**5w**	**10**
T20Is	9	186	188	13	3/18	3/18	14.46	6.06	14.3	0	0

MADY VILLIERS RHB / OB

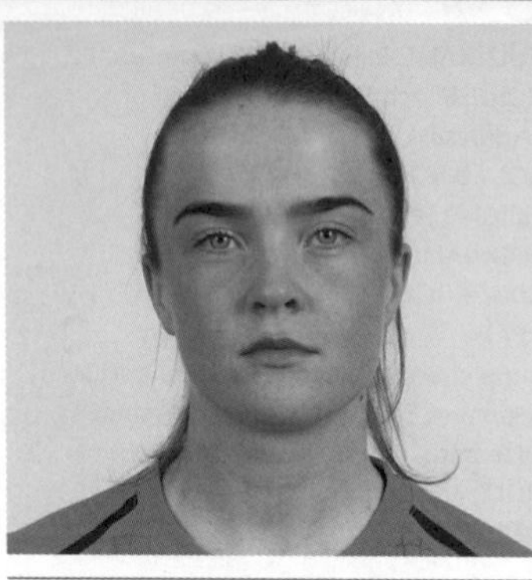

FULL NAME: Mady Kate Villiers
BORN: August 26, 1998, Havering, Essex
SQUAD NO: TBC
HEIGHT: 5ft 5in
NICKNAME: Mads, AB
EDUCATION: Shenfield High School, Brentwood, Essex
TEAMS: England, Essex, Trent Rockets, Surrey Stars
ROLE: Allrounder
DEBUT: T20I: 2019

WHAT WAS YOUR FIRST CRICKET CLUB? Bentley CC, Brentford, Essex
WHAT WERE YOU DOING WHEN ENGLAND WON THE WORLD CUP? I was in the car with my mum on the way home from an England Academy game
HOW WOULD YOU DISMISS STEVE SMITH? Bowl him a cheeky full toss and hope that he picks out a fielder
WHAT EXCITES YOU ABOUT THE HUNDRED? The opportunity to play at some of the best grounds in the country
BIGGEST TOPIC OF DISCUSSION IN YOUR DRESSING ROOM? Veganism and the environment
MOST INTERESTING TEAMMATE? Katherine Brunt – she has some amazing stories and is also a lunatic
CRICKET STAR OF THE FUTURE? Emma Jones (Essex) – very promising fast bowler
IF YOU WERE AN ANIMAL, WHICH WOULD IT BE? A panda – because they eat for 16 hours every day
TWITTER: @VilliersMady
NOTES: The 21-year-old off-spinner, who is also a useful bat, has been one of the Kia Super League's star performers and won the T20 title with Surrey Stars in 2018. Villiers made her international debut last summer and was chosen in England's squad for the T20 World Cup in Australia earlier this year

Batting	Mat	Inns	NO	Runs	HS	Ave	SR	100	50	Ct	St
T20Is	4	-	-	-	-	-	-	-	-	1	0
Bowling	**Mat**	**Balls**	**Runs**	**Wkts**	**BBI**	**BBM**	**Ave**	**Econ**	**SR**	**5w**	**10**
T20Is	4	96	109	5	2/20	2/20	21.80	6.81	19.2	0	0

FRAN WILSON RHB / OB

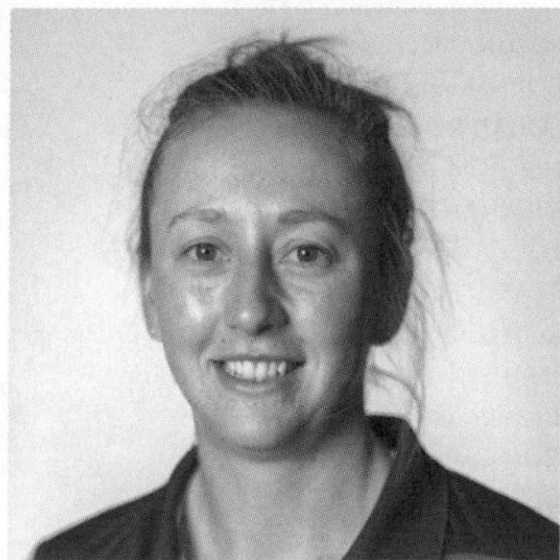

FULL NAME: Frances Claire Wilson
BORN: November 7, 1991, Farnham, Surrey
SQUAD NO: 35
HEIGHT: 5ft 4in
NICKNAME: Franki
EDUCATION: University of Bath; Loughborough University
TEAMS: England, Kent, Oval Invincibles, Hobart Hurricanes, Middlesex, Somerset, Sydney Thunder, Wellington, Western Storm
ROLE: Batsman
DEBUT: Test: 2017; ODI: 2010; T20I: 2010

BEST ODI BATTING: 85* England vs Pakistan, Kuala Lumpur, 2019

WHAT WAS YOUR FIRST CRICKET CLUB? Bath CC. Played alongside Anya Shrubsole throughout my youth and was coached by her dad
WHAT EXCITES YOU ABOUT THE HUNDRED? The crowds
BIGGEST TOPIC OF DISCUSSION IN YOUR DRESSING ROOM? How to pay our tax returns
CRICKETING HERO? Brett Lee – always competing and smiling
BEST INNINGS YOU'VE SEEN? Danni Wyatt's maiden T20 hundred against the Aussies in 2017 – because she's one of my best friends and helped us win the series
SURPRISING FACT ABOUT YOU? I didn't play international cricket for five years after my England debut. I have an MSc in Sport and Exercise Nutrition and run a business delivering nutrition workshops in schools
BIGGEST CRICKETING REGRET? Giving up leg-spin aged 13
WHICH BOOK MEANS MOST TO YOU? The Tale of Peter Rabbit by Beatrix Potter
IF YOU WERE AN ANIMAL, WHICH WOULD IT BE? A bird
TWITTER: @fwilson07

Batting	Mat	Inns	NO	Runs	HS	Ave	SR	100	50	Ct	St
Tests	1	1	0	13	13	13.00	24.52	0	0	0	0
ODIs	30	22	2	462	85*	23.10	88.33	0	2	13	0
T20Is	25	21	8	300	43*	23.07	97.08	0	0	5	0
Bowling	**Mat**	**Balls**	**Runs**	**Wkts**	**BBI**	**BBM**	**Ave**	**Econ**	**SR**	**5w**	**10**
Tests	1	-	-	-	-	-	-	-	-	-	-
ODIs	30	-	-	-	-	-	-	-	-	-	-
T20Is	25	-	-	-	-	-	-	-	-	-	-

LAUREN WINFIELD RHB / WK

ENGLAND WOMEN

FULL NAME: Lauren Winfield
BORN: August 16, 1990, York
SQUAD NO: 58
HEIGHT: 5ft 8in
NICKNAME: Loz
EDUCATION: Lougborough University
TEAMS: England, Yorkshire, Northern Superchargers, Adelaide Strikers, Brisbane Heat, Hobart Hurricanes, Yorkshire Diamonds
ROLE: Batsman
DEBUT: Tests: 2014; ODI: 2013; T20I: 2013

BEST ODI BATTING: 123 England vs Pakistan, Worcester, 2016

FAMILY TIES? My dad plays and we spent many a Saturday afternoon down at my local club Stamford Bridge
WHAT WERE YOU DOING WHEN ENGLAND WON THE WORLD CUP? I was there!
HOW WOULD YOU DISMISS STEVE SMITH? Have a bowl…
BIGGEST TOPIC OF DISCUSSION IN YOUR DRESSING ROOM? Love Island
CRICKETING HERO? Graham Dilley – my former coach at Loughborough, my mentor and a good friend
WHICH RULE WOULD YOU CHANGE ABOUT CRICKET? You can't be run out when the ball deflects off the bowler's hand at the non-striker's end
SURPRISING FACT ABOUT YOU? I love classical music
BIGGEST CRICKETING REGRET? Dropping a catch
CRICKET STAR OF THE FUTURE? Bess Heath (Derbyshire)
IF YOU WERE AN ANIMAL, WHICH WOULD IT BE? A penguin
TWITTER: @Lozwinfield

Batting	Mat	Inns	NO	Runs	HS	Ave	SR	100	50	Ct	St
Tests	3	6	0	94	35	15.66	25.06	0	0	1	0
ODIs	42	42	4	892	123	23.47	66.46	1	3	15	0
T20Is	40	31	6	552	74	22.08	111.29	0	3	16	0
Bowling	**Mat**	**Balls**	**Runs**	**Wkts**	**BBI**	**BBM**	**Ave**	**Econ**	**SR**	**5w**	**10**
Tests	3	-	-	-	-	-	-	-	-	-	-
ODIs	42	-	-	-	-	-	-	-	-	-	-
T20Is	40	-	-	-	-	-	-	-	-	-	-

DANNI WYATT RHB / OB

FULL NAME: Danielle Nicole Wyatt
BORN: April 22, 1991, Stoke-on-Trent, Staffs
SQUAD NO: 28
HEIGHT: 5ft 4in
NICKNAME: Chesney, Waggy
EDUCATION: St Peter's High School; Stoke-On-Trent Sixth Form College
TEAMS: England, Sussex, Southern Brave, Lancashire Thunder, Melbourne Renegades, Nottinghamshire, Staffordshire, Southern Vipers
ROLE: Batsman
DEBUT: ODI: 2010; T20I: 2010

BEST ODI BATTING: 110 England vs Pakistan, Kuala Lumpur, 2019
BEST ODI BOWLING: 3-7 England vs South Africa, Cuttack, 2013

FAMILY TIES? My older brother Ryan played but then he quit when I got better than him – whoops! Dad still rolls them over on a Sunday for the mighty Whitmore Third XI
WHAT WAS YOUR FIRST CRICKET CLUB? Whitmore CC, Staffordshire. Played there since I was 10 and still play there now. There's nowhere better
BEST ADVICE RECEIVED? Block the good 'uns, hit the bad 'uns (Charlotte Edwards, 2012)
WHAT WERE YOU DOING WHEN ENGLAND WON THE WORLD CUP? I was in the stands watching!
WHAT EXCITES YOU ABOUT THE HUNDRED? To be playing under Charlotte Edwards with a group of amazing players
BIGGEST TOPIC OF DISCUSSION IN YOUR DRESSING ROOM? Love Island
BIGGEST CRICKETING REGRET? Not believing in myself earlier and not listening to myself and doing what works for me
WHICH BOOK MEANS MOST TO YOU? The Subtle Art of Not Giving a F*** – A Counterintuitive Approach to Living a Good Life by Mark Manson
IF YOU WERE AN ANIMAL, WHICH WOULD IT BE? A dolphin
TWITTER: @Danni_wyatt

Batting	Mat	Inns	NO	Runs	HS	Ave	SR	100	50	Ct	St
ODIs	74	60	8	1028	110	19.76	80.56	1	1	16	0
T20Is	109	88	9	1588	124	20.10	123.10	2	7	27	0
Bowling	**Mat**	**Balls**	**Runs**	**Wkts**	**BBI**	**BBM**	**Ave**	**Econ**	**SR**	**5w**	**10**
ODIs	74	918	770	27	3/7	3/7	28.51	5.03	34.0	0	0
T20Is	109	759	715	46	4/11	4/11	15.54	5.65	16.5	0	0

The
Umpires

ROB BAILEY

NAME: Robert John Bailey
BORN: October 28, 1963, Biddulph, Staffordshire
HEIGHT: 6ft 3in
NICKNAME: Bailers
APPOINTED TO F-C LIST: 2006
INTERNATIONAL PANEL: 2011-2019
ELITE PANEL: 2014
TESTS UMPIRED: 1 (1 as TV)
ODIS UMPIRED: 34 (4 as TV)
T20IS UMPIRED: 36 (13 as TV)
COUNTIES AS PLAYER: Northamptonshire, Derbyshire
ROLE: Batsman; RHB OB
COUNTY DEBUT: 1982 (Northamptonshire), 2000 (Derbyshire)
TEST DEBUT: 1988
ODI DEBUT: 1985

Batting	Mat	Inns	NO	Runs	HS	Ave	SR	100	50	Ct	St
Tests	4	8	0	119	43	14.87	36.50	0	0	0	0
ODIs	4	4	2	137	43*	68.50	69.89	0	0	1	0
First-class	374	628	89	21844	224*	40.52		47	111	272	0
List A	396	376	65	12076	153*	38.82		10	79	111	0
Bowling	**Mat**	**Balls**	**Runs**	**Wkts**	**BBI**	**BBM**	**Ave**	**Econ**	**SR**	**5w**	**10**
Tests	4	-	-	-	-	-	-	-	-	-	-
ODIs	4	36	25	0	-	-	-	4.16	-	0	0
First-class	374	9713	5144	121	5/54		42.51	3.17	80.2	2	0
List A	396	3092	2564	72	5/45	5/45	35.61	4.97	42.9	1	0

NEIL BAINTON

NAME: Neil Laurence Bainton
BORN: October 2, 1970, Romford, Essex
HEIGHT: 5ft 8in
APPOINTED TO FIRST-CLASS LIST: 2006
ODIS UMPIRED: 8 (3 as TV)
T20IS UMPIRED: 5 (1 as TV)

WHAT ARE YOU LOOKING FORWARD TO IN 2020? Visiting some new venues, given that quite a few of the 50-over games will be played at club grounds
HIGHLIGHT OF YOUR PLAYING CAREER? I kept wicket for South of England U15 at the England Schools Festival in 1986
SURPRISING FACT? I have worked for the Royal Mail as a postman during the winter months
STRANGEST LOCATION WHERE UMPIRED? I'm lucky to have umpired in Mozambique and Uganda on MCC tours
FAVOURITE OUTGROUND? Colwyn Bay. Lovely little ground, great pitch, friendly people

PAUL BALDWIN

NAME: Paul Kerr Baldwin
BORN: July 18, 1973, Epsom, Surrey
APPOINTED TO FIRST-CLASS LIST: 2015
TESTS UMPIRED: 1 (1 as TV)
ODIS UMPIRED: 23 (2 as TV)
T20IS UMPIRED: 12 (1 as TV)

WHAT ARE YOU LOOKING FORWARD TO IN 2020? The warmth of summer, the food around the grounds, but mostly the people. No doubt 2020 will be the most memorable yet, with the dawn of The Hundred and a busier schedule for us umpires. I can't wait!
HIGHLIGHT OF YOUR PLAYING CAREER? Being selected to captain RAF Brüggen, my club side in Germany in 1996, which I captained for the next four years
FAVOURITE PASTIMES OUTSIDE OF CRICKET? Equestrian photography – mostly when our horses compete
SURPRISING FACT ABOUT YOU? I appeared as an extra in two films in Germany, one as an RAF pilot and the other as an American military policeman protecting Lyndon B. Johnson

IAN BLACKWELL

NAME: Ian David Blackwell
BORN: June 10, 1978, Chesterfield, Derbyshire
HEIGHT: 6ft 2in
NICKNAME: Blackdog
APPOINTED TO FIRST-CLASS LIST: 2014
COUNTIES AS PLAYER: Derbyshire, Durham, Somerset, Warwickshire
ROLE: Allrounder; LHB SLA
COUNTY DEBUT: 1997 (Derbyshire), 2000 (Somerset), 2009 (Durham), 2012 (Warwickshire)
TEST DEBUT: 2006
ODI DEBUT: 2002

Batting	Mat	Inns	NO	Runs	HS	Ave	SR	100	50	Ct	St
Tests	1	1	0	4	4	4.00	25.00	0	0	0	0
ODIs	34	29	2	403	82	14.92	86.66	0	1	8	0
First-class	210	319	26	11595	247*	39.57		27	64	66	0
List A	254	233	21	5765	134*	27.19		3	34	64	0
T20s	77	69	9	1281	82	21.35	131.79	0	5	17	0
Bowling	**Mat**	**Balls**	**Runs**	**Wkts**	**BBI**	**BBM**	**Ave**	**Econ**	**SR**	**5w**	**10**
Tests	1	114	71	0	-	-	-	3.73	-	0	0
ODIs	34	1230	877	24	3/26	3/26	36.54	4.27	51.2	0	0
First-class	210	31618	14295	398	7/52		35.91	2.71	79.4	14	0
List A	254	8885	7102	207	5/26	5/26	34.30	4.79	42.9	1	0
T20s	77	1273	1508	50	4/26	4/26	30.16	7.10	25.4	0	0

MIKE BURNS

NAME: Mike Burns
BORN: February 6, 1969, Barrow-in- Furness, Lancashire
APPOINTED TO FIRST-CLASS LIST: 2016
INTERNATIONAL PANEL: 2020-
TESTS UMPIRED: 1
ODIS UMPIRED: 3 (1 as TV)
T20IS UMPIRED: 4

COUNTIES AS PLAYER: Warwickshire, Somerset
ROLE: Allrounder; RHB RM
COUNTY DEBUT: 1992 (Warwickshire), 1997 (Somerset)

Batting	Mat	Inns	NO	Runs	HS	Ave	SR	100	50	Ct	St
First-class	154	248	14	7648	221	32.68		8	51	142	7
List A	221	207	21	4802	115*	25.81		3	31	101	15
T20s	9	7	0	108	36	15.42	108.00	0	0	3	0
Bowling	**Mat**	**Balls**	**Runs**	**Wkts**	**BBI**	**BBM**	**Ave**	**Econ**	**SR**	**5w**	**10**
First-class	154	4751	2885	68	6/54		42.42	3.64	69.8	1	0
List A	221	1844	1769	58	4/39	4/39	30.50	5.75	31.7	0	0
T20s	9	36	55	2	1/15	1/15	27.50	9.16	18.0	0	0

NICK COOK

NAME: Nicholas Grant Billson Cook
BORN: June 17, 1956, Leicester
NICKNAME: Beast
APPOINTED TO FIRST-CLASS LIST: 2009
TESTS UMPIRED: 1
ODIS UMPIRED: 4
T20IS UMPIRED: 7
COUNTIES AS PLAYER: Leicestershire, Northamptonshire
ROLE: Bowler; RHB SLA
COUNTY DEBUT: 1978 (Leicestershire), 1986 (Northamptonshire)
TEST DEBUT: 1983
ODI DEBUT: 1984

Batting	Mat	Inns	NO	Runs	HS	Ave	SR	100	50	Ct	St
Tests	15	25	4	179	31	8.52	23.58	0	0	5	0
ODIs	3	-	-	-	-	-	-	-	-	2	0
First-class	356	365	96	3137	75	11.66		0	4	197	0
List A	223	89	36	491	23	9.26		0	0	74	0
Bowling	**Mat**	**Balls**	**Runs**	**Wkts**	**BBI**	**BBM**	**Ave**	**Econ**	**SR**	**5w**	**10**
Tests	15	4174	1689	52	6/65	11/83	32.48	2.42	80.2	4	1
ODIs	3	144	95	5	2/18	2/18	19.00	3.95	28.8	0	0
First-class	356	64460	25507	879	7/34		29.01	2.37	73.3	31	4
List A	223	10077	6812	200	4/22	4/22	34.06	4.05	50.3	0	0

BEN DEBENHAM

NAME: Benjamin John Debenham
BORN: October 11, 1967, Chelmsford, Essex
APPOINTED TO FIRST-CLASS LIST: 2012
ODIS UMPIRED: 1
T20IS UMPIRED: 1

WHAT ARE YOU LOOKING FORWARD TO IN 2020? The same things I always look forward to: enjoying the company of my colleagues while watching vibrant limited-overs cricket and challenging Championship cricket
TRICKS TO MAINTAIN CONCENTRATION? Enjoying the cricket helps to retain focus
STRANGEST LOCATION WHERE UMPIRED? A coffee plantation in Arusha, north Tanzania
HIGHLIGHT OF YOUR PLAYING CAREER? Captaining MCC against Melbourne CC at the MCG
FAVOURITE PASTIMES OUTSIDE OF CRICKET? Skiing in Australia with my family

JEFF EVANS

NAME: Jeffrey Howard Evans
BORN: August 7, 1954, Llanelli, Carmarthenshire, Wales
HEIGHT: 5ft 8in
APPOINTED TO FIRST-CLASS LIST: 2001
ODIS UMPIRED: 5
T20IS UMPIRED: 5 (2 as TV)

WHAT ARE YOU LOOKING FORWARD TO IN 2020? This is quite a special season as it will be my last on the first-class umpires list. I've thoroughly enjoyed it and hope to continue to umpire locally
SURPRISING FACT ABOUT YOU? I hold a PCV (Passenger Carrying Vehicle) driving licence and regularly drive ski groups out to the Alps in the winter so that I can indulge my passion for skiing
MOST MEMORABLE DISMISSAL? Giving Brian Lara out first ball in the Indian Cricket League. Thankfully the replays showed the decision was correct
FAVOURITE OUTGROUND? Scarborough for its atmosphere and excellent support

MICHAEL GOUGH

NAME: Michael Andrew Gough
BORN: December 18, 1978, Hartlepool
HEIGHT: 6ft 5in
NICKNAME: Goughy
APPOINTED TO FIRST-CLASS LIST: 2009
INTERNATIONAL PANEL: 2013-2019
ELITE PANEL: 2019-

TESTS UMPIRED: 18 (5 as TV)
ODIS UMPIRED: 96 (28 as TV)
T20IS UMPIRED: 35 (10 as TV)
COUNTY AS PLAYER: Durham
ROLE: Batsman; RHB OB
COUNTY DEBUT: 1998

Batting	Mat	Inns	NO	Runs	HS	Ave	SR	100	50	Ct	St
First-class	67	119	3	2952	123	25.44	-	2	15	57	0
List A	49	45	4	974	132	23.75	-	1	3	14	0
Bowling	**Mat**	**Balls**	**Runs**	**Wkts**	**BBI**	**BBM**	**Ave**	**Econ**	**SR**	**5w**	**10**
First-class	67	2486	1350	30	5/66		45.00	3.25	82.8	1	0
List A	49	1136	947	21	3/26	3/26	45.09	5.00	54.0	0	0

IAN GOULD

NAME: Ian James Gould
BORN: August 19, 1957, Taplow, Buckinghamshire
HEIGHT: 5ft 7in
NICKNAME: Gunner
APPOINTED TO FIRST-CLASS LIST: 2002
INTERNATIONAL PANEL: 2006-2009
ELITE PANEL: 2009-2019

TESTS UMPIRED: 99 (25 as TV)
ODIS UMPIRED: 189 (47 as TV)
T20IS UMPIRED: 60 (19 as TV)
COUNTIES AS PLAYER: Middlesex, Sussex
ROLE: Wicketkeeper; LHB
COUNTY DEBUT: 1975 (Middlesex), 1981 (Sussex)
ODI DEBUT: 1983

Batting	Mat	Inns	NO	Runs	HS	Ave	SR	100	50	Ct	St
ODIs	18	14	2	155	42	12.91	63.78	0	0	15	3
First-class	298	399	63	8756	128	26.05		4	47	536	67
List A	315	270	41	4377	88	19.11		0	20	242	37
Bowling	**Mat**	**Balls**	**Runs**	**Wkts**	**BBI**	**BBM**	**Ave**	**Econ**	**SR**	**5w**	**10**
ODIs	18	-	-	-	-	-	-	-	-	-	-
First-class	298	478	365	7	3/10		52.14	4.58	68.2	0	0
List A	315	20	16	1	1/0	1/0	16.00	4.80	20.0	0	0

PETER HARTLEY

NAME: Peter John Hartley
BORN: April 18, 1960, Keighley, Yorkshire
HEIGHT: 6ft
NICKNAME: Jack
APPOINTED TO FIRST-CLASS LIST: 2003
INTERNATIONAL PANEL: 2006-2009
TESTS UMPIRED: 10 (9 as TV)
ODIS UMPIRED: 21 (10 as TV)
T20IS UMPIRED: 16 (6 as TV)
COUNTIES AS PLAYER: Warwickshire, Yorkshire, Hampshire
ROLE: Bowler; RHB RFM
COUNTY DEBUT: 1982 (Warwickshire), 1985 (Yorkshire), 1998 (Hampshire)

Batting	Mat	Inns	NO	Runs	HS	Ave	SR	100	50	Ct	St
First-class	232	283	66	4321	127*	19.91	-	2	14	68	0
List A	269	170	62	1765	83	16.34	-	0	4	46	0
Bowling	**Mat**	**Balls**	**Runs**	**Wkts**	**BBI**	**BBM**	**Ave**	**Econ**	**SR**	**5w**	**10**
First-class	232	37108	20635	683	9/41		30.21	3.33	54.3	23	3
List A	269	12636	9069	356	5/20	5/20	25.47	4.30	35.4	5	0

RICHARD ILLINGWORTH

NAME: Richard Keith Illingworth
BORN: August 23, 1963, Greengates, Bradford
NICKNAME: Harry, Lucy
APPOINTED TO FIRST-CLASS LIST: 2006
INTERNATIONAL PANEL: 2009-2013
ELITE PANEL: 2013-
TESTS UMPIRED: 67 (19 as TV)
ODIS UMPIRED: 126 (54 as TV)
T20IS UMPIRED: 37 (8 as TV)
COUNTIES AS A PLAYER: Worcestershire, Derbyshire
ROLE: Bowler; RHB SLA
COUNTY DEBUT: 1982 (Worcs), 2001 (Derbyshire)
TEST DEBUT: 1991
ODI DEBUT: 1991

Batting	Mat	Inns	NO	Runs	HS	Ave	SR	100	50	Ct	St
Tests	9	14	7	128	28	18.28	32.08	0	0	5	0
ODIs	25	11	5	68	14	11.33	57.14	0	0	8	0
First-class	376	435	122	7027	120*	22.45		4	21	161	0
List A	381	185	87	1458	53*	14.87		0	1	93	0
Bowling	**Mat**	**Balls**	**Runs**	**Wkts**	**BBI**	**BBM**	**Ave**	**Econ**	**SR**	**5w**	**10**
Tests	9	1485	615	19	4/96	6/150	32.36	2.48	78.1	0	0
ODIs	25	1501	1059	30	3/33	3/33	35.30	4.23	50.0	0	0
First-class	376	65868	26213	831	7/50		31.54	2.38	79.2	27	6
List A	381	16918	11157	412	5/24	5/24	27.08	3.95	41.0	2	0

RICHARD KETTLEBOROUGH

NAME: Richard Allan Kettleborough
BORN: March 15, 1973, Sheffield
HEIGHT: 5ft 10in
NICKNAME: Ketts
APPOINTED TO FIRST-CLASS LIST: 2006
INTERNATIONAL PANEL: 2008-2011
ELITE PANEL: 2011-
TESTS UMPIRED: 85 (23 as TV)
ODIS UMPIRED: 136 (43 as TV)
T20IS UMPIRED: 34 (10 as TV)
COUNTIES AS PLAYER: Yorkshire, Middlesex
ROLE: Batsman; LHB RM
COUNTY DEBUT: 1994 (Yorkshire), 1998 (Middlesex)

Batting	Mat	Inns	NO	Runs	HS	Ave	SR	100	50	Ct	St
First-class	33	56	6	1258	108	25.16	-	1	7	20	0
List A	21	16	4	290	58	24.16	-	0	1	6	0
Bowling	**Mat**	**Balls**	**Runs**	**Wkts**	**BBI**	**BBM**	**Ave**	**Econ**	**SR**	**5w**	**10**
First-class	33	378	243	3	2/26		81.00	3.85	126.0	0	0
List A	21	270	230	6	2/43	2/43	38.33	5.11	45.0	0	0

NIGEL LLONG

NAME: Nigel James Llong
BORN: February 11, 1969, Ashford, Kent
HEIGHT: 6ft
NICKNAME: Nidge
APPOINTED TO FIRST-CLASS LIST: 2002
INTERNATIONAL PANEL: 2002-2012
ELITE PANEL: 2012-
TESTS UMPIRED: 91 (29 as TV)
ODIS UMPIRED: 217 (75 as TV)
T20IS UMPIRED: 65 (14 as TV)
COUNTY AS PLAYER: Kent
ROLE: Allrounder; LHB OB
COUNTY DEBUT: 1990

Batting	Mat	Inns	NO	Runs	HS	Ave	SR	100	50	Ct	St
First-class	68	108	11	3024	130	31.17	-	6	16	59	0
List A	136	115	24	2302	123	25.29	-	2	8	41	0
Bowling	**Mat**	**Balls**	**Runs**	**Wkts**	**BBI**	**BBM**	**Ave**	**Econ**	**SR**	**5w**	**10**
First-class	68	2273	1259	35	5/21		35.97	3.32	64.9	2	0
List A	136	1317	1210	40	4/24	4/24	30.25	5.51	32.9	0	0

GRAHAM LLOYD

NAME: Graham David Lloyd
BORN: July 1, 1969, Accrington, Lancashire
APPOINTED TO FIRST-CLASS LIST: 2014
ODIS UMPIRED: 6 (2 as TV)
T20IS UMPIRED: 2
COUNTY AS PLAYER: Lancashire
ROLE: Batsman; RHB RM
COUNTY DEBUT: 1988
ODI DEBUT: 1996

Batting	Mat	Inns	NO	Runs	HS	Ave	SR	100	50	Ct	St
ODIs	6	5	1	39	22	9.75	48.75	0	0	2	0
First-class	203	323	28	11279	241	38.23		24	64	140	0
List A	295	258	48	6117	134	29.12		4	29	67	0
Bowling	**Mat**	**Balls**	**Runs**	**Wkts**	**BBI**	**BBM**	**Ave**	**Econ**	**SR**	**5w**	**10**
ODIs	6	-	-	-	-	-	-	-	-	-	-
First-class	203	339	440	2	1/4		220.00	7.78	169.5	0	0
List A	295	72	103	1	1/23	1/23	103.00	8.58	72.0	0	0

JEREMY LLOYDS

NAME: Jeremy William Lloyds
BORN: November 17, 1954, Penang, Malaysia
HEIGHT: 5ft 11in
NICKNAME: Jerry
APPOINTED TO FIRST-CLASS LIST: 1998
INTERNATIONAL PANEL: 2002-2006
TESTS UMPIRED: 16 (10 as TV)
ODIS UMPIRED: 43 (22 as TV)
T20IS UMPIRED: 4
COUNTIES AS PLAYER: Somerset, Gloucestershire
ROLE: Allrounder; LHB OB
COUNTY DEBUT: 1979 (Somerset), 1985 (Gloucestershire)

Batting	Mat	Inns	NO	Runs	HS	Ave	SR	100	50	Ct	St
First-class	267	408	64	10679	132*	31.04	-	10	62	229	0
List A	177	150	26	1982	73*	15.98	-	0	5	58	0
Bowling	**Mat**	**Balls**	**Runs**	**Wkts**	**BBI**	**BBM**	**Ave**	**Econ**	**SR**	**5w**	**10**
First-class	267	24175	12943	333	7/88		38.86	3.21	72.5	13	1
List A	177	1522	1129	26	3/14	3/14	43.42	4.45	58.5	0	0

NEIL MALLENDER

NAME: Neil Alan Mallender
BORN: August 13, 1961, Kirk Sandall, Yorkshire
HEIGHT: 6ft
NICKNAME: Ghostie
APPOINTED TO FIRST-CLASS LIST: 1999
INTERNATIONAL PANEL: 2002-2004
TESTS UMPIRED: 11 (5 as TV)
ODIS UMPIRED: 36 (10 as TV)
T20IS UMPIRED: 3 (1 as TV)
COUNTIES AS PLAYER: Northamptonshire, Somerset
ROLE: Bowler; RHB RFM
COUNTY DEBUT: 1980 (Northamptonshire), 1987 (Somerset)
TEST DEBUT: 1992

Batting	Mat	Inns	NO	Runs	HS	Ave	SR	100	50	Ct	St
Tests	2	3	0	8	4	2.66	36.36	0	0	0	0
First-class	345	396	122	4709	100*	17.18		1	10	111	0
List A	325	163	75	1146	38*	13.02		0	0	60	0
Bowling	**Mat**	**Balls**	**Runs**	**Wkts**	**BBI**	**BBM**	**Ave**	**Econ**	**SR**	**5w**	**10**
Tests	2	449	215	10	5/50	8/122	21.50	2.87	44.9	1	0
First-class	345	53215	24654	937	7/27		26.31	2.77	56.7	36	5
List A	325	15488	9849	387	7/37	7/37	25.44	3.81	40.0	3	0

DAVID MILLNS

NAME: David James Millns
BORN: February 7, 1965, Clipstone, Nottinghamshire
HEIGHT: 6ft 3in
NICKNAME: Rocket Man
APPOINTED TO FIRST-CLASS LIST: 2009
INTERNATIONAL PANEL: 2020-
TESTS UMPIRED: 1
ODIS UMPIRED: 12 (1 as TV)
T20IS UMPIRED: 8 (1 as TV)
COUNTIES AS A PLAYER: Nottinghamshire, Leicestershire
ROLE: Bowler; LHB RF
COUNTY DEBUT: 1988 (Nottinghamshire), 1990 (Leicestershire)

Batting	Mat	Inns	NO	Runs	HS	Ave	SR	100	50	Ct	St
First-class	171	203	63	3082	121	22.01	-	3	8	76	0
List A	91	49	26	338	39*	14.69	-	0	0	18	0
Bowling	**Mat**	**Balls**	**Runs**	**Wkts**	**BBI**	**BBM**	**Ave**	**Econ**	**SR**	**5w**	**10**
First-class	171	26571	15129	553	9/37		27.35	3.41	48.0	23	4
List A	91	3931	3144	83	4/26	4/26	37.87	4.79	47.3	0	0

STEVE O'SHAUGHNESSY

NAME: Steven Joseph O'Shaughnessy
BORN: September 9, 1961, Bury, Lancashire
APPOINTED TO FIRST-CLASS LIST: 2011
ODIS UMPIRED: 9 (1 as TV)
T20IS UMPIRED: 2 (1 as TV)
COUNTIES AS PLAYER: Lancashire, Worcestershire
ROLE: Allrounder; RHB RM
COUNTY DEBUT: 1980 (Lancashire), 1988 (Worcestershire)

Batting	Mat	Inns	NO	Runs	HS	Ave	SR	100	50	Ct	St
First-class	112	181	28	3720	159*	24.31	-	5	16	57	0
List A	176	151	23	2999	101*	23.42	-	1	15	44	0
Bowling	**Mat**	**Balls**	**Runs**	**Wkts**	**BBI**	**BBM**	**Ave**	**Econ**	**SR**	**5w**	**10**
First-class	112	7179	4108	114	4/66		36.03	3.43	62.9	0	0
List A	176	5389	4184	115	4/17	4/17	36.38	4.65	46.8	0	0

PAUL POLLARD

NAME: Paul Raymond Pollard
BORN: September 24, 1968, Nottingham
APPOINTED TO FIRST-CLASS LIST: 2018
T20IS UMPIRED: 1 (1 as TV)
COUNTIES AS PLAYER: Nottinghamshire, Worcestershire
ROLE: Batsman; LHB RM
COUNTY DEBUT: 1987 (Nottinghamshire), 2004 (Worcestershire)

Batting	Mat	Inns	NO	Runs	HS	Ave	SR	100	50	Ct	St
First-class	192	332	24	9685	180	31.44	-	15	48	158	0
List A	187	173	17	5233	132*	33.54	-	5	33	66	0
Bowling	**Mat**	**Balls**	**Runs**	**Wkts**	**BBI**	**BBM**	**Ave**	**Econ**	**SR**	**5w**	**10**
First-class	192	275	272	4	2/79		68.00	5.93	68.7	0	0
List A	187	18	9	0	-	-	-	3.00	-	0	0

TIM ROBINSON

NAME: Robert Timothy Robinson
BORN: November 21, 1958, Sutton-in-Ashfield, Nottinghamshire
NICKNAME: Robbo, Chop
APPOINTED TO FIRST-CLASS LIST: 2007
INTERNATIONAL PANEL: 2013-2019
TESTS UMPIRED: 1 (1 as TV)
ODIS UMPIRED: 27 (1 as TV)
T20IS UMPIRED: 29 (12 as TV)
COUNTY AS PLAYER: Nottinghamshire
ROLE: Batsman; RHB RM
COUNTY DEBUT: 1978
TEST DEBUT: 1984
ODI DEBUT: 1984

Batting	Mat	Inns	NO	Runs	HS	Ave	SR	100	50	Ct	St
Tests	29	49	5	1601	175	36.38	41.62	4	6	8	0
ODIs	26	26	0	597	83	22.96	58.18	0	3	6	0
First-class	425	739	85	27571	220*	42.15		63	141	257	0
List A	397	386	40	11879	139	34.33		9	75	120	0
Bowling	**Mat**	**Balls**	**Runs**	**Wkts**	**BBI**	**BBM**	**Ave**	**Econ**	**SR**	**5w**	**10**
Tests	29	6	0	0	-	-	-	0.00	-	0	0
ODIs	26	-	-	-	-	-	-	-	-	-	-
First-class	425	259	289	4	1/22		72.25	6.69	64.7	0	0
List A	397	-	-	-	-	-	-	-	-	-	-

MARTIN SAGGERS

NAME: Martin John Saggers
BORN: May 23, 1972, King's Lynn, Norfolk
HEIGHT: 6ft 2in
NICKNAME: Saggs
APPOINTED TO FIRST-CLASS LIST: 2012
INTERNATIONAL PANEL: 2020-
TESTS UMPIRED: 1 (1 as TV)
ODIS UMPIRED: 10 (3 as TV)
T20IS UMPIRED: 6
COUNTIES AS PLAYER: Durham, Kent
ROLE: Bowler; RHB RFM
COUNTY DEBUT: 1996 (Durham), 1999 (Kent)
TEST DEBUT: 2003

Batting	Mat	Inns	NO	Runs	HS	Ave	SR	100	50	Ct	St
Tests	3	3	0	1	1	0.33	3.33	0	0	1	0
First-class	119	147	43	1165	64	11.20		0	2	27	0
List A	124	68	34	313	34*	9.20		0	0	23	0
T20s	10	1	0	5	5	5.00	62.50	0	0	2	0
Bowling	**Mat**	**Balls**	**Runs**	**Wkts**	**BBI**	**BBM**	**Ave**	**Econ**	**SR**	**5w**	**10**
Tests	3	493	247	7	2/29	3/62	35.28	3.00	70.4	0	0
First-class	119	20676	10513	415	7/79		25.33	3.05	49.8	18	0
List A	124	5622	4229	166	5/22	5/22	25.47	4.51	33.8	2	0
T20s	10	186	256	6	2/14	2/14	42.66	8.25	31.0	0	0

BILLY TAYLOR

NAME: Billy Victor Taylor
BORN: January 11, 1977, Southampton, Hampshire
APPOINTED TO FIRST-CLASS LIST: 2016
TESTS UMPIRED: 1
ODIS UMPIRED: 1
COUNTIES AS PLAYER: Sussex, Hampshire
ROLE: Bowler; LHB RMF
COUNTY DEBUT: 1999 (Sussex), 2004 (Hampshire)

Batting	Mat	Inns	NO	Runs	HS	Ave	SR	100	50	Ct	St
First-class	54	68	26	431	40	10.26		0	0	6	0
List A	142	58	28	191	21*	6.36		0	0	26	0
T20s	37	9	8	22	12*	22.00	84.61	0	0	3	0
Bowling	**Mat**	**Balls**	**Runs**	**Wkts**	**BBI**	**BBM**	**Ave**	**Econ**	**SR**	**5w**	**10**
First-class	54	8412	4535	136	6/32		33.34	3.23	61.8	4	0
List A	142	6311	4699	182	5/28	5/28	25.81	4.46	34.6	1	0
T20s	37	713	883	30	2/9	2/9	29.43	7.43	23.7	0	0

RUSSELL WARREN

NAME: Russell John Warren
BORN: September 10, 1971, Northampton
HEIGHT: 6ft 2in
NICKNAME: Rabbit
APPOINTED TO FIRST-CLASS LIST: 2014
ODIS UMPIRED: 1
T20IS UMPIRED: 3
COUNTIES AS PLAYER: Northamptonshire, Nottinghamshire
ROLE: Wicketkeeper/batsman; RHB
COUNTY DEBUT: 1992 (Northamptonshire), 2003 (Nottinghamshire)

Batting	Mat	Inns	NO	Runs	HS	Ave	SR	100	50	Ct	St
First-class	146	238	26	7776	201*	36.67		15	41	128	5
List A	177	162	25	3363	100*	24.54		1	15	135	11
T20s	2	1	0	26	26	26.00	86.66	0	0	0	0
Bowling	**Mat**	**Balls**	**Runs**	**Wkts**	**BBI**	**BBM**	**Ave**	**Econ**	**SR**	**5w**	**10**
First-class	146	6	0	0	-	-	-	0.00	-	0	0
List A	177	-	-	-	-	-	-	-	-	-	-
T20s	2	-	-	-	-	-	-	-	-	-	-

ALEX WHARF

NAME: Alexander George Wharf
BORN: June 4, 1975, Bradford, Yorkshire
HEIGHT: 6ft 4in
NICKNAME: Gangster
APPOINTED TO FIRST-CLASS LIST: 2014
INTERNATIONAL PANEL: 2018-
TESTS UMPIRED: 2
ODIS UMPIRED: 13 (4 as TV)
T20IS UMPIRED: 34 (5 as TV)
COUNTIES AS PLAYER: Yorkshire, Nottinghamshire, Glamorgan
ROLE: Allrounder; RHB RMF
COUNTY DEBUT: 1994 (Yorkshire), 1998 (Nottinghamshire), 2000 (Glamorgan)
ODI DEBUT: 2004

Batting	Mat	Inns	NO	Runs	HS	Ave	SR	100	50	Ct	St
ODIs	13	5	3	19	9	9.50	67.85	0	0	1	0
First-class	121	184	29	3570	128*	23.03		6	14	63	0
List A	155	109	22	1411	72	16.21		0	1	42	0
T20s	34	20	7	157	19	12.07	120.76	0	0	5	0
Bowling	**Mat**	**Balls**	**Runs**	**Wkts**	**BBI**	**BBM**	**Ave**	**Econ**	**SR**	**5w**	**10**
ODIs	13	584	428	18	4/24	4/24	23.77	4.39	32.4	0	0
First-class	121	16825	10941	293	6/59		37.34	3.90	57.4	5	1
List A	155	6497	5552	192	6/5	6/5	28.91	5.12	33.8	1	0
T20s	34	644	1028	39	4/39	4/39	26.35	9.57	16.5	0	0

Roll *of*
Honour

SPECSAVERS COUNTY CHAMPIONSHIP TABLES

Division One

Team	Mat	Won	Lost	Tied	Draw	Aban	Pts
Essex	14	9	1	0	4	0	228
Somerset	14	9	3	0	2	0	217
Hampshire	14	5	3	0	6	0	176
Kent	14	5	5	0	4	0	172
Yorkshire	14	5	4	0	5	0	165
Surrey	14	2	6	0	6	0	133
Warwickshire	14	3	6	0	5	0	131
Nottinghamshire	14	0	10	0	4	0	67

Division Two

Team	Mat	Won	Lost	Tied	Draw	Aban	Pts
Lancashire	14	8	0	0	6	0	233
Northamptonshire	14	5	2	0	7	0	188
Gloucestershire	14	5	3	0	6	0	182
Glamorgan	14	4	3	0	7	0	167
Durham	14	5	5	0	4	0	157
Sussex	14	4	5	0	5	0	156
Derbyshire	14	4	6	0	4	0	145
Middlesex	14	3	5	0	6	0	133
Worcestershire	14	3	7	0	4	0	125
Leicestershire	14	1	6	0	7	0	107

GRAY-NICOLLS
SURRIDGE

North Group

Team	Mat	Won	Lost	Tied	N/R	Pts	Net RR
1 Nottinghamshire	8	6	1	0	1	13	0.619
2 Worcestershire	8	6	2	0	0	12	1.083
3 Lancashire	8	5	3	0	0	10	0.344
4 Durham	8	4	2	0	2	10	0.472
5 Derbyshire	8	3	4	1	0	7	-0.07
6 Yorkshire	8	2	3	2	1	7	-0.091
7 Warwickshire	8	2	5	1	0	5	-0.911
8 Northamptonshire	8	2	6	0	0	4	0.069
9 Leicestershire	8	2	6	0	0	4	-1.313

South Group

Team	Mat	Won	Lost	Tied	N/R	Pts	Net RR
1 Hampshire	8	7	1	0	0	14	1.02
2 Middlesex	8	6	2	0	0	12	0.135
3 Somerset	8	5	3	0	0	10	0.505
4 Gloucestershire	8	5	3	0	0	10	0.27
5 Sussex	8	4	4	0	0	8	0.013
6 Glamorgan	8	3	4	0	1	7	-0.298
7 Kent	8	2	5	0	1	5	-0.966
8 Essex	8	2	6	0	0	4	0.325
9 Surrey	8	1	7	0	0	2	-1.007

QUARTER-FINALS

Worcestershire v Somerset at Worcester

May 10 – Somerset won by 147 runs

Somerset 337-8 (50/50 ov); Worcestershire 190 (38/50 ov)

Middlesex v Lancashire at Lord's

May 10 – Lancashire won by 20 runs

Lancashire 304-4 (50/50 ov); Middlesex 284 (48.5/50 ov)

The two group winners progressed straight into the semi-finals; the second- and third-placed teams played two 'quarter-finals'

SEMI-FINALS

Hampshire v Lancashire at Southampton

May 12 – Hampshire won by 4 wickets

Lancashire 241 (47.4/50 ov); Hampshire 245-6 (49/50 ov)

Nottinghamshire v Somerset at Trent Bridge

May 12 – Somerset won by 115 runs

Somerset 337 (50/50 ov); Nottinghamshire 222 (38.2/50 ov)

FINAL

Hampshire v Somerset at Lord's

May 25 – Somerset won by 6 wickets

Hampshire 244-8 (50/50 ov); Somerset 245-4 (43.3/50 ov)

ROYAL LONDON
ONE-DAY
CUP
ROYAL LONDON

North Group

Team	Mat	Won	Lost	Tied	N/R	Pts	Net RR
Lancashire	14	8	2	0	4	20	0.755
Nottinghamshire	14	6	4	0	4	16	0.336
Derbyshire	14	7	5	0	2	16	0.022
Worcestershire	14	6	5	0	3	15	0.205
Yorkshire	14	4	5	1	4	13	0.339
Durham	14	5	7	0	2	12	-0.049
Northamptonshire	14	4	6	0	4	12	-0.543
Birmingham	14	4	7	1	2	11	-0.467
Leicestershire	14	4	7	0	3	11	-0.471

South Group

Team	Mat	Won	Lost	Tied	N/R	Pts	Net RR
Sussex	14	8	3	1	2	19	0.803
Gloucestershire	14	7	3	1	3	18	0.242
Middlesex	14	7	6	0	1	15	0.216
Essex	14	5	4	1	4	15	-0.464
Kent	14	6	6	0	2	14	0
Somerset	14	6	7	0	1	13	0.448
Hampshire	14	5	6	1	2	13	0.021
Surrey	14	5	7	1	1	12	-0.246
Glamorgan	14	1	8	1	4	7	-1.381

QUARTER-FINALS

Lancashire v Essex at Chester-le-Street
September 4 – Essex won by 6 wickets
Lancashire 159-5 (20/20 ov); Essex 165-4 (19.2/20 ov)

Nottinghamshire v Middlesex at Trent Bridge
September 5 – Nottinghamshire won by 10 wickets
Middlesex 160-8 (20/20 ov); Nottinghamshire 165-0 (16.2/20 ov)

Sussex v Worcestershire at Hove
September 6 – Worcestershire won by 8 wickets
Sussex 182-6 (20/20 ov); Worcestershire 187-2 (17.4/20 ov)

Gloucestershire v Derbyshire at Bristol
September 7 – Derbyshire won by 7 wickets
Gloucestershire 135-7 (20/20 ov); Derbyshire 137-3 (17.1/20 ov)

SEMI-FINALS

Worcestershire v Nottinghamshire at Edgbaston
September 21 – Worcestershire won by 1 run
Worcestershire 147-9 (20/20 ov); Nottinghamshire 146-5 (20/20 ov)

Derbyshire v Essex at Edgbaston
September 21 – Essex won by 34 runs
Essex 160-5 (20/20 ov); Derbyshire 126 (18.4/20 ov)

FINAL

Essex v Worcestershire at Edgbaston
September 21 – Essex won by 4 wickets
Worcestershire 145-9 (20/20 ov); Essex 148-6 (20/20 ov)

SEVEN

COUNTY CHAMPIONSHIP BATTING AVERAGES *Minimum of 500 runs*

Name	Mat	Inns	NO	Runs	HS	Ave	BF	SR	100	50	0	4s	6s
OJ Pope	5	8	1	561	221*	80.14	866	64.78	2	2	0	68	1
DJ Vilas	14	17	4	1036	266	79.69	1388	74.63	2	7	2	146	6
DP Sibley	13	21	2	1324	244	69.68	3024	43.78	5	5	1	151	1
M Labuschagne	10	18	1	1114	182	65.52	1462	76.19	5	5	1	154	8
RF Higgins	14	21	5	958	199	59.87	1250	76.64	4	3	2	124	9
JL Denly	6	11	2	504	167*	56.00	828	60.86	2	1	1	57	7
Hassan Azad	14	26	4	1189	137	54.04	2860	41.57	3	8	0	124	1
SR Hain	12	19	3	822	129*	51.37	1865	44.07	2	3	1	112	0
SA Northeast	13	22	3	969	169	51.00	1613	60.07	3	5	1	122	3
LA Dawson	8	12	1	561	103	51.00	1020	55.00	1	5	0	63	1
S van Zyl	12	20	3	820	173	48.23	1627	50.39	2	4	1	110	0
DJ Malan	13	22	1	1005	199	47.85	1728	58.15	4	2	2	124	4
CDJ Dent	14	24	1	1087	176	47.26	2204	49.31	4	4	2	142	3
R Vasconcelos	10	18	2	750	184	46.87	1400	53.57	2	3	0	105	2
GS Ballance	14	23	2	975	159	46.42	1970	49.49	5	3	1	144	1
AM Rossington	13	19	2	787	82	46.29	1274	61.77	0	8	1	92	13
LS Livingstone	11	14	1	599	114	46.07	954	62.78	1	5	2	85	6
AN Cook	14	24	4	913	125	45.65	2015	45.31	1	7	0	117	0
CT Bancroft	9	17	1	726	158	45.37	1607	45.17	2	3	1	76	2
BC Brown	14	22	3	812	156	42.73	1315	61.74	3	3	4	100	3
TC Lace	11	21	1	835	143	41.75	1671	49.97	3	4	1	111	1
JA Simpson	14	22	3	773	167*	40.68	1531	50.48	2	4	1	112	2
EJH Eckersley	13	22	4	720	118	40.00	1599	45.02	1	4	0	71	1
AHT Donald	9	15	1	554	173	39.57	665	83.30	1	2	0	74	9
JL du Plooy	10	17	3	554	118	39.57	1174	47.18	2	2	0	66	4
RS Bopara	10	14	1	514	135	39.53	991	51.86	2	2	3	60	2
T Kohler-Cadmore	14	22	1	828	165*	39.42	1539	53.80	2	3	1	118	3
BA Godleman	14	26	0	1008	227	38.76	1724	58.46	4	2	1	131	3
DW Lawrence	14	22	3	725	147	38.15	1391	52.12	1	5	3	97	2
T Bavuma	8	15	0	566	134	37.73	890	63.59	2	1	0	70	5
RJ Burns	8	16	0	603	107	37.68	1200	50.25	1	2	1	79	2
AZ Lees	14	25	1	899	181	37.45	1941	46.31	3	3	4	97	6
SD Robson	14	24	1	858	140*	37.30	1675	51.22	2	4	2	117	1
RR Rossouw	10	17	1	595	92	37.18	751	79.22	0	5	1	84	10
RP Jones	14	19	2	624	122	36.70	1547	40.33	1	4	1	85	0
WT Root	14	22	1	768	229	36.57	1199	64.05	2	1	2	99	1
AG Wakely	12	16	1	548	102	36.53	1147	47.77	1	2	1	72	2
LA Procter	14	21	7	510	86*	36.42	1022	49.90	0	2	2	46	5
T Westley	14	23	1	794	141	36.09	1666	47.65	1	3	0	113	2
DJ Bell-Drummond	14	26	1	892	166	35.68	1743	51.17	1	5	1	121	1
CN Ackermann	14	25	6	675	70*	35.52	1579	42.74	0	7	3	91	0
MJ Cosgrove	13	23	3	697	107*	34.85	1494	46.65	1	6	2	98	1
WL Madsen	13	24	1	794	204*	34.52	1308	60.70	1	3	4	119	1
NJ Selman	14	24	2	752	150	34.18	1617	46.50	1	6	3	95	0
JR Bracey	13	22	2	677	152	33.85	1276	53.05	2	2	1	88	0
RI Keogh	14	22	0	744	150	33.81	1468	50.68	2	2	2	100	1
PD Salt	10	19	1	603	122	33.50	777	77.60	2	3	2	75	7
WMH Rhodes	14	23	0	770	109	33.47	1422	54.14	1	5	2	106	10
OG Robinson	14	25	2	765	143	33.26	1290	59.30	2	3	1	93	2
DI Stevens	12	19	1	597	237	33.16	833	71.66	1	2	3	69	17

KIA
GM

COUNTY CHAMPIONSHIP BOWLING AVERAGES *Minimum of 20 wickets*

Player	Mat	Overs	Mdns	Runs	Wkts	BBI	BBM	Ave	Econ	SR	5	10
JM Anderson	6	159.4	61	281	30	5/18	9/47	9.36	1.75	31.9	2	0
KJ Abbott	13	362.5	78	1117	71	9/40	17/86	15.73	3.07	30.6	6	1
L Gregory	11	284.1	81	804	51	6/32	11/53	15.76	2.82	33.4	4	1
OE Robinson	11	380.3	83	1036	63	8/34	14/135	16.44	2.72	36.2	6	3
MJ Leach	9	250.3	71	596	34	6/36	7/121	17.52	2.37	44.2	2	0
DI Stevens	12	403	126	914	52	5/20	10/92	17.57	2.26	46.5	5	1
TJ Murtagh	11	295.3	93	757	43	6/51	8/76	17.60	2.56	41.2	4	0
SR Harmer	14	595.5	175	1518	83	8/98	12/61	18.28	2.54	43	10	2
C Rushworth	14	486.4	127	1271	69	14/37	10/67	18.42	2.61	42.3	4	1
J Overton	8	156.5	29	521	28	5/70	7/94	18.60	3.32	33.6	1	0
KA Maharaj	5	266	76	719	38	7/52	10/127	18.92	2.70	42	4	2
MW Parkinson	4	143.5	33	381	20	6/23	10/165	19.05	2.64	43.1	1	1
G Onions	10	306.1	66	881	45	5/38	8/57	19.57	2.87	40.8	3	0
BW Sanderson	14	448.2	118	1179	60	6/37	10/55	19.65	2.62	44.8	3	1
LM Reece	14	371	105	1022	52	6/58	6/62	19.65	2.75	42.8	3	0
A Virdi	5	140	34	452	23	8/61	14/139	19.65	3.22	36.5	2	1
BA Hutton	10	263.3	72	700	35	6/57	7/79	20.00	2.65	45.1	2	0
PM Siddle	8	263.4	72	683	34	6/104	7/80	20.08	2.59	46.5	2	0
RJ Gleeson	9	273.1	61	948	47	6/43	10/113	20.17	3.47	34.8	5	1
TE Bailey	9	289.2	81	777	37	5/41	10/119	21.00	2.68	46.9	3	1
LA Patterson-White	5	134.5	17	420	20	5/73	6/107	21.00	3.11	40.4	1	0
SJ Cook	9	235.5	61	673	32	7/23	12/65	21.03	2.85	44.2	3	1
MG Hogan	11	349	85	974	46	5/62	7/71	21.17	2.79	45.5	1	0
CAJ Morris	11	293	67	945	44	7/45	8/93	21.47	3.22	39.9	3	0
BA Raine	14	463.4	122	1179	54	6/27	9/96	21.83	2.54	51.5	3	0
C Overton	10	282.3	64	810	37	5/31	7/69	21.89	2.86	45.8	2	0
EG Barnard	14	371	100	993	44	6/42	8/121	22.56	2.67	50.5	1	0
WD Parnell	7	157.4	42	507	22	5/47	5/47	23.04	3.21	43	1	0
FJ Hudson-Prentice	7	148	38	465	20	3/27	6/69	23.25	3.14	44.4	0	0
RF Higgins	14	453.4	110	1182	50	5/54	8/89	23.64	2.60	54.4	2	0
R Clarke	14	332	73	1031	43	7/74	8/128	23.97	3.10	46.3	2	0
AP Palladino	10	282.5	99	652	27	5/29	7/59	24.14	2.30	62.8	1	0
J Shaw	9	225.2	43	737	30	4/33	6/102	24.56	3.27	45	0	0
R Ashwin	5	297.4	73	836	34	6/69	12/144	24.58	2.80	52.5	4	1
TG Helm	7	208	39	600	24	5/36	6/71	25.00	2.88	52	2	0
ME Milnes	14	386.4	68	1383	55	5/68	7/111	25.14	3.57	42.1	2	0
OJ Hannon-Dalby	12	399	108	1129	44	5/18	9/137	25.65	2.82	54.4	2	0
JA Porter	13	391.2	83	1234	48	5/51	9/73	25.70	3.15	48.9	2	0
Mohammad Abbas	9	281.5	81	747	29	4/72	6/88	25.75	2.65	58.3	0	0
BO Coad	11	340	82	955	37	6/52	9/118	25.81	2.80	55.1	1	0
FH Edwards	14	353.1	55	1240	48	5/49	8/100	25.83	3.51	44.1	4	0
R Rampaul	12	374	79	1139	44	5/77	8/130	25.88	3.04	51	2	0
DA Payne	12	403.5	94	1113	43	4/40	6/88	25.88	2.75	56.3	0	0
GJ Batty	8	234.3	43	678	26	8/64	10/111	26.07	2.89	54.1	1	1
DM Bess	11	271.3	68	681	26	5/59	7/93	26.19	2.50	62.6	1	0
MD Taylor	9	245	43	760	29	5/57	5/57	26.20	3.10	50.6	1	0
J Leach	12	384.4	83	1081	41	6/79	7/106	26.36	2.81	56.2	1	0
LJ Fletcher	12	326.4	68	926	35	5/50	6/113	26.45	2.83	56	2	0
HW Podmore	14	473.3	105	1380	52	5/41	8/123	26.53	2.91	54.6	2	0
KHD Barker	13	348	78	984	37	5/48	6/88	26.59	2.82	56.4	1	0

Specsavers
Garden

COUNTY CHAMPIONSHIP WICKETKEEPING *Minimum of 20 dismissals*

Name	Mat	Inns	Dis	Ct	St	Max Dis Inns	Dis/Inn
OG Robinson	14	26	54	54	0	6 (6ct 0st)	2.076
BC Brown	14	24	53	52	1	5 (5ct 0st)	2.208
SM Davies	14	27	50	47	3	5 (5ct 0st)	1.851
DJ Vilas	14	25	48	47	1	4 (4ct 0st)	1.92
BT Foakes	13	23	45	39	6	4 (4ct 0st)	1.956
TR Ambrose	12	22	42	39	3	4 (4ct 0st)	1.909
GH Roderick	14	20	42	41	1	5 (5ct 0st)	2.1
EJH Eckersley	13	23	42	42	0	4 (4ct 0st)	1.826
OB Cox	14	26	39	38	1	4 (4ct 0st)	1.5
JA Tattersall	14	24	35	32	3	4 (4ct 0st)	1.458
JA Simpson	14	24	35	35	0	3 (3ct 0st)	1.458
AM Rossington	13	22	34	32	2	4 (4ct 0st)	1.545
HR Hosein	14	24	32	30	2	4 (4ct 0st)	1.333
TJ Moores	13	21	30	29	1	4 (4ct 0st)	1.428
AJA Wheater	10	17	29	26	3	4 (4ct 0st)	1.705
TN Cullen	9	13	29	29	0	5 (5ct 0st)	2.23
LJ Hill	7	12	24	23	1	4 (4ct 0st)	2
LD McManus	7	11	21	20	1	4 (4ct 0st)	1.909
CB Cooke	7	11	20	18	2	4 (4ct 0st)	1.818

COUNTY CHAMPIONSHIP FIELDING *Minimum of 15 catches*

Name	Mat	Inns	Ct	Max	Ct/Inn
T Kohler-Cadmore	14	24	30	6	1.25
A Lyth	14	24	26	2	1.083
WL Madsen	13	23	21	3	0.913
MH Wessels	14	26	21	3	0.807
CN Ackermann	14	21	19	2	0.904
R Clarke	14	25	18	4	0.72
DKH Mitchell	14	26	18	3	0.692
JC Hildreth	14	27	17	3	0.629
CJ Jordan	11	20	17	2	0.85
DJ Malan	13	22	17	3	0.772
KK Jennings	14	27	17	3	0.629
J Overton	8	15	16	4	1.066
SR Hain	12	22	16	3	0.727
SG Borthwick	13	23	16	3	0.695
Z Crawley	13	24	16	2	0.666
CT Bancroft	9	17	16	3	0.941
DL Lloyd	14	24	16	4	0.666
AN Cook	14	25	15	2	0.6
SR Harmer	14	25	15	3	0.6

MVP TOP 100

#	Name	County	Batting	Bowling	Field	Capt.	Wins	Pld	Pts	Avg.
1	Simon Harmer	Essex	70.03	479.86	33.00	8	18	34	608.89	17.91
2	Kyle Abbott	Hampshire	39.00	481.10	4.00	0	18	36	542.10	15.06
3	Jeetan Patel	Warwickshire	68.03	417.63	15.00	9	9	34	518.66	15.25
4	Luis Reece	Derbyshire	226.74	236.68	13.80	0	15	36	492.22	13.67
5	Ryan Higgins	Gloucestershire	216.91	240.40	9.20	0	17	35	483.52	13.81
6	Lewis Gregory	Somerset	143.89	287.50	16.00	1	16	26	464.39	17.86
7	Craig Overton	Somerset	80.82	296.97	26.00	0	20	33	423.79	12.84
8	Billy Godleman	Derbyshire	367.76	0.00	15.40	15	15	36	413.16	11.48
9	Dane Vilas	Lancashire	272.42	0.00	89.60	22	22	36	406.02	11.28
10	Darren Stevens	Derbyshire	122.62	273.80	3.00	0	5	19	404.42	21.29
11	Liam Dawson	Hampshire	184.79	178.20	17.00	0	18	30	397.99	13.27
12	Colin Ackermann	Leicestershire	238.67	119.55	21.00	5	7	35	391.23	11.18
13	Wayne Madsen	Derbyshire	323.15	16.83	35.80	0	15	35	390.78	11.17
14	Ed Barnard	Worcestershire	95.83	243.00	20.80	0	17	37	376.63	10.18
15	Tom Abell	Somerset	251.44	47.85	30.00	22	23	38	374.29	9.85
16	David Wiese	Sussex	210.27	137.82	8.60	0	16	36	372.70	10.35
17	Dawid Malan	Middlesex	307.83	13.94	21.40	13	13	32	369.17	11.54
18	Ben Sanderson	Northamptonshire	24.27	327.01	2.00	0	10	31	363.29	11.72
19	Tom Banton	Somerset	301.58	0.00	35.00	0	20	34	356.58	10.49
20	Toby Roland-Jones	Middlesex	87.41	240.00	10.40	0	16	33	353.81	10.72
21	Sam Hain	Warwickshire	315.11	0.00	24.00	0	9	31	348.11	11.23
22	Daniel Bell-Drummond	Kent	255.42	62.29	9.00	6	13	30	345.71	11.52
23	Tom Kohler-Cadmore	Yorkshire	286.11	0.00	44.00	4	11	32	345.11	10.78
24	Matthew Milnes	Kent	40.43	287.61	10.00	0	7	23	345.04	15.00
25	Rikki Clarke	Surrey	123.17	191.75	24.00	0	4	24	342.92	14.29
26	Ravi Rampaul	Derbyshire	26.47	292.93	5.80	0	13	32	338.20	10.57
27	Harry Podmore	Kent	55.21	266.15	9.00	0	7	22	337.36	15.33
28	Dominic Sibley	Warwickshire	317.82	-1.40	12.00	0	7	29	335.42	11.57
29	Wayne Parnell	Worcestershire	95.32	221.19	4.60	0	14	28	335.10	11.97
30	James Vince	Hampshire	290.88	-0.28	15.00	14	14	26	333.60	12.83
31	Adam Lyth	Yorkshire	231.27	57.82	33.00	0	11	31	333.09	10.74
32	Ben Raine	Durham	81.84	226.18	7.60	0	13	31	328.62	10.60
33	Zak Crawley	Kent	290.48	-0.95	26.00	0	13	33	328.53	9.96
34	Ollie Robinson	Sussex	34.72	277.67	4.40	0	11	21	327.79	15.61
35	Sam Northeast	Hampshire	286.11	0.00	17.00	4	18	36	325.11	9.03
36	Tom Westley	Essex	283.24	1.96	20.00	0	19	36	324.20	9.01
37	Riki Wessels	Worcestershire	268.68	0.00	30.80	0	17	37	316.48	8.55
38	Luke Fletcher	Nottinghamshire	62.50	237.55	5.00	0	8	24	313.05	13.04
39	Will Rhodes	Warwickshire	186.71	98.14	19.00	0	9	34	312.85	9.20
40	Ravi Bopara	Essex	174.42	101.35	19.00	0	15	30	309.77	10.33
41	Rob Keogh	Northamptonshire	188.42	96.31	10.00	0	11	32	305.73	9.55
42	Marnus Labuschagne	Glamorgan	210.12	74.86	12.60	0	6	18	303.58	16.87
43	Dan Lawrence	Essex	241.39	24.14	16.00	0	19	36	300.53	8.35
44	Philip Salt	Sussex	257.77	0.00	26.40	0	16	31	300.17	9.68
45	Matthew Critchley	Derbyshire	109.90	153.79	19.20	0	15	36	297.89	8.27
46	David Payne	Gloucestershire	34.74	240.07	7.20	0	15	31	297.01	9.58
47	Steven Croft	Lancashire	213.06	33.49	16.20	0	19	33	281.75	8.54
48	Steven Mullaney	Nottinghamshire	181.26	69.84	17.00	6	6	23	280.10	12.18
49	Liam Livingstone	Lancashire	155.02	102.81	7.60	0	14	23	279.44	12.15
50	Fidel Edwards	Warwickshire	5.07	261.36	4.00	0	9	24	279.43	11.64

#	Name	County	Batting	Bowling	Field	Capt.	Wins	Pld	Pts	Avg.
51	David Lloyd	Glamorgan	212.60	35.60	19.80	3	8	34	279.01	8.21
52	Samit Patel	Nottinghamshire	121.10	132.92	9.80	0	14	34	277.82	8.17
53	Tom Helm	Middlesex	27.00	225.57	8.80	0	16	30	277.37	9.25
54	James Bracey	Gloucestershire	214.37	3.75	43.40	0	15	33	276.52	8.38
55	Saqib Mahmood	Lancashire	21.71	233.52	3.00	0	18	28	276.23	9.87
56	Jamie Porter	Essex	6.40	246.34	9.00	0	14	23	275.74	11.99
57	Ben Foakes	Surrey	148.86	0.00	116.00	0	6	30	270.86	9.03
58	Ollie Robinson	Kent	174.84	0.00	80.00	0	13	32	267.84	8.37
59	Steven Patterson	Yorkshire	43.93	198.37	7.00	7	7	21	263.30	12.54
60	Morne Morkel	Surrey	19.16	236.56	4.00	0	3	20	262.72	13.14
61	Chris Rushworth	Durham	6.86	246.39	3.40	0	6	15	262.64	17.51
62	James Hildreth	Somerset	215.49	0.00	23.00	0	23	38	261.49	6.88
63	Alex Lees	Durham	236.08	0.00	13.00	0	12	30	261.08	8.70
64	Glenn Maxwell	Lancashire	110.50	116.49	18.40	0	15	21	260.39	12.40
65	John Simpson	Middlesex	168.52	-0.16	75.00	0	16	37	259.36	7.01
66	Joe Clarke	Nottinghamshire	237.46	0.00	9.00	0	12	32	258.46	8.08
67	Nathan Sowter	Middlesex	34.96	186.60	20.20	0	16	30	257.76	8.59
68	Adam Rossington	Northamptonshire	183.36	-0.32	58.60	5	10	30	256.64	8.55
69	Oliver Hannon-Dalby	Warwickshire	16.60	228.84	5.00	0	6	21	256.44	12.21
70	Gary Ballance	Yorkshire	238.28	0.00	10.00	0	8	26	256.28	9.86
71	Henry Brookes	Warwickshire	50.11	193.30	6.00	0	6	26	255.41	9.82
72	Roelof van der Merwe	Somerset	55.96	154.81	27.00	0	16	28	253.77	9.06
73	Jamie Overton	Somerset	60.93	158.67	20.60	0	12	19	252.20	13.27
74	Gareth Batty	Surrey	22.88	215.39	5.00	0	8	27	251.27	9.31
75	Marchant de Lange	Glamorgan	52.80	182.51	9.60	0	6	28	250.91	8.96
76	Duanne Olivier	Yorkshire	22.57	216.06	4.00	0	7	23	249.63	10.85
77	Alastair Cook	Essex	220.65	0.00	17.00	0	11	22	248.65	11.30
78	Peter Siddle	Essex	33.84	202.56	3.00	0	8	14	247.40	17.67
79	Tim Murtagh	Middlesex	20.82	217.16	4.40	0	5	15	247.38	16.49
80	Benny Howell	Gloucestershire	98.79	122.01	14.60	0	11	25	246.41	9.86
81	Rilee Rossouw	Hampshire	222.95	0.00	8.00	0	15	32	245.95	7.69
82	Daryl Mitchell	Worcestershire	130.34	75.93	25.40	0	14	34	245.67	7.23
83	Chris Dent	Gloucestershire	212.16	-0.14	11.20	10	10	22	243.22	11.06
84	Brydon Carse	Durham	41.49	178.35	7.80	0	12	27	239.64	8.88
85	Richard Gleeson	Lancashire	3.56	215.40	6.60	0	13	20	238.56	11.93
86	Tom Moores	Nottinghamshire	153.03	0.00	70.00	0	13	34	236.03	6.94
87	Ben Brown	Sussex	149.65	-0.60	68.60	8	10	27	235.65	8.73
88	Ben Duckett	Nottinghamshire	197.73	-0.67	24.00	0	13	32	234.06	7.31
89	Charlie Morris	Worcestershire	13.28	207.27	2.00	0	10	22	232.55	10.57
90	Matthew Parkinson	Lancashire	3.85	203.43	7.40	0	16	25	230.68	9.23
91	Jordan Clark	Surrey	103.95	113.98	5.00	0	7	27	229.93	8.52
92	Keshav Maharaj	Yorkshire	50.24	170.58	3.00	0	6	10	229.82	22.98
93	Leus du Plooy	Derbyshire	192.62	5.20	18.20	0	12	29	228.02	7.86
94	Cameron Bancroft	Durham	189.87	0.00	21.80	8	8	17	227.67	13.39
95	Ben Cox	Worcestershire	135.36	0.00	74.40	1	16	36	226.76	6.30
96	Keith Barker	Hampshire	56.39	162.90	2.00	0	5	13	226.29	17.41
97	Alex Hughes	Derbyshire	99.15	93.37	20.80	0	12	31	225.32	7.27
98	Ravichandran Ashwin	Nottinghamshire	63.24	158.61	2.00	0	0	5	223.85	44.77
99	Ryan ten Doeschate	Essex	178.28	1.62	13.00	11	19	34	222.90	6.56
100	Keaton Jennings	Lancashire	169.57	4.28	26.60	0	22	36	222.45	6.18

NOTES

NOTES

NOTES